Steve Wheeler

RUNNERS AND RACES: 1500M./MILE

CORDNER NELSON & ROBERTO QUERCETANI

TAFNEWS PRESS
Book Division of
Track & Field News

First Published in 1973 by Tafnews Press
Book Division of Track & Field News,
Box 296, Los Altos, California 94022, U.S.A.

Copyright © 1973 by Track & Field News
All rights reserved.

Library of Congress Catalog Card Number: 72-90579
Standard Book Number: 0-911520-40-6

Printed in the United States of America

To Mary and Maria Luisa

The authors also wish to thank the following track nuts, who supplied valuable information and assistance: Ed Fox, Don Potts, Rooney Magnusson, Fulvio Regli, and Wally Donovan.

Production Staff: Dave Haugh, Grace Light. Jacket design: Dave Haugh.

CONTENTS

Foreword		v
I	A Bit of Ancient History	1
II	Rise of the Amateurs	13
III	Paavo Nurmi	30
IV	Renaissance (1929-1932)	49
V	The Time of Lovelock	66
VI	Gunder Hägg	118
VII	The Bannister Years	155
VIII	The Explosive Revolution	182
IX	The Elliott Interlude	205
X	The Reign of Peter Snell	222
XI	The Jim Ryun Era	252
X	Unfinished Symphony	287
All-Time World List, to 20 October 72		314
Index		319

ILLUSTRATIONS

Pekka Vasala	vi
Walter George	Opp. 48
Walter George-Will Cummings	Opp. 48
1912 Olympic final	Opp. 49
Joie Ray, Jules Ladoumègue, Paavo Nurmi	Opp. 49
Jack Lovelock	54
Jack Lovelock in Berlin	Opp. 106
Jack Lovelock in Mile of the Century	Opp. 106
Bill Bonthron, Luigi Beccali	Opp. 106
San Romani, Zamperini, Venske, Cunningham	Opp. 107
Arne Andersson, Gunder Hägg	Opp. 142
Wooderson, Ericksson, Strand, Dodds	Opp. 143
Don Macmillan, Josy Barthel, Gaston Reiff, Bob McMillen	Opp. 178
Bannister at Oxford	Opp 178A
Bannister vs. Landy at Vancouver	Opp. 178B
Wes Santee, Jungwirth and Iharos, Bailey and Landy	Opp. 179
Ron Delany, Don Bowden, Derek Ibbotson and Brian Hewson	Opp. 204
Herb Elliott	Opp. 205
Jim Beatty, Igloi's troops, Dyrol Burleson	Opp. 250
Tom O'Hara, 1964 US Olympic Semi-Trials	Opp. 250A
Michel Jazy, Peter Snell	Opp. 250B
Peter Snell at Tokyo	Opp. 251
Ryun at San Diego, Ryun at Berkeley	Opp. 272
1966 European Championships, 1965 Emsley Carr mile	Opp. 273
Keino wins at Mexico City	Opp. 286
1969 NCAA mile, Kip Keino	Opp. 287
Pekka Vasala conquers the field in Munich	314

FOREWORD

This book is about the most interesting runners and the most exciting races in the history of the mile run and its metric equivalent—1500 meters. Based on the principle that one snowflake seen under a microscope is far more interesting than a whole snowball, we have selected the most important runners and the most significant races for the enjoyment of anyone who likes foot racing.

Our emphasis on individual runners and races is intended to make history more clear, and if you will read from the beginning, without skipping ahead, you will discover a curious continuity, for no sooner is one great race ended than another begins to take shape for the future. One runner's career comes to an end while another's is gaining strength.

Thus, this book may seem to have hundreds of small chapters, but in reality it has only one. It may seem to have dozens of heroes . . . but it may have only one. Perhaps the hero is man himself, progressing eternally toward finer achievements, pushing ever onward toward greater goals. In a way, this book is a testimony to man's will to develop his speed and strength, to his determination and courage, to his intelligent application of his powers, and to his insatiable desire for progress.

Cordner Nelson

Roberto Quercetani

Pekka Vasala—1972 Olympic 1500-meter winner.
Don Wilkinson

1
A bit of ancient history

The first foot race undoubtedly took place many thousands of years ago, perhaps in a handicap race between a man and a sabre-toothed tiger. Homer described a close foot race in the Iliad, supposedly before the 11th century B.C., and after that, the Greek Olympics were held for almost twelve centuries, until 393 A.D. Some of their races approximated a mile distance, but none of these were timed, for watches had no second hands until almost 1700 A.D.

After the Dark Ages, foot racing between "footmen" became popular in England during the 17th century. A footman was a servant who ran on ahead of horse-drawn coaches to arrange accommodations at the inns for his master. These footmen began to race each other while their sedentary masters wagered on the outcome.

In the early 19th century, all races were held on roads or on courses designed for horse races. The winning times of these races were probably accurate to within a second, but the distances were badly measured, and so times are not considered accurate before running tracks were used in the mid-1800's.

In Britain, during the 19th century, foot racing was called "pedestrianism" and it was the most popular of all sports. Entertainment was wonderfully unsophisticated then, with few spectator sports and no radio, movies, nor television, and so large crowds gathered to watch head-and-head match races between the best runners.

These were professional races. As an indication of their popularity, it is reported that one James Metcalf won an 1825 mile race in 4:30 for a prize of 1000 guineas, enough to live on for years.

1865

THE CHAMPION MILER OF ENGLAND

On August 19, 1865, by far the greatest field of milers up to that time was assembled at the center of pedestrianism—Manchester, England. Fifteen thousand eager spectators were there to watch the best-known professionals compete for the title of The Champion Miler of England.

Among the nine pros warming up on the grass track were:

SIAH ALBISON, who had broken the world record in a sensational race on this same track almost five years before. On that date—October 27, 1860—the fastest mile of an acceptable nature was 4:23 (by Thomas Horspool, two years earlier). Albison garnered the world record by crossing the line in 4:22¼, most probably the fastest mile yet run on a properly measured track.

EDWARD MILLS, who had broken Albison's world record with a 4:20½ mile on April 23, 1863. Mills, a tiny 112-pounder only 5'4½" tall and called "Young England", lowered his own record to 4:20 on June 25, 1864, here at Manchester.

WILLIAM LANG, who lost a heartbreaker to Albison in the 1860 record race by only half a yard. Lang, however, had improved since then while Albison had not. A 5'9½" bearded 155-pounder known as the "Crowcatcher", Lang, had set world records for two miles (9:11½) and six miles (29:50) in 1863 as well as running a 4:21¾ mile. At 27, he was at his peak and anxious to win.

Other entrants included the fast Scot, McInstray, aggressive James Nuttall, and a lightly regarded darkhorse from Wales named William Richards.

Excitement was mounting and fans were still placing their bets when the shocking news spread that world record holder Mills was limping and could not run. This made Lang the favorite, with Scottish money taking the odds on McInstray.

The starting line was at the head of the backstretch of the 651-yard track. Nuttall set off at a reckless pace and the others strung out behind him. As Nuttall passed the 440-yard mark, ten yards short of the finish line, a timer called "60 seconds" and a cheer went up from the crowd.

Around the long turn and down the backstretch, Nuttall sped along in the lead. At the 880-yard mark, into the turn, his time was 2:05½ and a great excitement took hold of the crowd.

But the pace was too fast, and Nuttall slowed. In spite of the crowd's urging, the runners passed the finish line at a rapidly slowing pace. Even so, some of them fell back. At the three quarters, 18 yards beyond the starting line, Lang was leading. His time was 3:14, still fast enough to make this the first mile ever run under 4:20, and the fans shouted with anticipation.

Down the long backstretch, Lang tried to pull away. Most of

the runners could not stay with him but McInstray was still there, and so was the relentless Richards. Albison was out of it by now. Those who had bet on Lang feared the Scot. Those who had bet on McInstray implored him to hang on. The few who had their money on Richards took hope with every stride.

Around the long turn and into the homestretch they came, and the crowd roared with frenzy, for never had a race been so fast and so close. They were running faster than their starting pace now, driving for the finish, and McInstray began to lose ground. But Richards was amazing them all, actually gaining on Lang.

Rushing toward the finish in an all-out drive, Richards fought alongside, and they flashed across the finish line in a blur of pumping arms and sprinting legs, five yards ahead of McInstray. The judges called it a tie, and Lang's supporters howled with rage, but the judgment stood.

Their time was 4:17¼, so fast that no man was to better it for 16 years.

Postscript: The public wanted a run-off a week later, and "Crowcatcher" Lang beat Richards in 4:22.

THE AMATEURS

Amateurism, an ideal of the English gentlemen, did not take hold until the Victorian puritanical era, and amateur running became popular after 1860. So wide was the chasm between the gentlemen and the crass professionals that no man bridged the gap for a quarter of a century, and the amateurs were the worse for comparison. Here is the progression of the amateur record:

4:55   J. Heaviside of Ireland, at Dublin, April 1, 1861.
4:49   Heaviside lowered his own record at the Dublin Military Sports, May 27, 1861.
4:46   N.S. Greene of Ireland lowered Heaviside's record in another race in the same meet.
4:33   George H. Farran of Ireland, on Dublin University's 440-yard track, May 23, 1862.
4:29 3/5   Walter M. Chinnery of England, on March 10, 1868, at Cambridge.
4:28 4/5   William Gibbs of England, on April 3, 1868, at London. A great natural talent not yet 20 years old, Gibbs retired shortly after on the advice of his doctor.
4:28-3/5   Charles Gunton of England, at Lillie Bridge, London, on March 31, 1873.
4:26   Walter Slade of England, on May 30, 1874, at the Lillie Bridge Grounds in West Brompton (London). Slade won this handicap mile by 2½ yards.

4:24½ Slade, on June 19, 1875, at Lillie Bridge. He set an amazing pace of 60 and 2:03½.

WILLIAM J. CUMMINGS—THE GREAT PROFESSIONAL

Cummings made up his mind to take up the uncertain life of a professional pedestrian before his 18th birthday on June 10, 1876, and his first professional race came a few months later. The 5'6¼" 124-pound Scot ran 4:28½ on the day before his 19th birthday. In 1878, before he was 20, he ran a losing 4:25 and covered two miles in 9:20½.

He was so impressive that he was invited to Mecca—the race for the Champion's Belt at Lillie Bridge on July 1. A long shot in the betting, he won in 4:28 to become the 1878 Champion of England.

Back home in Glasgow on September 21, an enthusiastic crowd of 5000 watched him win from scratch in 4:18¼. Two weeks later he won in 4:19½. Not yet 21, he was at the top of pedestrianism.

Then, possibly because most of his training came from racing, he had two years of mixed fortunes. Running often, against tough opposition, he did not always win. In 1879, he ran four miles in 19:57¼, but he lost his cherished mile title to E. Dickenson's 4:20-4/5.

In 1880, Cummings regained the Champion's Belt in 4:22-2/5 and also won the Belt for 10 miles in 51:47-2/5. On July 17 he set a world record for 1½ miles in 6:43½, but on December 20 he was shocked to lose behind William Duddle's 4:19½.

Thoroughly chastened, Cummings set out to regain his superiority in 1881. On April 30, he raced Duddle over 1000 yards at Preston and won by 6 yards in world-record time of 2:17. Two weeks later on the same track, Cummings set out to retain his prized Championship Belt. Running in a steady rain on the 600-yard track, he won decisively in 4:16-1/5, the fastest mile ever run.

Now he was invincible. He beat Duddle in 4:18¼ and 4:20½, and in December he ran under 4:20 twice more. In the next four years he switched to longer races, but nobody could extend him. Professional running was beginning to die, partly because Cummings won so easily.

WALTER G. GEORGE—THE GREAT AMATEUR

Only three months younger than Cummings but five inches taller, Walter George did not begin running until Cummings had been a professional for two years. George was apprenticed to a chemist at 16 and he had to work from 7 a.m. to 9 p.m. Needing exercise on week-ends, he tried cycling races and then walking races.

1882

Before his 20th birthday, on September 9, 1878, he trained for three months and amused his teammates by predicting he would run a mile in 4:12. He even wrote in his notebook the pace for such a race—59, 2:02, 3:08. In his very first race, a mile handicap, he was given 45 yards and he won in 4:29. Startled officials withheld his prize for an hour while they checked to determine whether this 5'11½" stranger was a ringer. That race was the only one in which George was ever given a handicap.

Unable to train properly out of doors, he devised his famous '100-up", a form of running in place with high knee lifts and springing action. Within a year he won England's 1879 Amateur Championships in the mile (4:29) and 4-mile.

In 1880, the Amateur Athletic Association held its first championship meeting and George won the mile (4:28-3/5) and the 4-mile. On August 16 on the three-year-old Stamford Bridge cinder track not far from Lillie Bridge in the Chelsea district of London, George held his "ideal" pace of 59 for one lap, then slowed to 2:04½ and 3:14. He was disappointed in his 4:23-1/5, but it was fast enough to break Slade's world amateur record.

In 1881, while Cummings was rising to professional supremacy, George was injured and finished behind in both the 880 and mile at the AAA Championships. When he felt well again, he set a world amateur record of 14:42-4/5 for three miles.

In 1882, George was the toast of amateur racing. He won AAA titles in the 880, mile (4:32-4/5), 4-mile, 10-mile, and cross country. He lost the steeplechase, after building up a six-yard lead, because one shoe came off. He set world amateur records from ¾ mile to ten miles.

On June 3 he ran the mile in the Civil Service Sports at Stamford Bridge. He was close to his ideal schedule with 3:08¾, but he could not hold the pace. He finished in 4:19-2/5, lowering his own amateur record. Only three professionals had ever run faster.

Now only Cummings stood ahead of George, but the little Scot was a tainted pro. George applied to the new AAA for permission to race Cummings, with his share of the gate to go to charity, but the request was denied, and eager track fans had to wait three years for a race between the two great runners.

George sailed for America, and in November he ran a series of three races against Lon Myers. These duels were witnessed by the astonishing total of 130,000 people at the Polo Grounds in New York. George ran the 880 in 1:57 but lost in the stretch to the speedy Myers' 1:56-3/5. A week later, in the mile, George led all the way in 61½, 2:05-1/5, and 3:16, and he won in a comfortable 4:21-2/5. Myers, who was the best miler in America even though it was far beyond his best distance, faded on the last lap and almost quit near the end, but he finished in 4:27-3/5.

Two weeks later, in the deciding race, 60,000 people braved the cold to watch the ¾ mile showdown. On a bad track, George led by a narrow margin with times of 61-2/5 and 2:02¾. Myers hung on until the homestretch but he staggered in the last 25 yards. He finished in 3:13 but he collapsed and was unconscious for two hours. George won in 3:10¾, walked calmly to the dressing room, and fell unconscious for 20 minutes. He said it was "the most grueling race I ever ran."

In 1883, George suffered an illness and William Snook took over the mile championship. George won the cross country, and at the end of the year he lowered his amateur record for ten miles.

George's chance for revenge came on June 21, 1884, at the Astor Lower Grounds in Birmingham, when he met defending champion Snook in the AAA Championships. George was in great condition but he was saving himself for the 4-mile the same afternoon. Snook ran under George's world record, but George fought him down the homestretch and won in 4:18-2/5. It was the third time he had set a world amateur record for the mile.

He won the 4-mile that day in 20:12-4/5. Two days later he won the AAA 10-mile in a tranquil 54:02. He also won titles in the 880 and cross country. In a series of planned gallops, he broke world amateur records for the 2-mile (9:17-2/5), 3-mile (14:39), 6-mile (30:21½), 10-mile (51:20), and one hour (11 miles 932 yards).

In 1885, with no more worlds to conquer in amateur track and badly in debt, George turned professional and challenged Cummings to a series of races.

George had set many records through the conditioning he attained by running in place, but when he prepared for an important match he also trained twice a day outside. His workouts were mild compared with modern methods. He usually ran only one distance in a workout, at medium to fast pace, varying his distance according to pace—350 to more than a mile, with a little sprinting.

THE FIRST CHALLENGE RACE

The long-awaited challenge mile on August 31, 1885, incited fans to a fever pitch and preparations were made for 10,000 spectators at Lillie Bridge. But months of speculation had stirred up an interest unparalleled in athletic history. Special trains came from many cities, including Cummings' home, Glasgow.

In spite of occasional showers, more than 30,000 people turned out, causing massive traffic jams. The turnstiles were opened for business at 4:00 p.m., two hours before the competition, and yet they could not manage the crowd. Officials closed the gates at 5:00 p.m., and the angry thousands still outside broke down walls and surged inside. They lined the track all the way around, inside and out. Cummings arrived at 5:30 and calmly walked two laps of the track. George was caught in traffic, and when he arrived, shortly before 6:00, the crowd was too dense to risk pushing through. He climbed over them on a ladder to his dressing room at the back of the grandstand.

The two runners pushed through the dangerously thick crowd onto the track with their trainers. Masseurs loosened their leg muscles in lieu of a warmup, and they took off the coats and headgear which had given them some protection from the rain.

There were two tracks at famous old Lillie Bridge, the quarter-mile cycling track inside an almost rectangular third-mile track of worn and scattered cinders, loose and slow. It had been neglected because amateur runners now used the nearby Stamford Bridge track. Cummings had won the toss and, surprisingly, he chose the old cinder track.

Betting was heavy, with Cummings favored five to four because of his superior experience in tough pro races.

George, tall and lean, with a small mustache and his hair parted in the middle and curling above his ears, wore black, with a blue trim extending to his knees. Cummings, smaller and boyish-looking, wore all-white. It was raining when the gun sounded, and George broke to the front.

George set his usual wicked pace, with Cummings close behind. Around the sharp turns on the slow track, George ran 58-3/5 and the crowd cheered the sensational pace.

George concentrated on his long stride while Cummings followed close enough to use the old pro trick of touching George's heels with his finger tips. They passed the 880 mark in 2:01 and the spectators were delirious with excitement.

The pace had to slow, and at 1000 yards Cummings pulled even. George fought back and Cummings had to fall in behind. George passed the three-quarter mark in 3:07½, only half a second slower than the world record.

The rain was heavy now, and the sensational pace had the crowd screaming. Based on all previous running experience, both runners should have slowed gradually to the finish, but George kept the pace going, headed for his 4:12. Cummings was struggling now and his backers implored him to hang on.

Then, half-way through the last lap, Cummings gave up, knowing he was beaten. He walked, and half the crowd gasped while the others cheered for George. Nobody cared much about time. Winning was all that mattered. When George was far enough ahead, he slowed to a walk. Urged by his boosters, Cummings forced himself into a slow run. This caused George to run again and he coasted across the finish line 65 yards ahead. In spite of his lazy finish, his time was 4:20-1/5. Later, he said he could have run 4:12.

THE SECOND CHALLENGE MILE

Almost a year later (Aug. 23, 1886) the two great milers returned to Lillie Bridge for their second mile challenge.

In 1885 they had also run a 4-mile challenge at the famous Powderhall Grounds in Edinburgh, two weeks after their first mile race. In near-hurricane weather, George was badly beaten and some fans suspected a fixed race. The 10-mile challenge, two weeks after that, was run counter clockwise on Lillie Bridge's 440 track. George had fainted seven times two days before and claimed he had been poisoned. He disappointed 15,000 spectators and lost by almost a lap. That winter he lost all three duels to Myers on the sharp turns of Madison Square Garden in New York, but he was now out of debt.

Enthusiasm was thus not so frantic as for their first challenge match, but 20,000 spectators crowded into Lillie Bridge. And never before had two such good milers been so determined.

When Jack White, former 2-mile world record holder, fired the starting gun at 7:12 p.m., George set off with long striding purpose and he circled the 440-yard red brick dust track in 58¼. Behind him, relaxed and gliding, came the white-clad Cummings.

Concentrating fiercely, George sped around to the end of the second lap in 2:01¾, a quarter of a second faster than his ideal pace.

Around the third lap the spectators could see no sign of weakness in either runner. Coming down to three quarters in 3:07¾, Cummings pulled alongside and his fans went wild as he took the lead.

Suddenly, into the turn with 350 yards to go, Cummings launched his kick. He pulled away, opening a gap of eight yards. The crowd went berserk, and there were cries of "Cummings wins!"

But George was confident no man could hold that pace. He maintained his stride and, on the backstretch, he began to gain. He closed the gap. He pulled alongside. He moved two yards ahead into the homestretch. Then, with dramatic suddenness, it was all over. Cummings collapsed, and George coasted to the finish.

Instead of mobbing George as they had last year, the spectators waited in eerie silence for the time to be written on the blackboard. Then the chalked figures appeared—4:12¾.

Pandemonium broke loose and frenzied fans mobbed George, pounding him on the back until he could barely breathe. At 28 he had come within ¾ of a second for each 440 of the ideal pace he had outlined as a beginner of 19.

WALTER GEORGE—POSTSCRIPT

George had the worst of it in the 1886 4-mile challenge against Cummings, but in the 10-mile duel he passed six miles in 30:26-4/5, lapped Cummings, and forced him to quit. In 1887, George met Myers again in three different cities of Australia and lost only the 880. In 1888, far from good condition, he lost three encounters with Cummings . . . a ¾ mile in 3:13-3/5, and disappointing miles in 4:30-1/5 and 4:31-1/5.

Those two losses were his only outdoor defeats in the mile since his injury in 1881. He was probably the greatest miler of all time until well into the 20th century.

One of his best miles was in a time trial. Two weeks before his professional debut against Cummings in 1885, he ran 4:14½. Then, a few days before the race, he ran a time trial at Surbiton against three local runners with handicaps. His pace was a startling 58-1/5, 1:58-3/5, and 3:07, a time nobody had ever beaten. He took the lead then, but he was testing himself—something he rarely did when he ran against other men—and he finished in 4:10-1/5. The three timers could hardly believe their watches, and the track was immediately measured. He had run six yards too far! It was almost half a century before any man ran faster.

THOMAS P. CONNEFF—THE FIRST FAST AMERICAN

In 1886, a 20-year-old Irish runner named Tommy Conneff ran 4:32-3/5. In 1888, the short, stocky runner, who ran with his arms nearly straight, triumphed in the AAA mile in 4:31-3/5. Soon after that, he emigrated to the United States and joined the Manhattan Athletic Club. In the second national meet of 1888, he won the mile title of the NAAAA in 4:32-3/5 and the 5-mile in 26:46.

Conneff enjoyed longer distances, and he won three more national titles in the AAU 5-mile, with a best of 25:37-4/5. In 1890 he also won the 10-mile (55:32-3/5), but he lost the mile to A.B. George. In 1891 he won his second mile championship (4:30-3/5) and had a best time of 4:21-2/5. He was in poor condition in 1892 and failed to finish the AAU mile.

Then, in 1893, at the age of 27, he changed from a plodding distance runner to world record holder for the mile. Under the coaching of famed Mike Murphy, Conneff improved his speed and pacing ability, although he "fell in a faint" in the last straight of the AAU mile.

At Holmes Field, Cambridge, Mass., on August 26, the weather was clear and very warm, and the track was "in admirable condition." Conneff, representing Holy Cross Lyceum, started from scratch in the Boston AA handicap games and easily overtook runners with long starts.

He circled the first two laps in the exciting time of 59 seconds and 2:00. He stirred the spectators by continuing his George-like pace around the third lap in 67. On the last lap, with spirited encouragement from the fans, he fought a losing battle to hold the pace but he finished with the record he wanted—4:17-4/5, a new amateur record.

Conneff lost his record in the AAA Championships at Stamford Bridge, London, July 6, 1895. Frederick Bacon had won in 1893 (4:22-1/5) and 1894 (4:25-4/5) and he ran 4:18-1/5 in 1894. The pace was set by William Lutyens, who ran 4:19-4/5 in 1894. Bacon trailed Lutyens to the last backstretch, then shot into the lead. His excellent drive won by more than 10 yards in 4:17, breaking Conneff's amateur record.

Conneff wanted to regain his record. After a tune-up in 4:21 at Weehawken, New Jersey, on August 10, the popular little runner ran 3/4 mile at Travers Island, New York, 11 days later, in 3:02-4/5. This time was to remain the fastest ever run for 36 years!

He returned to the cinder track at Travers Island on August 28 for a special record effort. Paced by four-time AAU mile champion and 4:21-1/5 miler George Orton, Conneff passed the 440 in 62 2/5 and the 880 in 2:06-3/5. He held his pace to 3:10-4/5 for three quarters.

Eddie Carter, twice AAU champion, joined Conneff to set the pace in the last 300 yards. With people anxiously peering at watches, Conneff made his way around to the homestretch with agonizing slowness.

He crossed the line in 4:15-3/5 to regain his title of amateur world record holder.

On September 21, 1895, Conneff followed a 65, 2:10-3/5 pace by Orton, then forced Lutyens to drop out in an international dual meet against the London AC. It was a hot day and Conneff finished in a trot, 50 yards ahead of Orton in 4:18-1/5. Some idea of Conneff's fine potential can be found in these remarks by William B. Curtis, who reported the event:

"He never was in such fine fettle as during the past four weeks. He could at any time have beaten his own world's best amateur record of 4:15-3/5 and might have equalled or surpassed the world's best professional record, 4:12-3/4 ... He is one of those athletes who speedily make their handlers gray-haired, is restive under the restrictions of training, and prone to stray outside the bounds laid down for athletic aspirants. He is now 29 years old and can hardly hope to improve hereafter."

THE FIRST OLYMPICS

Held at Athens, April 7, 1896, this was far from being a

world championship meet. Most of the best milers were absent. Only 8 men entered the 1500 meter run, and there was no preliminary round. The ancient stadium, rebuilt at various periods for more than two thousand years, had a track of loose and slow cinders. The track was long and narrow between the marble seats, with extremely difficult bends, and runners ran clockwise.

Albin Lermusiaux of France, a willowy runner, set an indifferent pace around the hairpin turns of the old Greek track. In a wild spring down the last "stade", Arthur Blake (USA) and Edwin Flack (Australia) passed Lermusiaux. Flack, a resident of London who had won the 1893 Australasian mile title in 4:44 and who was to win the Olympic 800 meters two days later in 2:11, won out in the sprint. His time was a most unimpressive 4:33-1/5.

GEORGE B. TINCLER—THE SUPREME PROFESSIONAL

At 18, Tincler won the Irish Championship and he repeated at 19 in 1893. Disappointed in failing his law examinations, he turned professional and ran until 1916. Called "The Gander", Tincler competed with great success in Australia, South Africa, Canada, and the United States. Some say he never lost.

On August 21, 1897, at Worcester, Mass., Tincler met the new professional, Tommy Conneff. Tincler's wicked pace of 61, 2:04 1/2, and 3:08 crushed Conneff and Tincler coasted home in 4:15 1/5. He won again from Conneff in 4:17. He also beat Fred Bacon in 4:16 2/5 and P. Carroll in 4:17.

Tincler's remarkable ability was praised by U.S. Olympic coach Lawson Robertson:

"He had a faultless style of running and he was never extended in any of his races. While in this country he ran two tense (practice) heats at the mile distance—one in four minutes and nine seconds and one in four minutes and eight seconds."

FASTEST MILERS OF THE 19th CENTURY

4:12-3/4	Walter George, Eng. (Pro)	London	23 Aug 1886
4:15-1/5	George Tincler, Ire. (Pro)	Worcester, Ms.	28 Aug 1897
4:15-3/5	Thomas Conneff, USA	New York	30 Aug 1895
4:16-1/5	Wm. Cummings, Scot. (Pro)	Preston	14 May 1881
4:17	Frederick Bacon, Eng.	London	6 Jul 1895
4:17-1/5	Hugh Welsh, Scot.	London	2 Jul 1898
4:17-1/4	Wm. Lang, Eng. (Pro)	Manchester	19 Aug 1865
4:17-1/4	Wm. Richards, Eng. (Pro)	Manchester	19 Aug 1865
4:18-2/5	W.G. George (amateur)	Birmingham	21 Jun 1884
4:18-1/2 e	Wm. Snook, Eng.	Birmingham	21 Jun 1884
4:19-1/5	Harold Wade, Eng.	London	2 Jul 1892
4:19-1/2	Wm. Duddle, Eng. (Pro)	Manchester	20 Dec 1880
4:19-3/5e	Wm. Lutyens, Eng.	London	6 Jul 1895

THE 1500 METER RUN

This distance—199.57 yards short of a mile—was adopted on the European continent as a standard race, probably by the French who favored the metric system of measurement.

The first important race at 1500 meters was the French Championship in 1888. The earliest record holders were J. Borel, who ran 4:24 3/5 in 1892, F. Meiers, 4:21 in 1893, and F. Bourdier, 4:19 4/5 in 1895, poor times, indeed.

Michel Soalhat of France lowered the record to 4:16 4/5 on May 26, 1895, on Paris' Croix-Catelan track, which was to be the site of the 1900 Olympics. On June 28, 1896, after winning the bronze medal at the first Olympics, Lermusiaux gathered further honors with a world record 4:10-2/5, still much inferior to times for the mile distance.

The only other beginnings at this distance by the end of the 19th century were two weak national records set in 1898: Edvard Johansson of Sweden, 4:21-2/5, and Franz Dühne of Germany, 4:26-1/5.

II

Rise of the amateurs

Professional pedestrianism faded and the amateurs made slow progress at the beginning of the twentieth century, for the early Olympic Games were little more than a good idea and foot racing was still confined mostly to the English-speaking nations. For a decade, progress was slow or non-existent, but then the inevitable happened: The basic human interest in foot racing welled up again and the amateur milers became as exciting as their predecessors . . . and, eventually, they became faster.

1900 OLYMPICS

Like the first, this second Olympic 1500 is memorable only because it is part of Olympic history. Only nine men ran and the race was notable for those who were absent. Welsh of Scotland had retired. The U.S. champion, Orton, was busy winning the steeplechase. John Cregan of Princeton and Alex Grant of the New York A.C. (formerly of Canada) were in Paris for the Olympics but they withdrew from the 1500 because it was run on Sunday. Cregan had won the IC4A mile three times and the AAU mile in 1897 and 1898. Grant won the AAU mile in 1899. He won the indoor AAU 2-mile in 1899 and 1900.

France's favorite, running at home, was Henri Deloge. He ran away from everybody except Charles Bennett, who had won the British AAA mile championship a week before in 4:28-1/5. Bennett outkicked Deloge by two yards in 4:06-1/5, disappointing the Paris crowd. Well back in third place was John Bray, who had finished second to Cregan in the IC4A.

1902

BRITISH RECORD

In the 1902 AAA Championships at Stamford Bridge on July 5, 23-year-old Alfred Shrubb set an ambitious pace of 60-1/5 and 2:06-2/5 but he failed to finish. The race became a close battle through 3:14 between Lt. Henry Hawtrey, A.E. Barker, and 28-year-old Joe Binks, who took only one workout per week—half an hour of repeats—and raced almost every week. In an exciting finish, Binks came from behind in the homestretch to win by two yards in 4:16-4/5, a British record and second best amateur mile ever run. With Hawtrey's time estimated at 4:17 and Barker's at 4:19-1/5, a total of ten amateurs had now run under 4:20.

1904 OLYMPICS

The Olympic Games had still not caught the public's fancy. Held in St. Louis in September, 1904, they were called the Louisiana Purchase Exposition revival of the Olympic games, and the New York Athletic Club outscored the Chicago AA for the team title. Few athletes were interested enough to cross the Atlantic, and none of the good British milers appeared for the 1500 meters.

Absent were Henry Gregson, who ran 4:19-4/5 at Cambridge on March 14, 1903, and Alfred Shrubb, who emerged as a great distance runner in 1903, winning the AAA title from Joe Binks in 4:24, and again in 1904 with 4:22. Even Alex Grant was missing, although he was good enough to win the AAU mile championships in 1901, 1902, and 1903.

Only nine men ran, before a capacity crowd, and Chicago AA runners dominated the race. The gold medal was won by James Lightbody, who had won the Olympic 800 meters in 1:56.0 two days earlier. Lightbody collected a world record for 1500 meters in 4:05-2/5 although it was no better than a mile in 4:25.7. He had earlier won the 2500-meter steeplechase.

1906 OLYMPICS

Dissatisfaction with participation in the 1904 Olympics led to an unofficial Olympics at the Panathenaic Stadium, Athens, in April of 1906. The enthusiastic Greeks had no idea their Olympics was unofficial, for King George and royalty attended, 100,000 people crowded the stadium and hills above it, athletes came from 19 nations, and official reports and newspaper accounts made no mention that it was all unofficial. In fact, it was regarded as far more successful than the three previous Olympic Games.

There were 20 competitors in the 1500, but unfortunately many of the best British runners were absent: C.C. Henderson-

Hamilton, who won the 1905 Oxford-Cambridge Sports in 4:17-4/5 over A.R. Welsh (4:19-2/5), and George Butterfield, who won AAA titles in 1905 and 1906, the latter in 4:18-2/5.

The best British miler present at Athens was John McGough of Scotland, who had finished four steps behind Butterfield in an estimated 4:19-1/5 and set a Scottish record of 4:21-3/5 later in 1906. The 1904 Olympic champion, James Lightbody, had won both the 880 and mile in the 1905 AAU, and he had qualified here in the 800 and in the first round of the 400.

Entering the last lap of the 1500, the leader was George Bonhag of the U.S.A. who placed fourth in the Olympic 5-mile and won the 1500-meter walk. He was followed by G.A. Wheatley, a 4:23 miler from Australia. Lightbody was waiting patiently in fourth place and McGough was seventh.

Down the long homestretch, Lightbody's speed was too much for the others, who strung out behind him, disheartened, with several yards between runners. Lightbody's 4:12 was reasonably fair on the poor track. McGough was second, Kr. Hellström of Sweden third, and Wheatley fourth. The next day, Lightbody suffered defeat in the 800 meters by two feet.

AAU FIASCO

The 1908 AAU was held on the New York AC's five-lap track on Travers Island. An official rang the bell by mistake after three laps, and some runners stopped after one more lap. But the IC4A 2-mile champion, Harold L. Trube, one of the first of Cornell's great stable of runners, finished correctly in 4:16-4/5.[1] Officials called for a rerun an hour later, and again Trube won. But the same mistake was made again! Trube won the second rerun the following Wednesday in 4:25, which became the official time. Not only was Trube forced to win three races for one championship, but his time, equal to Binks' second-best ever, was not made official.

1908 OLYMPICS

The 1908 Olympics in London were the first truly international Games, but a vicious method of qualifying for the finals made the competition fierce. Eight heats were run in the 1500 meters and only *one* man qualified from each heat. To make matters worse, there was no seeding to separate outstanding runners.

In the very first heat, shortly after King Edward had declared the Games open, defending champion James Lightbody strode in calmly, as though two men qualified, and he was eliminated by teammate J.P. Sullivan.

The second heat was even worse, bringing together three of

[1] From eye-witness account by George P. Meade.

the best runners at London: J.P. Halstead, who had run the second fastest 1500 in history . . . 4:01-1/5 at Philadelphia on June 6; George Butterfield, who had won his third straight AAA championship in 1907.

MEL SHEPPARD

Mel Sheppard was far better known as a half-miler. Reared on a farm in New Jersey, he had progressed through sprinting, football, Brown Prep, and cross-country. He set an interscholarship 2-mile record of 9:57.4 in 1905 at the age of 21.

A 5'8½", 165 pounder, he trained hard and raced often, indoors and out. He trained six days a week except for two days rest before a meet. His training consisted of one spirited run a day at successive distances of 440, 600, 700, 1000, 880, and either a fast quarter or two fast 300's. He won the AAU 880 in 1906, 1907, and 1908, and in 1908 he won the indoor AAU 600. He had little experience at the mile distance, but he was known as a great tactician.

In the second heat of the 1500 at London, Butterfield made the mistake of allowing a relatively slow pace, and Halstead was able to run away from him, but Sheppard stayed close and calmly edged Halstead in Olympic record time of 4:05.

In the third heat, Norman Hallows, an English 3-miler, had a hard race against Emilio Lunghi of Italy, the unofficial world record holder at 1000 meters. Hallows won in 4:03-2/5. Lunghi's 4:03-4/5 was faster than any other runner in the qualifying rounds and yet he was not allowed in the final.

Winner of the seventh heat was Harold Wilson, a dangerous 5'4", 115-pounder who set a world record for 1500 meters in 3:59-4/5 on May 30 and won the AAA mile in 4:20-1/5 on July 4 in this same stadium.

The Shepherd's Bush stadium had been filled for the opening ceremonies and the 1500 heats on July 13 in spite of the rain, but scattered showers on July 14 held the crowd to 10,000 for the final. Wilson and Hallows were favored to beat Sheppard.

Fairbairn-Crawford, who had won his heat in 4:09-1/5, set a fast early pace. E.V. Loney tried to take over, but the pace lagged. Then Hallows went into the lead while Wilson bided his time and Sheppard seemed reluctant to make his move.

Wilson started his finishing drive with 300 yards to go and led Hallows into the homestretch, with Sheppard fourth. Sheppard moved smoothly and with confidence. He accelerated remarkably and took the lead with only 15 yards left. He won in 4:03-2/5 to equal Hallows' Olympic record. Wilson was only 1/5 back and Hallows was third in 4:04.

An amusing footnote to this race appeared in the *New York Times.* It was revealed that Sheppard had been rejected as a New York policeman because of a bad heart. The secretary to the Police Commissioner was quoted: "Most athletes have weak hearts ... We don't want a man on the force whose heart might give way under a sudden strain."

JOHN PAUL JONES

Conneff's world amateur record of 4:15-3/5 grew older with few to threaten it. Harold Trube became the first man to run under 4:20 indoors when he ran 4:19-4/5 on February 13, 1909, but he never developed. Best bet seemed to be Wilton Paull of Penn, who won the IC4A in 4:17-4/5 as a sophomore in 1909, but he lost in the 1910 IC4A. When the 1911 IC4A was held, few fans were ready for John Paul Jones.

At Phillips Exeter, Jones could not make the track team until his last year and he showed little promise until his last race. He entered Cornell in the fall of 1909 in mechanical engineering. His father had died and so he worked his way through college, first by manual labor in a fraternity house and then by operating his own laundry agency.

A well-built, handsome youth, 5'10½" and 145 pounds, he was extraordinarily popular. He worked long hours at his studies, played baseball and tennis each summer, and ran only as a pastime. But he was an extremely graceful runner, he worked hard at it when he trained, and he had the most successful coach of the time. Jack Moakley put Jones through a full cross country season in the fall. During track season, Jones took several sprint starts each day and worked hard at one run of from 300 to 880 yards. Once a week he ran three miles with six hard 50-yard bursts.

He won the freshman intercollegiates easily, and in the fall of his sophomore year he won the IC4A cross country championship, quite an achievement for a runner with excellent half-mile speed and barely 20 years old. Still, nobody knew how good he really was.

In 1911 IC4A at Soldiers' Field in Cambridge, Mass., on May 27, attracted 12,000 spectators in near-perfect weather. Boyle of Penn led at the quarter in 59-2/5, followed by his teammate, Paull. Jones, hoping to help Cornell win the team title by doubling in the 880, hung back in fifth place.

Hanavan of Michigan led at the half in 2:08-1/5. Jones ran easily in third place, behind Paull, and he made no effort to move up as Paull took over at 1000 yards and Hanavan regained the lead for a full lap.

With 220 yards to go, Jones lengthened his beautiful stride and glided away from them. He won by ten yards as Hanavan beat

Paull by inches. Jones had made no effort to run his fastest, and yet his 4:15-2/5 was a world amateur record. The 4:17.5 estimate for Hanavan and Paull tied them for seventh on the all-time amateur list.

1912 OLYMPICS—THE GREATEST RACE EVER RUN

The 1912 Olympic Games at Stockholm produced the greatest mile or 1500 meter race ever run from the standpoint of exciting competition between fast runners. The top contenders were:

JOHN PAUL JONES had won the 880 in 1:54-4/5 to give Cornell the IC4A championship half an hour after his world record mile. After a pleasant summer of baseball and tennis, he won his second IC4A cross country championship, the first man ever to win twice. In the IC4A, he tied for first in a 4:20-3/5 mile but won the 880 in collegiate record time of 1:53-4/5. He had no desire to run in the Olympics and he stopped training after the IC4A on June 1. But he was talked into running for his country and barely made the ship, where, of course, he could not do much in the way of training.

MEL SHEPPARD came back a week after his Olympic 1500 meter victory in 1908 to win another gold medal in the 800 meters in world record time of 1:52.8. He won the indoor AAU 600 in 1909. In 1910, he added to his prestige with official world records for 600 yards in 1:10.8 and 1000 yards in 2:12.4. He won the AAU 880 in 1911 and 1912. But his only 1500 meter time of note came on May 26, 1912, when he ran a non-winning 4:02. On July 8, two days before the 1500-meter final, he lost a heart-breaker to Ted Meredith by the width of his body in the 800 meters. His time was 1:52.0.

A.N.S. JACKSON. Arnold Nugent Strode-Jackson was the English counterpart of J.P. Jones. Intelligent and likable, he ran only to win and he had the short career of a true amateur. He was a natural runner with a long stride and he preferred to run from behind, like Jones. The only indication he gave of his great ability came at the age of 22 in the Oxford-Cambridge Sports of March 23, 1912, when he won in 4:21-2/5.

NORMAN S. TABER. A promising runner from Providence, Rhode Island, who placed third in the IC4A mile for Brown in 1910, Taber stayed out in 1911. He placed sixth in the IC4A cross country, and in the spring of 1912, at 5'8½" and 145 pounds, he emerged as one of the country's best milers.

He won the New England intercollegiates in 4:25-2/5. Then he surprised everybody in the IC4A by running a dead heat with Jones in 4:20-3/5. A week later, he ran his fastest race in a 1500 trial for selection of the Olympic team, finishing only ten feet behind in a world-record race. Two months before his 21st birthday he was one of the leading favorites for Olympic honors.

1912

ABEL KIVIAT was at once the youngest of the new American stars but also the most experienced. A sturdy 5'8" 146-pounder, he won the Canadian Championship in 1909 when barely 17. His time of 4:23-1/5 stamped him as a runner with great potential. Instead of attending college, he ran full seasons for the Irish-American A.C. In 1910, he won the indoor Baxter Mile in 4:22-1/5 and ran 4:20-2/5 outdoors.

In 1911 he was remarkably successful for his age. Before he was 19, he won both the Baxter and Hunter miles. In the indoor AAU meet, he won both the 600 and 1000. On June 4 he ran 1500 meters in 4:03-2/5 to equal Sheppard's national record, and he won the AAU mile in 4:19-3/5.

His sensational 1912 season was run as a teen-ager except for the Olympics, for he became 20 on June 23, 16 days before the Olympic heats. He triumphed in the BaxterMile again with 4:22-1/5. There was no AAU indoor championship meet that year, and so he waited for spring. He wanted Wilson's 1500-meter world record.

On May 26, at Celtic Park on Long Island, N.Y., Kiviat met Olympic champion Sheppard and beat him without strain in 3:59-1/5, a new world record. A week later, on the same track, Kiviat lowered his record to 3:56-4/5.

Six days later, at Cambridge, June 8, Kiviat ran in the all-important Olympic Trials against Taber and Oscar Hedlund, who had tied the indoor mile record of 4:19-4/5 on February 22. About 20,000 people were there to cheer them on.

Hedlund led for 500 yards. Then Kiviat took the lead, passing the 880 in 2:03-3/5, ahead of Hedlund and Taber. Kiviat, wearing all-white, passed three-quarters in an excellent 3:09-1/5 and Taber moved to second.

Running at world-record pace, Kiviat held onto his lead over Taber's courageous challenge and won by ten feet with Hedlund 18 yards back. Kiviat's time was 3:55-4/5, again a world record, and equivalent to Jones's mile record.

But Kiviat was not satisfied. He struggled on past the official distance toward the mile tape. Because of his battle with Taber he had nothing left and the 120 yards took him a painful 19.8 seconds. Still, he missed Jones' amateur mile record by only 1/5 of a second.

With Jones out of training, Kiviat seemed definitely the best in the world, and the USA was expected to win the first three or four places in the Olympic 1500 a month away.

And, indeed, seven of the 14 qualifiers on July ninth were from the United States. The others included Jackson, his unfortunate teammate Philip Baker, who ran with a dislocated bone in his foot bound with surgical tape, Henri Arnaud of France, who ran 4:04-2/5 in 1911, Erwin von Sigel of Germany, and three good Swedes. They were Ernst Wide, who ran 4:02.8 in 1909 and 4:02.7 in 1910, Evert

1912

Björn, who ran 4:04.6 and 4:03.8 behind Wide, and John Zander, a promising young runner who shared January 31, 1890, as a birth date with Jackson.

For the final on Wednesday, July 10, many spectators could not get inside the crowded gray-violet stadium shaped like a covered horseshoe with two square watch towers at the open end. The 27,000 spectators sat in excellent weather and saw the greatest 1500 meter race any crowd had ever seen.

Arnaud set the pace, ahead of von Sigel and Jones. Kiviat, who had lost a few precious yards starting on the outside, was close to Jones, as was Taber. Jackson ran toward the rear of the large pack. On the second lap there was little change of interest, although Wide moved to 7th place.

At the bell, Kiviat took the lead, followed by Taber and Jones. The two-week sea voyage had not agreed with Kiviat and he had run the fastest heat yesterday (4:04.4), but he made a race of it.

He led around the curve and down the last backstretch. Jackson moved ahead of Sheppard, but the wily defending champion stayed on his heels. Wide, who was 15 meters behind at the bell, began to gain on the backstretch and the Swedish crowd went wild.

Around the last curve, Kiviat held onto his precarious lead. On his heels was Taber, followed by kickers Jackson, Jones, and Sheppard, with Wide closing on the five runners ahead. Taber made his move before they reached the homestretch and he was nearly even with Kiviat when they straightened out for the stretch run.

Jackson was threatening them with bounding strides. Jones, unable to make his usual break on the backstretch because of the faster pace and his lack of condition, swung wide for his final spring. Sheppard, out of his class at this distance and almost 29 years old, faded badly. Wide kept gaining on everybody.

Down the stretch they sprinted. Kiviat, short and almost bow-legged, held onto his tiny lead over Taber. Jackson's long strides became faster and he gained steadily. Jones also gained on the two leaders, and Wide too, was coming swiftly, to impassioned Swedish cheers.

Jackson caught the two leaders, and for 50 yards they ran abreast, with Jones straining close behind and Wide's desperate sprint gaining on them all. First it became evident that Wide could not catch them. Then Jones's hopes faded. But they were ten yards from the tape before the winner was obvious.

Then Jackson summoned that raging strength which seemed then to be the private property of British middle-distance runners. He almost leaped ahead to win by two yards, then fell into the arms of his friends. Kiviat and Taber were so close together it took the official camera to award Kiviat the silver medal.

Results: Jackson 3:56.8, Kiviat 3:56.9, Taber 3:56.9, Jones 3:57.2, Wide 3:57.6, Baker 4:01e, Zander 4:02e, Arnaud 4:02.2e. Thus, eight of the ten best 1500's of all time had been run in 1912.

James E. Sullivan, American Olympic Commissioner, said: "We did not think there was any man living who could break up our wonderful combination of Sheppard, Kiviat, Taber, and Jones." And Jackson, who did it, said, "I am very grateful and proud to have run with Kiviat, Jones, Taber, and Sheppard."

OLYMPIC POSTSCRIPTS...

... JACKSON. The Olympic champion ran 4:22-3/5 on February 28, 1914. Then his strangely sparce career was cut short by World War I, where he was badly wounded three times and eventually became an acting brigadier general.

... KIVIAT. The Olympic silver medalist won the AAU championship from James Powers at Pittsburgh on September 21 in the time of 4:18-3/5. A week later he won the Canadian championship in 4:20-3/5.

Indoors in 1913, Kiviat again won the 600 and 1000 double in the indoor AAU. On February 12, Hedlund lowered the world indoor mile record to 4:18-4/5, but three days later Kiviat had the best of it, winning his fourth consecutive Baxter Mile in 4:18-1/5. Physical disability kept him out of the outdoor season and seemed to cut short his promising career.

He came back in the fall to win the AAU cross-country title and in 1914 he won his indoor encounters, including the AAU 1000. He beat Powers in the outdoor AAU in 4:25-1/5. Kiviat's best time was 4:20-4/5 on October 3 in the Metropolitan AAU.

He never lived up to his promise as a teen-ager. In 1915 he was second in the indoor AAU 1000 and fourth in the outdoor mile. In October he was suspended for excess demands for expense money. His seven-year championship career thus ended when he was 23.

... JONES. After the Olympics, Jones won his third consecutive IC4A cross country championship. In 1913, he traveled to Ann Arbor, Michigan, to win a 4:19-4/5 mile indoors.

On May 31, in excellent condition, he was once more at Cambridge, the site of his world record in 1911. In his last IC4A championship, he was menaced by Olympic bronze medalist Norman Taber, who had run 4:19-4/5 against Syracuse on May 3 and 4:18-3/5 in the New England Intercollegiates a week ago on this same track.

But Jones was confident. He had beaten Taber by 150 yards in the IC4A cross country and he was close to world record time for the 880. Surely he could handle Taber at a mile.

1913

Taber, unkindly called a plodder by some, pushed the pace after laps of 61.8 and 2:09.3. Taber led at three-quarters in 3:16.1, but as the gun sounded, Jones launched into his famous drive.

Taber ran well on that last lap, but Jones simply ran away from him, gaining all the way. Taber finished in 4:16-2/5, a time bettered by only three amateurs, but Jones finished serenely graceful in 4:14-2/5, one full second under his own world record.

A short time later Jones lost his first IC4A 880, and this race ended his career. He graduated soon after, voted by his classmates "most popular", "most respected", "best all-round", and "man who did the most for his college." Because of his lack of interest in record breaking, it is almost certain he could have run much faster.

... TABER. After his defeat by Jones, Taber won the AAU championship in 4:26-2/5, then went to Oxford as a Rhodes Scholar. In April of 1914 he ran poorly for the Oxford 4-mile relay team, with Arnold Jackson, in the Penn Relays. Taber lost 22 yards to Louis Madeira, who had run 4:21-1/5 and 4:20-1/5 behind Taber in the last two IC4A championships. Taber's only excuse was that he was up late the night before while becoming engaged. He returned to the United States in the summer and placed fourth in the AAU mile.

During the 1915 season, Taber did something fairly rare among milers of those days. Nearing 24 years of age, he made an all-out effort. At the urging of his coach, Eddie O'Connor, he had trained hard for six months with his goal a new mile record, and by June he was in great shape.

On June 26 in the Eastern Trials for the AAU meet, Taber finished ahead of Kiviat in a 4:15-1/5 mile, second best of all amateur miles. Two weeks later, Taber won the Millrose AA mile in 4:17-3/5.

On Friday, July 16, he traveled by train to Cambridge with his fiancée to make a special attempt on the mile record. He wanted Jones' amateur record, but his real target was George's professional record of 4:12¾ which had stood for almost 30 years as the best mile ever run.

The Harvard track was in extremely fast condition and the weather was perfect. Five expert timers were on hand for the record attempt. Three men were given handicaps to enable them to pace Taber to the best advantage. J.M Burke was given 355 yards, D.S. Mahoney 120, and J.W. Ryan ten yards.

Ryan set an ambitious pace for the first lap, carrying Taber through in 58 seconds. Then Taber followed Mahoney, who had loafed through the first lap. Taber was satisfied with a half in 2:05 and slowed to 3:13 for three quarters.

Burke was in the right place to coax Taber on the last lap and the crowd was worked up, sensing a record. Taber increased the pace, driving faster than ever before in his fastest race. He passed 1500 meters in an unofficial 3:55, faster than the world record, and the few watch holders knew Jones's amateur record was doomed. Taber shot around Burke into the homestretch. He slowed slightly, but his form held to the finish. The timers huddled, consulting their watches, while coach O'Connor fidgeted anxiously. Then it was official: 4:12-3/5. Taber had bettered George's record by 0.15 second. He was the fastest miler in history.

The special program also included a 440 intermediate hurdle race in which William Meanix ran 54-3/5, better than the world record. Then a 100-yard-dash was run in 10.2, after which Taber wanted to try for the 880 record, even though his fastest time was 1:55-3/5. He was talked out of the attempt, however.

Objections were raised about the record because it was a paced attempt rather than a race, but it gained approval by the IAAF.

Taber apparently rested on his laurels, for when the AAU meet was run in San Francisco a month later he was outkicked in a 4:23-1/5 mile after setting the pace all the way.

THIRD FASTEST AMATEUR

L. Vere Windnagle was a talented half-miler from Portland, Oregon, where he ran 1:56.8 in high school. In the Pacific Coast Interscholastics at Berkeley, California, April 27, 1912, he won the mile in 4:31.0. He ran at the University of Oregon but later transferred to Cornell and was a promising second in the 1915 IC4A mile.

On May 13, 1916, Windnagle met Ted Meredith in the dual meet with Penn. In a magnificent race, Windnagle equalled Meredith's world 880 record of 1:52.5, but Meredith won in 1:52.2.

Two weeks later, in the IC4A meet at Cambridge, Windnagle won the mile in 4:15.0, third best amateur time ever run. But like Jones, who held the Cornell record at 4:14.4, Windnagle retired.

THE WAR YEARS

During World War I, competitive standards dropped except for Sweden and the United States. Each had one outstanding miler who dominated throughout the war—Zander for Sweden and Ray for the U.S.

JOHN ZANDER

Seventh in the 1912 Olympics with a time of 4:02, Zander was still dominated by his countryman Ernst Wide in 1913, but the tall, lean Swede went to London and won the AAA championship in 4:25-4/5. Although primarily a longer distance runner, he ran 1000 meters in 2:34.4, an unratified world record.

In the 1914 Baltic Games, Zander won the 5000 and the 3000 meter team race. In 1915 he was acclaimed for another world record, 2000 meters in 5:37.2. In the 1916 Swedish Games he won the 1500, 3000, and 5000 and ran a steeplechase in 9:58.4. In the Fall he ran an interesting 1000 meters against Olympic 800-meter champion Ted Meredith. He beat Meredith without trouble, but he was edged at the tape by Anatole Bolin. Both were timed in 2:31.2, which equalled the unofficial world record.

In 1917, the ambitious Zander set world records for 2000 meters (5:31.0) and 3000 (8:35.7), but his most notable run was at 1500 meters at the Stockholm Championships on August 5.

He had run a mile in 4:18.6 on July 7 and now he wanted Kiviat's world record for 1500 meters. A large crowd in the Olympic "Stadion" cheered loudly as Zander ran almost alone, for his opponents could not keep up.

His first lap of the 385-meter track was 57-flat, which must have brought him past 400 meters in about 59.5. At two laps, his 1:57.5 stirred up the crowd. He had no more opposition when he passed 800 meters in an estimated 2:02.5, for he was more than a second faster than Kiviat's world-record pace. Zander feared he was going too fast. "Believe it or not, my legs began to go numb after the first lap."

Coming into the homestretch with more than a lap to go, Zander dropped his arms at full length for a few strides and the crowd was afraid he was giving up, but he returned to full action and completed three laps in 2:59.7. His estimated time for 1200 meters was 3:07.5, clearly faster than Kiviat had run.

Now it was a battle to stay ahead of his invisible opponent. The sympathetic crowd pleaded and cheered as he forced himself around the track. His pace was slowing. He was running slower than at any time during the race, but Kiviat had slowed, too, and Zander had enough endurance to hang on. The crowd whooped with relief and delight when he crossed the finish line in 3:54.7, a new world record.

Zander's time was as good as a mile in 4:14.2, making him second only to Taber as an amateur 1500/mile runner. Most remarkable of all, it was the first record made without competition, either real or paced.

Two weeks later, he won a fine double at the Swedish Championships. His 14:59.6 was a Swedish 5000 record, and he ran 3:57.6 for the 1500. No other runner had broken four minutes since the 1912 Olympics.

In 1918, Zander was better than ever. He set Swedish records for two miles (9:17.2) and 5000 (14:57.5) and world records for 2000 (5:30.4) and 3000 (8:34.8 and 8:33.1). On July 7 he won his fourth straight Dickson Cup mile. This is the most famous mile race outside the English-speaking countries, started in 1891 by James F. Dickson. Ernst Wide had won the Cup six years in a row, with a best time of 4:21-3/5, in 1910. Zander won in 1918 in 4:16.8,which equalled Joe Binks's time as the fastest mile ever run in Europe. His last good 1500 came on August 22, when he hit the tape in 3:58.0. Nearing 29 years of age, he retired.

JOIE RAY

Meanwhile, back in the States, a short, muscular, crew-cut distance runner from Illinois was moving up the ladder of all-time great milers. "Chesty" Joie Ray was only 5'5" tall, and when he began as a 5-miler, in 1912 at the age of 18, he weighed only 118 pounds, but he "bulked up" to 127 before he was through.

He was second to the great Hannes Kolehmainen in the 1913 AAU 5-mile. In 1914 he tried the mile for the first time, winning the Central AAU in 4:21. In the AAU Championships at Baltimore in September, he lost to Kiviat and Powers, but he was good enough to beat Taber for third.

He now had a reputation as a miler, but he still ran other distances. Indoors in 1915, he won the Central AAU in 4:22-1/5, and placed third in the AAU 2-mile. After a surprising loss in a 4:21-1/5 mile at the outdoor Central AAU, he won the western tryouts for the AAU in 4:16-2/5. He was now fifth fastest amateur miler of all time:

4:12.6	Taber	1915
4:14.4	Jones	1913
4:15.6	Conneff	1895
4:15.6	Kiviat	1912
4:16.4	Ray	1915
4:16.8	Binks	1902

Even so, it was a shock when he outkicked new world-record holder Taber in the 1915 AAU at San Francisco to win his first championship, in 4:23-1/5.

Ray had a bad year in 1916, losing three mile races indoors and one out. He turned to the 5-mile in the AAU and won.

In 1917, Ray came back strong, indoors. He set an indoor record of 6:46.6 in the Wanamaker 1½-mile. He set an indoor record of 9:11.4 for the 2-mile, only 1.8 seconds off Shrubb's world record. He lost only the AAU 1000 yards, to Overton's record 2:14.

Outdoors, Ray had a poor record when he went to San Francisco on September 1 to run in the AAU against Eddie Fall of Oberlin, who was regarded as the next great miler.

1918

Fall ran 4:15-4/5 at Chicago on June 9 and he won the Central AAU in 4.16, both faster than Ray's best. Fall was favored, but Ray beat him in 4:18-2/5 and came back in the 880 to place third behind Mike Devaney and John Overton, who had run 4:16.0 indoors.

In 1918, Ray was so good he lost only in 880 races. In the indoor AAU he tied the 1000-yard record of 2:14. Four days later he beat Devaney and Fall in an indoor 3:04.8 for three-quarters, the best time on record. He beat Fall in a 4:20 indoor mile and after Fall joined the army, Ray won the outdoor AAU in 4:20.0 at Great Lakes, Illinois. He placed second in the 880.

In 1919, Ray was great wearing a thick mustache, he won the indoor AAU 1000, and defeated Fall with a world indoor record mile of 4:14-3/5, lowered the indoor 1000 record to 2:13.4, and beat Fall twice more in outdoor miles. In the AAU at Philadelphia on September 13, Fall ran a 4:15.0 mile, but the confident little Ray beat him handily with 4:14-2/5, then came back to win the 880 title in 1:56.0.

Ray was now tied with Jones as the second fastest amateur of all time. Six days later he ran 4:15-3/5 and the next week he ran three-quarters in 3:04-1/5.

In 1920, hoping to reach his peak for the Olympic Games, Ray ran only to win indoors. He won another AAU 1000-yard title and set an indoor 1500-meter record of 3:57.0. Outdoors, he circled four laps at the midwest Olympic Tryouts in 4:16.0 and he triumphed for the fifth time in the AAU, with 4:16-1/5. No miler in history had run so many fast times. He was ready for the Olympics.

ALBERT HILL

Hill was born March 24, 1889, and so his career unfortunately spanned World War I. He was successful in cross country in 1907, and he won the British AAA 4-mile championship in 1910. In 1914, he placed second in the AAA 880, three yards behind Homer Baker's meet record 1:54-2/5. Then came the war. He fought with the Royal Flying Corps and had no athletic hopes again until 1919. Most men, at the age of 30, would never dream of renewing a career which had been little more than promising, but Hill was a rare man.

He sought coaching from Sam Mussabini, England's most famous coach. In an amazing comeback on July 5 during the one-day AAA Championships, he won the 880 in 1:55-1/5 and defeated Sweden's 4:00.1 1500-meter runner, Sven Lundgren, in a 4:21-1/5 mile.

This feat would have been remarkable enough, considering his age, but Hill was only beginning. On August 9, in Glasgow, he surprised the experts with 4:16-4/5 to tie the British and European records.

In 1920, Hill prepared for the Olympics by concentrating on speed work and pace running. He did not leave his best race on the track in early, unimportant meets. Even in the AAA Championships he ran only the 880, where he lost narrowly in 1:55-4/5 to Bevil Rudd, a Rhodes Scholar from South Africa. On August 17 at Antwerp, Hill became, amazingly, the Olympic 800-meter champion, defeating Earl Eby and Rudd in 1:53-2/5 on a slow track. The next day he qualified for the 1500 meter final.

1920 OLYMPICS

The British, as usual, were quietly confident of Hill. The Americans thought Ray would win, but disaster struck and Joie pulled a tendon in the calf of his right leg ten days before the Olympics. He could do little training, but he won his heat. John Zander had been talked into a comeback for the Olympics, but a fractured rib hurt his training. He, too, qualified for the final, however.

The fastest time in the heats was by Václav Vohralik of Czechoslovakia, who ran 4:02-2/5. Other finalists on that rainy August 19 included Sven Lundgren of Sweden, who ran 3:59.3 on August 1, and Philip Baker, the courageous sixth placer from 1912, and Larry Shields, a sophomore from Penn State who had won the IC4A in 4:22-2/5 and placed third in the AAU.

The track was slow and wet, but Ray boldly set the pace, followed by Vohralik. Zander dropped out about half way through the race. Ray led all the way to the bell, but around the curve, Hill and Baker went past.

Shields tried to pass on the backstretch as the bitterly disappointed Ray faded, Baker fought Shields off, and the fair-haired Hill had clear running room all the way to the tape. He pulled away in the last few yards and won in the slow time of 4:01-4/5. Baker, who had placed fifth in the IC4A for Haverford in 1907 at the age of 17½, was a good second in 4:02-2/5. Shields finished third in 4:03-1/5, Vohralik fourth, Lundgren next and Ray eighth.

Jack Moakley, coach of the U.S. team, said, "I regard Albert Hill as the wonder man of the meeting . . . he scalped young American athletes in two events . . . He is a grand chap."

SECOND FASTEST AMATEUR

The 1921 AAA Championships brought together 32-year-old Albert Hill, the double Olympic champion, and a prodigy of remarkable promise, Hyla (Henry) B. Stallard, barely 20 on April 28.

Stallard had run well in the United States in 1920 at the Penn Relays, where his combined Oxford-Cambridge team set a world

1921

record in the 4 x 880 relay, and he won the mile in the two duals, vs. Yale and Harvard and vs. Princeton and Cornell. He won the mile for Cambridge in both the 1920 and 1921 meets against Oxford.

He had excellent speed and only a broken bone in his foot kept him from running in the 1920 Olympics.

Hill began preparing for this AAA race right after the Olympics, and his mentor was none other than the great old pro, Walter George. Hill's last trial was three-quarters in 3:05-4/5.

The track at Stamford Bridge on July 2 was dry and dusty, and 44 competitors lined up a dangerous 20 yards from the first curve. When the gun sounded, Hill sprinted to avoid trouble and Stallard, from outside, did the same.

Hill led in 59-3/5, with two other runners contending. At the half, in 2:04, only Stallard challenged Hill, and as the pace slowed to 3:11-1/5, Stallard stayed menacingly on Hill's shoulder.

At the start of the backstretch, Stallard burst into sprint action and gained a slight lead. But Hill was no novice, and he, too, had half-mile speed and experience. His only hope was to stay ahead, and he managed to increase his speed enough to keep Stallard from cutting in to the lead before the last curve.

With the crowd aboil, they raced around the turn side by side, neither giving an inch but the 20-year-old was running three yards extra. In the homestretch, Hill swung out from the curb and Stallard tried to drop back and go inside him. This advantage was all the wily Hill needed, and he held it all the way to the tape.

His time was a new British record of 4:13-4/5, the second fastest amateur mile ever run, while Stallard's 4:14-1/5 moved him ahead of Jones and Ray into third place.

ALL TIME AMATEUR LISTS AT THE END OF 1919

1,500m:
(+ during mile)

Time	Athlete		Place	Date	
3:54.7	John Zander (Sweden)	(1)	Stockholm	5 Aug	1917
3:55-4/5+	Abel Kiviat (USA)	(1)	Cambridge, Mass.	8 Jun	1912
3:56-2/5+e	Norman Taber (USA)	(2)	Cambridge, Mass.	8 Jun	1912
3:56.8	Arnold Strode-Jackson (GB)	(1)	Stockholm	10 Jul	1912
3:57.2	John Paul Jones (USA)	(4)	Stockholm	10 Jul	1912
3:57.6	Ernst Wide (Sweden)	(5)	Stockholm	10 Jul	1912
3:59-4/5	Harold Wilson (GB)	(1)	London	30 May	1908

MILE:

Time	Athlete		Place	Date	
4:12-3/5	Norman Taber (USA)	(1)	Cambridge, Mass.	16 Jul	1915
4:14-2/5	John Paul Jones (USA)	(1)	Cambridge, Mass.	31 May	1913
4:14-2/5	Joie Ray (USA)	(1)	Philadelphia	13 Sep	1919
4:15.0	Vere Windnagle (USA)	(1)	Cambridge, Mass.	27 May	1916
4:15.0	Eddie Fall (USA)	(2)	Philadelphia	13 Sep	1919
4:15-3/5	Thomas Conneff (USA)	(1)	New York	28 Aug	1895
4:15-3/5	Abel Kiviat (USA)	(1)	Cambridge, Mass.	8 Jun	1912
4:16-4/5	Joe Binks (GB)	(1)	London	5 Jul	1902
4:16.8	John Zander (Sweden)	(1)	Stockholm	7 Jul	1918
4:16-4/5	Albert Hill (GB)	(1)	Glasgow	9 Aug	1919
4:17.0	Frederick Bacon (GB)	(1)	London	6 Jul	1895
4:17.0e	Henry Hawtrey (GB)	(2)	London	5 Jul	1902
4:17-1/5	Hugh Welsh (GB)	(1)	London	2 Jul	1898

1921

Time	Name		Pos	Location	Date	Year
4:17-4/5	C.C. Henderson-Hamilton (GB)		(1)	London	31 Mar	1905
4:17-4/5	Wilton Paull (USA)		(1)	Cambridge, Mass.	29 May	1909
4:18-2/5	Walter George (GB)		(1)	Birmingham	21 Jun	1884
4:18-2/5	George Butterfield (GB)		(1)	London	7 Jul	1906
4:18-2/5	James Powers (USA)		(1)	Masterton, N.Z.	5 Mar	1914
4:18-3/5e	William Snook (GB)		(2)	Birmingham	21 Jun	1884

Indoors:

Time	Name		Pos	Location	Date	Year
4:14-3/5	Joie Ray (USA)		(1)	Chicago	12 Apr	1919
4:16.0	John Overton (USA)		(1)	Philadelphia	10 Mar	1917
4:18-1/5	Abel Kiviat (USA)		(1)	New York	15 Feb	1913
4:18-4/5	Oscar Hedlund (USA)		(1)	New York	12 Feb	1913

1920
MILE:

Time	Name		Pos	Location	Date
4:16.0	Joie Ray (USA)		(1)	Chicago	26 Jun
4:21.0	William Curtis (USA)		(1)	New York	12 Jun
4:22.0	Harold Cutbill (USA)		(1)	Philadelphia	26 Jun
4:22-2/5	Larry Shields (USA)		(1)	Philadelphia	29 May
4:23.0	Armand Burtin (France)		(1)	London	3 Jul
4:23-2/5	Ray Watson (USA)		(1)	Ames, Iowa	29 May
4:23-4/5	Grant Swan (USA)		(1)	Pasadena	26 Jun
4:24.0	James Connolly (USA)		(1)	Boston	20 Jun

1,500m:

Time	Name		Pos	Location	Date
3:59.3	Sven Lundgren (Sweden)		(1)	Stockholm	1 Aug
4:01-4/5	Albert Hill (GB)		(1)	Antwerp	19 Aug
4:02-2/5	Joseph Guillemot (France)		(1)	Lyon	22 Jun
4:02-2/5	Václav Vohralik (Czechosl.)		(1)h	Antwerp	18 Aug
4:02-2/5	Philip Baker (GB)		(2)	Antwerp	19 Aug
4:03-1/5	Larry Shields (USA)		(3)	Antwerp	19 Aug
4:03-4/5	Armand Burtin (France)		(1)	Paris	18 Jul

Indoors:

Time	Name		Pos	Location	Date
3:57.0	Joie Ray (USA)		(1)	New York	30 May

1921
MILE:

Time	Name		Pos	Location	Date
4:13-4/5	Albert Hill (GB)	AAA	(1)	London	2 Jul
4:13.9	Paavo Nurmi (Finland)		(1)	Stockholm	10 Jul
4:14-1/5	Henry Stallard (GB)		(2)	London	2 Jul
4:14-4/5	Joie Ray (USA)		(1)	Berkeley, Cal.	9 Jul
4:15.0	Ray		(1)	Toronto	10 Sep
4:15-3/5	Ray		(1)	Dodge City	Sep
4:16-4/5	Ray	AAU	(1)	Pasadena, Cal.	4 Jul
4:17.0	Hill		(1)	London	14 May
4:17-1/5	Dennis O'Connell (USA)		(1)	Boston	21 May
4:17-1/5	James Connolly (USA)	IC4A	(1)	Cambridge, Mass.	28 May
4:18.0e	Lucien Duquesne (France)		(3)	London	2 Jul

1,500:
(+ during mile)

Time	Name		Pos	Location	Date
3:55.3/5+	Joie Ray (USA)		(1)	Dodge City	8 Sep
3:59.1+	Paavo Nurmi (Finland)		(1)	Stockholm	10 Jul
4:01-1/5	Sven Lundgren (Sweden)		(1)	Vienna	8 Sep
4:01.3	Nestori Järvelä (Finland)		(1)	Kotka	21 Aug
4:01-2/5	Friedrich-Franz Köpke (Ger)		(2)	Vienna	6 Sep
4:01-3/5	Václav Vohralik (Czech.)		(1)	Copenhagen	26 Jun
4:02.6	Matti Tala (Finland)		(2)	Kotka	21 Aug
4:03-2/5	Henry Stallard (GB)		(1)	Colombes	11 Sep
4:04.1	Emil Bedarff (Germany)		(1)	Berlin	3 Jul
4:04.4	Edvin Wide (Sweden)		(1)	Copenhagen	3 Jul

III

Paavo Nurmi

Imagine a nine-year-old boy peeping wistfully through a hole in a fence in Turku, Finland, watching a boys' club track meet in 1906 and deciding he wanted to be a runner. Imagine this unusual desire combined with great natural ability and you have Paavo Nurmi, the greatest distance runner of his time . . . or of any time before him.

Nurmi was not a specialist at 1500 meters or the mile. He ran only a few such races, but even without specifically training for the distance he produced remarkable results and so he must be regarded as a major miler.

At the age of ten and now a member of the club, he is supposed to have run 1500 meters in a "round-the-houses" event in 5:43, an astonishing time. He is supposed to have improved to an almost unbelievable 5:02 at 11 years. Then tragedy struck a blow which would have stopped an ordinary boy. His father died when Paavo was 12. The family of six had to live in one room, and Paavo had to give up the boys' club and go to work.

He worked as an errand boy, pushing a cart. There are hills in Turku, Finland, and pushing a loaded cart up a hill is no easy work. Nurmi credits that work for building some of the strength in his legs.

The grind of poverty shaped Nurmi's future in other ways. He grew into a grave, unsmiling, silent man who fought his battles with extreme mental and physical discipline. For example, he was a vegetarian not because he believed in it especially, but because his family could not afford meat.

At the 1912 Olympics in nearby Sweden, Hannes Kolehmainen won four races to become the hero of Finland and 15-year-old Paavo's idol. This inspiration led Nurmi to begin training again . . . and he joined another club. "All my spare time was used in walking through the woods or in running." His 1500-meter times improved. He ran 4:37.8 in 1915, at the age of 18, but he liked longer races. The year before he won the junior nationals at 3000 meters. His 1500 time, as a result, was an unpromising 4:29 in 1918 at 21 years of age. Other men had run much faster than that for a mile at the same age.

That year he was a mechanic in the army and he was so dedicated that he rose at 5:30 a.m. to walk the icy roads. In the afternoon, he ran. On the Russian front, later that year, he won two long races and he began to attract attention.

In 1920, he arrived as a distance runner. Although his 1500-meter time improved to 4:05.5, he set a Finnish record for the 3000 and began to rival Kolehmainen as a national hero at the Antwerp Olympics, where he barely lost in the 5000, then won gold medals in the 10,000, the cross country, and the 3000 team race.

He was not satisfied, however. His training had consisted of a fast morning walk for one hour with a few spurts of running. In the afternoon, during the months of April through September, he had done long, slow running. Now he felt the need for pace training.

He bought a stopwatch and carried it in his right hand to check his time at certain posts along the road. He continued to try for a long, smooth stride, heel touching first, his head erect and his elbows flying high and wide.

In 1921, now 24 years old, he improved some more. On June 22 he ran the fastest 10,000 meters ever run. With no speed training at all, he placed second in the Finnish 800 meters. On July 10, only eight days after the fast race between Hill and Stallard, Nurmi ran in the Dickson Cup in Stockholm. If there had been a longer race he would probably have won it instead, but he opened a few eyes when he ran 4:13.9, missing the new European record by less than one stride.

And yet, in 1922, Nurmi still preferred his longer races. He won the AAA 4-mile and steeplechase. Starting on August 27, he jolted the track world with three world records on consecutive weekends, at 3000, 2000, and 5000 meters. Five days after his 5000, he ran 1500 meters in a comfortable 3:59.8, his only major effort of the year at this distance.

In 1923, a Swede named Edvin Wide developed into a great runner, so good, in fact, that Swedes thought he could beat Nurmi, and a challenge was issued. Nurmi was willing, and his Finnish supporters expected him to ask for a race at 10,000 meters, a safe distance for him. But Nurmi surprised them by asking for Wide's best distance—one mile. The race was scheduled for August 23 in Stockholm. Early in August, Nurmi ran 1500 in 3:55.6, less than a second from Zander's world record. He was pleased with his condition.

EDVIN WIDE

No relation to Ernst Wide of the 1912 Olympics, Edvin was born in Kimito, Finland, February 22, 1896, part of the 7% of Swedish-language people living in Finland. He moved to Sweden in 1918 and became a Swedish citizen, but he would never run for Sweden in the important dual meet against Finland.

In sharp contrast to Kiviat or fast milers who developed in college by the time they were 21 or 22 years old, Wide made amazingly little progress at all until he was 24 years old. A 5'7", 138-pounder, he ran in the 1920 Olympics then, placing 15th in the 3000 team race. In 1921 he ran 1500 meters in a mediocre 4:04.4 and in 1922 he ran 4-flat.

It was only in 1923 that Wide developed into an interesting runner. The 27-year-old school teacher ran successive 1500's in 4:00.8, 3:59.5, and 3:58.1. Then, at Göteborg in July he ran 3:57.0 with a last lap in 59.0 to demoralize Otto Peltzer of Germany. After another 1500 in 3:58.4, he improved even more in the Swedish Championships on August 18: he set a new Swedish record of 14:44.1 for 5000 meters and the next day he won an easy 1500 in 3:56.7. He was eager for the clash with Nurmi four days later.

NURMI VS WIDE

The Swedes were confident of victory. One newspaper wrote: "People will go to the Stadium to see Nurmi break Taber's world record—and see Wide beat Nurmi!"

When a Swedish voice called, "Ready," Nurmi moved purposefully from the dim old dressing room under the Olympic stadium with his companions, including Finnish Olympic coach Jaakko Mikkola and Hannes Kolehmainen. They went through a small corridor to the track, all as serious and almost grim as Nurmi himself.

Wide came out a little later and the crowd of 18,000 welcomed him loudly. Preliminaries were brief and the two runners took their marks, with Wide on the pole. For a moment the Olympic stadium was tensely quiet.

Then the gun sounded and Wide led around the first curve, where the crowd in the standing section cheered him loudly. Wide led all the way around the 385-meter track with Nurmi content to follow close behind.

1923

Wide passed the first 440 in 60.1 with Nurmi in 60.3. Then Nurmi took the lead, calmly smooth, and Wide stuck close to his heels, his form slightly more jerky.

On the backstretch of the second lap, Wide moved alongside Nurmi, but the stolid Finn would not let him pass. Again, before the curve, Wide tried to pass, encouraged by thousands of pleading Swedes, but Nurmi held onto his narrow lead.

Coming down the homestretch for the second time, Wide was on Nurmi's shoulder and the crowd was loud with anticipation. Nurmi passed the 880 in 2:03.2, faster than most high-quality mile paces to that time and one tenth lead of his rival.

Now was the time when most runners would have eased up for a quarter in 67 or 68 seconds, but Nurmi kept the pressure on. Nobody in the crowd could detect any slowing of the pace. Wide was in trouble now, and a tiny gap was beginning to show. The crowd begged him in desperation, but he could not hold Nurmi's relentless pace.

At three-quarters, Nurmi led in 3:06.7 to 3:07.3 for Wide. A record seemed certain, unless both runners tied up. The crowd, still hoping against hope, cheered Wide so loudly the bell could barely be heard. Wide fought desperately around the turn past his standing rooters. Then, in the backstretch, Nurmi turned his head and looked back at Wide.

Satisfied, the cool Finn continued his steady run. He made no change in his stride, but the gap began to widen. Around the last turn to the 1500 meters mark, Nurmi led by eight yards. His time was 3:53.0 to Wide's 3:54.2, remarkably faster than Zander's world record.

Nurmi continued his even stride down the homestretch, while Wide, thoroughly beaten, had to let up. Nurmi won by 18 yards, and now only the small group of Finns cheered wildly.

The jubilant Finns rushed from the stands to congratulate Nurmi. Then the announcer silenced the crowd with his megaphone and gave them the time—4:10.4. Even the Swedes applauded, for Taber's eight-year-old record had fallen.

Nurmi jogged to cool down and allowed photographers, but he had nothing to say.

Wide, who finished in 4:13.1, third fastest amateur mile, said, "I felt I could break both Taber's and Zander's records, but I wondered if that would suffice to beat the Finn. I must train harder, and have a more intensive massage, then perhaps I'll be ready... With one lap to go my legs were as heavy as lead and I was in a psychic depression."

Coach Mikkola said, "We had respect for Wide and knew that he would be dangerous, but we had planned a schedule and Nurmi adhered to it almost without a fault."

1923

Rumor circulated that Nurmi had run a practice mile in 4:11 to be certain he was good enough for this race.

The next day, on the same track, Nurmi broke the world record for three miles on the way to beating Wide at 5000 meters. Three days later, Wide collected the Swedish 2-mile record with 9:12.8. On September 10, Nurmi added to his fame with a world 3000-meter record. But the two did not meet again at 1500 or a mile for three years.

1922
MILE:
4:17.0	Joie Ray (USA)	AAU (1)	Newark	9	Sep
4:18.4*	Larry Shields (USA)	IC4A (1)	Cambridge, Mass.	27	May
4:19.0	Ray Watson (USA)	(1)	St. Joseph, Mo.	4	Jul
4:19.2	Harold Cutbill (USA)	( )			
4:19.8	Billy Burke (USA)	(1)	Cambridge, Mass.	13	May
4:20.1	Malcolm Douglas (USA)	(1)	New Haven	7	May
4:21.0	Henry Stallard (GB)	(1)	Cambridge	9	Mar

*Timing to one-tenth adopted by IC4A for the first time.

1,500m:
3:59.8	Paavo Nurmi (Finland)	(1)	Helsinki	17	Sep
4:00.0	Edvin Wide (Sweden)	(1)	Stockholm	1	Jun
4:01.5	Matti Tala (Finland)	( )			
4:03.8	Otto Peltzer (Germany)	(1)	Duisburg	20	Aug
4:03.9	Eino Borg (Finland)	( )			
4:04-2/5	Henry Stallard (GB)	(1)	London	29	Jul
4:04-2/5	Ferruccio Bruni (Italy)	(1)	Busto Arsizio	17	Sep

1923
MILE:
4:10.4	WR	Paavo Nurmi (Finland)	(1)	Stockholm	23	Aug
4:13.1		Edvin Wide (Sweden)	(2)	Stockholm	23	Aug
4:15.5		Joie Ray (USA)	(1)	Des Moines	28	Apr
4:17.8		Edward Kirby (USA)	(1)	Philadelphia	26	May
4:18.0		Ray	AAU (1)	Chicago		
4:20.0		Walter Higgins (USA)				
4:21-3/5		Charles Blewitt (GB)	(1)	Manchester	23	Jun
4:21-3/5		Henry Stallard (GB)	AAA (1)	London	7	Jul
4:21-3/5		C.E. Davis (GB)	(1)	London	21	Jul

Indoors:
4:17.8	James Connolly (USA)	(1)	New York	3	Mar

1,500m:
3:53.0+	WR	Paavo Nurmi (Finland)	(1)	Stockholm	23	Aug
3:54.2+		Edvin Wide (Sweden)	(2)	Stockholm	23	Aug
3:55.6		Nurmi	(1)	Kotka (early in August)		
3:56.7		Wide	(1)	Stockholm	19	Aug
3:57.0		Wide	(1)	Göteborg	13	Jul
3:59.4		Otto Peltzer (Germany)	(2)	Göteborg	13	Jul
4:01-1/5		B. MacDonald (GB)	(1)	Paris	9	Jun
4:01.7		Erik Hulthin (Sweden)	(2)	Stockholm	17	Jun
4:01-4/5		René Wiriath (France)	(2)	Paris	9	Jun

NURMI AT THE 1924 OLYMPICS

As world record holder at six distances, from 1500 meters to 10,000 meters, Nurmi was regarded as the greatest runner in history and a favorite for any race he chose in the 1924 Olympics at Paris. He felt he could win five Olympic gold medals, but he was frustrated by several unrelated events.

1924

The IAAF schedule came out with only half an hour between the 1500 and 5000. Outraged Finns protested and the schedule was widened to a hardly generous 55 minutes.

Next, Nurmi fell during training on an icy road on Easter Sunday and hurt his knee on a sharp stone. For two weeks he could not walk at all, and then his leg was stiff. His first desperate effort to run resulting in a shocking 2:12 for 800 meters.

And Ville Ritola returned from the United States and broke Nurmi's 10,000 meter record. Nurmi was told he could not run the 10,000 at Paris, but he decided to try the all-but-impossible double of 1500 and 5000 on the same day.

Because he had lost some training, and because he had to be better than ever, he took grim measures and trained in a new way. After his usual morning walk of 10 to 12 kilometers and some work in the gym, he rested for an hour. Then, on a track, he ran four or five hard sprints, a high-quality 400 to 1000 for time, and a 3000 to 4000-meter run with "the last lap always very fast'" Each evening he ran 4000 to 7000 meters cross country, punishing himself at the finish. His day ended with four or five punishing sprints.

"This daily training helped me to attain the condition I had at the 1924 Olympic Games."

His condition was soon better than ever and he planned a dress rehearsal for June 19, six days after his 27th birthday and three weeks before his big day at Paris. The meet was organized by the HKV club at the Helsinki Zoological Garden grounds. He ran the 1500 at 7:05 p.m.

With only two poor runners opposing him, Nurmi was on his own. He sped around the first 400 meters in 57.3, far too fast, possibly as a result of his speed training. He reached 800 meters in 2:01 and 1200 meters in 3:06, slightly behind his 4:10.4 pace. Unworried, he made little effort to increase his speed, and he came in smoothly in world record time of 3:52.6.

He was angry with himself because of that 57.3 first lap. He had planned 61 seconds, and he felt he could have run two seconds faster than 3:52.6 if he had started more calmly.

At 8:10 p.m. he started the 5000 and he broke world records for three miles (14:02) and 5000 meters (14:28.2). Only then did he allow himself to talk . . . and reveal his sensitivity.

"Nobody can imagine how hard I trained after recovering from a leg injury. And nobody knows how nervous I was while recovering. Nor what times I turned in while preparing for today's races. I knew in advance that the records would fall; otherwise I wouldn't have let the newspapers play up these record attempts as strongly as they did."

At Paris, Nurmi qualified without care in the 5000 meters on July 8, winning the slowest heat in 15:28-3/5. The next day, he

1924

qualified in the 1500 by winning his heat in a leisurely 4:07-3/5. His opposition in the 1500 final on July 10 was not regarded as formidable. Wide and Ray ran longer distances. Stallard, now 23, had run no fast races, but he was undefeated in university competition, in international dual meets, and in the AAA, where he won the 1923 mile and the 1924 880. He crossed the finish line a good fourth with 1:53 in the Olympic 800 meters on the day before the 1500 heats. The other Englishman in the 1500 final was the exciting 21-year-old, Douglas Lowe, who had won the 800 in 1:52-2/5. Willy Schärer of Switzerland, only 21, was a "dark horse", having won the fastest heat.

The three U.S. runners in the final were not highly regarded, although Ray Buker tied Kiviat's American record of 3:55-4/5 at Cambridge on June 14. Buker was fourth in the 1924 indoor AAU 1000 (behind third-place Abel Kiviat, who was suspended in 1915!). Lloyd Hahn was a promising young runner with speed who placed third, right behind Buker, in the 1923 AAU and won the Baxter mile in 4:19.2 in 1924. Ray Watson, the third American, won the 1921 NCAA mile, ran 4:19 in 1922, and was 1923 AAU 880 champion.

The Olympic track in Stade de Colombes was 500 meters and Nurmi aimed for 75 seconds per lap for the first two laps, a bold 60 seconds per 400 meters. He carried a borrowed stop watch which he checked for four minutes by shaking it hard.

At his desired pace, Nurmi expected to be all alone in the Olympic 1500, but Watson stayed on his heels. Nurmi cocked his head to the right to check his time as he passed 400 meters in 58 and completed the first lap in 1:13.2. Too fast! He passed 800 meters in 1:58.5. He and Watson were 25 meters ahead of the field.

Then Watson could stand it no longer and he let go, and Nurmi was able to slow his reckless pace. He completed the second lap in 2:32, two seconds behind schedule, but several yards ahead of his 4:10.4 pace.

Casually, he tossed his watch aside. Now it was merely a race, and he had to conserve energy for the 5000. He looked back and saw his nearest pursuer 40 meters behind.

He slowed his pace and ran only to win. He looked back to keep close watch on his opposition, for a great battle developed behind him. Stallard and Lowe passed Buker and Hahn with half a lap to go. Then Schärer passed Stallard as Lowe faded in the home stretch. Stallard, who was in great pain because of an injured leg, fought back with all he had and drew abreast of Schärer ten yards from the line. But the effort was his last, for Schärer pulled away and Stallard fell across the line, unconscious for half an hour.

Results: Nurmi 3:53.6, Schärer 3:55.0, Stallard 3:55.6, Lowe 3:57.0, Buker 3:58.6, Hahn 3:59.0, Watson 3:59.9, Liewendahl (Finland) 4:00.3, Peussa (Finland) 4:00.6.

Nurmi ignored 25,000 cheering fans, on their feet in admiration. While some of his opponents collapsed, he stopped his job only to pick up his sweat clothes. He jogged to the dressing room and rested on a mattress. Some say he slept.

According to Joe Binks, who was now a sports writer, Nurmi was at the start of the 5000 only 42 minutes later. Ritola and Wide tried to break Nurmi with a fantastic pace, but Nurmi let them go 40 yards ahead, checking his pace with his watch until they faded back to him. He won while coolly watching Ritola over his shoulder.

The next day he ran a heat of the 3000 meter team race. The day after that came the fateful cross country run in which many runners collapsed. Nurmi deliberately ran Ritola into the ground and won by a large margin. When Ritola came dragging in, Nurmi allowed himself one of his few public smiles.

On July 13, Nurmi won his fourth race of the Paris Olympics in the 3000-meter team race. He was the athletic wonder of the world.

After the Olympics in 1924, Nurmi retained his great form, breaking world records at four miles (twice), five miles (twice), six miles, 10,000 meters, and one-half hour. He was still only a part-time miler.

Nurmi now had a lucrative job as a paper hanger, hired by wealthy families so they could point with pride to his work, but when an offer arrived to tour the United States during the 1925 indoor season he accepted eagerly.

Thousands of Americans were unable to get in to the packed arena to watch him run in his first meet. Those who did saw an unsmiling, balding man in blue sweats warm up for 2½ miles in preparation for his duel with Joie Ray.

JOIE RAY IMPROVES

After his Olympic disaster of 1920, Ray lost many more races in Europe because of his injured leg. Disheartened, he did not run indoors in 1921, letting his leg heal. He won the 1921 AAU mile at Pasadena, California, in 4:16-4/5 and ran 4:14-4/5 at Berkeley only five days later.

In 1922 he had shaved his mustache and let his hair grow longer, and his leg was in good shape. He set indoor records for 1½ miles, 3000 meters, and 1¼-mile, but he lost the indoor AAU 1000 to Harold Cutbill's record-tying 2:13-2/5. Outdoors, he lost a careless 4:24-3/5 mile at the Drake Relays to half-miler Ray Watson, but he won the AAU mile again in 4:17.0 and placed third in the 880.

He was still better in 1923. Indoors, he broke his record for the Wanamaker 1½, and ran two miles in 9:08-2/5, fastest ever run,

1924

indoors or out. He set records at several odd distances, and beat the great Ritola in the AAU two-mile in 9:10-2/5. Outdoors, he won at Drake in 4:15.5 over Ray Buker, and he beat Buker and Hahn in the AAU meet at Chicago with 4:18.0, his eighth AAU mile title.

Ray's bad luck struck again in the Olympic year. (He was born on Friday the 13th.) He had tonsillitis and had to have his tonsils removed before the trials. Then, three days before the Olympics, he pulled another calf muscle, and he ran only in the 3000 meter team race. But by the time the 1925 indoor season arrived, he was ready for Nurmi.

1924

MILE:

4:17-4/5	Thomas Cavanaugh (USA)	(1)	Newton, Mass.	17	May
4:20-1/5	Hill (USA)	( )			
4:20-2/5	Willie Goodwin (USA)	(1)	New York	21	Jun
4:21-1/5	William Seagrove (GB) AAA	(1)	London	21	Jun
4:21-1/5	Russell Payne (USA)	( )			

1,500m:

3:52.6	WR	Paavo Nurmi (Finland)	(1)	Helsinki	19	Jun
3:53.6		Nurmi	(1)	Colombes	10	Jul
3:55.0		Willie Schärer (Switzerland)	(2)	Colombes	10	Jul
3:55.6		Henry Stallard (GB)	(3)	Colombes	10	Jul
3:55-4/5		Ray Buker (USA)	(1)	Cambridge, Mass.	14	Jun

RAY VS NURMI

The series of races between the two great runners should have been the greatest series in history, but it turned out otherwise.

They met first on January 6 in New York's Madison Square Garden. Nurmi feared Ray's vaunted kick and set a blistering pace of 59 and 2:02-4/5. But Chesty Joie not only stayed with him, he took the lead in the third quarter and the crowd noise was deafening as they passed three-quarters in 3:08-3/5.

With 250 yards to go, Nurmi regained the lead and Ray pursued him around the last lap and a half. Ray's desperate sprint could not gain and Nurmi won by three yards in world indoor record time of 4:13-3/5. Ray's 4:14.0 was his fastest ever.

After Nurmi broke Ray's record in the Wanamaker 1½, with Ray absent, they were supposed to meet at Chicago for another mile race, but Nurmi kept increasing the distance he would run until it became 1-3/4 miles. Ray was angry and did not try.

Nurmi ran 4:12.0 alone on March 7 at Buffalo, New York, on a flat track, lowering his indoor record and giving him the two fastest miles ever run. Then he withdrew from their next scheduled races. Ray ran alone in the Columbian Mile in New York on March 17 and tied Nurmi's record 4:12.0. When they finally met in a mile race, Ray had a bad cold and had to drop out.

Thus, their rivalry resulted in two 4:12 miles and one good race, but nothing like the hoped-for competition.

Ray was suspended for accepting too much expense money and never ran the mile again. He came back as an Olympic marathoner in 1928.

1925
MILE:

4:15.2	Paavo Nurmi (Finland)	(1)	Cambridge, Mass.	22	May
4:16.9	Lloyd Hahn (USA)	(1)	Los Angeles	25	Apr
4:18.0	B. MacDonald (GB) AAA	(1)	London	18	Jul
4:18.2	James Connolly (USA)	(2)	Cambridge, Mass.	22	May
4:18.4e	Cyril Ellis (GB)	(2)	London	18	Jul
4:18.8	James Reese (USA)	(1)	Chicago	13	Jun
4:19.4	Nick Carter (USA)	(1)	Los Angeles	16	May
4:19.4	Ray Buker (USA) AAU	(1)	San Francisco	4	Jul

Indoors:

4:12.0	Paavo Nurmi (Finland)	(1)	Buffalo, N.Y.	7	Mar
4:12.0	Joie Ray (USA)	(1)	New York	17	Mar
4:13.0	Lloyd Hahn (USA)	(2)	New York	17	Mar

1,500m:

3:55.4	Edvin Wide (Sweden)	(1)	Stockholm	16	Jul
3:58.2	Roger Pelé (France)	(1)	Stockholm	30	Aug
3:59.4	Nils Eklöf (Sweden)	(2)	Stockholm	16	Jul
3:59.6	René Wiriath (France)	(1)	Colombes	5	Jul
3:59.8	Paul Bontemps (France)	(2)	Stockholm	30	Aug
4:00.2	Otto Peltzer (Germany)	(1)	Berlin	9	Aug
4:01.6	Ray Dodge (USA)	(1)	Oslo	14	Aug
4:01.9	Herbert Böcher (Germany)	(2)	Berlin	9	Aug

Indoors:

3:55.8	Lloyd Hahn (USA)	(1)	Washington, D.C.	21	Feb
3:56.2+	Paavo Nurmi (Finland)	(1)	New York	6	Jan
3:57.0	Joie Ray (USA)	(1)	New York	3	Feb

THE MILE TEST SERIES

Early in 1926, Lloyd Hahn travelled from the United States to New Zealand to run a series of miles against a raw talent named Randolph Rose.

Hahn had developed rapidly after his sixth place in the 1924 Olympics. Indoors in 1925, it is almost incredible, but he did not figure in the Nurmi vs. Ray rivalry. Hahn won the Baxter Mile on February 14 in a world indoor record 4:13.4 with laps of 59, 2:06, and 3:12. He won the indoor AAU 1000 in 2:13.8, ran 3:55.8 indoors at Washington, D.C., on February 21, a 4:16.9 in Los Angeles on April 25, and placed second in the outdoor mile, behind Buker's 4:19.4.

Rose was an amazing farmer who had never trained formally. He walked all day on the farm and ran back and forth from work and to lunch. Only after his first race with Hahn did he make an effort to develop speed by running 300's for a week.

Hahn and Rose raced in four separate miles early in 1926. Hahn surprised nobody when he won the first by 15 yards in 4:18-3/5, but Rose won a handicap in 4:26-2/5 with Hahn fourth, and Rose won the third in 4:19 by two yards. In their last race, at

1926

Masterton on March 4, Rose was about 15 yards ahead when he crossed the line in 4:13-3/5, and the crowd closed in on him before Hahn could finish. This was the fourth fastest outdoor amateur mile ever run. A few months later, Rose went to Europe for the AAA Championships. He placed only fourth behind Frenchman Georges Baraton's 4:17-2/5 race and gave up in discouragement.

A CLASSIC 1500 IN BERLIN

The organizers of the Charlottenburg club in Berlin became excited when they received a cable message reading:
"Saavun kilpalnikinne stop Nurmi"
Translated, this meant, "I'm coming to your meet," and it was signed by Nurmi. They had already lined up Wide and the great Dr. Otto Peltzer, and thus they had the ingredients for the greatest 1500 or mile race ever run. It was to be on September 11, 1926, at 1500 meters.

Unlike many planned races which turn out badly, this race fulfilled all their hopes. In fact, Torsten Tegnér, editor of the Swedish "Idrottsbladet" and probably the best-known sports journalist in the world, described the race as the most exciting he had ever seen.

NURMI had returned from his exhausting U.S. tour of 55 races with a best outdoor mile of 4:15.2 and he broke no outdoor records in 1925.

In 1926 he set a world record for 3000 meters on May 24, and continued his remarkable winning streak. He had not lost a race of longer than 1000 meters since the 1920 Olympics except for an indoor 5000 defeat by Ritola when he suffered from stomach cramps.

On July 12, he went to Stockholm for his second mile race against Wide. The great Swede , now 30 years old, was stronger than ever, but he had not yet sharpened his speed for the short mile distance and Nurmi was superior after the halfway point. The 385-meter laps were run in 58, 59.6, and 60.4. At three-quarters, Nurmi led in 3:06.6 and Wide was timed in 3:07.5. At 1500 meters, Nurmi's lead was insurmountable, 3:53.6 to 3:55.7.

Nurmi gained another three or four yards in the last 120, but the official time gave him a disappointing 4:11.9 to Wide's 4:13.7, which showed a gain for Wide over the last 120. A poll of expert unofficial timers found a dozen who caught Nurmi in 4:10.9 to 4:11.1, mostly 4:10.9. Thus Nurmi's true time was probably at least 4:11.0.

The next day, Wide showed his real strength by scaring Nurmi to a world-record 3000 meters, 8:20.4 to 8:20.8. Nurmi agreed to a 1500-meter race in his home town of Turku, to take place in nine days.

A strong wind killed any hopes for a record at Turku. Frej Liewendahl, the Finn who placed eighth in the 1924 Olympics, helped push the pace for three laps. Wide took the lead with 350 meters to go and Nurmi followed him to the homestretch. With 70 meters left, Nurmi sprinted furiously and won by five meters, 3:54.9 to 3:55.7.

WIDE had followed Ritola across the finish line in two Olympic races in 1924, second in the 10,000 and third in the 5000. In 1925, he continued his relentless progress with 5000 meters in 14:40.4 and world records at 2000 (5:25.9) and 3000 (8:27.5). He also recorded his fastest winning 1500 with 3:55.4. He was ready for a fast race in Berlin.

PELTZER was 26 years old in 1926, and he had almost no reputation at 1500 meters. A 6'1¼", 159-pound native of Holstein, (b. March 8, 1900) he did not start running until 1920. His chosen distance was 800 meters and he progressed slowly from 1:58.2 in 1921 to 1:54.7 in 1923. He ran his fastest 1500 that year, 3:59.4, behind Wide. He was ill in 1924 and failed to progress, missing the Olympics.

In 1925, Peltzer became internationally known with an 800 in 1:52.8, less than a second from the world record. But he was more the quarter-miler type than miler, for he ran 400 meters in 48.8 and 1500 meters in 4:00.2.

In 1926, Peltzer became great. On June 6, in Hungary, he set an official world record of 1:03.6 for 500 meters. On July 3, in the AAA Championships at Stamford Bridge, Peltzer's great finishing kick beat Olympic champion Douglas Lowe by three yards in a world record 1:51.6 880.

Peltzer wanted to run against Nurmi at Berlin on May 24, but Nurmi had switched to the 3000. Peltzer won the 1500 in 3:58.6, for a German record. This convinced him he could run well at that distance and he began to do some longer training. On August 22 in Switzerland, he won in 3:59.2.

Although his fastest time was far behind that of Nurmi and Wide, the Germans, especially, knew he could run much faster, and many people were unable to get inside the SCC Sportplatz, which held only 20,000.

At 6:10 p.m., the three runners were joined at the starting line by Herbert Böcher, a 23-year-old with a best of 4:00.3 and an estimated 4:17-4/5 in the AAA. It was partly cloudy, but otherwise the weather was good. The 400-meter track was in good condition.

A moment before the start, a small boy, climbing a pole for a better view, caused the Finnish flag to fall. Nurmi, a superstitious man, was too intent on the race to witness this bad omen.

1926

Peltzer, a high-strung, nervous athlete, jumped the gun twice before the race was underway. Wide, wearing a green jersey, went into the lead, followed by Peltzer who wore the black eagle of Germany on his white shirt. Nurmi, in somber black, was third.

Nurmi moved purposefully into the lead before 300 meters, and with three laps to go, he was followed by Wide, Peltzer, and Böcher. Nurmi's time at 400 meters was 61 seconds (Wide 61.2, Peltzer 61.5). After 500 meters Nurmi tried to get away and opened a small gap. At 800 meters, his time was 2:02.2, with Wide at 2:02.8 and Peltzer 2:03.0.

Then, down the backstretch, Peltzer moved ahead of Wide into second place and the German crowd came alive. Nurmi led at 1000 meters in 2:34.8, about 20 yards slower than his pace in the 1924 Olympics.

He was obviously not as good today, but he led down the homestretch and the bell clanged for the final lap. Around the curve, Wide surprised by passing Peltzer, to the dismay of the crowd.

Nurmi led past the starting line, timed in 3:05.6 for 1200 meters, close to his fastest pace. Wide was close in 3:05.8 and Peltzer crossed in 3:06.0. Suddenly, the unexpected happened. Wide charged past Nurmi down the backstretch, and Nurmi was unable to hold him off. Grimly, Nurmi held on, with Peltzer on his heels and Böcher dropping out.

Around the last curve they sped, in single file, and the crowd implored Peltzer to move. If past history meant anything, Nurmi would swing wide in the homestretch and sprint to victory. Instead, as they turned for home, Peltzer launched a drive and went past Nurmi.

Now the crowd was hysterical. Peltzer was beating Nurmi. He was gaining on Wide. The time was fast.

With 60 meters left, Peltzer caught Wide. His quarter-mile speed was gone now, and Wide's 10,000-meter endurance was beginning to count. For 20 meters they ran shoulder to shoulder while the German crowd screamed.

Then Peltzer drew on a small reserve he had not yet used, and he pulled away. He won by about three meters and the delighted Germans continued an ovation which lasted 15 minutes. Almost unseen, Paavo Nurmi strode in for the first third place of his career.

Peltzer was mobbed by athletes and spectators. A band played a victory march. An airplane buzzed low and dropped a bouquet of yellow flowers.

Sometime during the chaotic celebration came the announcement that Peltzer had run 3:51.0, his last 300 in 45.0. His new world record was equal to a mile in 4:10.2. Wide's time was a fast 3:51.8 and Nurmi's 3:52.8 ... although many said they were closer than that. When the din subsided, Peltzer left without taking his victory lap.

1926

The sports world was shocked by Nurmi's defeat, for he had been invincible for so many years. Some blamed the shin splints and other injuries he had picked up during his hectic tour of the United States a year before. One historian wrote, "It took Nurmi three years to recover his style." Another said Nurmi never recovered. The next day, September 12, Nurmi seemed to verify this when Wide beat him by 20 yards with a world record 2-mile of 9:01.4.

In any case, Nurmi's reign as king of the milers had ended.

1926
MILE:

Time	Athlete		Place	Date
4:11.9*	Paavo Nurmi (Finland)	(1)	Stockholm	12 Jul
4:13-3/5	Randolph Rose (NZ)	(1)	Masterton	4 Mar
4:13.7	Edvin Wide (Sweden)	(2)	Stockholm	12 Jul
4:15.9	Gunnar Sjögren (Sweden)	(1)	Stockholm	12 Sep
4:16.0	Lloyd Hahn (USA) AAU	(1)	Philadelphia	5 Jul
4:17-2/5	Georges Baraton (France) AAA	(1)	London	3 Jul
4:17.7	Nils Eklöf (Sweden)	(2)	Stockholm	12 Sep
4:17-4/5-e	Herbert Böcher (Ger) AAA	(2)	London	3 Jul
4:18.8	Eino Borg (Finland)	(1)	Jyväskylä	

*Time probably misread, supposedly no slower than 4:11.0.

1,500m

Time		Athlete		Place	Date
3:51.0	WR	Otto Peltzer (Germany)	(1)	Berlin	11 Sep
3:51.8		Edvin Wide (Sweden)	(2)	Berlin	11 Sep
3:52.8		Paavo Nurmi (Finland)	(3)	Berlin	11 Sep
3:53.6+		Nurmi	(1)	Stockholm	12 Jul
3:54.6		Séra Martin (France)	(1)	Colombes	26 Sep
3:54.9		Nurmi	(1)	Turku	22 Jul
3:55.7+		Wide	(2)	Stockholm	12 Jul
3:55.7		Wide	(2)	Turku	22 Jul
3:55.8		Eino Borg (Finland)	(1)	Helsinki	13 Jun
3:56.6		Roger Pelé (France)	(2)	Colombes	26 Sep
3:57.3		Gunnar Sjogren (Sweden)	(1)	Stockholm	19 Sep
3:57.6+		Nils Eklof (Sweden)	(2)	Stockholm	12 Sep
3:57.6		Folke Eriksson (Sweden)	(3)	Colombes	26 Sep
4:00.2		Georges Baraton (France)	(2)	Colombes	11 Jul

FASTEST COMBINED TIMES THROUGH 1926

3:51.0	(4:10.2)	Peltzer	1926
(3:51.2)	4:10.4	Nurmi	1923
(3:51.8)	4:11.0	Nurmi	1926
3:51.8n	(4:11.1)	Wide	1926
3:52.6	(4:11.9)	Nurmi	1924
(3:52.8)	4:12.0i	Nurmi	1925
(3:52.8)	4:12.0i	Ray	1925
3:52.8n	(4:12.1)	Nurmi	1926
(3:53.3)	4:12.6	Taber	1915
(3:53.4)	4:12¾	George (pro)	1886
3:53.6	(4:13.0)	Nurmi	1924
(3:53.6)	4:13.0ni	Hahn	1925
(3:53.7)	4:13.1n	Wide	1923
(3:54.0)	4:13.4i	Hahn	1925
(3:54.1)	4:13.6i	Nurmi	1925
(3:53.1)	4:13.6	Rose	1926
(3:54.3)	4:13.7n	Wide	1926
(3:54.4)	4:13.8	Hill	1921
(3:54.6)	4:14.0ni	Ray	1925
3:54.6	(4:14.0)	S. Martin	1926

43

WIDE VS HAHN

In 1927, Wide ran successfully indoors in the United States, setting records at odd distances. On March 17, he ran against Lloyd Hahn in the Columbian Mile of the Knights of Columbus Games in Madison Square Garden.

Hahn had won the 1926 AAU mile in 4:16.0 after his fast defeat by Rose in New Zealand. Indoors in 1927, he won the Wanamaker Mile in 4:15.6, the Baxter Mile in 4:14.8, and set an indoor record while winning the AAU 1000 in 2:12.8.

In the Columbian Mile, the rapid pace was set by Willie Goodwin, the AAU indoor 2-mile champion. He led in 58.3 and 2:05, but Wide held back in 62 and 2:07, while Hahn stalked Wide in 62.2 and 2:07.6. Wide led at three-quarters in 3:12 to 3:12.2, but on the last lap Hahn shot ahead amid loud cheers and led at 1500 meters in 3:56.3 to 3:56.5. Hahn led around the last curve and pulled away to win in 4:12.2 to 4:12.8, faster than anyone except Nurmi and Ray.

1928 OLYMPICS

In a strange exodus, most of the big name milers disappeared from Olympic contention at 1500 meters. Nurmi chose to run longer races, and he collected another gold medal and two silver. Wide was eliminated in a tactical heat of the 1500 but he won two bronze medals in longer races. Douglas Lowe was content to confine himself to the 800 and he won it again. Peltzer, now 28, was eliminated in both the 800 and the 1500. Lloyd Hahn, who won all the 1928 indoor miles including a 4:13.0 Columbian Mile after an ambitious 3:07.8 three-quarters, won the AAU 800 meters in 1:51.4 and placed fifth in the Olympic 800; then he dropped out of his 1500-meter heat. Joie Ray made a comeback but he lacked speed for the shorter race and placed fifth in the Olympic marathon. Séra Martin, a promising Frenchman who ran 3:54.6 in 1926 and 4:18.4 and 3:59.0 in 1927, set a world 800 record of 1:50.6 in 1928 and so ran the Olympic 800, placing sixth. Then he was eliminated in a 1500-meter heat. To fill this void, three interesting milers appeared:

JULES LADOUMÈGUE, born in Bordeaux on December 10, 1906, ran well in cross country and road races as a teen-ager. In 1926, not yet 20, he went to Paris and created a stir with a third in the French 5000-meter championship. Two weeks later he improved his time to 15:11-3/5 against Great Britain, making him No. 20 on the world list for 1926.

A French track expert discouraged him, however, saying Ladoumègue's long, galloping stride was not suited for long distances, and in 1927 Ladoumègue tried the 1500 meters. He was drafted into the army and stationed near Paris, where he was able to train, but his best time in 1927 was only 4:03.6 and he placed a disappointing sixth in the French Championships.

In 1928 he joined Séra Martin and ran for Stade Français under the tutelage of Charles Poulenard, one of France's best-known coaches. Ladoumègue's improvement was startling. On June 3, he ran 3:58.0 and a week later, 3:55.2. Two weeks later he ran 5000 meters in 15:03.2.

On July 1, he won the Paris Championships in 3:54.6. Two weeks later he stirred the crowd when he ran off by himself in the last half of the French Championship and finished in 3:52.2, third fastest of all time behind only Peltzer and Wide.

In one year, Ladoumègue came from nowhere to Olympic favorite.

EINO PURJE, who ran under the name of Borg until 1927, clocked 4:11 for 1500 meters in 1920 at the age of 20, and he showed little promise for several years after that. He was 25 years old when he set a Finnish record of 1:55.6 for 800 meters in 1925. He ran 1500 meters in a good 3:55.8 in 1926.

In 1927 he improved again. He ran 1:55.2 and 3:57.2 and won against Sweden. On August 9 he pleased the Finns by breaking Nurmi's world record for 2000 meters with 5:23.4.

On June 21, 1928, Purje ran 5000 meters in 14:39.3 behind Ritola and, at that time, he was a good bet for an Olympic medal. He did qualify for the Olympic 5000 meter final, but after his race in the Finnish Trials on July 7 against Larva, he preferred the 1500.

HARRI LARVA was three months older than Ladoumègue, 3½ inches taller at 5'10-7/8" and 20 pounds heavier at 150. His family name was Lagerström (Swedes living in Finland), but he changed to Larva in 1927. He played soccer as a boy, but he "fell in love with track" at 18 when he saw a race between Ritola and Nurmi.

He began as a better half-miler than miler and progressed to 1:57.5 and 4:07.1 in 1926. In 1927 he ran an encouraging 1:55.7 and 3:59.6. (This 1500 meter time placed him third at Viipuri on October 8, behind Peltzer's 3:57.0 and Purje's 3:57.9.)

Larva was more an English-type miler. He was tall, with half-mile speed, and he liked to win with a big kick. He also was able to rise to the big occasion.

At the trials for the Finnish team on July 7 at the Helsinki Zoological Garden ground, Larva used his big kick to great advantage. With Nurmi fading behind in 3:57.3, Purje ran a fast race in 3:53.1, but Larva outkicked him in 3:52.6 to tie Nurmi's national record.

THE OLYMPIC FINAL on August 2 saw the runners line up on the 400-meter track in the Grand Stadium of Amsterdam. The expectant crowd sat in covered stands on each side and stood at the end. The running track was encircled by a 500-meter cycling track, a moat, and a solid white fence.

Six heats the previous day had cut 54 hopefuls to 12 finalists. Wide was eliminated in a sprint finish by slim Ray Conger of the U.S., who had run 3:55.0 at Cambridge on July 7, and by Jean Keller of France. The fastest heat was 3:59.6 by Böcher, who had run in the world-record race in Berlin. The only British runner in the final was Cyril Ellis, who had won the 1927 AAA in a good 4:17.0. Sid Robinson, second in the AAU at 3:55.7e, dropped out of the third heat, and Nick Carter, 4:16.8 in 1927 and 3:55.9e in the AAU, barely missed qualifying in the sixth heat.

When the gun sounded, the tense finalists ran in a bunch, with many changes of position. Ladoumègue was caught in a box in the middle, but the two Finns took better care of themselves, with Larva leading until Purje took over at 400 meters.

At 800 meters, Purje led in 2:04. Many runners were giving up hope then but Ladoumègue went after the two Finns. On the backstretch of the last lap, Ladoumègue rushed past Purje into the lead. Purje could not hang on, but Larva pursued Ladoumègue and the crowd was in an uproar.

As Purje fell farther and farther behind around the last curve, it became a fierce duel. Larva followed Ladoumègue into the homestretch. Then he swung wide and tried to pass. With agonizing suspense, he pulled alongside, the tape rushing closer by the second and the howling crowd in doubt as to the winner.

Then, only 20 meters from the end, Larva pulled away. When Ladoumègue knew it was hopeless he eased up and lost by four yards.

Results: Larva 3:53.2, Ladoumègue 3:53.8, Purje 3:56.4, Hans Wichmann of Germany 3:56.8, Ellis 3:57.6, Paul Martin of Switzerland 3:58.4, Krause of Germany 3:59.0, Kittel of Czechoslovakia 4:01.4, Whyte of Australia, Conger, Keller. Böcher did not finish.

LARVA IMPRESSES HIS DOUBTERS

There were many who thought Larva was simply lucky to be the best on a given day, but in post-Olympic meets he set about to prove his true ability.

On August 25, he won the Finnish 800-meter title in 1:53.7, and on September 16, in Turku, he ran an outstanding mile against Purje. They stayed within 0.2 seconds of each other as Purje ran 61.4, Larva led in 2:03.7, and Purje passed three-quarters in 3:08.0. Then, once again, Larva's kick was superior and he won in 4:11.0, second fastest mile ever run. Purje's 4:11.6 was the fastest non-winning time ever.

1928

On October 7, Larva challenged the Germans in Berlin. He took the lead at 450 meters and led at 800 in 2:04, followed by Olympic fourth-placer Wichmann, Peltzer, and Böcher. The amazing Wichmann took the lead on the last backstretch, and the faster pace caused Peltzer to drop out in despair, while Böcher fell behind. But Larva hung on gamely to the homestretch and kicked past Wichmann to win in 3:52.0. Wichmann ran 3:52.6 and Böcher 3:55.0.

Larva was now very near the top in quality races, even though he held no world record. Consider this list of the fastest races of all time through 1928:

3:51.0	(4:10.2)	Peltzer	1926
(3:51.2)	4:10.4	Nurmi	1923
(3:51.8)	4:11.0u	Nurmi	1926
(3:51.8)	4:11.0	Larva	1928
3:51.8n	(4:11.1)	Wide	1926
3:52.0	(4:11.2)	Larva	1928
3:52.2	(4:11.5)	Ladoumègue	1928
(3:52.3)	4:11.6n	Purje	1928
3:52.6	(4:11.9)	Nurmi	1924
3:52.6	(4:11.9)	Larva	1928
3:52.6n	(4:11.9)	Wichmann	1928

One oddity of Larva's career was that he never won a Finnish Championship at 1500 meters. He won the 800 in 1928, 1929, 1930, and 1934.

In 1929, he ran two 1500 meter races of note. On August 4, in Berlin, he again outkicked Ladoumègue, 3:56.6 to 3:56.8. Four days later, in Stockholm, he met a good field which included Leo Lermond of the United States.

Lermond had placed fourth in the Olympic 5000, behind Ritola, Nurmi, and Wide. In 1929, he ran two strong miles—4:14.6 at the Penn Relays and 4:13.0 at New York on June 17—and he won the AAU in 4:24.6.

At Stockholm, Larva and Lermond ran neck and neck down the homestretch, with Lermond winning a thriller. Both were timed in 3:56.2.

1927

MILE:

4:16.8	Nick Carter (USA)		(1)	Los Angeles	28 May
4:17.0	Cyril Ellis (GB)	AAA	(1)	London	2 Jul
4:17.6	Ray Conger (USA)		(1)	Chicago	11 Jun
4:17.8e	Herbert Böcher (Germany)	AAA	(2)	London	2 Jul
4:18.4	Séra Martin (France)		(1)	Paris	28 Aug
4:18.8	Henry Stallard (GB)		(1)	Cambridge	11 Jun
4:19.0	Edvin Wide (Sweden)		(2)	Los Angeles	28 May
4:19.4	William Cox (USA)		(1)	State College, Pa.	21 May

Indoors:

4:12.2	Lloyd Hahn (USA)	(1)	New York	17 Mar
4:12.8	Edvin Wide (Sweden)	(2)	New York	17 Mar
4:18.6	William Cox (USA)	(1)	New York	5 Mar

1,500m:

3:56.6	Leo Helgas (Finland)	(1)	Helsinki	17 Sep
3:56.2	René Wiriath (France)	(1)	Colombes	21 Aug
3:56.6	Herbert Böcher (Germany)	(2)	Colombes	21 Aug

1928

3:57.0	Otto Peltzer (Germany)	(1)	Viipuri	8	Oct
3:57.2	Eino Purje (Finland)	(2)	Helsinki	17	Sep
3:57.7	Paavo Nurmi (Finland)	(1)	Helsinki	14	Aug
3:58.3	Armas Kinnunen (Finland)	(1)	Lahti	26	Jun
3:59.0	Séra Martin (France)	(1)	Paris		
3:59.0	John Moore (GB)	(1)	London	30	Jul
3:59.0	Nils Eklöf (Sweden)	(1)	Norrköping	7	Aug
3:59.4e	S.T. Ashby (GB)	(2)	London	30	Jul
3:59.6	Harri Larva (Finland)	(3)	Viipuri	8	Oct

Indoors:

3:56.3+	Lloyd Hahn (USA)	(1)	New York	17	Mar
3:56.5+	Edvin Wide (Sweden)	(2)	New York	17	Mar

1928
MILE:

4:11.0	Harri Larva (Finland)		(1)	Turku	16	Sep
4:11.6	Eino Purje (Finland)		(2)	Turku	16	Sep
4:15.4	Jules Ladoumègue (France)		(1)	Colombes	8	Jul
4:17.6	Rufus Kiser (USA)	NCAA	(1)	Chicago	9	Jun
4:17.7e	Leroy Potter (USA)	NCAA	(2)	Chicago	9	Jun
4:18.7	Joe Sivak (USA)		(1)	Chicago	9	Jun
4:19.6	R.S. Starr (GB)		(1)	London	26	May
4:19.8e	F. Tilbury (GB)		(2)	London	26	May
4:20.0e	J. Langridge (GB)		(3)	London	26	May
4:20.0	S.T. Ashby (GB)		(1)	Luton	23	Jun

Indoor marks:

4:13.0	Lloyd Hahn (USA) (60.8—2:04.2—3:07.8)	(1)	New York	29	Feb
4:20.0	William Cox (USA)	(1)	New York	3	Mar

1,500m:

3:52.0	Harri Larva (Finland)		(1)	Berlin	7	Oct
3:52.2	Jules Ladoumègue (Fr)	Fr Ch	(1)	Colombes	15	Jul
3:52.6	Larva		(1)	Helsinki	7	Jul
3:52.6	Hans Wichmann (Germany)		(2)	Berlin	7	Oct
3:52.8	Ladoumègue		(1)	Köln	7	Aug
3:53.1	Eino Purje (Finland)		(1)	Helsinki	7	Jul
3:53.2	Larva	OG	(1)	Amsterdam	2	Aug
3:53.8	Ladoumègue	OG	(2)	Amsterdam	2	Aug
3:54.6	Ladoumègue		(1)	Colombes	1	Jul
3:54.6	Ladoumègue		(1)	Colombes	8	Sep
3:55.0	Ray Conger (USA)	AAU	(1)	Cambridge, Mass.	7	Jul
3:55.0	Herbert Böcher (Germany)		(3)	Berlin	7	Oct
3:55.2	Séra Martin (France)		(1)	Paris	22	Jul
3:55.7e	Sid Robinson (USA)	AAU	(2)	Cambridge, Mass.	7	Jul
3:55.9e	Nick Carter (USA)	AAU	(3)	Cambridge, Mass.	7	Jul
3:55.9e	Orval Martin (USA)	AAU	(4)	Cambridge, Mass.	7	Jul

Left, Walter George, first amateur under 4:20.

Below, the start of one of the famous George-Cummings match races in 1886.

The finish of the 1912 Olympic 1500 final. Strode-Jackson defeats Kiviat, Taber, Jones and Wide.

Joie Ray

Jules Ladoumègue

Paavo Nurmi

IV

Renaissance (1929-1932)

The world-wide depression coincided with a tremendous surge of new interest and strength in the 1500 and mile. Otto Peltzer had already proved what a man with speed could do, but now runners with natural speed concentrated on the 1500 and mile as never before and the result was a golden decade erasing all previous concepts of how fast man could run.

First man to put the Finns into eclipse was a high-strung Frenchman.

LADOUMÈGUE SHOWS THE WAY

Five days after his Olympic disappointment, Ladoumègue ran 3:52.8 at Köln. On September 9, at the Olympic stadium of Colombes, he ran 800 meters in 1:52.0 for third place.

After the Olympics, some unkind experts said Ladoumègue lacked the kick necessary for winning close finishes ... that he had to run away with the race before the homestretch. An emotional man, he wanted to prove the experts wrong.

On the 28th of July, 1929, at Colombes, France met Great Britain in a dual meet, and Ladoumègue purposely allowed the pace to dawdle. He waited until the homestretch for Cyril Ellis to attack, and Ellis did exactly that, defeating the chagrined Ladoumègue 4:04 to 4:04.2. One week later, in Berlin, a stubborn Ladoumègue lost the close race to Larva.

Perhaps the experts were right! At any rate, when he ran against Böcher on September 1 in the Colombes stadium, Ladoumègue did not wait for the homestretch and he won as he pleased, 3:55.4 to 3:58.0.

1930

In 1930 the question became somewhat academic, for Ladoumègue was good enough to win any way he chose. After starting with 3:53.8 on July 13, he ran in the dual meet with Great Britain at London on August 2 against Reggie Thomas and Cyril Ellis, who had humiliated him in 1929. Thomas had won the AAA title in 4:15.2 and three weeks later he was to win the Empire championship in 4:14.0, but Ladoumègue beat him thoroughly, 4:15.2 to 4:17.2, with Ellis far back in 4:20.2.

At the end of August, Ladoumègue ran 3:54.6. On September 21 he went to Berlin and beat Peltzer badly, 3:53.7 to 3:59.0. One week later he ran 3:55.4 and in another week, on October 5, he was ready to attempt a record.

His effort was to be at 1500 meters on the 450-meter track at Stade Jean Bouin near Ladoumègue's home. Ladoumègue once recalled his nervous preparation in an interview with Marcel Hansenne:

"As was my custom on racing days, all I had for breakfast in the morning was a cup of black coffee. And I was to remain at that until the evening. It was impossible for me to eat anything on racing days. It just wouldn't go through. And it was worse than ever on that day. While waiting, I listened to the noise made by the rain falling on a nearby poplar. Then, suddenly, I saw my mother open a cupboard and surreptitiously collect a bottle of water. Intrigued by her behavior, I followed her from a distance. I saw her go to the track and pour water on the cinders, while saying a prayer.

"Only a while later did I learn it was a bottle of water from Lourdes. Then, believe it or not, the rain was off, and so was the wind. And I finally saw a ray of sunshine in the sky, the very thing I had been hoping for. A happy coincidence, no doubt, but that gave me confidence.

"Even so, I still had fears. I was telling myself: You are trying to do better than a man who on his day left the great Paavo Nurmi 15 meters behind. Due to such a state of mind, I had purposely refrained from training all through the week, for fear of putting too heavy a stress on my muscles. To get up to my bedroom I could, in preference to the stairs, use a big rope my father had fixed for me, so that my arms would take some labor away from my legs. Obsessed by the same fear, I limbered up just a little before entering the stadium, and even so I felt a twinge in my thigh, no doubt the fruit of my imagination. And I went back to the massage room so that my faithful Morizot could take the trouble off my muscles. This soothed me considerably and I thought I was back to a normal state until somebody summoned me to the starting line. It was like feeling a blade go through my flesh."

Séra Martin and Jean Keller wanted to help Ladoumègue until the last lap. Also in the contest were Coenjaerts of Belgium and a mediocre 3:57.2 man from Italy who had already lost a couple of races to Ladoumègue ... Luigi Beccali. Ladoumègue's ambitious schedule called for 500-meter times of 1:16, 1:17, and 1:17 for a total of 3:50.

1930

They started out in the order Keller, Martin, Ladoumègue, and Beccali, without any troublesome tactics. Keller passed 400 meters in 58.6 and 500 in 1:13.4. He slowed the pace, hoping to get back on schedule, but Ladoumègue felt so fresh he cried, "Plus vite, plus vite!" ("Faster, faster!"). Keller passed 800 meters in 2:00.4 and dropped out.

Ladoumègue was satisfied, however, when Martin reached 1000 meters in 2:33.0, exactly on schedule. He ran on for a few more yards and stopped before they reached 1100 meters. When the bell sounded its expectant warning, Ladoumègue and Beccali were alone.

Relentlessly, Ladoumègue increased the pace and Beccali fell back. Ladoumègue passed 1200 meters in 3:05.0—1.0 second faster than Peltzer's pace, but Ladoumègue lacked Peltzer's kick. He had to run hard all the way if he wanted the record.

He drove himself all the way around the big curve and down the long homestretch. "My legs were like lead in that final lap, and it looked to me as if there was one Ladoumègue nailed to the ground and another Ladoumègue trying to defy the law of gravity and lengthen his stride."

He fought to maintain his pace to the end, running the last 200 in 29.7, the last 300 in 44.7, and the last 400 in 60.4. Three watches caught him in 3:49-1/5, and two others in 3:49.0. The slower verdict was taken as official. He was the new world-record holder.

"I knelt down on the track and for the first time I felt so light . . . until my masseur put his hand on my shoulder and it felt so heavy. . ."

Two weeks later, on the same track, in another paced race, Ladoumègue ran the world's fastest 1000 meters, in 2:23.6.

In 1931, he was content to start slowly and by July his fastest time was 3:58.0. On July 2 he set his third world record. This was 2000 meters in 5:21.8 at Jean Bouin stadium.

After a 3:54.4 at Stockholm on July 10, he met Thomas again in the dual meet against Great Britain at friendly Colombes on August 2. Ladoumègue was satisfied to win, 3:53.6 to 3:55.0. Then, at the same stadium on September 13, he met dangerous Eino Purje, whose 2000-meter record he had broken, in a race at ¾ mile.

The usual eager hares were out in front but they were gone before two laps of the 500-meter track. Ladoumègue led at 1000 meters in 2:29.0 with tenacious Purje on his heels.

In the homestretch, Purje gained slowly. He caught up with Ladoumègue and inched ahead as 20,000 fans pleaded with their favorite. Then Ladoumègue proved he could race, too. He fought back, caught Purje, and won by about a foot. Both men were timed in 3:00.6, well under the world record.

1931

A year before, Ladoumègue had gained glory with his 1500-meter world record on the first Sunday of October, and he wanted to try again in 1931. On Sunday, October 4, he sought Nurmi's mile record in Stade Jean Bouin.

Paris' weather was perfect, with no wind, as the seven Frenchmen started... after two false starts, one of them by the highly nervous Ladoumègue. René Morel, a 1:54 800-meter runner, set a steady pace for 1000 meters, one of the best paces yet set in a record attempt. He passed 440 yards in a swift 60.8 and 880 in 2:04.2. After reaching 1000 meters in 2:34.6, Morel slowed and, at the bell, Ladoumègue was alone with his desire and his fatigue.

He kept up his purposeful, long-striding pace past three-quarters in 3:08.0. He was now 1.3 seconds behind Nurmi's record pace, but he was still full of ambition. As in his 1500 meter record race, he spread his remaining strength over the whole last quarter. He tried all the way.

When he came out of the last turn and passed 1500 meters in 3:52.4, he was 0.6 ahead of Nurmi's pace and still determined. Nurmi had run the last 120 yards in 17.4, and Ladoumègue wanted to prove he had a better finish. He pushed himself hard down the homestretch even though the second runner, Keller, was 100 meters behind.

Ladoumègue proved his point with the last 120 in a good 16.8. His time was 4:09.2, not as sensational as his 3:49.2 1500 time, but still a world record by 1.2 seconds.

He was a national hero and the logical choice to win the Olympic 1500 meters to be held in Los Angeles in 1932. But the French Federation, much to the disgust of the French public, disqualified him for life as a result of charges that he had received under-the-table payoffs on several occasions.

He was the fastest 1500-meter runner and miler in history, holder of world records at 1000, ¾ mile, 1500, mile, and 2000 meters, and he could not run in the Olympic Games.

1929
MILE:

4:13.0	Leo Lermond (USA)	(1)	New York	17	Jun
4:14.6	Lermond	(1)	Philadelphia	27	Apr
4:15.0e	Augustus Moore (USA)	(2)	New York	17	Jun
4:16.0	Orval Martin (USA)	(2)	Philadelphia	27	Apr
4:16.2	George Offenhauser (USA)	(1)	State College, Pa.	25	May
4:16.4	Vernon Morgan (GB)	(1)	Durban, S.A.	8	Sep
4:16.8	Rufus Kiser (USA)	(1)	Eugene	1	Jun
4:18.0	Nick Carter (USA)	(1)	Los Angeles	4	May
4:18.6	Jules Ladoumègue (France)	(1)	Paris	26	May
4:19.2	Birger Kraft (Sweden)	(1)	Stockholm	27	Oct
4:19.4	Wilbur Getz (USA)	(1)	Chicago	8	Jun

Indoor marks:

4:13.4	Ray Conger (USA)	(1)	New York	16	Mar
4:14.2e	Leo Lermond (USA)	(2)	New York	16	Mar

1929/31

1,500m:

3:55.4	Jules Ladoumègue (France)	(1)	Colombes	1	Sep
3:56.2	Leo Lermond (USA)	(1)	Stockholm	8	Aug
3:56.2	Harri Larva (Finland)	(2)	Stockholm	8	Aug
3:56.6	Reidar Jörgensen (Norway)	(3)	Stockholm	8	Aug
3:57.2	Birger Kraft (Sweden)	(4)	Stockholm	8	Aug
3:57.7	Bror Öhrn (Sweden)	(5)	Stockholm	8	Aug
3:57.8	Hans Wichmann (Germany)	(1)	Breslau	21	Jul
3:58.0	Herbert Böcher (Germany)	(2)	Colombes	1	Sep
3:58.4	Luigi Beccali (Italy)	(1)	Genova	20	Oct
3:59.0+	Stanislaw Petkiewicz (Poland)	(2)	Stockholm	27	Oct
	+during a 4:19.6 mile.				

1930
MILE:

4:12.4	Ralph Hill (USA)	(1)	Eugene	17	May
4:13.0	Rufus Kiser (USA)	(2)	Eugene	17	May
4:14.0	Reginald Thomas (GB) BCG	(1)	Hamilton	23	Aug
4:15.2	George Lermond (USA)	(1)	West Point, NY	24	May
4:15.2	Thomas AAA	(1)	London	5	Jul
4:15.2	Jules Ladoumègue (France)	(1)	London	2	Aug
4:15.8	George Bullwinkle (USA)	(2)	New York	7	Jun
4:16.0	Luigi Beccali (Italy)	(1)	Milan	15	Jun
4:16.6	Ray Swartz (USA)	(1)	East Lansing	17	May
4:16.6	Eino Purje (Finland)	(1)	Stockholm	12	Jun
4:17.0	Jerry Cornes (GB)	(1)	Oxford	21	Jun

Indoor marks:

4:15.2	Ray Conger (USA)	(1)	New York	12	Mar
4:15.6	Paul Martin (Switzerland)	(2)	New York	12	Mar

1,500m:

3:49.2 WR	Jules Ladoumègue (France)	(1)	Paris	5	Oct
3:53.7	Ladoumègue	(1)	Berlin	21	Sep
3:53.8	Ladoumègue	(1)	Colombes	13	Jul
3:53.9	Eino Purje (Finland)	(1)	Helsinki	25	May
3:54.6	Ladoumègue	(1)	Hannover	31	Aug
3:54.7	Purje	(1)	Helsinki	18	Jun
3:55.4	Ladoumegue	(1)	Colombes	28	Sep
3:56.7	Reidar Jörgensen (Norway)	(2)	Helsinki	18	Jun
3:57.2	Stanislaw Petkiewicz (Poland)	(1)	Warsaw	14	Jun
3:57.2	Luigi Beccali (Italy)	(2)	Colombes	13	Jul
3:58.0	Janusz Kusocinski (Poland)				
3:58.6	Toivo Loukola (Finland)	(1)	Viipuri	14	Sep
3:58.8	Hans Wichmann (Germany)	(1)	Stockholm	27	Jul
3:59.0	Otto Peltzer (Germany)	(2)	Berlin	21	Sep
3:59.2	Albert Larsen (Denmark)	(1)	Stockholm	21	Jul

1931
MILE:

4:09.2 WR	Jules Ladoumègue (France)	(1)	Paris	4	Oct
4:13.4	Reginald Thomas (GB)	(1)	London	25	May
	(British record: 61-63-65-64.4) won by 100y				
4:14.4	Frank Crowley (USA)	(1)	New York	20	Jun
4:14.7e	Gene Venzke (USA)	(2)	New York	20	Jun
4:15.0	Leo Lermond (USA)	(1)	New York	6	Jun
4:16.3	Ray Putnam (USA)				
4:16.8	Clark Chamberlain (USA)	(1)	East Lansing	16	May
4:17.0	Cyril Ellis (GB)	(1)	London	22	Aug
4:17.3	Ralph Hill (USA)	(1)	Seattle	30	May
4:17.4	D.W. Price (GB)	(1)	Cambridge	12	Jun

Indoor marks:

4:13.0	Carl Coan (USA)	(1)	New York	16	Feb
4:13.4	Gene Venzke (USA)	(2)	New York	16	Feb
4:13.6	Ray Conger (USA)	(1)	New York	7	Feb
4:14.4	Leo Lermond (USA)	(2)	New York	14	Mar
	(+ during mile)				

1931

1,500m:

3:52.4+	Jules Ladoumègue (France) (1)	Paris	4 Oct
3:53.6	Ladoumègue vs. GB (1)	Colombes	2 Aug
3:53.6	Eino Purje (Finland) (1)	Stockholm	30 Aug
3:54.1	Purje (1)	Turku	30 Jul
3:54.4	Ladoumègue (1)	Stockholm	10 Jul
3:54.6	Reginald Thomas (GB) (1)	Stockholm	6 Aug
3:55.0	Thomas vs. Fr (2)	Colombes	2 Aug
3:55.5	Harri Larva (Finland) (2)	Turku	30 Jul
3:55.5	Lauri Lehtinen (Finland) (3)	Turku	30 Jul
3:55.8	Eric Ny (Sweden) (2)	Stockholm	30 Aug
3:56.5	Martti Luomanen (Finland) (4)	Turku	30 Jul
3:57.5	Tarmo Pohjala (Finland) (2)	Helsinki	16 Aug
3:57.6	Reidar Jörgensen (Norway) (2)	Stockholm	10 Jul
3:57.6	Hans-Helmut Krause (Ger) (1)	Berlin	1 Aug
3:57.6	Hans Wichmann (Germany) (2)	Berlin	1 Aug

Jack Lovelock

1932

1932 BRINGS THE "NEW WAVE"

An astonishing turn in the history of the mile run took place in 1932. Never had so many new and great milers emerged in one year. And coupled with the shocking downfall of the best milers of 1931, the Olympic year presented a complete turnover in talented hopefuls.

Olympic fever reached a high pitch in the United States, with the Olympics scheduled for Los Angeles in August, and great new milers appeared. Since now only three runners could represent a nation in the Olympics, the U.S. Final Olympic Trials in July was full of suspense. In the meantime, at least four new milers emerged from other countries and their names were to be of supreme interest in international running for at least five years. They were Cornes, Lovelock, Beccali, and Edwards.

JERRY CORNES

Born John Frederick Cornes, Jerry was a dark-haired, determined runner who showed great promise in 1930 when he was barely 20. Running for Clifton College, Bristol, in the inter-varsity sports, he won in 4:22.4. On June 21, he ran a highly promising 4:17.0 and on July 5 he placed second to Thomas in the AAA Championships with 4:18.0. In August he placed third in the Empire Games. Exposed to the gentlemanly lethargy of Oxford, he ran only 4:01.2 for 1500 meters and 4:22.0 in 1931. But with the arrival of a promising freshman in 1932, he was pushed to greater glory.

JACK LOVELOCK

He was born John Edward Lovelock on January 5, 1910, at Greymouth, New Zealand, the first son of a delicate, sensitive mother and a thoroughly English father who loved sports but migrated to New Zealand for his health. At the age of 12 when his father died, Jack was a lazy dreamer, with a likable smile and no enthusiasm for any sports except horseback riding.

In school, Jack's impressive intelligence was used in a leadership capacity. He was head prefect, or monitor, at Timaru Boys' High, and at the same time he was a cool, poised prankster. His first running was done in pursuit of boys who had sneaked out to buy candy. Jack usually captured the guilty boys, gained favor with the Headmaster, and shared the candy with his friends.

He was not enthusiastic about Rugby and cricket, but he was a skillful boxer, calm and ruthless. He liked running because he could be alone and aloof. He lacked sprinting speed, but he soon found he could win at 880 yards. He enjoyed sneaking out early in the mornings for four-mile runs, and late at nights for a swim. When he was 17 he was enthusiastic enough to buy a stopwatch to time his runs.

Before he was 19, a brilliant student and champion boxer, winner of a 3-mile steeplechase, and a mysterious trainer, he ran three races in one day. He won the 440 in 54.0, the 880 in 2:05.2, and the mile in 4:44.4. The *Timaru Herald* commented, "He has a beautiful style, a long, springy stride, and runs without apparent effort."

He began medical studies in the university at Dunedin, but he also decided to become a great runner. His first race outside of school was a handicap 1000 which he won easily, but then he was outkicked in a mile and later broke an ankle bone in Rugby.

In early 1930 he won a handicap mile in time equivalent to 4:30, and he was delighted at an invitation to run against the touring American, Leo Lermond, a good 4:13 miler who had placed fourth in the Olympic 5000 meters. Lovelock finished only fourth, but he talked keenly about training with Lermond and wrote extensive notes.

Lovelock won the Otago championship in 4:30, then improved to 4:26 for fourth place in the New Zealand Championships. One veteran runner commented, "He's got a wonderful stride, hasn't he? If only he had a finish."

He lost another mile, again with a poor finish. Then he entered a 3-mile steeplechase against 157 others, including cross-country champions. He won easily in fast time. He obviously had great natural endurance, improved by his 4-mile training runs.

He worked hard on improving his form still further. Below average in height, he ran on one side of a stone wall with a friend running on the other side. His friend's job was to watch for Lovelock's head. Weeks of this sort of practice helped develop Lovelock's famous float, with his legs working like wheels of a clock beneath him.

But the next year he finished only third in the New Zealand Championship, disappointed again in the homestretch. In the fall of 1931 he went to Oxford as a Rhodes scholar, a freshman at almost 22 years of age. One of his first visits was to the famous track at Iffley Road, where three laps made a mile and races were run clockwise.

His first race at Oxford was a handicap 880 in which he was given a generous 25-yard start over Jerry Cornes and Jack won in two minutes flat.

In the Oxford trials he ran his first real race against Cornes, who had already won the 880 in 1:56 that day. Lovelock fought hard and ran 4:26, but Cornes ran 4:22. In the relay against Cambridge, Lovelock's 4:24.4 provided the winning margin.

He was in bed with the flu for a week and had only one week

1932

to train for the Oxford Sports. He felt weak, but he ran 4:28.4 behind Cornes' 4:22.4. He had qualified to run in the big race against Cambridge.

The track at the White City Stadium in London was new and it cut up early. There was a discouraging wind, and yet Lovelock stuck close to Cornes past three-quarters in 3:18. He ran well and Cornes staged a dead heat in 4:22.4 so Lovelock could win his full blue.

The Olympic Games in Los Angeles were five months away and Lovelock wanted to go. He rebuilt his strength with long walks and ran several small races. On a good track at Aldershot, he felt exceptionally full of energy and he pushed the pace alone to 4:20.8.

He attempted a dead heat with Cornes in the Universities Championship, but a third runner fooled him and he was third in 4:22. Shocked and bitter, he did not train all week, but toward the end of the week he began planning to run 4:18 in a meet at Iffley Road, May 26, against the AAA team. It was to be one of the most remarkable miles ever run.

He was full of energy from his long rest and he ran fast, so fast that he led his pacemaker for 150 yards. He felt no effort and he became impatient. He shouted, "Faster, faster!" so loud it was heard all around the track. The first 440 was run in 57.5.

The pacemaker struggled past the half in 2:02, then had to stop. Lovelock waited in vain for his next pacemaker, who could not force the pace. His speed slowed to 71 seconds, and Lovelock passed three-quarters in 3:13.0—laps of 57.5, 64.5, and 71.0. Dismayed, he opened up and ran faster than ever before on the last lap of a mile. Recklessly, he poured it on, down the backstretch and into the last curve. Then he felt tight but he kept going, and, miraculously, he felt better.

"I was feeling absolutely on top, as if running on air, in fact, no effort at all, an exhilarating feeling."

He concentrated on holding his form and he had more energy than he needed, so much so that he jumped at the tape. The 400 spectators were excited by the time, a new British record of 4:12.0.

Lovelock's first question was, "Do you think New Zealand will enter me in their team for Los Angeles?"

Since only one man had run faster in the past four years, Lovelock was assured he would be selected. The most remarkable part of it all was the potential it showed. Certainly, with a more even pace, he could have approached Ladoumègue's world record. But there were some who wished he had saved this astonishing effort for a more important occasion.

After two weeks of slacking off, he and Cornes tried to break the record for three-quarters, both Conneff's recognized 3:02.8 and Ladoumègue's 3:00.6. They went out too fast, in 56.5 and 1:57.5, and Lovelock had an agonizing struggle to win in 3:02.2. He called it, "...one of the worst acts of folly of my whole racing career."

In his first 1500 meter race, at Antwerp, he beat Miklós Szabó by a convincing 12 yards in 3:57.8. The next week he ran a 4:20.8 relay mile and it felt hard. He was losing his form.

He was favored in the AAA Championships, with defending champion Thomas out with an injury. Lovelock led after 59.5 and 2:05.5 and passed three-quarters in 3:11, his fastest pace. But Cornes followed him to the homestretch and outkicked him by more than a yard in 4:14.2. Worst of all, Lovelock felt much more tired than after his 4:12.0. He was not running well, and the Olympics came next.

LUIGI BECCALI

Like most great milers, Beccali began running at an early age. Born in Milan on November 19, 1907, he ran his first race at the age of 14—a 5000-meter race with poor results. Later in 1922, still not 15, he placed thirty-second in a 12,000-meter road race. He continued to run on the roads, but he tried to be a cyclist until 1925 when he joined the Pro Patria club and trained for track under Dr. Dino Nai.

"Nini" Beccali was short (only 5'6½") and muscular (139 pounds), with dark hair and a tough determination. In 1926, while still 18 years old, he made good progress with 800 meters in 1:57.2 and 1500 in 4:08.2. But in 1927 he served in the army's Bersaglieri and managed to run only a poor 4:21.4 for 1500 meters.

In 1928 he ran 1:56.6. Then, at Paris in June, against Ladoumègue, he cut his 1500 time to 3:59.6. This made him fast enough to run in the Olympics at Amsterdam, but to his great disappointment he could not qualify for the final.

In 1929, he ran 1:57.0 and improved his 1500 a little to 3:58.4, but in his search for success he also tried longer races. He ran a steeplechase in 9:38.4, only 17 seconds slower than the 1928 Olympic winner. Beccali ran 5000 meters against that steeplechase champion, Toivo Loukola, in Paris in October. Loukola barely beat him as Beccali ran 15:20.8, promising time.

In 1930, Beccali continued his determined improvement with 1:55.2 and a mile in 4:16.0. But in July he ran against Ladoumègue in Paris and although he ran his fastest 1500—3:57.2—he was badly beaten.

Determined to improve, he gave up cross-country racing, and trained hard in the open fields during the winter of 1930-31. The result was surprisingly improved speed for the 1931 season. He concentrated on 800 meters and lost narrowly in four races. He ran 1:53.8, 1:53.4, and 1:53.4. He was also frustrated in a close 880 loss

to Tom Hampson in 1:55.9. At 1500 meters, he ran 4:00.0 for a teasing loss to Janusz Kusocinski in Poland, and his best of the year was 3:59.4. None of this rather mediocre background prepared the track world for his explosive 1932 season. He began on April 21 with an easy 3:59.4. Then on May 15 on the 500-meter track of the Milan Arena, where Napoleon once paraded his troops, Beccali ran at a remarkably even pace for three laps in 1:17.0 (equal to 400m average of 61.6), 1:18.0, and 1:17.2 for 3:52.2. Only Ladoumègue had bettered Beccali's times since 1928, and this five-second improvement in his personal record, equal to a 4:11.5 mile, made him an Olympic threat.
Four weeks later he won easily in Germany in 3:54.1.

PHIL EDWARDS

A remarkable 1500-meter runner because he almost never ran the distance except in Olympic Games, Dr. Edwards was best known as a half-miler. He was a British Guiana Negro who became a citizen of Canada and attended New York University.

In 1927, at the age of 19, he was fourth in the indoor AAU 1000 and second in the outdoor 880. He won races indoors in 1928, most importantly the AAU 600. Outdoors, he became an excellent half-miler. He won the IC4A and AAU 880, ran a 1:52.0 800 in the Canadian Championships, and placed fourth in the Olympic 800.

In 1929 he equalled the fastest indoor record of 1:05 for 500 meters and repeated as AAU 600 champion. Outdoors, he was faster than ever. He won the IC4A 880 with a gallant all-out solo effort in 1:52.2, equaling Meredith's American record, and he won the AAU 880.

Out of college in 1930, he slipped to a poor fifth in the British Empire Games 880 and mile. In 1931 indoor competition he lost to Chapman's 1:52.4, but he maintained his indoor AAU 600 supremacy for the fourth consecutive year.

In 1932, he improved to third in the Olympic 800, with 1:51.5. The next day, possibly for something interesting to do while he waited for his heat in the 1600 meter relay, he entered the 1500-meter heats. Nowhere in his record is there evidence of serious training for this distance.

THE U.S. CONTINGENT

The United States had its fastest crop of milers of all time, even though the fastest men of recent years had left the scene. Lermond won the AAU in 4:15 in 1931 but he was out of the picture in 1932. Ralph Hill of Oregon, who had set a surprising

American record of 4:12.4 at Eugene on May 17, 1930, while threatened by former NCAA champion Rufus Kiser of Washington (4:13.0), ran only 4:17.3 in 1931 and made a successful switch to longer races. (He almost won the Olympic 5000.) Ray Conger was through after dominating indoor mile racing and winning the 1930 outdoor AAU title. He ran 4:13.4 indoors in 1929, swept the boards in 1930, and ran 4:13.6 in 1931.

Surprisingly enough, several fast milers developed in 1932:

GENE VENZKE

Venzke's parents moved from Minnesota to Pennsylvania when he was ten, and he did his first running in hobnailed boots on the three-mile road to school. He began as a road runner but he always wanted to be a miler. He dropped out of high school at 16, moved to New York on his own, and worked as an apprentice toolmaker. When he lost his job in the depression, he returned to high school after a five-year lapse.

He came to national attention in 1930, when he placed fourth in the indoor AAU two-mile and fourth in the outdoor AAU mile. In 1931, at 22, he became one of the fastest milers in the country, running 4:13.4 indoors and 4:14.7 outdoors, but he lost all except one race. He was second in the AAU mile.

He continued his long cross country running in the fall and tried everything anybody suggested to improve his speed. He was one of the first to use a type of interval training. In the 1932 indoor season he became the fastest miler in U.S. history. At 6'2" and 155 pounds, he was tall, bronzed, and handsome, the favorite hope for an American Olympic championship.

On February 6, as a 23-year-old high school senior, he ran 4:11.2 for a world indoor record, beating Lermond's 4:12.0. Eleven days later, in the Baxter Mile, he followed Lermond's 61.2 and Crowley's 2:06.2, then took the lead in 3:10.6. He ran hard and scared. "I was afraid of Lermond . . . I thought he was right behind me . . . I swear I almost felt his breath on my back." But Lermond was 50 yards back and Venzke won in 4:10.0, the second fastest race ever run.

Venzke set a world indoor 1500 record of 3:53.4 ten days later and won the indoor AAU in 4:15.0. Outdoors, he set an American record with a sparkling 3:52.6 for 1500 meters on June 18 at Cambridge. He was regarded as a sure Olympic team member and a hope for the gold medal.

GLENN CUNNINGHAM

Born August 4, 1909, Glenn went with his brothers to start a fire in the little country school at Elkhart, Kansas in 1917. They

1932

used kerosene to hasten the job, and there was a flash of flame and an explosion and the screams of young boys. Glenn's legs were so badly burned that amputation was proposed. But he and his mother would not stand for it.

He spent six painful months in a hospital while skin was grafted to his legs. Then his mother spent countless hours massaging strength back into the scarred legs. When he was able, Glenn began to run to strengthen his crippled legs. He did such a good job of overcompensating that he became a good runner. After an attempt at football, he devoted himself to track.

In 1929, as a 19-year-old junior in high school, he ran 4:36.5. The next year he went to the National Interscholastics in Chicago and his scarred legs carried him to victory in 4:24.7. But even at nearly 21, he was not the fastest high school miler in the nation and he did little to surprise anyone in 1931 as a freshman at Kansas.

He lost a race indoors in 1932 (to Chapman's 4:18.4), then won some small meets, but he aroused little interest until May 21 in the Big Six conference meet at Lincoln, Nebraska. Then Cunningham became an Olympic prospect. He won the mile in 4:14.3 and came back later in the day to win the 880 in 1:53.5.

On June 11 he was in Chicago again, this time for the NCAA championship. For the first time in important competition, the track world saw the barrel-chested figure quicken his stride at the half-way mark and run the last half of his race at surprising speed. Cunningham won in 4:11.1, a new American record and a time beaten only three times outdoors and once indoors in all track history.

PEN HALLOWELL

Norwood Penrose Hallowell of Harvard was a talented runner who remained hidden in Ivy League competition until 1932. As a sophomore in 1930 he was second in the IC4A mile behind Bullwinkle's 4:18.8, but he won in 1931 in 4:18.0.

He emerged as an Olympic threat indoors in 1932 when he won the IC4A title in an electrifying 4:12.4. He proved his speed outdoors with a 50.8 440 and a good 1:52.6 880, only 0.4 seconds off the American record, and he barely lost in the outdoor IC4A mile.

HENRY BROCKSMITH of Indiana placed second in the 1930 NCAA 2-mile and fourth in 1931. Turning successfully to the mile in 1932, he won at Chicago indoors in a startling 4:12.5. At the NCAA meet, he followed Cunningham to second place in 4:11.6, also breaking the American record. Two weeks later, at Evanston, Ill., he ran 3:53.9 to better the official American record for 1500 meters.

JOE MANGAN, a junior at Cornell, surprised by winning a

hard-fought IC4A mile at Berkeley, California, in 4:14.8, ahead of Hallowell and Crowley.

FRANK CROWLEY was chosen All-American high school miler the year Cunningham was a senior. In 1931, as a freshman at Manhattan, Crowley placed third in the AAU mile and beat Venzke on June 20 in 4:14.4. This year, his best was third in the IC4A in 4:15.1.

FINAL OLYMPIC TRIALS. The AAU meet at Stanford University near Palo Alto, California, served as the do-or-die Final Olympic Trials. The heats were run on July 15 and Frank Nordell, who had previously run 4:13.0 indoors, disappointed his followers and was eliminated.

In the finals, the next day, before 35,000 stirred-up spectators, Brocksmith led around the last curve. About 100 yards from the finish, Venzke passed Brocksmith convincingly and appeared momentarily to be the winner. Hallowell, though, was at Venzke's elbow, and the talented Crowley, in dark sun glasses, was close behind, followed by Cunningham.

Venzke fought desperately for 20 yards, then faded as all three rushed past him. There was no change in position among the first three, but the gaps widened between them. The poised Hallowell appeared well within himself as he won by five yards. Crowley beat Cunningham by three yards and a sorely disappointed Venzke was eight yards behind Cunningham. Hallowell's time was 3:52.7, and he now had to be considered a contender for the gold medal.

With the elimination of Venzke from the American team, the astonishing reversal was complete. In February of 1932, the experts thought of four or five runners as contenders in the Olympic 1500: Ladoumègue, the double world-record holder; Venzke, the 4:10 miler; Thomas, the British record holder, Empire champion, and two-time AAA champion; Purje, still good enough to run 3:53.6 in 1931 and almost beat Ladoumègue at three-quarters of a mile in a 3:00.6 world record; and the defending Olympic champion, Larva, with the fearsome kick, who had won two Finnish championships at 800 meters since 1928 and was still a threat.

But Venzke was out; Ladoumègue was declared a professional in March; Thomas suffered a split Achilles tendon; and the two Finns faded a bit more, although they were still feared by many.

In the meantime, there had been an equally astonishing emergency of new threats: Lovelock, who yelled for more speed while running an oddly-paced 4:12; Beccali, who suddenly cut five seconds off his fastest 1500; Cunningham, who made the big jump from obscure freshman to NCAA champion in 4:11.1; Cornes, who began to show his early promise with a 4:14.2 victory in the AAA and who had trained well in the month since then; Hallowell, whose first excursion into big-time racing had brought him a 4:12.4 indoors and a 3:52.7 victory in the U.S. Final Olympic Trials; and Edwards, a strong half-miler who looked dangerous in his 1500 meter heat.

1932 OLYMPIC GAMES

The heats on August 3 were won by Cunningham in 3:55.8, Lovelock in 3:58.0, and Beccali in 3:59.6. The famous former world record holder, Otto Peltzer, now 32 years old, was eliminated. But all the favorites were in, plus Eric Ny of Sweden, who ran 3:55.8 in 1931 and 3:55.6 on June 11, 1932; the third Finn, Martti Luomanen, who ran 3:56.5 in 1931; and the third American, promising Frank Crowley. Edward King of Canada qualified but he did not run in the final the next day.

They lined up tensely on the gray track at the head of the backstretch in the gigantic bowl of the Los Angeles Coliseum. Behind them, across the wide expanse of extra space where the water jump was located, beyond the high flight of stairs, above the peristyle entrance, on a concrete column atop the high rim of the stadium, burned the orange Olympic flame. And 65,000 spectators watched with suspense in the clear Los Angeles heat.

Luigi Beccali also felt the suspense. Before the gun could sound, he moved nervously across the starting line in a false start, and they had to line up again.

Jack Lovelock felt the suspense. This was the third time this year he had run a final the day after the preliminary heats, and he had lost both of the others. He had to feel fresh to do his best, and he had not run well in yesterday's heat. In addition, his Achilles tendon was sore from training on the hard tracks.

Glenn Cunningham was unsmilingly serious. Even Jerry Cornes, usually happy-go-lucky, who last night had said the Finns looked bad, today feared even the Finns.

When the gun sounded, it was an uncertain pack of runners with no clear plan. Edwards, with the greatest speed of all, led at the start, but Lovelock ran past him and cut in to the pole. Beccali secured the third position, followed by the three hopeful Americans.

After the curve, Ny moved into the lead with three laps to go, but his pace was unsatisfactory and Lovelock regained the lead. He completed the first 400 meters in 60.5.

On the backstretch, Cunningham strode past Lovelock, prematurely eager, followed by Larva and Edwards. Hallowell moved to Lovelock's heels, ahead of Beccali and Cornes. There was a continual uncertain shuffling and changing of positions and Edwards led at 800 meters in 2:04.5. Nobody took Edwards seriously at this point, for it was natural that so great a half-miler could lead for 800 meters.

Then Cunningham launched into the tactic he was already establishing as his trademark. He rushed into the lead with quick, powerful confident strides, his barrel chest thrust forward. He was three yards ahead of Edwards before the tall Negro matched his pace. Before they reached the curve a dismayed Beccali was ten yards behind Edwards, in third place.

Now the American crowd was howling, for they tasted victory. Even while Edwards closed the gap around the curve, they fancied a gold medal, for Cunningham was strong, while Edwards was only a half-miler and Beccali was falling farther behind.

Edwards pulled alongside Cunningham in the stretch and, in spite of the crowd's pleas, he nosed ahead as the bell clanged. Cornes had moved into third place, but he was 15 yards behind. Lovelock, dazed and desperate, followed Cornes around Beccali with his last strength.

Edwards passed 1200 meters in 3:07.0. Then, to the astonishment of everybody in the Coliseum, he began a drive which Cunningham could not match. Here was a rank novice winning the Olympic 1500!

Cornes, Lovelock, and Beccali were gaining, but they were too far back, and Cunningham looked beaten. Inch by inch, Edwards was opening a small but significant gap. But it was not over yet!

On the last curve, Lovelock began to tie up disastrously. Suddenly, Beccali shot past him with shocking speed, his blue shirt a blur and his slicked-down coal-black hair bouncing. Beccali was running with amazing speed as he passed the powerful Cornes. Hallowell and Ny swept past Lovelock.

Beccali, engaged in the fastest 1500-meter finish ever, rushed past Cunningham on the curve and caught Edwards with 100 yards to go. There was no stopping him as he sailed past and pulled away. He broke the tape with both hands, almost 10 yards ahead.

Cornes, also running the best race of his life, caught Edwards five yards from the finish line. The tall Canadian was flailing his arms in a desperate effort to salvage the silver medal, but Cornes opened a gap in the last steps.

Cunningham finished about four yards behind Edwards, thoroughly beaten. Hallowell's head was back as he strained down the stretch. He lost all form and Ny, running his fastest race, passed him for fifth place. Lovelock staggered in 15 yards behind Hallowell, completely exhausted and bewildered, in sharp contrast to the jubilance of Beccali, who was embraced by his enthusiastic countrymen.

Results: Beccali 3:51.2, Cornes 3:52.6, Edwards 3:52.8, Cunningham 3:53.4, Ny 3:54.6, Hallowell 3:55.0, Lovelock 3:57.8.

Beccali's Olympic record of 3:51.2 was the second fastest 1500 ever run. His last 300 meters was estimated in 41.7, easily the fastest ever run in a fast race. His last lap was guessed as about 57 seconds. Something new had been added to foot racing.

1932

MILE:

4:11.1	Glenn Cunningham (USA)	NCAA	(1)	Chicago	11	Jun
4:11.6	Henry Brocksmith (USA)	NCAA	(2)	Chicago	11	Jun
4:12.0	Jack Lovelock (NZ)		(1)	Oxford	26	May
4:14.2	Lovelock		(1)	Montreal	19	Aug
4:14.2	Jerry Cornes (GB)	AAA	(1)	London	2	Jul
4:14.3	Cunningham		(1)	Lincoln, Neb	21	May
4:14.4e	Lovelock	AAA	(2)	London	2	Jul
4:14.8e	Cyril Ellis (GB)	AAA	(3)	London	2	Jul
4:14.8	Joe Mangan (USA)	IC4A	(1)	Berkeley (4:14.70)	2	Jul
4:14.8	Norwood Hallowell (USA)	IC4A	(2)	Berkeley (4:14.72)	2	Jul
4:15.1	Frank Crowley (USA)	IC4A	(3)	Berkeley (4:15.04)	2	Jul
4:16.4	Ward Hardman (USA)		(1)	Annapolis	28	May
4:16.9	E.W. Barwick (Australia)		(1)	Melbourne	30	Jan

NB. Carl Coan, 4th at Berkeley, 10 yds. behind the winner.

Indoor marks:

4:10.0	Gene Venzke (USA)		(1)	New York	17	Feb
4:11.2	Venzke		(1)	New York	6	Feb
4:12.0	Leo Lermond (USA)		(2)	New York	6	Feb
4:12.4	Norwood Hallowell (USA	IC4A	(1)	New York	5	Mar
4:12.5	Henry Brocksmith (USA)		(1)	Chicago	12	Mar
4:13.0	Frank Nordell (USA)	IC4A	(2)	New York	5	Mar
4:14.8	William McKniff (USA)	IC4A	(3)	New York	5	Mar

1,500m:

3:51.2	Luigi Beccali (Italy)		(1)	Los Angeles	4	Aug
3:52.2	Beccali		(1)	Milan	15	May
3:52.6	Gene Venzke (USA)		(1)	Cambridge, Mass.	18	Jun
3:52.6	Jerry Cornes (GB)		(2)	Los Angeles	4	Aug
3:52.7	Norwood Hallowell (USA)		(1)	Palo Alto	16	Jul
3:52.8	Philip Edwards (Canada)		(3)	Los Angeles	4	Aug
3:53.1+	Glenn Cunningham (USA)	NCAA	(1)	Chicago	11	Jun
3:53.4	Cunningham		(4)	Los Angeles	4	Aug
3:53.6	Frank Crowley (USA)		(2)	Palo Alto	16	Jul
3:53.9	Henry Brocksmith (USA)		(1)	Evanston	25	Jun
3:54.0	Janusz Kusocinski (Poland)		(1)	Królewska Huta	12	Jun
3:54.1	Beccali		(1)	Frankfurt/M.	12	Jun
3:54.6	Eric Ny (Sweden)		(5)	Los Angeles	4	Aug
3:55.3	Eino Purje (Finland)		(1)	Helsinki	18	Jun

Indoor mark:

3:53.4	Gene Venzke (USA)		(1)	New York	27	Feb

V

The time of Lovelock

Following the great surge of new milers in 1932 came a period of fierce competition during which new super-stars fought for supremacy with first one and then another forging to the front.

The middle 1930's may well be the most exciting short period in the history of the 1500 and mile. It was a time of world records and surprises, a time of great improvement generally and uneasy uncertainty for individuals. But most of all, it was the time of Lovelock.

CUNNINGHAM MAKES HIS BID

In 1933, Glenn Cunningham began to earn the title, "Iron Man." He ran a full indoor season. And ran a difficult outdoor season while doubling in the 880. Furthermore, he ran 20 races in Europe during the summer.

Indoors, he won the Wanamaker Mile from Venzke in 4:13.0 and he beat Venzke by ten yards in the Baxter Mile in 4:14.6. But Venzke gained revenge a week later in the AAU 1500 as both runners crossed the line in 3:55.4.

Cunningham began the outdoor season as an unsuspecting victim of Dawson's kick in a 4:29.9 mile at Tulsa. It was his only mile defeat of the year. In the Big Six conference meet, he won a good double in 4:18.4 and 1:52.2, but that was nothing compared with his remarkable double in the NCAA meet at Chicago on June 17.

First he won the mile, all alone after his 62-second third lap. His time was 4:09.8, second best ever run. Then he came back in a sensational 880 against Charley Hornbostel, the defending champion.

He lost by a foot, but both men were timed in 1:50.9, equal to Ben Eastman's not-yet-recognized world record. In the AAU meet at Chicago on June 30, Cunningham won the 1500 in 3:52.3, another national record. Then, in a great double he won the 800 in 1:51.8 over Hornbostel.

On his first tour of Europe, he ran 20 races without defeat. He began in true iron-man style by running three fast races in three days at Stockholm, July 19-21. He won a 1000-meter race from Ny in 2:23.9, only 0.3 from the world record. He beat Ny in a 1:50.6 800 and then in a 3:53.0 1500. He ran another 1:51.0 800 on the tour, but his big race was at 1500 meters against Miklós Szabó at Budapest, on August 12. After setting a pace of 59, 2:02.2 and 3:08.0, Cunningham had to run 3:51.6 to beat the 25-year-old Hungarian's 3:52.6. Thus, Cunningham moved to fourth best on the all-time 1500-meter list.

LOVELOCK SETS A GOAL

After his poor race in the 1932 Olympics, Lovelock said, "I must have been overtrained," but his two post-Olympic races were good. At San Francisco, in a 4-mile relay against the USA, he started the third leg five yards behind Cunningham, trailed him for 3½ laps, and then overwhelmed him by 15 yards in 4:18. Five days later in Montreal, he ran what Jerry Cornes called an astonishing time.

After the long journey by rail, Lovelock spent the afternoon having tea and chocolates on a river cruise before being persuaded to run in the twilight meet. Then, on a poor track in cold weather, he ran a 2:10 half and finished in 4:14.2.

Cornes called him "the most amazingly gifted runner I've ever known," and said, "I believe that Lovelock's debacle was fundamentally due to nerves. He was certainly not over-trained—and he was running as well, if not better than me in practice."

At any rate, Lovelock chalked it up to experience. The most important lesson of all, he thought, was in the sprint finish Beccali displayed. "All I can hope for is to square my account with Beccali."

He returned to Oxford and answered a question about his future in medicine and athletics: "I can't do both things equally well. I'm going to aim at a second-class pass—and a gold medal at Berlin."

His philosophy valued poise and relaxation and avoidance of overtraining. He mixed boxing, some hard cross-country races, and a mixture of track races at all distances. During the Christmas holiday period he also had fun dancing, swimming, and fencing. In the Universities boxing tournament, after a midnight 400-yard race, he fought four matches in one day, losing the final.

He reached respectable running condition in early 1933, but he ran nothing faster than 4:18. Still he felt ready for the trip to

1933

America with the combined Oxford and Cambridge team.

He avoided running on the ship, but he combined exercise with fun by walking, swimming, dancing, and doing gym work. After two weeks away from competition, he ran 4:12.6 against Harvard and Yale with good form and a last lap in 60.

"A most satisfactory run in every way as it gave me the necessary confidence to meet Bonthron of Princeton."

BILL BONTHRON

A big, strong-looking 19-year-old with close-cropped black hair, Bill Bonthron did not wish to run in the big races in 1932. Although he was a sophomore at Princeton, he had neither the maturity nor the desire to break track records. In the IC4A meet he placed second in the 2-mile and that was the end of his season.

Like another promising sophomore, Glenn Cunningham, Bonthron was the victim of a childhood accident. At 12, one leg was severely burned by an electric wire while he was playing in a tree, and a doctor ordered running to restore his leg. Bonthron preferred other games, but he was good at running and so he competed for Princeton.

In 1933, he earned a reputation for doubling, at the same time Cunningham was building an iron-man reputation. Bonthron won the 1500 and 800 against Harvard, and against Yale he added the 3000. In the IC4A meet he won the 1500 in a good 3:54 and came back to win the 800 in 1:53.5. People began to compare him favorably with John Paul Jones.

THE GREATEST DUEL

The anticipated duel between Bonthron and Lovelock was to be on July 15 at Princeton's Palmer Stadium in the dual meet between Oxford-Cambridge and Princeton-Cornell. Early in the week, they met on the track and introduced themselves, jogging companionably until Bonthron's coach, Matty Geis, separated them.

Geis was quoted in the newspaper: "Bill is in grand shape. He's ready to run any pace Lovelock does. And I'm not disregarding the fact that Bill may also run in the half-mile. He has the greatest combination of stamina and speed I've ever come across."

Watching Bonthron train, hard and fast, Lovelock began to feel nervous and he believed Bonthron could break the world record. Still, Lovelock did little work during the week. What he wanted most was rest.

A threat of rain on the day of the meet held the crowd to 6,000, but rain did not fall, the temperature was warm, and there was no hindering wind. The track was hard and fast for the mile, first race on the program at 4:40 p.m.

Lovelock's teammate, Forbes Horan, wanted to set a pace of 3:06, but Bonthron shot into the lead at the start. Lovelock was overjoyed. And when Bonthron's teammate, Hazen, took over the lead on the backstretch, it was confirmed. Bonthron wanted a fast pace, too.

Around the curve, a groundskeeper wandered unconsciously in front of them. Hazen shouted and dodged, bumping him slightly, and the others were thrown off stride. But they were soon back in rhythm and they passed the 440 in time which suited Lovelock perfectly, 61.2 for Bonthron, 61.4 for himself.

They followed Hazen for one more lap. Then, just before the half-mile, Bonthron moved resolutely past his teammate and Lovelock was quick to follow. They passed the 880 in 2:03.5 and 2:03.6. Around the curve, Horan raced into the lead, trying to keep the pace to 3:06, but he could not hold it and Bonthron passed him.

Lovelock ran carefully behind Bonthron, watching the broad back... waiting. Around they went, up to the starting line. Bonthron was leading in 3:08.6, Lovelock's time was 3:08.7. Lovelock waited alertly around the curve, knowing Bonthron's famed charge would come soon.

Into the backstretch, 300 yards from the end, it came. Bonthron seemed to gather himself closer together, head down, arms swinging in tightly. Then, with shocking power, he exploded.

Lovelock was watching for the move and he swung into a faster stride immediately, but Bonthron's power was astonishing. A gap of three yards opened immediately, and for a moment Lovelock doubted he could keep up. Then Bonthron's surge eased and they were merely running at great speed.

Lovelock closed the gap and followed closely, feeling the cinders peppering his legs. Around the last turn, Lovelock poised himself expectantly. Then, as the homestretch appeared, he gathered his strength.

He gave it all he had, concentrating on high knee action, high arm action, head down to help with his balance, emphasis on form. He felt a great thrill as he shot past Bonthron. There was no answering effort from his opponent and he moved away, concentrating on holding his speed.

He was 20 yards from the tape before he felt his form go. He glanced back. He was safe. He concentrated harder, held his form fairly well, although he could feel his knees begin to turn out and his hands going too high. Then he hit the tape and he could relax.

He kept jogging, a full lap, while the standing crowd kept clapping and shouting. He was still jogging when the loud speaker crackled: "Time for Lovelock, four minutes seven-point-six seconds, which breaks the world record by one and three-fifths seconds."

The crowd was shrieking its admiration, but Bonthron said to his coach, "What's the use?"

Geis asked him if he knew he had run 4:08.7, also under the world record.

"Aw, nuts!" Bonthron said. "He beat me."

Later, when he spoke to the press,he said, "I was in the best shape of my life and did about what I hoped. I'm satisfied with my race and I'm satisfied that I was beaten by the greatest miler in the world."

Lovelock said, "I think I ought to be able to do the mile in 4:06 with a faster third quarter. If I could reach the three quarters in 3:06 I feel sure I could do the last quarter in an even 60 seconds."

Now the all-time mile list stood:

4:07.6	Lovelock	1933	4:10.4	Nurmi	1923
4:08.7n	Bonthron	1933	4:11.0	Larva	1928
4:09.2	Ladoumègue	1931	4:11.6n	Purje	1928
4:09.8i	Cunningham	1933	4:11.6n	Brocksmith	1932
4:09.8	Cunningham	1933	4:12.0i	Ray	1925
4:10.0i	Venzke	1932	4:12.0ni	Lermond	1932

Lovelock: "That is the sort of race which one really enjoys—to feel at one's peak on the day when it is necessary, and to be able to produce the pace at the very finish. It gives a thrill which compensates for months of training and toiling. But it is the sort of race that one wants only about once a season."

Lovelock had two weeks of deteriorating on the banquet circuit in the U.S. and then a week's trip by ship. He had almost no training when he ran in Glasgow on August 5 in the Ranger's Sports and he was up against dangerous Reggie Thomas who had won his third AAA championship on July 8 in 4:14.2.

It was a handicap race, with 12 starters, and 40,000 people were in Ibrox Park in anticipation. Lovelock followed Thomas all the way, through a 3:11 three-quarters, and waited until the last 50 yards to sprint past. He won, 4:13.6 to 4:14.2, and the next day he was sick in bed with the flu.

Five weeks later, on September 9, he was in Turin for the World Student Games. His opponent in the 1500 was the formidable Olympic champion.

BECCALI, THE CHAMPION

A few days after his Olympic victory, Beccali suffered a foot injury and ran no great late races as Larva had in 1928. In 1933, Beccali was content to build slowly toward a September climax. On June 11 he ran against France at Colombes, where he was cheered as Olympic champion while other fans cheered Ladoumègue, who was

1933

not allowed to run. Beccali won the 1500 in 3:55.4 and the 800 in 1:56.2.
Four days later, in Milan, he ran three-quarters in 3:03.4. Then he took a welcome rest during the hot summer weather and worked on his job as a draftsman for the city of Milan. On August 27, he ran 800 meters in 1:53.2.
On September 7, they ran in heats of the Student Games. Both Lovelock and Beccali placed fifth easily, to make the ten-man final. Beccali ran an 800-meter relay leg later in the day in 1:51.4, but Lovelock felt tired and stiff.
This had never happened to him before and Lovelock could not understand it. He tried to walk it off, but the next day he was stiff and sore.
He felt depressed on the day of the race. The weather was overcast, the track was too hard, and Beccali was obviously in high spirits. When Beccali tipped his hand with a false start, Lovelock knew he was in for a fast race.
Lovelock had to start on the outside and the line was not curved, and so he dropped in behind while Beccali raced off enthusiastically, behind his pace-setter. The first 400 meters on the 446-meter cinder track was in 59.8, with Beccali close behind.
Then Beccali took over full of energy at 675 meters, and Lovelock had to move up behind him. Beccali passed 800 meters in 2:04, then, apparently dissatisfied with the pace, he increased it. To Lovelock he looked smooth and very strong. Lovelock was uncomfortable with the pace, but he hung on past 1200 meters in 3:06.
The pace was faster than in his world record mile, but he was not thinking of records. With half a lap to go he surged to test Beccali and the Italian crowd fell silent with fear, but Beccali responded with enough speed.
In the middle of the last curve, Beccali started his drive. He opened a two-yard gap and the crowd began to cheer. Lovelock managed to go along with the swift Italian's drive and he prepared for a sprint in the homestretch. He launched his attack, but he could not gain. In fact, the strong Olympic champion pulled away still further.
Beccali won by more than three yards. Then officials carried him to the official box and many people received embraces, including Lovelock. Beccali's time tied Ladoumègue's world record of 3:49.2, and Lovelock ran 3:49.8.
Beccali said he was saving something for a challenge in the stretch. He thought he might have finished a mile under the record. Lovelock said : "Beccali is a great champion, and very strong. He was unbeatable today."
On September 17, both men made attempts on the 1500 meter record. Lovelock ran a special race in Colombes, on a cut-up

track against 13 opponents. All alone for the last 600 meters, he ran only 3:52.8, much slower than he had hoped.

That same day, at Milan's Arena, Beccali ran against Great Britain and Reggie Thomas. The powerful Beccali followed the second-strings past 60.0 and 1:59.4, with Thomas following him. Beccali took over at 1000 meters, letting the pace slow, but Thomas could not keep up.

After passing 1200 meters in 3:07, Beccali uncorked the fastest finish in history. He had run the last 300 against Lovelock in 43.2, and Ladoumègue had run it in 44.7 during his world record. But now Beccali ran down the backstretch and around the curve so fast that the crowd cheered with sheer excitement. He ran it in 42-flat and his time was 3:49.0.

He held the world record, and he had made it in an international dual meet, a rare occurrence in middle-distance running.

Beccali was in top form. A week later, at Florence, he ran 800 meters in 1:50.6 in a planned record attempt. On October 1 he ran 800 meters in a relay in 1:50.4. On October 15 in Turin, he ran 60 seconds, 2:05, 3:06, and finished 1500 meters in 3:49.6.

He now had run three of the four fastest 1500's ever run. After two more victories, he closed his season on November 4 at Milan with a world record of 2:10.0 for 1000 yards.

PAAVO NURMI (Postscript)

After Nurmi's defeat by Peltzer and Wide in Berlin, he was no longer the invincible Flying Finn, but he was hardly through. In 1927 he ran even more poorly (only a world record at 2000 meters). In 1928 he blamed illness for his disappointments at the Olympics, where he won only one gold medal and had to settle for two silver.

He moved up to longer distances with success, setting three world records in one day after the Olympics. But in 1929 he went to the U.S. again and lost a slow mile to Ray Conger. Embittered, he returned home and it seemed the great career was over.

His career as a miler may have been over, but he set world records for six miles and 20,000 meters in 1930, for the 2-mile in 1931, and in 1932 he was prepared to win the Olympic marathon when suddenly he was declared professional ... a tearful disappointment to the great Nurmi.

Yet he would not quit. He was still considered an amateur in Finland, and in 1933 he made one last effort at 1500 meters. In the Finnish Championships at Turku on August 6, he trailed Olympic 5000 meter champion Lauri Lehtinen to the homestretch, then burst past spectacularly to win in 3:55.8, to 3:56.8 for Paavo Mickelsson, 3:57.2 for Eino Purje, and 3:57.9 for Lehtinen. At 36 years of age, Nurmi still had some fight left.

1933

JULES LADOUMÈGUE (Postscript)

As a professional, Ladoumègue ran several "races" at friendly Jean-Bouin in Paris during late 1933. He beat Purje, who had turned professional, by 20 meters in a 2:29.4 1000 and ran 3:54.8 on October 1. Then he ran a great series of four races. On October 9 he ran ¾ mile in 2:59.2, better than the world record. On October 14 he ran 3:50.8, and four days later he ran 3:51.4. On October 21, after a pace of 61 and 2:03.4, he picked up to 3:05 and finished in 3:50.4. He was apparently as good as ever. However, all of these were paced record attempts.

Ten years later, when he was almost 37, Ladoumègue's amateur status was restored, and he still enjoyed running. At Stade Jean-Bouin he ran 3:58.4.

1933

MILE:
4:07.6	Jack Lovelock (NZ)	(1)	Princeton, N.J.	15	Jul
4:08.7	Bill Bonthron (USA)	(2)	Princeton, N.J.	15	Jul
4:09.8	Glenn Cunningham (USA) NCAA	(1)	Chicago	17	Jun
4:12.6	Lovelock	(1)	Cambridge, Mass.	8	Jul
4:13.6	Lovelock	(1)	Glasgow	5	Aug
4:14.1	Ray Sears (USA)	(1)	Milwaukee	2	Jun
4:14.2	Reginald Thomas (GB) AAA	(1)	London	8	Jul
4:14.2	Thomas	(2)	Glasgow	5	Aug
4:15.0	Tom Riddell (GB)	(3)	Glasgow	5	Aug
4:15.1	Charles Hornbostel (USA)	(1)	Lafayette, Ind.	6	May
4:15.7	William Lauck (USA)	(1)	Charlottesville, Va.	13	May
4:15.7	Herbert Lewis (USA)	(1)	Durham, N.C.	20	May
4:16.5	Frank Crowley (USA)	(1)	West Point, N.Y.	20	May

Indoor marks:
4:09.8	Glenn Cunningham (USA)	(1)	Chicago	25	Mar
4:12.0	Cunningham	(1)	New York	16	Mar
4:13.0	Cunningham Millrose G	(1)	New York		Feb
4:14.6	Cunningham	(1)	New York	18	Feb

1,500m:
3:49.0	Luigi Beccali (Italy)	(1)	Milan	17	Sep
3:49.2	Beccali	(1)	Turin	9	Sep
3:49.6	Beccali	(1)	Turin	15	Oct
3:49.8	Jack Lovelock (NZ)	(2)	Turin	9	Sep
3:51.0	Glenn Cunningham (USA)	(1)	Budapest	12	Aug
3:52.3	Cunningham AAU	(1)	Chicago	30	Jun
3:52.6	Miklós Szabó (Hungary)	(2)	Budapest	12	Aug
3:52.8	Lovelock	(1)	Colombes	17	Sep
3:53.0	Cunningham	(1)	Stockholm	21	Jul
3:53.3	Cunningham	(1)	Lawrence	22	Apr
3:53.6	Reginald Thomas (GB)	(2)	Milan	17	Sep
3:54.0*	Bill Bonthron (USA) IC4A	(1)	Cambridge, Mass.	27	May
3:55.0	Joe Mangan (USA) AAU	(2)	Chicago	30	Jun
3:55.0	Alfredo Furia (Italy)	(3)	Milan	17	Sep
3:55.3	Paavo Mickelsson (Finland)	(1)	Helsinki	6	Sep
3:55.5*	Frank Crowley (USA) IC4A	(3)	Cambridge, Mass.	27	May
3:55.5	Eino Purje (Finland)	(1)	Helsinki	15	Jun
3:55.5	Volmari Isohollo (Finland)	(1)	Oslo	2	Jul

*Electric times: Bonthron 3:53.2, (Mangan 2nd 3:53.82), Crowley 3:55.30.

1934

FASTEST RUNS THROUGH 1933:

(3:48.5)	4:07.6	Lovelock	1933
3:49.0	(4:08.1)	Beccali	1933
3:49.2	(4:08.3)	Ladoumègue	1930
3:49.2	(4:08.3)	Beccali	1933
3:49.6	(4:08.7)	Beccali	1933
(3:49.6)	4:08.7n	Bonthron	1933
3:49.8n	(4:09.0)	Lovelock	1933
(3:50.0)	4:09.2	Ladoumègue	1931
3:50.4	(4:09.6)	Ladoumègue (pro)	1933
(3:50.6)	4:09.8i	Cunningham	1933
(3:50.6)	4:09.8	Cunningham	1933
(3:50.8)	4:10.0i	Venzke	1932
3:50.8	(4:10.1)	Ladoumègue (pro)	1933

CUNNINGHAM–BONTHRON–VENZKE

The competitive level of racing at 1500 meters and one mile had been increasing constantly, and in 1933 it reached fever pitch. Still Cunningham and Bonthron had never raced each other. Their first meetings took place during the 1934 indoor season, with Venzke as a constant threat, and mile racing reached new heights of popularity.

Madison Square Garden had to turn away thousands of people who wanted to see them. Their exploits made headlines throughout the country. At New York's first big meet of 1934, the Millrose Games on February 3, 16,500 spectators crowded in and at least 5,000 more were turned away. Cunningham beat Venzke by 20 yards in 4:11.2.

A week later in Boston, Cunningham ran 4:18.4 against lesser opposition. Then, on February 17 the three fastest Americans in history met in the Baxter Mile of the NYAC Games.

Nobody cared about time; all three wanted to win. The pace dawdled through a 2:13.6 half. Then Cunningham decided he was playing into their hands and he reversed his waiting tactic. He took off at an unprecedented pace for a third quarter. Venzke was surprised and left behind, but Bonthron stuck to Cunningham all the way to the homestretch and his big kick brought him to the tape inches in front in 4:14.0. Venzke, after lagging behind, gained seven yards on both of them in a startling finish, running his last half under two minutes and his last 440 under 58.

Venzke was still the favorite of the New York fans, and in the AAU meet the next week many thought he would win the 1500. He trailed Cunningham's 62.2 by a full second, but ahead of Bonthron. At the half, Cunningham led in 2:09.4, with Bonthron at 2:09.9 and Venzke 2:10.2.

Then Venzke began to thrill his fans. He caught Cunningham at three-quarters in 3:09.6 (a 440 in 59.6!) and went into the lead with the crowd hysterically delighted. Bonthron was now a full second behind. With two laps to go, Bonthron seemed out of it,

1934

while Venzke was striding smoothly and gracefully.
On the last backstretch, Cunningham fought past Venzke to the dismay of the fans. Bonthron, three yards back, lowered his head as he gathered for his kick. Then he lifted his head and started.
On the turn, Bonthron was on Venzke's heels. In the 50-yard stretch he began to gain. He passed Venzke on the inside with 30 yards to go and almost caught Cunningham. In a sensational race, both men clocked 3:52.2, a new world indoor record, and Venzke was only a step behind.
The three men did not meet again until June. In the Columbian Mile on March 17, Cunningham ran his now standard type of race with laps of 62.6, 2:07.4, and 3:08.6 to set a world indoor record of 4:08.4, beating a discouraged Venzke by 30 yards. It was the second fastest mile ever run. In April he beat Venzke twice in special miles, 4:12.7 at the Kansas Relays and 4:11.8 at the Penn Relays.
Bonthron, meanwhile, ran a good 3:53.7 on May 19. In the IC4A he beat sophomore Venzke in 3:56.0, then took the 800 in 1:54.8. On June 16 he was on his home track at Palmer Stadium for the first Princeton Invitational Games.

THE FIRST PRINCETON INVITATIONAL GAMES

After the great Lovelock-Bonthron race of 1933 at Palmer Stadium, Princeton graduate manager of athletics Asa Bushnell conceived the brilliant idea of an annual invitational meet. This first meet had only four events, starting at 5:00 p.m. after the Yale-Princeton baseball game. About ten minutes before the mile started, Ben Eastman ran 1:49.8 for a world-record 880 on the fast cinder track.
Only three men were invited to run the mile—Bonthron, Cunningham, and Venzke. Up to 25,000 people were in the concrete stands flooded with sunlight. And most of them expected Princeton's Bonthron to thrash the others. Cunningham had strained his instep and ran with a heavily taped ankle, but it did not seem to bother him.
Venzke led for the first lap in 61.7 with Cunningham close behind in 61.8. After another half lap, Cunningham moved calmly past the taller man into the lead. Bonthron, who only had to be on Cunningham's heels around the last curve to be the winner, moved up behind Cunningham and the Princeton rooters were satisfied.
Cunningham sped past the 880 in 2:05.8. The pace was not exceptional, and Bonthron and Venzke were right behind him. Everything seemed to be going normally and the spectators waited in suspense.
But as soon as he started the third lap, Cunningham increased

his pace visibly. His scarred legs churned swiftly, and he looked as if he had started the last lap. Around the turn he opened an alarming gap of ten yards over Bonthron. On the backstretch the gap was 20 yards, and Cunningham was still gaining.

The partisan crowd gave up on Bonthron and began to watch the huge electric clock at the open end of the field. Cunningham flashed past the three-quarters in 3:07.6, and now the crowd was cheering him wildly.

All the way around that last lap they cheered, while the gap back to Bonthron widened to 40 yards and Venzke fell farther behind. As Cunningham rushed down the homestretch the fans glanced anxiously from him to the clock, trying to calculate how fast he was running.

Cunningham wanted the record, and he drove hard all the way through the tape. As soon as he hit the tape, the clock stopped and the impassioned spectators could see it read 4:06.7. Cunningham jogged 30 yards past the tape, then turned back to receive congratulations from Bonthron, who finished in 4:12.5, and Venzke, 4:16.0. And so, twice in 11 months, Bonthron had the mixed fortune of finishing second to a world record mile on his home track.

BONTHRON COMES BACK

The three met again one week later in the NCAA championships in the Los Angeles Coliseum. By now, Cunningham's deadly tactics were so well known that nobody was surprised when he broke away from the pack at the end of two laps. Bonthron and Venzke, especially, knew it, and they moved out with him resolutely.

The three ran away from the others during the fast third lap. Then Venzke had to let go, and in his discouragement he almost lost third place. But Bonthron was determined. Today Cunningham was not going to get away from him.

Around the gray track they raced with the crowd feverish, and Cunningham could not open a gap on his implacable pursuer. As they turned into the homestretch, Bonthron exploded with an unbeatable kick which shot him five yards past Cunningham in the space of about 30 yards. He won in 4:08.9 to Cunningham's 4:10.6.

Now Cunningham and Bonthron had each beaten the other twice. The vital rubber race was the next week end, June 30, in the Marquette University stadium in Milwaukee, Wisconsin. It was a hot, sultry day but 17,000 keyed-up people were in the big stadium when the 1500 began on the gray-black cinder track.

Optimistically, Venzke set the early pace. He came around to the starting line, just before the backstretch began, in 61.3. At the end of the backstretch, Cunningham moved, unexpectantly early. In spite of the heat he was running faster than ever before. As they

1934

came down the homestretch, with two laps to go, Bonthron moved ahead of Venzke into second place. Discouraged, Venzke began to drop behind.

Cunningham went past the 880 mark in 2:01.8 and the crowd gasped at the time. Cunningham had obviously changed tactics in hopes of shaking loose from Bonthron. Down the backstretch, Cunningham seemed to accelerate, but actually it was Bonthron, helplessly letting him go.

The gap widened to five yards on the backstretch, to eight yards around the curve. With one lap to go, Bonthron was an alarming 11 yards behind. Cunningham whirled around the curve to the starting line in 3:04.5, by far the fastest three-quarters ever accomplished, and he showed no signs of tiring. Bonthron crossed the line in 3:06.

He had come from that far back against Cunningham indoors, but not when Cunningham was running this mercilessly. It was almost like Princeton all over again. Around the last turn, Cunningham widened his lead to a safe 15 yards and there were few among the 17,000 who thought Bonthron had any chance.

But that was because they had never seen Bonthron unleash his thunderbolt kick. At the head of the stretch he lowered his head and a thrill ran through the few who knew him. When his head came up he exploded his thunderbolt.

The raging crowd saw him cut Cunningham's lead in half within 30 yards. He caught up with the dismayed Kansan 30 yards from the tape and ten yards later he was ahead. A few steps from the tape Bonthron looked over his shoulder at a defeated Cunningham and he flashed across the line two feet ahead. His astounding kick had won the rubber race.

His time was 3:48.8, a new world record. Cunningham's 3:48.9 was also under Beccali's record, and Cunningham said, "It's a strange feeling to break a world's record and still lose." Venzke was a poor third with a good 3:50.5.

It was revealed that on the Thursday before the race, Bonthron had said, "I don't care about records. Track doesn't mean anything to me. I'd rather play baseball." And yet he had run so hard that he collapsed and could not appear on the victory stand.

SYDNEY WOODERSON

When a man is only 5'6" tall, weighs only 125 pounds, wears glasses, has a chest expansion of only three inches, and appears frail and pale, he is not expected to possess one of the greatest running talents in the history of the sport, but such was the case with Sydney Wooderson.

Inside that deceptive body was an unprecedented combination of speed and endurance plus astonishing courage in the homestretch. All this was amply demonstrated in 1934 when he emerged as a top miler at the tender age of 19.

Sydney began running when he was 12, because he liked it and because he was good at it, and because his older brother, A.T. Wooderson, was a good schoolboy runner. Little Sydney placed third in the school mile at 15 when his brother won it in 4:49.8.

In 1931, at 16, Sydney bravely entered the Public Schools Championship and placed sixth against boys up to three years older. At 17, in 1932, running through pools of water on the track, he came from nowhere in the last 50 yards to miss victory by inches in 4:34.4. At 18, his last 220 in 30.2 won in 4:29.8, and impressed observers said he could have run much faster.

Then, following the then prevalent tradition in England of avoiding excess racing, he retired for the remainder of the 1933 season. He trained diligently, but he did not race again until June of 1934, when he won the championship of Kent County in 4:27.8.

None of this prepared anyone for his debut into big-time racing at the Southern Championships held on Guildford's grass track on June 30. He was only one of 30 hopefuls running against Jack Lovelock and Jerry Cornes.

JACK LOVELOCK (Part 3)

After his defeat by Beccali, Lovelock competed in cross-country, but his left knee began to pain and he had an operation for a bruised and split cartilage.

He ran erratically, hurting his knee again, and on June 23, in a handicap mile, he ran himself out, staggering at the finish in the slow time of 4:23. On the next week-end he ran at Guildford against Cornes and Aubrey Reeve, who had been running well, in the low 4:20's.

Lovelock had every reason to believe 4:19 would win this Southern Championship, for Cornes had been in Nigeria since the 1932 Olympics. Lovelock followed Cornes through the unwieldy field of runners. They were third and fourth, behind a 3:13 pace, but then Cornes let down and young Reeve rushed past.

Lovelock waited for Cornes to respond, but Cornes could not, and when Lovelock came out of the turn and moved past he was startled to see Reeve 12 yards ahead in the homestretch. Lovelock ran better than he expected in the stretch, but he tied up near the end and he was helpless, three yards behind Reeve.

And in the last five yards a black-clad figure hurtled past him, gasping and straining ... Wooderson!

Lovelock vomited, but his knee stood up and he had run 4:15.2, faster than he thought he could. He was surprised at

Reeve's 4:14.8 and Wooderson's 4:15.2, and at Cornes' lack of speed. They would all meet again in the AAA championships in two weeks.

After another ten days of training effort, Lovelock felt his spring and speed returning and he felt confident about the AAA. Fans were talking about a record race, but he had no desire for a fast pace, for he was scheduled to run against Bonthron the following week.

As they lined up for the AAA mile in the White City, Cornes told him mysteriously, "Somebody is going to learn a lesson today." And 50 yards beyond the start, Cornes slowed the pack to a 68 pace. The crowd hooted as they passed the 880 in an absurd 2:22.5.

Lovelock wanted to run faster, but if they wanted it this way... The pace picked up only slightly on the third lap. Just before the bell, Cornes tore off ahead in a mad sprint, passing three-quarters in 3:28. Lovelock moved easily behind him, catching the others napping.

Lovelock followed Cornes all the way to the homestretch, then went past easily and won in 4:26.6. Wooderson finished in his typically fast style and was second, eight yards back, in 4:27.8.

The third meeting between the three came in the British Empire Games at White City on August 7, but Lovelock first had to run the mile with Oxford-Cambridge against Princeton-Cornell, and Bonthron. This race was on July 21 at White City.

Four days before the race, Lovelock did something uncharacteristic. He ran a fast ¾ mile time trial. After a lap in 59, he was heard to shout, "Faster, Charles! Faster!", and he passed the 880 in 2:00.5. He felt as wonderful as he had in that 4:12 mile at Iffley Road in 1932. He finished the three-quarters in 3:00.5, world-record time. But that night he was tired and his weight was two pounds under. On Saturday, however, it was back within half a pound of the 132 he considered right.

Lovelock knew of Bonthron's great finish in his world-record 1500. Publicity for the race was overwhelming, and Lovelock expected a fast pace. But right from the start, to the disappointment of 20,000 spectators, the pace was slow.

Bonthron, obviously nervous, allowed the second strings to go around in 63 and 2:07, then actually allowed a gap to open. Prudently, Lovelock moved ahead of Bonthron and the leader passed three quarters in 3:12.0 before moving aside for Lovelock.

Lovelock made no effort to increase the pace. He waited for Bonthron's attack. It did not come at the head of the backstretch. Bonthron did not rush past to lead into the last curve. Lovelock prepared to keep Bonthron wide if he sprinted on the curve, but no sprint came.

Puzzled, Lovelock glanced back. Bonthron was still following

1934

placidly. The two world-record holders were running as if they had a lap to go. The attack could only come in the homestretch, and Lovelock knew what he must do.

Before they reached the straight, Lovelock started his own sprint. It was an explosion of his own, smooth and effortless as it appeared, but it surprised Bonthron and opened a gap of seven yards.

Then Bonthron bucked into his terrific drive and began to cut down Lovelock's lead. With the English crowd roaring, he gained rapidly on the unsuspecting Lovelock. He came rushing up to lose by only a yard.

It was only a 4:15.4 mile, but it is one of the few times in history that two such fast finishers waited to settle it in the homestretch.

Lovelock's comment about Bonthron was, "There was nothing wrong with him but his judgment."

In the British Empire Games at White City on August 7, Lovelock wore the black New Zealand uniform with its silver fern, unwilling to believe it brought bad luck. He had worn it while losing to Beccali in Turin, in his abortive record attempt at Paris, and he had failed in the 1932 Olympic Games.

Now he had to face Cornes as a rival from another country, and Cornes was in good shape. On July 29, Cornes had run 3:53.8 at Colombes to beat Reeve's 3:54.8. And Cornes' third English teammate was little Sydney Wooderson, dangerous even though still 23 days from his 20th birthday.

Lovelock had trained lightly for this race, but he was more nervous than for his races against Beccali and Bonthron. It was his most important race since the Olympics.

The first lap on the heavy track was run in 59.5 by the fourth Englishman, Craske, and Lovelock ran fifth in 60.2. Craske passed the half in 2:06 then faded away. Lovelock, at 2:07, followed Cornes confidently past Reeve, and Cornes reached three quarters in 3:12.5 with Lovelock at 3:12.8.

As the bell sounded behind them, Wooderson went past unexpectedly, into the lead. On the backstretch, Cornes went past Wooderson. Lovelock, fearing a trap, slipped past Wooderson so as to follow Cornes into the last curve.

Lovelock felt the threat of Wooderson behind him and realized he could be boxed on the curve. Abruptly, before they reached the homestretch, he launched into his sprint. He felt wonderfully light and quick as he rushed past Cornes and won in 4:12.8.

Behind Lovelock, Wooderson flung himself down the homestretch furiously and passed Cornes to equal the British record with 4:13.4 to Cornes' 4:13.6. It was a great first year for a miler not yet 20.

Lovelock said, "this was a very easy run for a British Empire Championship."

On August 12, Lovelock ran an interesting 1500 in the Olympische Stadium in Amsterdam against Cornes, who was running his last race before returning to Nigeria, and Bonthron, who had run a fast 3:00.8 three-quarters in Sweden on July 31.

Before the race, Lovelock and Bonthron jogged around the heavy, dead track to the applause of 20,000 people. Then Cornes set off to run a fast time in his farewell race, passing 400 meters in 58.0. Lovelock led the rest in 62. Cornes ran 2:02 and Lovelock 2:05. Lovelock set out to catch Cornes on the third lap and Bonthron's footsteps faded behind him. At three-quarters in 3:07, Lovelock had caught up and he followed with assurance until the homestretch. He won by six yards in 3:53.3 as Bonthron thundered past Cornes with his belated sprint, 3:54.1 to 3:54.9.

Lovelock agreed amiably to another race against Bonthron at Colombes in Paris the following week. He did little running, and he did not take the race seriously. He was content to run in the middle of the pack during a stiff breeze, with Bonthron on his heels. Lap times were 64, 65, and 66.

He had beaten Bonthron by surprising him with a sprint just before the straightaway. Now he wanted to see if he could let Bonthron get the jump into the stretch and beat him from behind. Only Lovelock would attempt such a reckless experiment.

Lovelock went into the lead on the last curve and waited for Bonthron. He turned to look for the big American and there he was, shooting past at frightening speed. Lovelock pursued him but he had no chance. He finished, laughing at himself, beaten 3:57 to 3:58.

Bonthron was delighted, and Lovelock said, "it taught me several lessons in training and tactics."

BECCALI IN THE EUROPEAN CHAMPIONSHIPS

After his great year in 1933, Beccali eased off in 1934. He was obviously not at his best when he went to Sweden to race against Eric Ny. At Malmö on July 22, he followed Ny's 2:01.2 pace, and his reputation scared Ny into running away from him on the last curve. Ny finished in 3:50.8, breaking Wide's Swedish record, and Beccali finished in a badly beaten 3:54.3.

At Budapest on August 19, in the dual meet against Hungary, Beccali and his teammate, Umberto Cerati, defeated Miklós Szabó, who had run 3:52.6 behind Cunningham the year before. Results: Cerati 3:54.0, Beccali 3:54.8, Szabó 3:55.4.

The European Championships, next greatest competition to the Olympics, were held for the first time in 1934, at Turin, on September 7. Ny chose the 800 and Beccali won the 1500 in the last

1934

300 meters in 3:54.6 with no English milers present. Szabó ran 3:55.2. Third in 3:57.0 was Roger Normand of France, who had finished only a yard behind Lovelock when Bonthron won at Colombes. Fourth was a promising German, Friedrich Schaumburg, in 3:57.8. Janusz Kusocinski, Olympic 10,000 meter champion, was fifth in 3:59.4.

1934
MILE:

Time		Athlete		Place	Date	
4:06.7	WR	Glenn Cunningham (USA)	(1)	Princeton	16	Jun
4:08.9		Bill Bonthron (USA)	NCAA(1)	Los Angeles	23	Jun
4:10.6		Cunningham	NCAA(2)	Los Angeles	23	Jun
4:11.8		Cunningham	(1)	Philadelphia	28	Apr
4:12.5		Bonthron	(2)	Princeton	16	Jun
4:12.6		Eric Ny (Sweden)	(1)	Göteborg	7	Oct
4:12.7		Cunningham	(1)	Lawrence	21	Apr
4:12.8		Jack Lovelock (NZ) Br Emp Gms	(1)	London	7	Aug
4:13.4 e		Sydney Wooderson (GB) d:o	(2)	London	7	Aug
4:13.6 e		Jerry Cornes (GB) d:o	(3)	London	7	Aug
4:14.5		Ray Sears (USA)	(1)			
4:14.8		Aubrey Reeve (GB)	(1)	Guildford	30	Jun
4:15.2		Gene Venzke (USA)	NCAA(3)	Los Angeles	23	Jun
4:15.2		Wooderson	(2)	Guildford	30	Jun
4:15.2		Lovelock	(3)	Guildford	30	Jun
4:15.3		Harry Williamson (USA)	NCAA(4)	Los Angeles	23	Jun
4:15.4		Lovelock	(1)	London	21	Jul
4:15.6 e		Bonthron	(2)	London	21	Jul

Indoors:

4:08.4	Glenn Cunningham	(1)	New York	17	Mar
4:11.2	Cunningham	(1)	New York	3	Feb
4:14.0	Bill Bonthron	(1)	New York	17	Feb

1,500m:

Time		Athlete		Place	Date	
3:48.8	WR	Bill Bonthron (USA)	AAU(1)	Milwaukee	30	Jun
3:48.9		Glenn Cunningham (USA)	AAU(2)	Milwaukee	30	Jun
3:50.5		Gene Venzke (USA)	(3)	Milwaukee	30	Jun
3:50.8		Eric Ny (Sweden)	(1)	Malmö	22	Jul
3:52.6		Luigi Beccali (Italy)	(1)	Milan	10	Jun
3:53.3		Jack Lovelock (NZ)	(1)	Amsterdam	12	Aug
3:53.4		Venzke	(1)		30	May
3:53.7		Bonthron	(1)		19	May
3:53.8		Jerry Cornes (GB)	(1)	Colombes	29	Jul
3:54.0		Venzke	(1)	Philadelphia	5	May
3:54.0		Bonthron	(1)	Oslo	6	Aug
3:54.0		Umberto Cerati (Italy)	(1)	Budapest	19	Aug
3:54.1		Bonthron	(2)	Amsterdam	12	Aug
3:54.3		Beccali	(2)	Malmö	22	Jul
3:54.6		Beccali European Ch.	(1)	Turin	7	Sep
3:54.8		Robert Goix (France)	(1)	Colombes	8	Jul
3:54.8		Aubrey Reeve (GB)	(2)	Colombes	29	Jul
3:54.8		Beccali	(2)	Budapest	19	Aug
3:54.9		Cornes	(3)	Amsterdam	12	Aug

Indoors:

3:52.2	Glenn Cunningham (USA)	AAU(1)	New York	24	Feb

1934, one of the most remarkable years in the entire history of the 1500 and mile, changed the all-time combined list considerably:

(3:47.7)	4:06.7	Cunningham	1934
(3:48.5)	4:07.6	Lovelock	1933
3:48.8	(4:07.8)	Bonthron	1934
3:48.9n	(4:08.0)	Cunningham	1934
3:49.0	(4:08.1)	Beccali	1933

3:49.2	(4:08.3)	Ladoumègue	1930
3:49.2	(4:08.3)	Beccali	1933
(3:49.3)	4:08.4i	Cunningham	1934
3:49.6	(4:08.7)	Beccali	1933
(3:49.6)	4:08.7n	Bonthron	1933
(3:49.7)	4:08.9	Bonthron	1934
3:49.8n	(4:09.0)	Lovelock	1933
(3:50.0)	4:09.2	Ladoumègue	1931

CUNNINGHAM–BONTHRON–VENZKE: ENCORE

Cunningham and Bonthron had graduated in June. Cunningham went to Iowa to work for his master's degree, while Bonthron, now 22, worked in New York as an accountant. He ran for the New York AC and did some half-hearted training during his lunch hour on the roof of a department store. Venzke was a junior at Penn, and he won the IC4A titles, indoors and out, in a leisurely 3:57.6 and 3:57.9.

Cunningham was in good condition for the indoor season and won easily. He won the Wanamaker Mile in 4:11.0 with Venzke second in 4:12.2 and Bonthron at 4:16.8. Eric Ny of Sweden was fourth. On February 16, the order was the same, but Cunningham won by an overwhelming 30 yards in 4:09.8. A week later, in the AAU 1500, Cunningham lead at the 880 in 2:01, then won by 30 yards from Bonthron in best-ever indoor time of 3:50.5. Venzke was two yards behind Bonthron, with Ny far back. On March 16, Cunningham won the Columbian Mile from Venzke in an easy 4:14.8, then came back to beat Hornbostel by three yards in a sizzling 2:10.1 for 1000 yards, a world indoor record.

They raced very little outdoors. Cunningham beat Venzke for the AAU title in 3:52.1, fastest 1500 of the year, but, before that, all three met Lovelock in the Princeton Invitational.

LOVELOCK AND THE SECOND PRINCETON INVITATIONAL

After a winter of light training, mixed with pleasure-oriented physical activities, Lovelock began serious training in mid-February. His goal was to be ready to run at Princeton on June 15. He ran many races against little opposition, at mixed distances, ending with the Universities Championship in a comfortable 4:19.8.

His final tune-up before leaving for the big race at Princeton, was the Kinnaird Trophy meet. After a pace of 63 and 2:07 in a strong wind, he worked to get away from Reeve and passed three-quarters in 3:10.5. He won in 4:13.8 and observers raved about his ability, considering the wind.

After the race, Lovelock trained deliberately hard for a week,

1935

then, on the first of June, he climbed aboard the Aquitania for a week's rest. His main goal was to win the race, but when he arrived in the U.S. he found the press building publicity about a new record.

A week before the race, Lovelock ran a ¾ trial in 3:02, and, at a different time, Bonthron ran one in 3:04. On Tuesday, Lovelock ran his fastest ever 660 trial—1:21.2. He was told Bonthron ran one in 1:20, but Bonthron's proved to be 21 yards short. It fooled Bonthron even more than it caused fear in Lovelock. Cunningham arrived late in the week, having run 1:52.2 for 800 meters on the previous Saturday.

Lovelock ran a few sprints, but for most of the week he rested, and waited. "No one who has not gone through such an ordeal can realize what a tremendous part one's nervous impulses play in tuning one's body to perfect pitch for intense competition."

The day of the meet was hot, even though the mile did not start until 6:00 p.m. There was an aroused overflow crowd of 40,000, most of them supporting Bonthron against his five opponents.

Venzke had the pole position, but he did not lead because Glen Dawson and Cunningham raced in ahead of him and then purposely slowed the pace. Lovelock moved ahead of Venzke, wanting to be on Cunningham's heels. They moved ahead of Dawson and came up to the quarter in a groan-producing 64.9.

Lovelock concluded, later, that the slow first lap was a deliberate attempt to protect Cunningham's record. In any case, as soon as the time was announced, Cunningham leaped into a much faster stride for the second lap. Now he was racing. With only Lovelock and Bonthron following him, Cunningham completed the lap in a sparkling 60.8 for 2:05.7.

Lovelock ran on Cunningham's shoulder, as close as possible. "The trick of shadowing an opponent within sight and hearing is one of the more maddening and distracting forms of tactics one can use in any race."

Cunningham's speed dropped, and they reached three-quarters in 3:08.9. Lovelock felt confident now, and Bonthron dropped back behind him even though there was little pressure from the pace. On the last backstretch, Lovelock estimated the pace at about 65. Cunningham was obviously in trouble.

Lovelock waited confidently until the homestretch, then burst past. When he had a safe lead he coasted in to the tape. Behind him, Bonthron came on with his wild charges of old and took second place. Results: Lovelock 4:11.2, Bonthron 4:12.6, Cunningham 4:13.0.

Bonthron said, "I thought Lovelock would win," and he announced he did not want to race anymore.

Lovelock traveled back across the Atlantic, won a 3:59 1500

in Antwerp, ran a relay leg in 4:23.5 which felt much harder than it should, and qualified for the AAA final with another uncomfortable run. He was not right and he had to run against Wooderson.

WOODERSON PROGRESSES

After his short but spectacular start in 1934, Wooderson stayed away from fast races until June of 1935. He was being advised by former Olympic champion and British record holder, Albert Hill. On June 22, Wooderson won the Southern Championship a few precious inches ahead of Reeve in 4:18.6.

The AAA meet on July 13 brought 40,000 spectators to White City, but a poor track and hot weather with gusty winds ruled out a fast race. Peter Ward ran the first 440 in 61, but Lovelock led the rest of the pack in 64. Wooderson stalked Lovelock with care.

Lovelock caught Ward at the 880 in 2:08. He felt tired and he was aware of Wooderson's strength behind him. Ward still led in the third lap, but the pace slowed to 68. Lovelock had the same mental weariness as in the 1932 Olympics, but he went past Ward at the bell.

Wooderson passed Lovelock and Roger Normand of France came alongside. Wooderson's pace was fast, and everybody else faded. Lovelock followed the black-clad 20-year-old around the last curve. At the start of the homestretch, he launched his sprint, without confidence, but Wooderson matched him and then began to pull away. Lovelock knew he could not beat Wooderson and his form was going bad, and so he slowed to 4:18.4 behind Wooderson's 4:17.2.

While Lovelock was in Stockholm on July 26, skillfully outkicking Venzke and Ny in a 3:57.6 1500, Wooderson ran against France at White City on July 27 and won the mile in 4:19 with his last lap in 60.6. Then the two great ones met in a special handicap race at the Rangers' meet at Glasgow's Ibrox Park on August 3.

The largest crowd to see a British meet—a wrought-up 50,000—came out to watch the two men race. Lovelock was feeling better, ready for 4:10 and there was much anticipation of a record pace, but a stiff wind ruled out a fast run.

And Lovelock knew he was in trouble early in the race. He had planned a pace of about 62½, but he ran 61.6. When he was sharp, his pace judgment was better. Then he slowed to 2:07.4, with Wooderson waiting patiently on his heels and Reeve and Riddell 30 yards ahead off their handicaps.

Lovelock forced himself to run 64.4 on the third lap but he felt it kill his chances. Wooderson went past him 300 yards from home and Lovelock could not hold him. Wooderson went hopelessly far ahead and placed third to Reeve in 4:12.7, while Lovelock finished in 4:15.5.

1935

Wooderson retired for the season, but Lovelock, stale and weary, ran two more easy races, in Budapest and Zagreb and "made up my mind to defeat Wooderson next year or die, but it is not going to be so easy now."

BECCALI BIDES HIS TIME

Once again, Beccali had an easy year, running only to win as he pointed for the 1936 Olympics. His first real race came on September 1 in Berlin after a 4:15.4 mile tune-up in Milan on August 25. In Berlin, during a meet between five nations, he was to run against the new German threat, Schaumburg.

This year, Schaumburg had won convincingly in 3:54.2, 3:54.0, and 3:54.5. Beccali showed Schaumburg a champion's kick and won in 3:54.0 to the German's 3:55.2. (Later in the season, Schaumburg beat lesser men in 3:53.6 and 3:54.4.)

Beccali ran again on September 22 in Turin, and defeated Normand, 3:53.0 to 3:53.6. Then he began to prepare for Berlin and defense of his Olympic title. Truly, he had no trouble!

1935
MILE:

4:11.2	Jack Lovelock (NZ)	(1)	Princeton	15 Jun
4:12.0	Robert Graham (GB)	(1)	Glasgow	20 Aug
4:12.6	Bill Bonthron (USA)	(2)	Princeton	15 Jun
4:12.7	Sydney Wooderson (GB)	*(3)	Glasgow	3 Aug
4:13.0	Glenn Cunningham (USA)	(3)	Princeton	15 Jun
4:13.8	Lovelock	(1)	London	25 May
4:14.4	Don Lash (USA)	(1)	Ann Arbor	25 May
4:14.5	Norman Bright (USA)	(1)	San Diego	27 Jun
4:14.8	Ray Sears (USA)	(1)	Milwaukee	7 Jun
4:15.0	Richard Bauer (USA)	(1)	Hanover, N.H.	4 May
4:15.4	Luigi Beccali (Italy)	(1)	Milan	25 Aug
4:15.5	Lovelock	*(4)	Glasgow	3 Aug

*Both lost to handicap men Reeve and Riddell

Indoors:

4:09.8	Glenn Cunningham (USA)	(1)	New York	16 Feb

(Gene Venzke apparently 2nd, 3 yds. back, Bonthron 3rd, Eric Ny of Sweden dropped out)

4:11.0	Cunningham	(1)	New York	5 Feb
4:12.2	Gene Venzke (USA)	(2)	New York	5 Feb

(Bonthron 3rd in 4:16.8, Ny fourth)

1,500m:
(+ during mile)

3:52.1	Glenn Cunningham (USA)	AAU(1)	Lincoln	4 Jul
3:53.0	Luigi Beccali (Italy)	(1)	Turin	22 Sep
3:53.6	Friedrich Schaumburg (Germany)	(1)	Colombes	15 Sep
3:53.6	Roger Normand (France)	(2)	Turin	22 Sep
3:54.0	Schaumburg	(1)	Munich	11 Aug
3:54.0	Beccali	(1)	Berlin	1 Sep
3:54.2	Schaumburg	(1)	Berlin	4 Aug
3:54.2	Aubrey Reeve (GB)	(2)	Munich	11 Aug
3:54.4	Schaumburg	(1)	Stuttgart	22 Sep
3:54.4	Umberto Cerati (Italy)	(3)	Turin	22 Sep
3:54.5	Schaumburg	(1)	Helsinki	25 Aug
3:54.7	Tommy Riddell (GB)	(3)	Munich	11 Aug
3:54.7	Ossi Teileri (Finland)	(2)	Helsinki	25 Aug
3:54.8	Gene Venzke (USA)	AAU(2)	Lincoln	4 Jul

1936

3:55.0+	Jack Lovelock (NZ)	(1)	Princeton	15	Jun
3:55.0	Eric Ny (Sweden)	(1)	Varberg	27	Jun
3:55.0	Martti Matilainen (Finland)	(1)	Stockholm	2	Aug
3:55.0	Ny	(2)	Stockholm	2	Aug
Indoors:					
3:50.5	Glenn Cunningham (USA)	AAU(1)	New York	23	Feb

IN QUEST OF A GOLD MEDAL

Unlike past Olympic 1500 meter races, the 1936 contenders were almost all veterans with great talent, valuable experience, and an unusual ability to bring themselves to a peak for the big race. Veteran runners eventually reach a stage of maturity which enables them to consider only a few races important, and the 1936 Olympics became the focal point for the greatest collection of milers in history. Nor was the result disappointing, for the Olympic final in Berlin turned out to be the greatest race ever run to that date.

After the 1935 season, the favorites for the Olympics would have to be chosen from (1) Lovelock, Cornes, and Wooderson in England, (2) the great defending champion, Beccali, (3) the Americans, Cunningham, Bonthron, and Venzke, for nobody yet foresaw the sensational emergence of Archie San Romani, and (4) promising continental Europeans such as Szabó, Ny, and Schaumburg. Virtually no one considered that gallant Canadian, Phil Edwards.

CUNNINGHAM HOLDS BACK

Cunningham was not impatient to reach a peak this year. August 6 was a long way off. He did his endurance running in the cold winter, but he made less effort than usual to sharpen his speed for the board track meets.

In his first race of the year, the Boston K of C on January 27, he barely won in 4:17.7 from Joe Mangan, who was making a determined comeback. In the Wanamaker Mile on February 1, Mangan outkicked Venzke in 4:11.0 with Cunningham four feet back. Then Venzke beat Cunningham again by three yards in the Baxter Mile in 4:10.2 and took the indoor AAU 1500 in a record 3:49.9 to Glenn's 3:50.1.

After two more frustrating losses, to Norm Bright in San Francisco and to Mangan in Providence, R.I., Cunningham took desperate measures. Tired of being outkicked, he refused to push the pace in the Columbian Mile on March 14. Venzke and Mangan allowed the pace to slow to an astonishing 3:52.6 for three-quarters. Then Cunningham blasted his last quarter in 54.2 to beat Venzke by five yards and Mangan by seven in 4:46.8. Before the race, Cunningham had said, "I'm going to win, no matter if it's going to take me the whole night." Sportswriters dubbed it "the typographical error mile."

Outdoors, Cunningham was still not at his best when he ran in the Princeton Invitational on June 13.

Bonthron was there in the horseshoe-shaped stadium, lured out of retirement for his Olympic bid on a rainy day before 30,000 fans. Cunningham took the lead at 600 yards and led Venzke and Bonthron until the start of the last lap when the poorly-conditioned Bonthron let them go.

Venzke stuck close to Cunningham all the way to the homestretch, then pulled even as Cunningham sprinted. Venzke fought his way ahead in the last 20 yards to win in 4:13.4, his first outdoor victory over Cunningham. Bill Daly edged Bonthron for third in 4:19.8.

Two weeks later in the Central Olympic Trials in Milwaukee, Cunningham was ready for a serious race against Archie San Romani, who was fast building a reputation.

ARCHIE SAN ROMANI

Another fast Kansan, running for Emporia State, San Romani was almost completely unknown when he ran in the 1935 NCAA mile at Berkeley. His only victory of note had been in a 1500-meter race in the Kansas Relays for runners not good enough for the Invitational mile. San Romani won in 3:57.2.

Absent from the 1935 NCAA were Venzke, who had won the Heptagonals in 3:52.6 and the IC4A in 3:58.8, Don Lash, the Big 10 champion at 4:14.4, and Ray Sears, the Central Collegiate champ at 4:14.8. In a mass finish which looked like a subway crush, San Romani was the NCAA winner in 4:19.1.

In 1936, San Romani did no fast running early, and when he reached the NCAA meet at Chicago on June 20, he was not favored against the two fast Big 10 milers, Lash and Chuck Fenske. Lash had beaten Fenske in a brilliant conference championship race at Columbus, Ohio, on May 23, 4:10.8 to 4:10.9. Then, in the Central Collegiates at Milwaukee on June 5, Lash won another thriller, 4:15.2 to 4:15.4. A week before the NCAA, Lash ran a startling 8:58.3 at Princeton to break Nurmi's world 2-mile record.

Against these two, San Romani won a decisive victory in the NCAA. He ran away in 3:53.0, to 3:56.7 for Fenske and 3:57.8 for Lash, who had been running too many fast races. San Romani was now a serious contender for the Olympic team and he entered the three races necessary for selection.

1936

THE AMERICAN TRIALS

Two significant qualifying meets were held on June 27. In the Eastern trials at Cambridge, Bonthron outkicked Venzke by one foot in 3:55.2, and his comeback was now taken seriously. At Milwaukee, Cunningham beat out San Romani, 3:53.2 to 3:53.6. The following week, they all gathered at Princeton for the AAU meet. If there was any doubt about San Romani's ability or Cunningham's condition it was removed when Cunningham won the coveted championship in 3:54.2 by two yards over San Romani, with Venzke another two yards back and an unhappy Bonthron four yards behind Venzke.

The third race actually selected the team. The Final Trials were held in hot, unpleasantly humid weather on New York City's brand new cinder track on Randall's Island in the East River. Over 21,000 intense fans filled the horseshoe stadium to capacity when the ten 1500 meter runners went to their marks.

The five serious contenders were in the pack for half the distance. Then, with two laps to go, Bonthron went to the front, afraid to lag behind as before because he knew he was not yet in top shape. Within the next half lap, the five contenders for the Olympic team were in front: Venzke, Cunningham, Bonthron, San Romani, and Fenske.

At the gun, a resolute San Romani was leading Fenske, followed by Venzke and Cunningham, with Bonthron laboring. Then Cunningham darted to second on the curve and followed San Romani. As the pace became extremely fast, first Fenske and then Bonthron fell away.

Cunningham kicked furiously coming into the homestretch and caught up with San Romani. As they sprinted together they pulled away from Venzke. For a few seconds of suspense, Bonthron's supporters still hoped his big kick would catch Venzke and take the third place on the Olympic team, but it never happened.

Cunningham barely edged San Romani with a last effort, and they were both timed in 3:49.9, with Venzke at 3:52.2 and Bonthron 3:53.7. The two leaders were immediately called contenders for the Olympic gold medal.

BECCALI PREPARES HIS DEFENSE

The man who proved himself to be the best racer in the world during 1932 and 1933, made every effort to defend his Olympic championship in 1936 at nearly 29 years of age. The veteran American track coach, Boyd Comstock, was hired to coach the Italian team, and he said Beccali trained harder than any man before him.

1936

Beccali worked out twice a day for a month before the Olympics, running as many as 15 dashes of 300 meters each. An impressed Comstock said:

"He has done three times as much work as I would recommend but I have kept my hands off. If he wins this meet—and I don't know who is going to beat him—I will have to alter every theory I ever had on conditioning. I can hardly wait to see that race."

Beccali ran 3:53.0 in Milan on May 30, then went to Budapest two weeks later for his only serious test before the Olympics. On June 14 he ran agaist Miklós Szabó, who set a determined pace of 59.2 and 2:00.4.

Beccali ran 0.4 seconds behind until the third lap when he was only one tenth behind Szabó's 3:04.2 for 1200 meters. Then, as Szabó faded from his excessive effort, Beccali ran his last 300 in 46.3 without any competition to spur him on. His 3:50.6 proved he would be a difficult man to beat in Berlin.

WOODERSON IS READY

The hopes of England lay with 21-year-old Wooderson, no longer merely a great prospect but a maturing runner with a devastating finish.

Wooderson tuned himself carefully again, but this year he would have to run many more races. He postponed his serious racing until the Inter-Counties mile on June 1 against Reggie Thomas and Jerry Cornes, who was back from Africa and training hard toward another great effort in the Olympics. Wooderson ran away in the last half lap, covering it in 30-flat for a time of 4:16.4.

On June 13, Wooderson won the Kinnaird Cup mile in an effortless 4:20.2 with Cornes second in 4:21.8. Wooderson's next race, one week later in the Southern Championships at Chelmsford, was treated as a serious time-trial. His coach, Albert Hill, wanted 4 laps of 62 seconds each.

Wooderson ran 60.6, slowed disappointingly to 2:05 and 3:08.8, then finished in 4:10.8 for a new British record. Observers were impressed with his smooth, powerful performance and with his poise in a solo effort, 45 yards ahead of Thomas and Cornes. He was ready for the AAA mile against Lovelock.

LOVELOCK WORRIES HIS FRIENDS

At the end of his 1935 season, Lovelock was tired, mentally and physically. No other miler had such ups and downs in performance and he was now as low as he could go. For four months he ran only once on a track and his only exercise was an occasional walk to the hospital or a swim. His friends were worried.

His escape from running lasted into February, 1936. He won the inter-hospitals featherweight boxing championship in March, then began training, but it was May before he trained seriously. He had convinced himself he could reach his best form for a single race in a short time.

He started gentle competition—4:53 plus a half-mile the same day, and 4:42 plus a half—but then he was beaten into third place while running 4:30 . . . and he was dead tired.

Now it was June, two months before the Olympics, and everybody else was worried about his condition, but he did not worry. Sometimes he was up all night, his sleep broken by maternity calls, and he had been without a holiday for nine months. He avoided hard competition and concentrated his efforts on long work.

He persuaded the New Zealand selectors to name him for the 5000 meters as well as the 1500 in the Olympics, and on June 13 he ran an eye-opening three-mile race in the Polytechnic Harriers' open meet. He ran away from two opponents with a last lap in 59.4 for a time of 14:20.8, only 3.6 seconds from Shrubb's British record.

At the Southern Championships the next week, while Wooderson was running 4:10.8, Lovelock lost a dismal half-mile race in which he ran only 1:55.0. Although track experts had been amazed at Lovelock's three-mile performance, they now said he had no chance against Wooderson.

Lovelock wanted to test himself against Wooderson, and he was relieved when Wooderson entered the AAA mile instead of the 880 on July 11. Also in the race were Cornes and Robert Graham, a formidable young Scot who had run 4:12.0 in 1935.

Graham led in 62.2 and 2:10, then Cornes led for half a lap at the same lazy pace. Suddenly Cornes burst into a fast run with 660 yards left to go. He covered the next 220 in 30-flat, enough to disturb most opponents. But Wooderson not only followed, he took the lead on the last lap, and Lovelock stayed close behind.

With 50,000 spectators at White City shrieking, Lovelock followed Wooderson to the homestretch, swung wide and gained a little. But in the last 50 yards his famous sprint could not make any headway against Wooderson's. He finished less than a yard back, smiling. Even though he had lost, 4:15.0 to 4:15.2, he was well satisfied with his progress.

Now Lovelock's training became more intense than ever before. He knew exactly what he wanted to do to be ready in Berlin on August 6. He did much intensive pace work, both in short bursts during longer runs and against a stop watch.

He ran a ¾ with Cornes in 3:05. A week later they ran another, and even Lovelock was surprised at his 3:01. His weight was now rising satisfactorily and he continued his hard work. On July 25, he ran in a two-mile race in Birmingham. It was a cold, wet, windy afternoon and the track was rough. After three laps he was on his own, at an unfamiliar distance, but he ran his last lap under 62 and finished in British record time of 9:03.8, only 5.4 seconds from Lash's new world record. He could have broken the world record if he had realized his strength, especially under good conditions.

He trained hard for a few more days and went to Berlin dead tired. He rested with light jogging and walking until five days before the 1500. Then he ran ¾ in 3:03 so easily that he wrote in his diary, "This is getting too easy." He finished that day with a two-mile jog, including several fast bursts. Then he rested for the Olympic competition.

Still, he had not decided between the 1500 and the 5000, and he needed tranquilizers to sleep. On August 4, the day before the 1500 heats, the 5000 heats were held, and Lovelock ended the suspense by withdrawing.

1936 OLYMPICS

A crowd of 100,000 watched the heats under threatening clouds in the Reich Sports Field Stadium. Cunningham had complained of leg trouble, but a doctor said it was from worry, and in the first heat Cunningham moved up from fourth place at the end to tie Ny in 3:54.8. Böttcher was the other qualifier, in 3:55.0. Eliminated were Mihály Iglói of Hungary and Paul Martin of Switzerland, the Olympic silver medalist in the 1924 800.

Lovelock and Cornes made a friendly agreement to control the second heat. Cornes kept the pace steady and comfortably slow, while Lovelock controlled the rest of the field. Venzke ran in third place, but in the homestretch he was scared by Scholtz of South Africa and burst to the front. He won the heat in 4:00.4 to 4:00.6 for Cornes and Lovelock. They finished a barely secure three yards ahead of the first non-qualifier.

In the third heat, Beccali and Szabó both ran 3:55.6 to qualify safely, but Graham's 3:56.6 was not good enough against the powerful finish of a man who had not been heard from at this distance since the 1932 Olympic final—Dr. Phil Edwards of Canada, who qualified with 3:56.2. Edwards had won his *fifth* Olympic bronze medal on August 4 with third place in the 800 final.

In the last heat, with the first lap in a snappy 59.6, San Romani ran ninth most of the way, and in the homestretch he was fourth, behind Wooderson—an uncomfortable position. But Wooderson, who had turned his ankle while walking cross country a few days before, was running in extreme pain. When three runners were ahead of him, going away, Wooderson stopped and walked, out of the Olympics. Later, x-rays showed a broken bone.

The heat was won by surprising Robert Goix of France in

1936

3:54.0, fastest time in the qualifying round. San Romani finished second in 3:55.0, ahead of the 3:55.2 by Schaumburg. Eliminated in 3:56.6 was promising Joseph Mostert of Belgium.

For the final on August 6, the weather was cold and dark and more than 100,000 curious people turned their heads to watch Hitler enter his box as the 12 runners lined up on the curve of the red clay track.

Beccali had predicted warily, "Any one of five men may win. It depends which one of us happens to be exactly right. But I don't think the time will be very fast. All of us will be too cautious."

And at the start the tense and nervous runners *were* cautious. Cornes led at first but Schaumburg took the lead in front of Hitler, and, with three full laps to go, Beccali was third, Lovelock was sixth, and Cunningham an uncertain seventh. The last three were Edwards, Venzke, and San Romani.

Feeling endangered, Cunningham made a move around the curve and took the lead at 400 meters in 61.5, and Lovelock moved vigilantly to second place. Schaumburg was alongside Lovelock, with Beccali right behind.

Around to the homestretch again, the pack bunched dangerously and Lovelock lost the position he wanted. With two laps to go, Cunningham led Ny, Schaumburg, Lovelock, and Beccali. As they reached the starting line in a satisfactory 2:05.2, Ny moved expectantly to Cunningham's shoulder. Lovelock and Beccali passed Schaumburg, and then San Romani came up threateningly from the rear, past the German into fifth place.

In a surprise move, Ny passed Cunningham on the curve and led into the stretch approaching the bell. Cunningham was not used to being passed while he pushed the pace in the third lap. Lovelock was concerned about Beccali behind him, and so he swung wide of Cunningham to avoid the perils of a box.

As the bell clanged its warning, Lovelock was outside Cunningham, boxing him in on the curve. Ny was bounding along with big strides, while Lovelock floated along with light, mincing steps. Cunningham, inside Lovelock, was running with great power in his longer strides, and Beccali behind him had the shortest stride of all. Lovelock had Cunningham boxed in, and he felt in control of the race. The low rumbling of the crowd was rising to a thunder of excitement as they raced around toward the starting line.

Lovelock moved quickly to Ny's shoulder and caught the answering movement of Cunningham, ready to follow him. Lovelock paused, as if reluctant to sprint. He shortened his stride and moved his weight forward, over his toes, as they reached 1200 meters in 3:05.4.

Then came a single instant when Olympic history was made. Lovelock eased into a sprint with the beautifully fluid motion he had

1936

practiced for so long. Almost instantly he shot past Ny and opened a devastating gap of more than four yards.

He had taken them by surprise by making a move earlier than ever before in his career. Now he must hold the lead. He concentrated on form, relaxing as he drove down the backstretch. Ny faded behind such speed, but Cunningham and Beccali set out after him with determination and power.

Around the last curve they raced, the huge crowd roaring with excitement. Lovelock's black figure led Cunningham's white by four yards. Beccali's blue shirt was almost on Cunningham's shoulder. The amazing Edwards, in the red pants of Canada, had closed to within six yards of Beccali, and behind him San Romani fought desperately to retain the ground he had lost. Cornes, once more running his best race where it counted most, was leaving the others behind as he pursued San Romani.

As he reached the homestretch, Lovelock took no chances. He launched into a full sprint, and his speed was remarkable. Cunningham and Beccali had been gaining on him, running the races of their lives, but now he opened the gap to six yards. He could feel his hands flapping at his wrists in a relaxed way and he could see the tape ahead. He knew he was safe, but he looked back automatically. He had won! He eased his sprint and coasted in.

Cunningham, who never let up, gained back two yards when Lovelock coasted, and he pulled away from the bitterly disappointed Beccali to secure the silver medal by more than five yards. San Romani roared home faster than any of them, passing Edwards in the stretch drive, and Cornes finished well.

Results: 1. Lovelock, 3:47.8; 2. Cunningham, 3:48.4; 3. Beccali, 3:49.2; 4. San Romani, 3:50.0; 5. Edwards, 3:50.4; 6. Cornes, 3:51.4; 7. Szabó; 3:53.0; 8. Goix, 3:53.8; 9. Venzke, 3:55.0; 10. Schaumburg, 3:56.2; 11. Ny, 3:57.6; 12. Böttcher, 4:04.2.

Lovelock was now the fastest man who ever ran 1500 meters, and Cunningham had broken Bonthron's U.S. record. Five of the first eight finishers ran faster than ever before in this fastest of all mile or 1500 meter races, and San Romani missed his personal best by only one tenth, Beccali by two, and Szabó by four tenths.

Five of the six place-winners were veterans of the 1932 Olympic final, but this time Edwards beat Cornes, Cunningham beat Beccali, and Lovelock beat them all.

Lovelock said, "It was the most perfectly executed race of my career."

Cunningham said, "He must be the greatest runner ever."

Perhaps the most remarkable part of Lovelock's victory was the fact that he was not under full stress at the finish. He said, "I think I could have sustained it for another 100 meters if necessary."

1936

If true, he could have run a mile close to 4:03.

Beccali was spiked early in the race and may have lost a little of his edge from the mishap, but he said, "I was spiked, but that did not affect my chances."

Cunningham and Beccali congratulated Lovelock enthusiastically after the race, along with Cornes, and the crowd kept thundering its approval. Lovelock said, "I'm very happy. Very happy indeed."

He explained his long drive, from 300 meters out: "That's what fooled Cunningham, Luigi Beccali and the others. They thought I would sprint only about the last 70 meters and were not prepared when I started my run."

But after his last 300 meters in 42.4 had defeated the fastest field in history, his immediate pleasure wore off, and Lovelock said, "It isn't the fun it used to be. I think it's about time to hang up my shoes."

But he did not retire immediately. He won a 3-mile a few weeks later in 14:14.8. Then, because he was to travel across the United States on his way home to New Zealand, a race was proposed for October 3. He accepted cheerfully, and he ran the last mile of his career at Princeton's Palmer Stadium before 40,000 people between halves of a football game.

The pace was peculiar. Dawson led in 62 and 2:02. Then, with Cunningham obviously not fit, the pace slowed to 3:12.2 before San Romani took off at great speed. Lovelock challenged with 300 to go, but he could do nothing with San Romani's great drive, which carried around the last lap in an exceptional 56.8 for a winning time of 4:09 to Lovelock's 4:10.1 and Cunningham's 4:13.0. Almost all of San Romani's superiority came in the last 120 yards.

And so, smiling, curly-haired Jack Lovelock retired, and one of his successors appeared to be young Archie San Romani.

1936
MILE:

4:09.0	Archie San Romani (USA)	(1)	Princeton	3 Oct
4:10.1	Jack Lovelock (NZ)	(2)	Princeton	3 Oct
4:10.8	Don Lash (USA)	(1)	Columbus	23 May
4:10.8	Sydney Wooderson (GB)	(1)	Chelmsford	20 Jun
4:10.9	Charles Fenske (USA)	(2)	Columbus	23 May
4:12.5	Robert Graham (GB)	(1)	Glasgow	27 Jun
4:13.0	Glenn Cunningham (USA)	(3)	Princeton	3 Oct
4:13.4	Gene Venzke (USA)	(1)	Princeton	13 Jun
4:13.5	Lash	(1)	Dual meet	
4:13.5 e	Cunningham	(2)	Princeton	13 Jun
4:14.0	San Romani	(1)	New Orleans	27 Dec
4:15.0	Tom Deckard (USA)	(3)	Columbus	23 May
4:15.0	Wooderson	AAA(1)	London	11 Jul
4:15.2	Lash	(1)	Milwaukee	5 Jun
4:15.2	Lovelock	AAA (2)	London	11 Jul

Indoors:

4:10.2	Gene Venzke (USA)	(1)	New York	15 Feb
4:10.7e	Glenn Cunningham (USA)	(2)	New York	15 Feb
4:11.0	Joe Mangan (USA)	(1)	New York	1 Feb
4:11.1	Venzke	(2)	New York	1 Feb
4:11.2	Cunningham	(3)	New York	1 Feb

1936

1,500m:

3:47.8	WR	Jack Lovelock (NZ)	(1)	Berlin	6	Aug
3:48.4		Glenn Cunningham (USA)	(2)	Berlin	6	Aug
3:49.2		Luigi Beccali (Italy)	(3)	Berlin	6	Aug
3:49.9		Cunningham	(1)	New York	12	Jul
3:49.9		Archie San Romani (USA)	(2)	New York	12	Jul
3:50.0		San Romani	(4)	Berlin	6	Aug
3:50.4		Philip Edwards (Canada)	(5)	Berlin	6	Aug
3:50.6		Beccali	(1)	Budapest	14	Jun
3:51.3		San Romani	(1)	Viipuri, Finland	24	Aug
3:51.4		Jerry Cornes (GB)	(6)	Berlin	6	Aug
3:52.2		Gene Venzke (USA)	(3)	New York	12	Jul
3:52.2		Eric Ny (Sweden)	(1)	Stockholm	10	Jul
3:52.4		Ny	(1)	Göteborg	2	Sep
3:52.4		Ny	(1)	Oslo	12	Sep
3:52.6		Venzke	(1)	Cambridge, Mass.	9	May
3:52.8		Cunningham	(1)	Stockholm	21	Aug
3:53.0		Beccali	(1)	Milan	30	May
3:53.0		Miklós Szabó (Hungary)	(2)	Budapest	14	Jun
3:53.0		San Romani	NCAA (1)	Chicago	20	Jun
3:53.0		Szabó	(7)	Berlin	6	Aug
3:53.0		Joseph Mostert (Belgium)	(1)	Warsaw	19	Sep

Indoors:

3:49.9	Gene Venzke (USA)	(1)	New York	22	Feb
3:50.1	Glenn Cunningham (USA)	(2)	New York	22	Feb

FASTEST 1500 METER RUNS:			FASTEST MILE RUNS:		
3:47.8	Lovelock	1936	4:06.7	Cunningham	1934
3:48.4n	Cunningham	1936	4:07.6	Lovelock	1933
3:48.8	Bonthron	1934	4:08.4i	Cunningham	1934
3:48.9n	Cunningham	1934	4:08.7n	Bonthron	1933
3:49.0	Beccali	1933	4:08.9	Bonthron	1934
3:49.2	Beccali	1933	4:09.0	San Romani	1936
3:49.2	Ladoumègue	1930	4:09.2	Ladoumègue	1931
3:49.2n	Beccali	1936	4:09.8i	Cunningham	1933
3:49.6	Beccali	1933	4:09.8	Cunningham	1933
3:49.8n	Lovelock	1933	4:09.8i	Cunningham	1935
3:49.9i	Venzke	1936	4:10.0i	Venzke	1932
3:49.9	Cunningham	1936	4:10.1n	Lovelock	1936
3:49.9n	San Romani	1936			

ANGLO-AMERICAN POWER STRUCTURE (1937-1940)

A curious phenomenon of dominance in foot racing was demonstrated during the 1930's. The most successful way in which one nation or group of nations can dominate is to build a strong base consisting of many good milers competing against each other. Out of this fierce competition, so the theory goes, the best of those runners should dominate the world.

But in the early 1930's, dominance belonged successively to three milers who were almost the lone representatives of their nations—Ladoumègue, Beccali, and Lovelock—a rather curious contradiction of the theory.

Then, in the last half of the decade, milers from the United States built a formidable base of strength, forecasting dominance at the 1940 Olympics. This strength stayed ahead of the slower progress in Europe, but it was challenged by another lone exception—Sydney Wooderson.

1937

FAST INDOOR MILERS

San Romani was supposed to be the top U.S. miler in 1937, but Cunningham disputed the claim. Now studying at New York University toward his doctor's degree, Cunningham won at Boston, beating back Lash's threat in 4:11.9. In the Wanamaker Mile, his skill and experience won in 4:14.4 from Venzke, San Romani, and Lash. He took the Hunter Mile, safely ahead of Venzke, in 4:12.3. Then, with the irrepressible Beccali making his indoor debut in the Baxter Mile, Cunningham continued his triumphant streak in 4:12.4, ahead of Venzke and Beccali.

Cunningham withdrew from the indoor AAU 1500 because of a bad cold, and San Romani won an exciting race in 3:51.2 from Beccali 3:51.3 and Venzke 3:51.4. Szabó of Hungary was ten yards back, ahead of Lash.

The scene was set for the Columbian Mile on March 17, to be the fastest mass mile yet run. San Romani set a determined pace in 61, 2:05, and 3:09, followed by Beccali, Cunningham, and Venzke. Cunningham moved to second on the tenth lap and followed San Romani confidently to the last backstretch. Then he sprinted into the lead, but San Romani and Beccali charged after him furiously. Results: Cunningham 4:08.7, San Romani 4:08.9, Beccali 4:09.0, Venzke 4:11.1.

A FAST MILE AT PRINCETON

An unusual race in the fourth Princeton Invitstional resulted in even a faster mass finish than the Columbian mile. Rain threatened and a cold wind blew through the open end of Palmer Stadium and down the homestretch as 20,000 people watched a select field of five milers on the black cinder track.

Venzke dashed off in front, intent on setting a new record for ¾ mile, and scurried around the first lap in 58.6, five yards ahead of Lash, who had run a good 4:09.7 on May 8. Another five yards behind Lash was Beccali. Behind Beccali were Cunningham, whose fastest outdoor mile so far in 1937 was 4:14.1, and San Romani, who ran 1500 meters in a quick 3:50.3 in Kansas City on June 5.

Lash lost no more ground, as Venzke's ambition faded on the second lap. Lash passed the 880 in 2:01 to Venzke's 2:00.2, but now there was a disquieting gap of 18 yards back to the others.

On the third lap, Lash reluctantly let Venzke go at least 20 yards ahead in 3:01.4. Cunningham and San Romani had moved away from discouraged Beccali and now they were only ten yards behind Lash. When Venzke dropped out, Lash was the leader around the curve, but he was tiring. He had run the third lap at about a 64 pace and now he was down to about 65. The rabid crowd now saw him as a loser.

On the last backstretch, into the face of the cold wind, Cunningham and San Romani passed Lash, who by staying with them around the curve showed the crowd he still had some strength and a lot of courage. At 1500 meters, Cunningham was timed in 3:52.2 with both San Romani and Lash at 3:52.3, and the crowd was going wild.

San Romani sprinted furiously as they turned into the homestretch, but Cunningham matched his speed and Lash was after both of them. San Romani gained slowly on his idol, Cunningham, while Lash, who had broken the world 2-mile record here last year, threatened to catch both of them.

About 40 yards from the tape, San Romani was alongside Cunningham, and Lash was out wide, trying to pass San Romani. Not since the 1912 Olympics had three top milers been side-by-side so close to the tape. The frenzied crowd sounded deranged.

Then, suddenly, Cunningham was a beaten man as the other two fought a bitter battle. First Lash's red shirt was ahead and then it was the mustard-colored shirt of San Romani. They finished about two yards ahead of Cunningham, and the dazed Beccali was another 15 yards back. The judges had difficulty picking the winner.

Results: San Romani 4:07.2, Lash 4:07.2, Cunningham 4:07.4, Beccali 4:09.6.

Only Cunningham's world record was faster than San Romani and Lash. Beccali may have been hampered by a leg injury in practice a few days before.

At this date, the six fastest outdoor miles in history had been run on the great Princeton track: these three, plus Cunningham's world record, plus Lovelock's 4:07.6 ahead of Bonthron's 4:08.7.

ARCHIE SAN ROMANI (Part 2)

Young San Romani now had some claim as the best miler in the world, and in the AAU 1500 at Milwaukee on July 3 he set out to prove it. Instead of waiting until the homestretch, he was in the lead and seemed a sure winner when disaster struck. He stepped on the curb and fell.

Cunningham could not avoid him, and was injured in the collision. Cunningham went on to win anyway, in 3:51.8, 15 yards ahead of James Smith. Chuck Fenske, who had come from behind in the homestretch to beat Smith in the NCAA mile in 4:13.9, finished third. San Romani climbed gamely to his feet and beat out Venzke for the fourth and last medal.

San Romani had more bad luck when he travelled to London for a race against Wooderson and Szabó on August 2. He was out of sorts from the trip and ran poorly.

San Romani had a third mishap at Stockholm on August 5, when he went after the world record. His main opponent was Henry Jonsson of Sweden, who had won the bronze medal in the Olympic 5000 in 1936. Jonsson, in excellent condition, had run 3000 meters in 8:16.2 on July 21, only 1.4 seconds from the world record.

Jonsson started too fast in Stockholm's Olympic stadium, with San Romani, as usual, content to trail by a few yards. Jonsson ran 59.0 for 400 meters, 2:03.2 for 800, and he continued his effort to about 3:07 for three-quarters.

Full of spirit, San Romani rushed past Jonsson on the last backstretch and was pulling away impressively when they reached 1500 meters in 3:52.2 and 3:53.4. San Romani was one tenth of a second faster than at Princeton, within range of a world record, but he made a blunder.

Confused by the markings on the 385-meter track, San Romani thought the race was over and he slowed to a jog. As Jonsson rushed closer, San Romani was alerted by team manager John Magee, who shouted, "Go on, go on!"

San Romani broke into a run again and beat Jonsson's good finish, 4:08.4 to 4:08.8. A very fast time had been spoiled by his error.

WOODERSON STRIKES BACK

With his broken bone healed and the disappointment of the Olympics behind him, Wooderson proved he was still improving in the first race of 1937, the Kinnaird Cup on May 29. He won in 4:17.1 with his last lap in a fast 57.7.

He won the Southern Championship in 4:14.6 and ran a 4:13 relay mile under poor conditions. On July 17, he won his third consecutive AAA Championship by more than 20 yards in 4:12.2, fastest ever run in that meet.

On July 24, in Colombes stadium near Paris, he beat France in 3:51.0. At White City on August 2, he beat Szabó and an ill San Romani in 4:15.8. On August 7, in the Rangers' Meeting in Glasgow, he ran ¾ mile in a thwarting wind and broke Lovelock's British record with 3:00.9. On August 14 he won the dual against Germany from Schaumburg with an easy 4:19.

He was in great shape, and in the Blackheath Harriers' Meeting at Motspur Park on August 28, he planned a record attempt. The weather was good, the track fast, and he was two days from his 23rd birthday.

Reggie Thomas was given a ten-yard handicap, and he started too fast. Wooderson went past the 440 in 58.6 and the half in 2:02.6. Then, on his own, he continued to slow the pace to 3:07.2 for three-quarters. Thus, he had actually received no important help from the handicap men.

At this point he was a mere four tenths of a second ahead of Cunningham's record pace. Startled into action, Wooderson almost sprinted into the last lap, covering his first 110 yards in 14.4. His legs protested that pace, and he slowed to 14.9 and 15.1. He passed 1500 meters in 3:50.3.

Now, with his devastating sprint yet to come, a world record was assured. But Wooderson did not have his usual sprint. The faster race, at a poorly judged pace, had taken all his reserves. He managed to keep running on raw courage, but there was no noticeable increase in speed and the 3000 spectators feared the worst.

When the tiny, black-clad figure struggled through the tape, there was a long moment of suspense while the timers consulted their watches. Then the time was announced as 4:06.6, one tenth of a second faster than Cunningham, but a world record nevertheless, and the small crowd cheered mightily. Later, one of the two watches which clocked 4:06.6 was found to be unofficial and so the two at 4:06.4 governed and that time became the new world record.

Among the spectators at this great run was a 79-year-old man who was once the best of all . . . Walter George. The mile record had returned to England for the first time in the twentieth century.

MIKLÓS SZABÓ

Before the 1937 season, Szabó's fastest time was his 3:52.6 when he lost to Cunningham in 1933. After his good seventh in the Olympics, behind a great field, his reputation increased and he was invited to the United States to run indoors. He lost there and he ran 4:16.2 in losing a big international mile in London on August 2. But he lost none of his reputation there, because Wooderson beat him by only three yards.

Six days later, in Budapest, the ambitious 29-year-old Hungarian ran 3:51.8 and on September 5 he ran 3:52.1. Then, on September 30, still in friendly Budapest, the 5'9¾", 143-pound runner broke the world record for two miles with 8:56 flat.

Now in great condition, he ran 1500 meters three days later, also in Budapest. He set a pace of 60.4 and 2:03.6. Then he ran what was probably the fastest third quarter ever run—60.4 for 400 meters. He finished gamely in 44.6 for a time of 3:48.6, second fastest winning 1500 meters ever run. (Second in 3:52.2 was Mihály Iglói, later to become a famous coach.)

1937

4:06.4	WR	Sydney Wooderson (GB)	(1)	Motspur Park	28	Aug
4:07.2		Archie San Romani (USA)	(1)	Princeton	19	Jun
4:07.2		Don Lash (USA)	(2)	Princeton	19	Jun
4:07.4		Glenn Cunningham (USA)	(3)	Princeton	19	Jun
4:08.4		San Romani	(1)	Stockholm	5	Aug
4:08.8		Henry Jonsson *(Sweden)	(2)	Stockholm	5	Aug
4:09.4		Lash	(1)	Los Angeles	26	Jun

1937

4:09.6	Luigi Beccali (Italy)	(4)	Princeton		19	Jun
4:09.7	Lash	(1)	Bloomington		8	May
4:11.0	James Smith (USA)	(1)	Notre Dame		29	May
4:12.2	Wooderson	AAA(1)	London		17	Jul
4:12.2	Olle Pettersson (Sweden)	(3)	Stockholm		5	Aug
4:13.0	Smith	(2)	Bloomington		8	May
4:13.4	Pete Bradley (USA)	(1)	Princeton		17	Jul
4:13.8	Jack Emery (GB)	(1)	Cambridge, Mass.		10	Jul
4:13.9	Charles Fenske (USA)	NCAA(1)	Berkeley		19	Jun

*changed his name to Kälarne in 1939.

Indoors:

4:08.7	Glenn Cunningham (USA)	(1)	New York	17	Mar
4:08.9	Archie San Romani (USA)	(2)	New York	17	Mar
4:09.0	Luigi Beccali (Italy)	(3)	New York	17	Mar
4:11.1	Gene Venzke (USA)	(4)	New York	17	Mar

1,500m:
(+ during mile)

3:48.6	Miklós Szabó (Hungary)	(1)	Budapest	3	Oct
3:50.3	Archie San Romani (USA)	(1)	Kansas City	5	Jun
3:50.3+	Sydney Wooderson (GB)	(1)	Motspur Park	28	Aug
3:51.0	Wooderson	(1)	Colombes	24	Jul
3:51.4	Henry Jonsson (Sweden)	(1)	Stockholm	11	Jul
3:51.8	Glenn Cunningham (USA)	AAU(1)	Milwaukee	3	Jul
3:51.8	Szabó	(1)	Budapest	8	Aug
3:52.1	Szabó	(1)	Budapest	5	Sep
3:52.2+	San Romani	(1)	Stockholm	5	Aug
3:52.2	Mihály Iglói (Hungary)	(2)	Budapest	3	Oct
3:52.2+	Cunningham	(1)	Princeton	19	Jun
3:52.3+	San Romani	(2)	Princeton	19	Jun
3:52.3+	Don Lash (USA)	(3)	Princeton	19	Jun
3:52.4	Ake Jansson (Sweden)	(1)	Berlin	18	Sep
3:52.8	Lennart Nilsson (Sweden)	(1)	Stockholm	24	Sep
3:53.0	Jansson	(2)	Stockholm	24	Sep
3:53.1	Iglói	(2)	Budapest	5	Sep
3:53.2	Friedrich Schaumburg (Ger)	(1)	Warsaw	22	Aug
3:53.2	Hans Lehne (Nor)	(1)	Oslo	12	Sep
3:53.2	Schaumburg	(2)	Berlin	18	Sep

Indoors:

3:51.2	Archie San Romani (USA)	AAU(1)	New York	27	Feb
3:51.3e	Luigi Beccali (Italy)	AAU(2)	New York	27	Feb
3:51.4e	Gene Venzke (USA)	AAU(3)	New York	27	Feb

The fast races of 1937 changed the all-time combined list:

(3:47.4)	4:06.4	Wooderson	1937
(3:47.7)	4:06.7	Cunningham	1934
3:47.8	(4:06.8)	Lovelock	1936
(3:48.2)	4:07.2	San Romani	1937
(3:48.2)	4:07.2n	Lash	1937
3:48.4n	(4:07.4)	Cunningham	1936
(3:48.4)	4:07.4n	Cunningham	1937
(3:48.5)	4:07.6	Lovelock	1933
3:48.6	(4:07.7)	Szabó	1937
3:48.8	(4:07.8)	Bonthron	1934
3:48.9n	(4:08.0)	Cunningham	1934
3:49.0	(4:08.3)	Beccali	1933
3:49.2	(4:08.3)	Ladoumègue	1930
3:49.2	(4:08.3)	Beccali	1933
3:49.2n	(4:08.3)	Beccali	1936
(3:49.3)	4:08.4i	Cunningham	1934
(3:49.3)	4:08.4	San Romani	1937
(3:49.6)	4:08.7n	Bonthron	1933
3:49.6	(4:08.7)	Beccali	1933
(3:49.6)	4:08.7i	Cunningham	1937
(3:49.7)	4:08.8n	Jonsson	1937
(3:49.7)	4:08.9	Bonthron	1934
(3:49.7)	4:08.9in	San Romani	1937
3:49.8n	(4:09.0)	Lovelock	1933
(3:49.8)	4:09.0	San Romani	1936
(3:49.8)	4:09.0in	Beccali	1937

1938

CUNNINGHAM GOES ON AND ON

Cunningham admired endurance. Speaking of the longevity type of endurance, he once said, "If you stay in the running—if you have endurance—you are bound to win over those who haven't."

Cunningham had that type of endurance. He had lost many important races to runners who were no longer competition for him in 1938. And, at the age of 28, he was faster than ever.

On January 2, at New Orleans' Sugar Bowl meet, he beat San Romani and Lash in a mediocre 4:13.1. He beat all comers indoors, running gradually faster races, through 4:11.9 in the Wanamaker Mile, 4:10.1 at the Boston AA, and 4:08.6 in the Baxter Mile.

On February 26, in the indoor AAU, he wanted to run in the distance medley relay after the 1500 meters, but he went out and pushed the pace by himself, running away from Venzke and San Romani, who had suffered an ankle injury.

He ran 61.6, 2:04.8, 3:05.2, and won in 3:48.4, time bettered only by Lovelock's Olympic record. Venzke was second in 3:50.8. Then Cunningham came back and anchored his team to victory in the relay.

Only five days later, March 3, on Dartmouth's large track at Hanover, New Hampshire, he tried for a record in a special handicap race. The track was wonderfully fast and springy and it was only 6-2/3 laps to a mile, giving more speed on the wide turns.

One Dartmouth runner started five yards ahead of Cunningham and dropped out at the 880. Four runners started 260 yards ahead, and one, with a 600-yard start, ran slowly so as to urge Cunningham on in the last quarter.

"I planned to do my first three-quarters miles in 60, 63, and 61 seconds and then run the last one as fast as I could."

Cunningham reached the 440 in 58.5. When he heard the time, "I thought I ran my first quarter too fast." He slowed down deliberately and passed the 880 in 2:02.5. "I was back on my schedule at the half-mile."

Cunningham passed all except the last handicap man before the three-quarters, which he reached in 3:04.2. "I felt quite fresh." He pushed himself over the last quarter, with 3,000 spectators noisily aware he was making history. He passed the last runner on the last lap and charged through the tape in 4:04.4.

The time, two seconds faster than anybody else ever ran, made the front page of the New York Times. Cunningham said: "It's a great track and those wide turns helped me a lot . . . conditions were ideal."

Many experts discounted his time because it was made on a large track and in a handicap race, but outdoor tracks were larger and many records were made in handicap races. Actually, the amazing

time did not surprise real insiders, such as San Romani, who had predicted Cunningham could run 4:03 outdoors in 1938.
On March 12, Cunningham ran 4:07.4 in the Columbian Mile. This was hailed as an indoor record, for the Hanover track was deemed too large to count. In a remarkable double little over an hour later, Glenn tied the world 600 record of 1:11.3 but placed third to Jim Herbert's 1:11.1.

The Chicago Relays on March 26 was run on boards for the first time. Cunningham was challenged by Chuck Fenske, now a senior at Wisconsin and maturing strongly. Fenske had won the Big Ten indoor mile in 4:11.1 and a week before had run a sparkling 4:08.9 on a dirt track indoors in Chicago.

Cunningham barely survived Fenske's challenge in the Bankers Mile with 4:09.9. Already the young milers were after him.

Cunningham lost a slow 4:23 mile to San Romani in the Kansas Relays, April 23, and one other unimportant race, his only losses before he ran in the Princeton Invitation on June 18.

At the now-famous Palmer Stadium meet he was running against San Romani, Pete Bradley of Princeton, a 4:13.4 miler in 1937, Blaine Rideout, who had run some fast relay legs for North Texas State, and Joseph Mostert of Belgium, who ran 3:53.0 in 1936 and bettered all known records for ¾ mile with 3:00.4 on September 26, 1937, in Paris.

A determined San Romani led in 61.2, 2:05.8, and 3:09.0, although Rideout took the lead temporarily on the third backstretch. San Romani passed 1500 meters in 3:50.9 with Cunningham on his shoulder with 3:51.0 and Rideout hopelessly beaten in 3:53.9.

Cunningham began to gain with agonizing slowness. With 50 yards to go he pulled even, and they ran side by side for several strides with the crowd blaring. Then San Romani made another mistake. He turned to inspect Cunningham's fatigue and once again he stepped on the curb. He fell and Cunningham went on to win a hollow victory. Mostert, ten yards behind Rideout at 1500 meters, beat him by over five yards.

Results: Cunningham 4:07.2, San Romani 4:10.4, Mostert 4:11.6, Rideout 4:12.4, Bradley 4:13.9.

Not content with equalling the third fastest mile time ever run outdoors, Cunningham had a massage and a short rest, then came onto the track to attack the pending record for ¾ mile. He ran in fourth place until the last lap, trailed Wayne Rideout, Blaine's twin brother, by several yards in the homestretch, and lost by three yards. Rideout bettered Mostert's "world record" with 3:00.3, while Cunningham completed his extraordinary double in 3:00.8. Venzke was third.

In the AAU championships, held at Buffalo, New York, on July 3, Cunningham lined up with his rivals from the Princeton race

1938

plus the two best college runners. Fenske had won the Big Ten race in 4:10.9 and the Central Collegiates in 4:10.6, but he lost in the NCAA meet, held in Minneapolis on the same day as the Princeton race, to a new star from the University of Southern California.

LOUIS ZAMPERINI was a juvenile delinquent, a bad-tempered misfit, until his older brother, Pete, forced him into a 660-yard race in 1932 at the age of 15. Louis crossed the line third and the attention he received made him want more. He placed fifth in the Los Angeles class C 660 that season. This caused him to give up smoking, start studying so he would be eligible to run, and start training.

So great was his natural talent that he was undefeated in his last three years of high school. As a sophomore he ran the fastest ¾ mile in state history. As a junior in 1934, aged 17, he broke the interscholastic mile record with 4:21.2. As a senior he ran only to win, saving himself for future glory. He was also elected president of the student body.

He graduated from high school in January of 1936. Instead of going on to college, he trained for the Olympic Games. On July 12, in the Final Trials at Randall's Island, he surprised by tying for first with Don Lash in the 5,000 meters and made the team. Although overweight, he placed eighth in the Olympics.

A skiing injury set him back in 1937, but in 1938 he was better than ever. Running only to win, he had times of 4:14.0 and 4:13.7 before the NCAA meet. There, he outkicked Fenske's 4:08.8 with 4:08.3, fastest college mile ever run. He was rightfully regarded as one of the truly great prospects for the mile distance.

But Zamperini celebrated by getting drunk and a few days later, in a dual meet against the Big Ten, Fenske avenged his defeat by five yards.

In the AAU meet, at Buffalo, N.Y., on July 3, 15,000 people saw a thrilling 1500 meter race but the time was slowed by the track, which was built of black cinders on top of the concrete slab covering a reservoir.

On the all-important last lap, Ray Mahannah of Drake was leading by five yards over Cunningham and Fenske. San Romani and Blaine Rideout were close behind, and Mostert and Zamperini were as close as they could get.

On the last backstretch, Cunningham moved into the lead and Fenske was on his shoulder. With the crowd clamoring, they raced that way all around the turn and down the homestretch, and Cunningham won his fifth title by one foot in 3:52.5. San Romani showed a spark of his old power to beat Zamperini for third. Mostert was fifth and Rideout sixth.

1938

WOODERSON CARRIES ON

Because of routine business commitments, Wooderson did not compete in the British Empire Games at Sydney, Australia, on February 12. (James Alford was the surprise winner in 4:11.5 over Gerald Backhouse of Australia, 4:12.3, and Pat Boot of New Zealand, 4:12.6.)

Wooderson's goal for 1938 was the world record for 880 yards, and he started with slow 880's in June. On July 2, he ran a good 4:11 in a relay. On July 9 he won an easy 1500 in 3:58.6 against Norway. On July 16, he won another AAA Championship in 4:13.4.

On August 1, in a big international meet at White City, he ran the 880 against the 1936 Olympic runner-up at 800 meters, Mario Lanzi of Italy. Wooderson outkicked Lanzi spectacularly in British record time of 1:50.9.

On August 6, in a handicap race in Glasgow, he tried to break Lovelock's world 1500 record of 3:47.8. Wooderson ran 58.0, 2:05, and 3:05.4, but he was too tired to finish faster than 43.6, and he settled for a time of 3:49.0.

After an easy win against France in 1:55.8, Wooderson made his 880 attempt at Motspur Park on August 20th in the Blackheath Harriers' meeting where he broke the mile record in 1937. He started too fast and slowed down all the way to the finish, proving once more that his famous sprint could come only with a relatively slow pace. He passed the 440 in 52.6, then set brilliant world records of 1:48.4 for 800 meters and 1:49.2 for 880 yards.

On September 5, the second European Championships were held at Colombes, near Paris. Main threats to Wooderson were Beccali, who was not at his best, Mostert, Empire champion Alford, Goix, Niilo Hartikka of Finland, who ran 3:52.0 and four other races under 3:53, and Toivo Sarkama of Finland, who ran 3:52.2 behind Hartikka.

Against this reasonably strong opposition, Wooderson ignored record possibilities because of a strong wind and he ran with the pack, timed in 61.2, 2:06, and 3:10. He did not kick until the homestretch, where he looked back several times as if expecting more of a challenge.

Results: Wooderson 3:53.6, Mostert 3:54.5, Beccali 3:55.2, Hartikka 3:56.5, Sarkama 3:56.7, Jan Staniszewski of Poland 3:58.4.

On September 11 at Milan, Wooderson ran an interesting 1500 on a track made very slow by a heavy rain. His opponents were Beccali and Chuck Fenske, who had run a fast 1500 on July 20 at Stockholm, 2½ weeks after the AAU meet. In that race, Fenske lagged well back in the pack while Henry Jonsson blistered the track in 57.2 and 1:58.5. At the bell, Fenske was 15 meters behind, but he

1938

finished with power in 3:49.4, 20 yards ahead of Jonsson and Hartikka. But here at Milan, Fenske could not hold off Wooderson's great sprint in the homestretch and the little Englishman won in 3:58.4 and Beccali nipped Fenske in 3:58.8. Wooderson ran one more good race: at Oslo on September 15, he followed a fast pace by Kauko Pekuri of Finland, with Mostert following Wooderson. After running 60.0, 2:02.5, and 3:05, Wooderson needed his good finish to beat Mostert, 3:48.7 to 3:50.0.

1938

4:07.2	Glenn Cunningham (USA)	(1)	Princeton	18 Jun
4:08.3	Louis Zamperini (USA) NCAA(1)		Minneapolis	18 Jun
4:08.8	Charles Fenske (USA) NCAA(2)		Minneapolis	18 Jun
4:10.4	Archie San Romani (USA)	(2)	Princeton	18 Jun
4:10.6	Fenske	(1)	Milwaukee	10 Jun
4:10.9	Fenske	(1)	Columbus	21 May
4:11.4	San Romani	(1)	Memphis	13 May
4:11.4	Mel Trutt (USA)	(2)	Columbus	21 May
4:11.5	James Alford (GB) Br Emp Gms	(1)	Sydney	12 Feb
4:11.6	Joseph Mostert (Belgium)	(3)	Princeton	18 Jun
4:11.7	Cunningham	(1)	Pottstown, Pa.	28 May
4:12.0	Trutt	(1)	Bloomington	28 May
4:12.3	Gerald Backhouse (Australia)	(2)	Sydney	12 Feb
4:12.4	Blaine Rideout (USA)	(4)	Princeton	18 Jun
4:12.5	James Smith (USA)	(2)	Bloomington	28 May
4:12.6	Pat Boot (NZ)	(3)	Sydney	12 Feb
4:13.0	William Southworth (USA)	(3)	Bloomington	28 May
4:13.0	Greg Rice (USA)	(4)	Bloomington	28 May
4:13.1	Cunningham	(1)	New Orleans	2 Jan
4:13.1	Gene Venzke (USA)	(2)	Pottstown, Pa.	28 May

Indoors:

4:04.4	Glenn Cunningham (USA)	(1)	Hanover, N.H.	3 Mar
4:07.4	Cunningham	(1)	New York	12 Mar
4:08.6	Cunningham	(1)	New York	19 Feb
4:08.9	Charles Fenske (USA) dirt track	(1)	Chicago	19 Mar
4:09.9	Cunningham	(1)	Chicago	26 Mar

1,500m:
(+ during mile)

3:48.7	Sydney Wooderson (GB)	(1)	Oslo	15 Sep
3:49.0	Wooderson hdcp race	(2)	Glasgow	6 Aug
3:49.4	Charles Fenske (USA)	(1)	Stockholm	20 Jul
3:50.0	Joseph Mostert (Belgium)	(2)	Oslo	15 Sep
3:50.9+	Archie San Romani (USA)	(1)	Princeton	18 Jun
3:51.0+	Glenn Cunningham (USA)	(2)	Princeton	18 Jun
3:52.0	Niilo Hartikka (Finland)	(1)	Helsinki	11 Jul
3:52.0	Hartikka	(1)	Kouvola	17 Jul
3:52.2	Toivo Sarkama (Finland)	(2)	Kouvola	17 Jul
3:52.2	Henry Jonsson (Sweden)	(2)	Stockholm	20 Jul
3:52.2	Hartikka	(1)	Tampere	11 Aug
3:52.5	Cunningham AAU	(1)	Buffalo	3 Jul
3:52.5	Kauko Pekuri (Finland)	(2)	Tampere	11 Aug
3:52.6	Hartikka	(3)	Stockholm	20 Jul
3:52.7	Fenske AAU	(2)	Buffalo	3 Jul
3:52.8	Luigi Beccali (Italy)	(1)	Milan	29 May
3:52.8	Hartikka	(1)	Viipuri	14 Jul
3:52.8	Mihály Iglói (Hungary)	(3)	Kouvola	17 Jul
3:52.8	Sarkama	(3)	Tampere	11 Aug

Indoors:

3:48.4	Glenn Cunningham (USA)	AAU(1)	New York	26 Feb
3:50.8	Gene Venzke (USA)	AAU(2)	New York	26 Feb

Two of Jack Lovelock's greatest victories: Left, 1936 Olympic Games, over Cunningham. Above, winning the 1933 "Mile of the Century" at Princeton in a world record 4:07.6.

Below, Bill Bonthron. Right, Luigi Beccali, 1932 Olympic 1500 champion.

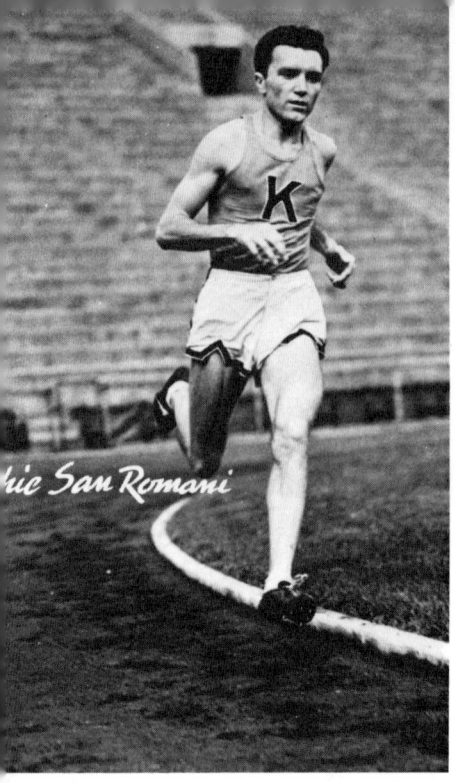

Four American mile aces of the mid-thirties.

PREPARATION FOR PRINCETON

WOODERSON ran cross country during the winter. In 1939 he wanted to be ready early, for he was going to Princeton in June to run against the Americans. On April 29, he ran a self-paced mile in 4:14.8, and on May 20, 4:12.0. The Inter-Counties Championships were held at White City on May 29, and 50,000 people hoped for a record. Wooderson ran the mile as an all-out time trial, leading all the way in 61.2, 2:05, and 3:08.0. He finished with an excellent 4:07.4.

On June 6, in Manchester, he ran ¾ mile with the aid of pacemakers in 2:59.5, the best on record. The next day he boarded the Normandie for his trip to Princeton. He was full of confidence, as was his coach, Albert Hill, who said Wooderson could make any pace he wanted against the Americans. He said Wooderson could run 4:03, but Wooderson said, "Hang the time. I am going to concentrate on beating Cunningham."

CUNNINGHAM won at the Sugar Bowl on January 1, 1939, beating Blaine Rideout by a yard in 4:10.7. He won indoors consistently, but his best time was 4:10.8 and that beat Wayne Rideout by only two precarious feet. After a triumph in the AAU, he surprised the best two-milers—Lash, Rice, and Deckard—by beating them in 9:11.8.

In the New York K of C Games, Cunningham had a fever, yet he tried a courageous double. He ran 2:09.2 in the 1000, but lost to John Borican's record 2:08.8. He was doomed in the mile and finished fourth.

CHUCK FENSKE was only a 4:39 miler in high school, for he had never even seen a track meet until his senior year, in 1933. In 1935, as a freshman at Wisconsin, he ran 4:28 indoors and 4:23 outdoors.

Fenske's coach, Tom Jones, wanted him to be a two-miler because of Fenske's cross-country ability, but Fenske asked to run the mile in the Big Ten indoor meet of 1936. When he defeated Lash, his mile career was launched. It was held back though while Fenske was an undergraduate because he doubled in the 2-mile in all meets except the big ones, and in his senior year he tripled, adding the 880!

Early in 1939, Fenske, now in graduate school, won the Columbian Mile (with Cunningham fourth) in 4:11.1. Then he won convincingly from behind at Chicago to beat Cunningham in 4:12.8. Outdoors, he was beaten by Cunningham's greater sprint speed in 4:29.2 at the Kansas Relays.

At Memphis in May, Fenske beat San Romani, 4:11.5 to 4:11.7, showing a strong kick. On June 2, Fenske set an American record of 2:09.3 for 1000 yards.

1939

THE PRINCETON INVITATIONAL OF 1939

Wooderson's opponents on that memorable June 17 were Cunningham, Fenske, San Romani, and Blaine Rideout, whose best times in 1939 were 4:10.9 and 4:11.4. On a time basis, the Americans seemed inferior to Wooderson.

After weeks of intense publicity, the five men lined up before 28,000 spectators at 6:20 p.m. of a hot Saturday. A wind whipped the American flag and the Union Jack on the rim of Palmer Stadium.

Wooderson took the lead, and nobody contested him, although his pace was slow. The calm little man in black passed the 440 in 64 and the 880 in 2:08, with Fenske wasting yardage on his shoulder. Cunningham ran easily behind Wooderson, with Rideout alongside, and San Romani was content to run a close fifth.

Wooderson passed the three-quarters in 3:14 and the crowd was puzzled. With the Americans poised behind him for a big sprint, Wooderson increased the pace little if any around the curve to the backstretch. Then, Fenske says, "the race really started."

Down the backstretch they moved at a fast pace. Rideout's white shirt moved ahead of Fenske's red, up alongside Wooderson as they reached the last curve. Cunningham was badly boxed behind Wooderson and San Romani still trailed.

Rideout "tried to race past Wooderson twice in the backstretch, and he bore out on me and forced me back. Then I decided to go right on through, for I had clear racing room on his outside. He reached out and pushed me as I passed him."

Wooderson, who, curiously enough, was not able to stay ahead by running faster, said, "I was fouled . . . Rideout cut across in front of me and forced me onto the rail." Wooderson stumbled, then regained his stride. Coincidentally, at the same moment, Cunningham stumbled on the curb behind Wooderson.

Rideout said, "Wooderson was a beaten runner when I passed him. I cut in too quickly. I'm sorry. That's the last thing I'd want to do to a beaten runner."

In a flash, Rideout was in the lead. Fenske whipped into unusually fast sprint action and overhauled Rideout. Cunningham swung out of the box, intent on following Fenske. And San Romani swept past Wooderson. Within the space of 50 yards, to the 1500-meter line, Wooderson was last, at least seven hopeless yards behind Fenske.

A crew of eight timers caught these times at 1500 meters: Fenske 3:57.0, Cunningham 3:57.2, San Romani 3:57.3, Rideout 3:57.5, Wooderson 3:58.1.

In the last 120 yards, Wooderson finished as fast as ever before, covering the distance in 14.9, but the only man he gained on was Rideout. Ahead of him, Fenske, Cunningham, and San Romani finished faster than any milers in history, with Fenske pulling away in the stretch with an unprecedented kick.

Results: Fenske 4:11.0, Cunningham 4:11.6, San Romani 4:11.8, Rideout 4:12.8, Wooderson 4:13.0. The foul by Rideout was unfortunate, but it is a matter of speculation as to whether Wooderson could withstand last 120's in 14-flat, 14.4, and 14.5 by the three leaders. Fenske's last lap was in 56.8. The British press was understandably furious, having already predicted the Americans would gang up on Wooderson.

The foul definitely had an adverse effect on Wooderson, but so did those blazing sprints of the Americans. Joe Binks, the former British record holder and now a reporter, wrote: "Sydney just wasn't himself today. I think he would have lost anyway. He was not the Wooderson he was in England. I believe he did too much work the last three weeks before he sailed for the Princeton race."

The history of foot racing shows many upsets. A runner may have an off day for many reasons. Perhaps the hot weather or the long trip hurt Wooderson. Surely he did not fail entirely because of the slight incident. Cunningham, behind him at the time, also stumbled and still finished much faster than Wooderson.

Wooderson had a difficult race for his fifth consecutive AAA title on July 8. (Note: this was the last AAA meet held until after World War II, thus ending Wooderson's string of victories.) He won the 1939 title from Denis Pell, 4:11.8 to 4:12.0, with a last lap in 57.4 and last 220 in a sizzling 27.9.

On July 16 at Brussels, Wooderson edged Mostert by an unimpressive yard in 3:54.8. (A month later in Helsinki, Mostert ran a 4:10.4 mile.) Wooderson ended his frustrating season prematurely on July 26 when he injured a calf muscle while winning a handicap mile in 4:15.

THE AMERICANS ran another upsetting race on July 4, in Lincoln, Nebraska, for the AAU 1500 championship. Added to the field was Zamperini, who had won the IC4A in 4:11.2 and the NCAA in 4:13.6 as well as a 4:11.9 mile on June 21 in Berkeley.

The upset began when they were on the backstretch of the second lap. Blaine Rideout moved into the lead with surprising speed and gradually pulled away. The temperature was 100 degrees and Cunningham felt no need to go after Rideout. (Greg Rice had collapsed after the 5000 meters.) The others trusted Cunningham's judgment, and so when the gun sounded, Rideout had a 20-yard lead which suddenly looked dangerous.

On the last backstretch, Cunningham moved to second, with Fenske on his shoulder and Zamperini close behind. They gained rapidly on Rideout, but he was not tying up. Fenske, worried now, broke away from Cunningham with 80 yards to go and went after Rideout.

At the finish, Fenske was still five feet behind. Zamperini edged Cunningham, three yards back of Fenske. Unplaced and bewildered were Venzke, San Romani, and Walter Mehl. The experts recovered from their shock to realize Rideout's time was a good 3:51.5 and he was from Texas and thus accustomed to heat.

ARNE ANDERSSON

Born at Trollhättan, Sweden, on October 27, 1917, Arne Andersson was encouraged by his father to compete in sports. He tried swimming first, played other games, and then discovered his love for running when he was 16.

Unlike many great milers, he showed no sign of great talent in his early days. He was a good student and his studies, combined with the long winters, made for slow progress. In 1937, at the age of 20, he ran 1500 meters in 4:04.2 and the next year he cut his time to 3:58.6. Only ten months younger than talented Zamperini, he was about ten seconds slower.

In 1939, Andersson began to show interesting improvement. Early in the season, in June, he took almost five seconds off his personal record with a startling 3:53.8. Then, in a 4 x 1500 relay for the national team title, he ran the anchor leg for his club, Örgryte of Göteborg, against Ake Jansson, a 3:53.4 runner. Andersson won, and the two were selected to run for Sweden in the big dual meet against Finland in Stockholm on July 28.

The Finns were Hartikka and Sarkama, and the young Swedes were given little chance. Sarkama, who had run 3:51.9 five days before, set the pace for two laps of the 385-meter track, with Andersson passing 400 meters in 59.3. Then Hartikka took the lead in 2:00.6 for 800 meters, with Andersson second in 2:00.9.

Andersson "thought the speaker was joking when he called the 800 meter time. I am used to slower time, and normally I thought I would die under such a rhythm. Somehow I didn't, and I still wonder why."

When the bell clanged, Andersson astounded the crowd by taking the lead. The Swedish crowd watched in joyous amazement as Andersson pulled away in the last lap and Jansson placed second.

Results: Andersson 3:48.8, Jansson 3:49.2, Hartikka 3:50.0.

Swedes were filled with wonder, for 21-year-old Arne Andersson was only one quick breath away from the world record. One Swedish commentator described Andersson as a man with great physical qualities, "an abnormal chest, strong elastic muscles, a heart in the very style of his chest, and a steel-hard will." Then the commentator picked Andersson as a possible winner in the 1940 Olympics.

1940

1939

4:07.4	Sydney Wooderson (GB)	(1)	London	29	May
4:10.4	Joseph Mostert (Belgium)	(1)	Helsinki	18	Aug
4:10.7	Glenn Cunningham (USA)	(1)	New Orleans	1	Jan
4:10.9e	Blaine Rideout (USA)	(2)	New Orleans	1	Jan
4:11.0	Charles Fenske (USA)	(1)	Princeton	17	Jun
4:11.2	Louis Zamperini (USA)	IC4A(1)	New York	27	May
4:11.4	B. Rideout				
4:11.5	Fenske	(1)	Memphis		May
4:11.6	Cunningham	(2)	Princeton	17	Jun
4:11.7e	Archie San Romaní (USA)	(2)	Memphis		May
4:11.7	Walter Mehl (USA)	(1)			
4:11.8	San Romani	(3)	Princeton	17	Jun
4:11.8	Wooderson	AAA(1)	London	8	Jul
4:11.9	Zamperini	(1)	Berkeley	21	Jun
4:12.0	Wooderson	(1)	Birmingham	20	May
4:12.0	Denis Pell (GB)	AAA(2)	London	8	Jul
4:12.0	Taisto Mäki (Finland)	(2)	Helsinki	18	Aug

Indoors:

4:10.8	Glenn Cunningham (USA)	(1)	Boston	11	Feb
4:10.9e	Wayne Rideout (USA)	(2)	Boston	11	Feb
4:11.1	Charles Fenske (USA)	(1)	New York	11	Mar

1,500m:
(+ during mile)

3:48.8	Arne Andersson (Sweden)	(1)	Stockholm	28	Jul
3:49.2	Ake Jansson (Sweden)	(2)	Stockholm	28	Jul
3:50.0	Niilo Hartikka (Finland)	(3)	Stockholm	28	Jul
3:50.2	Ludwig Kaindl (Germany)	(1)	Cologne	20	Aug
3:50.2	Denis Pell (GB)	(2)	Cologne	20	Aug
3:51.1+	Sydney Wooderson (GB)	(1)	London	29	May
3:51.5	Blaine Rideout (USA)	AAU(1)	Lincoln	4	Jul
3:51.9	Toivo Sarkama (Finland)	(1)	Terijoki	23	Jul
3:52.0e	Charles Fenske (USA)	AAU(2)	Lincoln	4	Jul
3:52.0	Herbert Jacob (Germany)	(3)	Cologne	20	Aug
3:52.4	Harry Mehlhose (Germany)	GerCh (1)	Berlin	9	Jul
3:52.6e	Louis Zamperini (USA)	AAU(3)	Lincoln	4	Jul
3:52.8e	Glenn Cunningham (USA)	AAU(4)	Lincoln	4	Jul
3:52.8	Joseph Mostert (Belgium)	( )			

FENSKE REACHES THE TOP

Good enough to win the NCAA mile as a junior and place second as a sophomore, Fenske was close to the top as a senior in 1938 when it took a great run by Zamperini to beat him. He barely lost to Cunningham twice, once indoors and once in the AAU.

In 1939, when his fastest-ever finish won the Princeton Invitation, he was near the top of the world milers, but his record was marred when he let Rideout steal the AAU title.

In 1940, Fenske finished fourth in a slow Sugar Bowl 1500 behind San Romani, Rideout, and Cunningham. Still not in top shape, he was only third at Boston on January 13 when the ever-hopeful Venzke edged Cunningham in 4:13.1.

Fenske's next race was the Wanamaker Mile on February 3 against the fastest field of indoor milers ever assembled. Fenske's indoor spiked shoes had been burned in a fire and he spent his day in New York filing the spikes on new outdoor shoes.

1940

Rideout tried another steal, and they let him go as much as 25 yards ahead in 56.8 and 2:01. In the third quarter, Fenske passed Rideout and began to build up a big lead. With 3½ laps to go, he was ten yards ahead, and Cunningham faltered and faded to fourth. With two laps to go, Fenske led by 25 yards. Then he began to lose his lead and the crowd of 16,000 was delirious.

Cunningham, who was determined to make his last indoor season a good one, led the pursuit. He was followed by Venzke, who had said, "I'm in the best shape of my life," and Zamperini, who also wanted to prove himself. With one lap to go, Fenske still led by 17 yards. But his lap times of 60, 2:03, and 3:04, had taken too much and he was staggering in the homestretch. Cunningham came within three yards of catching him.

Results: Fenske 4:07.4, Cunningham 4:07.7, Venzke 4:08.2, Zamperini 4:08.2.

Fenske's time tied the official indoor record, and all except Cunningham ran faster than ever. Now Fenske was the man to beat.

He beat Cunningham at Philadelphia, and at Boston his last quarter in a fast 58.5 beat Zamperini by five yards, 4:11.2. Cunningham, suffering from a cold, was another three yards back.

In an exciting Baxter Mile, Zamperini took over the lead at 8½ laps. Fenske challenged twice but could not get past until the last backstretch. Having put in two weeks of speed training, his last quarter was in 58.2 and Fenske won by three yards, 4:07.4 to 4:07.9, while a delighted Venzke edged Cunningham by one foot in 4:08.8.

In the AAU meet on February 24, Fenske had an easy victory. Cunningham, his only pursuer with a lap to go, fell after stepping on Fenske's heel. Fenske won—eased up after 3:08.5—eight yards ahead of Venzke and 14 ahead of Zamperini in 4:08.8.

The Columbian Mile on March 9 was supposed to be a record attempt, with John Borican as pace-maker, but Borican's wild 58.2 pace slowed to 2:07 and 3:14.4. Fenske passed him on the last backstretch and beat Cunningham by six yards in 4:13.2. Cunningham, bidding a sad farewell to New York's indoor circuit, edged Venzke, while Zamperini fell.

At Chicago, on March 23, Fenske's last lap in 59.9 won another fast one, in 4:07.9, 12 yards ahead of Venzke, with Cunningham third. Fenske had won eight straight mile races and nobody questioned his superiority. There was still talk, in March of 1940, of holding the Olympic Games in Finland, but the war soon caused cancellation, and many runners saw no future. Fenske proved his condition with 4:08.3 outdoors at Memphis on May 11, but a throat infection culminating in a tonsillectomy in September ended his racing and training for the year. Although out of condition, he attempted some indoor races in 1941. Fenske volunteered for military service and his career ended.

CUNNINGHAM'S FAREWELL

This was his last year. He had been the man to beat for eight years, and few milers had outkicked him, but most of them were gone now—Bonthron, Lovelock, San Romani, Lash, Fenske—and Cunningham wanted to retire as a winner. He trained carefully and avoided racing, aiming for the AAU championships to be held in Fresno, California.

But the parade of great milers never stands still. No matter who is on top, ambitious young men are plotting to overthrow him.

One was tall Walter Mehl of Wisconsin, who had an impressive record in the two-mile. He beat Greg Rice for the 1938 NCAA title, won a fine Sugar Bowl 3000 meters over Rice and Lash on the last day of 1939, and finished second to Rice in the indoor AAU three-mile. Mehl ran 8:58.2 behind Rice's world indoor record 8:56.2, then won in 9:05.5 at Kansas City over sensational world record holder Taisto Mäki of Finland. In that race, Cunningham finished ten yards back.

Mehl tried the mile in 1939, winning the Big Ten title and he finished second to Zamperini in the NCAA. Helpless against Rice at longer distances in 1940, he was forced back to the mile.

Another young prospect was Paul Moore of Stanford. Unheard of in 1939, Moore developed under the stimulus of fast teammates and Dink Templeton's intensive coaching. On April 17, at Stanford, he ran the fastest ¾ mile ever run. With a pace of 57.8 and 61.4, he finished in 2:58.7. Then, when he beat Zamperini in Los Angeles in 4:11.5, he was recognized as a threat to anyone.

A third college miler of dangerous talents was John Munski of Missouri. His experience in big races had been limited to third place in the tough 1939 NCAA mile, behind Zamperini and Mehl, but in 1940 he won so convincingly, including 4:11.6 in a dual meet, that he was invited to the Princeton Invitation.

This was also the farewell to a great track meet, for it was never held again. Blaine Rideout, who had beaten his twin by two yards in 4:10.1 on April 20, set a leisurely pace through three-quarters in 3:14.4. Then Munski bolted to the front and the small crowd of 10,000 screamed with excitement at the fast pace.

Munski built up a ten-yard lead while running that last lap in 56.6 and only Mehl's great kick could gain on him in the homestretch. Mehl finished in 4:11.6 to Munski's 4:11.0. Newcomer Leslie MacMitchell, only 20, improved to 4:12.0, and Zamperini was fourth.

Cunningham, on that same day in Kansas City, ran a purposeful 1500 meters in 3:49.0. He was ready, and on June 29 he was in

1940

the hot San Joaquin Valley town of Fresno, nervously intent on winning in the last race of his great career.

That evening, under the floodlights, he led the pack from the start, running his chosen pace, letting the youngsters do what they chose. Venzke and Rideout, the defending champion, stayed close for awhile, along with Munski, Moore, and Mehl, but the excited capacity crowd of 14,000 had eyes only for Cunningham.

This was the master, at his peak for his last race, running with the grace and power of old, setting a pace as stiff as any he had ever run except for his "freak" 4:04.4. Actually, the spectators were surprised to see anyone staying close behind.

And yet, in the homestretch, Mehl and Moore challenged Cunningham. Moore could not continue his drive and dropped back, but Mehl's long strides carried him past a disappointed Cunningham in the last few steps and he won by a yard.

Results: Mehl 3:47.9, Cunningham 3:48.0, Moore 3:48.5, Munski, Venzke, Andy Neidnig, Rideout.

Mehl missed Lovelock's world record by only one tenth of a second! Cunningham ran his fastest 1500 in his gallant farewell. Moore was now fourth fastest of all time. Oddly enough, Cunningham's three fastest outdoor 1500's had come in second place.

1940

MILE:

4:08.3	Charles Fenske (USA)	(1)	Memphis	11	May
4:09.4	Ake Jansson (Sweden)	(1)	Helsinki	1	Aug
4:10.1	Blaine Rideout (USA)	(1)	Lawrence	20	Apr
4:10.4	Wayne Rideout (USA)	(2)	Lawrence	20	Apr
4:10.6	Henry Kälarne (Sweden)*	(2)	Helsinki	1	Aug
4:10.8	Arne Andersson (Sweden)	(3)	Helsinki	1	Aug
4:11.0	John Munski (USA)	(1)	Princeton	8	Jun
4:11.0	Sydney Wooderson (GB)	(1)	Glasgow	3	Aug
4:11.2	Niilo Hartikka (Finland)	(4)	Helsinki	1	Aug
4:11.2	Toivo Sarkama (Finland)	(5)	Helsinki	1	Aug
4:11.5	Paul Moore (USA)	(1)	Los Angeles	4	May
4:11.6	Munski	(1)	(dual meet)		
4:11.6	Louis Zamperini (USA)	(1)	Los Angeles	25	May
4:11.6	Walter Mehl (USA)	(2)	Princeton	8	Jun
	*formerly Jonsson.				

Doubtful:

4:08.7	Blaine Rideout (USA)	(2)	Memphis	11	May

Indoors:

4:07.4	Charles Fenske (USA)	(1)	New York	3	Feb
4:07.4	Fenske	(1)	New York	17	Feb
4:07.7	Glenn Cunningham (USA)	(2)	New York	3	Feb
4:07.9	Louis Zamperini (USA)	(2)	New York	17	Feb
4:07.9	Fenske	(1)	Chicago	23	Mar
4:08.2	Gene Venzke (USA)	(3)	New York	3	Feb
4:08.2	Zamperini	(4)	New York	3	Feb
4:08.8	Venzke	(3)	New York	17	Feb
4:08.8	Cunningham	(4)	New York	17	Feb
4:08.8	Fenske	AAU(1)	New York	24	Feb

1,500m:

3:47.9	Walter Mehl (USA)	AAU(1)	Fresno	29	Jun
3:48.0	Glenn Cunningham (USA)	AAU(2)	Fresno	29	Jun
3:48.5	Paul Moore (USA)	AAU(3)	Fresno	29	Jun
3:48.7	Henry Kälarne (Sweden)	(1)	Göteborg	7	Aug

1940

3:48.8	Gunder Hägg (Sweden)	(2)	Göteborg	7	Aug
3:49.0	Cunningham	(1)	Kansas City	8	Jun
3:49.0	Ake Jansson (Sweden)	(1)	Stockholm	13	Sep
3:49.0	Hägg	(2)	Stockholm	13	Sep
3:51.0	Arne Andersson (Sweden)	(3)	Göteborg	7	Aug
3:51.2	Toivo Sarkama (Finland)	(4)	Göteborg	7	Aug
3:51.2	Kälarne	(3)	Stockholm	13	Sep
3:52.8	Lennart Nilsson (Sweden)	(2)	Gävle	17	Jul
3:52.8	Miklós Szabó (Hungary)	(1)	Budapest	22	Sep

LES MACMITCHELL

A New York city boy with remarkable talent, MacMitchell set a meet record in the indoor national interscholastic meet in each of the three years he ran. In 1936, at 15, he surprised in the 1000 with 2:22.9. In 1937, he won the mile in 4:23.6 at the tender age of 16. In 1938, he won the 880 in 1:58.0. That year, he set an indoor high school mile record of 4:21.7. In June, barely 18, he ran in the ¾ mile race in the Princeton Invitation and placed sixth in a respectable 3:04.5.

In 1939, the 5'10½", 154-pound NYU freshman lost to Venzke by one foot in 3:07.2 for ¾ mile, fastest flat floor time ever run. At Princeton in June, he placed third in the ¾, behind Wayne Rideout's world record, and Venzke.

As a sophomore in 1940, not quite 20 years old, he ran a good 9:09.7 two-mile on a flat floor, behind Lash's 9:08.6. He won the IC4A mile with no difficulty in 4:19.4 and was third behind Munski and Mehl in the Princeton Invitation with a highly promising 4:12.0. He was second to Munski in the NCAA, again ahead of Zamperini.

MacMitchell started his drive to the top in the 1941 season by running 4:10.2 at Boston, but he lost to AAU champion Mehl and NCAA champion Munski, both timed in 4:09.7. In the Wanamaker Mile, he beat Munski and Chuck Fenske—out of retirement—but he lost to Mehl's big kick. Then, on February 8, in Boston, he won his first major victory with 4:10.7, beating Mehl, Fenske, Munski, Beccali, and Borican.

In the Baxter Mile on February 15, 33-year-old Beccali set a fast pace for three quarters. Then Venzke forged ahead, but Mehl soon passed the other 33-year-old veteran. MacMitchell shot ahead of Mehl as the gun sounded and held off his powerful finish in the homestretch. Both were timed in 4:07.4, equalling the best competitive indoor record. At the age of 20, MacMitchell was as fast as any miler in the world.

He lost once more in 1941, to Mehl's 4:10.4. He won the indoor IC4A in 4:12.0 and doubled well in the outdoor IC4A—4:16 and 1:53. The Compton Invitation replaced the Princeton Invitation and MacMitchell won the 1500 as he pleased in 3:51.4.

In the NCAA at Palo Alto, he won by two feet in 4:10.4 over

1941

tough Leroy Weed, who had run 4:09.7 behind Phil Leibowitz's 4:09.3 at Berkeley on May 31. On June 29, at Philadelphia's Franklin Field, he established superiority over Mehl and won the AAU in 3:53.1.

In his senior year, MacMitchell continued undefeated in cross country, winning his third IC4A championship. Indoors, he began where he left off in 1941, at the top. He won the Metropolitan Collegiates in 4:08.0. He was the conqueror in the Wanamaker Mile, the Hunter Mile in Boston, and the Baxter in 4:09.8. When he reached the AAU indoor he had 26 consecutive victories.

GIL DODDS

Born in Kansas, Dodds went to high school in Nebraska. It is said his first "race" was when he threw a rock at a farmer, who turned out to be former star miler Lloyd Hahn. Dodds ran an 880 in 2:00.1 and a mile in 4:28.2 in 1937. As a freshman at Ashland College (Ohio) in 1938, he ran only 4:24. By choice a two-miler in college, although he ran some mile races, he placed fourth in the 1939 NCAA two-mile behind Rice and third in 1941 behind Fred Wilt. In 1941 he won the Beloit Relays mile in a promising 4:13.7.

His great natural endurance was increased by many three- to five-mile runs at a stiff pace of 5:15 to 5:20 per mile. He walked six-eight miles to and from workouts each day for awhile, and he walked two to four miles before bed each night.

After graduation from Ashland, he wanted to follow his father's footsteps and he became a divinity student in Boston. His training included some repetition-type track training before his competitive season. As he matured, with even greater endurance, he also learned to run faster and he eventually began to run in the popular mile races during the eastern season.

In 1942, after running very fast two-miles in 8:53.6 and 8:53.7 only to lose to Rice, Dodds decided to try the mile in the indoor AAU championships. This provided something of a shock to track experts, for he stayed ahead of MacMitchell to win in 4:08.7 to MacMitchell's 4:08.9.

Properly warned, MacMitchell came back to beat Dodds in a good Columbian Mile, 4:08.0 to 4:08.4, and in a special meet in the nine-lap track of the Bronx Coliseum, 4:07.8 to 4:08.7. Then his impending entry into the U.S. Navy hurt MacMitchell. Outdoors, he won the IC4A, but he lost to Bobby Ginn of Nebraska and Weed in a 4:11.1 race at the NCAA.

The AAU was in New York, June 20, and Dodds won by a large margin in 3:50.2, ahead of Weed, MacMitchell, Culp, and Ginn.

As had happened so many times before, the top miler of the previous year was beaten at the start of the new season. On February

6, 1943, Dodds ran 4:08.9 in the Wanamaker Mile but lost to Earl Mitchell's surprising 4:08.6. Mitchell was Indiana state high school champion in 1938 with 4:34.5, but his limited career at Indiana was confined mostly to longer races. His fastest two-mile was 9:13.1 in winning the 1942 Indiana Intercollegiates. In the fall of 1942, he won the Big Ten cross country title and placed second in the NCAA Championships.

Third in the Wanamaker, in 4:10.6, was young Frank Dixon, an amazing Negro freshman at NYU who had run 4:14.1 in 1942 while in high school.

Indoor honors were mixed between those three:
Boston: Dixon barely beat Mitchell in 4:11.4.
Baxter Mile: Dodds won in 4:08.8.
AAU: Dixon beat Dodds, 4:09.6 to 4:09.9.
Columbian Mile: Dixon beat Dodds by three yards in 4:09.6.
Chicago: Dodds 4:08.5, Mitchell 4:09.9e, Dixon 4:10.0e.
Cleveland: Dodds 4:08.7.

Dodds' record was not a particularly impressive one to take into competition against a great touring Swede named Gunder Hägg, whose first race was the 5000 meters of the outdoor AAU championships in New York. Dodds refused to run on Sunday, and so the 1500 was switched to Saturday and he beat Bill Hulse by 30 yards in 3:50.0.

VI
Gunder Hägg

On the last day of 1918, in Jämtland, Central Sweden's great forest country, Nils and Selma Hägg became the parents of a boy who was to become the wonder of the track world, and they named him Gunder.

Life was hard. Food and pleasures were unsophisticated. Gunder lived mostly on soup and hard Swedish rye bread, and, as a child of nature, he loved to run in the woods.

He often raced other boys for short distances in the woods, losing more often than not, for he was a poor start. He was tall and lean, reaching 5:10¾" and 150 pounds when mature. When he was ten years old he was proud to work with his father in the forest, helping to trim trees after the adults had felled them.

Sports were the chief group pleasure of those hard-working people, and Gunder's parents approved his efforts at soccer, skiing, and running. At the same time, he progressed to a man's work in the forest.

His sports career took a turn for the better in a local meet when he won the high jump at 4'10", the pole vault at 7'2", the 1500 meters (in something near five minutes), and placed second in both the 100 and 400. His father was so delighted that he spent hard-earned money on a pair of track shoes for Gunder.

In the summer of 1936, Nils Hägg was sent deeper into the forest to work, and Gunder took along his prized shoes. Each evening, after a day's work, he ran joyfully along the springy forest floor. His father measured a 750-meter course along a road and sat on the porch of their hut with his big alarm clock while Gunder ran 750 meters out and then back, as hard as he could go.

1941

Nils told Gunder he had run 4:45, and they stayed up late that night planning a future for Gunder as glorious as that of his idol, 1936 Olympic medalist Henry Jonsson. This was the stimulus Gunder needed to take his running seriously, and it was not until years later that his father admitted he had shaved half a minute off the time for the trial.

In a happy quirk of fate, there lived in the nearby village of Kälarne a farmer named Fridolf Westman who loved track and who had coached Henry Jonsson in his early efforts. Westman offered Gunder a job on his farm, and Gunder accepted eagerly. He joined the local club and began running immediately.

In 1936, at the age of 17, Hägg won the junior championship of Jämtland at 1500 meters in 4:22.2 and 5000 meters in 16:11. He was on his way.

In 1937, amazingly enough, he beat Olympic 5000 meter champion Gunnar Höckert of Finland in a 2000 meter race, 5:39.6 to 5:45.4. Even though Höckert was obviously in poor shape and not serious about the race, the news made headlines. Sweden's famous coach, Gösse Holmér—inventor of "Fartlek"—who had advised Westman on Hägg's training by mail, said anything could be expected from Hägg in years to come. And Hägg was invited to run in Stockholm's Olympic stadium on August 4, where he placed fourth at 3000 meters in 8:36.8, seventh fastest Swedish time of the year.

In 1938, when he was 19, Hägg wanted to run the steeplechase in the Swedish Championships at Stockholm on August 14. He placed second to Lars Larsson, who was soon to be crowned European Champion. Hägg's time was 9:28.4, which turned out to be faster than the fourth finisher in the European Championships. Later that year, Hägg cut his time to a good 9:23.0. He also ran his first race abroad, at Trondhjem, Norway, and won at 5000 meters in 15:00.7. That year, he ran 1500 in 4:04.6 and two miles in a good 9:16.6. In the two-mile he set the pace and finished fifth, ahead of another famous Olympic champion, Volmari Iso-Hollo.

In 1939, the year Arne Andersson lowered the Swedish 1500 record to 3:48.8, Hägg was stunned by a severe case of double pneumonia. When he left the hospital late in the summer, the doctor warned, "Whatever you do, you can regard your athletic career as finished."

But Hägg loved to run, and he would not quit. He began training for 1940. In December, he entered the military service and during the war he spent some bitterly cold days guarding the frontier. Wherever he was, he measured off a 5000-meter course, preferably in the forest with some hills. When necessary he ran in the snow.

He trained with the method now called "Fartlek" (Speed play). He would run so hard up a hill he was almost exhausted. Then he would coast down the other side while he recovered. All his running was in bursts of good speed rather than steady-pace runs. His 5000 meters took up to 20 minutes and he often ran it twice a day. He recovered by sleeping 10 to 12 hours each night and he liked to take an hour's nap before a race.

He raced again on June 23 in a significant 3000 against Ake Jansson, who had pushed Andersson with a 3:49.2 1500 the year before. Hägg lost by inches in 8:32.4. One who was impressed with Hägg was Arne Andersson, who said, "What a stride and rhythm!"

A week later, Hägg ran against Jansson in a 1500. Also present was Hägg's idol, Henry Jonsson, who had changed his name to Kälarne in honor of his home town. The two veterans paid little attention when Hägg raced off in front in 60, 2:02, and 3:06 for 1200 meters. Then it was too late and they fought each other for second in 3:56.2. Hägg won in 3:51.8, and now he was recognized as a threat to anyone.

On August 7 at the famous Slottsskogsvallen track in Göteborg, the same three ran again, with an added starter in the person of Arne Andersson. After Jansson led in 60.0, Hägg took the lead in 2:01 and 3:06. With half a lap to go, Kälarne passed Andersson and cut down Hägg's lead. He won narrowly in 3:48.7 to Hägg's 3:48.8, with Andersson at 3:51.0. Rounded off to 3:48.8, both men became official co-holders of the Swedish record along with Andersson.

Andersson's coach said, "Of this race, I'll remember only Hägg. It was an experience to see him. He's the greatest talent Sweden has ever had."

A week later, in Stockholm, Hägg bettered the world record for 3000 meters with 8:11.8, but Kälarne won in 8:09.0. While Kälarne was winning the 1940 Swedish championship in 3:52.4, Hägg barely lost the 5000 title to Bror Hellström while running 14:40.4. He beat the great Kälarne in 14:38.2 and in his second 1500 against Andersson, he won 3:52.4 to 3:52.6.

Praise for the 21-year-old Hägg rang out. Finnish expert Martti Jukola wrote: "Hägg is the ideal runner of our time. He runs in such an effortless manner, and his movements show perfect coördination."

Another Finn, Laaksonen, wrote: "In two years Hägg will be ready to break all world records between 1500 and 5000 meters, possibly 10,000 meters as well. He is more of a natural runner than Kälarne and has plenty of stamina."

Kälarne said, "My time is over; now comes the Hägg era."

But Andersson liked competition and he trained hard to catch up with Hägg. Their first meeting of 1941 came in a 4000-meter cross country race for the Swedish championship on May 11. Andersson won by 17.2 seconds.

1941

On June 29 Hägg, now a fireman in Gävle, ran 3:51.4. Two days later, Andersson ran a good 3:49.8. Three days after that, Hägg ran the same time. Four days later, Andersson ran 3:50.0. Their remarkable see-saw rivalry was underway.

They raced each other on July 18 in the dual against Hungary. Miklós Szabó was in Göteborg for the race and he ran a creditable 3:52.6, but he was outclassed by the two Swedes. On a heavy track, Hägg outlasted Andersson, 3:50.2 to 3:50.4. Three days later, all by himself, Hägg ran 3:48.6 at Malmö for a new Swedish record and equal to Szabó's European record.

Excitement was high for the Swedish Championships in Stockholm on August 10. Gösse Holmér wrote: "A reservation on the world record is made for 10 August." Another sportswriter wrote: "All Stockholm knew that Lovelock's record was trembling."

Hägg won his heat on August 9 in 3:53.0 while Andersson qualified in 3:58.4. The next morning, Hägg slept until 8:30, enjoyed a visit with Henry Kälarne, ate over a pound of strawberries for breakfast, lunched mostly on fish, and napped for three hours. He went to the Olympic stadium at 5:00 p.m., ready for his best.

The 1500 meters was saved for the last event, as the most popular, and it was cold when they started. Arne Ahlsén set the pace, with Hägg close. After 400-meter times of 59.0 and 2:02.1, Hägg went through the third 400 in 61.4 for a sensational 3:03.5. Kälarne and Andersson worked hard to stay with Hägg but they eventually had to give up, even though Hägg's last 300 was no faster than 44 seconds.

When the announcer told the crowd Hägg had broken the world record, a ten-minute ovation began. When it was quiet enough, he said, "Maybe we should talk about the time, too. It was 3:47.6."

Hägg's time was really 3:47.5. Andersson's 3:48.6 equalled the old Swedish record. Kälarne's 3:49.2 was half a second off his 1940 best, and Ahlsén's 3:50.4 was a personal record.

Hägg beat Andersson twice more in exciting duels: 3:58.4 to 3:58.6 at 1500 meters, and 4:09.2 to 4:09.6 in a mile race. Then Hägg was suspended from competition for ten months because of excessive travel expenses. Andersson was upset by Hellström in 4:09.6, set a Swedish mile record of 4:08.6, and ran the fifth fastest 5000 in history, with 14:18.2 behind Hellström's 14:15.8.

A ten-month suspension seems severe—almost a year—but actually it ran only through June, leaving Hägg plenty of time to run during the 1942 season. And, after his best training winter, he was ready and eager on July 1. There followed 82 days of some of the greatest running in the history of track.

His first race was a mile against Andersson at Göteborg. Andersson had run 3:49.0 in June and he was at his best weight of 154 pounds. A capacity crowd of 19,769 were in the stands and

1942

many others could not get inside.

Hägg said, "I have no chance so early in the season and with no racing behind me over the past ten months, but I'll come later."

Andersson said, "Gunder wins by a couple of decimeters."

Olle Pettersson, a 4:12.2 miler in 1937, set the early pace with Hägg timed in a fast 59.4 and 2:01.2. Andersson stuck close behind Hägg, obviously determined. Hägg had only Andersson with him when he passed 1200 meters in 3:04.8.

The crowd was cheering their fellow townsman, Andersson, who lost not an inch. Hägg passed 1500 meters in 3:50.4. Then, in the stretch, Andersson gamely caught up and the crowd roared, but Hägg had a little more than ever before and he pulled ahead.

Results: Hägg 4:06.1, Andersson 4:06.4, Hellström 4:15.4.

Hägg's world record was rounded off at 4:06.2, while Andersson equalled Wooderson's record. Hägg said, "Tonight I looked better than I am."

Andersson said, "Gunder just flows along. I labor."

The great rivalry between them developed further on July 3, although not at the mile distance. Andersson ran two miles in 8:51.4, two seconds faster than the world record, but for the second time in three days, Hägg set a faster world record—8:47.8. Then, two days later, on July 5, Hägg ran 1500 meters in 3:48.4.

On July 10, Hägg ran an 880 in 1:53.5. In the same meet, Andersson followed a pace of 58.5 and 2:01 in troublesome windy weather, then poured it on to pass 1500 meters in 3:49.8. This was a mile race, however, and Andersson finished in 4:06.2, equalling Hägg's world record!

Hägg was to run against Andersson at 1500 meters on July 17 in Stockholm. As preparation for the race, the amazing Hägg raced on Sunday, Monday, Tuesday, and Wednesday, turning in respectable times of 8:25.1 (3000), 3:53.4, 8:22.6, and 3:54.5.

To provide the runners with better footing, pipes were put in the Olympic track between lanes two and three, making the track about 400 meters. Hägg moved even with Ahlsén at 400 meters in a fast 58.0, then pulled away.

He ran at a pace no man had ever attempted, and the lap times drove the crowd wild. He passed 800 meters in 1:58.2. Then, instead of slowing to about 3:04 as usual, he kept driving and passed 1200 meters in 2:58.9. Needless to say, he had no competition left in the race, even from a dejected Andersson.

Hägg tired on the last lap and his pace dropped to 31.8 for the last 200 meters, but he finished in 3:45.8, 1.7 seconds faster than his world record. He had proved his courage, along with his ability. Andersson, very discouraged, had to fight in the home stretch to beat out Ahlsén, 3:49.2 to 3:49.4.

Hägg's 3:45.8, as good as a mile in 4:04.7, was his third world record in 17 days. And still he kept trying. He went to Malmö,

1942

and after 800 meters in 1:53.3 on July 20, he tackled Andersson at 2000 meters the next day. This time Andersson gave him a real battle, and Hägg barely won in 5:16.4. Andersson's 5:16.8 tied San Romani's world record, making the third time in three weeks he had run world record time only to lose to Hägg.

But now Hägg was running down, physically and mentally. The next two days he won slow 1500's, in 4:02.4 and 3:55.6. Almost a week's rest restored some of his vigor, and on July 29 at Gävle, he beat Andersson at 3000 meters, 8:09.4 to 8:11.4 (with Bror Hellström at 8:10.4). Hägg had missed Kälarne's world record by only four tenths of a second and the disappointed crowd did not cheer him.

Hägg said, "They wanted it too badly . . . I prefer to do it the playful way whenever I can."

Indisposed and uninspired, Hägg ran in a 4 x 1500 relay on August 2 and was outkicked on his leg 3:55.0 to 3:55.8. It was time for a rest, to rebuild the stores of energy he had squandered so recklessly in a wonderful month of record breaking. He returned to Valadalen.

This idyllic resort and training center in Jämtland, run by Gösta Olander, allowed Hägg to enjoy the beauty of lakes and forest while he restored his energy and desire to race. After three weeks of inspiring atmosphere, Hägg was ready again.

On August 23 he raced Andersson at 2000 meters. Andersson, who ran 800 meters in 1:50.8, was now run out, and Hägg beat him by almost 19 seconds in 5:11.8, almost five seconds faster than Hägg's own world record. This was an average pace of a 4:11.2 mile with almost another quarter added at the same pace.

After running 3:55.0 the next day, Hägg went after Kälarne's 3000 meter record at Stockholm on August 28. That evening a curious fan phoned the Swedish sports paper, *Idrottsbladet*, wanting to know Hägg's time.

"8:01.2" was the answer.

"Is that possible?" asked the startled fan.

"No, it isn't, but he did it anyhow."

After a 3:54.4 on August 30, Hägg prepared for a big mile effort at Stockholm on September 4. In spite of the rainy weather, the Olympic stadium was packed. Long lines of people tried in vain to get inside and tickets were sold on the black market. Nils and Selma Hägg were inside, to watch their famous son surpass those dreams of six years ago.

It was twilight when the race started at 8:00 p.m. Hägg's young teammate from Gefle IF, one Henry Eriksson, generously set a blistering pace for the first quarter, while Hägg stayed a few yards back in 57.2. When Eriksson was too tired, in the second quarter, Hägg moved into the lead, allowing the pace to drop to 2:00.2 and

1942

3:04.2. Now hopelessly out of it were Ake Spangert (formerly Jansson) and Rolf Seidenschnur, a German 3:51.4 man.

Everybody in the crowd knew Hägg had a chance to break the record of 4:06.2 he shared with Andersson, and some of the wildest cheers came from Selma Hägg as her son flowed around that last quarter, his long blond hair bobbing with each beautiful stride. Hägg raced past 1500 meters in 3:48.8 and now a new record seemed certain. As usual, Hägg was unable to produce a real kick, but he finished strongly. His time was 4:04.6.

One enthusiastic spectator was a German paratrooper named Rudolf Harbig, world record holder at 400, 800, and 1000 meters. Harbig said, "He is fantastic. One should have seen him in this race to believe his unbelievable times. His form is perfect—smooth and flawless all the way through the race."

During the next week, Hägg won comfortable 1500's in 3:56.8 and 3:51.8. Then, again in the Olympic stadium, he broke the world record for three miles with 13:35.4. Two days later he ran 3:50.4. After 3:56.0 on September 18, he came back zealously two days later at Göteborg with what some people call his greatest race.

On a cold autumn day he lowered his own brand-new three-mile record to 13:32.4, then finished strongly for 13:58.2 at 5000 meters, more than ten seconds better than Mäki's world record. It was Hägg's tenth world record, at seven distances, in 82 days.

The rest of his season was an anti-climax. After 1500's in 3:54.8 and 3:54.2, he met Andersson, his most dangerous opponent, in Budapest on September 27. Andersson, who had said, "Believe it or not, we are good friends off the track and foes only when racing each other," was in no condition to contest Hägg. He was well back, 3:53.2 to 3:50.6, his seventh loss of the year to Hägg and his third at 1500 or a mile.

Hägg closed out his great year with four slow victories, 2000 in 5:28.4, 1500 in 3:56.8, and 3000's in 8:19.6 and 8:40.8. He had won the remarkable total of 32 races between July 1 and October 11. It was surely one of the greatest years any runner had ever had. Yet Swedish observers claimed he reached his potential only in his 8:01.2 for 3000 meters.

After a good rest and then resumption of winter training in the snow, Hägg began serious spring training. Dan Ferris of the AAU wanted Hägg to run in the United States in 1943 as a quasi official Swedish ambassador. His eight-race tour raised $150,000 for the U.S. Army Air Forces Aid Society.

Hägg left Sweden aboard a tanker on May 11. The only training he could do, in addition to uninspiring gymnastics, was in a corridor only 30 meters long. He reached New Orleans on June 5 and immediately limbered up at 2000 meters. He said it "didn't feel so good."

Two weeks later he ran in the AAU championships in New

York. His opponent at 5000 meters was great little Greg Rice, who had won more than 60 races since his last defeat. But Rice was in the service and not at his best. Hägg won easily, 14:48.5 to 14:53.9.

At Chicago on July 2, Hägg ran against Gil Dodds for the first time. On a track "as soft as a potato field" in Soldiers Field, Hägg won at two miles, 9:02.8 to 9:06.3. All he needed was a last lap in 66.8. When he won at Los Angeles on July 10, 8:53.9 to Dodds' 9:12.8, and a San Francisco mile on July 17 by an overwhelming 25 yards in 4:12.3, the tour seemed more like an exhibition. But he had not yet seen the best of Gil Dodds.

The next race was a mile at Cambridge on July 24. Since nobody was giving Hägg any competition, this was to be a handicap. One man was given 25 yards, while Dodds and NCAA champion Don Burnham of Dartmouth were honored to be on the scratch line with Hägg. Bill Hulse of NYU was given ten yards, but he refused to run unless he could start from scratch.

Hulse's best mile was 4:15.9, on June 5, but he knew he was better than that. Second to MacMitchell in the 1941 IC4A mile, but only third in 1942, he dropped down to the 880 in the 1942 NCAA for a disappointing fifth. In the 1943 AAU, he was second to Dodds in the 1500 on Saturday and won the 800 in 1:53.4 on Sunday.

With Dodds more at home in the Boston area, Hägg soon found himself pressed a little. He went past the handicap runner before he reached the 440 in 58.4. He slowed to 2:01.9, but when Dodds challenged him, he ran his third quarter in 60 flat for 3:01.9. Then he pulled away on the last turn with a 63.4 lap for a new American record of 4:05.3, his second fastest mile. Dodds finished in 4:06.5, breaking Cunningham's U.S. national record, and Hulse amazed everyone with 4:07.8.

Suddenly, interest in the American milers picked up, and they ran another mile at Baldwin-Wallace College in Berea, Ohio, on July 31. Les Eisenhart, a half-miler, led for 700 meters, passing the 440 in 59.0. Hägg took over in 2:02 and a very fast 3:03, but Dodds was right on his heels and the amazing Hulse was as close to Dodds as he could get.

Hägg's last lap was not inspired, but Dodds slowly lost ground. Then, in the homestretch, Hulse fought past Dodds. Results: Hägg 4:05.4, Hulse 4:06.0, Dodds 4:06.1. Thus, the surprising Hulse now held the U.S. national record.

On August 7, in Cincinnati, Hägg ran two miles in 8:51.3, but he lost to a man with a 440-yard handicap. Behind Hägg, Hulse ran 9:09 and Dodds a poor 9:18.

Hägg's last race of his successful tour was at Randall's Island, New York, on August 11. Only 5500 spectators watched the three rivals start off after a handicap man at 105 yards. Hulse set the pace in 59.6 and 2:03.5. On the third lap, Hägg wanted a faster pace, for he tapped Hulse on his pants and said, "Faster, faster."

Hägg led Hulse by one foot at three-quarters in 3:06.5. On the backstretch, Dodds drew applause as he raced past both men into the lead, but Hägg responded with a pick-up which left no doubt as to the best man. Without going all out, he held off Dodds, 4:06.9 to 4:07.2, while Hulse faded to 4:08.2.

Afterwards, as a farewell gift, Hägg presented his running shorts to Hulse, one shoe to Dodds, and the other to Greg Rice. Hägg had a good time in the United States, attending banquets and making speeches. He was enthusiastic enough about the country to consider living there, but he flew back to Sweden on September 26.

He had missed an interesting Swedish season, although, on October 10, he did run an exhibition 1000 meters.

MEANWHILE... ANDERSSON!

After his frustrating defeats of 1942, it was a new Arne Andersson in 1943. He was now teaching school in Göteborg, and so his mind was on track only when training or racing. He was married to Karin, "a wonderful girl," who was an athlete and approved his efforts. He was careful not to reach peak form too early as in previous years. And it could not hurt his confidence to have Gunder Hägg far away in the United States.

But best of all, he had learned a new running form. Ever since the fall of 1942 he had worked on form with a friend who was a 400-meter runner and a keen student of the sport. Andersson's wildly exuberant way of running, with bounding strides, was wasting energy. He learned to bring his arms up and shorten his stride, and the difference was wonderful. He had much more speed.

His training was now similar to Hägg's, with much of his running in a natural setting, but he also worked hard on sprints. He won four easy 1500's between May 27 and June 27 of 1943, in 3:52.2, 3:54.6, 3:56.6, and 4:01.0. On July 1, exactly one year after his frustrating 4:06.4, he ran at Göteborg against a strong field of Swedish milers.

Arne Ahlsén set a fast pace. He was a short man with ungainly form, who ran 3:49.4 in 1942 and 3:50.4 already in 1943. He led with 400m times of 58 flat and 1:59.8 and the crowd became excited.

Andersson trailed a few yards back with estimated 440 times of 59.4 and 2:00.8, followed by tall, smooth-striding Rune Gustafsson. A fast half-mile type, Gustafsson's best time was 3:51.2 behind Ahlsén, but like Hulse in the United States, he knew he could run faster.

Bringing up the rear were 32-year-old Ingvar Haglund, who ran 3:52.6 in 1942, and Rune Persson, not yet 21, a promising runner who had improved 13.2 seconds in 1942, to 3:54.0.

As they reached the bell, Andersson went past Ahlsén in 3:04.0, followed by Gustafsson. The crowd was a little disappointed in the time, for Andersson had run behind Hägg in similar times last year and failed to win.

But Andersson was moving well. It was going to be a personal record. And it was a good race, for Gustafsson was hanging on down the backstretch.

Around the curve, Andersson began to pull away. He flew past 1500 meters in a sensational 3:47.4 to Gustafsson's 3:48.4. Now the crowd was roaring, for that was the second fastest 1500 ever run, and Andersson was finishing with his great newly-found power. Never had they seen a miler come off a fast 1500 and lift into a sprint finish, for it had never been done before.

Down the homestretch Andersson sprinted, powerful shoulders rolling, arms struggling forcefully. He raced through the tape and the enthusiasm of his home crowd was "beyond description."

Results: Andersson 4:02.6, Gustafsson 4:04.6, Ahlsén 4:06.6.

It was easily the greatest mile race yet run, with Gustafsson equalling Hägg's world record 15 yards behind Andersson.

Across the war-torn Atlantic, in the United States, Gunder Hägg heard the news and said, "I want to meet him before the season is over."

After an easy 3:55.2 three days later, Andersson went after Hägg's 1500-meter record at Stockholm on July 8. On a heavy track in the rain, he beat Ahlsén 3:48.8 to 3:50.8. He was three seconds behind Hägg's record, but Henry Kälarne said of him, "This guy is fantastic."

In the next ten days, Andersson won in 3:55.0, 3:52.0, and he beat the dangerous Ahlsén 3:49.4 to 3:49.6 in Copenhagen. Two days later, on July 20 in Malmö, he ran an excellent ¾ mile race in 2:58.8, defeating Gustafsson, 2:59.6, and Ahlsén, 3:00.5. Andersson's time was only one tenth short of Paul Moore's best-on-record.

Andersson won two more slow races. Then, in poor conditions at Stockholm on August 6, he ran 3:47.8. On August 15, he won the Swedish championship in 3:50.4. Ahlsén, who ran 3:47.8 on July 26, was only a poor fifth. Then, only two days later, Andersson made another attempt on Hägg's 1500-meter record of 3:45.8.

This was on August 17 at his home track in Göteborg in balmy weather, with no wind. Three men were given ten-second starts, and two others started with Andersson. One of them led him through nicely-paced 400-meter times of 58.5 and 2:01, but

1943

Andersson was all alone before he passed 1200 meters in 3:00.8. His time was 1.9 seconds slower than Hägg's pace in his world record race, but Hägg had finished slowly and Andersson had demonstrated greater finishing speed in his record mile. Where Hägg had finished in 46.9 for the last 300 meters, Andersson's raw power took him around in 44.2 and he had another world record of 3:45.0.

As soon as he stopped, his club manager hugged him and the crowd of 10,258 knew. They cheered him wildly.

Over in New York, Hägg was awakened very early. Without being told anything, he asked, "Which of my records was beaten?"

When told, he said, "Glad it was Arne who broke it." Then he added, "I'd better pack up and go home or he'll break all my other records."

But Andersson was worn out. After slow wins in 3:57.4 and 3:55.8, he was nipped in 3:57.4, by Lennart Nilsson, the same man who had conquered Hägg in a relay in 1942. Andersson won in 3:50.8 against Denmark, then lost at 1000 meters, dropped out of a 5000-meter race, and ended with a two-mile in 9:26.8.

It was time to rest and regain his strength for his battles with Hägg in 1944.

1941
MILE:

Time	Athlete		Place	Date
4:08.6	Arne Andersson (Sweden)	(1)	Stockholm	19 Sep
4:09.2	Gunder Hägg (Sweden)	(1)	Gävle	30 Aug
4:09.3	Phil Leibowitz (USA)	(1)	Berkeley	31 May
4:09.6	Andersson	(2)	Gävle	30 Aug
4:09.6	Bror Hellström (Sweden)	(1)	Stockholm	5 Sep
4:09.6	Andersson	(2)	Stockholm	5 Sep
4:09.7	Leroy Weed (USA)	(2)	Berkeley	31 May
4:10.1	Robert Ginn (USA)	(1)	Berkeley	19 Apr
4:10.4	Leslie MacMitchell (USA) NCAA(1)		Palo Alto	21 Jun
4:10.4	Henry Kälarne (Sweden)	(3)	Stockholm	5 Sep
4:10.5e	Weed (2 ft. back) NCAA(2)		Palo Alto	21 Jun
4:11.0	Ake Jansson (Sweden)	(3)	Gävle	30 Aug
4:11.0	Andersson	(1)	Göteborg	14 Sep
4:11.1	Dick Peter (USA)	(2)	Berkeley	19 Apr
4:11.2	Sydney Wooderson (GB)	(1)		

Indoors:

Time	Athlete		Place	Date
4:07.4	Leslie MacMitchell (USA)	(1)	New York	15 Feb
4:07.4	Walter Mehl (USA)	(2)	New York	15 Feb
4:09.7	Mehl	(1)	Boston	25 Jan
4:09.7	John Munski (USA)	(2)	Boston	25 Jan
4:10.2	MacMitchell	(3)	Boston	25 Jan
4:10.4	Mehl	(1)	New York	8 Mar
4:10.7	MacMitchell	(1)	Boston	8 Feb
4:10.9	Mehl AAU(1)		New York	22 Feb
4:11.0	Campbell Kane (USA)	(1)	Chicago	22 Mar

1,500m:

Time	Athlete		Place	Date
3:47.5	Gunder Hägg (Sweden) Swd. Ch.	(1)	Stockholm	10 Aug
3:48.6	Hägg	(1)	Malmö	21 Jul
3:48.6	Arne Andersson (Sweden) Ch.	(2)	Stockholm	10 Aug
3:49.2	Henry Kälarne (Sweden) Ch.	(3)	Stockholm	10 Aug
3:49.8	Andersson	(1)	Göteborg	1 Jul
3:49.8	Hägg	(1)	Stockholm	4 Jul
3:50.0	Andersson	(1)	Gävle	8 Jul
3:50.2	Hägg	(1)	Göteborg	18 Jul

1943

3:50.4		Andersson	(2)	Göteborg	18	Jul
3:50.4		Arne Ahlsén (Sweden) Ch.	(4)	Stockholm	10	Aug
3:51.0		Bror Hellström (Sweden)	(2)	Stockholm	4	Jul
3:51.2		Ahlsén	(1)	Motala	5	Oct
3:51.4		Leslie MacMitchell (USA)	(1)	Compton	6	Jun
3:51.4		Hägg	(1)	Oestersund	29	Jun
3:51.4		Kälarne	(2)	Gävle	8	Jul
3:51.8		Ake Jansson (Sweden)	(1)	Södertälje	25	Jul
3:52.2		John Isberg (Sweden)	(1)	Sundbyberg	3	Aug
3:52.6		Miklós Szabó (Hungary)	(3)	Göteborg	18	Jul
3:52.6		Olle Akerberg (Sweden) Ch.	(5)	Stockholm	10	Aug

1942
MILE:

4:04.6	WR	Gunder Hägg (Sweden)	(1)	Stockholm		4	Sep
4:06.1		Hägg	(1)	Göteborg		1	Jul
4:06.2		Arne Andersson (Sweden)	(1)	Stockholm		10	Jul
4:06.4		Andersson	(2)	Göteborg		1	Jul
4:11.1		Robert Ginn (USA) NCAA	(1)	Lincoln		13	Jun
		(Weed 2nd, MacMitchell 3rd, times not known)					
4:12.2		Leslie MacMitchell (USA) IC4A	(1)	New York		30	May
4:12.5		Don Burnham (USA) IC4A	(2)	New York		30	May
4:13.0		Gil Dodds (USA)	(1)	Newton, Mass.		6	Jun
4:13.8e		Bill Hulse (USA)	(3)	New York		30	May
4:14.0		Campbell Kane (USA)	(1)	Evanston	15 or	16	Jun
4:14.4*		Ake Spangert (Sweden)	(2)	Stockholm		4	Sep
4:14.6		Burnham	(1)	New York		6	Jun
4:14.7		William Tribou (USA) IC4A	(4)	New York		30	May
4:14.8		Kane	(1)	Memphis		10	May

*Formerly Jansson.

Indoors:

4:07.8	Leslie MacMitchell (USA)	(1)	New York	25	Mar
	(This was on a 9-lap track in the Navy Relief meet)				
4:08.0	MacMitchell	(1)	New York	12	Feb
4:08.0	MacMitchell	(1)	New York	14	Mar
4:08.4e	Gil Dodds (USA)	(2)	New York	14	Mar
4:08.7	Dodds AAU	(1)	New York	28	Feb
4:08.7e	Dodds	(2)	New York	25	Mar
4:08.9	MacMitchell AAU	(2)	New York	28	Feb
4:09.8	MacMitchell	(1)	New York	21	Feb

1,500m:

3:45.8	WR	Gunder Hägg (Sweden)	(1)	Stockholm		17	Jul
3:48.4		Hägg	(1)	Oestersund		5	Jul
3:48.8+		Hägg	(1)	Stockholm		4	Sep
3:49.0		Arne Andersson (Sweden)	(1)	Linköping		16	Jun
3:49.2		Andersson	(2)	Stockholm		17	Jul
3:49.4		Arne Ahlsén (Sweden)	(3)	Stockholm		17	Jul
3:49.8		Ahlsén	(2)	Linköping		16	Jun
3:49.8+		Andersson	(1)	Stockholm		10	Jul
3:50.2		Gil Dodds (USA) AAU	(1)	New York		20	Jun
3:50.4+		Hägg	(1)	Göteborg		1	Jul
3:50.4		Hägg	(1)	Boras		13	Sep
3:50.6		Ake Spangert (Sweden)	(1)	Stockholm		16	Aug
3:50.6		Hägg	(1)	Budapest		27	Sep
3:51.4		Leroy Weed (USA) AAU	(2)	New York		20	Jun
3:51.4		Rolf Seidenschnur (Ger)	(1)	Berlin		2	Aug
3:52.5		Leslie MacMitchell (USA) AAU	(3)	New York		20	Jun
3:52.6		Ingvar Haglund (Sweden)	(2)	Boras		13	Sep
3:53.2		Edward Culp (USA) AAU	(4)	New York		20	Jun
3:53.2		John Isberg (Sweden)	(3)	Boras		13	Sep

1943
MILE:

4:02.6	Arne Andersson (Sweden)	(1)	Göteborg	1	Jul
4:04.6	Rune Gustafsson (Sweden)	(2)	Göteborg	1	Jul
4:05.3	Gunder Hägg (Sweden)	(1)	Cambridge, Mass.	24	Jul
4:05.4	Hägg	(1)	Berea, O.	31	Jul
4:06.0	Bill Hulse (USA)	(2)	Berea, O.	31	Jul

1943

4:06.1	Gil Dodds (USA)	(3)	Berea, O.	31	Jul
4:06.5	Dodds	(2)	Cambridge, Mass.	24	Jul
4:06.6	Arne Ahlsén (Sweden)	(3)	Göteborg	1	Jul
4:06.9	Hägg	(1)	New York	11	Aug
4:07.2	Dodds	(2)	New York	11	Aug
4:07.8	Hulse	(3)	Cambridge, Mass.	24	Jul
4:08.2	Hulse	(3)	New York	11	Aug
4:11.2	Sydney Wooderson (GB)	(1)	Manchester	26	Jun
4:11.8	Wooderson	(1)	London	2	Aug
4:14.0	Doug Wilson (GB)	(2)	London	14	Jun
4:15.0	James Alford (GB)				
4:17.2	Robert Porter (USA)	( )			
4:17.6	Clarence Dunn (USA)	(1)	Milwaukee	29	May

Indoors:

4:08.5	Gil Dodds (USA)		(1)	Chicago	20	Mar
4:08.6	Earl Mitchell (USA)		(1)	New York	6	Feb
4:08.7	Dodds		(1)	Cleveland	27	Mar
4:08.8	Dodds		(1)	New York	20	Feb
4:08.9	Dodds		(2)	New York	6	Feb
4:09.6	Frank Dixon (USA)	AAU(1)		New York	27	Feb
4:09.6	Dixon		(1)	New York	13	Mar
4:09.9	Dodds	AAU(2)		New York	27	Feb
4:09.9e	Mitchell		(2)	Chicago	20	Mar
4:10.0e	Dixon		(3)	Chicago	20	Mar
4:10.1e	Dodds		(2)	New York	13	Mar
4:10.6	Dixon		(3)	New York	6	Feb
4:11.4	Dixon		(1)	Boston	13	Feb
4:11.5e	Mitchell		(2)	Boston	13	Feb

1,500m:

3:45.0	WR	Arne Andersson (Sweden) hdcp	(1)	Göteborg	17	Aug
3:47.4+		Andersson	(1)	Göteborg	1	Jul
3:47.8+		Gunder Hägg (Sweden)	(1)	Cambridge, Mass.	24	Jul
3:47.8		Arne Ahlsén (Sweden)	(1)	Oerebro	26	Jul
3:47.8		Andersson	(1)	Stockholm	6	Aug
3:48.4+		Rune Gustafsson (Sweden)	(2)	Göteborg	1	Jul
3:48.5+		Gil Dodds (USA)	(2)	Cambridge, Mass.	24	Jul
3:48.7+		Hägg	(1)	Berea, O.	31	Jul
3:48.8		Andersson	(1)	Stockholm	8	Jul
3:49.4		Andersson	(1)	Copenhagen	18	Jul
3:49.6		Ahlsén	(2)	Copenhagen	18	Jul
3:50.0		Dodds	AAU(1)	New York	19	Jun
3:51.0		Aage Poulsen (Denmark)	(2)	Stockholm	29	Aug
3:51.4		Bertil Andersson (Sweden)	(2)	Stockholm	6	Aug
3:51.6		Ake Spangert (Sweden)	(1)	Stockholm	2	Jul
3:51.8		Hans Liljekvist (Sweden)	(1)	Stockholm	10	Oct
3:52.0		Ake Durkfeldt (Sweden)	(2)	Oerebro	26	Jul

DODDS IMPROVES INDOORS

Most of the good runners were occupied with the war, and only Dodds and Hulse seemed likely to run well during the 1944 indoor season.

In the Wanamaker Mile on February 5, Dodds ran his second quarter in a startling 59.9 to reach the 880 in 2:01.3. Then he passed three-quarters in 3:04. His last 440 was only 66.6, but he beat Hulse, 4:10.6 to 4:11.0.

At Boston on February 12, Dodds used the same odd pace: 63.6, 58.7, 61.7. He beat Hulse by 20 yards in 4:09.5, the fastest mile ever run in Boston.

Dodds won the Baxter Mile without Hulse in 4:08.0, after another hard pace of 58.6, 1:59.7, and 3:03.3. Then, in the AAU meet, he ran 1:58.8 and 3:01. His last quarter in a slow 67.3 gave

1944

him a mile in 4:08.3.
On March 11 in the Columbian Mile, he tried his desperate pace again. After 60.8, he ran 59.8 for 2:00.6. He reached three-quarters in 3:03.4, but this time he finished better and set a new indoor record of 4:07.3.
Hulse was back in competition at Chicago on March 18, after an illness, and he clung to Dodds' 60-flat, 2:01 and 3:04 until the last lap. Then he faded 20 yards back while Dodds completed a last quarter in 62.4 for a record 4:06.4 to Hulse's 4:09.6.

HÄGG vs ANDERSSON

Hägg did not want to continue his job as a fireman after his tour of the United States, and so he became a salesman in a Malmö clothing store where the pay was good and the hours extraordinarily lenient.
Andersson, now teaching in Stockholm, shortened his training hours—he had spent as many as four hours in one workout—and increased his speed. Not quite ready, he lost at 1000 meters in June, then spent ten days sharpening for his first race against Hägg.
Hägg's preparation for the race was more confident, if less wise. Three days before, at Oestersund on June 25, he broke the world record for two miles with 8:46.4.
They ran at Stockholm and interest among the sports fans was great, but a slow first 400 in 62.9 ruined any chances for a fast race. Hägg, knowing he had to get away from Andersson's big kick, stepped it up to 2:03. But he was probably still feeling the effects of his record two-mile and he ran only 3:05.7 for 1200 meters.
Andersson followed him to the homestretch, then showed Hägg his beautiful new finishing kick. He won by ten yards. Results: Andersson 3:48.8, Hägg 3:50.2, Ingvar Bengtsson 3:50.6, Gustafsson 3:50.6, Persson 3:51.6, Erik Ahldén 3:51.8.
Reporters asked Hägg if he was sorry his long winning streak had ended, and he said, "I feel neither glad nor disappointed. I know however that Arne will be all the more glad for it ... and one can wish success to a good friend."
On July 2, Hägg ran 3:48.2, and on July 5 he ran 2000 meters in 5:19.0. In the same Stockholm meet, Andersson looked unbeatable as he smashed all records for ¾ mile. After a pace of 59 flat and 1:59.2, he ran a powerful 440 in 57.4 to finish in 2:56.6.
Now Andersson was feared by all of Hägg's supporters when they met only two days later in Göteborg. The weather was good when they reached the starting line at 7:47 p.m. Gustafsson and Persson were in the race, but the capacity crowd had eyes only for Hägg, in his black-green-and-white club colors, and the hometown favorite Andersson, in the green of his new Stockholm club.

1944

The early hot pace was set by a young unknown runner named Lennart Strand, who stepped off the track after 800 meters. Hägg followed the fast pace, passing 400 meters in 56.7. Andersson lagged five meters behind, at a wiser pace.

With Hägg passing 800 meters in a sensational 1:56.5, Andersson had closed the gap slightly to 3½ meters and his fans were loud in their encouragement. He closed the gap in the next 100 meters and ran on Hägg's heels around to 1200 meters in a sensational 2:58.0.

At this point, Andersson said, "I almost felt like quitting. My arms were heavy and my legs like lead." He was paying for his great ¾ mile record of two days before.

Hägg increased his pace slightly and began to pull away. Andersson fought courageously, but he was losing his form and the gap opened gradually. Hägg looked back and saw the gap, but Andersson was running too well for him to ease his hard pace. Still, Hägg was running smoothly at the end.

Results: Hägg 3:43.0, Andersson 3:44.0, Gustafsson 3:48.2, Persson 3:51.8.

Hägg's new world record was equivalent to a second faster than Andersson's mile record. Now the two were even again . . . but not for long.

A week later, they raced at 1500 meters again, in Stockholm. The slow pace favored Andersson and his kick was too much for Hägg. Andersson won, 3:48.4 to 3:49.2.

Four days later, at Malmö Idrottspark, a capacity crowd of 14,279 came to watch the two great runners compete at the mile distance, and another four or five thousand stood outside to listen to the loudspeaker.

Andersson had sharpened his spikes, as he liked to do before a race, and in the morning he enjoyed a run in the woods. He thought of his terrible mistake in letting Hägg get away from him and he was determined to stick to Hägg today no matter what the pace.

The 393-meter track was fast, the weather was good, and three other milers were capable of making it interesting—Gustafsson, Persson, and a last-minute entry, Strand. Again young Strand set a fast pace of 56.8 and 1:56.0. Hägg was close behind, hoping to run away again, but Andersson was on his heels.

Then Strand dropped out and Hägg "felt a bit dull and not really in the mood. Never before did I find myself thinking, when will it be over?" He let the pace slow to 31.0 for the next 200 meters, then 31.5, reaching 1200 meters in a tiring 2:58.5.

Gustafsson and Persson were forced to let go, but Andersson stayed on Hägg's heels. The pro-Hägg crowd shouted desperate encouragement to Hägg. They feared Andersson and they felt he was doing something unfair when he merely followed Hägg's pace.

Hägg could not hold the pace. He slowed some more, to 31.8 for the next 200. Around the last curve they raced, Andersson awkward and determined compared to the graceful Hägg. They sped past 1500 meters in almost unbelievable times of 3:46.0 and 3:46.1. They could not help breaking the record, but which one would it be? Turning into the homestretch, Hägg gave all he had. He had some power left and he ran the next 100 meters in 14.2, his fastest since the fifth 100 of the race. He turned to look for Andersson and Andersson was alongside, looking at him! Desperately, Hägg fought, and the crowd pleaded with him, but Andersson was too fast. Hagg's dark-haired friend went past and won by three yards. Hägg finished pale and well-beaten.

Results: Andersson 4:01.6, Hägg 4:02.0, Gustafsson 4:05.6, Persson 4:06.8.

Andersson, who said he felt very strong in the stretch, ran his last 120 yards in 15.5. His splits were 57.1, 59.6, 62.9, and 62.0.

That evening, Hägg and his parents invited Andersson and his wife, Karin, to dinner. Hägg smiled. "It's not every day that I can invite a world champion to dinner."

Andersson said, "If ever we could get together and help each other, the four-minute mile would be ours for the asking." Then he offered Hägg some important advice. "And you, Gunder, why do you run so wide around the curves? I always gain on you there."

Over in the United States, a bemused Greg Rice commented, "I never thought that a man brought forth by a woman would be able to beat Hägg."

Paavo Nurmi explained that Andersson's and Hägg's superior times were because of their better build-up in the winter.

On July 25, Hägg missed his two-mile record by only 0.8 seconds with 8:47.2, but he reached his goal at Stockholm on August 4 with 8:42.8. His last mile was in 4:19.8. In the same meet, Andersson set a Swedish 1000-meter record of 2:21.9. On August 11 in Stockholm, Andersson attempted a 1500-meter record in a handicap, but he ran only 3:49.8.

The next anxiously-awaited race between Andersson and Hägg came in the Swedish Championships at Stockholm on August 20. Hägg carelessly allowed the pace to dawdle and he was outsprinted. Andersson won in 3:49.6 and Hägg had to work to nip Bertil Andersson in 3:50.0.

That was the end of their fierce competition at 1500 and a mile during 1944, but they met twice more at longer distances. Andersson trailed Hägg confidently in a hot 2000 at Stockholm on August 30 and outkicked him again, 5:12.6 to 5:13.2. Then, at Malmö on September 3, Hägg made little effort to get away in a 3000, and Andersson sprinted away at the finish, 8:20.8 to 8:22.4.

Hägg's fans were bitter, an attitude reflected by a Malmö

1944

sportswriter who wrote that Hägg, always leading for most of the race and always losing, was a man subjected to torture.

In September, the strong Finn, Viljo Heino, holder of the world record for 10,000 meters, toured Sweden. He ran 5000 meters in 14:09.6, forcing Andersson to drop out, but Hägg beat him three times. The shoe was on the other foot now, and Hägg was the "torturer" with his speed at the finish. Although Heino set Finnish records at 3000 and two miles, Hägg won convincingly in 8:09.8 and 8:51.2. Hägg finished the season at 5000 meters, beating Heino 14:24.4 to 14:24.8. There were no complaints from Swedes that Heino was being tortured.

In 1944, Andersson defeated Hägg in six races out of seven, losing only to Hägg's great 3:43.0. This brought the score between them to 14 victories for Hägg and seven for Andersson. At the 1500-mile distance, Hägg still held a commanding lead of ten to four. But Andersson was gaining. The year 1945 caused excited conjecture even before it started, and Hägg's fans were afraid of what would happen.

1944
MILE:

Time		Athlete		Place	Date	
4:01.6	WR	Arne Andersson (Sweden)	(1)	Malmö	18	Jul
4:02.0		Gunder Hägg (Sweden)	(2)	Malmö	18	Jul
4:05.6		Rune Gustafsson (Sweden)	(3)	Malmö	18	Jul
4:06.8		Rune Persson (Sweden)	(4)	Malmö	18	Jul
4:12.0		Gustafsson	(1)	Karlstad	2	Jul
4:12.2		Persson	(2)	Karlstad	2	Jul
4:12.8		Sydney Wooderson (GB)	(1)	Manchester	24	Jun
4:13.4		Doug Wilson (GB) hdcp race	(1)	Glasgow	5	Aug
4:14.2		Bill Hulse (USA)	(1)			
4:14.6		Bob Hume (USA))twins	(1T)	Great Lakes, Ill.	3	Jun
4:14.6		Ross Hume (USA)	(1T)	Great Lakes, Ill.	3	Jun
4:17.0		Don Burnham (USA)	(1)	Philadelphia	20	May

Indoors:

4:06.4	Gil Dodds (USA)	(1)	Chicago	18	Mar
4:07.3	Dodds	(1)	New York	11	Mar
4:08.0	Dodds	(1)	New York	13	Feb
4:08.3	Dodds	AAU(1)	New York	26	Feb
4:09.5	Dodds	(1)	Boston	12	Feb
4:09.6e	Bill Hulse (USA)	(2)	Chicago	18	Mar
4:10.2	Dodds	(1)	New York	4	Mar

1,500m:

3:43.0	WR	Gunder Hägg (Sweden)	(1)	Göteborg	7	Jul
3:44.0		Arne Andersson (Sweden)	(2)	Göteborg	7	Jul
3:46.0+		Hägg	(1)	Malmö	18	Jul
3:46.1+		Andersson	(2)	Malmö	18	Jul
3:48.2		Hägg	(1)	Hälsingborg	2	Jul
3:48.2		Rune Gustafsson (Sweden)	(3)	Göteborg	7	Jul
3:48.4		Andersson	(1)	Stockholm	14	Jul
3:48.8		Andersson	(1)	Stockholm	28	Jun
3:49.2		Hägg	(2)	Stockholm	14	Jul
3:49.6		Andersson Swd Ch.	(1)	Stockholm	20	Aug
3:49.8		Andersson (hdcp race)	(7)	Stockholm	11	Aug
3:50.0		Hägg Ch.	(2)	Stockholm	20	Aug
3:50.0		Bertil Andersson (Sweden) Ch.	(3)	Stockholm	20	Aug
3:50.6		Ingvar Bengtsson (Sweden)	(3)	Stockholm	28	Jun
3:50.8		Sven Malmberg (Sweden)	(1)	Göteborg	17	Sep
3:51.6		Rune Persson (Sweden)	(5)	Stockholm	28	Jun

3:51.8	Erik Ahldén (Sweden)	(5)	Stockholm	28	Jun
3:53.2	Aleksandr Pugachovskiy (USSR)	(1)	Moscow	18	Jun
3:53.2	Roland Sundin (Sweden)	(1)	Härnösand	6	Aug

(Bill Hulse won the AAU title in 3:54.3)

HÄGG'S INDOOR FIASCO

Promoters in the United States tried to strengthen the 1945 indoor season by inviting Hägg again. Dodds was missing, and nobody else could run fast races.

Unprepared to run that early in the year, Hägg tried to make up for lost time and ran into trouble. He caught the flu and used a "prescription for horses." He was still weak when he left for the United States.

On March 1, Hägg staggered off a freighter after 23 days at sea. Two days later he tried to run his first indoor mile, but he finished a dismal last in 4:31. He improved to 4:19.1 a week later in the Columbian Mile after working out all week in Central Park, but he was still fifth.

At Chicago on March 17, Hägg tried hard. He led until the last lap and ran 4:14.5, but he lost by four yards to James Rafferty's 4:13.7. After winning in 4:16.7 at Cleveland, Hägg stole off to San Francisco to visit a girl. He was to meet Rafferty at Buffalo on March 31 but he could not make it in time. Rafferty won in 4:10.9, fastest time of the season.

To make amends for his escapade, Hägg offered to compete in an outdoor meet "under any conditions" and so he was entered in a handicap mile at the Penn Relays. He ran a respectable 4:12.7 and finished fourth.

He returned to Sweden to a cold reception and began to train hard. He did not race against Andersson until July 17.

LENNART STRAND

Almost unnoticed by the Swedish public, who had Hägg and Andersson to idolize, Strand's sudden emergence in 1945 was almost an intrusion. Although both Hägg and Andersson said later that Strand had the most natural talent of any runner, he had little inclination to race and train at first.

In 1941, at the age of 20, he was competing in canoe races, and his best running mark was 52 seconds for 400 meters. He showed his talent by running 800 meters in 1:54.5 the very next year, but he ran only 1:56.3 in 1943 and 4:04.0 for 1500 meters. "I was too lazy to really try."

After Hägg moved to Malmö at the end of the 1943 season, Strand received advice from him and became his friend and team-

1945

mate. In 1944, Strand sacrificed himself by setting a fast pace for Hägg and so his best times, even though he was much faster, were only 1:53.1 and 3:55.4.

In 1945 this 5'8", 134-pound athlete who was also a talented pianist began to train seriously. At the end of June, Hägg revealed that he was unable to shake off Strand in their recent workouts. "He's the one who will beat us all."

Strand's emergence as a real threat came at Stockholm on June 29. In a 1500-meter race against all the best Swedes except Hägg, Strand raced past Andersson on the last backstretch with a long-striding drive which appeared effortless and incredibly efficient. Andersson was scared and it took his strong finish to win in 3:46.8. Strand was nipped at the finish by little Rune Persson in 3:47.0, but he had cut more than eight seconds from his best time and observers knew he was now a threat to the best.

ANDERSSON PREPARES

After beating Hägg in six out of seven races in 1944, Andersson was regarded as the best miler in the world, even though Hägg's one victory resulted in 3:43.0 for a world record at 1500 meters.

Andersson started moderately in 1945, with a best of 3:51.8 before his 3:46.8 on June 29, but he wanted the 1500 meter record, and on July 4 he made an effort at Göteborg. In a handicap race, he passed 800 meters in 1:58.0, but toward the end he admitted defeat and he settled for 3:45.0. Only Hägg had ever won a faster 1500.

On July 13, in a dual meet against Denmark in Stockholm, Andersson won easily from Gustafsson, 3:47.0 to 3:48.2, with a last 300 in 42.0. He was ready for the big race four days away . . . against Gunder Hägg.

HÄGG vs. ANDERSSON

They met at Malmö on July 17 . . . the world record holder for 1500 meters against the world record holder for the mile. Also in the race were Strand, Persson, and Ake Pettersson, a teammate of Hägg and Strand. An hour before the race, a sign reading "Utsalt" (sold out) was posted outside the stadium. Inside, 14,087 paying spectators waited eagerly for the greatest mile ever run.

Hägg's fastest time of the year was 3:51.4, made at Trelleborg on July 9, but he had been training with determination. His face was pale and he had secret thoughts of a time under four minutes. The favorite, Andersson, had an intent look on his dark face as he drew air into his huge chest. Strand had red patches on his usually pale cheeks. At 7:55 p.m. the temperature was 71 degrees.

1945

They were so nervous that all five runners jumped the gun. Next time they were off well and Pettersson immediately went into the lead to do his assigned task, and he passed the 440 mark on the 393.05-meter track in 56.5. Pettersson slowed and Hägg urged him to go faster, but he passed the 880 in 1:59.2. Then he stepped off the track.

Hägg knew what he wanted to do and he increased the lagging pace. Strand could not keep up, but Andersson and Persson followed closely. Hägg passed three quarters in 3:01.4 with Andersson close on his heels. Persson had to let them go, even though he was running the fastest race of his career.

Hägg tried harder, driving the whole last lap, but Andersson remained close to Hägg's flying heels and a great fear built up in Hägg's home-town fans. All last year, Andersson had followed Hägg and outkicked him and he was about to do it again. Only a few neutral fans were completely happy as Hägg hit the 1500-meter tape in a startling 3:45.4 with Andersson at 3:45.8.

In Andersson's world-record race, one day less than a year ago, Hägg led past 1500 meters in 3:46.0, and so a new world record was possible today. But in that race, Andersson was only one tenth of a second behind at 1500 meters. His rooters, remembering Hägg's 3:43, were none too hopeful of victory.

Hägg turned and looked anxiously at Andersson. "He looked like having his hands full. That gave me new confidence and more strength."

Andersson had been irritated throughout the distance by what he thought was a twisted spike on his right shoe, but what turned out to be a starter's cartridge impaled upon a spike. But now he forgot his irritation as he began his final kick.

He fought his way closer as they turned into the homestretch. With 75 meters to go, he pulled alongside while the crowd shrieked for Hägg to hold him off.

At that moment, heading for a world record, all mile history hung in the balance. The winner would be recognized as the greatest miler of all time, for this was fated to be the last of their great duels.

It was Andersson, with his big kick, against front-runner Hägg, who had not run faster than 3:51.4 this year. It was the two fastest men in history side by side in the deciding battle of their careers. Now only the homestretch was left.

Slowly, but with definite superiority, Hägg inched ahead. The crowd, surprised and deliriously happy, saw him pull away and then Andersson had to give up and let the margin grow to six yards at the finish.

Results: Hägg 4:01.3, Andersson 4:02.2, Persson 4:03.8, Strand 4:09.2.

Officially rounded off at 4:01.4 in spite of two faster official watches at 4:01.3 and one at 4:01.2, this gave Hägg both the mile and 1500 record. The starter fired his gun to salute Hägg's record.

Hägg told Andersson, "You're a great opponent. I was really scared!"

Andersson answered, "I can only return the compliment." Later he admitted, "I was, if anything, overconfident."

Hägg joked, "Now I have qualified for the MAI relay team." (And indeed, his club team won the Swedish 4x1500 championship 12 days later with a new world record.)

Hägg, expansive in victory, had further comments: "At the start, it looked like a bad day for me. Very few customers showed up at the shop. Seeking a better mood, I slept a few hours after lunch, but apprehension was still in my limbs when I woke up . . . I never thought I would break both tapes first, so I concentrated on the 1500 meter tape. After that I feared that Arne would outkick me, as usual . . . The four-minute mile. It should well be possible."

WOODERSON'S REMARKABLE RETURN

The war ended most formal track races in Britain. The AAA Championship was not held after Wooderson's 1939 victory until 1946. Wooderson's poor eyesight kept him from active duty, but he served the army in a clerical job. He continued to train and he managed to run at least one respectable mile each year.

In 1940, at the Rangers Sports in Glasgow on August 3, he won in 4:11.0. In 1941, his best was 4:11.2. In 1942, he lost his world mile record and ran no faster than 4:16.4. In 1943, he ran 4:13.8 at London on June 14 and a good 4:11.2 at Manchester on June 26.

On June 24, 1944, he won in Manchester in 4:12.8. Soon after, he was disabled by severe rheumatic trouble which struck first one part of his body and then another. He was in the hospital for almost four months, and his doctor told him he must give up any hope of every running again.

During his two-month convalescence, Wooderson felt himself wanting to run. He began to jog gently, for the pleasure of it, and for mild exercise. Gradually, he began to increase his speed, and with it, his desire to compete again.

One sports writer called his recovery "one of the most remarkable in medical history." Less than four months after his convalescence ended he ran a mile under 4:25.

With typical understatement, Wooderson called it "rather encouraging." He began to train harder and his recovery was amazing. Only eight months after his convalescence, he was in White City, ready to compete against Arne Andersson!

THE END OF ANDERSSON

In a busy season, Andersson's next important race was in London on August 6. A tremendous crowd of 52,000 crowded White City to see Wooderson, only 24 days from his 31st birthday, run against Andersson. After a pace of 60.8 and 2:02, Wooderson had the temerity to forge into the lead at three quarters in 3:09.0. But Andersson was too strong for him and won, 4:08.8 to 4:09.2. The crowd was loud in its praise of Wooderson's gallant comeback.

In the Swedish Championships, held in Stockholm only six days later, Andersson was described as a "lifeless runner" as he lost to Strand, 3:47.6 to 3:49.6. With Hägg in the 5000 and Persson not up to his earlier speed, this was something of a letdown in a country which admired the 1500 meters so much that 60 Swedes ran under four minutes in 1945.

Andersson continued to run in too many meets, including a 4:06.2 mile on August 30. He lost again to Strand on September 2, 3:49.4 to 3:50.0, as if he did not care. After a 4:08.8 mile on September 5, he brought himself to a peak for a mile test on September 9.

A capacity crowd of 19,993 was a record for Göteborg. The attraction was Sydney Wooderson, who had given Andersson a good fight on the slow White City track.

A hare set the pace at 58.5, then Andersson took over at 800 meters in 1:59.5 and 1200 meters in 3:02. In spite of the unaccustomed pace, Wooderson moved to second, followed by Gustafsson. Then, with 220 yards to go, the amazing Wooderson went into the lead.

Looking frail in contrast to the big-chested Swede, Wooderson pattered determinedly around the last curve and passed 1500 meters in 3:48.4, his best time ever! Gustafsson was falling behind.

Andersson was not at his best, but he put on a fast finish, covering the last 120 yards in 15.3. He won by less than three yards from a man who had been given up years before.

Results: Andersson 4:03.8, Wooderson 4:04.2, Gustafsson 4:05.8.

Andersson regained more of his waning stature at Hälsingborg on September 15 when he defeated Strand 3:46.0 to 3:48.6. Andersson ran the last race of his great career on October 14—winning a 3000-meter event in 8:31.6—but the last 1500 or mile of any note was, suitably enough, against Hägg on September 21.

1945

HÄGG STOPS TRYING

Consciously or unconsciously, Hägg retired from mile racing after his 4:01.3. After a poor start with consequent loss of background endurance, it is possible his all-out effort in his 4:01.3 mile was his last gasp and he needed more training instead of racing. Or, it is possible that he grew mentally stale, aided by either satisfaction that he was on top or fear that he would be beaten. Or, the fact that he was being investigated for professionalism may have reduced his desire.

In any case, he never again ran up to his high standards. In the Bank Holiday Meeting in London, he won the two-mile in 9:00.6 instead of battling Wooderson and Andersson. In the Swedish Championships, he preferred the 5000 and he won uncomfortably in 14:29.0. Thus, he came down to September 21 and his last mile with only the one good time to his credit.

A crowd of 19,643, a record for Stockholm, came to see Hägg run against Andersson, Strand, and Marcel Hansenne of France, who had run 3:49.4 behind Wooderson's 3:48.9 on September 2. A hare led in 57.5 and 2:00.4 before he tired. After another half lap, Hägg gave a signal to Strand, who obediently took the lead.

Strand led at the bell in a surprisingly slow 3:05.8, but Hägg lost contact and dropped behind. It was a sad end to the holder of seven world records and a few spectators were unkind enough to boo.

Andersson tried a while longer. It was not until the last 200 meters that he had to let Strand run away from him.

Results: Strand 4:04.8, Andersson 4:07.2, Hansenne 4:08.2, Hägg 4:12.2. Hansenne thus broke Ladoumègue's French record, the famous 4:09.2.

And so the two great milers finished together in defeat. Hägg said, "Arne may not agree with me, but our best days are over. We have taken so much out of ourselves, and out of each other, for years . . . I believe Strand can beat us every time from now on."

Hägg's last race was a close 3000-meter victory in 8:33.4 on October 7. On March 17, 1946, the Swedish federation completed its long and thorough investigation of "excess expense accounts" and passed sentence on nine runners.

Three were suspended for one year, three were suspended for two years, and suspended from all further amateur competition were Henry Kälarne (already retired), Arne Andersson, and Gunder Hägg. It was a melancholy end to a glorious era.

News had filtered from Russia that any future world record breakers would be paid 25,000 rubles. Hägg's laughter was poignant: "Under the Russian system I would have made 300,000 rubles. But I don't regret being a Swede."

1945

ALL-TIME COMBINED LIST AT THE END OF 1945

(3:42.7)	4:01.3	Hägg	1945
(3:42.9)	4:01.6	Andersson	1944
3:43.0	(4:01.7)	Hägg	1944
(3:43.3)	4:02.0n	Hägg	1944
(3:43.6)	4:02.2n	Andersson	1945
(3:44.0)	4:02.6	Andersson	1943
3:44.0n	(4:02.7)	Andersson	1944
3:45.0	(4:03.8)	Andersson	1943
3:45.0	(4:03.8)	Andersson	1945
(3:45.0)	4:03.8	Andersson	1945
(3:45.0)	4:03.8n	Persson	1945

1945
MILE:

4:01.3 WR	Gunder Hägg (Sweden)	(1)	Malmö	17	Jul
4:02.2	Arne Andersson (Sweden)	(2)	Malmö	17	Jul
4:03.8	Rune Persson (Sweden)	(3)	Malmö	17	Jul
4:03.8	Andersson	(1)	Göteborg	9	Sep
4:04.2	Sydney Wooderson (GB)	(2)	Göteborg	9	Sep
4:04.8	Lennart Strand (Sweden)	(1)	Stockholm	21	Sep
4:05.8	Rune Gustafsson (Sweden)	(3)	Göteborg	9	Sep
4:06.2	Andersson	(1)	Stockholm	30	Aug
4:07.2	Andersson	(2)	Stockholm	21	Sep
4:08.2	Marcel Hansenne (France)	(3)	Stockholm	21	Sep
4:08.8	Andersson	(1)	London	6	Aug
4:08.8	Andersson	(1)	Stockholm	5	Sep
4:09.2	Strand	(4)	Malmö	17	Jul
4:09.2	Wooderson	(2)	London	6	Aug
4:11.4	Douglas Wilson (GB)	(1)	Cowley	11	Aug
4:12.4	Erik Ahldén (Sweden)	(3)	Stockholm	30	Aug
4:14.6	Roland Sundin (Sweden)	(2)	Stockholm	5	Jul
*Ratified as 4:01.4.					

Indoors:

4:10.9	Jim Rafferty (USA)	(1)	Buffalo	31	Mar

1,500m:

3:45.0	Arne Andersson (Sweden) hdcp	(1)	Göteborg	4	Jul
3:45.4+	Gunder Hägg (Sweden)	(1)	Malmö	17	Jul
3:45.8+	Andersson	(2)	Malmö	17	Jul
3:46.0	Andersson	(1)	Hälsingborg	15	Sep
3:46.2+	Rune Persson (Sweden)	(3)	Malmö	17	Jul
3:46.8	Andersson	(1)	Stockholm	29	Jun
3:47.0	Persson	(2)	Stockholm	29	Jun
3:47.0	Lennart Strand (Sweden)	(3)	Stockholm	29	Jun
3:47.0	Andersson	(1)	Stockholm	13	Jul
3:47.5+	Strand	(4)	Malmo	17	Jul
3:47.6	Strand	(1)	Stockholm	12	Aug
3:47.6	Strand	(1)	Helsinki	23	Sep
3:48.2	Erik Ahldén (Sweden)	(4)	Stockholm	29	Jun
3:48.4+	Sydney Wooderson (GB)	(1)	Göteborg	9	Sep
3:49.2	Rune Gustafsson (Sweden)	(2)	Göteborg	4	Sep
3:49.4	Sven Malmberg (Sweden)	(3)	Goteborg	4	Sep
3:49.4	Marcel Hansenne (France)	(2)	Colombes	2	Sep
3:49.9	Henry Eriksson (Sweden)	(1)	Gävle	12	Sep

LENNART STRAND

With Hägg and Andersson unwelcome and Persson not up to his 4:03.8 of early 1945, Strand was left as the world's fastest miler. As such, he was invited to the United States for three races. He began on June 7 by winning the Compton Invitational 1500 by an absurd 60 yards in 3:51.6.

141

1946

The AAU meet was run in uncomfortably hot weather at San Antonio, Texas, on June 29. Strand appeared on the infield a few minutes before race time and ran a lazy 1000 yards for a warm-up. His most dangerous American opponent was Les MacMitchell, who had run every day possible during the war but lost much of his condition. MacMitchell won all eight of his indoor races in 1946, but his best time was 4:12.3. His bubble was burst outdoors in New York on June 15 by Tommy Quinn, 4:12.6 to 4:13.7.

In the AAU 1500, the pace was a ridiculous 66 and 2:16, with the Americans either afraid of the heat or of the blond, frail Swede. After two laps, Strand ran off by himself with a nearly unbelievable lap in 58 and he beat MacMitchell by 40 yards in 3:54.5. Strand's last sizzling 440 was in 56.5 and his last 880 in 1:56.5.

In New York on July 2, Strand took the lead with over two laps to go, passed three-fourths mile in 3:08.9, and won easily in 4:09.0 to 4:17.1 for Quinn and 4:25.8 for MacMitchell in fourth place.

Back to reality on July 23, in Malmö, Strand had to run 3:48.4 to beat Gustafsson's 3:49.8. On August 11, in Stockholm, he won his second Swedish Championship in 3:48.2, securely ahead of Henry Eriksson's 3:51.6 and Persson's 3:55.2.

HENRY ERIKSSON

A year and a half older than Strand, Eriksson was remarkably slow developing. He ran 3:59.8 in 1940, at the age of 20, but after training with Hägg and three years of military service, his best after 1943 was only 3:57.0. In 1944, now a fireman at Gävle, he improved to 3:53.8, and in 1945 he broke through with 3:49.8 in beating Hansenne. The first inkling of his great competitive ability came in 1946 when he finished second to Strand in the Swedish Championships.

In the European Championships at Oslo on August 25, Eriksson gave Strand his only competition. Eriksson took the lead after a pace of 59 and 2:02 and led at 1000 meters in 2:35. At the bell, only Václav Cevona of Czechoslovakia was able to stay with the two blond Swedes.

Strand glided away with 300 meters to go, but he thought he had one more lap to go! When Eriksson realized Strand was not running hard it was too late and his belated sprint left him five yards behind.

Results: Strand 3:48.0, Eriksson 3:48.8, Erik Jörgensen of Denmark 3:52.8, Cevona 3:53.0, Sándor Garay of Hungary 3:53.0, Douglas Wilson of GB 3:53.2.

OTHER RUNNERS

SYDNEY WOODERSON ended his great career as a miler

Arne Andersson

Gunder Hägg

Sidney Wooderson

Henry Ericksson

Peddy-Foto

Acme

Lennard Strand

Gill Dodds

after his 4:04.2 in 1945, but he continued to compete for one more year. In 1946 he tried longer races, beginning with a two-mile in 9:05 on July 10. In the AAA, he won the three-mile with a courageous last lap in 58.4 and set a new British record of 13:53.2. His only other test before the European Championships was a 13:57 three-mile against France.

In the European Championships 5000, Wooderson calmly ran with the pack until the last backstretch, then kicked so hard that he won by 5.4 seconds in 14:08.6, second fastest ever run.

1946
MILE:

4:06.6	Lennart Strand (Sweden)	(1)	Malmö	27 Aug
4:09.0	Strand	(1)	New York	2 Jul
4:09.4	Erik Ahldén (Sweden)	(2)	Malmö	27 Aug
4:12.1	Gil Dodds (USA)	(1)	Brookline, Mass.	2 Sep
4:12.3	Edward Walsh (USA)	(1)	Annapolis	25 May
4:12.6	Tommy Quinn (USA)	(1)	New York	15 Jun
4:13.0	Rune Gustafsson (Sweden)	(1)	Copenhagen	9 Aug
4:13.7	Leslie MacMitchell (USA)	(2)	New York	15 Jun
4:15.0	Roland Sink (USA)	(1)	Los Angeles	24 Mar
4:15.2	Robert Rehberg (USA)	NCAA (1)	Minneapolis	22 Jun
4:15.8	Don Wold (USA)	NCAA (2)	Minneapolis	22 Jun

Indoors:

4:11.5	Edward Walsh (USA)	(1)	Cleveland	22 Mar
4:12.3	Leslie MacMitchell (USA)	(1)	New York	16 Feb
4:13.2	Tommy Quinn (USA)	(2)	New York	16 Feb
4:15.8	Marcel Hansenne (France)	(2)	New York	9 Mar
4:15.9	Forrest Efaw (USA)	(3)	New York	16 Feb

1500m:

3:48.0	Lennart Strand (Sweden)	Eur. Ch. (1)	Oslo	25 Aug
3:48.2	Henry Eriksson (Sweden)	(1)	Helsinki	1 Aug
3:48.2	Strand	Swd. Ch. (1)	Stockholm	11 Aug
3:48.4	Strand	(1)	Malmö	23 Jul
3:48.5	Marcel Hansenne (France)	(1)	Strasbourg	15 Sep
3:48.8	Eriksson	Eur. Ch. (2)	Oslo	25 Aug
3:49.8	Rune Gustafsson (Sweden)	(2)	Malmö	23 Jul
3:50.0	Thorild Ringvall (Sweden)	(1)	Lulea	18 Aug
3:50.4	Eriksson	(1)	Stockholm	28 Jun
3:50.4	Wim Slykhuis (Holland)	(1)	Stockholm	30 Aug
3:50.4	Erik Ahldén (Sweden)	( )		
3:51.0	Rune Persson (Sweden)	(3)	Malmö	23 Jul
3:51.4	Bertil Andersson (Sweden)	(2)	Stockholm	12 Jul
3:51.6	Lars-Erik Georgsson (Sweden)	(3)	Stockholm	12 Jul
3:51.6	Gaston Reiff (Belgium)	(2)	Stockholm	30 Aug

STRAND: "OUR OLYMPIC BET"

Two days after his 1946 European Championship victory, Strand ran a mile in 4:06.6 at Malmö, beating Ahldén's 4:09.4. Then Strand suffered his only two losses of the year, both to Gustafsson, who had won the European Championships at 800 meters. Strand was humbled at 1000 meters, 2:22.2 to 2:23.8 and at 880 yards, 1:51.9 to 1:52.7.

In 1947, Strand continued to live up to the glowing predictions made for him by Hägg and Andersson. After two early victories in 3:52.6 and 3:52.2, he raced Eriksson at Gävle on July 4. After following a hare around the 375.47-meter track in 58 and 2:00.4,

1947

Eriksson and Strand went ahead by themselves with surprising Gösta Bergkvist in their wake.

The real battle came on the long backstretch where Strand forced Eriksson to drop back. Strand won, 3:44.8 to 3:45.4, a break-through for both runners. Bergkvist accomplished even more of an improvement. At 27 years of age, he was never considered a threat, but now he ran 3:46.6.

Eriksson ran 3:48.8 on July 8, and then they met again on July 15 at Malmö. Strand, unusually nervous, forgot to bring his sweat shirt and had to borrow one for his warmup. Seven runners lined up on the Idrottspark 393.05-meter track at 8:00 p.m. on a perfect, windless evening.

Börje Karlsson, the same willing hare as in the previous contest, spurted off at 13.8 for the first 100 and passed 400 meters in 57.8. With Bergkvist and Eriksson behind him, the first three men all wore the pretty light blue of the Gefle IF. Strand ran fourth.

After they reached 800 meters in 1:59.3, Eriksson took the lead and set a pace worthy of Hägg himself. In fact, it was almost Hägg vs. Andersson all over again, with Strand following Eriksson's strong pace.

Eriksson went past 1200 meters in 2:59.6 with Strand running smoothly behind, flittering along as if it cost him no effort. They rounded the curve in tandem, and the crowd roared with excitement at one of the greatest races ever run.

Strand pulled alongside in the homestretch. Eriksson, like Hägg before him, made a total effort until Strand pulled away and settled the issue. When it was hopeless, Eriksson eased off.

Results: Strand 3:43.0, Eriksson 3:44.4, Bergkvist 3:50.2, Torben Jörgensen of Denmark 3:52.8, Kaare Vefling 3:53.0 (Norwegian record).

Strand had equalled Hägg's world record. Eriksson retained fourth on the all-time list. Experts predicted more records from the pair, and people felt sorry for Eriksson.

As soon as Strand heard his time, he said, "Tack Henry!" (Thank you, Henry.) It was all friendly fun, and as they jogged a lap of honor, the announcer said, "The runner in lane one is Strand." And at the victory ceremony, "Prizes to be presented by salesman Gunder Hägg from Malmö".

On July 31, Strand out-fought Eriksson again, in the dual meet against Finland, 3:46.8 to 3:47.0. On August 5, Strand won the mile in 4:07.0 with his last lap in a good 58 flat. Olle Aberg was second in 4:09.4 and Karl-Erik Karlsson had 4:09.8, his best.

In the Swedish Championships, at Stockholm on August 17, Strand won another close victory over Eriksson, 3:49.6 to 3:50.0. Hägg warned Strand about racing too often, but Strand was undefeated at a mile or 1500 meters in the past two years and he had

no fear.
He ran a poor 4:07.6 for 1500 meters on the sharp turns at Athens on September 20. Flying to Paris a week later, his plane flew through winds of gale force and they made an emergency landing. He arrived at Paris late, but he tried to pass Hansenne after a 3:01 pace at Jean-Bouin Stadium. Then, suddenly, he had to give up and jog in. Results: Hansenne 3:47.9 (French record), Reiff 3:48.4 (Belgian record), Josy Barthel 3:51.0 (Luxemburg record), André Wartelle 3:51.6, Strand 3:53.0.

Hägg commented, "They're spoiling our surest Olympic bet by letting him into so many races, big and small."

DODDS THE UNDEFEATED

The Reverend Dodds returned to competition after an absence in 1946 and continued his indoor winning streak which began in 1943. The 28-year-old minister won two-mile races in 9:05.6 and 9:10.1. Gustafsson was brought over from Sweden, but, like Hägg in 1945, he could not offer much competition, his best being only 4:16.1.

Dodds won by 20 to 40 yards in 4:08.9 (Hunter Mile) to 4:12.7 (AAU). Then, in the Columbian Mile, he slowed badly to a last quarter in 64.5 for a time of 4:07.1.

On March 28 he ran 4:08.5 in Cleveland and the very next night, before 17,632 fans in Chicago, the rugged reverend passed three quarters in 3:05 and finished in 4:06.8.

He ran little outdoors in 1947, with a best of 4:09.2 in the New England AAU, but he was back stronger than ever for the 1948 indoor season. In his opener at the Boston KC, he crushed Hulse by 50 yards in a meet record 4:08.4.

The next week, in the Wanamaker Mile on January 31, Dodds ran away from his opponents with an unusually fast first quarter in 58.4. He passed the half in 2:00.8 and three-quarters in 3:03.9. With one of his best finishes, he toured the last quarter in 61.4 for a time of 4:05.3. Only Hägg, Andersson, and Strand had ever won faster competitive miles.

The next week, in Boston's Hunter Mile, Dodds tried a faster pace of 60, 1:59.7, and 3:02.2, but he faded to 4:08.1. Then he was sick with the mumps and was out for the rest of the indoor season. He came back in May with half miles in 1:57 and 1:54.6, plus a good 3/4 mile workout in 3:03. He won the New England AAU in 4:12.5. Then, when he ran 4:08.8, unpressed, in Bloomfield, N.J., on June 26, he seemed ready for the Olympics.

But he injured a heel, barely won the AAU in 3:52.1, and had to withdraw from the Final Olympic Trials. The career of the fastest pace-pusher outside of Hägg was finished. His winning streak

1947

remained at 35 straight.

1947
MILE:

Time	Athlete	Pos	Location	Date
4:07.0	Lennart Strand (Sweden)	(1)	Stockholm	5 Aug
4:08.8	Gösta Bergkvist (Sweden)	(1)	Göteborg	22 Aug
4:09.2	Gil Dodds (USA)	(1)	Brookline, Mass.	21 Jun
4:09.4	Olle Aberg (Sweden)	(2)	Stockholm	5 Aug
4:09.8	Karl-Erik Karlsson (Sweden)	(3)	Stockholm	5 Aug
4:10.4	Jean Vernier (France)	(2)	Göteborg	22 Aug
4:10.6	Sándor Garay (Hungary)	AAA(1)	London	19 Jul
4:10.6	Thorild Ringvall (Sweden)	(4)	Stockholm	5 Aug
4:10.6	Strand	(1)	Malmö	8 Aug
4:11.2	Bergkvist	(2)	Malmö	8 Aug
4:11.6	Gerald Karver (USA)	(1)	State College, Pa.	10 May
4:12.0	Jack Dianetti (USA)	(2)	State College, Pa.	10 May
4:12.0	Erik Jörgensen (Denmark)	(1)	Copenhagen	26 Aug

Indoors:

Time	Athlete	Pos	Location	Date
4:06.8	Gil Dodds (USA)	(1)	Chicago	29 Mar
4:07.1	Dodds	(1)	New York	8 Mar
4:08.5	Dodds	(1)	Cleveland	28 Mar
4:08.9	Dodds	(1)	Boston	8 Feb
4:09.1	Dodds	(1)	Boston	25 Jan
4:09.2	Dodds	(1)	New York	1 Feb
4:12.4	Tommy Quinn (USA)	(2)	Boston	8 Feb

1,500m:

Time	Athlete	Pos	Location	Date
3:43.0 eq.WR	Lennart Strand (Sweden)	(1)	Malmö	15 Jul
3:44.4	Henry Eriksson (Sweden)	(2)	Malmö	15 Jul
3:44.8	Strand	(1)	Gävle	4 Jul
3:45.4	Eriksson	(2)	Gävle	4 Jul
3:46.6	Gösta Bergkvist (Sweden)	(3)	Gävle	4 Jul
3:46.8	Strand	(1)	Göteborg	31 Jul
3:47.0	Eriksson	(2)	Göteborg	31 Jul
3:47.9	Marcel Hansenne (France)	(1)	Paris	27 Sep
3:48.4	Gaston Reiff (Belgium)	(2)	Paris	27 Sep
3:48.8	Eriksson	(1)	Stockholm	8 Jul
3:49.6	Strand Swd. Ch.	(1)	Stockholm	17 Aug
3:50.0	Eriksson Swd. Ch.	(2)	Stockholm	17 Aug
3:50.2	Olle Aberg (Sweden)	(1)	Stockholm	29 Aug
3:50.6	Václav Cevona (CSR)	(1)	Prague	15 Aug
3:50.6	Sven Gottfridsson (Sweden)	(2)	Stockholm	29 Aug
3:51.0	Joseph Barthel (Luxemburg)	(3)	Paris	27 Sep
3:51.2	Rune Persson (Sweden)	(1)	Halmstad	30 Jul

STRAND WORRIES

Almost everybody predicted Strand would have little trouble winning the Olympic gold medal. Only Strand was nervous about his chances, and his nerves became increasingly more of a problem. Swedish writers called them "French nerves" and one commentator said, "minor jolts in life had the effect of an earthquake on his inner seismograph."

He started too early in 1948, with 3:51.4 on May 11. On June 16, in a handicap event in Malmö, he finished with an excellent last 400 meters under 56 for a time of 3:47.6. Now there was little doubt that he would win easily at London.

But after the trials for the Swedish team, doubts began to rise. Strand won his heat on July 1 in 3:56.2. The following day, the Stockholm crowd expected another victory for Strand, although

they were interested in Eriksson, whose best so far was 3:51.6, and Bergkvist, with a fastest time of 3:53.2 in 1948. The first 400 of the final was run in 57.5 and Strand lagged far behind. At 800 meters in 2:00.6, with Persson leading, Strand was at least 25 meters behind and the spectators were puzzled. Eriksson took the lead at 1200 meters, ahead of Bergkvist and Aberg. Strand began to gain, but Bergkvist pulled away from Eriksson on the last lap. Strand caught Eriksson as usual, but he was badly beaten by Bergkvist.
Results: Bergkvist 3:48.0, Strand 3:49.8, Eriksson 3:50.0, Aberg 3:51.4, Rolf Andersson 3:52.4, Stig Lundqvist 3:52.8, Persson 4:00.0.
Three weeks later, Strand stayed away from a hard race and won in 3:52.4. The Olympics were only two weeks off and he was nervous.

ERIKSSON PERSISTS

After losing to Strand again in the Swedish trials, Eriksson despaired of ever beating him. At Gävle on July 21, Eriksson tried to run away from Bergkvist and barely beat him, 3:47.8 to 3:48.0. His last 300 meters took him 45.8 seconds, and his prospects did not seem overly bright.
He qualified easily in the Olympic heats on August 4th. "Before falling asleep on the eve of the final, I ran the race again and again in my thoughts—and won it regularly. I tried to convince myself that I wanted to win, could win, and would win, in spite of the irritating weather conditions."
On the day of the final, Eriksson ate an omelette, meat balls, and potatoes, 4½ hours before the race. Then, calmly, he went back to sleep, à la Hägg. "I was calm and confident, but I got nervous as we approached the stadium."

1948 OLYMPIC GAMES

Because of World War II, the 1948 revival of the Olympic Games, in London, showed a shortage of strong 1500-meter runners. Former hotbeds of mile racing such as Great Britain and the United States had been completely stripped of their best runners. The last American succumbed when Dodds was injured. The last British chance went when Wooderson retired.
Only the Swedes had progressed during the war, but Hägg and Andersson were no longer eligible. Still, the Swedes made plans to collect all three Olympic medals. In fact, Arne Andersson wisecracked, "Why don't they send the medal to Sweden and save Strand the trip?"

1948

Fastest of the non-Swedes was Hansenne, with his 3:47.9 in 1947, and he had already won the bronze medal in the Olympic 800 meters. Reiff, who ran 3:48.4 behind Hansenne last year, entered the Olympic 5000 instead and won the gold medal. Third fastest active runner outside of Sweden was Václav Cevona of Czechoslovakia, who ran 3:50.6 in 1947 and 3:49.4 on June 23, 1948. Best of the British was Bill Nankeville, who won the AAA mile in 4:14.2.

Willem Slykhuis of Holland was something of a threat. He ran 3:50.4 in 1946 and 3:51.9 in 1947, but he was impressive in longer races. He placed second in the European Championships 5000 in 1946, ranked second best in the world at 3000 meters in 1947, and placed third in the Olympic 5000 two days before the 1500 meter heats.

Bergkvist won the fastest heat, in 3:51.8. The only American to make the final was promising Don Gehrmann, the NCAA champion and Final Trials winner at 3:52.2.

Wembley Stadium's cinder track was badly soaked and the final on August 6 was run during a discouraging downpour. Strand predicted nobody would run under 3:50 in those conditions.

Hansenne, however, started off at a furious pace. Even after he slowed down he passed 400 meters in 58.3. He led at 800 meters in 2:02.6, with Eriksson still out in lane two to avoid trouble.

The Swedes, who had wished each other luck before the race, went into the lead on the third lap. The formidable trio in pale blue trunks pulled away from Hansenne, and everybody despaired of beating them.

The tall, 165-pound Eriksson led by three yards at 1000 meters but Strand closed up emphatically, flittering through the puddles as if he would handle Eriksson again as he had every time they had ever raced. With 300 meters to go, Eriksson looked back and was happy to find only Strand still with him in 3:05.0.

Strand followed Eriksson relentlessly down the backstretch and around the curve. Then, as they entered the long homestretch, he pulled alongside, ready for the kill. For 20 yards, the two blonds ran shoulder to shoulder, and it appeared to be a repetition of every race they had ever run before, but Eriksson says, "I still felt very confident."

Then, surprisingly, with 50 yards to go, Strand could no longer put up a fight and he dropped behind. He looked back and saw Slykhuis, "The King of the Finish", gaining on him like a wild man. Slykhuis tried to pass Strand on the inside, but Strand moved over and closed the space. The two runners collided and Slykhuis was knocked off the track for a step or two. Strand managed to stay ahead until they crossed the line.

Results: Eriksson 3:49.8, Strand 3:50.4, Slykhuis 3:50.4, Cevona 3:51.2, Bergkvist 3:52.2, Nankeville 3:52.6, Garay 3:52.8,

1948

Jörgensen, Barthel, Gehrmann, Hansenne, Johansson of Finland.

ERIKSSON THE CHAMPION

Eriksson's first victory over Strand came at an opportune time! From that time on, he was distinguished from the many other Erikssons by calling him "Guld-Eriksson" (Gold Eriksson). On August 22, in Stockholm, Eriksson set about to prove his victory was no fluke because of the weather. In the Swedish Championships, he ran easily while Strand appeared to be nursing his right arm. Strand finally dropped out, and Eriksson won in 3:49.0 to 3:49.6 for Persson. A newcomer of note, Ingvar Ericsson, was third in 3:50.2, and Aberg was fourth in 3:51.4.

1948
MILE:

4:08.8	Gil Dodds (USA)	(1)	Bloomfield, N.J.	26 Jun
4:09.4	Wim Slykhuis (Holland)	(1)	Malmö	29 Sep
4:11.8	Lennart Strand (Sweden)	(2)	Malmö	29 Sep
4:12.4	Gerald Karver (USA)	(1)	State College, Pa.	15 May
4:12.6	Roland Sink (USA)	(1)	Los Angeles	28 May
4:12.8	Denis Johansson (Finland)	(3)	Malmö	29 Sep
4:13.4	Karl-Erik Karlsson (Sweden)	(4)	Malmö	29 Sep
4:13.5	Clem Eischen (USA)	(2)	Los Angeles	28 May
4:13.8	Anders Svensson (Sweden)	(5)	Malmö	29 Sep
4:14.2	Bill Nankeville (GB)	AAA(1)	London	3 Jul

Indoors:

4:05.3	Gil Dodds (USA)	(1)	New York	31 Jan
4:08.1	Dodds	(1)	Boston	7 Feb
4:08.4	Dodds	(1)	Boston	24 Jan
4:12.0	Don Gehrmann (USA)	(1)	Chicago	20 Mar
4:13.1	John Twomey (USA)	(1)	New York	6 Mar
4:13.2	Tommy Quinn (USA)	AAU(1)	New York	21 Feb
4:13.7	Browning Ross (USA)	(1)	Washington	3 Jan
4:13.9	Bill Mack (USA)	(1)	Cleveland	19 Mar
4:14.1	Gerald Karver (USA)	(3)	New York	6 Mar

1,500m:

3:47.6	Lennart Strand (Sweden)	(1)	Malmö	16 Jun
3:47.8	Henry Eriksson (Sweden)	(1)	Gävle	21 Jul
3:48.0	Gösta Bergkvist (Sweden)	(1)	Stockholm	2 Jul
3:48.0	Bergkvist	(2)	Gävle	21 Jul
3:48.2	Marcel Hansenne (France)	(1)	Colombes	19 Sep
3:49.0	Eriksson	Swd. Ch.(1)	Stockholm	22 Aug
3:49.2	Eriksson	vs Finl(1)	Helsinki	11 Sep
3:49.4	Václav Cevona (CSR)	(1)	Prague	23 Jun
3:49.4	Rune Persson (Sweden)	vs Finl (2)	Helsinki	11 Sep
3:49.6	Persson	Swd. Ch. (2)	Stockholm	22 Aug
3:49.6	Wim Slykhuis (Holland)	(1)	Louvain	7 Sep
3:49.6	Denis Johansson (Finl)	vs Swd. (3)	Helsinki	11 Sep
3:50.2	Ingvar Ericsson (Sweden)	Swd Ch (3)	Stockholm	22 Aug
3:50.4	Erik Jörgensen (Denmark)	(1)	Oslo	5 Jul
3:50.4	Gaston Reiff (Belgium)	(2)	Louvain	7 Sep
3:50.4	Ingvar Bengtsson (Sweden)	(1)	Stockholm	17 Sep

Indoors:

3:49.7+	Gil Dodds (USA)	(1)	Boston	7 Feb

WIM SLYKHUIS: KING OF THE FINISH

Nine days after winning his second Olympic medal, Slykhuis

ran 3000 meters in 8:10.2. On September 7, at Louvain, he beat Reiff, 3:49.6 to 3:50.4, and then suffered a tactical defeat by 800-meter runner Bengtsson. On September 29, at Malmö, Slykhuis won the Dickson Cup in 4:09.4 as Strand showed little spirit in 4:11.8.

Early in 1949, Slykhuis ran indoors in the United States. He ran only 4:21.7 in his frustrating debut on the boards and in his second race he was nipped by Gehrmann in 4:09.5. But he was unbeaten in his other five races, although he did not face Gehrmann again. Slykhuis beat Hansenne 4:09.2 to 4:10.3 in the Baxter Mile and won the AAU easily from Bengtsson in 4:11.2.

An injury kept Slykhuis out of competition during the early outdoor season and he was unable to run satisfactorily until August 14 when he won a 1500 in 3:53 in Amsterdam. A week later, at Antwerp, he ran 1500 meters against Reiff, who set a world record of 7:58.7 for 3000 meters only nine days earlier. Not at his best so early, Reiff had lost to Hansenne on June 2, 3:47.4 to 3:48.2.

The Belgian tried to run away from Slykhuis with a first lap in 56 and Reiff led at 800 meters in 1:56. Still trying to pull away, the Olympic 5000 meter champion passed 1200 meters in 2:59, but Slykhuis stayed within striking distance.

Reiff managed to open a small gap several times on the last lap, but Slykhuis fought back and closed it each time. In the homestretch, they ran together for about 30 meters and then Slykhuis summoned his remarkable kick and spurted away and Reiff eased up.

Results: Slykhuis 3:43.8, Reiff 3:46.0.

Slykhuis' time had been bettered only by Hägg and Strand. Reiff was now sixth fastest of all-time.

Slykhuis ran 3000 meters in 8:13.8 on August 26. Running again only two days later, in Göteborg, he placed only fourth with a mediocre 3:50.2. He finished his odd season on September 18 with a mile in 4:12.4.

STRAND: OFF-AGAIN ON-AGAIN

After four easy victories early in 1949, Strand ran 3:48.6 at Stockholm on July 7 to defeat two of the most promising of the new Swedish milers: Aberg 3:49.6 and Sture Landqvist 3:51.6.

The important Dickson Cup Mile was run at Gävle on July 19 with all the best Swedish milers present. Guld-Eriksson was trying to swallow something in his throat as the starting gun fired and he had trouble breathing, but he took over the lead and passed three quarters in 3:03.6.

Then, suddenly, the spectators received a shock. Both Eriksson, who was still having trouble, and Strand slowed their pace and lost contact. Then Landqvist let go and the race was between

1949

Olympian Bergkvist and half-miler Aberg. In a fine battle, Aberg won in the homestretch.
  Results: Aberg 4:05.4, Bergkvist 4:05.8, Landqvist 4:10.2, Strand 4:13.6, Eriksson dnf.
  A week later, Strand beat Eriksson in a tactical thriller, 3:49.0 to 3:49.2, in the Norden vs USA dual meet. On August 9, Strand dropped out of a race at Malmö, but on August 21, the same day as Slykhuis' great 3:43.8, Strand ran a good one in the Swedish Championships in Stockholm.
  Nils Toft set a typical sensational Swedish pace of 56 and 1:59, and Strand was back to sixth place. Aberg took the lead, but he could not shake off his persistent rivals, and Bergkvist was leading at the bell. Around the curve, he was pursued by Aberg, Eriksson, Strand, and Landqvist.
  Going into the last turn, Strand put on his devastating kick. Surprisingly, it was Landqvist who made the best effort to follow Strand, and it was Eriksson who gave up in discouragement.
  Results: Strand 3:45.2, Landqvist 3:46.6, Bergkvist 3:47.4, Aberg 3:48.6.
  Strand won in 3:51.0 on September 4, then defeated the rest of Scandinavia comfortably in 3:50.0 on September 9, ahead of Johansson and Landqvist, who had won impressively in 3:48.4 at Göteborg on August 28, ahead of Slykhuis in fourth place.
  A big contest was arranged for Brussels on September 27, but several runners failed to appear. Then Strand ruined the race when he stepped on the curb and fell, failing to finish. Reiff ran away with a ridiculously easy victory in 3:45.8 to 3:51.2 for Aberg and 3:52.2 for Bergkvist.
  Strand made a good comeback in his last race of the year, against France in Paris' Colombes Stadium on October 2. Strand won in 3:46.2 to 3:47.2 for France's Algerian newcomer, promising Patrick El Mabrouk.
  The most consistently fast runners of all-time, at the end of 1949, were:

1500's under 3:50*		Miles under 4:10	
Arne Andersson	19	Arne Andersson	13
Lennart Strand	18	Gunder Hägg	7
Henry Eriksson	13	Lennart Strand	5
Gunder Hägg	10	Gil Dodds	5
Marcel Hansenne	7	Glenn Cunningham	4
Glenn Cunningham	5	Sydney Wooderson	4
Gaston Reiff	5	Dodds (indoors)	22
*Excluding times in mile races		Cunningham (indoors)	10

1949
MILE:

4:05.4	Olle Aberg (Sweden)	(1)	Gävle	19	Jul
4:05.8	Gösta Bergkvist (Sweden)	(2)	Gävle	19	Jul
4:08.6	John Joe Barry (Eire)	(1)	Dublin	27	Aug
4:08.8	Bill Nankeville (GB)	AAA(1)	London	16	Jul
4:09.4	Barry	(1)	Dublin	13	Jul
4:09.6	Don Gehrmann (USA)	NCAA(1)	Los Angeles	18	Jun
4:09.7	Jerry Thompson (USA)	(1)	Inglewood	4	Jun
4:09.8	Marcel Hansenne (France)	(1)	London	6	Jun

1949

<u>4:10.0</u>	Jean Vernier (France)	vs GB (1)	London	1	Aug
4:10.2	Sture Landqvist (Sweden)	(3)	Gävle	19	Jul
4:10.4	Fred Wilt (USA)	(1)	Dublin	8	Jun
4:10.4	Ilmari Taipale (Finland)	(1)	Pori	26	Aug

Indoors:
4:09.2	Wim Slykhuis (Holland)	(1)	New York	12	Feb
4:09.5	Don Gehrmann (USA)	(1)	New York	29	Jan
<u>4:09.5</u>	Slykhuis	(2)	New York	29	Jan
4:10.2	Ingvar Bengtsson (Sweden)	(1)	New York	26	Feb
4:10.3	Marcel Hansenne (France)	(2)	New York	12	Feb
4:10.9	Fred Wilt (USA)	(1)	Cleveland	18	Mar

Slykhuis won the indoor AAU title in 4:11.2.

1,500m:
3:43.8	Wim Slykhuis (Holland)	(1)	Antwerp	21	Aug
3:45.2	Lennart Strand (Sweden) Swd Ch.(1)		Stockholm	21	Aug
3:45.8	Gaston Reiff (Belgium)	(1)	Brussels	27	Sep
3:46.0	Reiff	(2)	Antwerp	21	Aug
3:46.2	Strand	vs Fr(1)	Colombes	2	Oct
3:46.6	Sture Landqvist (Sweden)Swd Ch.(2)		Stockholm	21	Aug
3:47.2	Patrick El Mabrouk (Fr)	vs Swd (2)	Colombes	2	Oct
3:47.4	Marcel Hansenne (France)	(1)	Paris	2	Jun
3:47.4	Gösta Bergkvist (Sweden)SwdCh.	(3)	Stockholm	21	Aug
<u>3:48.2</u>	Reiff	(2)	Paris	2	Jun
3:48.4+	Olle Aberg (Sweden)	(1)	Gävle	19	Jul
3:48.6	Jean Vernier (France)	(3)	Paris	2	Jun
3:48.6	Ingvar Bengtsson (Sweden)	(2)	Göteborg	28	Aug

GASTON REIFF

The Olympic 5000 meter champion, now 29 years old, continued to add a little more to his reputation as a miler even though he made his main emphasis in longer races.

At Paris, on May 21, Reiff ran a mile in Jean Bouin Stadium against the best France could offer. After a pace of 60 and 2:02, Reiff took the lead. Hansenne challenged him on the third lap, but Reiff accelerated and moved away to win by an overwhelming 20 yards.

Results: Reiff 4:06.2, El Mabrouk 4:09.2, Hansenne 4:11.2. Reiff slowed to 17.7 for his last 120 yards and yet his 4:06.2 was the fastest mile ever run anywhere in Europe outside of Sweden.

A big 1500 meter race was scheduled for Malmö on June 7. Reiff took the lead after 800 meters in 2:00.6 and ran a cruel third lap in 58.4 to shatter his opponents. Strand had arrived by air only a few hours earlier from the United States, where he won an easy Compton Invitational Mile in 4:07.3. When Reiff put on the pressure, Strand gave up and finished sixth in 4:03.6.

Results: Reiff 3:46.6, El Mabrouk 3:48.4, Hansenne 3:49.8, Landqvist 3:50.2, Jean Vernier of France 3:50.4.

Reiff ran only two more 1500's in 1950, winning easily with poor times. In the European Championships he took third in the 5000.

EUROPEAN CHAMPIONSHIPS

As in their triumphant 1948 Olympics, this event seemed to

1950

shape up as a challenge between the Swedes and the rest of Europe. The Swedes felt somewhat handicapped because they could enter only two men, and then Henry Eriksson and Bergkvist retired and Aberg and Landqvist suffered unexpectedly poor years.

Lennart Strand, however, was undefeated except for his poor race at Malmö, too soon after an air trip. He ran miles in 4:07.3 and 4:07.2 and 1500's in 3:47.4 and 3:47.0, the last in the Swedish Championships on August 6.

Strand's teammate in the European Championships was 22-year-old Ingvar Ericsson, whose fast 3:47.2 behind Strand placed him eleventh on the all-time list.

With Reiff in the 5000 and Hansenne in the 800, the rest of Europe could offer no favorites for the 1500 championship.

El Mabrouk seemed the most consistently good, having won four tactical races after his two losses to Reiff. Bill Nankeville of Great Britain was another consistent runner but not fast enough to beat the Swedes. After his sixth place in the 1948 Olympics, he won the AAA in a good 4:08.8 in 1949 and 4:12.2 in 1950, but he lost three tactical races in 1950.

One man with the necessary talent was Slykhuis, still the third fastest 1500-meter runner of all time. But he had run only four indifferent races all this year. His fastest time in 1950 was 3:52.8 when El Mabrouk beat him by ten yards, and he had no good races at longer distances.

The best of the others were Cevona with 3:50.4 in 1949, Jean Vernier with 3:48.6 in 1949 and 3:50.4 this year, Ilmari Taipale who broke Nurmi's 27-year-old Finnish record this year with 4:09.4, and British Empire 3-mile champion Len Eyre with a best mile of 4:11.8.

The final was run in good weather on August 27. The 60,000-seat Heysel Stadium in Brussels was not quite full as twelve runners went to their marks. The starting line was straight and since the race started on the curve, Strand and El Mabrouk on the outside were at a disadvantage.

Of the two possible tactics, El Mabrouk tried to sprint up toward the front, while Strand chose to start slowly and move over to the curb behind the pack.

Nankeville set an indifferent pace down the backstretch and around the curve. Then Taipale took the lead and increased the pace. Strand still ran last, and now he was completely defeated by his nerves. He lost more ground and dropped out on the first lap.

Taipale passed 400 meters in 61.0 and 800 in 2:01.0. Then Jean Vernier took the lead as the pace slowed to 2:32.6 at 1000 meters. Coming out of the turn before the bell, Ingvar Ericsson moved into the lead. As he led past the clanging bell and around the curve, Sweden's superiority seemed to continue without Strand.

1950

But on the last backstretch, Nankeville went past Ericsson with obvious power, followed relentlessly by El Mabrouk. As they pulled away from Ericsson, Slykhuis managed to follow them. El Mabrouk fought his way past Nankeville, running wide on the curve, and led into the homestretch. Then Slykhuis turned on his famous sprint finish. Within a few yards he closed on Nankeville, pulled even, and went past. Nankeville's fight to hold off Slykhuis gained a little on El Mabrouk. Slykhuis' flashing legs sent him past El Mabrouk to an impressive victory in meet record time.
Results: Slykhuis 3:47.2, El Mabrouk 3:47.8, Nankeville 3:48.0, Taipale 3:50.4, Eyre 3:51.0, Cevona 3:51.4, Ericsson 3:52.4, Vernier 3:53.2, Otenhajmer of Yugoslavia 3:53.4, Janssens of Belgium 3:56.8, Herman of Belgium 4:05.2.
These were personal records for Nankeville, Taipale, and Eyre.

OTHER RUNNERS

EL MABROUK won more races against top milers after his good show in the European Championships. Against Great Britain, he won in 3:49.8 to 3:50.6 for Nankeville and Eyre. Against Sweden, he won easily in 3:51.3 with both Strand and Ericsson absent. Against Finland, El Mabrouk won in 3:53.8 to 3:54.6 for Taipale.

1950
1,500m:

3;46.6	Gaston Reiff (Belgium)	(1)	Malmö	7 Jun
3:47.0	Lennart Strand (Sweden)	(1)	Stockholm	6 Aug
3:47.2	Ingvar Ericsson (Sweden)	(2)	Stockholm	6 Aug
3:47.2	Wim Slykhuis (Holland)	(1)	Brussels	27 Aug
3:47.8	Patrick El Mabrouk (France)	(2)	Brussels	27 Aug
3:48.0	Bill Nankeville (GB)	(3)	Brussels	27 Aug
3:48.8	Sven Gottfridsson (Sweden)	(3)	Stockholm	6 Aug
3:49.8	Marcel Hansenne (France)	(3)	Malmö	7 Jun
3:49.8	Sándor Garay (Hungary)	(1)	Moscow	30 Jul
3:49.8	Karl-Erik Karlsson (Sweden)	(4)	Stockholm	6 Aug

Mile:

4:06.2	Gaston Reiff (Belgium)	(1)	Paris	21 May
4:07.2	Lennart Strand (Sweden)	(1)	Göteborg	11 Aug
4:07.7	Jim Newcomb (USA)	(1)	Los Angeles	9 Jun
4:07.8	Bob McMillen (USA)	(2)	Los Angeles	9 Jun
4:08.4	Rune Persson (Sweden)	(2)	Göteborg	11 Aug
4:09.2	Patrick El Mabrouk (France)	(2)	Paris	21 May
4:09.2	Karl-Erik Karlsson (Sweden)	(3)	Göteborg	11 Aug
4:09.4	Ilmari Taipale (Finland)	(1)	Helsinki	10 Jul
4:09.8	John Twomey (USA)	(3)	Los Angeles	9 Jun
4:09.9	Roger Bannister (GB)	(1)	Christchurch, NZ	30 Dec
4:10.0	Olle Aberg (Sweden)	(4)	Göteborg	11 Aug
4:10.0	Sven Gottfridsson (Sweden)	(5)	Göteborg	11 Aug

Noteworthy Indoor Marks:

4:09.3	Fred Wilt (USA)	(1)	New York	28 Jan
4:09.3	Don Gehrmann (USA)	(2)	New York	28 Jan
4:09.6	Bill Mack (USA)	(1)	East Lansing	18 Feb

VII

The Bannister years

After a decade of Swedish dominance, other runners had their chance. They learned about Holmér's "Fartlek" and saw the results of Emil Zátopek's hard repeat training, and gradually they began to evolve a form of interval training.

Just as an embryo is supposed to go through the stages of human evolution, a beginning miler in those days had to go through various evolving forms of training until he hit upon what was best for him. Nowhere has this ever been better demonstrated than in the career of a young Oxford runner with enormous talent.

ROGER BANNISTER

As a boy, "I just ran anywhere and everywhere—never because it was an end in itself, but because it was easier for me to run than to walk." He won his school's junior cross-country run three years in a row, at ages 12 to 14.

Inspired by Wooderson's comeback at White City in 1945, he decided upon a career as a runner, and yet, when he began at Oxford in the fall of 1946 at the age of 17, he had never worn spikes nor run on a track.

His training consisted of one workout each week, plus a 7½-mile cross-country race, yet in March of 1947 he won against Cambridge in 4:30.8 with a strong finish, and in June, with his training increased to half an hour, three or four times a week, he ran 4:24.6.

1951

So great was Bannister's promise that he was selected as an Olympic "possible" for 1948, but he declined the honor because he felt he was not physically nor mentally ready.

His first major race was the Kinnaird Cup in June of 1948, where he placed fourth in 4:18.7. Then he finished fifth in the AAA in 4:17.2. He watched the 1948 Olympics in London and was further inspired to become a great miler.

"New targets had to be set and more vigorous training programs prepared . . . I was restless and anxious to compete. There were four years to wait before my chance would come at Helsinki in 1952."

On June 1, 1949, he proved his speed with a 1:52.7 880. He traveled to the United States as captain of the combined Oxford-Cambridge team, and he won in 4:11.1 and 4:11.9. At the age of 20 he was now more than a good prospect, but he did no training for six weeks and placed third in a race at White City in 4:14.2.

In the fall, he learned about Fartlek and began using it, but he trained lightly because of his medical exams. Even so, his improvement was obvious. On July 1, 1950, he ran only 4:13, but his last lap was 57.5. He was beginning to develop his devastating kick.

Two weeks later, in the AAA, he ran a 1:52.1 880 behind Arthur Wint, and on August 26 at Brussels, he ran the 800 in the European Championships, losing the title by only one foot. His 1:50.7 placed him third and he decided he was "ill prepared" and needed more training. In the fall of 1950 he began to train seriously. His goal . . . the 1952 Olympics.

He took time off to beat Slykhuis in the mile at New Zealand's Centennial Games in 4:09.9 on December 30. Then he put in three months of "severe" training, doing five to ten miles of intervals, five days a week. This resulted in an encouraging time trial over three laps at Motspur Park in 2:56.8.

Ten days later, on April 28, he was in the United States for a mile race at the Penn Relays against Gehrmann and Wilt, who had both run faster than Bannister's best. The pace was slow and Bannister trailed in 62.8 and 2:06.4. He took the lead at 2½ laps and passed three-quarters in 3:11.6. He impressed 40,000 Americans with his last lap in 56.7, leaving Wilt 15 yards behind his 4:08.3. "I knew from my fast finish that I was now capable of a time near four minutes five seconds."

Two weeks later, in the British Games at White City, Andrija Otenhajmer of Yugoslavia came up to Bannister's shoulder on the last lap. Once again, Bannister burst away from the field. His last lap was 56.9 and he finished in 4:09.2. He was deliberately developing his finishing speed.

With his light background of running and his philosophy of "freshness," like Lovelock, he could not stand a long season, and he felt himself slipping, but he beat Taipale in Helsinki on July 5 in 3:52.4.

His next race, on July 14, was his biggest test to date, the AAA mile before 47,000 people at White City. "I was worried, lest I had done too much racing and traveling ... I knew I was not at my best."

Bannister followed the leader all the way to the bell in 3:08.6, but John Parlett was on Bannister's shoulder. Parlett was a 1948 Olympic finalist at 800 meters and 1950 European champion. He ran 4:09.2 in May.

Bannister broke through the box with a hard burst, then coasted the curve before beginning a steady drive on the backstretch. He ran a 59.1 last lap to win in a meet record 4:07.8 to 4:08.6 for defending champion Bill Nankeville and 4:09.2 for Parlett.

He said, "I had never been so exhausted before."

He stopped "regular" training for five weeks after his AAA victory. Then, on August 25, he ran in Belgrade in the dual meet with Yugoslavia against Otenhajmer.

The 24-year-old Yugoslav had been a soccer player until he was 19, when he entered the army, and it was 1950 before he broke through in international competition. In August he placed ninth in the European Championships in 3:53.4, then ran 3:53.2. In his first 1951 race he was badly beaten by Bannister's 4:09.2. On June 16, he lost a close one to Zdravko Ceraj of Yugoslavia in 3:50.7. In July, he ran 3:51.2 and 3:51.4.

Otenhajmer obviously remembered Bannister's 56.9 last lap in London, for he set out to take the sting out of that kick. Otenhajmer's pace of 59.0 and 2:01.6 left Bannister ten yards behind. Bannister fought back and caught Otenhajmer at the bell, but the stocky runner pulled away to win in a surprising 3:47.0. Bannister's 3:48.4 was a personal record but his invincibility had been shattered.

THE FASTEST RACE IN TWO YEARS

On Sunday afternoon, August 26, Gaston Reiff was in Göteborg for his only serious short race of the year. His opposition included Landqvist, Aberg, and Rune Persson, the 4:03.8 miler of 1945, now 29 years old, who was still fast enough to run 3:50.0 and 4:08.4 the previous year.

Sture Landqvist, after his fast 3:46.6 in 1949, had an off season in 1950, with a best of 3:50.2. This year, his fastest times were 3:50.8 and 4:09.0.

Olle Aberg, who was No. 4 in World Ranking for 800 meters in 1949 and seventh in the 1500, also had an off-year in 1950, with best times of 3:51.8 and 4:10.0. He ran 3:49.8 and 4:08.8 in 1951,

1951

including three tactical victories over Landqvist, but in his last race, he lost a close one to Landqvist, 3:51.0 to 3:50.8.

Reiff set a wicked pace, with the intention of running his Swedish rivals into the ground as he had last year. He ran the first 400 in 57.7 and 800 meters in 1:58.5. His 1200 meters in 2:58.0 excited the crowd and it should have been enough to shake off his opponents.

Instead, Landqvist passed him, followed by Aberg. Reiff, as was his habit when beaten, eased off, but Landqvist had to fight all the way to stay ahead of Aberg.

Results: Landqvist 3:44.8, Aberg 3:45.4, Reiff 3:49.0.

Only five men had ever won faster races than Landqvist's, and some Swedes began to hope that their domination had not ended, after all.

1951
1,500m:

3:44.8	Sture Landqvist (Sweden)	(1)	Göteborg	26	Aug
3:45.4	Olle Aberg (Sweden)	(2)	Goteborg	26	Aug
3:47.0	Andrija Otenhajmer (Yugoslavia)	(1)	Belgrade	25	Aug
3:47.8	Ilmari Taipale (Finland)	(1)	Kotka	2	Sep
3:48.2	Patrick El Mabrouk (France)	(1)	Belgrade	28	Sep
3:48.4	Roger Bannister (GB)	(2)	Belgrade	25	Aug
3:48.8	Stanislav Jungwirth (Czechosl.)	(1)	Budapest	25	Aug
3:49.0	Gaston Reiff (Belgium)	(3)	Göteborg	26	Aug
3:49.2	Alf Holmberg (Sweden)	(1)	Stockholm	3	Jul
3:49.4	Werner Lueg (Germany)	(2)	Stockholm	3	Jul
3:49.8	Ingvar Ericsson (Sweden)	(2)	Belgrade	28	Sep

Mile:

4:07.8	Roger Bannister (GB)	(1)	London	14	Jul
4:08.6	Patrick El Mabrouk (France)	(1)	Paris	27	May
4:08.6	Bill Nankeville (GB)	(2)	London	14	Jul
4:08.8	Warren Druetzler (USA)	(1)	Seattle	16	Jun
4:08.8	Olle Aberg (Sweden)	(1)	Malmö	13	Aug
4:08.9	Don Macmillan (Australia)	(1)	Melbourne	24	Nov
4:09.0	Don McEwen (Canada)	(1)	Evanston	25	May
4:09.0	Bob McMillen (USA)	(1)	Compton	1	Jun
4:09.0	Sture Landqvist (Sweden)	(2)	Malmö	13	Aug
4:09.1	Alf Holmberg (Sweden)	(2)	Compton	1	Jun
4:09.2	John Parlett (GB)	(2)	Paris	27	May
4:09.4	Wim Slykhuis (Holland)	(3)	Compton	1	Jun

Noteworthy Indoor Marks:

4:07.5	Don Gehrmann (USA)	(1)	New York	27	Jan
4:08.3	Fred Wilt (USA)	(2)	New York	10	Feb
4:10.4	Len Truex (USA)	(1)	Champaign, Ill.	3	Mar

1952 OLYMPIC GAMES

No single runner was an outstanding favorite for the Olympic 1500-meter championship, for this had the greatest depth of any race in history. About 25 runners had times faster than 3:50 or 4:09.2, and a 3:48.2 man, Sune Karlsson, could not make the Swedish team.

Gaston Reiff and Ilmari Taipale confined their efforts to the 5000, and Wim Slykhius was injured and could not qualify for the semi-finals. Two others surprised by failing in the first round—

1952

Otenhajmer and the 3:48.2 Hungarian, Sándor Garay.
Among the contenders, the most interesting were Bannister, El Mabrouk, McMillen, Barthel, and Lueg.

ROGER BANNISTER caused much controversy in England by avoiding racing after his great 1951 season. True to his plan, he trained half an hour daily during the winter, except for a month off because of a leg injury, and he saved his nervous energy for Helsinki. He did not race at all until May 28 when he ran an 880 in 1:53.0. On June 7 he ran a mile, with no competition, in 4:10.6. He was satisfied with his workouts, but nobody else in England agreed. In the AAA, he stayed out of the mile and won the half in 1:51.5, ten yards ahead of Albert Webster, who later placed fifth in the Olympic 800.

After losing a slow 880 to Webster, Bannister ran in a secret time trial at Motspur Park ten days before the Olympic final. He ran ¾ mile with laps of 58.5, 57.5, and 56.9 for a fantastic 2:52.9. His confidence rose, for he considered it equal to a four-minute mile.

Then came the announcement that semi-finals would be run in the Olympic 1500 meters. Bannister said, "I knew the change would hit me harder than the other competitors, most of whom had been training for an hour or so daily, with very severe interval running. With three races their tougher training gave them an advantage."

BOB McMILLEN was national junior college champion in 1948 but his best mile was 4:23.6. Only 19, he tried the steeplechase with some success. He placed second in the AAU and won the Final Trials in 9:18.7, but he fell three times in his Olympic heat and vowed never to run another steeplechase.

In 1949, McMillen won 2-mile races in 9:16.3 and 9:12.9, and in 1950 he won the 2-mile in the Coliseum Relays in 9:02, the fastest time by any western American. Two weeks later, in the Compton Invitational, McMillen made his debut to big-time mile racing by attempting to pass Lennart Strand on the last backstretch. Strand's 58.5 last lap left McMillen 12 yards behind, but McMillen had a time of 4:09.5.

A week later, in a district AAU meet in Los Angeles, McMillen took the lead at the gun in 3:08.3 and ran a 59.5 lap only to lose by two feet to the 4:07.7 by Jim Newcomb, a 21-year-old Shawnee-Delaware Indian who was a sophomore at Southern California. Newcomb, who ran 9:06.5 behind McMillen's 9:02 2-mile, had improved his mile time from 4:22.9 to 16th on the all-time list.

McMillen dropped out of the AAU 1500 in 95-degree heat and high humidity. In 1951 he ran for Occidental College and won a close Compton victory over Alf Holmberg and Slykhuis in 4:09.0, with Newcomb well back.

1952

In the 1951 NCAA mile, McMillen led at three-quarters in 3:06.4, but his 4:09.5 lost to 4:08.8 by Warren Druetzler, a consistent place-winner in the NCAA 2-mile and cross-country as well as 1951 AAU steeplechase champion.

Obviously lacking the necessary finishing kick, McMillen changed his tactics and mental attitude during the spring of 1952 in a series of experiments. In the Coliseum Relays 1500 he stayed too far back and his fast finish could gain him only fourth place in 3:54.9. At the Compton Invitational mile, he used good tactics but lost to Druetzler by one foot with a time of 4:10.9. In the SPAAU 1500, he tried his old tactics again, with a pace of 58, 2:01, and 3:06. He faded badly to 3:53.8 in third place.

In the NCAA 1500 at Berkeley, McMillen ran easily in last place for the first two laps, then moved up quickly and took the lead before the gun. He ran his last 440 in 57.7 and won in 3:50.7.

In the Final Olympic Trials in the Los Angeles Coliseum, McMillen ran in the middle of the pack behind a 2:04 half, then barely escaped from a box to lead on the last turn. Druetzler, who was the leading indoor miler in 1952 with 4:08.2, challenged on the curve, but McMillen sprinted away to win by ten yards in 3:49.3.

McMillen's last 400 meters in 58.3 and his last 300 in 42.8 led his coach, Payton Jordan, to predict, "He'll run 3:46 in Helsinki."

PATRICK EL MABROUK, after his strong second to Slykhuis in the 1950 European Championships with 3:47.8, lost only two races during his long 1951 season—to Reiff and to Nankeville. He was under 3:50 in four races, with a best of 3:48.2, and he defeated the best Swedes in 3:51.6. He won a mile in 4:08.6.

In 1952, he went into the Olympics undefeated, with times of 3:49.8 and 3:49.4.

JOSY BARTHEL set a national record of 3:55 for Luxemburg in 1946. He became internationally known in 1947 when he ran 1:51.0 and 3:51.0. In 1948 he placed second in the AAA mile in 4:15.4 and ninth in the Olympic 1500. In 1950 he ran 800 meters in 1:51.7 to qualify for the final of the European Championships, but he finished ninth in the final.

In 1951, he ran only 3:52.6, demonstrating how three years of intensive chemical engineering studies had prevented him from improving on his encouraging 1947 times.

Then Woldemar Gerschler became Luxemburg's national coach. Gerschler had coached Harbig to an amazing world record for 800 meters in 1939, but his methods had not yet revolutionized training. The 5'8" Barthel trained so hard on interval work that he lost 22 pounds, to 145. He also improved his speed enough to defeat Olympic medalist Heinz Ulzheimer at 800 meters. And his endurance was enough to defeat Herbert Schade, Olympic 5000 meter medalist,

1952

at 2000 meters.

And yet the experts, unaware of his training, did not take him seriously, for the only evidence of his improvement at 1500 meters came in a solo race in 3:48.5 on June 19.

WERNER LUEG ran 3:54.4 in 1950 at the age of 19. In 1951 he set a German record of 3:49.4. On May 10, 1952, now 21 years old, he ran in a great mile race at Bremen. Günther Dohrow, a half-miler, set the pace with 60.2 and 2:04.4, while Lueg ran last. Lueg moved to the front at 1200 meters in 3:07.0, equal to about 3:08.2 for three-quarters. He finished well in 4:06.4, with his last 120 yards in 15.4. He said, "Is that possible? Am I really faster than Bannister?"

In the German Championships at Berlin on June 29, Dohrow, who had run 4:07.7 behind Lueg, set off at a frantic pace of 56.6. Unable to shake off his pursuer, Dohrow slowed to 1:58.8 for 800 meters and 2:31.0 for 1000 meters. At 1200 meters, Lueg led in a fast 3:00.2 and he pulled away over the last 300 meters to win by 12 yards in 3:43.0, equalling the world record! Dohrow ran 3:44.8 and Rolf Lamers 3:47.4.

Lueg, at 21, was now an Olympic favorite.

THE OLYMPIC SEMI-FINALS were great races in themselves. On July 25, 12 men ran in each heat to qualify the first six to the final, and some superb runners were shut out.

The pace-setter in the first semi-final, with laps of 60.2, 2:05 and 3:07.4, was Denis Johansson, the popular Finnish champion and record holder at 3:47.4. A student at Purdue in the United States, Johansson brought forth great Finnish cheers with a last lap in 56.7 to win the heat in 3:49.4.

Lueg followed easily behind Johansson in 3:49.8, but a fierce fight developed for the other four qualifying places. Fading on the last curve and eliminated were Bill Nankeville, who ran 3:49 in May and won his fourth AAA title in 4:09.8, Mikhail Velsveebel, Soviet record holder with a fast 3:48.2, George Hoskins, New Zealand record holder at 4:11.6, and Bill Parnell, the Canadian record holder at 4:09.6.

Don Macmillan, the gigantic Australian champion who ran 4:08.9 in 1951, finished with power in 3:50.8 along with Druetzler, another tall runner. El Mabrouk, always reliable, was fifth in 3:51.0 alongside Audun Boysen of Norway, a fast half-miler who ran 3:50.2 in 1951 at the age of 22.

Cevona, who ran 3:49.6 in June, and Landqvist, in shape to run 3:48.0 in June, were others who disappointed their followers, both eliminated with 3:51.4.

In the second semi-final, John Ross, a promising Canadian sophomore at Michigan who won the Big Ten indoor and outdoor miles in 4:09.4 and 4:10.7, set the early pace with 62.0 and 2:07.6

before fading badly. Nikolay Byelokurov of the USSR, a 3:48.6 man, led at 1200 meters in 3:07.6 then dropped to the rear as the pace quickened.

Dohrow also faded unexpectedly. Next to lose out were Vilmos Tölgyesi, Hungary's 3:50.2 man, and Frans Herman, the Belgian champion who had run 3:49.2 in June. Into the homestretch, seven men fought for six places. All of them finished within four yards of Barthel's winning 3:50.4. The unlucky non-qualifier, in 3:51.0, was Stanislav Jungwirth, the 21-year-old Czech comer who had run 3:47.2 on June 15. Bannister, fourth alongside Aberg, Ericsson, and McMillen, felt "blown and unhappy." The sixth finisher was Rolf Lamers.

THE OLYMPIC FINAL

The 12 finalists, surely below their best after two days of hard heats, lined up on a curved track at the beginning of the backstretch of the red-brick track not far from the majestic statue of Paavo Nurmi.

Johansson, in the blue shirt of Finland, had the pole position, but the eager Boysen broke to the front. Lamers, from lane ten, forged into the lead, followed by Lueg.

Lamers passed 400 meters in 57.8, far too fast. He slowed, and ran the next lap in 63.6 for an 800 time of 2:01.4. Lueg was close behind, followed by Boysen, Druetzler, El Mabrouk, and Bannister, who says, "I was content to keep to the inside, because I was too tired to struggle."

Then, on the backstretch, Lueg moved into the lead. At 1000 meters in 2:32.8, he began to push the pace faster. Barthel was poised on his shoulder, full of run. Aberg was running outside Lamers. Behind them came three runners in tandem—Johansson on the pole, Boysen alongside, and El Mabrouk out in the second lane, eager to race. Behind them came another trio—side-by-side— Druetzler badly boxed on the pole, then Bannister, and Ericsson. Behind Druetzler came the Australian, Macmillan. Still running last, relaxed and saving ground, came the American hope, McMillen.

Thus, they were all bunched aggressively within about six yards as they ran down the stretch toward the corner of the stadium where the Olympic torch burned on top of the 22-story tower . . . and toward the bell.

As the rabid crowd thundered, Aberg moved ahead of Lamers and El Mabrouk moved up before the bell clanged. Around the turn they were poised for their final drive and when Lueg passed the starting line in 3:03, the action became almost chaotic.

Aberg made a run at Lueg, but the young German held him

1952

off and Aberg fell back, a beaten man. El Mabrouk drove for the lead, but he could not get past Lueg. Then came Bannister, and for a moment it looked as if he had the race under control. "But my legs were aching, and I had no strength left to force them faster. I had a sickening feeling of exhaustion and powerlessness."

The speed of the front runners cracked Druetzler, and he fell behind. Also hopelessly out of contention were Boysen, Johansson, and Macmillan.

Lueg led safely into the last turn and began a hard drive which opened a lead of three yards. Barthel, unnoticed in the middle of the pack since the backstretch action began, moved suddenly and surprisingly into second place. McMillen was moving impressively, too, and he passed Bannister and El Mabrouk on the inside.

As they turned into the homestretch, Lueg maintained his lead and seemed victorious. Barthel, three yards back, was full of fight, as was McMillen behind him. Bannister was on McMillen's shoulder, in good position but exhausted. El Mabrouk was also in contention on Bannister's shoulder, but all he had left was courage. Lamers was sixth, three yards behind McMillen, with no chance.

Down the stretch, with the crowd wildly excited, Barthel and McMillen were gaining while Bannister and El Mabrouk were losing with extreme reluctance. Suddenly, 50 yards from the beckoning tape, Lueg began to tie up and Barthel gained more rapidly. The crowd was raving mad as McMillen was in full sprint now, gaining very slowly on Barthel.

Both men swept past the unfortunate Lueg, with McMillen obviously catching Barthel. It became a dramatic race to determine whether McMillen could catch Barthel before the tape, but the tape came first and Barthel won Olympic glory by almost two feet in one of the most exciting of all the great races.

Five yards behind, Bannister barely fought off El Mabrouk for fourth, while Lamers held off Aberg for sixth. Don Macmillan finished with a frenzied rush which left Boysen far back and cut down Johansson before the finish line.

Results: Barthel 3:45.1 (officially rounded off at 3:45.2), McMillen 3:45.2, Lueg 3:45.4, Bannister 3:46.0, El Mabrouk 3:46.0, Lamers 3:46.8, Aberg 3:47.0, Ericsson 3:47.6, Macmillan 3:49.6, Johansson 3:49.8, Boysen 3:51.4, Druetzler 3:56.0.

Thus, the first eight finishers bettered Lovelock's Olympic record. McMillen's last lap was well under 57 seconds. Barthel's last 300 meters was in 41.7 and McMillen's about 41.3. National records were set by Barthel, Bob McMillen, Bannister, El Mabrouk, and Don Macmillan.

Barthel mounted the victory stand, heard the national anthem of his nation of 300,000 people, and shed tears of joy.

1952

REIFF, THIRD FASTEST

Six days after the Olympic 1500 meter final, the famed Dickson Mile was run in Gävle, Sweden. Reiff, who had dropped out of the Olympic 5000, followed a pace-setter through the 440 in 61 and the 880 in 2:02. Then he pushed the pace hard to get away from a fast field and he passed three quarters in 3:03.8. Even at that pace, Aberg challenged on the last turn, but Reiff held him off. In the homestretch, Ericsson made a run at Reiff while the Swedish crowd roared, but the strong Belgian stayed ahead for a close victory.

Results: Reiff 4:03.4, Ericsson 4:03.6, Aberg 4:04.2, Sune Karlsson 4:05.8, Herman 4:05.9.

Only Hägg and Andersson had run faster than Reiff and Ericsson—Hägg twice and Andersson three times.

This race, along with the Olympics, proved beyond question that 1952 was a turning point in the history of mile racing. Harder training, especially of the interval type, was changing all concepts of how fast a mile could be run.

Reiff lowered the world 2-mile record to 8:40.4 on August 26. After a big race against Barthel, he ran a mile on September 13 in Antwerp against Macmillan, the tall Australian. Macmillan, who had run 4:08.8 three days before, pushed the pace sensationally with converted times of 59.5, 2:00.2, and 3:02.3. While Macmillan faded to 4:12.0, Reiff passed 1500 meters in 3:47.6, then finished fast in 4:02.8, solidifying his position as third fastest miler of all time. Three weeks later, however, he ran against Nielsen.

GUNNAR NIELSEN was near the top as a half-miler, running 1:49.7 for fourth in the Olympics and 1:49.9 in defeating Boysen. He lost to Aberg's world record for 1000 meters at Copenhagen on August 10, 2:21.8 to 2:21.3. In Paris on October 4, he ran a mile against Reiff and Boysen.

Reiff was favored off his 4:02.8 and his world record for two miles and Boysen was an Olympic finalist while Nielsen was unknown as a miler. Reiff set the pace at 3:05.6, with Nielsen third. Reiff and Boysen passed 1500 meters in 3:49.6, but Nielsen finished in 15.0 for a 4:04.8 victory.

BARTHEL IS INVINCIBLE

Winner over Lueg at Zurich on August 12, 3:45.6 to 3:47.0, Barthel's biggest race was on August 20, when 4000 spectators at the Luxemburg Stadium saw their Olympic champion seriously challenged at 1500 meters by Olympic runner-up Bob McMillen and 4:03.4 miler Gaston Reiff.

Barthel trailed an impulsive hare who ran 57.6 for the first

400 meters and 2:01 for 800. Reiff and McMillen, who calmly held back through the fast first lap, almost closed the gap, with Druetzler and Herman farther back.

Predictably, Reiff wanted the lead and he passed 1200 meters in 3:02. McMillen, who had been racing every other day, passed Reiff and led around the last curve. Into the homestretch, the fearful crowd saw Reiff second, but Barthel was on his shoulder.

The little Olympic champion rushed past both runners to a decisive victory, while McMillen barely held off Reiff.

Results: Barthel 3:44.6, McMillen 3:45.2, Reiff 3:45.2, Herman 3:47.6, Druetzler 3:47.8.

These times were national records for Barthel and Reiff, and McMillen tied his own record. Druetzler moved to second on the U.S. all-time list, ahead of Walter Mehl.

With no real opposition, running in Luxemburg in cold, windy weather on September 4, Barthel followed pace-setters through laps of 56.5, 1:56.5, and 2:59.3 in a world-record attempt. All he needed was 43.5 for the last 300 meters, compared to his 41.7 in the Olympics, and about 42.4 in his 3:44.6 race. But the pace was too fast and he could finish no faster than 44.8 for a time of 3:44.1. This moved him up one place on the all-time list, to sixth.

In his last race of the year, on September 24 in Brussels, Barthel ran 3:45.8 to beat Karlsson and Ericsson by 20 yards. Thus, he completed a wonderful season undefeated.

JOHN LANDY

No better than a 4:38 miler at 19 and 4:19 at 20, Landy ran 4:11 at 21. He was eliminated in a heat of the 1952 Olympic 1500 at the age of 22. Then he went to work.

He trained hard—two to three hours a day—for four months. His favorite workout was 600 yards at a pace of about 65 seconds per 440 yards. He repeated this eight to 12 times with a four-minute jog in between for recovery. This was done five times a week. He also ran seven miles at an easier pace at least three times a week. While spending long hours on his studies, he usually had to train around midnight.

Toward the end of this intensive training program, Landy ran 4:17 on October 25 and 4:14.8 on November 15. On December 13, 1952, he was ready to surprise the track world.

At Olympic Park in Melbourne, before a crowd of 2000, Landy ran against Les Perry, good enough to place sixth in the Olympic 5000 meters. Landy took the lead at 300 yards on the cinder track and passed the first quarter in 59.2.

Nobody seemed excited at the pace, but when the 5:11½", 154-pounder passed the half in 2:01, interest picked up. And when he passed three quarters in 3:03 and showed no sign of fatigue, the few knowledgeable fans became excited. Macmillan's Australian record of 4:08.9 seemed certain to fall.

Then the few experts present—and in retrospect, the whole world—watched in amazement as this slim, dark-haired miler, who had never bettered 4:11, accelerated his pace. He actually ran faster! His speed was as great as at the start, and he completed the last lap in 59.1. His time was a startling 4:02.1, bettered only by Hägg and Andersson. Perry finished in a personal record 4:13.

On January 3, 1953, on Melbourne's Olympic Park's hard and dry cinder track, Landy made a serious attempt to run a mile under the coveted four minutes.

After his 4:02.1 three weeks earlier, he said he needed to pass the 880 in 1:59 to run four minutes, and in this race Les Perry paced him to 58.6 and 1:59.4. Landy took over by himself on the difficult third lap and passed three quarters in 3:01.

Around the turn he ran well, and down the backstretch he increased his pace with the wind at his back. He raced into the turn and passed 1500 meters in 3:44.4, a time bettered by only six men. He needed to run 15.6 for a four-flat mile.

But those last 120 yards proved Landy's limit in this race was 1500 meters. Heading into the wind he tied up badly in the homestretch and struggled home with a slow 18.4. His mile time was 4:02.8.

Landy thus proved to be a remarkable solo runner. No other runner had ever run so well without the spur of competition on the last lap. He said, "I have conditioned myself to think in terms of solo running, as there is no alternative to record-breaking in Australia."

1952
1,500m:

Time	Runner	Place	City	Date
3:43.0	Werner Lueg (Germany)	(1)	Berlin	29 Jun
3:44.1	Josy Barthel (Luxemburg)	(1)	Luxemburg	4 Sep
3:44.8	Günther Dohrow (Germany)	(2)	Berlin	29 Jun
3:45.2	Bob McMillen (USA)	(2)	Helsinki	26 Jul
3:45.2	Gaston Reiff (Belgium)	(3)	Luxemburg	20 Aug
3:46.0	Roger Bannister (GB)	(4)	Helsinki	26 Jul
3:46.0	Patrick El Mabrouk (France)	(5)	Helsinki	26 Jul
3:46.4	Ingvar Ericsson (Sweden)	(2)	Düsseldorf	14 Sep
3:46.8	Olle Aberg (Sweden)	(1)	Stockholm	4 Jul
3:46.8	Rolf Lamers (Germany)	(6)	Helsinki	26 Jul
3:47.2	Stanislav Jungwirth (Czechosl)	(1)	St. Boleslav	15 Jun
3:47.2	Sune Karlsson (Sweden)	(2)	Malmö	6 Aug

Mile:

Time	Runner	Place	City	Date
4:02.1	John Landy (Australia)	(1)	Melbourne	13 Dec
4:02.8	Gaston Reiff (Belgium)	(1)	Antwerp	13 Sep
4:03.6	Ingvar Ericsson (Sweden)	(1)	Gävle	1 Aug
4:04.2	Olle Aberg (Sweden)	(2)	Gävle	1 Aug
4:04.8	Gunnar Nielsen (Denmark)	(1)	Paris	4 Oct
4:05.8	Sune Karlsson (Sweden)	(4)	Gävle	1 Aug
4:05.9	Frans Herman (Belgium)	(5)	Gävle	1 Aug
4:06.4	Werner Lueg (Germany)	(1)	Bremen	10 May
4:07.2	Audun Boysen (Norway)	(3)	Paris	4 Oct
4:07.7	Günther Dohrow (Germany)	(2)	Bremen	10 May
4:08.0	Rolf Lamers (Germany)	(3)	Bremen	10 May

1952

Noteworthy Indoor Marks:
4:08.2	Warren Druetzler (USA)	(1)	New York	22 Mar
4:08.4	Don Gehrmann (USA)	(1)	Milwaukee	1 Feb
4:09.4	John Ross (Canada)	(1)	Champaign	8 Mar

BANNISTER SETS A NEW GOAL

On June 27, 1953, at the famous Motspur Park track, an almost secret mile run was inserted into the Surrey Schools athletic meeting. Bannister made an attempt to run the four-minute mile, aided by Chris Brasher, a close friend who had placed eleventh in the 1952 Olympic steeplechase, and Don Macmillan, now living in England.

Bannister had spent two months deciding whether he wanted to continue running after the Olympics. Then, in his half hour a day, he intensified his training to a hard interval type. He decided to try to become the first man to run a mile in less than four minutes, and his effort was to be made at Oxford. In the meantime he made an attempt on the British record at Oxford on May 2, paced by Chris Chataway, and ran 61.7, 2:04.1, 3:05.2, and 4:03.6. "This race made me realize that the four-minute mile was not out of reach."

On May 23, he won the mile in the British Games in 4:09.4 with a last lap in 56.6. A week later he suffered a muscle injury while running a fast 440, and he was required to rest. But, "In eight days I was dancing, and after ten days I was running gently." After a few days of slow running he ran two half-miles under two minutes each. Friends then talked him into this paced mile, but he knew nothing of the details.

Macmillan set a stiff pace, with Bannister timed in 59.6 and 1:59.7. Macmillan had to give up after 2½ laps, but Brasher had run at a more moderate pace and now, a lap behind, he was there to aid Bannister the rest of the way.

Bannister passed three quarters in 3:01.8. He finished in 4:02.0, faster than anyone since Hägg and Andersson, but British officials did not allow it as a British record. Bannister said, "My feeling as I look back is one of great relief that I did not run a four-minute mile under such artificial circumstances." He won the AAA mile in 4:05.2 and finished 1953 undefeated.

WES SANTEE

Nationally known as a freshman at Kansas in 1951 after running 4:23.8 and 9:21.6 in postal meets, the tall, thin, short-striding farm boy entered the AAU meet at Berkeley. He set a new record of 15:03.4 in the junior 5000 meters, then ran in the senior race the next day. He beat Semper and Capozzoli for second in 14:52.4. At 19, he was America's premier distance prospect.

1953

On April 25 and 26, 1952, he became its major mile prospect. The 6'1", 140-pounder started his anchor leg at the Drake Relays 40 yards behind Joe LaPierre. Santee was still 20 yards behind with 150 yards to go, but his sensational finish won by four yards. He was timed by the meet referee in 4:06.7 and by Coach Bill Easton in 4:07.5. The next day he started an anchor leg 45 yards behind and won overwhelmingly by 50, with a mile timed in 4:07.4 and 4:08.3.

He ran 4:08.8 in a dual meet with Kansas State on May 3. His next good race came in the NCAA, where he won the 5000 meters in 14:36.3, with his last 880 in 2:10.3. This made him the fourth fastest American and he said, "I could have cut many seconds off this particular race."

In the AAU 1500, the pace was slow and with two laps to go, Santee took off in the exciting manner of Cunningham and left the field behind. He ran that lap in 61 and the last in 59.8 to win in 3:49.3, fastest American time in 12 years.

Santee was eliminated in a heat of the Olympic 5000, then showed talent with a 1:51.2 800 in Vienna on August 6. In 1953 indoor meets he was undefeated in both 880 and mile races. He won the Big 7 meet in 4:08.3 and completed a great double with a 1:52.5 880. In the outdoor Big 7, at Ames, Iowa, on May 23, he set a collegiate mile record of 4:06.3, to break Cunningham's 19-year-old mark. Then he came back with a 1:50.8 victory in the half. A week later he won in the Missouri Valley AAU with 4:07.4 and 1:54.5.

Santee ran a stunning mile at the Compton Invitational in Compton, California, June 5, against Reiff, who had been bothered by a hairline fracture in his foot, and Johansson, who won at the Coliseum Relays in 4:08.6 three weeks ago.

A high school runner acted as hare and led by a ridiculous 50 yards at the half. Reiff set the real pace with 62.7, followed by Santee with his short, choppy stride. The slow pace continued and they passed the half in 2:05.2 and the crowd groaned. The slow pace did not change around the turn and nobody had any reason to believe they were about to see something startling.

Into the backstretch, Santee burst into a hard drive. Caught napping, Johansson took up the pursuit five yards behind, and Reiff followed. Johansson gained a yard and at the ¾ pole Santee led in 3:03.5. His third lap was a powerful 58.2 even after a slow first curve.

Santee pulled away and on the backstretch he led Reiff by 15 yards. He had run a lap in about 55 seconds! Into the turn, Johansson flew past Reiff and began to gain. Santee's flowing stride began to drag and he slowed a little, but he won by more than ten yards.

Results: Santee 4:02.4, Johansson 4:04.0, Reiff 4:05.7.

1953

Santee could not stop smiling. He jogged a lap of honor in acknowledgement of the fourth fastest winning mile of all time. His last 880 in 1:57.1 and last three quarters in 2:59.5 were unprecedented. He said, "I didn't think it was so fast."

In unpleasantly hot weather at Lincoln, Nebraska, on June 20, Santee was in sixth place in 59.5 as the runners completed the first lap of the important NCAA mile. On the second lap, Santee was third in 2:04.2. Exactly as at Compton, Santee waited until he had completed the next curve before he launched into his killing drive. He built up a 25-yard lead on second-place Fred Dwyer at the three quarters in 3:04. Dwyer, who had run 4:08.1 indoors, gained a little on the last lap.

Santee's good 4:03.7 broke Zamperini's 15-year-old meet record. Dwyer's 4:07.1 moved him ahead of San Romani and Lash to fifth on the U.S. list.

The AAU mile was run in the sweltering heat of Dayton, Ohio. Santee was in the lead by 660 yards and he led in 2:04.3 and 3:05.5, but the heat was too high for fast times. He won in 4:07.6 to 4:12.1 for Dwyer.

Santee ran too many races in Europe after the AAU meet—thirteen 1500/mile races and seven 800's. He lost twice to Johansson, although he ran 3:47.6 in the third race. He ran a fast half-mile in 1:49.9, losing to Whitfield on July 17. On July 21, he won a mile in 4:06.6 from Ericsson.

On July 23, at Göteborg's famous Slottsskogsvallen, rain had soaked the track and it was apparently not as fast as usual. Nils Toft, a 3:49.0 runner, started at a fast pace, passing 400 meters in 57.5. Only Sune Karlsson, the latest fast Swede, would follow him. Karlsson had run 3:47.2 and 4:05.8 in 1952 and in 1953 he was undefeated with times of 3:46.4, 3:46.0 and 3:44.2.

At 800 meters in 1:57.5, Santee and Ericsson were 12 meters behind. Toft had to give up, but Karlsson carried on alone, passing 1200 meters in 2:58.4. Santee was still ten meters behind, with Ericsson on his heels. The knowledgeable crowd, accustomed to fast battles, cheered what appeared to be a world record in the making.

Santee began to gain on both his opponents, and Ericsson was gaining slowly on Karlsson. To the dismay of the crowd, Santee closed the distance between them around the last curve, and into the homestretch he pulled alongside Karlsson.

Karlsson increased his speed desperately, and the two runners ran side by side in one of the most savage of all duels. At the finish, Santee managed to fight his way four inches ahead.

Results: Santee 3:44.2, Karlsson 3:44.2, Ericsson 3:45.2.

Santee's new American record made him seventh on the all-time list, along with Karlsson.

1953

OTHER RUNNERS

SUNE KARLSSON lost again after his disappointing loss to Santee. Then he came back courageously with a 4:04.4 mile at Gävle on August 7 and he won the Swedish Championship in 3:45.6. Against Great Britain he was pushed to 3:45.8 by Nankeville's bestever time of 3:46.6. He lost his last two races of the year, to Ericsson. No other runner in history had ever run the fast 3:46—4:04.8 equivalents more than the five times recorded by Arne Andersson in 1945 until Karlsson did it six times in 1953.

DENIS JOHANSSON had a badly mixed year. In addition to his non-winning 4:04.0 mile at Compton he had a non-winning 3:45.2 behind Karlsson at Gävle. Following that race, he defeated Santee twice in a row, running 3:44.8 at Pori on July 10. He triumphed over both Ericsson and Karlsson in the Finnish-Swedish dual meet in 3:48.6. And he won against Yugoslavia in 3:46.6. On the negative side, he lost seven races, including his eleventh place when he fell in the Finnish Championships.

WERNER LUEG lost only one race all season, an unimportant tactical contest. He won miles in 4:06.6 and 4:07.8, and 1500's in 3:48.0, 3:47.0, and 3:48.4. He edged Santee in Berlin on August 2, 3:52.4 to 3:52.6.

COMBINED LIST THROUGH THE 1953 EUROPEAN SEASON:

(3:42.7)	4:01.3	Hägg	1945
(3:42.9)	4:01.6	Andersson	1944
3:43.0	(4:01.7)	Strand	1947
3:43.0	(4:01.7)	Lueg	1952
(3:43.3)	4:02.0	Bannister	1953
(3:43.5)	4:02.1	Landy	1952
(3:43.7)	4:02.4	Santee	1953
3:43.8	(4:02.5)	Slykhuis	1949
(3:44.1)	4:02.8	Reiff	1952
3:44.1	(4:02.8)	Barthel	1952
3:44.2	(4:03.0)	Karlsson	1953
3:44.4n	(4:03.1)	Eriksson	1947

1953
1,500m:

3:44.2	Sune Karlsson (Sweden)	(1)	Gävle	23	Jun
3:44.2	Wes Santee (USA)	(1)	Göteborg	23	Jul
3:44.4+	John Landy (Australia)	(1)	Melbourne	3	Jan
3:44.8+	Roger Bannister (GB)	(1)	Motspur Park	27	Jun
3:44.8	Denis Johansson (Finland)	(1)	Pori	10	Jul
3:45.0	Stanislav Jungwirth (Czechosl.)	(1)	Opava	30	May
3:45.2	Ingvar Ericsson (Sweden)	(3)	Göteborg	23	Jul
3:46.6	Ernö Béres (Hungary)	(2)	Bucharest	9	Aug
3:46.6	Bill Nankeville (GB)	(2)	Stockholm	3	Sep
3:46.8	Ilmari Taipale (Finland)	(2)	Pori	10	Jul
3:47.0	Werner Lueg (Germany)	(1)	Gelsenkirchen	18	Aug

Mile:

4:02.0	Roger Bannister (GB)	(1)	Motspur Park	27	Jun
4:02.0	John Landy (Australia)	(1)	Melbourne	12	Dec
4:02.4	Wes Santee (USA)	(1)	Compton	5	Jun
4:04.0	Denis Johansson (Finland)	(2)	Compton	5	Jun
4:04.4	Sune Karlsson (Sweden)	(1)	Gävle	7	Aug

1953

4:05.7	Gaston Reiff (Belgium)	(3)	Compton	5	Jun
4:06.6	Werner Lueg (Germany)	(1)	Vienna	16	Jun
4:06.8	Gordon Pirie (GB)	(1)	London	8	Aug
4:07.1	Fred Dwyer (USA)	(2)	Lincoln	20	Jun
4:07.4	Bill Nankeville (GB)	(1)	London	9	Sep
4:07.4	Audun Boysen (Norway)	(2)	London	9	Sep

Noteworthy Indoor Marks:

4:07.8	Len Truex (USA)	(1)	Milwaukee	14	Mar
4:08.1	Fred Dwyer (USA)	(1)	New York	21	Feb
4:08.3	Wes Santee (USA)	(1)	Kansas City	28	Feb

LANDY TRIES FOR FOUR MINUTES

At Melbourne, on December 12, 1953, Landy made an all-out effort in a solo mile where the only other finisher was 200 yards behind. After a year of training 50% harder than ever before, and after three easy races, he was ready to take advantage of some rare weather.

He ran his first lap in 58.2 and reached the half in 1:58.6. Excitement grew as he passed the three quarters in 3:00.2. He slowed slightly on the last lap, but he reached 1500 meters in an excellent 3:44.4, equal to his pace of January 3. He could equal the world record with 17 seconds over the last 120 yards.

But he was nearly exhausted and a stiff breeze had developed during the race, blowing against him at 6.1 meters per second in the homestretch. He slowed woefully to 17.6 seconds for a mile time of 4:02.0.

This made him equal to Bannister in third place on the all-time mile list, but he was pessimistic about his chances . . . up against a psychological barrier. He said, "If Hägg and Andersson, with several years of hectic rivalry, couldn't go below 4:01.4, what hope have I got here, with *no* competition at all? . . . I can see now what a colossal task it is. Perhaps I can reduce my time by half a second, but more likely it will be by only a fifth."

Three more times, early in 1954, Landy made a serious assault on the four-minute mile:

1. On January 21, in Melbourne's first twilight meet, 20,000 people jammed Olympic Park in excellent weather. Landy ran 59.0, 2:00.3, and 3:02.2. He passed 1500 meters in 3:45.8 and finished in 16.6 for 4:02.4.

Disappointed and depressed, he said, "I thought I had it. I couldn't hear the lap times above the roar of the crowd."

2. On February 23, after winning the Australian Championship in 4:05.6 12 days earlier on a wet grass track, he tried again in another Melbourne twilight meet before 5000 spectators. In spite of a cold 30-mile wind, he followed a pace-setter through optimistic laps of 57.5 and 1:59.0. On his own, he passed three quarters in 3:01.0 and 1500 meters in 3:45.4. But those last miserable 120 yards took him 17.2 seconds, for 4:02.6.

1954

This was definitely a better effort, considering the wind, but pessimism took over. He felt stymied above 4:02.

3. Aftet four more miles under 4:10, with one at 4:05.9, Landy made his last effort of the Australian season on Bendigo's fast grass track in perfect weather on April 19. His only handicap was a football boot-stud which caught on one of his spikes for most of the distance.

He trailed a hare again, paced well this time at 59.0 and 1:59.4. On his own, he ran 3:02.0. His 1500 meter time was a disappointing 3:46.4, but he had been working on some suggestions from Percy Cerutty and he finished faster than before in 16.2, for 4:02.6.

With his new faster finish, and fast conditions in Finland ahead of him, he still hoped to be first under four minutes.

BANNISTER MAKES HIS EFFORT

Bannister read reports of Landy's efforts with interest and suspense. He expected Landy to break four minutes each time. This was to be Bannister's last season of racing and he felt certain he could run under four minutes.

He trained seriously for an hour each noon with Brasher. He spent one evening a week with Franz Stampfl, and his training followed Stampfl's principles of careful improvement. He trained weekends with Chataway. Doing repeat quarters and sprints, he reached a frustrating peak where he could run ten quarters in 61 with two minutes rest between, but he could run no faster. Needing a change, he and Brasher went mountain climbing for three days. On his return, properly rested, Bannister could run those quarters in 59.

His attempt was scheduled for May 6 on the Iffley Road track at Oxford when the British AAA team met Oxford, and he rested luxuriously for five full days before the race. "I had reached my peak physically and psychologically. There would never be another day like it."

The momentous day started with his usual morning at the hospital. Then he rode the train to Oxford, talking with Stampfl. His main concern was the strong wind, for the Iffley Road track was open on all sides. But after lunch with friends, Chataway convinced him he should not make a decision until time for the race.

At 5:15 p.m. a light rain fell. As they warmed up, still in doubt, the wind began to gust and it slowed hopefully. At race time the wind was about 15 miles per hour and Bannister decided to try.

Six runners started, and Brasher set the pace with Bannister close behind. After 220 yards, Bannister felt effortless and he called, "Faster," but his time was 28.7 and Brasher calmly continued the pace. Bannister passed the 440 in 57.5 and felt relieved that Brasher

had retained his poise.
Stampfl yelled, "Relax," and Bannister relaxed. He felt no strain as the next two 220's slowed to 30.0 and 30.7 for 1:58.2. Around the turn, Chataway sprang purposefully to the lead and continued the pace with 220's in 31.4 and 30.9. Bannister passed three quarters in 3:00.5 and felt it was a barely perceptible effort, so complete was his mental control.
Patiently, he followed Chataway's lead around the curve and then, on the last backstretch, he started his drive. His determined pace took him past the 1540-yard mark in 3:30.5. He had to break 29.5 to reach his goal, but his body was rapidly losing its strength.
He passed 1500 meters in an unofficial 3:43, equal to the world record. Only will power drove him now. "Those last few seconds seemed never-ending." His face was contorted with agony as 1200 spectators screamed themselves hoarse. He did not let down until he reached the tape and fell into waiting arms. "It was only then that real pain overtook me."
The announcement in the solemn voice of Norris McWhirter was a classic of planned understatement and suspense: "Ladies and gentlemen, here is the result of event number nine, the one mile: First, number 41, R.G. Bannister, Amateur Athletic Association and formerly of Exeter and Merton Colleges, Oxford, with a time which is a new meeting and track record, and which, subject to ratification, will be a new English Native, British National, British all-comers' European, British Empire, and World's Record. The time was THREE..."
Further words were drowned by a roar from the spectators.
The four-minute mile had been run. The 25-year-old, 6'1¼", 154-pound medical student had run 3:59.4. He broke Hägg's nine-year-old record by two seconds, the most the mile record had been lowered since 1874.
For a few moments, Bannister slumped, barely conscious. But after the announcement, he grabbed Chataway and Brasher, and the three trotted a lap of honor.
"I felt suddenly and gloriously free of the burden of athletic ambition that I had been carrying for years. No words could be invented for such supreme happiness, eclipsing all other feelings. I thought at that moment I could never again reach such a climax of single-mindedness."
He slept only two hours that night, and next day he was back at work at St. Mary's hospital, which had hoisted the Union Jack.

SANTEE HAS HIS TURN

After Landy's "failures" and Bannister's success, Santee had his chance. Ineligible for the NCAA in his senior year at Kansas

1954

because he had competed in the AAU as a freshman representing Kansas, he had to report to Marine camp before the 1953 AAU meet.

In the Sugar Bowl on December 31, he ran 4:04.2 with a last lap in a sensational 55.0. Indoors in 1954, he ran 4:04.9 and 4:06.5 with a relay leg in 4:02.6. Outdoors, against the University of California on April 10 in Berkeley, he had a spectacular day. He won the mile in 4:05.5, the half in 1:51.5, and ran a 48-flat relay leg. The next week he ran 4:03.1 at the Kansas Relays. By the end of May he was ready to try his best. Here is what happened on three exciting week-ends:

1. At Kansas City on May 29, he complained of a strained muscle in his left leg before the Missouri Valley AAU meet. He followed Kansas teammates while running 58 flat, 2:00.2, and 3:02. Then he finished with a good 59.3 for 4:01.3, equaling Hägg's actual time in his official world record. Only Bannister's time was faster than Santee's.

2. At the Compton Invitational on the night of June 4, Santee was ready for a new record. Ingvar Ericsson was in the competition but his condition was too poor to give Santee any help. Santee was in front at 2½ laps, having passed the 440 in 58.1 and the half in a promising 1:58.7.

At three quarters, Santee's time was a startling 2:59.0, 1½ seconds faster than Bannister's pace. Santee maintained his speed around the curve and down the backstretch. With half a lap to go his time was 3:28.7—1.8 seconds faster than Bannister—and the crowd of 8000 was nearly mad with excitement.

Then Santee's normally short stride became even shorter as he began to tie up. He was struggling when he reached the 1500 meter tape on the curve. His time was 3:42.8, a new world record.

He was still trying, but his pace was slowing with every stride. He strained down the homestretch with the 1500 tape flying behind him and the crowd screaming for a record, but he could not do it. His last agonizing 120 yards required 17.8 seconds and his time was 4:00.6 . . . only the second best in history.

Santee's coach, Bill Easton said, "Wes has a tendency to tie up in cold weather . . . Considering the existing weather conditions, that was probably the greatest mile ever run." The temperature was 63 degrees and the crowd had not considered the wind strong, but meet director Herschel Smith insisted it was the coldest, windiest Compton Invitational of them all.

3. The night after his great Compton race, Santee beat Mal Whitfield in the Pacific AAU meet in Stockton, Calif. On a hard dirt track, sticky from a surprise shower, Santee ran 1:50.0 to hand Whitfield his first defeat in more than three years. Six days later Santee was in the Los Angeles Coliseum for a serious SPAAU mile against Josy Barthel.

The little Olympic champion had never returned to his 1952 form. His fastest 1500 in 1953 was a non-winning 3:49.2. In 1954 he was studying at Harvard and he ran indoors. Undefeated, he had good times of 4:07.7, 4:07.5, 4:08.5, and then won the AAU in 4:11.7. On May 15 in a special mile at the Heptagonal Games, he beat Dwyer by more than five yards in 4:06.3.

At the last moment before the race started, Barthel generously volunteered to help push the pace on the last lap. Santee followed a pace-setter who ran 59.5. At the half he trailed a 1:59.5 by the formerly fast Swede, Sture Landqvist, now a student at Oklahoma A&M. Barthel came alongside Santee as they started the last lap in three minutes flat.

The gallant little Luxemburg runner took the lead and pushed the pace around to the backstretch. Then Santee went into the lead and Barthel faded uncomfortably to 4:09.9. Santee had more left than at Compton, but his pace had been slower. He passed 1500 meters in 3:43.6 and finished in 17.1 for a 4:00.7 mile, third fastest ever run.

Santee said the weather was too cold, and Whitfield said the track was dead, but the fact remained that Bannister was the only one of the big three to run under four minutes. Santee had now run three of the five fastest miles ever run.

LANDY MAKES HIS PILGRIMAGE

After his 4:02.6 at Bendigo, Landy traveled with hope in his heart to Turku, Finland, and the fastest distance track in the world. He arrived on May 3 and put in 25 days of intensive interval training. After this fast work, he rested two days for his effort on May 31.

Denis Johansson, Landy's host, was his main opposition, but Johansson could run no faster than 4:11.8, and so Landy set his own pace. The track was faster than he realized, and in spite of cold, windy weather, he ran 56.5 and 1:55.8 (estimated from metric times). He reached three quarters in 2:58, broke the 1500 meter tape in 3:43.4, and struggled to the end in 18.2 seconds for a 4:01.6 mile. It was his fastest time, but not what he had come to Finland to achieve. His last 440 was only 63.6.

On June 8 in Stockholm, Landy ran in very cold weather (48 degrees) on a wet track in the 1912 Olympic Stadium. His opposition was supposed to come from fast Sune Karlsson, but Karlsson was in poor early-season condition and once again Landy was on his own.

After more sensible quarters of 59.7 and 1:59.7 (calculated) behind Toft, Landy passed three quarters in 3:01 and then slowed to 1500 meters in 3:45.6. He showed 8,125 spectators his greatest ever kick as he finished in 16 flat. His time was again 4:01.6. Although the weather and his faster finish contained elements pointing to further improvement, he could not help thinking he had reached his limit.

Landy ran an unimportant solo race at Helsinki on June 11 in wind and rain, winning the 1500 in 3:46.4. On June 16, at Imatra in good weather, he ran the equal-fifth fastest 2000 meters ever, in 5:12.6, but this was not why he had come.

On Monday, June 21, at 7:00 p.m. in Turku, the weather was ideal, and Chris Chataway had come from England to help Landy. The leader at 400 meters clocked 58 flat. Landy, close behind, probably ran about 58.5 for 440 yards.

Landy took the lead at 700 meters and passed 800 in 1:57.9, followed by Chataway. Feeling stronger than ever before, Landy picked up the pace. His next 200 meters took only 29.3 seconds and he passed 1200 meters in a sizzling 2:56.0—a 400-meter lap in 58.1. (His three-quarters time is estimated at 2:57.2.)

With Chataway on his heels, Landy tried to accelerate around the curve, and he pulled ahead rapidly. But he could not hold such a pace, and he slowed. Once again he felt fatigue dragging him down, but he fought with all his considerable courage.

He passed 1500 meters in 3:41.8, one wonderful second under Santee's 17-days-old record. Now he only had to run those last cruel 120 yards in 18 seconds to be under four minutes. But he had run slower than that before and he had never attempted a pace as fast as this.

He fought down the homestretch with the Finns cheering wildly, and miraculously he was not tying up. His slender legs kept moving in tempo and he gave it everything he had. His long, hard training—surely the hardest of any miler before him—paid off, and he ran those last 120 yards in 16.1.

His time was 3:57.9.

In one jump he had broken his barrier by 3.7 seconds and passed Andersson, Hägg, Santee, and Bannister. He no longer had reason for pessimism.

Results: Landy 3:57.9, Chataway 4:04.4 (1500 in 3:45.4), Vuorisalo of Finland 4:07.0, Johansson 4:07.6, Taipale 4:10.6. Landy's time became the official world record at 3:58.0.

THE MIRACLE MILE

It was the mile championship of the British Empire Games in Vancouver, Canada, on August 7, but they called it the "Miracle Mile" because it was Bannister and Landy, the only two sub-four-minute milers, running against each other in top condition.

Bannister had felt let down after his 3:59.4 on May 6 and he had lost a half-mile and a two-mile. But after Landy's world record, he recovered his desire. In order to force Landy to set a stiff pace at

1954

Vancouver, Bannister showed what he could do in a slow race in the AAA Championships on July 10. His time was only 4:07.6, but he sprinted the last 330 so fast that his last lap was an amazing 53.8.

Landy, in contrast to Bannister's resting, had run hard. Four days after his record mile, he ran two miles in 8:42.4, only two seconds from the world record. Six days later he ran 1500 meters in 3:43.2. At Vancouver, he trained hard with fast intervals.

Bannister had a cold for a week before the race. Landy suffered a minor cut on his foot from a flash bulb while strolling barefoot the day before the race. Both qualified easily in heats two days before the final, Bannister in 4:08.4 with a 60.2 last lap, and Landy in 4:11.4 with a last lap of 58.8.

An eager crowd filled the new stadium as the eight finalists toed the starting line. Landy was on the pole, with Bannister in lane five, but little Bill Baillie of New Zealand grabbed the lead from the outside lane and overeager David Law took it from him.

In the middle of the second turn, Landy darted into the lead, running fast and smoothly. He began to pull away, and he passed the 440 in 58.2, about four yards ahead. Bannister moved warily to second alongside young Murray Halberg, in 58.8.

Landy continued to gain alarmingly as he ran the second lap in 60 flat. On the last turn he had an imposing lead—at least ten yards—but Bannister thought it was 15! Landy passed the half in 1:58.2, eight yards ahead of Bannister's 1:59.4.

Bannister's plan called for him to relax through this third lap, to save everything for his finishing drive. But his confidence wavered. Landy was not slowing and his lead was too great. Bannister increased his pace and began to gain. With great poise, he spread his effort evenly over the entire third lap. In the middle of the backstretch he had cut Landy's frightening lead in half. As they reached the bell he had closed the gap.

Landy's time for three quarters was a fast 2:58.4, although more than a second slower than his world-record pace. Bannister's 59.3 lap brought him around in 2:58.7, grimly close to Landy's heels.

They ran around the curve and then Landy began to run faster, and Bannister followed. "It was all I could do to hold him."

All down the backstretch and around the last turn of the race, 35,000 fans yelled and wondered if Landy had succeeded in running the kick out of Bannister. Landy flashed past 1500 meters in 3:41.9, only one tenth slower than his world record. He was definitely finishing faster than ever before. Bannister, still three tenths of a second behind, thought he could not win unless Landy slowed soon.

In the last stride before he turned into the home straight the roar of the crowd prevented Landy from hearing his pursuer, and he peeked over his left shoulder to find Bannister. But, as luck would have it, Bannister had chosen that very moment to launch his attack. The result was that Landy did not see him until he had inched ahead.

Then came the moment the 35,000 spectators awaited, along with millions of television viewers, and track fans all over the world. The two fastest milers of all time battled each other in the stretch. Bannister shortened his stride and appeared far superior as he won by five yards.

Landy's shock when he saw Bannister ahead of him may have had something to do with his poor finish, but actually he was run out. They had run 330 yards of the last lap at an average speed of 7.36 yards per second, a 59.9 pace. Bannister slowed in the last 120 yards, to 7.23 yds/sec., but Landy slowed badly, to 6.77 yds/sec., a 65.0 pace! What appeared to be a mighty Bannister sprint finish was only relative.

Results: Bannister 3:58.8, Landy 3:59.6, Ferguson of Canada 4:04.6, Milligan of Northern Ireland 4:05.0, Halberg 4:07.2, Boyd of England 4:07.2.

At that moment in history, Bannister and Landy were the two greatest milers of all time, and there was no doubt as to who was No. 1.

SÁNDOR IHAROS

Six feet tall and weighing only 132 pounds, Iharos was conspicuous for his long legs, but from the time he began regular training in 1948 at the age of 18 he seemed to have a good running style.

He joined the Honvéd Club in Budapest to train under Mihály Iglói, but military service delayed his progress in spite of his hard work. He became an officer and a physical education instructor, but his best result in 1951 was second place in the Hungarian 1500, his fastest time, 3:54.2.

In 1952 he ran 3:49.4, but he was eliminated in his heat in the Olympics. In 1953 he ran 3:48.8, but he was still not regarded as much of a threat. His philosophy was that a fast time was as important as a victory, and he was unusually nervous before a race.

In 1954, Captain Iharos was married and had a son, and he broke through into international prominence. He ran 3:49.0 on June 13 and 3:48.2 six days later. He won a close battle against Jungwirth in 3:46.4 on July 3. He ran a good 3:46.0 against Sweden, but he lost to Ericsson's 3:45.0.

Then, in a dual meet against Norway on August 3, came the bombshell. At Bislet Stadium, Oslo, the 24-year-old Iharos followed as Hamarsland set a foolish pace of 56.0 and then slowed to 1:59. At 1000 meters, the lead was taken by Boysen, a 1:48.1 and 3:46.0 man. Boysen passed 1200 meters in 3:01, with Iharos pursuing closely.

Don Macmillan

Josy Barthel

Gaston Reiff

Bob McMillen

Probably the most memorable event in track history: Bannister approaches the tape in the first sub-four minute mile ever run.

The Miracle Mile: Above, Landy has a big lead after two laps. Right, the gap is closed at the start of the bell lap. Below, at the finish it's Bannister convincingly.

H.O. Hacker

Left, Wes Santee.

Below, Jungwirth and Iharos, with Mihaly Igloi in background.

Below, Jim Bailey breaks through against countryman John Landy with a 3:58.6 in the Los Angeles Coliseum.

Suddenly, Iharos began to sprint. He passed Boysen on the backstretch, astounding everyone. He pulled away and won by ten meters in 3:42.4, a new European record. He had broken the former world mark held by Hägg, Strand, and Lueg, and, unofficially, Bannister. His last 300 meters was close to 41 flat.

STANISLAV JUNGWIRTH

Ill after the 1952 Olympics, Jungwirth ran only a few races until late in the year. On October 26, in the same meet at Stará-Boleslav Houstka where the fabulous Zátopek broke three world records in a 30,000 meter race, Jungwirth ran a laudable 800 meters in 1:48.7, moving him to fifth on the all-time list. The next day, on the 363.8 meter track, he broke the world record for 1000 meters with 2:21.2.

In 1953, he was good enough to win every 800 until his last test of the season. He ranked No. 6 with a best time of 1:48.6. In the 1500 he lost only once—to a surprise Hungarian named István Rózsavölgyi. On May 30 at Opava, after a 3:47.8 solo the previous week, he ran his best time—3:45.0—to reach eleventh place on the all-time list. He won the CSR Championship in 3:48.2 plus a great victory in the World Youth Festival meet at Bucharest on August 9. He ran 3:46.2, ahead of two Hungarians, Béres 3:46.6 and Iharos 3:48.8.

In 1954, Jungwirth won decisively in 3:47.6 and 3:48.4, then ran 3:46.4 behind Iharos and a fast but inadequate 3:46.2 behind Nielsen and Boysen.

EUROPEAN CHAMPIONSHIPS

On August 29, in the small Neufeld Stadium in Bern, Switzerland, the fastest field of 1500-meter runners ever assembled walked to the starting line. Missing were the injured Barthel, Slykhuis (able to run only 3:53 this year), Karlsson (below form at 3:48.4), and Boysen, who chose to run the 800. Three who failed to qualify were Reiff, Rózsavölgyi (a 3:46.6 man), and Zvolensky of Czechoslovakia, a 3:47.6 runner. Alfred Langenus of Belgium qualified for the final but withdrew because of an injury.

Roger Bannister had not raced since his victory at Vancouver and he worried about his ability in a jostling match with so many fast runners. Six of his opponents had run 3:46.2 or faster. The fastest, next to Iharos, was Ericsson at 3:45.0.

Iharos was nervous as they lined up on the curved starting line around the bend from the backstretch. The 11 runners burst forward at the gun and crowded together as they tried to stay close to the curb. Iharos was toward the rear, with Bannister.

1954

Almost immediately, Yugoslavia's 3:47.8 man, Mugosa, fell. and Bannister had to hurdle over him. Dohrow, with a best of 3:46.4, took the lead and passed 400 meters in 58.2, followed by Jungwirth, Lueg, and Nielsen. Bannister ran last, knowing the pace was too fast.

Then came one of those situations in championship races when some of the runners are frozen into a pattern of impassive indecision, while others are content with a slow pace because of confidence in their finishing kicks. Among the latter were Bannister and Nielsen, who had run 1:48 for 800 meters. But it is poor tactics when milers who are not good half-milers allow the pace to lag.

And lag it did. Jungwirth took the lead by default when Dohrow slowed. The Czech passed 800 meters in 2:02.0, a preposterous 63.8 lap, and he was followed by Dohrow, Johansson, and Lueg, who had run 3:45.4 on August 8. Bannister moved to sixth, patiently waiting.

At 1200 meters, with only 300 meters to go, the pace was only a little faster. A 62.3 lap had produced a time of 3:04.3, and yet there was little competition for Jungwirth. Johansson was second, with Bannister now third, in excellent position.

Down the last backstretch the pace still dawdled. Bannister was poised on Jungwirth's shoulder, ready to go, only waiting for the last 200 meters. He was afraid of Iharos if he started too soon and Nielsen if he started too late.

On the backstretch, Nielsen moved up, not yet sprinting, merely threatening Bannister. Still Bannister did not accelerate, and the crowd of 30,000 was in an uproar of suspense.

Suddenly Bannister struck. A dismayed Jungwirth saw him go past into the curve before he could increase his speed. A surprised Nielsen found himself left four yards behind. The others were immediately out of contention unless Bannister fell.

Around the bend, Bannister sprinted as never before. Nielsen surged past Jungwirth and took up the pursuit. Lueg moved behind Jungwirth, four yards back. Ericsson passed Johansson, and they were followed by Kakko and Dohrow. Iharos, suffering from tension, was out of it.

Then Nielsen was gaining! Into the stretch the Dane came closer and the crowd went mad. Bannister continued to sprint, cool and detached. He looked up at the clock and thought, "What a pity. No world record today." He actually drew away from the speedy Dane and won by four yards. Lueg faded while Iharos finally came to life with a powerful finish.

Results: Bannister 3:43.8, Nielsen 3:44.4, Jungwirth 3:45.4, Ericsson 3:46.2, Lueg 3:46.4, Iharos 3:47.0, Johansson 3:47.4, Dohrow 3:48.2, Boyd 3:49.2, Kakko 3:51.8.

Bannister ran his last lap in 54.7 after the first 100 meters in

15.4 and the second in 14.3. His blistering last 200 meters in 25 flat averaged 12.5 per 100 meters, by far the fastest finish in any significant mile or 1500 meter race. His last 300 meters took only 39.3. And yet there are some who wonder what would have happened if Nielsen had jumped Bannister first.

1954

1,500m:

3:41.8+	John Landy (Australia)	(1)	Turku	21	Jun
3:42.2+	Roger Bannister (GB)	(2)	Vancouver	7	Aug
3:42.4	Sándor Iharos (Hungary)	(1)	Oslo	3	Aug
3:42.8+	Wes Santee (USA)	(1)	Compton	4	Jun
3:43.4	Stanislav Jungwirth (Czech.)	(1)	St. Boleslav	9	Sep
3:44.2	Audun Boysen (Norway)	(2)	Oslo	3	Aug
3:44.4	Gunnar Nielsen (Denmark)	(2)	Bern	29	Aug
3:45.0	Ingvar Ericsson (Sweden)	(1)	Stockholm	28	Jul
3:45.4+	Chris Chataway (GB)	(2)	Turku	21	Jun
3:45.4	Werner Lueg (Germany)	(1)	Hamburg	8	Aug
3:46.2	Denis Johansson (Finland)	(1)	Helsinki	9	Jul
3:46.4	Günther Dohrow (Germany)	(2)	Hamburg	8	Aug

MILE:

3:57.9	John Landy (Australia)	(1)	Turku	21	Jun
3:58.8	Roger Bannister (GB)	(1)	Vancouver	7	Aug
4:00.6	Wes Santee (USA)	(1)	Compton	4	Jun
4:04.4	Murray Halberg (NZ)	(1)	Auckland	13	Feb
4:04.4	Chris Chataway (GB)	(2)	Turku	21	Jun
4:04.6	Rich Ferguson (Canada)	(3)	Vancouver	7	Aug
4:04.8	Ken Wood (GB)	(1)	London	14	Aug
4:05.0	Victor Milligan (N. Ireland)	(4)	Vancouver	7	Aug
4:05.2	Gordon Pirie (GB)	(1)	New Beckenham	19	Jun
4:05.2	László Tábori (Hungary)	(2)	London	14	Aug
4:05.4	Brian Hewson (GB)	(2)	New Beckenham	19	Jun
4:05.8	Fred Wyatt (GB)	(3)	London	14	Aug

Noteworthy Indoor Marks:

4:04.9	Wes Santee (USA)	(1)	East Lansing	15	Feb
4:07.5	Josy Barthel (Luxemburg)	(1)	New York	6	Feb
4:09.0	Len Truex (USA)	(2)	Boston	30	Jan

ALL-TIME COMBINED LIST:

(3:39.6)	3:57.9	Landy	1954
(3:40.5)	3:58.8	Bannister	1954
(3:42.0)	4:00.6	Santee	1954
3:42.4	(4:01.0)	Iharos	1954
(3:42.7)	4:01.3	Hägg	1945
(3:42.9)	4:01.6	Andersson	1944
3:43.0	(4:01.7)	Strand	1947
3:43.0	(4:01.7)	Lueg	1952
3:43.4	(4:02.1)	Jungwirth	1954
3:43.8	(4:02.5)	Slykhuis	1949

VIII
The explosive revolution

Now a dam seemed to burst and fast milers poured through the four-minute barrier in ever increasing numbers. This was caused by enlightened training methods as well as by removal of the psychological barrier, and the result was complete revolution of past concepts.

WES SANTEE

Indoor track was still confined mostly to the United States, but in 1955 two runners had the necessary training and determination to go after Santee and his indoor record of 4:04.9 . . . and even Cunningham's 4:04.4 made on a larger track.

Fred Dwyer had increased his training load and he was confident of running faster than his indoor 4:08.1 and his outdoor 4:07.1, both of 1953. Gunnar Nielsen was inexperienced indoors, but he had a kick everyone feared. At 800 meters, Nielsen ranked second in the world for 1954.

At Boston on January 15, Nielsen, in the United States only two days and a hopeless 40 yards behind with 240 yards to go, won with 4:07.9 to Dwyer's 4:08.7.

Six nights later, on Philadelphia's slow 12-lap track, Santee trailed Nielsen's 3:11.3 pace and outkicked him easily, 4:10.5 to 4:12.0. The next evening, on Washington's difficult flat track, Nielsen ran his last 440 in 56.8, coming from behind in the last 100 yards. His 4:09.5 beat Santee's 4:11.5. This was Santee's first mile loss in America since he was in high school, and he called his tactics, "stupid."

At the Boston AA on January 29, Santee changed tactics and ran 57.6, 2:00.3, 3:02.1, and 4:03.8, the fastest mile ever run indoors. Nielsen ran 4:08.2.

In a peculiar Wanamaker Mile in Madison Square Garden on February 5, Santee led in 3:03.6 but Dwyer and Nielsen were on his heels into the last lap, where Santee broke Cunningham's indoor 1500 meter record with 3:48.3; Nielsen's big kick on the backstretch was too much and he won in 4:03.6, breaking Santee's record. Dwyer and the tired Santee had a wrestling match on the last turn and Dwyer was disqualified after running 4:06.0 to Santee's 4:06.5. Bob McMillen, returned from overseas duty, ran 4:10.6.

In the Baxter Mile, a ridiculous situation developed, with the hare repeatedly passing Santee and *slowing* the pace. Santee and Nielsen, who tried to stick close to him, were both worn out by the shifting pace and Nielsen beat Santee, 4:16.5 to 4:17.0. Dwyer, however, had run the pace he wanted, and he won in 4:06.2. Dwyer said: "I think Santee is finished for the season. I think he has burnt himself out trying for records." Nielsen said: "I think Dwyer will win next time we race."

One week later, in the AAU, Dwyer led in 3:09.7 with Nielsen threatening from three yards back. On the last backstretch, Santee surprised them both to win by three yards in 4:07.9, while Nielsen barely beat Dwyer by a foot, although official times were 4:08.1 to 4:08.4.

The all-time indoor list was thus revised:

4:03.6	Nielsen	1955	4:07.4	Fenske	1940
4:03.8	Santee	1955	4:07.4	MacMitchell	1941
4:04.4	Cunningham	1938	4:07.4n	Mehl	1941
4:05.3	Dodds	1948	4:07.5	Gehrmann	1951
4:06.2	Dwyer	1955	4:07.5	Barthel	1954

In spite of Dwyer's dire prediction, Santee continued to race after Dwyer and Nielsen stopped. Santee won the Columbian Mile in an easy 4:10.4 and at Milwaukee in 4:08.6. Four days after that he was in Mexico City for the heat of the 1500 in the Pan American Games. Two days later, he lost a frustrating final by one yard to Juan Miranda of Argentina. The 7300-foot altitude held their time to 3:53.2. Dwyer was over 15 yards back, and McMillen was a poor fourth.

Only six days later, on Cleveland's 12-lap track, Santee ran a solo 4:04.6 with his last quarter in 58.6. The next night, far from burned out, Santee ran hard in Chicago. He trailed in 2:04 and 3:07.2 before driving to the tape in 4:04.2—a 57-flat last quarter. He now had to his credit four of the six indoor miles run under 4:05.

One week later, in the Texas Relays at Austin, Santee was tired and underweight for his first outdoor mile, but he went for a record. With no opposition at all, he ran 59.2, 2:00.0, and 3:01.0. He struggled to the tape in 4:00.5, breaking his own American record, but short of his goal.

Santee was subsequently banned as an amateur for accepting excess expenses.

THREE MORE UNDER FOUR MINUTES

At the British Games on May 28, 30,000 grateful spectators saw one of those totally unexpected fast miles resulting from stiff competition. The field included Chataway, Tábori, and Hewson.

CHRIS CHATAWAY ranked No. 9 in the world in 1954 for his second places behind world records by Bannister and Landy, but he was best known as a 5000-meter runner. He had been in the thick of the fight for the 1952 Olympic 5000 until his disastrous fall on the last curve. He ran an 8:49.6 2-mile in 1953 and 8:41.0 in 1954, ranking second best in the world both years.

In 1954, Chataway broke the world three-mile record with 13:32.2 for a close second in the AAA, won the British Empire title, and placed second in the European Championships 5000. In October, he beat Kuts by inches in a great 5000 to set a world record of 13:51.6.

His fastest mile was 4:04.4 behind Landy's world record. This was his first race since he was in South Africa in January.

LASZLO TÁBORI was only the third best miler in his club. But his club was the famous Honvéd, of Budapest, coached by Iglói. At 18, Tábori was a worker in a leather factory and he competed in two races, but it was not until he was doing his military service that he came under the masterly control of Iglói and became serious about running. He became a close friend of Iglói and worked extremely hard to be a good runner.

He did not break into international prominence until he was 23, in 1954. He was good enough to rank No. 7 at 3000 meters with times of 8:06.8 and 8:08.0. He ran 3:47.0 for 1500 meters, and he ran a 4:05.2 mile in losing at White City in August, 1954. He ran a 3:46.8 1500 the week before this race.

BRIAN HEWSON was painfully inexperienced at the mile distance and this was his first real race of the year. He was a fair sprinter at an early age, and he received some "training" by racing another boy half a mile each lunch period because he wanted to be first in line. At 14 he started competing in 440 races, and he joined a club so as to receive free coaching.

The son of a tailor, he wanted to learn tailoring and went to technical school at 16. He ran an 880 in 1:59.4, and at 17 he won the junior AAA championship with a record 1:55.3. He won again at 18 and joined the army for three years. He was allowed to train and race.

In 1953, at the age of 20, he became army champion at half a mile and won the British Championship in 1:54.2. His best time for 880 yards was 1:51.9 behind Bannister against France.

In 1954, Hewson repeated his AAA victory, in 1:52.2, placed second in the Empire Games in Vancouver, and ran 1:50.2 in his heat of the European Championships. Unfortunately, he was bumped and eliminated in the semi-finals.

His coach died and in 1955 he began to train under Franz Stampfl. He had run few miles but he conspired, with Chataway and Stampfl, to run under four minutes in this race. Their plan was for Alan Gordon to set the pace. The White City track, always fast after a rain, allowed Gordon to run 59.9. Chataway ran 60.4, Tábori 60.5, and Hewson 60.6. The weather, cold to the spectators, was right for the runners, and Gordon passed the half in 2:00.8. Hewson ran 2:01.2, Chataway 2:01.4, and Tábori 2:01.6.

On the backstretch of the third lap, Gordon's pace faltered. Hewson was supposed to take over, but he delayed uncertainly for a few yards. Then he went ahead, and when the bell clanged his time was 3:02.0, ahead of Chataway's 3:02.5 and Tábori's 3:02.7.

Hewson pushed the pace around the turn and down the backstretch. Chataway moved alongside, trying to pass, and Tábori ran on Chataway's shoulder. The crowd came to its feet, roaring for its favorite. Hewson had enough left to hold them off and they dropped back around the turn.

Hewson appeared to have the best chance, for at 1500 meters his time was 3:43.2. Chataway and Tábori were timed in 3:43.8, although they seemed more threatening than that. Tábori was beginning a fast sprint, and as Hewson straightened for home, Tábori burst past him and pulled away.

Tábori gained all the way to the tape and won impressively by five yards. Chataway fought his way alongside Hewson and edged him at the tape.

Results: Tábori 3:59.0, Chataway 3:59.8, Hewson 3:59.8.

They had become the third, fourth, and fifth four-minute milers!

HONVÉD STRIKES AGAIN

Two months after Tábori's great victory in London, his two most famous partners in the Honvéd Club represented Hungary in the dual meet with Finland in Helsinki on July 28.

SÁNDOR IHAROS was having a great year. Now 25, but still

1955

thin and frail-looking, he broke the world record for 3000 meters on May 14 in Budapest with 7:55.6. One week later, again on his club track, he ran a speedy 1500 meters in 3:42.6, almost equaling his own European record. He was too air-sick to run in the British Games mile on May 28, but on May 30 he entered the two-mile on the second day of the meet. He set a world record of 8:33.4. Then he lost a 2000 meter race to Pirie and Rózsavölgyi and he was forced to ease off in his training in order to recover. He beat Rózsavölgyi in a slow 1500 on July 2 and Tábori in 3:46.4 on July 16. In mid-July he had a 1200 meter workout in 2:52.4.

ISTVÁN RÓZSAVÖLGYI was now 26 years old, and, like his Honvéd teammates, at the top of his career. Iglói's training did not bring "Rózsa" around until 1953, when he ran 3:47.4. In 1954 he improved only a little, to 3:46.6, and so his running this year was a surprise.

His big breakthrough came on May 21 when he pushed Iharos to 3:42.6. Rózsa finished second in 3:43.2. One week later, while his teammates were in London, he ran the second fastest 2000 in history, 5:08.8. One June 4, in Budapest, he beat the third fastest miler of all time, Tábori, 3:42.8 to 3:45.0.

Then, at Belgrade on June 16, he beat Jungwirth and others after a startling first lap of 55 and 1200 meters in 3:00.0. His time was 3:42.2, a new European record. The day before, in the 800 meter race of this meet, he ran 1:49.7, losing a close battle with European champion Szentgáli's 1:49.5.

Helsinki's weather was ideal, and Rózsa set a wicked pace against the Finns, Vuorisalo and Huttunen. He passed 400 meters in 56.9. Then Iharos took over and passed 800 meters in a sensational 1:55.7. Iharos slowed, of course, and Rózsa led for 200 meters in 30.5. Then Rózsa could hold the vicious pace no longer, and Iharos became the leader while running even slower. The sixth 200 was run in 31 flat.

Rózsa could no longer stay close and Iharos reached 1200 meters in 2:57.2. Iharos finished the last 300 on strength and courage in 43.6 and won by about 13 yards.

Results: Iharos 3:40.8, Rózsavölgyi 3:42.8, Vuorisalo 3:46.2, Huttunen 3:46.4.

Iharos was the new world-record holder, one stupendous second under Landy's mark of last year. Iharos was definitely better than a four-minute miler.

GREAT 1500 AT OSLO

The international meet at Bislet Stadium, September 6, matched three fast runners:

AUDUN BOYSEN, who had been concentrating on the 800

meters so well that he broke the world record behind Roger Moens with 1:45.9 on this same track, August 3. On August 30 he lowered his own world record for 1000 meters to 2:19.0. His best 1500 this year was 3:48.0.

LASZLO TÁBORI had lost to Rózsavölgyi and to Iharos after his 3:59 mile, and he won some longer races, including a threemile victory over Chataway. August 6 saw him beat Rózsa at the Warsaw Youth Festival in a fast 3:41.6. On August 12, he beat Iharos and Chataway in a 4:05.0 mile. At Stockholm on September 2 he won another close victory in a 4:03.6 mile, with Iharos clocking the same time and Nielsen 4:03.8.

GUNNAR NIELSEN had shifted his main emphasis to the 1500 this year, although he set a new European 880 record of 1:48.2 on August 4. He was undefeated until his fast loss to the two Hungarians on September 2. He ran 3:44.2 and 3:42.9, plus a 4:03.4 mile.

Boysen, who preferred to be in front, followed Nielsen's 1:59.2 behind a hare's 1:58.0, then dropped back after three laps. Nielsen led at 1200 meters in 2:59.2, with Tábori apparently suffering in 3:00.0.

Tábori, who had stayed in the pack until the last lap, passing 400 meters in approximately 58 flat, and 800 in 2:00.0, made a run at Nielsen on the last backstretch, but few men ever passed the flying Dane in the stretch. Around the last turn, with the crowd roaring, Tábori was on Nielsen's heels, and into the straight he swung wide and fought his way up, inch by inch. He caught Nielsen and they battled shoulder to shoulder to the tape, where Tábori won the judge's decision.

Results: Tábori 3:40.8, Nielsen 3:40.8, Boysen 3:48.4.

Both received IAAF recognition as having equaled the official world record, the only time this ever happened in a 1500 or mile. Three men now held the record, all made in this one great year.

Four days later, Rózsa beat Tábori, 3:41.2 to 3:41.8 and the all-time list now read:

3:40.8	Iharos	1955	3:42.6n	Herrmann	1955
3:40.8	Tábori	1955	3:42.8+	Santee	1954
3:40.8n	Nielsen	1955	3:43.0	Hägg	1944
3:41.2	Rózsavölgyi	1955	3:43.0	Strand	1947
3:41.8+	Landy	1954	3:43.0	Lueg	1952
3:42.2+n	Bannister	1954	3:43.2+	Hewson	1955

1955
1,500M:

3:40.8 WR	Sándor Iharos (Hungary)	(1)	Helsinki	28	Jul
3:40.8 EWR	László Tábori (Hungary)	(1)	Oslo	6	Sep
3:40.8 EWR	Gunnar Nielsen (Denmark)	(2)	Oslo	6	Sep
3:41.2	István Rózsavolgyi (Hungary)	(1)	Budapest	10	Sep
3:42.6	Siegfried Herrmann (Germany)	(3)	Warsaw	6	Aug
3:43.2+	Brian Hewson (Great Britain)	(1)	London	28	May
3:43.4	Stefan Lewandowski (Poland)	(3)	Budapest	10	Sep
3:43.6+	Chris Chataway (Great Britain)	(1)	Aldershot	2	Jul
3:43.8	Stanislav Jungwirth (Czechosl.)	(3)	Bratislava	24	Sep
3:44.4	Werner Lueg (Germany)	(1)	Frankfort/M.	7	Aug

1955

3:44.4	Ernö Béres (Hungary)	(3)	Budapest	22	Oct
3:44.6	Olaf Lawrenz (Germany)	(2)	Frankfort/M.	7	Aug

MILE:

3:59.0	László Tábori (Hungary)	(1)	London	28	May
3:59.8	Chris Chataway (Great Britain)	(2)	London	28	May
3:59.8	Brian Hewson (Great Britain)	(3)	London	28	May
4:00.5	Wes Santee (USA)	(1)	Austin, Tex.	2	Apr
4:01.4	Bob Seaman (USA)	(2)	Compton, Cal.	3	Jun
4:01.6	Ken Wood (Great Britain)	(2)	Aldershot	2	Jul
4:01.8	Fred Dwyer (USA)	(3)	Compton, Cal.	3	Jun
4:02.1	Murray Halberg (New Zealand)	(1)	Auckland	28	Dec
4:03.0	Gunnar Nielsen (Denmark)	(1)	Copenhagen	1	Oct
4:03.0	István Rózsavölgyi (Hungary)	(1)	Melbourne	21	Dec
4:03.4	Siegfried Herrmann (Germany)	(1)	London	21	Sep
4:03.6	Sándor Iharos (Hungary)	(2)	Stockholm	2	Sep

Noteworthy Indoor Marks:

4:03.6	Gunnar Nielsen (Denmark)	(1)	New York	5	Feb
4:03.8	Wes Santee (USA)	(1)	Boston	29	Jan

1956 OLYMPIC GAMES

So rapid was improvement under severe interval training that each heat of the 1956 Olympic 1500 at Melbourne had a faster field of milers than in all previous Olympics combined. The competition was fierce, for only four runners from each of the three heats could qualify for the final.

THE FIRST HEAT included defending champion Josy Barthel, no better than 3:47.0 this year, Michel Jazy, a 20-year-old Frenchman of bright promise with a best of 3:49.8, and Mamo Wolde, an Ethiopian destined to win the Olympic marathon in 1968. But the really fast runners were Rózsavölgyi, Halberg, Jungwirth, Richtzenhain, and Bailey.

JIM BAILEY was the big surprise of 1956. An Australian attending the University of Oregon, he won the 1955 NCAA mile in 4:05.6. On May 5, 1956, less than three months from his 27th birthday, he ran in a special mile as part of a showcase for John Landy. Bailey stayed back in 61.0 and 2:03.0, and when Landy passed three quarters in 3:01.5 (after 60.6 and 2:02.3), Bailey was obscure in third place with 3:03.1, and he stayed there until the last backstretch.

Then, in full view of 38,543 shocked spectators in the Los Angeles Coliseum and a nationwide television audience, Bailey completely astounded the viewers with a sprint which seemed unbelievable. On the last curve he caught up with Landy and pulled alongside at 1500 meters in 3:43.3.

Surprised at his own power, Bailey still thought Landy was far superior. He slapped Landy on the rear and yelled: "Go," but when Landy did not go, Bailey himself increased his speed and won by five feet in 3:58.6.

Bailey was now second best only to Landy on the all-time

1956

mile list and he had beaten Landy with a last lap in 55.5. In half a lap he had jumped from near-obscurity to an Olympic favorite.

Since that race, Bailey had run only 3:44.4 and 4:06, and he lost the NCAA title to a better sprinter. Here at Melbourne, he was eliminated in the semi-finals of the 800 meters.

KLAUS RICHTZENHAIN of Germany, barely 22 years old, was improving rapidly. He had reached international class in 1955 with 1:50.0 and 3:45.6. This year he started with a fifth place in London even though he ran 3:46.6. His record suffered further when he lost to Pirie by five yards, although he ran a good 3:44.5. On July 7, he lost a close 1500 to Nielsen, 3:44.2 to 3:44.4. He was badly beaten by a great 3:41.8 in the East German Championships.

Then he began winning in faster times until he won in London in 3:43.0. On September 17 he beat Nielsen in a good mile race, 4:01.8 to 4:03.8. He sharpened his speed at 800 meters in 1:49.2 and 1:48.9, but lost out in a heat of the Olympic 800.

STANISLAV JUNGWIRTH, the speedy Czech, failed to keep up with progress in 1955, although he ran 3:43.8 behind Rózsavölgyi and Iharos. This year he ran a series of fast times, including miles in 4:04.5, 4:04.0, and 4:04.4. His fastest 1500's were 3:44.8 in April, 3:42.4 and 3:43.6 in June, 3:43.0 in September, and 3:42.4 on October 20. He ran an 800 in 1:49.2.

MURRAY HALBERG of New Zealand was running in formal races as long ago as 1947, when he was only 14, and he triumphed in his school mile three years in a row. A serious rugby accident in 1950 left him with a withered left arm. In late 1951 he came under the influence of Arthur Lydiard, but it was not until early in 1954 that he made international news with a 4:04.4 mile at the age of 20.

Halberg developed slowly under Lydiard's careful training, but early in 1956 he won miles in 4:02.4 and 4:01.8.

ISTVÁN RÓZSAVÖLGYI finished 1955 as a truly great runner. That year, he ran nine races of 3:44 or faster, six under 3:43. He ran two fast 1000's, on September 17 and 21, clocking 2:19.3 and then tying the world record with 2:19.0. On October 2 in Budapest, he set a world record for 2000 meters with 5:02.2.

And he was even better through September of 1956. On August 3 at Tata, site of the Hungarian training camp, he and Tábori made an assault on the world 1500 record. Rózsa had already run a 4:01.4 mile on July 3 at Göteborg, and he passed the 400 in a swift 55.7.

Curly-headed Tábori took over for part of each lap, but Rózsa led in 1:59.2 and 2:59.8. Then the slim blond army captain ran away from Tábori with a blistering 40.8 for his last 300 meters and won in 3:40.6, a new world record.

He came back 23 days later on Budapest's fast Népstadion track in an attempt to break the world mile record. It was the only event of the evening, yet 10,000 people watched as Tábori led in 57.2 and 1:57.6. Rózsa took over at 1200 meters in three-flat and 1500 in 3:43.0. He finished in 3:59.0 to equal the European record, Bannister's 3:58.8 having been run in Canada. In September Rózsa ran 3:41.4 and 3:41.0. No runner had been so consistently fast.

Then, on October 20, in the match against Finland, he suffered an attack of asthma and finished sixth. Next came the bloody revolt against the USSR and Rózsa stopped training. Two weeks before the Games, coach Iglói said Rózsa did not have a chance at the gold medal.

Bailey failed to show up at the starting line for his 1500 meter heat on November 29. He was suffering from hay fever and a warm-up lap in 66 exhausted him.

Jonas Pipyne, the Russian 3:44.6 man, went to the front and passed the 400 in an ambitious 57.1 and the 800 in 2:00.2. Then Richtzenhain moved easily from two seconds back and took the lead. At the bell, he was followed by Ian Boyd, now a 3:45.2 runner, Pipyne, Jungwirth, and Halberg.

Down the backstretch, the pale Rózsavölgyi made an effort, his wispy blond hair flying. He moved to fifth, but he was struggling, and he began to fade, only a shell of the magnificent runner he was during the regular season. When Pipyne faded, too, only four runners were left in contention for the four qualifying positions. Halberg was "flat out" and said, "It was bloody hard."

Results: Richtzenhain 3:46.6, Jungwirth 3:46.6, Boyd 3:47.0, Halberg 3:47.2. Non-qualifying: Rózsavölgyi 3:49.4, Ballieux of Belgium 3:49.8, Jazy 3:50.0, Ted Wheeler of USA 3:50.0, Pipyne, Barthel, Wolde.

THE SECOND HEAT contained some slow runners, but it also had Delany, Salsola, Wood, Dohrow, Lincoln, Ericsson, and Tábori.

GÜNTHER DOHROW's erratic career surged in 1956. He ran 800 meters in 1:48.2 and in October he ran 3:42.8, only three yards behind Jungwirth. He failed to qualify in a heat of the Olympic 800.

RON DELANY of Eire made the final of the 800 in the 1954 European Championships at the promising age of 18. In 1955, as a 19-year-old freshman at Villanova, he won two indoor 1000's, in 2:10.2 and 2:10.1. Outdoors, he met with more success in the Coliseum Relays 880 with a 1:50.5 victory.

That summer, in Dublin, he ran 1:50.0 and 4:05.8. Indoors in 1956, he won every race of a full mile schedule. His best was 4:06.3 in the Boston AA, where Santee was fourth in 4:08.9 shortly before he was barred from amateur competition. On April 14, Delany started his outdoor season with a good 4:04.9.

He ran at the Los Angeles Coliseum when Bailey surprised with 3:58.6 and finished third in 4:05.5. The next week, at Fresno,

1956

Delany finished hopelessly far back of Landy in 4:09.2. After a 4:14.4 victory in the IC4A and a loss in the 880, Delany showed his true speed at the Compton Invitational on June 1. He followed Gunnar Nielsen past three quarters in 3:02.5 and 1500 meters in 3:44.2. Then came one of the fastest finishes in mile history. Rosy-cheeked Delany gained inch by inch on the speedy Dane. His shoulders shrugging with each stride, he went past Nielsen with 20 yards to go and won a thriller by half a yard. Results: Delany 3:59.0, Nielsen 3:59.1, Dwyer 4:00.8, Bobby Seaman 4:01.4, Wheeler 4:04.7.

Now a contender for the gold medal, Delany almost faded away after his 3:59 and his sprint-finish NCAA victory over Bailey in 3:47.3. He returned to Eire and trained, suffered an injury, and ran only two races, losing both. On June 25, in Dublin, he was nipped at the tape in a 4:07 mile by Hewson. On August 6, in London, he ran 4.06.4 and placed third, badly beaten by Derek Ibbotson's 3:59.4 and Boyd's 4:03.2. He was thought to be unready for the Olympics. A week before, he said, "My best time since my injury last summer is 4:06. However, I feel I'm running somewhat better than that . . . Any one of at least 20 runners has the speed to win."

OLAVI SALSOLA, Finland, was one who had winning speed. He came out of nowhere in 1955 to run 1:49.1, 2:21.5 for 1000 meters, and 3:45.8. In 1956, his early improvement made him a contender for the gold medal. He won a 3:42.0 race at Gävle on July 23 and two weeks later he won a mile in 4:03.0. But on August 26 he lost in the coveted Finnish Championships, although he came back the next day with a 1:48.3 800. His 3:43.8 against Sweden on September 8 lost to Dan Waern's 3:43.6.

LÁSZLÓ TÁBORI was making a good comeback after his slow start in 1956. On September 15 he ran 3:42.6 against Czechoslovakia, losing to Rózsa's 3:41.4, but he beat Jungwirth's 3:43.0. Two weeks later, against Great Britain, he ran a commendable 3:42.0, behind Rózsa's 3:41.0 and ahead of Hewson's 3:43.2. Tábori won against Finland on October 21, a few days before Soviet tanks rolled into Hungary. In spite of his training difficulties since then, he placed sixth in the Olympic 5000 meter final the day before this heat.

INGVAR ERICSSON, Sweden, a veteran of 29, was better than ever. (He was seventh in the 1950 European Championships and fourth in 1954. He was eighth in the 1952 Olympics.) His best in 1954 was 3:45.0, with 3:45.8 in 1955. This year he ran 3:45.8, lost his Swedish Championship in a tactical race, and was only fourth against Finland, but he came to life with a 4:02.6 mile in Stockholm on September 14.

At Göteborg on September 30, he took part in a declared attempt on the world 1500 record by Dan Waern. The pace was typical Swedish record, with Waern's 55.5 trailing veteran Olle

Aberg. Waern ran a greedy 1:56.0 behind Gottfridsson. Meanwhile, Ericsson ran 56.5 and 1:57.0. He was still a full second behind Waern's extraordinary 2:26.0 at 1000 meters, but at 1200 meters he was timed in 2:57.4 behind Waern's 2:57.0. It was certainly a record pace, but both runners were spent. Ericsson pulled ahead in the homestretch battle to win by over a yard in 3:41.2, a new Swedish record.

MERV LINCOLN, Australia, was only third best in his country, but running at home helped make him a contender. Training under Franz Stampfl, now in Australia, Lincoln had cut a remarkable 11.4 seconds off his mile time early in 1956 when he ran 4:00.6 behind Landy. Barely 22 years old at the time, he had great prospects, but he ran only 4:08.8 in the Australian Championships, for third.

He began Australia's spring season with 4:05.8 on September 8, then failed to finish one encounter. On October 20, in the Australian Olympic Trials, he ran a satisfactory 3:45.0 behind Bailey's 3:44.4.

KEN WOOD, Great Britain, the No. 9 miler of 1955, had a strong finish which made him a great competitor. He was almost unknown until the 1954 season when he ran 4:04.8 at the age of 23. In 1955 he became known after his first race, a world record breaking two-mile in 8:34.8 behind Iharos. On July 2 he ran a 4:01.6 mile behind Chataway. He ran 4:06.2 in the AAA to finish five yards behind Hewson's big kick.

Wood was undefeated in 1956. After early May miles in 4:06.6 and 4:06.2, he won an important race in London on May 19. His kick took the others by surprise and he won in 3:43.4 from Rózsa, Tábori, Pirie, and Richtzenhain.

In the AAA Championships on July 14, Wood outkicked Hewson 4:06.8 to 4:07.4. In the important dual mile against Czechoslovakia on August 4 in London, Wood trailed Jungwirth and Hewson into the homestretch and his strong finish beat them in 4:03.8. He left for Melbourne on October 4, determined to train on the site.

Yevgeniy Sokolov, a Russian 3:45.4 runner, led the second Olympic heat in a fast 57.1 and 1:58.5. He was followed by an overweight Dohrow, Lincoln, and Emile Leva of Belgium, who had placed seventh in the Olympic 800 final. Then Lincoln moved ahead and ran hard enough to lead by five yards at the bell. He passed 1200 meters in 3:00.2 and pressed all the way, with the Australian crowd cheering as if he had a gold medal in sight.

Sokolov was passed, one at a time, by Wood, Delany, and Tábori, all running under control. Ericsson was hopelessly far behind and his sprint was not enough to get him a place in the finals. Lincoln's last lap was 62.3 compared with 59.0 for Richtzenhain in

the easier first heat.
Results: Lincoln 3:54.4, Wood 3:46.6, Delany 3:47.4, Tábori 3:48.0, Non-qualifiers: Ericsson 3:49.0, Sokolov 3:49.2, Depastas 3:52.0, Salsola 3:55.0, Dohrow 3:58.0, Sandoval 3:58.0, Don Bowden 4:00.0.
Lincoln said, "I've never had such a relaxed race in my life."
THE THIRD HEAT was a battle between, among others, Landy, Nielsen, Hewson, Waern, Herrmann, and Scott.
NEVILLE SCOTT, a tall, slim New Zealander only 21 years old, improved sensationally—more than ten seconds in 1956—to 4:02.5 behind Halberg's 4:01.8. He was regarded as one of the best prospects in the world.
JOHN LANDY ran well in Los Angeles, May 5, but he was shocked by Bailey's finish. Landy ran his last lap in 57.2 and last 120 in 15.4 for his 3:58.7, and still he had no confidence in his finishing speed.
He ran a 3:59.1 solo mile at Fresno the week after his defeat by Bailey and then retired for more training. He did not run in the Australian trials. His training was hampered by a sore tendon, and he was undecided whether to run the 5000 or 1500. Two weeks prior to this race he had finished twelfth in a two-mile race and said, "I've had it."
SEIGFRIED HERRMANN of East Germany ran 1:51.4 and 3:50.0 in 1953 at the tender age of 20, and he improved to 3:48.8 in 1954. His breakthrough came in 1955 when he barely lost to Nielsen, 3:44.4 to 3:44.2. Then, in Warsaw, he ran an excellent 3:42.6 behind Tábori and Rózsavölgyi. At London, in September, he won a mile in 4:03.4.
Herrmann improved impressively again in 1956, with 800 meters in 1:48.5, 3000 in 7:59.0 and 5000 in 14:08.0. At 1500 meters, he won the East German Championship in a startling 3:41.8. His only loss was when he ran 3:44.6 to Rózsa's 3:44.2. He defeated both Jungwirth and Nielsen.
GUNNAR NIELSEN continued to show his power after his 3:59.1 behind Delany at Compton. At Copenhagen on June 28, he beat Rózsa by three yards in 3:44.2. On July 7, he outfought Richtzenhain, 3:44.2 to 3:44.4. At Turku, on July 17, he ran 3:43.4 to beat Vuorisalo (3:43.8) and Salonen. That was his last victory, however, for injuries cut him down. On September 17, he ran a 4:03.8 mile behind Richtzenhain's 4:01.8. His best 800 was 1:48.0 on July 8. He won his heat of the Olympic 800 in 1:51.2, then scratched from the semi-final.
BRIAN HEWSON, only 22 in 1955, showed great promise. He lost only three times—when he ran 3:59.8, when Rózsa beat him 3:44.0 to 3:45.6, and on October 1 when he ran 4:03.6 behind

Nielsen. He won the prestigious AAA title in 4:05.4 with a great last lap in 53.5. Ten days after his 3:59.8, he set a "world record" of 2:55.4 for three laps. Two weeks after that he ran 1000 meters in 2:20.2, passing 1000 yards in a "record" 2:08.0. Against Germany he won a mile in 4:21.6 with an unprecedented last lap in 51.2. In the same meet he ran 1:48.9 in the half-mile. He later ran 880 yards in 1:48.6 and 1:48.8 to rank as eighth-best half-miler in the world. He won in 3:45.0 against Russia and finished the season with a 4:04.8 mile.

Hewson held back his training in 1956 so as to be ready for the Olympics. He cut a heel in Trinidad in March and lost some training, and he lost most of his races. He lost while running 1:49.8 and 4:04.8. Then he was boxed on the last lap of the AAA mile and failed to catch Wood. In August he ran 4:04.0 but lost to Wood and Jungwirth. In September, he ran a fine 1:47.5 for 800 meters and 2:19.9 for 1000, but he was edged by Pirie in a 3:49.2 race. On September 29, he ran 3:43.2 but he was well back of Rózsavölgyi and Tábori. Then he left for Melbourne, where he trained hard under Stampfl for four weeks. He ran an easy 1:49.7 800 as a test, and then, in practice, ran three quarters in 2:52.0, fastest ever known. He had come along exactly as he wanted. He felt he could win the gold medal.

DAN WAERN of Sweden ran 3:49.8 in 1954 at the age of 21, after 4:03 at 19 and 3:58.6 at 20. He slipped back to 3:53.4 because of injuries in 1955, but in 1956 he proved he would be Sweden's fastest middle-distance runner. He ran a whole series of losing 800 meter races faster than 1:49.7, with three at 1:48.6. He also set a Swedish 1000 meter record of 2:20.9. He began his 1500 meter season with a fourth in the Copenhagen race of June 28, running 3:48.0 behind three great runners—Nielsen, Rózsavölgyi, and Tábori. Then he lost a 4:03.2 mile to Rózsa's 4:01.4. He lost only three more races all season. Salsola beat him with an excellent 3:42 to his 3:43.8 on July 23. He lost to Tábori on September 2 as both men clocked 3:46.4. And he ran 3:41.3 in losing to Ericsson's startling 3:41.2. On the winning side, he broke the Swedish record with 3:41.9 on August 6 and ran 3:44.4 two days later. He won the Swedish Championship in 3:46.8 and then won the big dual against Finland in 3:43.6, beating Salsola's 3:43.8, his only victory of the year in a close stretch battle.

Nobody was anxious to set a fast pace in the third Olympic heat, and so the closely bunched pack reached 400 meters in 62.1, with Waern, Nielsen, and Herrmann up front. Landy looked unhappy in next to last place.

Gianfranco Baraldi, who broke Beccali's Italian record with 3:47.8 in August, took the lead on the second lap and the pack reluctantly lengthened out to single file. Waern led at 800 meters in

2:05.2, ahead of Herrmann. Waern wanted to stay in front and he held off Herrmann's bid to pass. At the bell, Landy had moved to third, ahead of Scott, Sergey Sukhanov, Russia's 3:45.0 man, and Nielsen.

Then came an accident which eliminated one of the best runners in the Games. Landy spiked Herrmann, and the unfortunate German was forced to drop out.

Scott powered into the lead on the backstretch and the field was down to five potential qualifiers when Sukhanov faded. Nielsen seemed the likely victim because he was obviously struggling.

Scott and Hewson pulled away easily in the stretch. Landy attempted to stride in and barely made third place. Nielsen put on one of his courageous finishes and edged Waern for fourth.

Results: Scott 3:48.0, Hewson 3:48.0, Landy 3:48.6, Nielsen 3:48.6, Non-qualifiers: Waern 3:48.8, Baraldi 3:52.0, Sukhanov 3:53.0, Jerome Walters of USA 3:55.0, Papavassiliou of Greece 3:57.0, Fontecilla of Chile 3:58.0.

Scott ran his last lap in an impressive 57.1 and Hewson ran about 56.9.

THE FINAL was run two days later on December 1, in the best weather of the Games, warm and windless. More than 100,000 people sat in the three-decked Melbourne Cricket Ground. Halberg had the pole on the starting line at the head of the backstretch.

Halberg and Hewson broke to the front when the gun sounded. At the rear, trying to get in on the curb, were Landy, Nielsen, and Lincoln, who had a pain-killer for his injured foot.

Halberg, with his all-black uniform and his withered arm, led past 400 meters in 58.4 followed by Hewson and Jungwirth. Delany was next to last in a calm 60 flat. On the backstretch, Nielsen moved up to seventh, but he could not get in to the pole. Around the curve they went, and a great Australian cheer went up as Lincoln rushed up to third.

With two laps to go, Lincoln took the lead and Boyd moved in behind him around the curve. Hewson, determined to stay close, was third, followed by Halberg, Jungwirth, and Scott. Landy was last but still dangerous in the bunched pack.

Lincoln's time at 800 meters was 2:00.1 while Delany, still next to last, ran 2:01.4. The pace slowed, the hopeful runners bunched up even more closely behind Lincoln, and the suspense and tension built. It was developing into a kicker's race, favoring such runners as Hewson, Wood, Richtzenhain, Delany, Nielsen—if he had been right—Landy—at his best—and possibly Scott.

Now was the time to maneuver for position, and down the homestretch Wood worked up to fourth, Hewson poised himself on Lincoln's shoulder for a big effort, Richtzenhain was on Hewson's shoulder, and Landy was on Richtzenhain's shoulder. Nielsen, struggling in last place, was only eight yards behind. Everybody still had a chance.

With 400 meters to go, the bell failed to sound, but Hewson began to move faster. He led into the curve, and Lincoln faded back through the pack. Nielsen, too, was finished and lost ground.

Hewson flashed past the starting line in 3:01.3 and struck out for gold. He intended to lead the rest of the way, but he was tense and running hard already. Richtzenhain had moved perfectly and was second down the backstretch. Boyd had come through the curve in third place. Landy, who was in good position with a lap to go, had lost ground on the curve in a tactical blunder caused by his lack of confidence. Delany moved to fifth around the curve, but he lost ground to Hewson's astute move.

Down the backstretch, with Hewson trying to break away, his closest pursuer was, surprisingly, Ian Boyd. Richtzenhain ran well in third place. John Landy, with the crowd screaming his name, was indecisive in fourth place. Halberg was letting go, back with Lincoln and Nielsen. Wood, who hoped to kick, found himself boxed in behind everybody on the bell turn and lost hope. But there were still eight contenders.

Sometimes a runner moves so fast past his opponents that the spectators immediately see he is the strongest in the race, and his opponents are disheartened. Such a move came on the backstretch by a black-haired, red-cheeked youth in a green jersey, running with mincing steps and a strange shoulder shrug. Ron Delany was moving!

He gained five important yards on the backstretch, and he rushed madly into the turn only three yards behind Hewson. Around the curve the flying Irishman sped past Richtzenhain and Boyd. Into the stretch, he ran past Hewson with startling speed. He said later, "I felt I had the race won." Hewson, terribly disappointed, began to struggle. "I could feel my body tensing."

Delany kept gaining. Richtzenhain went past Hewson and seemed to have the silver medal. Landy, whose inferiority complex had beaten him, finally came to life and showed a great finish, probably the fastest in the race. He sped past Hewson and almost caught Richtzenhain for second place, six yards back of the grinning Delany. Hewson slowed slightly at the end and Tábori nipped him and Jungwirth barely missed. Scott caught the gallant Boyd, who had run by far his greatest race.

Results: Delany 3:41.2, Richtzenhain 3:42.0, Landy 3:42.0, Tábori 3:42.4, Hewson 3:42.6, Jungwirth 3:42.6, Scott 3:42.8, Boyd 3:43.0, Wood 3:44.8u, Nielsen 3:45.7u, Halberg 3:45.9u, Lincoln 3:51.9u.

Delany, in coming within 0.6 of the world record, had run the last 100 meters in 12.9 and last 300 in 38.8, by far the fastest finish ever. (60.0, 2:01.4, 3:02.4). He fell to his knees and offered a

prayer of thanks. "I never felt better in my life."
Landy, who might have altered history with one of his typical races, said, "I did not think I would be in the finish at all... Most of the starters today would have beaten me anytime except that the weather here has upset their form."

ALL-TIME COMBINED LIST:

(3:39.6)	3:57.9	Landy	1954
(3:40.2)	3:58.6	Bailey	1956
(3:40.5)	3:58.8	Bannister	1954
3:40.6	(3:59.0)	Rózsavölgyi	1956
(3:40.6)	3:59.0	Tábori	1955
(3:40.6)	3:59.0	Delany	1956
(3:40.7)	3:59.1n	Nielsen	1956
3:40.8	(3:59.3)	Iharos	1955
(3:41.0)	3:59.4	Ibbotson	1956
3:41.2	(3:59.7)	Ericsson	1956

1956

3:40.6 WR	István Rózsavölgyi (Hungary)	(1)	Tata	3	Aug
3:41.2	Ingvar Ericsson (Sweden)	(1)	Göteborg	30	Sep
3:41.2	Ron Delany (Eire)	(1)	Melbourne	1	Dec
3:41.3	Dan Waern (Sweden)	(2)	Göteborg	30	Sep
3:41.8	Siegfried Herrmann (Germany)	(1)	Erfurt	20	Jul
3:42.0	Olavi Salsola (Finland)	(1)	Gävle	23	Jul
3:42.0	László Tábori (Hungary)	(2)	Budapest	29	Sep
3:42.0	Klaus Richtzenhain (Germany)	(2)	Melbourne	1	Dec
3:42.0	John Landy (Australia)	(3)	Melbourne	1	Dec
3:42.4	Stanislav Jungwirth (Czechosl.)	(1)	Prague	16	Jun
3:42.6	Brian Hewson (GB)	(5)	Melbourne	1	Dec
3:42.8	Günther Dohrow (Germany)	(2)	Prague	20	Oct
3:42.8	Neville Scott (New Zealand)	(7)	Melbourne	1	Dec

MILE:

3:58.6	John Landy (Australia)	(1)	Melbourne	28	Jan
3:58.6	Jim Bailey (Australia)	(1)	Los Angeles	5	May
3:59.0	Ron Delany (Eire)	(1)	Compton, Cal.	1	Jun
3:59.0	István Rózsavölgyi (Hungary)	(1)	Budapest	26	Aug
3:59.1	Gunnar Nielsen (Denmark)	(2)	Compton, Cal.	1	Jun
3:59.4	Derek Ibbotson (GB)	(1)	London	6	Aug
4:00.6	Mervyn Lincoln (Australia)	(2)	Melbourne	28	Jan
4:00.8	Fred Dwyer (USA)	(3)	Compton, Cal.	1	Jun
4:01.4	Bob Seaman (USA)	(4)	Compton, Cal.	1	Jun
4:01.8	Murray Halberg (New Zealand)	(1)	Auckland	11	Feb
4:01.8	Klaus Richtzenhain (Germany)	(1)	Bergen	17	Sep
4:02.2	Gordon Pirie (GB)	(1)	Croydon	28	Jul

Noteworthy Indoor Mark:

4:06.3	Ron Delany (Eire)	(1)	Boston	28	Jan

DON BOWDEN

In high school, Bowden was a long-striding half-miler who set a national record of 1:52.3 in 1954. As a freshman at California, in a restricted season, he ran 1:51.5 and 4:11.7, plus a relay leg in 1:48.9. As a sophomore he concentrated on the mile in 1956, and ran an early 4:08.2. He faded to seventh in the NCAA 1500, then made the Olympic team with a courageous stretch drive in 3:48.6, In October he ran 3:46.6 but then he was slowed by mononucleosis before the Olympics.

Called "divinely gifted" by his coach, Brutus Hamilton,

1957

Bowden ran 1:49.7 half-miles twice in 1957 and 4:09.9 and 1:50.0 on the same day. He broke through to international attention in May when he ran a mile relay leg in 4:01.5 and he beat Jim Bailey with an 880 in 1:47.8. On May 27 he ran three quarters with Tom Courtney in 2:57, and then he was concerned with final examinations and did not train.

After his final exam on June 1, he said, "I felt dead. I almost didn't come." But he rode the 65 miles to Stockton, Calif., for a twilight meet, thinking, "I'm just going to run a four-minute pace as long as I can."

Only five runners started in the PA AAU mile, before only 2500 spectators, and Bowden led every step of the way. His amazingly long strides—he was 6'3" tall and weighed 160 pounds—took him around the first lap in 59.7. "I began to feel good."

With his competition far behind, he passed the 880 in 2:00.8, and he kept trying. He came around in 3:00.6. "After three laps I felt great."

His gigantic stride never faltered as he swept around the last lap on the hard clay track. "I gave it all I had. I felt strong." His time was 3:58.7, bettered only by Landy and Bailey, and at last an American runner had bettered four minutes.

At the age of 20 Bowden was certainly the greatest prospect yet to appear.

THE RACE OF THE THREE OLAVIS

At 7:00 p.m. of July 11, on the fast cinder track in Turku's pure cool air, many of the world's fastest milers were ready for a record-breaking 1500:

DON BOWDEN, after his 3:58.7 mile, extended his unblemished career as a half-miler by winning the NCAA 880 in 1:47.2. This was the second fastest of all time and it ended Ron Delany's 25-race winning streak. Then Bowden ran only 4:07.2 for third in the AAU mile. At the last moment, here in Turku, he decided he was too tired, and he withdrew from the race.

DAN WAERN, the fastest-ever Swede, began his season eight days previously in Göteborg with a mile in 4:00.1, last 120 in 15.7. On July 6 he ran an 800 in 1:49.7 and yesterday in Stockholm he ran a good 1:48.9 at the same distance.

OLAVI SALONEN of Finland, a 23-year-old newcomer to international class, ran 3:44.6 in 1956. He started this year by winning in 3:48.8. Ten days before, in Helsinki, he ran 3:44.6 again, but he was disappointed with his third place behind two others also named Olavi.

OLAVI SALSOLA, six days younger than Salonen, came into prominence in 1955 with 1:49.1, 3:45.8, and the Finnish 800 meter

championship. In 1956 he ran well, with times of 1:48.3, 3:42.0, and 4:03.0. He lost the Finnish 1500 title to Vuorisalo but he was Finland's only 1500 meter runner in the Olympics. His first race of 1957 was a 3:44.0 victory by four yards over his "Olavi" opponents.
OLAVI VUORISALO improved from 3:50 and 4:07 in 1954 to 1:50.2 and 3:45.0 in 1955. He won the Finnish 1500 title in 1955 and repeated in 1956, when his fastest times were 3:43.8 and 4:03.2. This year he barely beat Salonen for second in 3:44.6 on July 1.

A field of 14 runners cluttered the track, and 5000 spectators cheered them on. Vuorisalo had difficulty with the large field on the first lap, but he moved up to fifth as the leader ran an optimistic 56.8.

Waern took the lead, followed by Salonen, Salsola, Jorma Kakko, and Vuorisalo. Waern passed 800 meters in 1:57.8, a record pace, and at 1000 meters his time was 2:29. At 1200 meters, Waern led in 2:58.4, but he was closely pursued by Salsola, Vuorisalo, and Salonen. Waern led around the final curve, and then the three Olavis struck.

Salsola stormed past Waern, followed by Vuorisalo and then Salonen. Vuorisalo gained on both of them. With the Finnish crowd in a frenzy of excitement while they watched three Finns and their stopwatches, Salonen went past Vuorisalo and caught Salsola at the tape. The photo timer failed to determine a winner and it was some time before the harried judges gave their decision.

Results: Salsola 3:40.2, Salonen 3:40.2, Vuorisalo 3:40.3, Waern 3:40.8.

The three Olavis had broken the world record! And Waern had a new Swedish record for his trouble.

Spectator Don Bowden said, "I didn't know that these guys were so good. If I had known . . ."

Salsola said, "Somebody will run under 3:40 *soon.*"

SOONER THAN HE THOUGHT

The very next day, on the famous forest track at Houstka Spa near Stará Boleslav in Czechoslovakia, 421 spectators watched Stanislav Jungwirth make his attempt.

Jungwirth, almost 27, expected to improve on his No. 7 ranking of last year, and he started the year early with 800 meters in 1:47.5 on May 19. During June, in excellent condition, he won in 3:42.0, 3:43.4, and 3:40.9.

Five runners started the 1500 at 5:30 on the 364-meter track. A good half-miler set the pace, with Jungwirth two or three steps behind. Jungwirth passed 200 meters in 26.2, obviously too fast, but he kept going. He passed the 400 in 54.9, full of determination. At 800 meters in 1:54.2 he was far ahead of any previous pace.

1957

His pace-maker dropped back and Jungwirth was on his own. He reached 1000 meters in 2:24.0. With nobody near him—even in history—he pushed on to 1200 meters in an amazing 2:53.4, five seconds faster than the pace in the Olavis' world record.

He did not slow down appreciably, nor could he increase his speed. He held a hard, awkward run all the way to the tape. His time was 3:38.1, the fastest race ever run . . . at either 1500 meters or the mile.

DEREK IBBOTSON

A carefree type who, nevertheless, trained extremely hard, Ibbotson began with cross country races at the age of 11. At 16, he left school to be an apprentice electrician. He trained haphazardly, once or twice a week, but won junior mile races.

So great was his talent that he ran a three-mile in 14:09.4 before the age of 20, placing second in the Northern Championships.

He wanted to take exams for the Higher National Diploma and so he missed the 1952 AAA Championships. In 1953 he tore ligaments in his ankle in a coal mine, and in 1954 he had not improved. At year's end, he joined the Royal Air Force and for the first time he learned about scientific training.

After a good cross-country season in 1955, he showed his first promise as a miler when he ran 2000 meters against Pirie. Ibbotson, now 5'9½" and 147 pounds, passed the mile mark in 4:08.8 before losing on the last lap.

A little later he won the Inter-Counties three-mile at White City in 13:34.6, 7.4 seconds from the British record. Then he lost the AAA three-mile to Chataway and decided he needed a faster finish.

Over the winter he trained with that purpose in mind, and in his first race of 1956 he finished a two-mile with a lap in 56. He beat favored Chris Chataway from behind in the stretch of the AAA three-mile, clocking 13:32.6. Against the Czechs on August 4, he won in 13:28.2.

Two days later he was persuaded to run in the Emsley Carr Mile on Bank Holiday, even though he said, "I am not really a miler." His best was 4:07 and he was to run against Delany, among others. He trailed a pace of 59.2 and 2:00.2, then took the lead in 3:02.4. With Delany no threat because of his injury, Ibbotson passed 1500 meters in 3:44.4 and sped home in 15 flat for 3:59.4. He had equalled Bannister's British record. "I did not feel exhausted and I knew then I could run faster."

He went on to place third in the Olympic 5000 meters. Then, over the winter, he trained very hard in the style of Vladimir Kuts—reducing the time he jogged between his intervals of faster running.

1957

He claimed such a workout as 20 to 25 440's in 60 seconds with no more than a 50-second jog between.

Ibbotson was in great shape when the 1957 racing season began, and he ran 4:00.6 in his first race, at Oxford, on May 14. Ten days later, in the Coliseum Relays in Los Angeles, he set all the pace (3:04) but he was cut off on the last curve and thrashed by Lincoln, Tábori, and Hewson. He finished fourth in 4:02.1. A little carelessness or overconfidence had proved dangerous, and so the next night, in Modesto, he ran a tactical race and beat Lincoln in 4:06.4, with a fast last lap of 55.2.

Back in London on June 8, he beat Richtzenhain in 4:03.2 with a 56-flat last lap. The next day he suffered a defeat in Amsterdam because a septic leg prevented him from bending his knee. The next Saturday he ran a noteworthy mile in the Police Sports at Glasgow's Ibrox Park.

Anxious to break the world record on this day his daughter was born, Ibbotson followed a pace of 57.2, passed the half in 1:58.0 and resolutely took the lead with a lap and a half to go. The temperature was near 90, but he passed three quarters in 2:59.8. Completely exhausted, he finished in 3:58.4, second fastest mile ever run.

Four days later, he beat Pirie in an 8:46.6 two-mile with only five minutes for warm-up before the race. His carelessness caught up with him again in the AAA Championships. Qualifying for the mile final was on a time basis and he failed to qualify by one tenth of a second. He made up for his mistake by winning the three-mile in British record time of 13:20.8.

Although Bannister had advised him to limit his racing, Ibbotson ignored him. Six days after the AAA, he was in London for the greatest mile race ever run.

Seven runners were in the mile on July 19 at White City Stadium where a rain had worked its peculiar magic on the cinder track. An expectant crowd of 30,000 watched world-recordman Jungwirth run against Wood, Delany, Ibbotson, and Stefan Lewandowski, a 27-year-old doctor from Poland, who had run 3:42.3 in June and a fast 1000 meters in 2:19.4 only three days earlier.

Ken Wood was training better than ever, although his only race was won in 4:11.7 two weeks ago. And Ron Delany, the Olympic champion, was the No. 1 indoor miler in the USA, undefeated with a best of 4:03.8 at Chicago. He was also undefeated outdoors, with a fastest of 4:04.7 at Dublin on July 5.

Ibbotson felt supremely confident and he asked Mike Blagrove, a 4:07.1 miler but a better half-miler, to set a fast pace ... "about one minute fifty-six or one minute fifty-seven seconds."

Blagrove started at a Jungwirth-like pace of 55.3 and 1:55.8.

201

Jungwirth rolled awkwardly along behind in 55.7 and 1:56.1. Ibbotson was third in 56.0 and 1:56.4. "I was now feeling very tired." Delany hung back, understandably reluctant, and Wood moved to fourth on the second lap.

Around the curve, Blagrove dropped out. Jungwirth now had the lead, but he could not force the record pace he had run the previous week. Ibbotson welcomed the slower pace. "Life was flowing back into my limbs."

Jungwirth passed three quarters in 3:00 flat, with Ibbotson at 3:00.3 and the others scattered behind. Ibbotson concentrated on relaxing until the last backstretch. Then he launched into a strong drive and ran away from Jungwirth. Ibbotson feared Delany's kick, but he forced himself to relax in the homestretch. "My body ached, I seemed to be suffocating, sweat blurred my vision."

Delany went past Jungwirth in the stretch, but he could not keep up with Ibbotson. Wood came from far back with a typical finish which almost caught Jungwirth.

Results: Ibbotson 3:57.2, Delany 3:58.8, Jungwirth 3:59.1, Wood 3:59.3, Lewandowski 4:00.6, Alan Gordon 4:03.4.

All six had set personal records. Ibbotson's last lap was in 56.9, his last 120 in a fast 15.3 to 16.4 for Delany and 17.0 for Jungwirth. Landy's world record had lasted only three years. The more arduous training methods were causing amazing progress.

Bannister commented enthusiastically: "Because of the uneven running in this mile he is at this moment capable of a time of three minutes fifty-five seconds."

Delany said, "It was a fabulous race, and a pleasure as well as a privilege to run in it. I shall dream about it for years."

Jungwirth said, "I was disappointed that I did not add the world mile record to my 1500 meters record time."

Bannister's statement was rather ironic in view of the controversy which arose. The IAAF balked at ratifying Ibbotson's record because it was a paced race. The new rules stated that the IAAF "will consider whether the claimant was unfairly assisted towards the time accomplished by pacing from another competitor apparently designed to assist him to achieve a record."

Ibbotson was bitter about a ruling he considered unfair. "If Jungwirth or Delany had won, would there have been the same fuss? I doubt it because neither spoke to Blagrove." It was small consolation to Ibbotson when the IAAF finally made his record official, but such recognition is retroactive, and so he was actually the mile record holder until his time was bettered.

Everybody treated Ibbotson as the record holder, and he accepted too many invitations to run. Ten days later, after two more races—one a mile in 4:03.3—he ran against Delany in Dublin. The pace dragged to 3:09, exactly right for Delany, who outkicked him,

4:05.4 to 4:05.9.

Nine days after that defeat, in Naantali, Finland—four days after an easy 5000 against France on a badly blistered foot and only two days after an 8:44.0 two-mile victory—Ibbotson ran another fast mile. Naantali is a seaside resort near Turku with a population of about 1000, but there were 10,000 spectators, some from as far away as 600 miles.

Ibbotson's only serious opponent was Olavi Vuorisalo. A pace setter ran 56 and 1:56, and then left Ibbotson in the lead. "I was in no mood for a fast race." But Ibbotson had to stay ahead of Vuorisalo, and it required 3:58.7 to do so, for Vuorisalo ran 3:59.1.

At this moment in history, Ibbotson had run the fastest mile ever (3:57.2), the third fastest (3:58.4), and he was tied for seventh (3:58.7).

But Bannister's warning was correct. Ibbotson should have limited his racing, for he lost six of his last seven 1500-mile races and also lost three races at longer distances.

OTHER RUNNERS

DAN WAERN lost only once, to Vuorisalo, after his fourth in the world record 1500 against the three Olavis. He ran 1500's in 3:43 twice and 3:42.6 twice, and he had the fastest series of miles since Landy. He won in 3:59.3, 4:01.1, 3:59.7, 3:59.6, and 3:58.5. His finishing kick, now called the best in Europe, kept improving; his last 120's in his four sub-four miles were 15.4, 15.5, 15.1, and 14.6. In between all these races, he ran a full season of 800 meter contests. With six under 1:49 and a best of 1:48.1, he ranked eighth in the world.

MERV LINCOLN ran 4:02.6 for second in the Australian Championships. Two weeks later, again in Melbourne, he was paced by a youngster named Ron Clarke to quarters of 59.2, 2:00.3 and 3:00.6. He ran himself out, struggling the last 120 in 16.9, but his time was 3:58.9,

In May he went to California for five encounters. In the Coliseum Relays, he beat a strong field—Hewson, Tábori, and Ibbotson—in 4:01.0. The next night, at Modesto, he lost a tactical race to Ibbotson. Six nights later he won easily at Compton in 4:05.0 over Bobby Seaman and Tábori. He won at Bakersfield in 4:04.4 over Tábori and Seaman. In the AAU Championships at Dayton, Ohio, he ran only to win, beating off-form Seaman and Bowden in 4:06.1 with a last lap in 56.2.

ROGER MOENS of Belgium was a great runner, but this was his first effort at 1500 meters or one mile. He ran 400 meters in 47.7 as early as 1953, and 47.3 in 1955. He lost only four 800 meter duels in five seasons, 1953 through 1957, ranking as best in the world in

1957

1955 and 1957. He set the world 800 meter record of 1:45.7 in 1955. This year, in addition to going undefeated at 800 meters, with a best of 1:46.0, Moens ran some excellent longer races. After a 3:50.8 debut at Antwerp on May 30, he ran 3:45.6 three days later in Brussels. He won convincingly in 3:44.1 on June 23, again in Brussels, and he won some slower races. On August 26, he was in Göteborg to run against Waern. He lost, as expected, but he ran 4:01.8. He tackled Waern again, at Malmö on September 4. Waern was forced to run his last 120 yards in 14.6 to defeat Moens, 3:58.5 to 3:58.9. Behind Moens in that fine race were Ericsson, 4:00.4, and Pirie, 4:00.9.

ALL-TIME COMBINED LIST

3:38.1	(3:56.4)	Jungwirth	1957
(3:38.9)	3:57.2	Ibbotson	1957
(3:39.6)	3:57.9	Landy	1954
(3:40.2)	3:58.5	Waern	1957
(3:40.2)	3:58.6	Bailey	1956
3:40.2	(3:58.6)	Salsola	1957
3:40.2n	(3:58.6)	Salonen	1957
(3:40.3)	3:58.7	Bowden	1957
3:40.3n	(3:58.7)	Vuorisalo	1957
(3:40.5)	3:58.8	Bannister	1954
(3:40.5)	3:58.8n	Delany	1957

1957
1,500m:

3:38.1 WR	Stanislav Jungwirth (Czechosl.)	(1)	Stará Boleslav	12	Jul
3:40.2	Olavi Salsola (Finland)	(1)	Turku	11	Jul
3:40.2	Olavi Salonen (Finland)	(2)	Turku	11	Jul
3:40.3	Olavi Vuorisalo (Finland)	(3)	Turku	11	Jul
3:40.8	Dan Waern (Sweden)	(4)	Turku	11	Jul
3:41.1	Jonas Pipyne (USSR)	(1)	Moscow	4	Aug
3:41.7	Yevgeniy Sokolov (USSR)	(2)	Moscow	4	Aug
3:41.9+	Derek Ibbotson (GB)	(1)	London	19	Jul
3:42.0+	Mervyn Lincoln (Australia)	(1)	Melbourne	23	Mar
3:42.0	Siegfried Valentin (Germany)	(4)	Moscow	4	Aug
3:42.3	Stefan Lewandowski (Poland)	(2)	Cracow	29	Jun
3:42.3+	Ron Delany (Eire)	(3)	London	19	Jul

MILE:

3:57.2 WR	Derek Ibbotson (GB)	(1)	London	19	Jul
3:58.5	Dan Waern (Sweden)	(1)	Malmö	4	Sep
3:58.7	Don Bowden (USA)	(1)	Stockton	1	Jun
3:58.8	Ron Delany (Eire)	(2)	London	19	Jul
3:58.9	Mervyn Lincoln (Australia)	(1)	Melbourne	23	Mar
3:58.9	Roger Moens (Belgium)	(2)	Malmö	4	Sep
3:59.1	Stanislav Jungwirth (Czechosl.)	(3)	London	19	Jul
3:59.1	Olavi Vuorisalo (Finland)	(2)	Naantali	7	Aug
3:59.3	Ken Wood (GB)	(4)	London	19	Jul
4:00.2	Olavi Salsola (Finland)	(1)	Turku	12	Aug
4:00.4	Herb Elliott (Australia)	(1)	Melbourne	9	Mar
4:00.4	Ingvar Ericsson (Sweden)	(3)	Malmö	4	Sep

Noteworthy Indoor Mark:

4:03.8	Ron Delany (Eire)	(1)	Chicago	16	Mar

Above, Ireland and Villanova's Ron Delany, 1956 Olympic champion, shown here winning the 1958 NCAA half-mile championship.

Don Bowden, first American under four minutes.

Derek Ibbotson and Brian Hewson
Ed Lacey

Herb Elliott, considered by many to be history's greatest miler.

IX

The Elliott interlude

All logic would suppose that the next dominant miler would emerge from the explosive turmoil of the mid-1950's. Surely, the best of those would be the new record holder. But such was not the case.

An entirely new runner appeared . . . a youth with more talent, determination, and knowledge than anyone before him. Never in the history of the 1500 and mile has so much news been made in such a short time. And by one man.

HERB ELLIOTT

Born at Subiaco, Perth, on February 25, 1938, Herb Elliott showed great promise as a child. He played many sports, won age-group sprints at eight, won a half-mile at ten, and ran his first mile (5:35) at 14. He was so good that he lost only once in a mile race, to a boy three years older.

He won the state schoolboy 880 in 2:10.4 at 15. Twenty days before turning 17, he won the junior national in an Australian junior record of 1:55.7. Two days after that, he crushed Ron Clarke in a record 4:20.8. At 17, Elliott ran 4:22 in his school sports, along with winning six other events, and an excited coach Percy Cerutty told him, "There's not a shadow of a doubt that within two years you will run a mile in four minutes."

Elliott was willing, and a few days later, in October, 1955, he won the state mile in 4:20.4. In December, he broke two bones in his foot while moving a piano, and he missed the entire 1955-56 season. He quit training, but his worried parents took him to the Olympic Games across Australia in Melbourne, and his interest was restored. Inspired by Kuts' double victory, Elliott talked with Cerutty and moved to the training camp at Portsea, Victoria.

Cerutty worked Elliott to exhaustion, at the same time force-feeding him his own philosophy: "Thrust against pain. Pain is the purifier. Walk toward suffering. Love suffering. Embrace it."

Elliott's foot still pained him, but he worked as hard as Cerutty told him, running long miles, sprinting up sandhills, and lifting weights. "I wanted to be the best miler in the world."

After only two months of such intensive training, he ran a mile at Olympic Park Stadium on January 12, 1957, in 4:06.0, breaking Clarke's world junior record by 0.8 seconds. Landy watched the race and said, "Elliott is the most fantastic junior I have ever seen."

In the next few weeks, Elliott broke all of the world junior records from half a mile to three miles, with best times of 1:50.8, 4:04.4, and 9:01. He ran three other fast miles, in 4:06.0, 4:06.2, and 4:06.4.

On February 25 he had his 19th birthday and was no longer a junior. On March 9 he tried for the Australian Championships in Melbourne against Merv Lincoln, the powerful Olympic finalist who ran 4:00.6 a year ago and 4:01.8 already this year.

Elliott followed Lincoln doggedly for three laps, then ran away to win in 4:00.4 to 4:02.6, with his last 120 in 15.4. Barely 19, he had beaten one of the best milers in the world in very fast time. And two days later he won the 880 title in 1:49.3.

On May 1, 1957, he began training for 1958. During the Australian winter and spring he ran 2,500 miles and lifted tons of weights. In his first race of 1958, on January 25, he ran 3:59.9. Not yet 20, he had a great future.

Five days later he raced Lincoln, who had improved to 3:58.9. After 3:02.6 for three quarters and a strong last lap, Lincoln challenged him in the stretch and Elliott won by only two yards, 3:58.7 to 3:59.0, last 120 in 14.6. Their next race was even closer. Elliott caught Lincoln at the tape in a thriller to win n 3:59.6.

In the Australian Championships, Elliott ran his last 880 in a remarkable 1:52.8, last 440 in 52.8 for 4:08.8, then won the 880 in 1:49.4. His Australian season was over but it was only the first stage of an astonishing year.

While training at Portsea, he took time off to rescue Cerutty from the treacherous surf, the third life he had saved.

His second 1958 "season" started in California, in May. Now a strong, lean, 20-year-old with a hawk nose, 5'11½" tall and 150 pounds, he drew 34,000 to the Los Angeles Coliseum. He set a pace of 3:00.3 and won over Lincoln's 4:01.0 in 3:57.8, second fastest mile ever. After a 4:02.7 race at Modesto, he went to the little Compton stadium for a race against Delany.

After 3:01.4, he began to pull away from Delany on the backstretch and his last 120 in 14.7 beat Tábori's 4:00.5 with 3:58.1. Delany, who jogged in at 4:10, said, "Sure, I'll thrash the pants off you in Dublin town."

Two weeks later, Elliott ran in the AAU at Bakersfield. After a totally unnecessary heat in 4:01.4 the first night, he beat Lincoln in the final, 3:57.9 to 3:58.5.

Elliott said, "I have never been in such bad physical shape in my life. I felt weak. I haven't eaten well and I ran too fast last night."

He had five weeks until his third "season" started with the British Empire Games. He relaxed and "indulged my long-neglected taste for high living," to such an extent that he placed a dismal third in the AAA 880.

On July 22, at Cardiff, Wales, he ran the Empire 880 against Hewson, who had beaten him in the AAA. After a slow 58.8, Elliott shot ahead and held on to win by two yards in 1:49.3. Four days later, in the rain, he won the mile over Lincoln by a staggering margin, 3:59.0 to 4:01.9.

He was to meet Delany's challenge in Dublin on August 6, but he spent much of his time at his "high living." On August 4, though, he beat Hewson by ten yards in a 1:47.3 880. On the same day, across London, he had to run another 880 and he worked hard to win in 1:50.7.

Two days later he was at the new Santry track in Dublin. The low stands were crowded with 20,000 people and others pushed to get in. The air was moist and cool and there was no wind.

It was raining when they lined up nervously on the red track, and an Irish spectator yelled, "Do him, Ronnie."

Little Albie Thomas, a 5'5½", 124-pound Australian, set the pace. Thomas was good enough to have placed fifth in the Olympic 5000, and less than a month earlier on this same track he broke the world record for three miles with 13:10.8. His best mile was 4:01.5, and he hustled around the first lap in 56 flat.

Lincoln followed cautiously in 56.2, and Elliott remained third in 56.4. "They got off a little too fast for me." Elliott was followed by black-clad Murray Halberg, now Empire three-mile champion over Thomas.

On the second lap, Elliott moved to second and ran on Thomas's shoulder, afraid the pace would slow. But Thomas passed the half in 1:58. On his heels in 1:58.2, Elliott thought, "I don't even feel I've been running."

1958

Mentally soaring, Elliott raced past Thomas on the backstretch. "I knew I was running the fastest race of my life." But on the curve he heard footsteps and Lincoln went past. "I was thunderstruck."

The bell clanged at 2:59 and Elliott (2:59.2) moved ahead into the turn. The others were close behind and the impassioned Irish crowd were screeching for their boy, Delany.

Elliott felt invincible even though he could still hear Lincoln behind him. He drove hard down the backstretch and around the curve to the 1500 meter timers. He passed in an unofficial 3:39.6, second only to Jungwirth's world record.

Elliott sprinted the last 120 in 14.9 and finished ten yards ahead of Lincoln. He felt great.

An excited timer rushed to Elliott. "Fantastic," he cried. "It's just fantastic. Your time is 3:54.5."

He had lowered Ibbotson's record by 2.7 seconds.

Lincoln, who ran 3:55.9, joked with Delany about taking up tennis. Delany, third in 3:57.5, was violently ill, but later he regained his humor: "There is only one way to beat Elliott. That's to tie his legs together." Halberg kept shaking his head and muttering about running 3:57.5 and placing only fourth. And Thomas, fifth in 3:58.6, was exuberant.

The five men in this one astonishing mile had moved to first, second, two tied for fourth, and equal to eighth on the all-time list.

Elliott went happily off to a pub, phoned his fiancée in Australia, "and then I sat down and got a little drunk."

The next night Elliott helped pace Thomas to a world two-mile record of 8:32.0. Elliott's 8:37.6 made him fourth fastest of all-time, behind Iharos and Wood.

Elliott wanted to race in Stockholm in 18 days, starting the fourth phase of his great year. He and some other athletes drove Pirie's Volkswagen bus on a carefree trip to Sweden. They camped out, drank beer and ale, and trained sporadically. "It provided the relaxation that was desperately needed before I could train intensely again."

He was an almost-bored spectator at the European Championships and stayed at an athletic camp outside Stockholm. Refreshed and enthusiastic again, he trained hard for several days with Ibbotson, who had done little winter training after his great year and was not selected to compete in the European Championships.

1958 EUROPEAN CHAMPIONSHIPS

While Elliott and Ibbotson watched, along with Hägg and a capacity crowd at the old Olympic Stadium in Stockholm, a fast

1958

field of 1500 meter runners qualified twelve in four heats run on Friday, August 22. The first was the fastest heat ever run. After a 1:59.5 pace, the lead was taken by Hewson, running his first 1500 after his disastrous eighth place in the Empire Games. He had been shattered by his loss to Elliott in the 880 after concentrating on the half-mile this year. Then the British selection board had named him for the 1500 here and he almost quit. Only a long pep-talk from the American coach, Joe Yancey, restored his desire to run.
Vuorisalo and Rózsavölgyi followed Hewson's fast pace. Vuorisalo went on to win in 3:40.8 to 3:41.1 for a coasting Hewson and 3:41.5 for the pale Hungarian officer. Among the unfortunate non-qualifiers were new national records by Hamarsland of Norway (3:41.9), Baraldi of Italy (3:42.3), and Verheuen of Belgium (3:43.0).
In the second heat. Delany, fresh after his 3:57.5 behind Elliott, won in a rational 3:47.0, while two big-name runners showed little life and were eliminated—Richtzenhain and Ingvar Ericsson.
The third heat was won by Waern, the Swedish favorite, in 3:42.3. Waern had lost many early-season races but a training session at idyllic Vålådalen had brought him to a peak and Hägg predicted Waern would win. Qualifying second behind Waern was Siegfried Herrmann (3:42.5), making a good comeback after his disappointment in the 1956 Olympics. Herrmann had run a good 3:42.7 this year in barely losing the East German title to Richtzenhain (3:42.6).

The fourth heat was easy for Jungwirth in 3:49.0. He had started slowly this year, pointing for late season. Undefeated, he had a best of 3:43.7.

Two days after the heats, the final was run in cool weather, threatening rain. Lajos Kovács of Hungary led for the first lap in 58.0. Waern was third while Delany and Hewson were far back.
The pace slowed too much on the second lap and Waern became a reluctant leader in 2:01.4. The Swedish crowd cheered him with louder and louder, "Heja, heja, heja," as he passed 1000 meters in 2:31.0 and still led past the clanging bell (3:00.3).
With one lap to go, Waern's closest challengers were Vuorisalo, Herrmann, and Rózsavölgyi. Hewson was seventh and Delany was eleventh, waiting patiently for the sprint finish.
On the backstretch, Waern started his strong drive, but Vuorisalo tried to pass and Rózsa moved up. From the rear of the bunched pack, Delany began to pass runner after runner, just as in his exciting Olympic victory.
Around the last turn, Waern was running strongly in the lead, but the pack was at his heels. Vuorisalo began to lose ground. Into the stretch, Delany swung wide, into the third lane, and began his feared kick. It looked as if he would win as he moved past Herrmann,

1958

Vuorisalo, and Rózsa.

Hewson was in poor position, seventh going into the homestretch, but he was full of run and his kick was faster than any. He had to swing into the fourth lane to see running room ahead, but his violent sprint took him past runner after runner. He caught Delany and was surprised to edge past. Only Waern was still ahead. Waern had fought off Delany's potent kick, to the joy of the crowd, but now Hewson rushed forward, caught Waern with only five yards to go, and won going away. Hewson exulted, "My morale was completely recovered."

Results: Hewson 3:41.9, Waern 3:42.1, Delany 3:42.3, Rózsavölgyi 3:42.7, Vuorisalo 3:42.8, Herrmann 3:43.4, Orywal of Poland 3:43.7, Jungwirth 3:44.4, Lundh of Norway 3:44.7, Jazy 3:45.4, Kovács 3:51.6, Salsola 3:53.9.

Waern's last 300 in 41.8 had not been fast enough to hold his lead, for Hewson ran his last 400 in 55.5. Delany's last lap was a speedy 54.6, but he started from too far back.

ELLIOTT'S FOURTH "SEASON" OF 1958

Rested and restored, Elliott ran in a small meet outside Stockholm on the day after the European Championship 1500. He won easily from Halberg in 3:41.7. Three days later, August 28, he was in Göteborg's new Ullevi stadium to run 1500 meters against a strong field.

As he warmed up, Mike Agostini, Trinidad's friendly sprinter, called, "Hey, there, Herb, I bet you one bottle of vodka you can't break another world record today."

Elliott's great confidence spoke for him. "You're on."

Albie Thomas had promised Elliott a fast pace, but Jungwirth set out at a 56 pace. Elliott carelessly allowed himself to be boxed at the start and he was only seventh in 58 flat. Thomas took over the lead and Elliott punished himself to catch up.

Elliott caught Thomas in 1:57.5 at 800 meters. "Suddenly my limbs and lungs were being tortured no longer. I felt strong and confident."

He ran the third lap at an awe-inspiring pace and the stunned runners strung out far behind. He reached the bell in 2:42, and there was Cerutty, wildly waving a white towel to signal Elliott he was at a record pace. Now he needed a lap in 56 to break Jungwirth's excellent record and he ran hard for the whole last lap.

He passed 1200 meters in 2:55.5 and kept going, swifter than any other man had ever run. Behind him, one of the fastest fields in history seemed hopelessly outclassed even though most of them were running better than ever before.

Elliott sprinted down the homestretch, feeling elated, and

won by close to 20 yards. The crowd of 35,000 continued to applaud for a full minute before the results could be announced:
Elliott 3:36.0, Jungwirth 3:39.0, Halberg 3:39.4, Rózsavölgyi 3:40.0, Waern 3:40.9, Lewandowski 3:41.1, Lundh 3:42.1, I. Ericsson 3:47.3, Ibbotson 3:50.8, Thomas 3:55.1, Holmestrand 3:56.8.

Elliott had destroyed Jungwirth's record by 2.1 seconds with a time superior to his mile record. As at Dublin, this race completely changed the all-time list. These runners were now the four fastest 1500 meter runners of all time.

Elliott was given a bouquet and he jogged a lap of honor before tossing the flowers to the crowd. Agostini ran up to him and said, "What some people will do for a bottle of vodka!"

Elliott was scheduled to run a mile in Malmö the very next day, but he objected to plans for a four-minute mile. "I'm not a machine that can be wound up every day."

Nevertheless, he overcame his fatigue and ran a last lap in 56 to beat a disappointed Waern, 3:58.0 to 4:02.0.

Five days later he was in London for a mile under the lights at White City. European Champion Hewson was there to menace the Australian. At the three quarters in 2:59.8, Hewson was a threat on his shoulder and Elliott was having a crisis. But he put all he had into it and ran away from Hewson's 3:58.9. Tired of running, he celebrated at a night club, went to bed at 3:30 a.m., and did not hear until the next noon that his time was 3:55.4, second fastest of all time.

Two days later he was in Oslo's Bislet Idrettsplass for his last race of the year. He felt listless at the start and glad to be so near the end. But after 800 meters in 1:59 he astounded Halberg with a lap in 56.5.

Elliott was "flagging badly at the end." He lost 20 yards of his lead as Halberg ran a strong 3:38.8 and Norway's amazing Arne Hamarsland ran 3:39.8. Elliott's head throbbed and his whole body ached. His time was 3:37.4, second only to his own record, and yet the crowd applauded only mildly. It was time to quit. "I'd strained my body to the bounds of endurance and running had become a nightmare."

In the past nine days he had run four races including the two fastest 1500's of all time, the second fastest mile of all time, and the tenth fastest mile. In only 32 days he had also run the fastest mile in history, the third fastest 880, and the fourth fastest two-mile. And he was only 20 years old!

The impact of Elliott and his pursuers in 1958 can be seen by looking at the year in which the fastest combined times were run:

1958

ALL-TIME FASTEST RACES THROUGH 1958:

3:36.0	(3:54.1)	Elliott	1958
(3:36.5)	3:54.5	Elliott	1958
(3:37.2)	3:55.4	Elliott	1958
3:37.4	(3:55.5)	Elliott	1958
(3:37.8)	3:55.9n	Lincoln	1958
3:38.1	(3:56.4)	Jungwirth	1957
3:38.8n	(3:57.1)	Halberg	1958
(3:38.9)	3:57.2	Ibbotson	1957
3:39.0n	(3:57.3)	Jungwirth	1958
(3:39.2)	3:57.5n	Delany	1958
(3:39.2)	3:57.5n	Halberg	1958
3:39.4n	(3:57.7)	Halberg	1958
(3:39.6)	3:57.8	Elliott	1958
(3:39.6)	3:57.9	Landy	1954
(3:39.6)	3:57.9	Halberg	1958
(3:39.7)	3:58.0	Elliott	1958
3:39.8	3:58.1	Elliott	1958
3:39.8n	(3:58.1)	Hamarsland	1958
3:40.0n	(3:58.3)	Rózsavölgyi	1958
(3:40.1)	3:58.4	Ibbotson	1957

1958
MILE:

3:54.5 WR	Herb Elliott (Australia)	(1)	Dublin	6	Aug
3:55.9	Mervyn Lincoln (Australia)	(2)	Dublin	6	Aug
3:57.5	Ron Delany (Eire)	(3)	Dublin	6	Aug
3:57.5	Murray Halberg (New Zealand)	(4)	Dublin	6	Aug
3:58.6	Albie Thomas (Australia)	(5)	Dublin	6	Aug
3:58.9	Brian Hewson (Great Britain)	(2)	London	3	Sep
3:59.7	Zbigniew Orywal (Poland)	(3)	London	3	Sep
4:00.0	Derek Ibbotson (Great Britain)	(4)	London	3	Sep
4:00.0	Mike Blagrove (Great Britain)	(5)	London	3	Sep
4:00.5	László Tábori (Hungary)	(2)	Compton, Cal.	6	Jun
4:01.0	Dan Waern (Sweden)	(1)	Bergen	25	Sep
4:01.1	Stefan Lewandowski (Poland)	(6)	London	3	Sep

Noteworthy Indoor Mark:

4:03.4	Ron Delany (Eire)	(1)	Chicago	14	Mar

1,500m:

3:36.0 WR	Herb Elliott (Australia)	(1)	Göteborg	28	Aug
3:38.8	Murray Halberg (New Zealand)	(2)	Oslo	5	Sep
3:39.0	Stanislav Jungwirth (Czechosl.)	(2)	Göteborg	28	Aug
3:39.8	Arne Hamarsland (Norway)	(3)	Oslo	5	Sep
3:40.0	István Rózsavölgyi (Hungary)	(4)	Göteborg	28	Aug
3:40.8	Olavi Vuorisalo (Finland)	(1)h	Stockholm	22	Aug
3:40.9	Dan Waern (Sweden)	(5)	Göteborg	28	Aug
3:41.1	Lajos Kovács (Hungary)	(2)	Budapest	5	Aug
3:41.1	Brian Hewson (Great Britain)	(2)h	Stockholm	22	Aug
3:41.1	Stefan Lewandowski (Poland)	(6)	Göteborg	28	Aug
3:41.5	Bill Dellinger (USA)	(3)	Budapest	5	Aug
3:41.5	Olavi Salsola (Finland)	(2)	Turku	29	Aug

EXODUS

After the great races of 1958, the next year was a distinct letdown. Perhaps the presence of Elliott discouraged some milers, or perhaps they began a careful build-up to the 1960 Olympic Games in Rome. In any case, several big-name milers did not contest the 1500 meter championship in the Olympics.

Murray Halberg, who had run three of the twelve fastest races ever run, without winning, toured and raced half-heartedly for 5½ months before returning to New Zealand. He was married in August of 1959 and began full training again in September, but he did not

1959

return to the mile distance. He changed to longer races and won the Olympic 5000. Derek Ibbotson never really came back after his fine 1957 season, although he managed to run 4:00.0 near the end of 1958. (The first four-*flat*!) He switched to longer races in 1959 and 1960 but his best race was 3000 meters in eight minutes flat.

Lázsló Tábori went to the United States with Iglói after the 1956 Olympics. He ran 4:01.6 in 1957, 4:00.5 in 1958, 4:06.2 in 1959, and 4:00.0 in 1960, but, unfortunately, as a displaced person he was not eligible for the Olympics. He won the 1960 AAA title in 4:01.0 from Wiggs and Jazy.

Siegfried Herrmann made a fine comeback in 1959 with 1500's in 3:40.9, 3:41.2, and 3:42.5 and miles in 4:00.2, 4:02.7, and 4:02.8. In 1960 he ran 3:41.3 but failed to make the German Olympic team.

Sándor Iharos was never again the super runner who set world records at seven distances before the Hungarian revolution. In the 1960 Olympics, he placed tenth and eleventh in the 5000 and 10,000.

Roger Moens gave up the mile after his great beginning in 1957 except for one 3:41.4 1500 in June of 1960 before his surprising defeat in the Olympic 800 meters.

Brian Hewson paced himself slowly in 1959, but he won the AAA 880 championship. He was pointing for the Olympics, but he injured his leg and failed to qualify in the Olympic 800.

Ron Delany, the defending Olympic champion, ran better than ever indoors in 1959. Undefeated in ten meets, he broke his indoor mile record with 4:02.5 in the AAU, with a last quarter in 57 flat. In the Columbian Mile, he again lowered the world record with 4:01.4, last 440 in 57.5. That was the last of Delany as a great miler, for he was stopped by an injury to his Achilles tendon. He tried the 800 in the Olympics but was eliminated in the second round.

1959
1,500m:

3:38.9	István Rózsavölgiy (Hungary)	(1)	Budapest	22	Aug
3:39.3	Siegfried Valentin (Germany)	(1)	Oslo	17	Jul
3:40.7	Dan Waern (Sweden)	(1)	Göteborg	8	Sep
3:40.9	Siegfried Herrmann (Germany)	(2)	Erfurt	6	Jun
3:41.0	Stefan Lewandowski (Poland)	(2)	Göteborg	8	Sep
3:42.1	Michel Jazy (France)	(3)	Göteborg	8	Sep
3:42.2	Michel Bernard (France)	(1)	Göteborg	4	Aug
3:42.4	Stanislav Jungwirth (Czechosl.)	(2)	Ostrava	12	Sep
3:42.9	Olavi Salonen (Finland)	(1)	Turku	12	Jun
3:42.9	Derek Johnson (Great Britain)	(2)	Turku	7	Aug
3:43.0	Zoltan Vamos (Rumania)	(1)	Bucharest	15	Aug
3:43.2	Hans Grodotzki (Germany)	(3)	Erfurt	6	Jun
3:43.2	Béla Szekeres (Hungary)	(2)	Budapest	20	Jun
3:43.2	Marian Jochman (Poland)	(2)	Stockholm	9	Jul

MILE:

3:56.5	Siegfried Valentin (Germany)	(1)	Potsdam	28	May
3:58.9	Herb Elliott (Australia)	(1)	Brisbane	14	Mar
3:59.2	Dan Waern (Sweden)	(1)	Västeras	12	Aug

1959

4:00.2	Siegfried Herrmann (Germany)	(2)	London	30	Sep
4:00.6	Stefan Lewandowski (Poland)	(2)	Västeras	12	Aug
4:00.8	Arne Hamarsland (Norway)	(3)	Västeras	12	Aug
4:01.0	Jim Grelle (USA)	(4)	Västeras	12	Aug
4:01.8	Michel Jazy (France)	(4)	London	30	Sep
4:02.1	Ed Moran (USA)	(1)	Univ. Park, Pa.	9	May
4:02.3	Zbigniew Orywal (Poland)	(1)	Zurich	7	Jul
4:02.6	Mervyn Lincoln (Australia)	(1)	Melbourne	7	Feb
4:02.8	Lajos Kovács (Hungary)	(2)	London	16	May
4:02.8	Olavi Salonen (Finland)	(5)	London	30	Sep

Noteworthy Indoor Marks:

4:01.4	Ron Delany (Eire)	(1)	New York	7	Mar
4:01.8	István Rózsavölgyi (Hungary)	(2)	New York	7	Mar

1960 OLYMPIC HEATS

Competition in the Olympic 1500 heats was less fierce than in 1956 because of uneven seeding and a few failures, but the overall speed of the entrants was, as expected, far faster than ever before.

THE FIRST HEAT, to qualify three runners to the final, was held on September 3. Of the 13 hopefuls, only Elliott, Salonen, Rózsavölgyi, and Burleson were considered threats.

DYROL BURLESON of USA changed from a five-foot high jumper in the eighth grade and he was an immediate success as a miler. In 1955, as a freshman at Cottage Grove High School in Oregon, barely 15, he ran 4:43.2. He trained on a mixture of Fartlek and fast interval runs, improving only to 4:33.4 as a sophomore, and 4:24.4 as a junior. On April 25, 1958, two days before his 18th birthday, he set a new high school mile record of 4:13.2. In the AAU meet in June, he ran 4:12.2 in a heat.

As a freshman at Oregon, coached by Bill Bowerman, Burleson's first big victory came in the 1959 Drake Relays. He outkicked Tábori at the tape in 4:06.7, a new freshman record. He won at Modesto in the same time, again with his strong finish.

Burleson's "big brother" at Oregon, Jim Grelle, won the NCAA in 4:03.9 with a good last lap in 56.6, but at the AAU in Colorado's mile-high altitude, Burleson demolished Grelle over 1500 meters, 3:47.5 to 3:48.4. He said, "I was real surprised when I passed Jim," but experts suspected they had seen the emergence of a major star.

In 1960, after barely losing to Jim Beatty indoors (4:05.4 for both), Burleson broke Bowden's national mile record with 3:58.6 in a dual meet against Stanford. Pushed by half-miler Ernie Cunliffe's 4:00.4, Burleson's last lap was in 57.4. He lost at Modesto to Iglóitrained Jim Beatty. Burleson's inexperience hurt him as Beatty won, 3:58.0 to 3:59.2. (Beatty, the new national record holder, chose to run the 5000 in the Olympic Games.)

Burleson won the NCAA and the Final Olympic Trials, and his fastest 1500 was 3:41.3 on August 12.

OLAVI SALONEN was fading out of the 1500 picture. He

ran 3:42.9 and 4:02.8 in 1959, but slipped to 3:44.7 and 4:05.2 in 1960.
ISTVÁN RÓZSAVÖLGYI continued to improve. He ran five good races indoors in the United States in 1959. He lost them all, but Delany was the winner by close margins. Rózsa's best time indoors was 4:01.8, bettered only by Delany's world record.
Rózsa was undefeated outdoors in 1959 and ranked as the best miler in the world. He ran 3:39.3 at Turku on August 7 and he won the Hungarian Championships in 3:38.9 on August 22. This gave him two of the five fastest winning times ever run. He also ran four other 1500's between 3:41.0 and 3:42.3.
In 1960, Rózsa lost only once, to giant-killer Gordon Pirie, who was in great early-season condition. After that, Rózsa ran 3:40.4, 3:41.1, and won the Hungarian Championships in 3:38.8. Holder of the world record for 2000 meters and former holder at 1000, he appeared to be Elliott's strongest opponent at Rome.

HERB ELLIOTT all but retired after his unparalleled feats of 1958. He began studying for Cambridge, was married in May of 1959, and liked to play golf instead of training. "The old dedication to running had vanished."
Even so, he won. He ran miles in 4:02.4, 4:07.2, and 4:04.1. His only real test came in his last mile of 1959, against Lincoln in Brisbane, March 14. He rode with Lincoln on the five-hour journey and roused Lincoln's hopes by drinking a bottle of beer and smoking several cigarettes.
Lincoln pushed the pace past three quarters in 3:02.8 and ran hard to the last curve. Then Elliott exploded past the second-fastest miler in history and won, 3:58.9 to 4:04.8. Soon afterwards, Elliott was bent over in pain, dry retching. Completely shocked by such speed from a man obviously out of condition, Lincoln never ran well again.
As 1959 ended, Elliott thought about the Olympics, only eight months away. "On 26th December I stopped smoking and started serious training at Portsea."
When he began racing again, early in 1960, he lost two shorter races, then won his first mile impressively in 3:59.8 on the grass track at Bendigo. He traveled across Australia to his home in Perth and won the Australian Championship in 4:02.1 in spite of the high temperature. "The pain was excruciating. My stomach was convulsing and I felt every moment I would vomit."
He won the 880 championship, ran 5000 meters in 14:09.9 on April 2, and punished himself with a 33-mile run at the end of April. He went to California again and won at the Coliseum Relays 1500 in 3:45.4. His last lap in 55.9 after loafing until the backstretch proved he was still the formidable Elliott.
Then a sore knee forced him out of the California Relays at

Modesto. At Compton he ran his last lap in an easy 57 flat to win in 3:59.2 over Grelle. He returned to the Australian winter, knowing he had to improve in the three months left to him. "There were days when I was filled with self doubt."

He ran faithfully before daybreak in the streets of Melbourne, and he cut short his lunch hour because he wanted to train earlier in the afternoon. Twice a week he lifted weights instead of eating lunch, and once again he listened to Percy Cerutty. "He is like an oasis in the desert of my lost enthusiasm."

On July 23, his wife and baby son left for Rome. Elliott received a leave of absence from his job with Shell Chemical and, eager for help, joined Cerutty at Portsea. "I needed Percy's inspiration more than I could remember needing it when I was a young and dedicated athlete."

He trained hard, but there were discouragements. He ran a 2:06 half which left him gasping. And yet he broke the course record for the Hall circuit at Portsea. He ran a poor relay leg in 4:15. He wanted to break the Australian 1500 record at Newcastle, N.S.W., on August 14, but he felt ill in the morning and ran only 3:48.2. Two days later, he lost to Tony Blue in an 800. And so, after two days of hard traveling to reach Rome, Elliott arrived in doubtful condition.

But in Rome he trained easily except for one all-out day on August 30 when he finished gasping for breath as if he had run a hard race. Then he did little more than warm up until time for his heat on September 3.

The pace was startlingly fast for a heat. Salonen was out of it on the last lap. When Burleson started a drive on the last backstretch, Russia's 3:42.7 man, Yevgeniy Momotkov, had no choice but to fall back. Last to go was Terence Sullivan of Rhodesia, a tall, strong-looking runner who had never bettered 4:06.6.

Results: Elliott 3:41.4, Rózsavölgyi 3:42.0, Burleson 3:42.2. Non-qualifiers: Sullivan 3:42.8, Momotkov 3:43.6, Salonen 3:46.4.

THE SECOND HEAT was definitely weaker even though it contained Thomas, Bernard, Hamarsland, and Valentin.

SIEGFRIED VALENTIN was the runner Elliott regarded as his most threatening opponent. After winning junior races in East Germany, Valentin ran 3:52.4 in 1955 at the age of 19. He improved rapidly, to 3:47.0 at 20, and a most promising 3:42.0 at 21. But in 1958 he ran only 3:42.9.

Valentin startled the track world early in 1959. On May 28 at the Peoples Army track in Potsdam, the 5'8", 139-pound runner led from 950 meters and circled the last lap in a fast 55.8 to finish a mile in 3:56.5. This new European record had been bettered only by Elliott and Lincoln.

Valentin ran 3:39.3 on July 17. He lost form at the end and was defeated three times in September, but he came back faster than ever in 1960. He ran 800 meters in 1:46.8, broke the world record for 1000 meters with 2:16.7, and, only seven days before the Olympic heats, he ran 3:38.7 at his favorite site, Potsdam.

ALBIE THOMAS was no longer the record breaker of 1958. His fastest mile in 1959 was 4:06.2, but in January of 1960 he came back surprisingly with 3:58.8 plus an 8:35.4 two-mile.

MICHEL BERNARD was French record holder at both 1500 and 5000 meters. Now 28 years old, he had progressed slowly, with a best 1500 of 3:46.1 in 1957, 3:44.7 in 1958, and 3:42.2 in 1959. This year he had run 3:42.0 and 5000 meters in 13:55.6.

ARNE HAMARSLAND was the mystery man of the race. He ran the 1500 in 4:04 in 1956 and 4:03.8 in 1957, then produced that fantastic 3:39.8 behind Elliott and Halberg in 1958. In 1959 he ran 3:44.5 and a 4:00.8 mile. So far in 1960 he had done nothing of note.

Bernard had run a hard 5000 final the day before his 1500 heat, but he set a fast pace to win all alone. Grelle, who had run 4:00.1 behind Elliott at Compton and won the AAU 1500 in 3:42.7, ran himself into wobbly-legged exhaustion to place safely second. Hamarsland was an easy third. Valentin was obviously not himself, victim of nerves, according to German writers.

Results: Bernard 3:42.2, Grelle 3:43.5, Hamarsland 3:44.4. Non-qualifiers: Kent-Smith of GB 3:46.1, Thomas 3:46.8, Valentin 3:46.9.

THE THIRD HEAT included six runners: Lincoln, Vuorisalo, Waern, Jazy, Lewandowski, and Vamos.

ZOLTAN VAMOS of Rumania preferred the 400 and 800 until 1957, when he increased his distance. In 1958, at the age of 22, he ran 3:44.9. He improved to 3:43 in 1969 and 3:40.5 this year.

STEFAN LEWANDOWSKI of Poland became a top middle-distance runner in 1959 with 1:46.5, 3:41.0, and 4:00.6, but this was a bad year for him, with no time better than 3:44.3.

MICHEL JAZY set a French record of 1:47.9 in both 1959 and 1960. His fastest 1500 was 3:42.1 in 1959. Known as a runner with talent and courage, he had never run up to his potential, preferring to win from behind.

DAN WAERN set a world 1000 meter record of 2:18.1 after his last frustrating race against Elliott in 1958. In 1959 he ranked second in the world with a 1500 in 3:40.7 and miles in 3:59.2 and 3:59.7. In the 800, he ran 1:47.8 twice and 1:48.2 or better a total of seven times. He lowered his own world record for 1000 meters to 2:17.8. He was indisposed for part of the 1960 season but he was ready now.

OLAVI VUORISALO ran only 3:45.2 in 1959 and 3:43.4 this year.

MERV LINCOLN ran 4:02.6 before his shattering loss to

Elliott in March of 1959, but his best 1960 time was 4:03.5.

Nor did Lincoln, Lewandowski, or Vuorisalo run well in this heat. Lincoln was seventh in 3:46.8, Vuorisalo tenth in 3:52.2, and Lewandowski a poor eleventh in 3:59.3.

Results: Waern 3:43.9, Jazy 3:44.9, Vamos 3:44.9. Nonqualifiers: Schwarte of Germany 3:45.3, Kovács 3:46.0, Wiggs of GB 3:46.5.

THE OLYMPIC FINAL

On Tuesday, September 6, Elliott, who had to take penicillin for a sore throat on September 4, awakened early. He went to mass, ate breakfast, tried to sleep some more, tried to read, tried to plan his race ... At 11:30 he went out and jogged easily on grass. He ate a light salad and tried to sleep. He lay awake, with his eyes closed, until 3:00 p.m.

"My nerves and muscles were screaming for action."

He rode a bus to Stadio Olimpico and went to the dressing room. He still had to wait half an hour before his warmup. "Even the worst pain of a mile race is preferable to the two hours anxiety experienced beforehand."

He went through the tunnel to the adjoining Stadio dei Marmi and warmed up between the huge statues. When the fateful call came, the nine finalists were marched into the beautiful flag-rimmed stadium like Christians being led to the lions, and they lined up at the head of the backstretch of the red track. Elliott, in the green and yellow stripes of Australia, had the pole position he did not want.

When the gun sounded, Elliott let the others break ahead of him. Bernard took the lead and set a fast pace, and nobody disputed him. Waern ran second and Vamos third. Elliott was an uncomfortable fourth around the curve, but down the stretch to where the finish judges perched he let Hamarsland pass, and then Jazy came alongside. Bernard's fast time for 300 meters was 43.0 and Elliott thought, "I feel as though I've run two laps already. I'm more tired than I should be."

Bernard passed 400 meters in 58.2. Elliott was sixth down the backstretch and into the curve. Disliking that position, he moved to fourth. "I shouldn't feel as tired as this."

Bernard passed 800 meters in 1:57.8 with the pack crowding anxiously behind him. Elliott in fourth place was timed in 1:58.0 and it was time to make a break. He felt too tired, but he had to do it. Their last 100 meters had been run in 15.3, but Elliott rushed into the lead and ran his next 100 meters in a startling 13.2.

Behind him, the discouraged runners strung out in single file. Rózsa, who had been following Elliott all the way, stayed grimly on his heels. Jazy came next, ahead of the other blue-clad Frenchman, Bernard. A disheartened Hamarsland drifted back to last place, behind Burleson and Grelle.

Around the curve, Elliott eased his pace and he ran the next 200 meters in 28.8. Vamos was fourth, on Jazy's heels, and there was a significant gap behind him to Bernard. Burleson was on Bernard's heels, six yards ahead of Waern.

The bell clanged and Elliott went into the curve afraid of what was happening behind him. "I drove in my strides even harder, panic squeezing some additional pace out of my tired body." He sped around the curved 100 in 14 flat. "I badly wanted that medal." He reached the starting line—1200 meters—in 2:54.0. He had completed a full lap in 56 seconds and now, at last, there was a three-yard gap back to the pale, wispy Hungarian. There was no change in the order behind Rózsa, but important little gaps were appearing between runners.

Down the backstretch, Elliott sped, once more a "scared bunny." He ran that 100 in a cruel 13.6 and increased his lead to eight yards as Jazy slipped ahead of Rózsa. There at the end of the backstretch, a wild-eyed Cerutty waved his white towel. Elliott knew what it meant—a record was within his grasp—but he did not know if he had the race won.

He punished himself around that last curve, running the 100 meters in 13.6. His margin over Jazy was now an awesome 15 yards and Jazy was three ahead of Rózsa. Vamos was a hopeless seven yards behind Rózsa and three ahead of Bernard, who was struggling just ahead of Waern and Burleson.

Elliott began to tie up slightly. His time slowed to 14.4 for the last 100 meters of that torturous homestretch. "The finishing straight appeared to stretch into eternity. And trying to reach the tape was like one of those nightmares in which you run frantically from a terror behind you, never making headway."

Jazy, not knowing what was happening behind him, could only see Elliott disappearing 20 yards ahead. "I suffered the woes of hell down the homestretch, yet I think I would have tortured myself to go a bit faster if I had known I was that close to the European record."

Five yards behind Jazy, Rózsa ran another of his fast times, working to stay ahead of Waern for the bronze medal. Waern, who was six yards behind Burleson at 1200 meters, rushed past him furiously on the backstretch and went into the last curve in sixth place, nine yards behind Vamos and 14 behind Rózsa. Around the curve, Waern gained four yards. And in a mad homestretch drive, he passed Vamos by five yards and gained five on Rózsa. Burleson belately followed Waern's strong pace and almost caught Vamos as Bernard faded. Too far back to be significant, Grelle outsprinted

1960

Hamarsland for eighth place.
Results: Elliott 3:35.6, Jazy 3:38.4, Rózsavölgyi 3:39.2, Waern 3:40.0, Vamos 3:40.8, Burleson 3:40.9, Bernard 3:41.5, Grelle 3:45.0, Hamarsland 3:45.0. Another world record for Elliott. Personal and national records for Elliott, Jazy, Waern, and Burleson. A personal record for the courageous Bernard.

Elliott's last 200 was run in only 28.0 and his last 300 in 41.6, but his finishing pace becomes more impressive for longer distances. His last 400 was 55.6, his last 600 in 1:24.4, his last 800 in an excellent 1:52.8, and his last three laps in about 2:52.

On the victory stand, Elliott saw his flag and heard his national anthem, and his sophistication gave way. "The tears welled up..."

ELLIOTT RETIRES AT 22

After the Olympics, Elliott ran too hard again—eleven races in 19 days. He began at London on September 14 with a mile in 3:58.6, beating Terence Sullivan's 4:00.9.

After an easy 880 on September 17, he flew to Göteborg to race Waern in Ullevi Stadium. He got off the plane the next day only 2½ hours before the race. He ran 56 and 1:56 behind his countryman, Tony Blue, and put in a hard burst on the next lap, but he could not get away from Waern. After a neck-and-neck battle, Elliott pulled ahead desperately in the last ten meters to win, 3:38.4 to 3:38.6.

Two days later, at Malmö, an unwilling Elliott stayed behind in fourth place while an even pace was set by Blue—60.5, 2:01, 3:01.5. Waern put on his strong drive on the last lap, but Elliott held on and barely inched ahead in the homestretch until Waern gave up in the last few yards. Their times were 3:58.6 and 3:59.0. Elliott complained that the track was too heavy and the weather too cold. Gunder Hägg said Elliott showed no improvement since 1958, while Waern was better. "He brought Elliott down to earth."

After one day of rest, Elliott was back in Dublin for a big 880 race at Santry Stadium. He ran 1:48.4 but lost to the surprise Olympic champion, Peter Snell, 1:47.9, Delany 1:48.2, and Blue 1:48.2.

The very next day, Elliott followed Thomas' fast 57 and 1:57 and Tábori's 2:59, then won decisively. Results: Elliott 3:57.0, Sullivan 3:59.8, Pirie 3:59.9, Tábori 4:00.7, Snell 4:01.5, Thomas 4:02.6.

Running a third day in a row, in Glasgow, Elliott beat Blue at 1000 meters in 2:20.7. Then, four days later, in London, Elliott ran the last real mile race of his great career. He followed Bernard's

3:04.6, then sprinted one last fast half lap to finish in 3:59.8 to 4:01.6 for Bernard, 4:03 for Pirie, and 4:03.7 for Sullivan. Elliott finished the short but intense season by racing three days in a row. He beat Blue in another 1000 at Manchester, won a three-fourths mile race in Birmingham in 2:57.8, and raced the dangerous Waern again, at 1000 meters, in Stockholm on October 2. Waern had beaten Rózsavölgyi a week before, 3:45.0 to 3:46.1, but Elliott came from behind the former world record holder to win, 2:19.1 to 2:19.4.

At Cambridge, in 1961, Elliott made a half-hearted effort to run again. On May 4 he ran 9:01.2 for two miles. On May 13, he doubled in a 1:49.9 880 and a 4:07.2 mile. Then he gave it up. He had actually retired as a miler in 1960 at the age of 22, undefeated and surely unparalleled.

When he retired, Elliott had run the two fastest miles ever run and the three fastest 1500's. He ran under four minutes 17 times in mile races and five more times in 1500 equivalents. Most impressive of all, he obviously never reached his potential.

1960
1,500m:

Time	Athlete	Place	City	Date
3:35.6 WR	Herb Elliott (Australia)	(1)	Rome	6 Sep
3:38.4	Michel Jazy (Francia)	(2)	Rome	6 Sep
3:38.6	Dan Waern (Sweden)	(2)	Göteborg	18 Sep
3:38.7	Siegfried Valentin (Germany)	(1)	Potsdam	27 Aug
3:38.8	István Rózsavölgyi (Hungary)	(1)	Budapest	30 Jul
3:40.5	Zoltan Vamos (Rumania)	(1)	Prague	18 Jun
3:40.9	Dyrol Burleson (USA)	(6)	Rome	6 Sep
3:41.3	Siegfried Herrmann (Germany)	(2)	Rostock	10 Jul
3:41.4	Roger Moens (Belgium)	(1)	Antwerp	19 Jun
3:41.5	Lajos Kovács (Hungary)	(2)	Budapest	30 Jul
3:41.5	Michel Bernard (France)	(7)	Rome	6 Sep
3:41.6	Hans Grodotzki (Germany)	(3)	Rostock	10 Jul

Noteworthy Indoor Mark:

Time	Athlete	Place	City	Date
3:44.6	Siegfried Herrmann (Germany)	(1)	Berlin	28 Feb

MILE:

Time	Athlete	Place	City	Date
3:57.0	Herb Elliott (Australia)	(1)	Dublin	23 Sep
3:58.0	Jim Beatty (USA)	(1)	Modesto, Cal.	28 May
3:58.6	Dyrol Burleson (USA)	(1)	Eugene, Ore.	23 Apr
3:58.8	Albie Thomas (Australia)	(1)	Sydney	6 Jan
3:59.0	Dan Waern (Sweden)	(2)	Malmö	20 Sep
3:59.8	Terence Sullivan (Rhodesia)	(2)	Dublin	23 Sep
3:59.9	Gordon Pirie (Great Britain)	(3)	Dublin	23 Sep
4:00.0	László Tábori (D.P. Hungary)	(3)	Modesto, Cal.	28 May
4:00.1	Jim Grelle (USA)	(2)	Compton, Cal.	3 Jun
4:00.2	Dave Power (Australia)	(2)	Sydney	6 Jan
4:00.4	Ernie Cunliffe (USA)	(2)	Eugene, Ore.	23 Apr
4:00.7	Brian Kent-Smith (Gt. Britain)	(1)	London	25 Jun

Noteworthy Indoor Marks:

Time	Athlete	Place	City	Date
4:03.8	Phil Coleman (USA)	(1)	Boston	6 Feb
4:04.0	Ed Moran (USA)	(2)	Boston	6 Feb

X

The reign of Peter Snell

When Elliott abdicated in 1961, there was no dominant miler on hand to take his place, but a remarkable Olympic 800 meter champion from New Zealand was already casting his shadow on the throne.

Those who knew Peter Snell's basic speed and long endurance training marked time, waiting . . .

BURLESON MOVES TO THE TOP

After his good sixth place in the Olympics, Burleson ran one more mile in 1960. Against the British Commonwealth team in London, he ran 4:02.1 behind Elliott's easy 3:58.6 and Sullivan's 4:00.9. Grelle and Lincoln finished behind Burleson.

Coach Bill Bowerman became enthusiastic about Arthur Lydiard's training of Olympic champions Snell and Halberg, and he experimented carefully with Burleson during the fall of 1960. On January 14, Burleson had to run his first indoor race without doing any speed work, and his opponent was tough little Jim Beatty. Burleson was outkicked, 4:07.4 to 4:08.7.

Then Burleson went to New Zealand for a hectic tour of six races in 19 days. In his first, at Auckland on January 21, he edged Halberg 3:47.4 to 3:47.7. Four days later, at Napier, he won a mile against easier opponents in 4:04.0.

At Auckland on January 28, he won again in 4:05.6, barely

edging Peter Snell, who had been badly boxed behind Halberg in the stretch. On February 1 at Dunedin on a poor track, Burleson ran away from Halberg, 4:01.2 to 4:03.6.

If there was now any doubt as to Burleson's great condition it was dramatically dispelled in an 880 race at Christchurch on February 4. On a wet and soft grass track, the three medal winners from Rome finished in the same order again—Snell 1:50.1, Moens 1:50.4, and Kerr 1:50.6—but Burleson charged powerfully past them all at the end to win in 1:50.0.

In a mile at Wellington on February 8, Burleson complained of too much racing and he was too tired to overhaul Halberg at the end of a mile, 4:04.2 to 4:04.8.

Burleson ran one good indoor race before the U.S. outdoor season. At Portland, Oregon, on March 3, he ran 4:03.8, with his last 440 in 61.1, to equal the U.S. citizen's indoor record.

After winning four dual meet miles, with a best of 4:04.2, Burleson ran two excellent relay legs on the same day at Fresno on May 13. In the afternoon, he ran 4:00.4 all alone as Oregon broke the American four-mile relay record. In the evening, 8½ hours later, he ran an anchor 4:01.0 to miss the distance medley record by only one tenth. He ran first laps of 57.2 and 58.5 in his two solo runs, putting pressure on himself, and he finished in 59.7 and 59.1.

On the following Wednesday, May 24, Burleson ran in a low-pressure twilight meet on Oregon's track at Eugene. He followed while running 60 and 1:59, then led in 2:58. With the home-town crowd roaring, he finished in 3:57.6 to break Beatty's American record.

On Saturday, at Modesto, Burleson started the anchor leg of the four-mile relay twelve yards behind dangerous Mike Wiggs of Southern Illinois, a strong Englishman who had run 4:01.2 the previous year. Burleson closed the gap with a first lap in 57.7, then outkicked Wiggs in the homestretch to complete another fast leg in 4:00.5.

After a 4:05.0 mile three days later, Burleson prepared for the NCAA at Franklin Field, Philadelphia, on June 17. He ran an easy heat in 4:09.8, then won the final the next day in 4:00.5 with a fast lap in 54.7. He was ready for the AAU encounter with Jim Beatty, who had beaten him in all three of their races.

JIM BEATTY

Seven and a half inches shorter than Burleson, at 5'6", Beatty was more than five years older. His first success came at the age of 17 when, after only one month's training, he won the North Carolina state high school championship in 4:40. He repeated his victory in his senior year, with four months of training, in 4:31. As a freshman

1961

at the University of North Carolina in 1954, he ran an unsensational 4:22 and 9:44 for two miles.

He showed great promise as a sophomore by placing second in the NCAA two-mile in 9:07.6. His fastest mile was 4:15.8. In 1956, he ran 4:09.4 and 9:05.8 and placed second in the NCAA 5000. In 1957, he ran 4:06.5 and 9:01.7 to continue his progress. Then he injured an arch and placed eleventh in the NCAA two-mile. He came back well in the AAU mile for sixth place in 4:09.8.

A truly promising career all but ended in 1958 after he placed a disappointed fifth in the Drake Relays mile in 4:13.4. After missing the entire 1959 season, he moved to California to train under Mihály Iglói, who had spent a short time at North Carolina after the 1956 Olympics.

Beatty's progress accelerated under Iglói's "tempo" training. After several months of running long mileage every day in short bursts, Beatty became an exciting runner. His first race in 1960 was an indoor two-mile in 8:57.0. He raced Burleson for the first time in the Baxter Mile and came from behind the 19-year-old sensation on the last curve to win narrowly in 4:05.4.

He beat Burleson again at Modesto in an American record 3:58.0. On June 3, at Compton, he beat Tábori in an American record 13:51.7 for 5000 meters. He lost a close 5000 to Oregon's Bill Dellinger in the AAU, then won the Final Trials 5000. Foot trouble prevented a full effort at the Olympics.

He began the 1961 season with his third victory over Burleson, in 4:07.4. He also won the indoor AAU mile in 4:09.3 from Rózsa (4:10.8). Outdoors, he won an easy 4:04.9 victory over Tábori at the Mt. San Antonio Relays. At the California Relays on May 27, he crushed Grelle in the last half lap to win in 3:58.8. His last lap was 56.6.

Beatty did not endanger his reputation again until the AAU meet before 20,000 fans at Downing Stadium on Randall's Island, New York. The pace was ridiculously slow—67.2 for the first lap and the same pace for half a lap more—but Beatty seemed unconcerned.

Burleson suddenly moved faster and they passed the 880 in 2:09.2. Beatty stayed in the pack and before the last lap started, Burleson burst away with a fast drive. Beatty made no move to follow until the backstretch when he was eight yards behind. He was a hopeless twelve yards back in the homestretch and he had to sprint hard to hold off Grelle for second.

Burleson's 4:04.9 was accomplished with a last 440 in 55.3, last 880 in 1:55.7, and last ¾ in 2:57.7. Of the crestfallen Beatty, who ran 4:06.5, coach Iglói said, "I think that he did a big mistake."

In Europe, Beatty beat Salonen in the Helsinki World Games in 3:42.4 to 3:44.4, beat the Russians easily in 3:43.8, won the mile against Great Britain in 3:59.7, and then ran against Poland and

Witold Baran. Baran suddenly broke through as an international star in 1961, opening with 3:42.7 on May 20. On June 17, he won the Kusocinski Memorial from highly-regarded Vamos in 3:41.2. Baran ran a 1:48.4 800, then lost a close 1500 to Jazy in the Znamenskiy Memorial. He ran well against the USA at Warsaw on July 29, but Beatty's strong finish beat him, 3:40.9 to 3:41.9. Beatty's next race was against big kicker Waern, at Göteborg, August 3.

DAN WAERN

After his fast post-Olympic losses to Elliott, Waern beat Rózsavölgyi, 3:45.0 to 3:46.1. In 1961 he started poorly and placed eighth in the World Games, behind Beatty. He ran 3:44.3, then was suspended by the Swedish Federation pending charges of professionalism. He was exonerated in time to run a 1:49.3 880 on July 25. On August 1, at the Nordic Championships in Oslo, he won the 800 in 1:48.9. The next day he won the 1500 in 3:44.8. The following day, probably tired, he ran the race against Beatty at Göteborg and lost, 3:44.8 to 3:45.5. Then he began to improve.

On August 10 (three days after Beatty ended his successful tour by beating Roger Verheuen of Belgium 3:40.2 to 3:42.4), Waern beat Jazy in a 1:48.3 800. The next day he crushed Jazy by 15 yards in 3:42.7.

Only two days after that he ran 1:48.8. The next day he beat Jazy again in 1:49.5. Two days later he ran 3:42.3 and his big sprint beat Pirie and Jazy. After a day of rest he beat the-by-now-resigned Jazy for the fifth time in nine days. Moens was third in the 2:20.4 1000 meters.

On August 24, the busy Waern won an easy Swedish Championship in 3:46.6. The next day, at Boras, he ran a fast 800 in 1:47.5. After two more victories, he ran his last mile in Stockholm on September 1.

This race, at the Olympic Stadium, was the best European mile of the year. Waern wanted only to win. He took the lead from Pirie with a lap to go, and his times were estimated at 59.3, 2:02.2, and 3:07 (3:05.5 for 1200 meters). Then Waern shot away and ran the fastest sub-four-minute-mile last lap ever recorded—51.9. His last 120 was in 14.6.

Results: Waern 3:58.9, Valentin 4:00.2, Baran 4:00.5, Bernard 4:01.7, Pirie 4:03.2.

Then the Swedish Athletic Federation shocked Swedish fans by disqualifying Waern from further running. They were forced into action by fiscal authorities who learned that Waern owned far more newly-acquired land than he should as a young man without a profession. A French paper revealed that Waern charged for his races like a taxi, so much per meter ... according to attendance.

1961

OTHER RACES

Dublin, Aug. 10—Delany tried a comeback in the mile and beat Ken Wood 4:04.3 to 4:04.9 with a last lap in 55.3.

OTHER RUNNERS

Rózsavölgyi ran on the banked boards in the United States early in 1961 and won six mile victories while losing only a tactical race in the AAU to Beatty. The following week, Rózsa took no chances. In the Columbian Mile, he went past 1500 meters in 3:46.6 and won in 4:01.8. Outdoors, the great Hungarian began to fade away at the age of 32. His best race was 3:44.6 for third in the World Games.

1961
1,500m:

3:39.8	Siegfried Valentin (Germany)	(1)	Potsdam	5	Oct
3:40.0	Witold Baran (Poland)	(1)	Walcz	10	Aug
3:40.2	Jim Beatty (USA)	(1)	Oslo	7	Aug
3:42.0	Olavi Salonen (Finland)	(1)	Helsinki	25	Jul
3:42.2	Sándor Iharos (Hungary)	(1)	Budapest	22	Jul
3:42.3	Dan Waern (Sweden)	(1)	Lund	15	Aug
3:42.4	Roger Verheuen (Belgium)	(2)	Oslo	7	Aug
3:42.5	Michel Jazy (France)	(1)	Moscow	2	Jul
3:42.5	Michel Bernard (France)	(1)	Hässleholm	17	Aug
3:42.5	Gordon Pirie (Great Britain)	(1)	Oslo	28	Aug
3:42.6	Zoltan Vamos (Rumania)	(2)	Warsaw	17	Jun
3:42.6	Attila Simon (Hungary)	(2)	Budapest	22	Jul

Noteworthy Indoor Mark:

3:45.4+	Siegfried Herrmann (Germany)	(1)	Berlin	26	Feb

MILE:

3:57.6	Dyrol Burleson (USA)	(1)	Eugene, Ore.	24	May
3:58.8	Jim Beatty (USA)	(1)	Modesto, Cal.	27	May
3:58.9	Dan Waern (Sweden)	(1)	Stockholm	1	Sep
4:00.2	Siegfried Valentin (Germany)	(2)	Stockholm	1	Sep
4:00.5	Witold Baran (Poland)	(3)	Stockholm	1	Sep
4:01.3	Derek Haith (Great Britain)	(1)	London	22	May
4:01.3	Jim Grelle (USA)	(2)	Modesto, Cal.	27	May
4:01.4	Mike Berisford (Great Britain)	(2)	London	22	May
4:01.7	Michel Bernard (France)	(4)	Stockholm	1	Sep
4:01.8	Ken Wood (Great Britain)	(1)	Chiswick	13	May
4:01.9	Stan Taylor (Great Britain)	(3)	London	22	May
4:02.9	Bill Dotson (USA)	(2)	Philadelphia	17	Jun

Noteworthy Indoor Marks:

4:01.8	Siegfried Herrmann (Germany)	(1)	Berlin	26	Feb
4:01.8	István Rózsavölgyi (Hungary)	(1)	New York	3	Mar
4:03.6	Jim Grelle (USA)	(1)	Milwaukee	11	Mar
4:03.8	Dyrol Burleson (USA)	(1)	Portland, Ore.	3	Mar
4:04.0	Hermann Buhl (Germany)	(2)	Berlin	26	Feb

PETER SNELL

At the tender age of 12, Snell set school records in both the 440 and 880, and at 13 his talent extended to a junior cross country record. At 15 he set a school mile record of 5:21 and ran a 2:16 880. And at 16 he ran 2:01.6 and 4:48.4. Barely 18, he ran 1:59.6 early

1961

in 1957.

Snell had done his running with no specialization whatever. His best sport was tennis, where he was good enough to reach the quarter-finals of the national under-17 tournament, but he also liked cricket, the high jump and long jump, golf, badminton, rugby, and hockey.

The little running he did was discouraged by one short-sighted teammate who said, "Pete, you'll never do any good. You haven't got a finishing sprint."

Around his 19th birthday (Dec. 17, 1957), Snell surprised everyone by running 1:54.1. Lydiard became his coach, and Snell improved rapidly to 1:52.9 for third in the national championship 880. Then he began the true Lydiard training, running long distances to build his heart and capillaries for the next season. This was hard work for a muscular 5'10½" 176-pounder, and after his first agonizing run over Lydiard's hilly, 22-mile "Waiatarua", he burst into tears.

But gradually he cut his time down below three hours, to 2:40. He ran well in cross country races, and in the 1958-59 season he made a national reputation by beating Halberg at 2000 meters in 5:15.8. He won both Auckland titles, in 1:51.6 and 4:12.4, and at the New Zealand Championships on March 7 he was supreme in both events, winning the mile in 4:10.3 and the 880 in 1:52.4 less than an hour later.

Later in 1959 he continued to improve and placed fourth in the national cross country. But then he suffered a stress fracture of the tibia and he was frustratingly idle for two months. He started running again at about the same time he was 21, eight days before Christmas of 1959, but he lost twice. He won the Auckland 880 on Feb. 13, 1960, in 1:49.2 but ran a poor 4:24.8 in losing the mile, and he ran only 1:53.9 plus a 47.9 relay leg in the national championships.

On March 14, he ran an 800 in Melbourne against Elliott and Blue. After a slow start, Snell surprised the two stars in 1:51.3. That was his last race until he ran in the Olympic Games at Rome in August.

He put in six important weeks of long running and set a personal record for Waiatarua of 2:12:45. Then he began shorter training—a week of circuit running, then three weeks of hard hill running—with a fast Waiatarua on week-ends, and he took five minutes off his record. Then, in spite of the unpleasantly wet and cold winter, he began his track training.

He ran no fast trials until he was in Rome, where he ran three laps in 2:57 with the final lap of 55. Then he ran 800 meters in 1:48. Lydiard told him: "This is going to be a test of stamina and you are probably the only athlete sufficiently prepared to stand four races in three days."

1962

Snell stood them exceptionally well, for he won the Olympic championships in an Olympic record 1:46.3. Twelve days later, against the USA in London,Peter ran an 880 relay leg in an amazing 1:44.8, and he said, "In Rome, I realized I just hadn't appreciated my own capabilities."
Eight days later, in Dublin, Snell won an important 880 in 1:47.9 over Delany, Blue, and Elliott. The next night he showed there was a good mile in his future when he ran 4:01.5 for fifth place. After another good 880, in 1:47.5, he went home to a heroe's welcome.

In January and February, 1961, he lost four times, including a close mile loss to Burleson when he was badly boxed in the homestretch and finished close to Burleson's 4:05.6. But losses did not bother Snell. He used races as part of his training and he knew he could not be as sharp as he desired every week of the year.

In June he went to Europe again. He won an 800 in 1:47.6 and an 880 in 1:47.2. An hour after that good 880 he came back with a mile relay leg in 4:01.2, helping New Zealand set a world record. That run "proved to me what an athlete is capable of doing in an inspired moment," and for the first time "steered my thoughts toward more concentration on mile running."

But the next day he was disappointed with his third in 4:10.0.

Still, that was the real beginning of his great career as a miler. He beat Waern in Sweden with a 2:20.4 1000, won an 880 from the Swede in 1:48.8, and went home to rest for six weeks. By November he was in excellent shape, good enough to run Waiatarua in 2:11 and a full marathon in 2:41. The afternoon of the marathon he tried to play cricket, and that evening, worn out, he went to a party where he met Sally Turner, later to become his wife.

On January 1, 1962, he lost a handicap mile, but his time was 4:01.3, with a last lap in an impressive 56.3. He knew he was on his way to something big in the mile.

On January 20, he ran 1:48.2, and four days later, 1:47.1. He was sharp and determined to run a fast mile at Wanganui on January 27. His secret goal was to better Halberg's national best of 3:57.5.

On the morning of the competition, he jogged for half an hour. He flew to Wanganui, was pleasant at afternoon tea with relatives, and went to a hotel for privacy. He lay on the bed and ate a package of barley sugar for energy and worried about Lydiard's prediction that he would run 3:55. At six o'clock he went out and looked at the grass track, bare in spots. At 8:55 he began to warm up, nervously. At 9:30 they lined up on the backstretch of the 385-yard track.

The grounds were jammed with people anxious to see Snell run against Halberg, Thomas, and British three-mile champion Bruce

1962

Tulloh.
 Snell started too slow and he was seventh at the 220 in 31.7. He moved up to third at the 440 in 60.7. Halberg, unfit to run because a friend had died that day, nevertheless set up the pace and Snell passed the 880 in 2:00.6.
 Snell went into the lead, anxious to reach three quarters in 3:00. Just before he made it in 2:59.6, Tulloh shot past and led into the last lap. Snell ran easily, poised on Tulloh's shoulder around the curve. Then, at the start of the backstretch, he let go a tremendous drive.
 "At this point I abandoned the studied relaxation. This is the moment when you stop consciously controlling what you are doing and pour everything into driving out the utmost speed."
 And what speed it was! The crowd exploded into a roar of joy and excitement as he left Tulloh behind. "I don't think I've ever felt such a glorious feeling of strength and speed without strain."
 He raced into the curve and passed 1500 meters in 3:39.3. Now he needed only 15.7 seconds to run 3:55. Lydiard had been right all along. Snell sprinted out of the curve and down the stretch, remarkably far ahead of Tulloh, who was in the process of running 3:59.3.
 Snell was still running hard when he hit the tape and the crowd poured down on the track, almost ending the meet.
 After several minutes of joy and confusion it was determined that he had broken Elliott's world record by one tenth of a second. 3:54.4.
 His quarters had each been faster than the one before—60.7, 59.9, 59.0, and 54.8. In one race he had moved from a best of 4:01.3 to fastest miler of all time. It took a few days for him to realize the wonder of it.
 On the next Wednesday, he ran an 880 in 1:52.2. Then, on Saturday, February 3—one week after his world record mile—he ran an 880 at Christchurch before 12,000 people. After a 440 in 51 he kept pushing the pace. He passed the 660 in 1:16.9. He tied up in the stretch, but his endurance work and his courage brought him to the finish with world records of 1:44.3 and 1:45.1 for the 800 and 880.
 He was the first man in 24 years to hold both the 880 and mile records, and he was invited to Los Angeles for an indoor 1000. He broke the indoor record by almost two seconds with 2:06.0, but the award as outstanding athlete went to Jim Beatty for a record mile and Beatty's happy prancing soured Snell. "If I ever meet him on the track, it will be my pleasure to beat him."
 He returned to New Zealand and ran 3:56.8, the sixth fastest mile ever run. He won the national 880 in 1:53.9 in mud. On March 17, he ran indoors in Tokyo's new Metropolitan Gymnasium near the Olympic stadium. He beat Halberg handily in 4:06.7 and the next

night set a world indoor record of 1:49.9 for the 880.

He took a hard-earned rest for four days, then did some winter training. On April 23, he ran a mile in 4:00.5, stopped in Hawaii for a 1:47.8 half, and reached California again, keen to run in the Coliseum Relays. But when he learned he was to run against Burleson he was afraid.

Burleson, the world's best miler of 1961, had lost a slow indoor mile to Grelle, but he won dual meet miles in 4:02.5 and 4:01.2. Then, on May 12, at Fresno, Burleson ran another fast mile leg in 3:57.7—first lap in 56.4, last in 58.2—as Oregon lowered New Zealand's world record for the four-mile relay by 14.9 seconds. And Snell, afraid he was not in top shape, worried about Burleson's kick.

A crowd of 40,000 in the Los Angeles Coliseum watched the good field go through an unexciting pace. Snell followed close to the leader in 59.0 and 2:01.8, and Burleson ran close behind, intent on beating Snell.

Snell passed three quarters in 3:02.1 behind Cary Weisiger, a fast-improving former Duke miler. The suspense continued around to the last backstretch. Then, surprising each other, both Snell and Burleson moved at the same time.

Burleson's good sprint covered the last 220 in 26 flat, one of the fastest of all time, but Snell brought gasps of amazement from the crowd by running away from Burleson at a speed never before seen in a mile race.

He finished faster than most quarter-milers—24.5 for the last 220, and a record 13.4 for the last 120. He sprinted through the tape in 3:56.1, fastest mile ever run in America. Nobody who saw that finish had any doubts as to Snell's superiority over any miler in the world.

Burleson approached his US record with 3:57.9, Grelle improved to 3:58.9, as did Seaman (4:00.6), Weisiger (4:01.5), and Milt Dahl of UCLA (4:02.3). Snell's last lap was a speedy 54 flat. He was content to end his season and return to long running.

BEATTY SETS RECORDS

Able to adapt well to the sharp turns of the banked indoor tracks, Beatty ran faster than any other indoor miler. After a 4:04.8 in Los Angeles, he ran there again on February 10. He followed Tábori's 59.1, led in 1:59.6, and followed Grelle confidently past three quarters in 3:01.2, then ran away with it. He passed 1500 meters in a new indoor record time of 3:43.2 and finished well to run 3:58.9, the first indoor mile ever run under four minutes.

In great shape, he won the Baxter Mile in 4:00.9, the AAU championship in 4:00.2, and the Chicago Daily News mile in 3:59.7.

He ran little in the early outdoor meets because of injuries.

1962

He clocked 4:02.6 in a relay, then did not race for ten weeks. When he did run, however, he was ready. In the SPAAU meet in Los Angeles on June 8, he broke the world two-mile record with 8:29.8. His last lap was in 59.6.

In the AAU meet at Walnut, east of Los Angeles, Beatty had a hard fight as four U.S. runners finished under four minutes for the first time in one race. Beatty fought from behind in the stretch to win in 3:57.9. Grelle, who deserved better after leading at 1500 meters in 3:41.5, barely inched ahead of Weisiger's fine run in 3:58.1. Fourth in 3:59.0 was Bill Dotson of Kansas, who had finished third in the NCAA with 4:00.5, behind Burleson (3:59.8) and Bill Cornell of GB (4:00.5). John Davies of New Zealand was a baffled fifth in 4:00.2.

Beatty won against Poland in 3:41.9, with Weisiger second and Baran third. Beatty ran a good 3:39.9 against Russia. Then, on August 9, at Oslo, he ran a national record 3:39.4 to beat Grelle's 3:40.2.

At London, on August 18, only three days after an American record 3000 in 7:54.2, Beatty ran against a strong field. He was first at ¾ mile in 2:58.8, but Grelle passed him. They were even at 1500 meters in 3:41.3 and Beatty had to fight hard to win by two yards.

Results: Beatty 3:56.5, Grelle 3:56.7, Stan Taylor of GB 3:58.0, Seaman 3:58.0, Mike Berisford of GB 3:59.2.

Both Beatty and Grelle had broken Burleson's national record, and five men once more ran under four minutes in one race. The four-minute mile had lost its glamour.

Only three days later in Helsinki, the eager Americans ran again. All four of them, including Tábori, were members of the Los Angeles Track Club, coached by Iglói. In the Helsinki mile they ran against Olavi Salonen, who had made a good comeback last year, with 3:42.0.

Seaman led in an overly ambitious 54.5 for the 440 with Beatty in 55.5. Grelle took over the lead and Beatty caught up at the 880 in 1:55.6. Then the others could not stand the pressure and Beatty pulled away, passing three quarters in 2:58.0 and 1500 meters in 3:40.8.

Results: Beatty 3:56.3 (US record), Grelle 3:58.8, Salonen 3:59.1 (ties Finnish record), Seaman 4:01.8.

Three days after that, the irrepressible Beatty won a 5000 at Turku in US record time of 13:45.0. He also set a three-mile record of 13:19.2. His tour was completed five days later in the mud when he ran 5:10.9 for 2000 meters. On September 29, in Bakersfield, he ran an easy mile in 4:02.7.

1962

MICHEL JAZY

Born in Oignies (Pas-de-Calais), June 13, 1936, of Polish extraction, Jazy was called Michal by his relatives. His father died while Michel was young and he worked as a lift boy and as a printer's hand. On November 24, 1952, he competed in his first race and won the cross-country event by 150 meters. The next day, Paris Presse carried his picture and a caption: "Maybe he'll be famous one day."

He worked as a printer for L'Equipe and trained in the forest of Marly. In 1958 he met Woldemar Gerschler and was influenced by his theories on interval training, but later he did more varied training, including longer runs.

He ran in the 1956 Olympics at the age of 20. In the next three years, he improved to 3:43.6, 3:42.5, and 3:42.1, with 1:47.9 for 800 meters in both 1959 and 1960. His second to Elliott in the 1960 Olympic 1500 was a major triumph as well as a surprise.

After a let-down in 1961, Jazy came back strong in 1962. On May 16, he ran a 4:01.9 mile and on May 26, he set a French record of four minutes flat. The next day he ran 3:43.3.

In June, he ran other distances with great success. After warming up with a 1:48.6 800 on June 3, he ran two good 1000's in 2:19.3 and 2:20.0 on June 6 and 9.

On June 14, in the Charléty Stadium in Paris, the determined 5'8-7/8", 143-pounder started a 2000 meter test at 10:00 p.m. He led at 400 meters in 60.3, followed a 2:00.4 pace, then led at 1200 in 3:02.2. He passed 1500 meters in 3:47.7 and 1600 in 4:03.1, equivalent to about 4:04.6 for a mile. He ran an excellent last 400 in 58.4 for 5:01.5, breaking Rózsavölgyi's world record.

On June 17, at Warsaw, Jazy beat some of the best of Europe's distance runners with 3000 meters in 7:59.6, but he knew he could do better and he planned a record attempt on June 27 at Saint-Maur in another night race. He took the lead at 1400 meters, ran his last lap in 60.2, and set a world record of 7:49.2.

After some good 800's, Jazy ran a fast 1500 at Zurich on July 10. He followed Michel Bernard's 3:01.2, then sprinted away from Cary Weisiger with a brilliant last 300 in 38.6 (last 200 in 24.8) to win, 3:39.9 to 3:42.1.

Jazy won the French 800 championship in 1:48.2. After a 4:01.4 mile, 800 in 1:47.8, and a fast 880 in 1:48.0, plus lesser victories, he reached the European Championships at Belgrade undefeated.

Jazy's competition had faded away, and Baran was the main threat. After his third against the USA in Chicago on June 30, Baran was undefeated, with a 3:40.8 1500 against Great Britain. The only other likely threat was a slender 20-year-old West German named Harald Norpoth who had surprised Herrmann with his long drive in

the German trials, winning in 3:42.0. Valentin was injured. Jazy qualified in 3:47.7 on September 14, while Baran ran 3:44.1. In the final, two days later, a confident Jazy took the lead before 400 meters in 59.8, but Baran led at 800 in 2:01. Approaching the start of the last lap, one threat vanished when Norpoth fell. Jazy was content to follow Baran past the 1200-meter mark in 3:00.8. Approaching the last curve, Jazy launched his speedy attack and ran away from Baran.
Results: Jazy 3:40.9, Baran 3:42.1, Salinger of CSR 3:42.2, Böthling of Germany 3:42.7.
It was a curiously weak European Championship. The depth had swung to the United States, where seven milers ranked among the world's ten best... behind Snell.
At the end of September, Jazy won a good 800 against Germany in 1:47.3 and came back the next day in the 1500. He won an interesting tactical race in 3:45.3 to 3:45.7 for Bernard and 3:46.3 for Norpoth, who had won ten days before in 3:41.2.
On October 3, Jazy was pleased with his first sub-four mile, in 3:59.8. Four days later, at St. Maur, he made a serious effort to break Jungwirth's European 1500 record of 3:38.1. Jazy followed some fast hares while running 58.0, 1:57.0, and 2:55.1. His last 400 meters was in 57.8, but his time was 3:38.3, breaking his own French record by one tenth of a second.
Jazy closed out an undefeated season with two easy 1500's and an 800 in French record time of 1:47.1.

1962
1,500m:

Time	Athlete	Place	Location	Date
3:38.3	Michel Jazy (France)	(1)	St. Maur	7 Oct
3:39.3+	Peter Snell (New Zealand)	(1)	Wanganui	27 Jan
3:39.4	Jim Beatty (USA)	(1)	Oslo	9 Aug
3:40.2	Jim Grelle (USA)	(2)	Oslo	9 Aug
3:40.8	Witold Baran (Poland)	(1)	London	4 Aug
3:41.0	Ivan Byelitskiy (USSR)	(2)	Palo Alto, Cal.	22 Jul
3:41.1	Vasiliy Savinkov (USSR)	(1)	Moscow	13 Aug
3:41.2	Keith Forman (USA)	(3)	Palo Alto, Cal.	22 Jul
3:41.2	Harald Norpoth (Germany)	(1)	Hamburg	20 Sep
3:41.7+	Cary Weisiger (USA)	(3)	Walnut, Cal.	23 Jun
3:41.8	Karl Eyerkaufer (Germany)	(1)	Rome	23 Jun
3:41.9+	**Bob** Seaman (USA)	(3)	London	18 Aug
3:41.9+	Stan Taylor (Great Britain)	(4)	London	18 Aug

Noteworthy Indoor Marks:

Time	Athlete	Place	Location	Date
3:43.2+	Jim Beatty (USA)	(1)	Los Angeles	10 Feb
3:44.5+	Siegfried Herrmann (Germany)	(1)	Berlin	25 Feb

MILE:

Time	Athlete	Place	Location	Date
3:54.4 WR	Peter Snell (New Zealand)	(1)	Wanganui	27 Jan
3:56.3	Jim Beatty (USA)	(1)	Helsinki	21 Aug
3:56.7	Jim Grelle (USA)	(2)	London	18 Aug
3:57.9	Dyrol Burleson (USA)	(2)	Los Angeles	18 May
3:58.0	Stan Taylor (Great Britain)	(3)	London	18 Aug
3:58.0	Bob Seaman (USA)	(4)	London	18 Aug
3:58.1	Cary Weisiger (USA)	(3)	Walnut, Cal.	23 Jun
3:58.3	Keith Forman (USA)	(1)	Modesto, Cal.	26 May
3:59.0	Bill Dotson (USA)	(4)	Walnut, Cal.	23 Jun
3:59.1	Olavi Salonen (Finland)	(3)	Helsinki	21 Aug
3:59.2	Mike Berisford (Great Britain)	(5)	London	18 Aug

1962

3:59.3	Bruce Tulloh (Great Britain)	(2)	Wanganui	27	Jan
3:59.8	Michel Jazy (France)	(1)	Lille	3	Oct

Noteworthy Indoor Marks:

3:58.9	Jim Beatty (USA)	(1)	Los Angeles	10	Feb
3:59.9	Siegfried Herrmann (Germany)	(1)	Berlin	25	Feb
4:01.4	Jim Grelle (USA)	(1)	Milwaukee	10	Mar
4:01.7	Tom O'Hara (USA)	(2)	Chicago	9	Mar

SNELL PROVES HIMSELF

Early in June of 1962, soon after his victory over Burleson, Snell began training for the British Commonwealth Games to be held in Perth, Australia. He won an exciting Auckland cross country championship, beating Bill Baillie by three yards over 10,000 meters. Then Snell won the national cross country by a remarkable 41 seconds.

He suffered an inevitable slump in August. And in September he broke a bone in his foot and had to rest for a month. On October 22, five weeks before important competition, he ran a hard 880 and could clock only 1:56 in a losing effort.

And yet, on November 26, he won the Commonwealth title in the 880 by edging George Kerr in 1:47.6. On November 29, he qualified for the mile in 4:02.4. "It was just no trouble at all."

On the morning of the mile final, December 1, he ran a hard 440 trying to qualify New Zealand in the mile relay. In the mile, he was content to disappoint the crowd of 45,000. After three quarters in 3:09, he won by four yards in 4:04.6.

Early in December, Snell had trouble beating Baillie in a 4:03 mile. On December 15, in Upper Hutt, he ran a satisfying 880 in 1:47.4, but the distance was doubtful. The Oregon team arrived for a tour and Snell beat Keith Forman and Burleson under poor conditions, with John Davies, the new New Zealand hope, fourth. After a day of water skiing which left him stiff and sore, Snell edged Burleson in a 1:48.8 half-mile. Then, in a four-mile relay, Snell held his lead on the anchor leg with an easy 4:02.2 mile.

After a 4:03 mile on February 4, he had to run indoors in Los Angeles five days later and he lost to Grelle, 4:04.7 to 4:06.4. Snell knew he was past his peak, but he agreed to run against Davies on the new all-weather track at Dunedin on February 15 before the Queen of England. Snell felt tired all the way and barely pulled even at 3:02. He won an agonizing duel by two feet in 3:58.6 to 3:58.8.

Snell won the Auckland 880, but he did not feel well enough to run in the nationals. "I was concerned to put something back into the bank to wipe out the overdraft on which I had been operating." He trained with long, gentle runs until May, when he was married and left for a honeymoon which was to include three races in California.

After a pleasant stop in Hawaii and a 1:49.5 880 time trial,

1963

Snell raced first in the Coliseum Relays, against Burleson and a new rising star, Tom O'Hara. Burleson had not run indoors and he lost at the Texas Relays when young John Camien proved a better mudder, 4:02.6 to 4:02.9. Burleson did win at the Drake Relays though in 4:05.4.

Tom O'Hara, a small fiery redhead from Loyola of Chicago, ran 4:01.7 indoors in 1962 at the age of 19. He won the NCAA cross country championship in the fall and lost a poor tactical mile in the Sugar Bowl at year's end. Indoors in 1963, he won the Wanamaker Mile in 4:01.5, was an admirable second to Beatty's 3:58.6 in the Baxter Mile with 3:59.2, and won at Chicago in 3:59.5.

O'Hara set a reluctant pace in the Coliseum in 62.1, 2:04.2, and 3:06.5. He led to the homestretch, then Snell struggled past. Burleson, with a shoe full of blood from a spike wound, gave Snell the jump and then gave him a fright, losing by four feet.

Results: Snell 4:00.3, Burleson 4:00.8, O'Hara 4:02.0, Seaman 4:04.1.

Snell's last lap in 53.1 had the fans shaking their heads.

Beatty, who had run 3:58.6 and 3:59.0 indoors, and set a two-mile record of 8:30.7 at Chicago, looked great in the Coliseum 5000, outkicking Halberg, and he decided the time had come to challenge Snell. The big race was to be at Modesto on May 25. Also in the race would be Grelle, who ran 4:00.0 and 3:59.8 indoors and then outsprinted a dismayed Beatty in the Pan-American Games 1500, John Camien, Bobby Seaman, and Cary Weisiger, who ran a solo 3:59.2 on May 4.

The publicity build-up was the greatest Snell had ever known, and 40 million people wanted to watch on television. Snell said of Beatty, "If he won, I felt, I was done."

Weisiger said wryly, "If we can't beat this guy on his honeymoon, we never will."

Snell was tense until the race started. "I was so nervous I couldn't finish my warmup."

Snell, still relatively inexperienced in mile racing, stayed safely in the middle of the pack, passing the 440 in 59.3 in sixth place. Beatty led at the half in 1:59.1, while Snell was fourth in 1:59.7. Weisiger led aggressively past three quarters in 2:59.4, followed by Grelle, Beatty, and Snell in 3:00.2.

Snell moved alongside Beatty around the curve to shut off Beatty's long drive. Then he moved ahead of Beatty on the backstretch and waited for the little runner's big kick. But it never came, and Beatty did not look especially dangerous as they approached the last turn.

Then, as sudden as a flash of lightning, Snell moved into high gear and took the lead as they reached the curve. Such speed has never been seen before on the last turn of any mile. Within 50 yards he had gained ten yards on some very fast milers. He gained another five yards on the astonished Americans before the stretch. Then he looked back and, satisfied, coasted to the finish.

Results: Snell 3:54.9, Weisiger 3:57.3, Beatty 3:58.0, Grelle 3:58.0, Camien 4:00.7, Seaman 4:05.3.

Snell's time was only half a second from his world record, quite surprising after a moderate pace. Some experts declared that Snell was unbeatable with such a fast finish (last 120 in 14.0). Others said he was not as much better than the Americans as it appeared on the last curve, because part of his victory was the result of surprise. They looked forward to a closer race on June 7 at Compton.

Only O'Hara was missing from the Compton race, and Snell had both Beatty and Burleson to worry about, especially since he felt "about raced out for the season."

Young Morgan Groth set a fast pace in 57.8, followed by Beatty and Grelle, with Burleson and Snell (58.7) in seventh and eighth places. Beatty took the lead at the half in 1:59.0, followed vigilantly by Grelle, Weisiger, Snell (1:59.5), and Burleson. With the pace slowing and the nine-man field bunched, it looked as if it would be another thrilling finish.

But Weisiger changed things dramatically in the middle of the third lap. He pulled away from the others, opening a five-yard lead over Snell and stringing out the discouraged field. Weisiger passed three quarters in 2:57.8—a lap in 58.6—and Snell was second in 2:58.7, faster than he wanted to run.

As Snell calmly cut down Weisiger's lead, Grelle and Burleson followed the black-clad New Zealand figure closely but Beatty surprised everyone and fell behind. As they reached the backstretch Weisiger's lead had vanished, but Beatty was 15 yards back.

Around the last turn, Snell waited on Weisiger's shoulder and glanced back at the others. Weisiger became the official American record holder when he passed 1500 meters in 3:39.3. Snell (3:39.4) felt, "I couldn't sprint as I wanted to," but he surged past Weisiger and opened a gap.

Burleson shot after Snell and finished well, but he could not gain. When he saw he could not win he eased off from the agonizing effort, unaware of Beatty, whose belated sprint brought him up from far behind. Beatty passed Burleson near the end to steal an American record, and Grelle beat out Weisiger.

Results: Snell 3:55.0, Beatty 3:55.5, Burleson 3:55.6, Grelle 3:56.4, Weisiger 3:56.6, Seaman 3:59.1, Groth 4:00.8.

Snell had now run three of the four fastest miles ever run. The runners behind him ran faster than any other defeated runners in history for their respective places.

Snell (last 120 in 15.6) said, "I didn't have my usual kick. I had more left but I couldn't use it. It was a real hard race." He returned to New Zealand for a rest, his season ended for the year.

JAZY COLLECTS EUROPEAN RECORD

Having taken his place as one of the all-time great middle distance runners while a 26-year-old in 1962, Jazy began to increase his reputation early in 1963. In May he ran a French record 1000 in 2:19.1 and another in 2:19.6.

On June 6, one week before his 27th birthday, Jazy, already holder of two world records, went after the two-mile record at Charléty Stadium to add to his collection. At 3000 meters he was 2.6 seconds behind Beatty's world-record pace, but he sprinted the last 200 in 26.5 to set a new world mark of 8:29.6.

Jazy ran a fast 3:39.5 1500, beat Norpoth by more than 20 yards in an 8:06.4 3000, and beat Bernard at 5000 meters in 14:02.4. He won a 1500 in 3:49.6 with his last 400 in a sizzling 51.7. On July 2 in the Znamenskiy Memorial in Moscow, he defeated a strong field in the 5000 in 13:50.2. Now he was a contender at both Olympic distances.

In the French Championships at Colombes Stadium on July 28, young Jean Wadoux led in 58.2. At 800 meters in 1:57.1, the leader was Bernard, who had set a French mile record of 3:58.2 on July 8. Jazy led at 1000 meters in 2:26.4, but Bernard led again at 1200 meters in a startling 2:55.7.

With the crowd howling from excitement and anticipation of a fast time, Jazy went ahead on the backstretch and won with a new European record of 3:37.8. Bernard's time was a fine 3:38.7.

Jazy spent almost a month at the famous Swedish training center, Våladalen, and injured an ankle. But he ran a 4:00.8 mile on September 3. Two days later he raced Bernard, who had failed to break Jazy's two-mile record when he ran 8:34.8 a few days earlier. Jazy barely beat Bernard in 4:03.7, ahead of Norpoth and Wadoux.

Jazy's ankle bothered him and he barely beat Wadoux in the 1500 against the Russian Republic. Doctors advised him to retire for the season, but he was stubborn and ran a 1500 in a small meet a month later, suffering his first outdoor defeat since August of 1961. He ran only 3:50 and lost to an unknown Swiss.

SIEGFRIED VALENTIN

After his injury in 1962, with an extremely poor competitive record alongside his fast times at Potsdam, Valentin came back strong in 1963. He started with five fast races in 13 days near the end of June.

He ran first on June 18 at Potsdam, with 1000 meters in 2:17.9, a time bettered by only one other man. On June 22, in East

1963

Berlin, he squeaked past Vamos 3:43.0 to 3:43.1. The next day, at Halle, he beat Herrmann, 3:39.4 to 3:41.7. Three days later, again at Potsdam, he narrowly missed his own European mile record of 1959 when he ran 3:56.9, last 120 in 15.9. Not content, he ran 3:39.7 four days later at Potsdam.

Valentin avoided fast running for about a month, but he ran a good 3:40 on August 3, ahead of dangerous newcomer Jürgen May and Herrmann, and won at Göteborg in a 4:04.8 mile on August 16. In the national championships at Jena, September 1, he foolishly allowed a slow pace and was outkicked by a half-miler.

At Moscow on September 14, he beat Baran handily, 3:43.9 to 3:44.4. Then came a good race at Varna, Bulgaria, on October 9. Valentin ran his last 300 in 42.9 to win a great race in 3:38.9 from 21-year-old Jürgen May (3:39.3) and Herrmann (3:39.8).

Valentin lost another poor tactical race to Alan Simpson of Great Britain, 3:46.3 to 3:46.0, then closed his season by beating Herrmann in a crowd-pleasing 3:41.4 to 3:41.5.

1963
1,500m:

3:37.8	Michel Jazy (France)	(1)	Colombes	28	Jul
3:38.7	Michel Bernard (France)	(2)	Colombes	28	Jul
3:38.9	Siegfried Valentin (Germany)	(1)	Varna	9	Oct
3:39.3+	Cary Weisiger (USA)	(1)	Compton, Cal.	7	Jun
3:39.3	Jürgen May (Germany)	(2)	Varna	9	Oct
3:39.4+	Peter Snell (New Zealand)	(2)	Compton, Cal.	7	Jun
3:39.8	Siegfried Herrmann (Germany)	(3)	Varna	9	Oct
3:40.5	Witold Baran (Poland)	(1)	Bydgoszcz	12	May
3:41.0	Dyrol Burleson (USA)	(1)	Moscow	21	Jul
3:41.3	Tom O'Hara (USA)	(2)	Moscow	21	Jul
3:41.7	Jean Wadoux (France)	(3)	Colombes	28	Jul
3:42.2	Volker Tulzer (Austria)	(3)	Halle	23	Jun
3:42.2	Tomáš Salinger (Czechoslovakia)	(1)	Ljubljana	31	Aug

1 MILE:

3:54.9	Peter Snell (New Zealand)	(1)	Modesto, Cal.	25	May
3:55.5	Jim Beatty (USA)	(2)	Compton, Cal.	7	Jun
3:55.6	Dyrol Burleson (USA)	(3)	Compton, Cal.	7	Jun
3:56.1	Jim Grelle (USA)	(2)	Toronto	25	Jun
3:56.6	Cary Weisiger (USA)	(5)	Compton, Cal.	7	Jun
3:56.9	Tom O'Hara (USA)	(2)	St. Louis	22	Jun
3:56.9	Siegfried Valentin (Germany)	(1)	Potsdam	26	Jun
3:58.2	Michel Bernard (France)	(1)	Cambrai	8	Jul
3:58.8	John Davies (New Zealand)	(2)	Dunedin	15	Feb
3:59.1	Bob Seaman (USA)	(6)	Compton, Cal.	7	Jun
3:59.1	Siegfried Herrmann (Germany)	(1)	Erfurt	24	Sep
3:59.2	Witold Baran (Poland)	(2)	Toronto	12	Jul
3:59.6	Albie Thomas (Australia)	(1)	Sydney	9	Feb

Noteworthy Indoor Marks:

3:58.6	Jim Beatty (USA)	(1)	New York	15	Feb
3:59.2	Tom O'Hara (USA)	(2)	New York	15	Feb
3:59.8	Siegfried Herrmann (Germany)	(1)	Berlin	24	Feb
3:59.8	Jim Grelle (USA)	(2)	Chicago	8	Mar
3:59.8	Bill Dotson (USA)	(3)	Chicago	8	Mar
4:01.8	Cary Weisiger (USA)	(2)	New York	1	Feb

THE AMERICANS

Fortunes of the milers from USA were rising in the early

1960's. As a result of their fast finish behind Snell's 3:55.0 at Compton in 1963, four of them were among the fastest eight milers of all time, and O'Hara was not in the Compton race.

O'Hara joined the battle at the AAU championships on June 22 after running 4:02.5 at Chicago on June 8 and winning the NCAA in 4:04.8 only to be disqualified for a doubtful infraction which gained him no advantage.

The AAU was held on a springy rubber track in St. Louis in weather which was mercifully cooler and less humid than expected. Only twelve men were optimistic enough to enter the mile, but heats were run on Friday before 7500 people.

Only 10,000 watched on Saturday as Beatty set a first-rate pace of 58.1, 1:59.5, and 3:00.0. Grelle, who had a troublesome cyst removed from his foot three weeks before, dropped out after the half. He seemed to be running well when his foot started hurting and he said, "I knew right away I should have kept running."

Weisiger was poised expectantly on Beatty's heels at the start of the last lap, followed by O'Hara and Burleson. The others were at least a hopeless ten yards behind Beatty.

An exciting race developed on the backstretch as Weisiger edged ahead of Beatty for a moment. On the last curve, all four were bunched, with O'Hara unhappily boxed inside Burleson. Suddenly Burleson cut loose with a Snell-like drive and broke up the battle.

Only O'Hara tried to catch Burleson. His pale legs flashing in the sun, O'Hara sprinted beautifully, gaining on Burleson, and he lost by only two feet. Weisiger fought past Beatty on the inside about 40 yards from the finish line.

Results: Burleson 3:56.7, O'Hara 3:56.9, Weisiger 3:58.5, Beatty 3:59.2, Camien 4:01.2, Seaman 4:05.6.

Burleson said, "I don't know if I could have lasted another couple of yards," and O'Hara added, "I might have caught him in another couple of yards."

Beatty complained of a knee injury, but three days later he ran in Toronto against Grelle, whose foot did not bother him. Beatty pushed the pace hard for three laps with Grelle close behind. Beatty pulled away slightly at the start of the last lap, but Grelle closed in the stretch to run his fastest mile. His 3:56.1 barely lost to Beatty's 3:56.0.

On July 4, in Oregon, Burleson trounced Weisiger, 4:00.3 to 4:01.9. At Toronto again, on July 12, Baran of Poland led at three quarters in 3:01, but Weisiger's surprise drive gave him a five-yard lead at the head of the backstretch. Grelle fought alongside Weisiger in the homestretch, but Weisiger pulled away to win by four yards. Beatty hobbled in fourth, his knee hurting.

Results: Weisiger 3:58.8, Baran 3:59.2, Grelle 3:59.3, Beatty 3:59.7, Cornell 4:00.8.

1964

The USA team went to Russia for the big dual meet in Moscow on July 21, and Burleson had to struggle from behind O'Hara in the stretch to win, 3:41.0 to 3:41.3.

In the dual meet against Poland, at Warsaw on July 26, the early pace was very slow and Burleson was forced into the lead. Baran jumped him on the last backstretch, followed by O'Hara, but Burleson fought back to win in 3:50.0 to O'Hara's 3:50.2 and Baran's 3:50.4.

The next week, against West Germany at Hanover, Burleson had gone home and O'Hara won the 800 in 1:49.3. In an upset, Morgan Groth won the 1500 over Weisiger, 3:42.4 to 3:43.1.

Against Great Britain at the famous White City in London, on August 3, O'Hara won the mile handily in 4:03.0 to Weisiger's 4:04.9. Alan Simpson dropped out.

This ended the important racing for the Americans, and five of them ranked among the seven best in the world for 1963. And young milers were improving rapidly. John Camien, not yet 20, was second in the NCAA cross country race in November. Morgan Groth's enthusiastic coach at Oregon State, Sam Bell, who had coached Burleson in high school, said Groth had as much potential as Burleson. And Bill Bowerman said one of his young runners "has the greatest potential of any runner that has ever come to Oregon." This was the son of a former great miler, Archie San Romani, Jr.

O'Hara won easily at the 1964 Boston KC in 4:06.3. Then he ran the fastest Wanamaker Mile in history (4:00.6) to beat Camien (4:02.6). Camien ran a good 4:01.9 mile and in the Baxter Mile he led O'Hara (60.0 and 2:01.5) in 2:01.3. But O'Hara was on top at three quarters in 3:01.6 and shattered Camien with a great 55 flat quarter for a world indoor record of 3:56.6.

In the Columbian Mile, O'Hara ran 3:58.5 all alone, with his last 440 in 56.6. At Chicago, on March 6, the tough little Irishman followed a fast 58.1 and 1:58.8 and then led in 2:59.8 with Grelle close behind. "I was afraid of him, O'Hara said. "He has that kick, too."

O'Hara passed 1500 meters in 3:41.6, fastest ever run indoors, and pulled away to break his own record in 3:56.4. Grelle was well beaten in 3:58.9.

With O'Hara injured, Grelle won at Cleveland the next week in 4:02.3, a record for a twelve-lap track. Outdoors, Grelle began with 4:01.3 at San Diego on March 23. At the Mt. San Antonio Relays on April 25, he was scared by San Romani, who finished only one tenth of a second behind Grelle's 4:01.1.

O'Hara won at Drake in 4:01.0, but he needed a 56.8 last lap to beat Camien by four yards. On May 13, Burleson ran 3:57.5 in another fast solo mile at Eugene. Two days later, in the Coliseum Relays, Camien outkicked Grelle in a good race, 4:00.7 to 4:01.4.

1964

The next day, in Raleigh, North Carolina, Weisiger ran 3:59.5. Groth and San Romani took turns beating each other. With the serious racing about to begin—at the California Relays—only one good prospect was not being considered.

JIM RYUN

As a boy, Jim Ryun enjoyed the usual boyish activities, including Little League baseball, basketball, and bowling in his hometown of Wichita, Kansas. He was taller and skinnier than most and somewhat awkward and frail-looking, but he was determined to be an athlete.

He first tried track in junior high school at about the time he was 15 years old on April 29, 1962. After some light sprint training he was able to run a 440 in 58.5, but that was not fast enough to make the team.

That summer, in the Junior Olympics program, he trained himself. "I'd run from my house down two blocks and back, and then lie down on the ground and die." He only improved to 56.4, but he had established a pattern of punishing hard work.

In the fall, a gangling 6'1" tall, he entered East High School and, almost by accident, tried out for the cross country team coached by Bob Timmons. Jim could not complete the workouts assigned and after a week he tried to run a mile. He finished 13th in 5:38, far behind another sophomore's 5:13. Nobody was impressed.

Coach Timmons, echoing Percy Cerutty, said, "Champions have the ability to battle pain," and Jim was good at that. He suffered through long interval workouts in which he covered ten to 15 miles. His mother said, "Sometimes he'd come home so sick he wouldn't want to eat."

As it turned out, Jim had exceptional talent, and the hard work developed him in rather amazing fashion. At first, he barely made the "B" team in cross country. By October 5 he was good enough to surprise everybody by winning a "B" race in Kansas City. But his time would have placed only 41st in the "A" race.

And yet, in only one month, he improved so much that he placed sixth in the state championship "A" race. Jim trained only about twice a week through the unkind Kansas winter, but when track season began, his improvement continued.

After practice miles in 4:48, 4:49.5, and 4:45, he was on the track excited about the first mile race of his career, in March, 1963. Against the defending state champion, Charles Harper, Jim ran 4:32.4 and barely lost. Timmons said, "I just couldn't believe it."

The very next week, Jim beat Harper in 4:26.4 and Timmons realized Jim's potential. He told Jim, "You've got a chance to run under four minutes in high school."

241

1964

Nobody else thought so, including Jim, but he kept working and improving. On April 6 he beat Tom Yergovich, the state cross country champion, in 4:21.7, with a surprising last lap in 60.7. He kept winning, and ran 4:19.7 on April 24. Two days after his 16th birthday, he came into national prominence with 4:16.2. And on May 18 he won the state championship in the same time.

Both Timmons and Jim were disappointed with his time, and Timmons entered him in the Missouri Valley AAU meet on May 25 against formidable Cal Elmore of Wichita University, who was later to place second in the NCAA mile.

On a damp and drizzling night in Shawnee Mission, Kansas, Elmore set a fast pace and Jim stuck to him doggedly. Jim passed three quarters in 3:07.7, five seconds faster than any pace he'd ever tried. Three weeks before, when he tried his fastest pace, he could finish no faster than 64.8 for the last lap, but he had improved astonishingly, and he finished in 60.5.

His time behind Elmore's 4:06.1 was 4:08.2, faster than the national high school record, and he had only finished his sophomore year. That time, and his 1500 meter time of 3:49.7, were world bests for 16-year-olds.

This rapid development was one of the most remarkable happenings in the entire history of track and field, yet Jim had no time to appreciate it. He was sick after the race, and then Timmons had him run the 880 an hour and 45 minutes later. Jim was fifth in 1:54.5.

The next week he disappointed the unenlightened with another fifth in an 880, but this time he ran 1:53.6, a world best for age 16. And the following week he placed sixth in the first national Federation Championships with his best-ever time of 4:07.8.

Jim continued his hard running in the summer and recorded the fastest two-mile ever run by a U.S. schoolboy—9:13.8. He had finished an amazing season for a 16-year-old, but many a great prospect has failed to develop.

In the fall he won the state cross country championship in record time. He suffered only one defeat—third in the district AAU cross country over four miles. Then he ran an indoor two-mile in San Francisco but he fell at the start and finished second behind a fast 9:00 by another amazing schoolboy, Gerry Lindgren, in Gerry's first major breakthrough.

Jim trained hard all winter and in the spring of 1964. His goal was a 4:02 mile, and he ran 4:11 easily at the Kansas Relays. The next day he ran an 880 relay leg in 1:51.9. On May 1, he ran 4:09.6 with a satisfying last lap in 59.3. In the regional meet he ran 4:12.6. In a workout, he ran ¾ mile in 2:58 with his last lap in 55. "I felt real good."

On May 15, in the state meet at Manhattan, Kansas, he ran a

fast 880 relay leg in 1:51.0. The next day he won the mile championship in 4:06.4, an official national high school record, and he was invited to California to run against the best milers in the United States.

THE AMERICANS (Part 2)

On the night of May 23, at the California Relays in Modesto, a capacity crowd of about 8,000 anticipated the first mile race of the season between Burleson and O'Hara. Also of interest were Weisiger, Camien, Seaman, and young Ryun. Jim Beatty had returned to North Carolina. Training on his own, away from Iglói, he was in poor shape and he declared he could try for the 5000 meters this year.

The Modesto mile was disappointing from a time standpoint, because Burleson was content to run in the middle of the pack in 62.7, 2:04.3, and 3:05.8. O'Hara waited patiently behind Burleson, and Ryun was close in 3:06.0.

In the middle of the last backstretch, O'Hara accelerated with a burst almost as fast as one of Snell's. He sped away, with only Burleson after him. He let down at the end and Burleson gained about two yards in the last ten. Burleson was awarded a disputed decision in 4:00.2.

Meanwhile, Ryun saw Burleson shoot away from him with bewildering speed on the backstretch. He had been running the same pace as in his state meet 4:06.4 when he could finish no faster than 60.5. But now, suddenly, he came to life with a fast drive of his own. He ran past Seaman immediately, and a few fans began to notice his speed. He rounded the curve as never before and he passed Camien going into the homestretch.

Now the fans were torn between watching the great duel for first place or this new athletic wonder bearing down on Weisiger for third place. Weisiger let up at the end and Ryun went past him for third in 4:01.7. Ryun's last lap was a startling 55.7.

Timmons said, "I nearly fell out of the stadium." This age-17 world best was within the fastest 75 one-miles ever run, and Ryun was less than a month past his 17th birthday.

Burleson said, "Isn't that amazing? . . . When I was a junior in high school my best time was 4:24."

Two weeks later, at the Compton Invitational on June 5, they all tried again. Grelle, who beat Baillie in four-flat on May 29, joined them, as did the three top collegians, San Romani, Groth, and Bob Day, who had a best of 4:01.8 and an eye-opening half-mile relay leg in 1:46.1.

With so many fast milers in the race, the pace could hardly be slow, but a hare was added to make certain. Bob Delaney ran 57.9 and 2:00.2 before dropping out. The pack was bunched behind

Grelle, who ran 58.6 and then caught Delaney. Unfortunately, Ryun was knocked off the track on the curve before the half-way point and lost time and position, but he kept trying.

Groth, in the orange and black of Oregon State, led at three quarters in 3:01.6, but so eager were the others that Weisiger, the only runner behind seventh-place Ryun, was timed in 3:02.8. Then, as the pace became faster, the pack bunched ever more.

At 1500 meters, Grelle led in 3:42.9 with Burleson threatening on his shoulder and O'Hara close behind. Weisiger, still in eighth place, was now only 0.8 seconds behind. It was an amazing battle.

Then the sprint started. Grelle finished with a reasonable 15.6 for those last 120 yards, but Burleson and O'Hara rushed away from him, San Romani sprinted past, faster than anybody, and Groth pulled away in the stretch. Ryun fought hard, finishing in 15.5. He almost caught Day, but Weisiger edged past him and Ryun finished a strong eighth.

Results: Burleson 3:57.4, O'Hara 3:57.6, San Romani 3:57.6, Groth 3:57.9, Grelle 3:58.5, Day 3:58.9, Weisiger 3:58.9, Ryun 3:59.0.

Grelle, not yet at his peak, ran the slowest last lap, in 56.6. Ryun ran 56.2. San Romani ran the fastest, with 54.9. Both Burleson and San Romani ran the last 120 in a sizzling 14.4.

Eight men ran under four minutes in the one race, and four of them did it for the first time. Out of such a mass of fine performances, much was overlooked. Perhaps the most perceptive statement was made by Burleson, who was usually taciturn:

"There was nothing unusual about my victory. The entire story was back in eighth place. There is simply no way to imagine how good Jim Ryun is or how far he will go after he becomes an adult. What he did was more significant than Roger Bannister's first mile under four minutes."

Eight days later, in San Diego, the strong 5000-meter runner, Bob Schul, who had run miles in 4:01.6 and 4:00.9, beat Weisiger, 3:59.1 to 4:00.0. This made the remarkable total of eleven active U.S. milers who had run under four minutes, including Beatty and Bill Dotson, who were not running well this year. Camien had not yet made it.

At this point in history, a total of 48 runners had broken four minutes and 33 of them had run 3:59 or faster. Only 17 had run 3:58 or faster.

Elliott led the list of sub-four miles with an imposing total of 17, followed by Beatty with eleven, Grelle with ten, Burleson and Snell with nine, and Waern eight.

The nine milers who had run 3:57.0 or faster had accomplished the feat a total of 24 times, including twice indoors. Snell led with five such fast runs, Beatty had done it four times,

1964

Elliott, Grelle, and O'Hara three times, and Burleson and Valentin twice.

Thus, the Americans were in the thick of it, but at that point they changed to 1500 meters for the remainder of the Olympic year. In the NCAA, at Eugene, San Romani's big sprint started from too far back and he lost to Groth, 3:40.4 to 3:40.8, with Camien third in 3:41.0 and Day a disappointed sixth in 3:42.1.

The AAU final was held at New Brunswick, New Jersey, on June 28. O'Hara rested for a race for the first time, anxious to beat Burleson. In hot, humid weather, the first lap in 58.1 was led by speedy John Boulter, a 1:47.8 half-miler from England.

Weisiger led at 880 yards in 1:59.5. O'Hara impatiently grabbed the lead with a lap and a quarter to go and passed the 1320 mark in 2:59.1. Going into the last curve, the 6'2" Ryun delighted his fans when he passed Weisiger and set out grimly after O'Hara and Burleson. The doughty high school junior actually edged ahead of Burleson on the curve.

Then O'Hara exploded with a great finish, running away from everybody.

Results: O'Hara 3:38.1, Burleson 3:38.8, Grelle 3:38.9, Ryun 3:39.0, Camien 3:39.9, Boulter 3:40.4, Ben Tucker 3:40.8, Weisiger 3:40.9, Peter Keeling of GB 3:44.3.

O'Hara's new American record had been bettered only by Elliott and Jazy. Burleson was now tied for eighth fastest of all-time, with Grelle at eleventh and Ryun twelfth. Boulter's 3:40.4 was a British national record. Tucker's 3:40.8 was equivalent to a mile in 3:59.3. And once again, 17-year-old Jim Ryun was amazing, for his 3:39 was equivalent to a mile in 3:57.3.

They ran a useless race the following week, at Randall's Island, New York. This was a semi-final meet to choose six men to run in the all-important Final Trials in September. With heats cutting the field to eight runners, they ran the final like another heat, to eliminate two more.

The pace was a lazy 60.8 and 2:07.2 and then it increased only a little for the next 300. Unexpectedly, Weisiger fell almost 20 yards behind.

Then came a very fast finish, with Burleson edging ahead of O'Hara in the stretch, and Grelle fighting past Ryun while Camien faded.

Results: Burleson 3:45.4, O'Hara 3:45.6, Grelle 3:46.1, Ryun 3:46.1, San Romani 3:46.4, Day 3:46.6. Non-qualifiers: Weisiger 3:46.7, Camien 3:48.5.

Burleson's last lap was in 52.5 and O'Hara's 52.9.

Waiting for September, Ryun trained especially hard in Kansas. Grelle won easily against the USSR in Los Angeles with 3:41.3 to Byelitskiy's 3:42.3 and 3:45.7 for Groth who preferred the

800 in the Final Trials. Grelle was outkicked by Schul in a good race, 3:58.9 to 3:59.0, then won in 4:00.1. Day won an 880 in 1:50.7 and a two-mile in 8:53.4.

On September 13, the six best met in the Los Angeles Coliseum before about 19,000 people to choose three for the Olympic team. Day led in 59.8, then they slowed somewhat surprisingly and O'Hara led in 2:04. At three-fourths mile in 3:04, the order was O'Hara, Grelle, Ryun, Burleson, and San Romani all packed into four yards. A discomfited Day had to let them go.

San Romani surprised by making the first break, into the backstretch, and he gained a strong position for his dangerous finishing kick. Grelle tried to get past O'Hara, but the little redhead held him off around the curve. Ryun swung wide, ready to pass, and Burleson moved into the box.

In a dangerous position, Burleson shoved Ryun aside and burst through. He went into the lead in the homestretch. O'Hara followed him in a fast sprint, and San Romani began to fade.

With Burleson and O'Hara now assured of a place on the team, the whole race came down to the battle between Grelle and Ryun. With 40 yards to go, Grelle was two feet ahead but Ryun "thought I could get him. I was still moving fast and I wasn't tired."

With the crowd screaming, Ryun cut down the margin with long, slow strides. Ten yards from the finish he caught Grelle, and he moved a foot ahead. But Grelle dived desperately for the tape and almost beat Ryun before he sprawled forlornly on the track.

Results: Burleson 3:41.2, O'Hara 3:41.5, Ryun 3:41.9, Grelle 3:41.9, San Romani 3:43.0, Day 3:46.1.

Out of a dozen "four-minute" men, there were three exceptional milers to carry the USA on their chests at Tokyo.

SNELL "STILL DANGEROUS"

After his Compton victory in 1963, Snell trained poorly and irregularly for several months. He was hindered by his adjustment to marriage, a temporary break with Lydiard, and his need for rest. On October 18, he ran a mile right in the midst of his hill training. He said before the race he hoped to run about 4:15, and he ran 4:12, behind John Davies' 4:06 and Ron Clarke's 4:09. After the race, a satisfied Snell went out for a 15-mile run.

He refused to take racing seriously until the time came. In January he ran 4:23.3 for third place, lost another mile to Davies with 4:07.8, and let Davies win a 1000 after he had tripped him. But then his speed work began to take effect, and on February 1 at Wanganui, he ran a mile in 3:57.7 with his last 120 in a fantastic record 13.1.

On February 3, he ran 1:50.8 in an exhibition. Two days

later he ran a half-mile while sick and placed fifth in 1:55.7. Ten days after that, still not well, he could run only 4:07.9 behind Davies and Weisiger.

He recovered enough to win the New Zealand championship at half a mile in 1:53.2. People thought he was all through as a champion, but he resolved to show them "I was still around and still dangerous."

He toured South Africa in March. He ran a good 3:59.6 on March 18, then won South African championships in 1:50.4 and 4:06.2. On April 11, back in Auckland, he struggled to beat Davies, 3:58.5 to 3:58.6.

That was his last race before the Olympics in October. He knew he was not right and he settled down to serious training. Never before had he been able to maintain a schedule of 100 miles a week for more than three weeks, but now he did ten weeks, and every Sunday night he ran the difficult 22-mile course.

Next, he labored through six weeks of hill training—springing uphill in long bounds. His goal in the Olympics was the 1500 meters because, "I felt that some of my sharpness, which was necessary for 800 meters, had gone."

After the hill training, he moved onto the track, and his speed work went well. For the first time in his career he trained straight through Lydiard's program. He was ready.

Arriving at Tokyo, he caught the flu, like many of the athletes, but he ran three-fourths mile in 2:56 and a mile in 4:02 in workouts. In a trial against Davies and O'Hara, he ran a fast 1:47.1 for 800 meters and decided he wanted to run the 800 as well as the 1500. Watching that time trial, Roger Moens, now a TV commentator, said, "Now I know you can win both medals."

Snell ran in his heat, semi-final and final on three consecutive days, and he won his second Olympic gold medal handily in 1:45.1.

"I subconsciously held just a little back for the 1500." He was ready for the first heat, the very next day.

1964 OLYMPICS

Four heats were run on October 17 to qualify four each to the semi-finals. Among the unfortunates were Olavi Salonen, Albie Thomas, and, once again, Siegfried Valentin. Choosing the 5000 instead were Norpoth and Jazy, who had run a 3:57.9 mile in September.

In the first semi-final, on October 19, Bernard, whose best was 3:40.9 this year, set another fast pace of 56.5, 1:55.8, and 2:55.8. Snell coasted in to win in 3:38.8. On his shoulder was Baran (3:38.9), who was much stronger this year at 3000 meters and who had set a new European mile record of 3:56.0 at London on August

3, with a second half a bit faster than the first.

The third qualifier, in 3:39.3, was Josef Odlozil of Czechoslovakia, something of an unknown quantity. Primarily an 800-meter runner, he barely lost to Baran in 1961 in 1:48.2 and won a race in the same time in 1962. His best 1500 in 1961 was 3:47.4, and he improved only slightly to 3:46.3 in 1962 and 3:43.6 in 1963. He ran 3:41.9 in 1964 at the age of 26. The only indication that he was better than these times came from some hard workouts he ran at Tokyo.

Bernard qualified in fourth place with 3:39.7, while John Whetton of England made the final in fifth place by running 3:39.9, faster time than the other fifth-place finisher. Whetton had run 3:41.0 and 3:58.9 in 1964. Far back in last place was Ryun, suffering from a cold or the flu.

In the second semi-final, the pace was slower. Burleson ran his last 300 meters in 41.3 to finish first in 3:41.5. An impressive second, in the same time, with a 41.0 finish, was Alan Simpson of Great Britain. Simpson was not considered a contender before this year. He ran 3:44.1 in 1961 at the age of 21, but he improved slowly, like Odlozil, to 3:44.0 in 1962 and 3:43.3 in 1963. His fast finish won some races in 1964, including the AAA Championship in 4:01.1, but his one great race was against Baran in London on August 15. Baran ran the third lap in a fantastic 57.2 and Simpson came from 15 yards behind at the bell to win a great battle, 3:39.1 to 3:39.8.

The next four finishers came in almost even at 3:41.9 and a photo was needed to choose the two qualifiers. Davies, whom the New Zealanders touted as second only to Snell, won the decision, and the fourth qualifier was Jean Wadoux of France, a 22-year-old who improved suddenly to 3:41.7 in 1963 and 3:40.8 this year. He broke Jazy's French record for 1000 meters this year with 2:18.6.

Failing to qualify, in fifth place was an ambitious Kenyan named Kipchoge Keino, who had placed fifth in the 5000 final on the day of "rest" between his 1500 heat and semi-final. O'Hara, who thought he had a chance to break the world record because of great workouts at home, caught a bad cold in Tokyo and finished seventh in this semi-final in 3:43.4. He said he would never run again.

THE FINAL was run two days later, on October 21, a cloudy day with a temperature of 67 degrees. A polite crowd of 75,000 sat in the National Stadium, and a gentle breeze fluttered the flags of all the competing nations while the flag-cords beat rhythmically against the metal poles. The nine finalists lined up tensely on the red track in lanes marked with white plastic strips.

Snell felt reasonably fresh, but he had decided that "in no circumstances would I attempt to run a record. It was going to be a matter of waiting as long as possible and concentrating purely

on winning."
 Bernard, as usual, enjoyed the early lead, passing 400 meters in 58.0. Davies moved up, and Snell was shunted back to sixth place. Then Bernard slowed, and Davies accepted the lead willingly at 700 meters. He passed 800 meters in 2:00.5, and then, down the backstretch, Snell moved to second place with masterly ease.
 But the relatively poor pace allowed much changing of position and both Baran and Whetton passed Snell on the curve. Whetton dropped back in the home straight, suddenly debilitated, but Burleson moved up to third and Simpson came alongside Snell at the bell, threatening a box.
 Around the curve they ran, toward the curved starting line, running at an excellent 14.5 pace for 100 meters (58.0 per 400). Davies' time at 1200 meters was a mild 2:59.3. Snell had moved ahead of Burleson to third, and Odlozil, who had been next to last for the first 800, continued to move up persistently until he was on Burleson's heels.
 Snell looked awkward at that pace, a little too muscular, but suddenly all that changed. His stride became beautiful—long, powerful, and *fast*. He shot into the lead and ran the 100 meters along the backstretch in an astonishing 12.7 seconds.
 Behind him, frantic runners fought to hang on. Davies was safely on Snell's heels, closely followed by Baran. Burleson was behind Baran and he wanted to go after Snell, but at that moment Odlozil appeared beside him and he was boxed. He gave up the effort to pass Baran and relaxed. "I just hung back and watched the race."
 Thus, with his fastest-finishing opponent boxed in, Snell was in a good position, but he did not know it. Everybody else thought he was making his final drive, but, as he approached the last curve, he was only gathering for the kill. He sprinted around the curve faster than it had ever been run before—12.3 seconds for 100 meters—and he opened a gap of six yards.
 He could not hold that pace, nor did he want to. He glanced back, saw he was safe, and eased off to 13.6 for the final 100 meters. "I felt that I could renew my effort if I needed to." Even so, he widened his lead to about ten yards at the end. "My run down the straight was a little easier than it had been in the 800 meters."
 Davies led the pursuit into the homestretch, but Baran was on his shoulder and closing. A frustrated Burleson was on the pole, on Davies' heels, and Simpson was outside him.
 Baran caught Davies, but he had no more left and he began to fade. Simpson came up on the inside of Davies as Odlozil pulled even. Burleson finally launched his sprint and passed Baran and gained on the others, but he was well beaten, two yards behind Simpson at the finish line.
 Results: Snell 3:38.1, Odlozil 3:39.6, Davies 3:39.6, Simpson

1964

3:39.7, Burleson 3:40.0, Baran 3:40.3, Bernard 3:41.2, Whetton 3:42.4, Wadoux 3:45.4.

Snell's explosive last 200 meters of the only 1500 final he had ever run, was 25.9, his last 300 in a breathtaking 38.6, and his last 400 in 52.7. More impressive was the middle 200, in 25.0. His last 600 meters was also impressive—1:22.7 unofficially. His last 800 was about 1:52.0.

SNELL THE INVINCIBLE

Back in New Zealand, Snell ran a good 1000 meters against Odlozil and Davies at Auckland on November 12. At 200 meters he heard a call of "26" and thought he was running too fast. He relaxed and passed 400 meters in 55.0. "Immediately I had to put on the pressure." He passed 800 meters in 1:49.5 and barely broke the world record with 2:16.6. He now held the world record at four distances outdoors.

Five days later he set out to break his own mile record on the same fast cinder track at Western Springs Stadium in Auckland. He had never set a fast pace and he wanted to know what would happen. He followed the pace-maker, but ahead of Odlozil and Davies, and passed the 440 in 56.4. The pace slowed, but "I yielded to an urge to continue at the same rhythm."

This resulted in an unprecedented 1:54.1 880. Snell kept the pressure on, pulling away with a lap in 60.2. He led at three quarters in a super-fast 2:54.3, 15 yards ahead of Odlozil and Davies.

The crowd of 25,000 yelled itself hoarse for a sensational record, but Snell was already in trouble. With a lap and a half to go his legs began "to cry out for relief."

He forced himself through the last lap, but his rhythm was gone, along with his energy reserve, his concentration, and his leg speed. All he had left was his basic endurance and his courage.

No matter how the crowd screamed, he could not increase his pace. "It was mechanical desperation running, completely without inspiration."

He passed 1500 meters in 3:37.6—a time run by no other runner except Elliott—and he ran the last agonizing 120 yards in 16.5, his slowest ever. Davies, who had run 3:58.6 three days previously, led Odlozil past the 1500 in 3:40.2, but the Czech outfought him.

Results: Snell 3:54.1, Odlozil 3:56.4, Davies 3:56.8.

"It was one of the hardest last laps of my life," Snell said. "I felt so good beforehand I just wanted to see what it would be like to lead from the front . . . but never again. I felt really good during the fast early stages. That's why I stayed with it, but my legs shouldn't have gone so dead later. They just wouldn't respond."

Left, Jim Beatty.

Coach Mihaly Igloi and protégés. Front: Beatty, Igloi, Max Truex. Rear: Seaman, Tabori, Grelle.

Left, Dyrol Burleson.

Left, Tom O'Hara.

Below, 1964 US Olympic Semi-Trials, 200m. to go. From left, Day, Grelle, San Romani, Ryun, Burleson (behind Ryun), O'Hara.

Don Sparks

Fionnbar Callanan

Left, Michel Jazy.

Shirner *Ed Lacey*

Right, Peter Snell.

Ed Lacey

Snell completes his Tokyo double, with plenty of daylight between him and the field at the tape in the 1500m. final.

1964

Lydiard said: "Peter reached his peak at Tokyo. If he had run for time there, the mile record would be lower than it is tonight. Also, he has had many late nights since Tokyo with social engagements, and this hasn't helped." But that fast early pace was excuse enough for barely breaking the world record.

On November 28, at Wanganui, Snell ran against Davies. Troublesome wind prevented a record attempt, and Snell won with a fast last 220 in 25.7—4:03.9 to 4:04.5.

On December 3, at Melbourne, Snell—seeking an Australian record—passed three quarters in three-flat with Davies only three yards back. Snell finished in 3:57.6 while Davies faded badly to 4:08.2 and fourth place.

1964
1,500m:

Time	Athlete	Place	Location	Date
3:37.6+	Peter Snell (New Zealand)	(1)	Auckland	17 Nov
3:38.1	Tom O'Hara (USA)	(1)	New Brunswick, N.J.	28 Jun
3:38.8	Dyrol Burleson (USA)	(2)	New Brunswick, N.J.	28 Jun
3:38.9	Jim Grelle (USA)	(3)	New Brunswick, N.J.	28 Jun
3:38.9	Witold Baran (Poland)	(2)sf	Tokyo	19 Oct
3:39.0	Jim Ryun (USA)	(4)	New Brunswick, N.J.	28 Jun
3:39.1	Alan Simpson (Great Britain)	(1)	London	15 Aug
3:39.3	Josef Odlozil (Czechoslovakia)	(3)sf	Tokyo	19 Oct
3:39.6	John Davies (New Zealand)	(1)	Dunedin	8 Feb
3:39.7	Michel Bernard (France)	(4)sf	Tokyo	19 Oct
3:39.8	Michel Jazy (France)	(1)	Alfortville	17 Jun
3:39.9	John Camien (USA)	(5)	New Brunswick, N.J.	28 Jun
3:39.9	John Whetton (Great Britain)	(5)sf	Tokyo	19 Oct

Noteworthy Indoor Mark:

Time	Athlete	Place	Location	Date
3:41.6+	Tom O'Hara (USA)	(1)	Chicago	6 Mar

Note: This time was registered by an insufficient number of watches; O'Hara's official best, still during a mile race, was 3:43.6+ (1) New York, 27 February

MILE:

Time	Athlete	Place	Location	Date
3:54.1 WR	Peter Snell (New Zealand)	(1)	Auckland	17 Nov
3:56.0	Witold Baran (Poland)	(1)	London	3 Aug
3:56.4	Josef Odlozil (Czechoslovakia)	(2)	Auckland	17 Nov
3:56.8	John Davies (New Zealand)	(3)	Auckland	17 Nov
3:57.4	Dyrol Burleson (USA)	(1)	Compton, Cal.	5 Jun
3:57.6	Tom O'Hara (USA)	(2)	Compton, Cal.	5 Jun
3:57.6	Archie San Romani II (USA)	(3)	Compton, Cal.	5 Jun
3:57.9	Morgan Groth (USA)	(4)	Compton, Cal.	5 Jun
3:57.9	Michel Jazy (France)	(1)	St. Maur	20 Sep
3:58.3	Albie Thomas (Australia)	(1)	Melbourne	21 Mar
3:58.5	Jim Grelle (USA)	(5)	Compton, Cal.	5 Jun
3:58.9	Bob Day (USA)	(6)	Compton, Cal.	5 Jun
3:58.9	Cary Weisiger (USA)	(7)	Compton, Cal.	5 Jun
3:58.9	Bob Schul (USA)	(1)	Los Angeles	12 Aug

Noteworthy Indoor Marks:

Time	Athlete	Place	Location	Date
3:56.4	Tom O'Hara (USA)	(1)	Chicago	6 Mar
3:58.9e	Jim Grelle (USA)	(2)	Chicago	6 Mar

XI
The Jim Ryun era

After another year of doubt, during which faster milers than ever before made their power plays, once again a single runner established himself as supreme beyond any question. But only for the usual short period.

MICHEL JAZY

In 1964, Jazy wanted to run the 5000, although he ran 3:39.8 on June 17 and won the French Championship from Wadoux and Bernard in 3:41.5 on July 26. Jazy was invincible at 5000 meters before the Olympics except for an acceptable loss to Ron Clarke at Cologne on July 8, 13:45.2 to 13:49.4, a French record.

On September 20, at St. Maur, Jazy broke the French mile record with 3:57.9, last lap in 57.9. Six days later, he lowered his 5000 meter record to 13:46.8. He chose to run the 5000 in the Olympics and was disappointed in his close fourth place.

He talked of retiring, but he continued to train, using his version of Fartlek in a Paris park. Early in 1965 he found himself in such good condition that he declared the first two weeks in June would be his.

After some 3000's, he beat Odlozil and Baran in 3:43.7 on May 14, but he chose the Paris suburb of St. Maur for his first real effort, on June 2. In a mile test, Jazy held back in 58.5 and 1:59.5. Baran passed the bell in 3:00.4 with Jazy (3:00.5) on his heels. Jazy sprinted away with 300 to go, passed 1500 meters in 3:40.6 and finished strong.

Results: Jazy 3:55.5, Wadoux 3:57.2, Baran 3:57.4, Claude Nicolas of France 3:59.1, Miroslav Juza of CSR 3:59.2, Bernard 4:03.3.

It was a new European record for Jazy, but only the beginning of his astonishing success.

Only four days later, at Lorient, the day after an easy 3:46.8 1500, Jazy beat Olympic silver medalist Mohamed Gamoudi at 5000 meters in 13:34.4 to break Kuts' European record.

Jazy felt in top shape, and so only three days went by before he attacked the mile record at Rennes on June 9 after an easy 4:08.5 mile on June 7. The weather was a pleasant 60 degrees, but the track was only mediocre. Eight other runners were in the field, but they helped set up a fast pace.

Jazy remained in fourth place at 440 yards in 57.3. Wadoux led at 880 yards in 1:55.7, but Jazy held back in third in 1:56.5 with great poise. As they reached the bell, Jazy moved into the lead in 2:57.4, full of run.

He pulled away with a strong last lap and passed 1500 meters in 3:38.4, the same as his 1960 Olympic runner-up time and 0.8 seconds slower than Snell's pace in his 3:54.1 world record.

But Jazy was still strong. He whirled out of the curve and into the homestretch with good speed, actually sprinting after such a pace. His last 120 yards took only 15.2 seconds and he was the new world record holder.

Results: Jazy 3:53.6, Gérard Vervoort 3:59.9, Bernard 4:00.9, Nicolas 4:03.2.

Jazy thought he had broken the European record, but when the world record was announced he jumped for joy and all nine runners took a victory lap. Once again, in an all-French effort, the world record had returned to France.

Jazy said, "Naturally I am delighted at this record, but I believe I could have gone a full second faster if the race had been held at the start of the meet tonight. After an hour of running on the track it got churned up and definitely slowed down. Certainly 3:52 is not impossible. On the contrary, it is quite certain. I would like to thank all the others who sacrificed their own chances to help me get this record. The greatest help was not having to lead at all until the bell but still reaching it in a fast enough time to smash the record."

Only two days later, in the Charléty Stadium, Jazy said, "I am in great form," and then beat Gamoudi again at 5000 meters. On the way he lowered the European three-mile record to 13:05.6 and he finished in 3:29.0, only 3.2 seconds from Clarke's world record.

The very next day he ran five fast laps for 2000 meters in 5:04.4, only 2.8 seconds from his own world record. And the next day,

1965

June 13, on his 29th birthday, he ran an easy 2000 in 5:21.2. Then he went on a holiday with his family.

But he was too full of energy to stay away, and after six days of rest he returned to action with a 1500 in 3:40.9, On June 23, he beat Ron Clarke with a new world record of 8:22.6 for the two-mile. Along the way he lowered his own world 3000 record to 7:49.0.

After a day of rest he ran a relay leg in 3:39.9 as France broke the world record for 4 x 1500. And the next day he ran 3000 meters in 8:04.2.

On June 30, Jazy ran against an all-star field in the 5000 at the Helsinki World Games. In a great race, he lowered his European records to 13:04.8 for the three-mile and 13:27.6 for 5000 meters and he beat Keino and Clarke. During twelve races in June he broke six European records and three world records plus one in a relay.

Then he quit running super-fast races, although he won all the rest of his competitions, including a 3:39.6 against Portugal on July 11. He was unbowed in all his mile and 1500 races in 1965.

SNELL'S DOWNFALL BEGINS

Snell was supposed to start training for his farewell tour in 1965, but he rested for most of December, 1964. He began his long training after New Year's Day, but he interrupted it to fly to Los Angeles, where he won the 1000 indoors in 2:07.9. He tried to mix a maximum of training with a minimum of racing during the New Zealand spring, but he did run one mile in close to four-flat.

He was injured in April and had trouble recovering. In Hawaii, on his way to begin his tour, he barely beat Schul in the 880 with a slow 1:53.8. He went to the Compton Invitational, now held in the Los Angeles Coliseum, on June 4, unsure of his ability to run well.

After a 3:01 pace, Snell started his feared drive with 300 to go, but into the last curve he realized he could not hold it. He eased off until Grelle pulled alongside in the homestretch and then won by six inches in an all-out effort. His time was 3:56.4.

After losing a 1:48.4 880 from Canada's Bill Crothers in 1:48.6, Snell suffered from gastritis and ran last in a mile in Vancouver. He took medication and recovered his strength in time for the AAU championships.

RYUN MATURES

After his disappointment in the Olympics, Ryun returned to high school in time for the end of the 1964 cross country season. Under a new coach, he trained at shorter distances, with faster speeds, and he climaxed his high school career with 3:58.3 in the

1965

state championships.

Two weeks later he began his 1965 open races at Modesto. He was almost surprised from behind in the stretch, but he won in 3:58.1 over astonishing John Garrison, whose 3:58.1 was 12.5 seconds under his previous best. Grelle was third in 3:58.2.

At the Compton Invitational on June 4, Ryun was third at three-fourths mile, trailing Snell intently, but on the backstretch, Snell's early burst of speed took him by surprise and both Snell and Grelle got away from him. Ryun gained a little when Snell eased up on the curve, but his 3:56.8 was only good enough for third place, behind Snell and Grelle (both 3:56.4) but ahead of Odlozil's 3:57.8.

This was Ryun's fastest mile, but he was disappointed. He knew what he had to do to stay in contention against Snell, and he determined to do it in the AAU meet at San Diego on June 27.

As they lined up on the black all-weather track, Ryun knew Grelle was also a threat, for he had run an American record 3:55.4 at Vancouver on June 15 in the race where Snell was ill. And Olympic runner-up Odlozil was not to be taken lightly.

Weisiger led for an uneventful 2½ laps, passing the 440 in 59.2 and the 880 in 1:59.7. With a lap and a half to go, the patient waiting game ended when Odlozil burst out of fourth place into a startling five-yard advantage.

At three quarters in 3:00.2, Grelle was Odlozil's closest pursuer, with Ryun and Snell close behind. Around the curve, Ryun coasted, preparing for his move. It came before they reached the backstretch, and he went into the lead. But he did not continue his drive. "It scared me to death."

He ran at a faster pace, waiting for Snell's burst. But it was Grelle who challenged him, going into the last turn. Ryun increased his pace enough to keep Grelle outside him and the veteran was forced to drop back.

In the homestretch, Snell rushed past Grelle and gained ominously on Ryun, but Ryun held his form all the way to the finish and won by one hard-earned yard.

Results: Ryun 3:55.3, Snell 3:55.4, Grelle 3:55.5, Odlozil 3:57.7, Weisiger 4:04.9.

Ryun's American record had been bettered by only three runners, and his last lap in 53.9, fastest ever run in such a fast mile, indicated a greater potential. Ryun's last 220 was in 26.6—an endurance finish rather than acceleration.

Snell threw his arm around Ryun's shoulders as they slowed to a stop. His comments included: "Ryun's got it—the quality which goes to make a champion... Ryun ran a perfect tactical race. Frankly, I did not think he could run that fast. I thought he would probably run 3:56. I thought Grelle would win it and I would be third behind Ryun... I personally ran a poor race. I gambled on the sprint. I was not able to explode like I used to. With 110 yards to go I was running in trouble. I could tell my legs were not going to go any faster."

At this point in history, the ten fastest 1500 or mile runs of all time had been accomplished by four men—one each by Jazy and Ryun and four each by Elliott and Snell. A time of 3:38.1 or 3:56.4 had been accomplished 30 times by twelve runners. Only five of them had done it more than once: Snell eight, Elliott five, Grelle four, Beatty three, and Jazy two.

Ryun injured his foot and training on it caused an injury to his knee. He ran two poor races, but he was taken with the team to Kiev to run against the USSR. He beat the Russians in 3:40.4, but he had to let Grelle win in 3:39.2.

Against Poland a week later, the pace was slow and Ryun's fast kick beat Baran by three yards in 3:49.9. On August 30, against West Germany, Ryun outsprinted Grelle in 3:41.6, with Bodo Tümmler 30 yards behind.

JÜRGEN MAY

In 1962, at the age of 20, May showed great promise by running 800 meters in 1:48.8 and 1000 meters in 2:20.4, second fastest in the world that year. He also ran 3:43.8. In 1963, the stocky, muscular East German nicknamed "The Toiler", proved his worth with 1:47.8 and 3:39.3 and appeared on his way to the top.

But 1964 was an off-year. His best times were 1:48.1 and 3:41.6, and he ran only 3:46.8 while being eliminated in a tough semi-final of the Olympic 1500 at Tokyo.

In 1965, however, he had better endurance and he started the season with 3000 meters in 8:04.4 and 5000 in 14:08.8 in May. He ran his best 1500, in 3:40.2, and then 3:40.7, and on June 27, in Potsdam, he ran a fast 800 meters in 1:46.8.

He won the Znamenskiy Memorial in 3:42.3. Then, in Prague, on July 9, he triumphed over the three Olympic medalists: May 3:42.1, Odlozil 3:42.3, Snell 3:42.6, Davies 3:42.7. May's last 300 was a fast 38.7.

On his home track at Erfurt on July 14, May followed a fast pace by Herrmann—57, 1:56, and 2:24—then shot ahead and ran a great 3:36.4, a European record and a time bettered only by Elliott. His last 300, after a killing 1200 meters in 2:53.5, was 42.9.

After an easy 1500 on July 17, he went after Snell's 1000 meter record on July 20, again at Erfurt. With Snell in the audience, May passed 800 meters in 1:47.8 and finished in 2:16.2, a new world record.

He finished the month by winning the East German Championship in 3:40.0, the dual meet against Finland in an excellent

3:38.4, and a very fast 1:46.5 800 meters. He continued his heavy running schedule after a welcome layoff in the first part of August. He ran 1:46.5 again, barely held off Simpson in 3:41.3, and then ran 1:47.0 and 1:46.3. His next race was against the amazing Keino.

KIPCHOGE KEINO

Hezekiah Kipchoge Keino was born on January 17, 1940, in the small village of Kipsamo near Nandi Hills township in Kenya. At the sensitive age of four, he was on the hill slopes with the other herd-boys when his mother died. At the age of ten he was experienced enough to tend the flock of goats all by himself. Soon he had the fastest run of his young life when he came face to face with a leopard which was eating a goat.

He had other adventures uncommon to most runners, including beatings from his uncle, sleeping in a tree and fighting off an unknown beast, malaria, and a 16-mile journey through dangerous country to his father's house. Then, at 11, he learned about school and he sneaked off to attend. But he had no money and he returned home to a thrashing. On one journey with his father, they were attacked by a leopard, and Kipchoge watched with apprehension while his father killed it.

Kipchoge was allowed to attend school when he was 12, and in his second year he entered the school cross country race. He placed fourth against much older boys, and his prize was a bar of soap. Later that year, he placed second in a 440. He liked to run and it was a blow when he had to give up school.

At the age of 16 he was on his own. He built a hut and grew vegetables. Looking for a job, he walked 40 miles to a train to Fort Ternan, but jobs were not easy to find. He returned and worked on a farm, clearing brush. On his way home one weekend, he was attacked by robbers and escaped by running one of his best races.

Kipchoge's father, Kipkeino Arap Kurgat, had won races of four and ten miles at the age of 45, before Kipchoge was born, and he encouraged his son to train on their home-made track. Kipchoge entered his first formal race when he was 16 and finished fifth in a three-mile.

He placed well in other senior events and in the district meeting he tried the marathon. He took the lead at the half-way mark and five miles from the finish he was second, but he accepted a soft drink and he was soon flat on his back, too sick to run.

He tried to join the Police, but he was rejected as too young. He finally slipped in when he was almost 19, and he was a conscientious student. He ran in more races and in August, 1959, he won a mile in 4:38 and a three-mile in 16:17.

He wanted to be assigned to his home district, but his

superiors assigned him to the Police Training School, where he could find good training and competition. After about a month he went to a district meet with one of the most famous runners in Kenya, Arere Anentia. Kipchoge was advised to run the steeplechase, but he ran in the three-mile and beat Anentia. Then he ran in the steeplechase and won. But in his next meet, he fell in the water jump and gave up steeplechasing in disgust.

With only his natural ability, hardened by his rough life and aided by only the most primitive training, Kipchoge won the three-mile in a big meet in 14:09.2 and finished second in the mile in 4:21. In August of 1962, now 22 years old, he improved to 4:17.

The 1962 Kenya Championships were held at Nakuru, and Kip (as he was affectionately called) won the three-mile by 40 yards in 14:09.7. He was sent by airplane to the East Africa Championships in Dar es Salaam, and he won the three-mile with a personal record 13:46.8.

He was happy to be selected to compete in the Commonwealth Games and he felt fortunate to have a month of training under a coach. The coach had him run 15 miles a day, hardly the kind of training he needed. At Perth, watching other runners, he began to learn something about interval training, and he planned to develop more speed.

He ran a two-mile in 8:52.2 before the Games, behind Bruce Tulloh and Ron Clarke. He qualified easily for the three-mile final, but his 4:07 was not good enough in the mile. In the three-mile final, he finished an exhausted eleventh in 13:50.0.

In 1963, he took a month's leave, married a girl he had known in his school days, and built a house and fence. He was kicked by an ox on his left knee, and the whole year was ruined. He became a father in December and began preparing for the Olympics.

The training schedule he wanted to follow called for three or four workouts a day for the first four days of the week. Then he needed a rest before competition. One workout was usually a long run of up to ten miles. Others were interval training, moderate because of the mile-high altitude.

He worked on lengthening his seven-foot stride, smoothing out his form, relaxing, and acceleration. In the Kenya Championships, he won the three-mile in 13:47.2 and his fastest mile—4:06.6. In the East Africa Championships, he won in 13:57 and showed promise as a miler with 4:03.8.

In the Olympic trials he ran 4:03.3, but when he was not chosen for the team, he asked for a special trial and he ran 4:01.5.

At the Olympics he startled the track experts by competing in both the 5000 and 1500. On October 16, he ran in a 5000 heat, forcing a faster pace than necessary. He ran 13:49.6 for second place, equivalent to some 25 seconds faster than he had ever run before.

The next day, he pushed the pace in his 1500 heat and won it in 3:45.8. People wondered how he could even attempt 5000 meters the next day, but he hung on, even though bewildered by the surging changes of pace by Ron Clarke. Inexperienced, Keino finished with startling speed to place fifth in 13:50.4. He was not as tired as he should have been from a full effort.

The next day, in the semi-final of the 1500, he made the mistake of running with the others at a tactical pace. Even without great speed, he was in the fight for the last two qualifying spots. Four runners excited the crowd when they reached the line in 3:41.9, but two of them beat Keino.

He was bitterly disappointed, but he was determined to do better, and people who had seen his potential invited him to compete in races all over the world. His first race was the famous midnight run at São Paulo, Brazil, on New Year's Eve. He led Olympic steeplechase champion Gaston Roelants by 40 yards with only half a mile to go when he had the bad luck to run into a motorcycle.

He changed his training schedule again, running only three days a week. But he put in three high-quality workouts each day. On other days he was busy playing games.

He was invited to the World Games in Helsinki in June of 1965, but first he won a triple with 4:05.5, 13:54.3, and a promising 29:46.8 for six miles. After a 4:03 mile, he won in the Kenya Championships in 4:05.5 and 13:33.3.

At Helsinki, Keino ran in a great 5000 meter race in which he beat world record holder Ron Clarke but lost 13:28.2 to 13:27.6 in the homestretch to Jazy. Only two days later, at Turku on July 2, Keino improved his time by two full seconds to 13:26.2 in defeating Clarke. He was now only 0.4 seconds from Clarke's world record. A third fast 5000 was run at Stockholm on July 6—three in one week!—when Keino led to the three-mile tape in 13:01.8, then slowed. When he saw Clarke race past, toward the 5000 meter tape, he resumed running but he lost, 13:26.4 to 13:30.4.

Keino returned to Africa as one of the three greatest 5000 meter runners of all time. In the All-Africa Games in the Congo, Keino showed his astonishing energy and lack of experience by running amazing heats. On July 20, he ran a 1500 heat in 3:39.6, his best time. The next day, he won the fastest 5000 heat in history—13:38.0. In the finals his times were 3:41.1 and 13:44.4.

Back to Europe went the ambitious Keino. In Stockholm on August 25 he ran his fourth great 5000, beating Roelants in 13:29.4. Only two days later, Keino ran one of the best times ever produced on a track. At Hälsingborg, he lowered Herrmann's world record for 3000 meters by nearly six seconds, to 7:39.6, equivalent to a two-mile in about 8:17.6. One Swedish sports writer called him "the new wonder runner."

1965

The very next day, the untiring Kenyan ran 3:39.5. And two days later he ran in a great race at White City, London—his first major mile race. He had no intention of winning the event, for he was running against May, Odlozil, and Simpson, but he wanted to become the first non-white to run under four minutes.

Odlozil, whose next race after the AAU in San Diego was a noteworthy 3:56.7 to 3:56.8 victory over John Davies here in London on July 3, had lost to May the next week and ran 3:58.7 on August 8 to edge Simpson by one tenth in a thriller. Simpson had lost two exciting races, to Odlozil and to May, but he was very strong—3:56.6 on June 7 and 3:56.9 on July 5—and he won the AAA in 4:01.9.

Old Derek Ibbotson set up a fast pace of 56.4 and 1:58.3, then dropped out. Olympic 800-meter medalist Wilson Kiprugut of Kenya had followed Ibbotson and now he faded away. Keino was surprised to be in the lead, after running 57.6 and 60.7, and he increased the pace to 59.9, trying to get away from his strong rivals, but May, second only to Elliott at 1500 meters, was on Keino's heels throughout that third lap.

But Keino appeared to be a super runner. He threw away his orange cap, and his green-clad figure simply moved farther and farther ahead as he toured the last lap in 56 flat and the crowd roared with amazement.

Results: Keino 3:54.2, Odlozil 3:55.6, Simpson 3:55.7, May 3:55.9, Juza 4:00.9, Whetton 4:01.7.

Keino had improved, in one race, from 4:01.5 to a time only six-tenths from the world record. The place times were the fastest of any race ever run.

Perhaps the surprise of the experts was best expressed by J.L. Manning, hailing Keino in the London Daily Mail: "If a Nandi tribesman can drop out of a police station 7,000 feet up Mount Kenya, run a mile 'just to get up some speed,' and miss the world's most sophisticated record by only six-tenths of a second because he does not 'understand lap times and all that sort of thing,' what next will come from the Dark Continent?"

Keino returned to Kenya for a tremendous welcome, including one from President Kenyatta. He was promoted three ranks, to Assistant Inspector, and a street was named Kipchoge Road.

Reporters from all over the world were curious about his life style. They learned that his principal food had been milk—mother's milk, cow's milk, and then murzik, a thick, curdled milk which could be stored in good condition for weeks without refrigeration. Later he ate fresh fruits and vegetables and roasted meat, but the reporters were more interested in stories about fresh blood mixed with milk. Actually, Keino only drank blood at special traditional ceremonies in his home area.

1965

During September and October, 1965, Keino recovered from his hard running, but in November he increased his training in preparation for a tour of Australia and New Zealand. On November 27, he ran in an unscheduled exhibition in Auckland. He did not extend himself and his time was a mere 3:41.9.

On November 30, in Western Springs Stadium in Auckland, Keino pushed the pace all by himself to set a new world record of 13:24.2 for 5000 meters. He now led Ron Clarke, five to four, in times of 13:30.4 or faster.

At the same meet, Davies beat May, 3:59.0 to 3:59.5. In the next meet, at Napier on December 4, May continued to sharpen his speed with an 880 in 1:48.9. Keino, running alone, won the mile in 3:56.9.

Two days later, he beat Davies by 20 yards in the same fast time. At the next night he beat Davies at 3000 meters in 7:50.4, excellent time on a muddy track in a strong wind. He appeared to be unbeatable as the time came for two mile duels against May.

They met first on December 11 at Cook's Gardens 386-yard grass track in Wanganui, made famous by Snell's world record of 3:54.4. May was well rested and ready, but it was Keino who set a fantastic pace. He raced past the first 220 too fast, in 27.4, and the 440 in 56.4. He passed the half-mile in 1:55.6, then slowed to 30.5 for the next 220. May, who had fought to hang on five yards behind, closed the gap.

Keino tried to break away again, running the sixth 220 in 28.8. He passed three-fourths mile in a startling 2:54.9, but May would not quit. Now Keino had to slow his pace. He ran the next 220 in 29.6 and went around to 1500 meters in an astonishing 3:38.0, but May followed him in 3:38.2.

With the crowd screaming at the fastest competitive mile ever run, May slowly moved past the fading Keino and won the battle comfortably.

Results: May 3:53.8, Keino 3:54.9, Davies 4:00.6.

May needed only a last 120 in 15.6 for his decisive victory, for Keino struggled through his last 120 in 16.9. Keino's last 220 was 30.4. He had a limit, after all.

Four days later, December 15, they raced again at Auckland's Western Springs Stadium. Keino tried to run closer to an even pace and yet still run away from May. He passed the 440 in 58.0 and the 880 in 1:57, but May was still on his heels. Keino increased the pace to 58.5 on the third quarter, but at 2:55.5 May was still threatening.

Keino's time was 0.6 seconds slower than in their last duel, but he had more left. He passed 1500 meters in his fastest-ever 3:37.6 to May's 3:37.8, and he had little power left in the homestretch. He ran his last 120 in 16.8 and May struggled past with 40 yards to go.

1965

Results: May 3:54.1, Keino 3:54.4, Davies 3:59.1.

May said, "I thought I'd never catch him, especially with 150 to go."

Now, of the ten fastest miles ever run, Keino had three of them to his credit. Snell also had three, with May two.

In two years the list of best milers was much changed:

3:53.6	Jazy	1965	3:55.3	Ryun	1965
3:53.8	May	1965	3:55.4	Grelle	1965
3:54.1	Snell	1964	3:55.5n	Beatty	1963
3:54.2	Keino	1965	3:55.6n	Burleson	1963
3:54.5	Elliott	1958	3:55.6n	Odlozil	1965

OTHER RUNNERS

PETER SNELL never fully recovered from his hard race at San Diego on top of an illness. He made the long trip to Helsinki and ran in the World Games on July 1. He placed fifth in 3:43.7 behind Grelle's 3:40.8 and blamed the hard San Diego track. Two days later he ran 3:59.8 in London and placed only seventh behind Odlozil's 3:56.7. Two days later, at Dublin, he still did not have time to recover and he placed third in 3:59.9 behind Simpson's 3:56.9.

Four days after that, at Prague, the bewildering losses continued when he could run only 3:42.6 behind May's 3:42.1 and Odlozil's 3:42.3. He was losing to good runners, but he never had time to recover. His unbeatable finishing kick no longer existed.

He enjoyed Czechoslovakia, especially Odlozil's hospitality in return for Snell's in New Zealand. He won an easy 800 in 1:50.4. Then he helped Odlozil break the Czech record for 2000 meters. Snell finished about six seconds behind.

Snell lost to Crothers' good 1:47.1 in Oslo. At Berlin on July 17, he was third to Grelle's 3:44.0. That was his last race. He retired with the sad conclusion "that it is possible to run yourself out of condition."

1965
1,500m:

3:36.4	Jürgen May (E. Germany)	(1)	Erfurt	14	Jul
3:37.6+	Kipchoge Keino (Kenya)	(1)	Auckland	15	Dec
3:38.4+	Michel Jazy (France)	(1)	Rennes	9	Jun
3:39.0	Jim Grelle (USA)	(1)	Cologne	7	Jul
3:39.5	Bodo Tümmler (W. Germany)	(2)	Cologne	7	Jul
3:39.7+	Josef Odlozil (Czechoslovakia)	(3)	London	30	Aug
3:39.8	Harald Norpoth (W. Germany)	(3)	Cologne	7	Jul
3:40.4	Jim Ryun (USA)	(2)	Kiev	1	Aug
3:40.6+	Alan Simpson (Great Britain)	(4)	London	30	Aug
3:40.7	Bob Schul (USA)	(4)	Cologne	7	Jul
3:40.7	Dyrol Burleson (USA)	(1)	Kouvola	19	Jul
3:40.8	Gérard Vervoort (France)	(5)	Cologne	7	Jul
3:40.8	Constantin Blotiu (Rumania)	(1)	Timisoara	16	Jul

Noteworthy Indoor Marks:

3:42.0+	Siegfried Herrmann (E. Germany)	(1)	Berlin	21	Feb
3:42.2	Jürgen May (E. Germany)	(1)	Berlin	14	Feb
3:42.6d	Michel Jazy (France)	(1)	Paris	5	Feb

1965

3:42.8	Dyrol Burleson (USA) d=dirt track	(1)	Stockholm	18	Mar

MILE:

3:53.6 WR	Michel Jazy (France)	(1)	Rennes	9	Jun
3:53.8	Jürgen May (E. Germany)	(1)	Wanganui	11	Dec
3:54.2	Kipchoge Keino (Kenya)	(1)	London	30	Aug
3:55.3	Jim Ryun (USA)	(1)	San Diego	27	Jun
3:55.4	Jim Grelle (USA)	(1)	Vancouver	15	Jun
3:55.4	Peter Snell (New Zealand)	(2)	San Diego	27	Jun
3:55.6	Josef Odlozil (Czechoslovakia)	(2)	London	30	Aug
3:55.7	Alan Simpson (Great Britain)	(3)	London	30	Aug
3:56.4	Bob Day (USA)	(1)	Bakersfield, Cal.	12	Jun
3:56.8	John Davies (New Zealand)	(2)	London	3	Jul
3:57.2	Jean Wadoux (France)	(2)	St. Maur	2	Jun
3:57.4	Witold Baran (Poland)	(3)	St. Maur	2	Jun

Noteworthy Indoor Mark:

3:58.6	Siegfried Herrmann (E. Germany)	(1)	Berlin	21	Feb

RYUN TAKES CHARGE

As a freshman at the University of Kansas, Ryun was back under the friendly guidance of coach Bob Timmons. One of the first things Timmons did was hospitalize Ryun for two weeks to check the dizziness he sometimes felt when he ran. The dreaded words "brain tumor" were spoken, and Ryun knew real fear, but the cause turned out to be a diminished function of the balance nerve in his inner ear.

Ryun ran little cross country, but his training mileage went as high as 120 miles a week and he ran a two-mile time trial in 8:51.1. He lost two long cross country races, won an easy Sugar Bowl 1500 in 3:42.7 on December 30, then began the indoor season.

Ryun beat Whetton, Europe's finest indoor miler, by three yards in 4:02.1 at San Francisco. On February 5, in a hectic freshman meet, he ran 4:04.5, 1:53.2, and 50.1 for a 440 relay leg. He won the Federation championship with an easy 4:01.6 in New York.

The following week, he raced in the Baxter Mile against Jim Grelle, who was undefeated this year indoors with a best of 4:00.9. Ryun's sudden spurt with two laps to go surprised Grelle and gained a five-yard lead. Ryun, not at his best on an indoor track, barely won in 4:02.2.

The next week in Kansas City, Ryun set a new indoor record for a twelve-lap track with 3:59.6. After miles in 4:00.5 and 4:03.3, he put in a real evening's work at Manhattan, Kansas, on March 19. He ran a 4:02.2 leg in a relay, a great indoor 1:47.9 880 leg, and a 48.5 440 leg.

He did not point for his first outdoor race of the season, at the Texas Relays on April 2. His last lap in 54.7 beat Camien by ten yards in 4:03.9. The next week he ran an 8:47.4 two-mile without special effort. On April 16 at the Emporia Relays, he ran a mile leg in 3:58.0, a three-fourths mile leg in 3:07.2, and a 440 leg in 47.9. He was ready.

1966

Ryun wanted to run a fast mile at the Kansas Relays, and Timmons cut his early training load in half, but on Thursday, Ryun ran a 3:59.0 mile leg with a good last lap in 53.5. On Saturday, he wanted a new American record, and he was paced to 57.6, then took the lead in 1:58.7, his fastest half. He slowed to 3:00.7 and then slowed even more. He sprinted in, with his last 220 in 26 flat, and his time was 3:55.8, disappointing in a way.

Still, he smiled about it for a long time after the race because it felt so easy. He confided to his friend, photographer Rich Clarkson, "I think there are going to be some very fine times this year." He ended the day with a fast 47-flat relay leg.

The next week was spent in hard training to make up for all that rest, and he went into the Drake Relays mile tired. He had to run an agonizing battle to beat Camien by two feet in 4:05.6.

Ryun did not race again until the Coliseum Relays on May 13. He entered the two-mile to compete against Keino, Grelle, and Burleson although his best time was far behind theirs. Keino set the pace, passing the mile in 4:13.6, and Ryun ran easily in the pack. With a little over a lap to go, Burleson had to let go and Keino threw his orange cap into the infield. In the middle of the last curve, Ryun dashed past Keino and Grelle went after him. The two milers sprinted beautifully down the homestretch two feet apart, and Ryun won a great race in 8:25.1.

There had been a debate as to which was Ryun's second-best distance, and it appeared to be the two-mile, since he was now the American record holder. His time was third on the all-time list, and close to Jazy's world record of 8:22.6. This race increased his confidence and he wanted to break the world mile record at Compton on June 4.

The competition was again in the Los Angeles Coliseum, his first mile in more than a month. Steeplechaser George Young pushed the pace after Ryun passed the 440 in 59.9, and Ryun's time at the half was 1:58.5.

On the backstretch of the third lap, Ryun pushed the pace faster, something he had never tried before. He came around to three quarters in 2:58.5. Approaching the last backstretch, Grelle was close behind, running one of his fastest miles—3:56.0—but Ryun simply ran away from him. Not since Snell's fast finishes of 1963 had the fans seen such running, and never in such a fast race.

Ryun's powerful last 440 was 55.2, his last 220 26.4, and his last 120 was in 14.4. He ran 3:53.7, only one tenth of a second from Jazy's world record. He was well pleased with his effort. "In the last 150 yards when I was blasting full out it never felt at all heavy. It was just almost too easy."

The following week, in the U.S. Track and Field Federation Championships at Terre Haute, Indiana, Ryun shocked the track world in the half-mile event. He felt tired after his heat on Friday, in 1:51.0, and the final came only two hours later. The weather was hot and sticky and the track was "just a quarter-mile strip of asphalt." Nobody expected much, for there were only about 1000 people in the stands.

Ryun passed the 440 in 53.3, and then, on the backstretch, he exploded. He had "the feeling of having all this tremendous strength." His last 220 was in 25.5 and he broke Snell's world record with 1:44.9.

Over in New Zealand, Snell said, "Now that Ryun has reeled off this half-mile, the 1500 meter and the mile records must be his for the asking."

The next day, Ryun had to run a mile and he barely won in 4:02.8. Spectators thought he merely ran to win, but he said, "I was really hurtin' bad. This was the worst I had ever felt in a race." Like Snell, Ryun did not favor an asphalt track.

Ryun trained hard for ten days, then eased off for the AAU meet in New York. He had to be ready for Grelle, who had run 3:55.4 at San Diego the week before, and the dangerous Burleson was there.

Burleson had gone into semi-retirement in 1965 while living in Sweden. He lost two races to two fast milers: Grelle beat him at the World Games in Helsinki, 3:40.8 to 3:41.4, and Odlozil beat him 3:49.0 to 3:49.1 at Hässleholm on July 30. His fastest time was 3:40.7, but he beat Odlozil and Tümmler with 3:42.1 at Stockholm on July 28.

In 1966, Burleson again avoided the big events, but he ran 3:57.5 on April 2 and 3:59.1 a week later. He won at Mt. San Antonio in 4:01.4, then jogged in disconsolately for a two-mile in 8:39.6 in the Coliseum Relays, behind Ryun's 8:25.1. Three weeks before the AAU meet, Burleson ran 3:57.3 in friendly Eugene.

The weather was far too hot for a record attempt and Ryun's main concern was Burleson, whom he had never beaten. He was content to follow a slow pace of 63.8 and 2:05.8, while the spectators booed to show their disappointment.

Ryun increased the pace enough to stay ahead in 3:06.0, and he accelerated into the last lap. Only Grelle and Burleson could stay with him. Then Ryun put on a Snell-like burst into the last curve and opened a gap of 13 yards. Into the stretch, Burleson passed Grelle and gained a little on Ryun.

Results: Ryun 3:58.6, Burleson 4:00.0, Grelle 4:00.6.

Ryun's last lap was in 52.6, after an ordinary first curve.

He had only one more mile race in 1966. There was no European trip scheduled, for the strong Polish and Russian teams were to come to the United States. But the Russians caused consternation by cancelling and the Poles followed the leader. A substitute

1966

meet was held at Berkeley on July 17.

Ryun had rested enough, mentally and physically, and he felt ready for a record attempt. He stopped his workouts out on Wednesday, July 13—except for warmups and a few easy springs. On Saturday, he watched the first day of the meet, completely relaxed.

About 2:30 p.m. on Sunday, he had hot salve applied to a sore knee and tape put on the two blisters on his right foot. He looked at the gray track in Edwards Field, then went to the baseball diamond next to it and rest. "I almost went to sleep before the race because it was so nice."

The weather seemed perfect, and he jogged into the stadium 15 minutes before race time. He sat calmly on the grass at the end of the stands on the backstretch side of the track and put on his spikes. "I was nervous, some, but so much less than in previous races."

He took off his blue USA sweat suit and lined up with five other runners, including Weisiger and the good half-miler Wade Bell, who had run 3:59.8. The clay and decomposed granite track felt hard and fast. "I knew this was my last chance."

After the starting gun cracked, Ryun saw the lead taken by Tom Von Ruden, another good half-miler, who had placed second with 1:47.9 in Ryun's world-record 880. Ryun was third, behind Richard Romo, a prospective four-minute miler from Texas.

Ryun passed the 220 in 29.3 and worried a little about the pace. But Romo passed Von Ruden on the curve and the pace seemed right. Ryun moved to second in 57.9. "I felt pretty good the first quarter."

Romo made an effort to increase the pace and Ryun's third 220 was in 28 flat, much too fast. "I felt a kind of heaviness."

They slowed, and Bell charged past before the 880, and Ryun followed. He passed the 880 in 1:55.5 and 15,000 spectators roared their approval. "I felt good again. I didn't think the first half would be that fast."

Around the curve, Ryun felt the excitement of a possible record, but then the pace slowed dangerously as Bell tired. On the backstretch, Ryun went past Bell, and Bell thought, "Man, he must have an awful good kick."

Ryun looked over one shoulder, then the other, surprised that nobody was following him. "I felt real good."

For a few seconds of suspense it was not apparent to the spectators whether Ryun would be content to win or whether he could push the pace all alone. Then, abruptly, he showed his intention. He thrust himself forward at greater speed and completed the slowest 220 of the race in 30.3.

The fans were already on their feet, knowing they were seeing history made, roaring encouragement in a mounting frenzy. They wanted a world record. They watched the slim figure in blue pace rapidly along the homestretch to the three-quarters pole, and when they heard the time—2:55.3—their shouts turned to screams and their voices became hoarse.

But a few of the experts watched carefully for signs of fatigue. Snell had tried that pace and slowed to 59.8 for the last lap, and Ryun needed 58.3 for a world record.

Ryun was feeling it now. "I didn't feel like I was tying up, but it didn't feel like I was picking it up, either." He pressed around the curve, trying to use all of his strength over the whole last lap instead of saving it for the finish."

On the backstretch, "I kept trying to pick it up, and I kept telling myself, 'Sprint,' but it didn't work."

He held good form into the last curve and the crowd was half mad with excitement. He needed only a 30-second 220 to break the record. Only one man in history had ever run faster than this. Elliott, in the Rome Olympics, would have been almost a second faster than Ryun's time for 3½ laps, but Elliott had tied up in his last 100 meters. And Ryun had 220 yards to go. "I didn't explode."

Ryun held his incomparable pace around the curve, but it became more difficult with each step. At any moment he might tie up and lose the record, but his hard training over the past four years had given him the ability to keep going in the face of extreme fatigue, and keep going he did.

With the crowd almost hysterical, Ryun forced himself past 1500 meters in 3:36.1, a time bettered only by Elliott. He had gained half a second on Elliott's world record pace in the last 100, but he still had that last agonizing 120 yards to run.

But he was running freely, not tying up, and now it was obvious a new world record was being set. The crowd was wild with joy. But Ryun still had to run the homestretch, and he forced his weary body as hard as he could. "You get used to the pain."

He drove his arms hard, leading his tired legs, "hoping I wouldn't tie up." He drove all the way past the finish line before he allowed himself to relax.

He walked slowly around the curve while photographers snapped his picture over and over again and the delighted crowd still stood and applauded. "I wasn't doing too much actual thinking after the race, just sort of walking in a daze." He was on the backstretch when the announcer gave the official time.

"3:51.3."

Ryun threw up his arms and the crowd's roar was loud with approval. "I didn't know it was a world record until they announced it over the loud speaker. I was surprised."

At the incredible age of 19 years, 2 months, and 18 days, Ryun was what might be called a good prospect. His last 120 was in 15.2, his last 220 in 28.0, his last lap in 56.0. Most impressive of all was his last three-fourths mile in 2:53.4. Weisiger was second in 3:58.0.

The next week he beat some great half-milers in the Los Angeles Coliseum in 1:46.2. In two months he had to his credit two of the three fastest half-miles ever run, two of the three fastest miles, and one of the three fastest 1500's and two-miles.

KEINO BECOMES NUMBER TWO

Four days after his second fast losing mile against May, Keino was in Australia trying to break the world record for two miles. It was windy at the Sydney Sports Ground, but he ran 8:25.2, third fastest on record. Two days later in Melbourne, he ran away from Ron Clarke in the last 300 of a 5000 and won by 40 yards in 13:40.6.

Now an experienced world traveler, the ex-tribesman went to Los Angeles for his first indoor competition on January 19, 1966. He had practiced carefully on a 160-yard track marked off around some tennis courts and shortened his stride on advice from Mal Whitfield, but his time trials were run in disheartening times of 4:22, 4:12.3, and 4:10.4.

Afraid he would be knocked off the track in Los Angeles, he set a pace nobody would follow. After 1:58.5 he led Grelle by ten yards. He held the same lead at 2:59.8, but Grelle passed him on the last turn and won, 4:00.9 to 4:01.8. To everybody's surprise, Keino announced he would try the two-mile 90 minutes later. Having learned another lesson, he followed to the last lap and then sprinted home to win in 8:42.6.

Keino enjoyed visits to Disneyland and the Empire State Building, and won the Wanamaker Mile by two feet from Bob Day in 4:03.9. Then he flew home, only to return for another Los Angeles meet on February 10, where he was badly beaten at two miles.

Back home, he still considered himself primarily a 5000 meter runner, but he did some sprint training to improve his speed and his finish. Then, in May, he made his third trip of the year to Los Angeles and placed third in the two-mile behind the great sprints of Ryun and Grelle.

Then he flew to Hamburg to take part in a Police Festival. While there, he ran in a mile race and underestimated Harald Norpoth's strong finishing kick. Norpoth, who had placed second in the Olympic 5000 in 1964, had one of the fastest finishes in the history of track, and he won 3:58.8 to 4:00.2.

Back to Kenya went the irrepressible Keino for a 4:02 mile in Nairobi on June 4. Then, still doing more traveling than training, he was in East Berlin on June 24. In a poorly-paced run on a muddy track, he lost again to Norpoth and May. Surprisingly enough, he had

1966

now lost five of his last six 1500-mile races on foreign soil, plus one two-mile.

Undaunted, he ran two days later, in the Berlin Olympic Stadium. He returned to his favorite distance and beat Clarke and Norpoth in a fast 13:26.6 5000. Then he went home and won the Kenya Championships in 4:00.9 (Jürgen May third in 4:12.0) and 13:35.1 for three miles at Nairobi's near-6000-foot altitude. For the first time in too long, he had time to rest and train properly for the Commonwealth Games in Kingston, Jamaica.

On August 8, Keino ran in the three-mile championship against Clarke, who had lowered Keino's 5000 meter record to 13:16.6 a month previously. But Clarke had lost surprisingly in the six-mile to Temu of Kenya only two days ago. Keino followed confidently until the last lap, finished in 56.4, and won by ten yards in 12:57.4, time bettered by only two men.

Keino proved he had learned little about pacing or running heats or, possibly, about loafing, when he won his mile heat on August 11 in 3:57.4, easily the fastest heat ever run. Two days later, in the final, he pushed the pace hard with 59.2 and 1:58.7.

At three quarters in 2:56.6, Keino was 20 yards ahead of Simpson. Keino tired and lost half of his lead, but he won.

Results: Keino 3:55.3, Simpson 3:57.1, Ian Studd of New Zealand 3:58.4, Wilkinson of Great Britain 3:59.3, Graham of Northern Ireland 3:59.4, Wheeler of Australia 3:59.8.

On the way home, Keino, with his abundant energy, stopped off in London to run the Emsley Carr Mile in the British Games on August 20. Although bothered by gusty winds, Keino led from 370 yards and ran away from Graham (3:59.2) and Simpson (3:59.8) with a pace of 58.9, 1:58.1, and 2:55.0—a third lap in 56.9! He used his strength to finish in 3:53.4, second only to Ryun's world record.

After two weeks back in Kenya, Keino traveled again, this time to Wales. In the difficult winds of Cardiff, he followed a pace of 58.2 and 1:57.2, then once again ran a strong third lap. His 58.8 brought him around in 2:56.0, but he could finish no better than 61.6 for a "disappointing" time of 3:57.6.

After beating Norpoth at 5000 meters three days later, he went to the Santry track in Dublin for a record attempt on September 18. A hare ran the first lap in a ridiculous 53 seconds and Keino seemed to confirm the fact that he did not know pace by following in 54.1.

The crowd was delirious throughout the race as Keino passed the half in 1:53.1 and three quarters in 2:53.2, the fastest pace ever attempted. But it was too much for him and he faded to 64.2 on the final lap, for a time of 3:57.4. This was his last trial of the year and he gave some thought to retiring as a miler. "The mile is fast becoming just a sprint and I am really more of a distance runner."

1966

EUROPEAN CHAMPIONSHIPS

The Eighth European Athletic Championships were held in Budapest's famous Népstadion, and Europe had several 1500-meter runners of exceptionally high quality—May, Jazy, Norpoth, Tümmler, Simpson, and Odlozil.

JOSEF ODLOZIL, after his strong running in 1965 when he dipped under 3:58 four times and broke the world record for 2000 meters, ran only one good race in 1966. At Prague on August 13, he came from behind in the last 50 meters to beat Jazy in 3:37.6. Unfortunately, a sore throat returned him to near-obscurity and he failed to qualify for the final in the European Championships.

MICHEL JAZY continued his great running of 1965 with some fast early-season runs in 1966. As early as May 14, he ran 3000 meters in 7:56.2. Then, after a fast relay leg in 47.9, he beat Baran in 3:41.8, beat Bernard with a 7:53.4 3000, and ran 5000 meters in 13:38.2 at Lorient on June 3.

He continued running varied distances with great success. On June 9, he ran 13:50.6. On June 12, he missed Odlozil's 2000 meter record by only 0.2 seconds. In a 1500 at Rennes on June 15, he followed a pace of 58.5 and 1:58.5, then led in an ambitious 2:55.6. He finished with 300 meters in 40.8 (last lap in 54.3) to equal the European record of 3:36.4. On June 19, he ran 3000 meters in 7:51.8 to win the Kusocinski Memorial from Herrmann.

Jazy tried to break Elliott's 1500 meter record at Sochaux on June 25. He followed a pace of 56.4 and 1:56.2, then led in 2:54.5, but he could not finish fast enough. His last 300 was in 41.8 (last lap in 56.1) and he broke the European record by one tenth with 3:36.3.

Then, once again, Jazy proved that such fine running cannot be continued without paying the price. He lost a tactical race to Tümmler on July 9, won the French Championships at 5000 meters in 13:49.8 on July 24, and, surprisingly, was outkicked by Odlozil and Wadoux at Prague on August 13, even though he ran a good 3:38.3.

BODO TÜMMLER, now 22 years old, was developing a great finishing kick. He beat a strong field of 800 meter runners in 1:47.0 flat at Berlin on June 26. On July 9 the big West German went ahead of the great Jazy with a little over a lap to go in a tactical 1500 and stayed ahead with a final lap of 53.5. His fastest time was 3:40.8, but he ran only to win.

HARALD NORPOTH was now regarded as a top racer, with his strong finishing drives. On May 19, he beat a tired Keino, 3:58.8 to 4:00.2. On May 25, the tall, thin (6 feet, 134 pounds), 24-year-old outkicked two great finishers, May and Tümmler, in 3:41.2 after a 2:08 800. On June 24, he edged May and Keino on a muddy track in East Berlin. Two days later, he lost a 5000 to the two fastest in history, Keino and Clarke, but his only 1500 meter loss was to Tümmler on August 20, when both ran 3:40.8.

ALAN SIMPSON, after his sharp 3:57.1 for second place in the Commonwealth Games, ran 3:59.8 and 3:58.8.

JÜRGEN MAY had a mixed season after his great victories over Keino in New Zealand the previous year. After his two frustrating losses to Norpoth, May ran 3:38.0 at Potsdam on June 26. A trip to Kenya taught him about altitude when he ran only 4:12 and collapsed. But he came back with two fine 3:38.2 races in July.

At Budapest, the heats for the European Championships on August 30 eliminated Olyeg Raiko and Mart Vilt of USSR, who had recorded impressive times of 3:38.7 and 3:39.0. Tiny André De Hertoghe of Belgium set a new meet record by winning the second heat in 3:40.7.

The final, on September 1, disappointed people who wanted to see a fast race. After a lap in 59.5 by De Hertoghe, Norpoth took the lead with May on his heels, but he passed 800 meters in 2:03.4. Norpoth pressed into the wind and increased the pace to 3:02.5 at the bell.

Behind him, smug as a cat about to pounce, came big Bodo Tümmler. May, who had run little since July, dropped back, and defending champion Jazy moved into position. Wadoux, who with 3:37.7 had almost beaten Odlozil in that 3:37.6 race, made no effort to push the pace.

Norpoth ran his race, with a long, fast drive, and Jazy could barely catch him, but Tümmler followed Norpoth to the stretch and powered past. His last 300 was a fast 38.8, and his last 400 was an overpowering 52.7.

Results: Tümmler 3:41.9, Jazy 3:42.2, Norpoth 3:42.4, Simpson 3:43.8, May 3:44.1, De Hertoghe 3:44.3, Wadoux 3:44.5, Szordykowski of Poland 3:45.8.

OTHER RACES:

HARALD NORPOTH placed a good second to Jazy in the European Championships 5000 only three days after the 1500 final. Another three days later, in Cologne, he ran his last kilometer in a strong 2:32.8 and lowered the European record for 5000 meters to 13:24.8. Now at his very best, he went after the world 2000 record only three days later, at Hagen, West Germany, on September 10.

He followed a hare in 58.7 and 1:59.7. Then Tümmler took over without much desire to hurry and Norpoth passed 1200 meters in 3:02.7. Norpoth stepped up the pace and passed 1500 meters in 3:48.0, 3.9 seconds slower than Odlozil's world-record pace. But Norpoth passed 1600 meters in 4:02.2 and the mile in 4:03.6, and sped a last lap in 55.6 for a world record 4:57.8.

1966

On September 17, against Poland, Norpoth lost a good 1500 to Tümmler's 3:39.1. Norpoth beat Baran for second, 3:39.7 to 3:39.8. The next week, against Norway, Norpoth took revenge against Tümmler, 3:50.2 to 3:51.6.

MICHEL JAZY attempted the 5000 in the European Championships only three days after the 1500, and hung onto Norpoth's great drive until the homestretch. Then Jazy kicked and won by eight meters in 13:42.8. His last 1000 meters was in an astonishing 2:28.

The day after Norpoth broke the world record for 2000 meters, Jazy tried it, but he finished in 5:05.0. Then on September 24, he ran 4:58.4. After two 5000 victories, Jazy's farewell to track was to be at St. Maur on October 12, in a meet called the Michel Jazy Jubilee. In a 2000 meter race, the 30-year-old veteran followed a pace of 58.0 with 58.4 and 1:58.7 with 1:59.0. The crowd chanted, "Jazy, Jazy," and he followed Wadoux's 2:59.6 with the same time and 3:44.5 for 1500 meters, only one tenth back.

Then Jazy roused the crowd at the bell in 3:58.6 (equivalent to a mile in 4:00.1). The crowd was on its feet screaming throughout the entire last lap, and Jazy forced himself around in 57.5.

The time was 4:56.1 and Jazy gasped, "Not possible. I'm dead. Ready to burst. Nothing left. I can't go another step. It's not true."

This gave Jazy four of the six fastest times ever run for 2000 meters, which is 13 yards short of 1¼ miles. In his career he broke world records nine times, including two relays, and European records 17 times, plus one tie. He ended as the third fastest ever at both one mile and 1500 meters.

1966
1,500m:

3:36.1+	Jim Ryun (USA)	(1)	Berkeley	17	Jul
3:36.3	Michel Jazy (France)	(1)	Sochaux	25	Jun
3:36.8+	Kipchoge Keino (Kenya)	(1)	London	20	Aug
3:37.6	Josef Odlozil (Czechoslovakia)	(1)	Prague	13	Aug
3:37.7	Jean Wadoux (France)	(2)	Prague	13	Aug
3:38.0	Jürgen May (E. Germany)	(1)	Potsdam	26	Jun
3:38.7	Olyeg Raiko (USSR)	(1)	London	17	Jun
3:39.0	Mart Vilt (USSR)	(2)	London	17	Jun
3:39.1	Stanislav Hoffman (Czechosl.)	(4)	Prague	13	Aug
3:39.1	Bodo Tümmler (W. Germany)	(1)	Warsaw	17	Sep
3:39.5	Witold Baran (Poland)	(1)	Poznan	6	Aug
3:39.7	Harald Norpoth (W. Germany)	(2)	Warsaw	17	Sep
3:39.8	Alan Simpson (Great Britain)	(3)	London	17	Jun

Noteworthy Indoor Marks:

3:40.7	Michel Jazy (France)	(1)	Lyons	27	Feb
3:41.7	Jürgen May (E. Germany)	(1)	Berlin	27	Feb

MILE:

3:51.3WR	Jim Ryun (USA)	(1)	Berkeley	17	Jul
3:53.4	Kipchoge Keino (Kenya)	(1)	London	20	Aug
3:55.4	Jim Grelle (USA)	(1)	San Diego	11	Jun
3:56.1	Neill Duggan (Great Britain)	(2)	San Diego	11	Jun
3:57.1	Alan Simpson (Great Britain)	(2)	Kingston	13	Aug
3:57.3	Dyrol Burleson (USA)	(1)	Eugene	2	Jun
3:58.0	Cary Weisiger (USA)	(2)	Berkeley	17	Jul

Jim Ryun upsets Snell and Grelle at the 1965 AAU in a U.S. record time of 3:55.3.

Below, Ryun en route to his world record mile at Berkeley in 1966.

Alan Shapiro

Mark Shearman

Top, 1966 European Championships. From left, Michel Jazy, Bodo Tümmler (winner in 3:41.9) and Harald Norpoth. Below, Jim Grelle leads the 1965 Emsley Carr mile. Odlozil and Simpson (the eventual winner) follow.

Fionnbar Callanan

1966

3:58.4	Bob Day (USA)	(1)	Los Angeles	2 Apr
3:58.4	Ian Studd (New Zealand)	(3)	Kingston	13 Aug
3:58.8	Harald Norpoth (W. Germany)	(1)	Hamburg	19 May
3:58.8	Richard Romo (USA)	(1)	Los Angeles	10 Aug

Noteworthy Indoor Marks:

3:58.2	Jürgen May (E. Germany)	(1)	Berlin	20 Feb
3:59.6	Jürgen Haase (E. Germany)	(2)	Berlin	20 Feb
3:59.6	Jim Ryun (USA)	(1)	Kansas City	26 Feb
4:00.3	Jim Grelle (USA)	(1)	San Francisco	25 Feb

RYUN IS EVEN BETTER

An injury kept Ryun out of most cross country meets, and he avoided most indoor meets in 1967. At Los Angeles on January 21, he was passed by Tom Von Ruden with a lap and a half to go. Von Ruden had developed into a strong runner. Ryun passed him with a lap to go and won in 4:02.6 to 4:03.3 for Von Ruden. Burleson, in a rare appearance, ran 4:03.8.

Ryun ran an 8:44.2 two-mile and then a great 1:48.3 for 880 yards on a 220-yard flat clay track, second fastest ever indoors.

On March 4, Ryun won the Big 8 Conference mile in 3:58.8, a record for a twelve-lap track. A week later, in the indoor NCAA, he ran an 880 heat on Friday, then a mile heat in 4:08.0, and 90 minutes later, overworked, he lost the 880 final to Dave Patrick, 1:48.9 to 1:50.7. It was his first loss between the 880 and two-mile distances since 1965, and he said, "I'm exhausted," but the next night he won the mile in 3:58.6.

He looked strong in his first outdoor meet on March 25 at Los Angeles when he ran a sharp double, 4:05.1 and then 1:48.1 within an hour. On March 31, he ran an 880 relay leg in 1:46.1 as Kansas broke the all-time record in the sprint medley relay.

Ryun's first major mile effort was in the Kansas Relays on April 22. He followed in 58.6 and 1:59.4, then went far ahead in 2:59.6. His fast last lap of 55.1 gave him a time of 3:54.7, and Timmons said, "I think he ran a great time for this early."

On the next week-end, he won the four-mile relay for Kansas at the Drake Relays with his easy anchor leg in 3:59.1. The next day was his 20th birthday, and he celebrated with a 3:55.6 anchor leg which brought Kansas a best-on-record 9:33.8 for the distance medley relay. After a conference meet on May 21 in which he ran 4:08.5, 1:49.1, and 47.7 for his relay legs, Ryun was ready for the big meets.

He was still short of peak condition when he ran at Los Angeles on June 2 in the Coliseum-Compton combination meet. He was pulled to 57.6 for the first lap, faster than he liked, and his pace slowed to 1:58.2 and 2:58.0. He ran the last 440 in 55.2 and the last 120 in 14.6 to finish in 3:53.2, second fastest mile ever.

He went to Colorado for a week's training at high altitude, for his next two meets were to be well above sea level and he wanted to start thinking about training for the Olympics the next year in Mexico City.

On June 9 and 10, in mile-high Albuquerque, he successfully defended his Federation championships with 1:47.2 and 4:09.3. In the NCAA at Brigham Young University in Provo, Utah, everyone was slow starting, fearing the altitude. Ryun ran his last lap in 52.5, with most of his speed in his fantastic 23.9 last 220. He won by 20 yards in 4:03.5.

The AAU was a pleasant night meet in Bakersfield, California, and Ryun wanted to break 3:50. Half an hour before race time, he felt well and he decided to run for time. He told Grelle he planned to set his own pace, and Grelle quipped, "Fine. I'll see you later."

The crowd of 11,600 on Friday, June 23, saw Ryun's gaudy Kansas uniform of blue and fluorescent red move in front at the starting gun, and they became interested in the lap times immediately.

Ryun passed the first 220 in 28.4, fast time with the standing start. "My legs felt heavy at the beginning." He made an effort to slow down and he overdid it, passing the 440 in 59 flat.

He had planned to run the half in 1:56, but he was timed in 1:58.9. "When I heard the timers say 1:59 when I passed the first half, I didn't think I could get the record. As for the 3:50 mile, I felt there wasn't any chance."

He increased his pace, leaving his strong opposition far behind with a third lap in 58.5. His 2:57.4 was 2.1 seconds slower than he ran in his world record 3:51.3, but he was full of strength and he set out to make up the deficit.

He ran the next 220 in 27.4 and now he was only 1.5 seconds slower than his world record pace. He continued his fast stride around the last turn, and then, in the homestretch, he sprinted along the pale red track as no man has ever finished before in a fast mile.

His last 120 yards must have been run in close to 14 flat as he caught up with his world record pace a few steps before he hurtled through the white tape.

Results: Ryun 3:51.1, Grelle 3:56.1, Dave Wilborn of Oregon 3:56.2, Von Ruden 3:56.9, Roscoe Divine of Oregon 3:57.2, Sam Bair of Kent State 3:58.7, Martin Liquori of Essex High School, Newark, N.J. 3:59.8.

Grelle, almost 31 years old, said, "Everybody in the race was a kid but me."

Ryun's world record, after a slow first half, came about because of his last 220 in 26.3, his last 440 in 53.7, last 660 in 1:22.9, last 880 in 1:52.2, and final three-fourths mile in a great 2:52.1.

Ryun said: "I wasn't nearly as tired after it was over as I was

1967

last year at Berkeley."

Grelle said, "It's very hard to run by yourself, like he did tonight. His build-up on that last lap was amazing."

Now Ryun was confident he had a chance to break Elliott's world record of 3:35.6 for 1500 meters and he prepared for it in the meet against the British Commonwealth at Los Angeles on July 8. But when Keino entered the competition, Ryun changed his plans to a tactical effort.

Keino's first race of 1967 was indoors at Vancouver. He was boxed in with four laps to go and, disgusted, he dropped out of the race, which Burleson won in 4:03.4. Only 24 minutes later, Keino returned to the track in the two-mile, and he won a rousing battle in 8:37.6. Then he caught a bad cold and returned to Kenya.

He won two easy races in Madagascar early in April, then took over two months leave to work on his house and farm, where he planted 35 acres of tea and did little training. When the invitation came to run against Ryun in Los Angeles, he declined it because he felt he was not fit.

But on June 24, at Nyeri's 6000-foot altitude, he was given a time of 3:55.0 (after 56, 1:54, and 2:55), and experts thought something must be wrong with the measurement of the track, for nothing approaching this feat had ever been accomplished at high altitude. Keino himself was amazed, but now the officials were able to talk him into running 1500 meters against Ryun.

It was hot down on the floor of the Coliseum, but the track had been resurfaced and it seemed fast. The other runners, however, felt no great urge to try to run away from Keino and Ryun, and so they started much too slowly. After dawdling for half a lap, Dave Bailey of Canada showed some ambition and Keino and Ryun followed him past the 440 in 60.9.

Keino was never one to fool around with slow paces. One moment his maroon jersey, green shorts, and blue shoes were behind Bailey, and the next moment he startled everybody by streaking away in front faster than any miler ever ran during the second lap. He used only 56 seconds to complete the circuit, and Ryun, close behind, reached the 880 in 1:57.0. The 23,786 spectators were excited now.

Ryun ran behind Keino with intense purpose. They came around to the gun lap, with 440 yards to go, and Ryun's time was 2:39.2. He needed only 56.2 to break Elliott's record, but could he win this duel? Keino was still moving strongly, past three quarters in a fast 2:55.0.

At this point, going into the last backstretch, Ryun was alongside Keino, ready for his drive. The real racing was about to start. Ryun says, "At that time I knew I could get the record because I was feeling strong, especially in the legs."

And he looked strong! Suddenly he was racing away from

Keino at almost unbelievable speed. He gained a yard in every ten on the great Kenyan. Ryun's next 210 yards took only 24.6 seconds, about twelve yards faster than Elliott ran in his hitherto fantastic record surge in the 1960 Olympics.

Ryun looked back twice for Keino, but "I didn't see him at all," for Keino was far behind although still running his best. Ryun continued the fastest long finish of all time with a last 100 meters in 13.5, although he said later, "Coming around to the tape, I tended to tie up."

The crowd knew it was a record when Ryun flashed across the finish line, and they roared mightily.

Results: Ryun 3:33.1, Keino 3:37.2, Simpson 3:41.7, Bailey 3:41.7, Grelle 3:43.6, Wilborn 3:51.2.

Ryun refused an immediate television interview. "I'm definitely tired... although I've felt sick before. I can't explain it because I felt real strong all through the race." He had the worst headache since his 1965 AAU victory over Peter Snell, possibly because of the excessive heat.

Ryun's last 320 yards took only 38.1 seconds (equivalent to 300 meters in 39.3). His last 440 was a good 53.9, not quite as fast as in his 3:51.1 mile. But his last 880 was in 1:51.3, fastest ever recorded. His last 1000 meters took him only about 2:18.7, equal to Wade Bell's new American record. And Ryun's last three-fourths mile was in about 2:48.7, far faster than any man had run for that distance alone.

Keino was heard to exclaim, "Oh, that Jim Ryun. He run too fast."

The two great milers raced again a month later. Ryun did not run before then, and Keino ran only twice. Keino ran the 5000 on the day after the world-record 1500 and beat Clarke in 13:36.8. On July 22, in Nairobi, he ran an easy 4:04.5.

They met in the Emsley Carr Mile during the USA vs Great Britain match before 35,000 at London's White City Stadium on August 12. Hindering winds of 20 mph ruled out a record attempt.

Once again, the first lap was boringly slow and both men were well behind 60.7. Then, to the crowd's dismay, Keino did not spurt out ahead as he had in Los Angeles. Instead, Ryun eased into the lead at the half in a dull 2:03.0. At three quarters in 3:02.2, Whetton was second to Ryun and Keino was third.

On the last backstretch, Keino moved to a threatening position on Ryun's shoulder and Ryun showed the crowd some real speed at last as he sprinted away to win by ten yards in 3:56.0. Keino, second in 3:57.4, said, "I had no plan. I didn't want to go in front and was hoping to come through very fast, but I was a bit too far behind at the start of the last lap."

Ryun ran one more race, five days later against West

1967

Germany in Düsseldorf. His opponents were Grelle, Tümmler, who had been slowed by an injury, and Norpoth, who had run 3000 meters in a very fast 7:45.2, two miles in 8:25.6, and a mile in 3:59.6. With four of the fastest finishers of all time in the battle, the pace was extremely slow. At the bell, Tümmler jumped into the lead, while Norpoth delayed Ryun. But Ryun swung around Norpoth on the curve, with the German crowd roaring loudly. Then came the fastest burst of speed ever recorded in any mile or 1500 meter race. Ryun accelerated so fast and left Tümmler behind so rapidly that the German crowd was stunned into silence. One expert observer timed Ryun's 100 meters along the backstretch in a nearly incredible 11.6 seconds.

Ryun continued to pull away, although naturally not quite so fast. His last 200 meters averaged 12.4 seconds for each 100, a total of 24.8. Thus his last 300 meters took only 36.4, easily the fastest ever run. His last 400 was also fastest on record—50.6. (One report gave his last 400 as 49.7.)

Results: Ryun 3:38.2, Tümmler 3:42.3, Norpoth 3:42.5, Grelle 3:42.8.

Ryun finished the season with a clear-cut superiority in speed over all other milers in history.

KEINO IS ASTOUNDING

Four days after losing to Ryun, Keino ran 3:57.2 at Belfast. He flew home and ran an astonishing four times in one day at Nyeri. He won the mile in 3:58.7, beat the great Kiprugut in a 1:49.0 880, was third in the three-mile, and ran a leg in the winning mile relay.

Commuting back to London, he ran in the Morley Mile at White City on August 28. He was fast all the way, in 56.0, 1:56.9, and 2:56.1, and his legs almost buckled under him as he finished in 3:53.8. Simpson, who had run 3:58.1 two days before, was a poor second in 4:00.4.

Back to Nairobi for the Kenyan Championships, Keino won easily in 3:59.5, while Simpson struggled in ninth in 4:19.2, gasping for oxygen. At Kisumu's 3,720-foot altitude during the East African Championships on September 10, Simpson made a real effort. Keino led in 56.2 and 1:56.1, and Simpson stayed with him. Then Keino ran the third lap in 58.1, for 2:54.2. Simpson managed to hang on that far, but then he fell behind rapidly, and Keino won, 3:53.1 to 3:57.6.

Keino's 3:53.1, third fastest mile ever run, was only part of his day's running. He came back later and won the three-mile, completing an amazing double in 13:31.6. Six days later, in Zambia's Matero Stadium, Keino won the Zambian Championship in 3:38.1.

OTHER RUNNERS

ANDRÉ DE HERTOGHE, the 5'6-1/8" Belgian, had progressed no farther than 3:41.8 in 1965 at the age of 24, and in 1966 he ran only 3:40.7. He had a good year in 1967, undefeated until the October Olympic Preview at Mexico City where he ran a poor 3:52.1 for seventh in that high altitude.

He won the 1967 World Games in June with 3:41.9, and ran a 3:57.3 mile a week later in Stockholm. His fastest 1500 of the year was 3:39.5 at Karlstad on August 25, where he narrowly defeated Anders Gärderud (3:39.6), who was running his sixth race in seven days, including a mile in 3:58.6 the day before, Wadoux, who had run 3:38.4, and Ulf Högberg, who had run 3:39.3. De Hertoghe also ran an excellent 1:46.7 for 800 meters.

TOM VON RUDEN made a hurried trip to Helsinki, and six days after his exciting 3:56.9 in the AAU, he placed only fifth in the World Games. Then he was undefeated for the rest of the year, winning with a long drive on the last lap. He won the Pan American Games easily in 3:43.4. Four days later, on August 9 in Montreal, he ran for the Americas team against Europe and out-drove Wadoux impressively, 3:41.0 to 3:42.3.

FASTEST COMBINED RACES OF ALL-TIME:

3:33.1	(3:51.0)	Ryun	1967
(3:33.2)	3:51.1	Ryun	1967
(3:33.5)	3:51.3	Ryun	1966
(3:35.2)	3:53.1	Keino	1967
(3:35.2)	3:53.2	Ryun	1967
(3:35.4)	3:53.4	Keino	1966
3:35.6	(3:53.6)	Elliott	1960
(3:35.6)	3:53.6	Jazy	1965
(3:35.7)	3:53.7	Ryun	1966
(3:35.8)	3:53.8	May	1965
(3:35.8)	3:53.8	Keino	1967
3:36.0	(3:54.1)	Elliott	1958
(3:36.1)	3:54.1	Snell	1964
(3:36.1)	3:54.1	May	1965

1967
1,500m:

3:33.1 WR	Jim Ryun (USA)	(1)	Los Angeles	8	Jul
3:36.7+	Kipchoge Keino (Kenya)	(1)	London	28	Aug
3:38.4	Jean Wadoux (France)	(1)	Sochaux	17	Jun
3:39.3	Ulf Högberg (Sweden)	(1)	Oslo	21	Jun
3:39.5	André De Hertoghe(Belgium)	(1)	Karlstad	25	Aug
3:39.6	Anders Gärderud (Sweden)	(2)	Karlstad	25	Aug
3:39.7	Claude Nicolas (France)	(1)	Monaco	9	Jul
3:40.2	Manfred Matuschewski (E. Ger)	(1)	Kiev	16	Sep
3:40.4	Arne Kvalheim (Norway)	(2)	Oslo	21	Jun
3:40.4	Igor Potapchenko (USSR)	(1)	Kiev	9	Sep
3:40.5	Francesco Arese (Italy)	(1)	Viareggio	20	Aug
3:40.5	Bodo Tümmler (W. Germany)	(2)	Kiev	16	Sep
3:40.6	Olyeg Raiko (USSR)	(2)	Kiev	9	Sep

Mile:

3:51.1 WR	Jim Ryun (USA)	(1)	Bakersfield, Cal.	23	Jun
3:53.1	Kipchoge Keino (Kenya)	(1)	Kisumu	10	Sep
3:56.1	Jim Grelle (USA)	(2)	Bakersfield, Cal.	23	Jun

1967

3:56.2	Dave Wilborn (USA)	(3)	Bakersfield, Cal.	23	Jun
3:56.9	Tom Von Ruden (USA)	(4)	Bakersfield, Cal.	23	Jun
3:57.2	Roscoe Divine (USA)	(5)	Bakersfield, Cal.	23	Jun
3:57.3	André De Hertoghe (Belgium)	(1)	Stockholm	4	Jul
3:57.6	Alan Simpson (Great Britain)	(2)	Kisumu	10	Sep
3:57.7	Dave Bailey (Canada)	(1)	Toronto	22	Jul
3:58.6	Anders Gärderud (Sweden)	(1)	Malmö	24	Aug
3:58.7	Sam Bair (USA)	(6)	Bakersfield, Cal.	23	Jun
3:58.7	Allan Rushmer (Great Britain)	(2)	Duston	26	Aug

Noteworthy Indoor Marks:

3:58.6	Jim Ryun (USA)	(1)	Detroit	11	Mar
3:59.3	Dave Patrick (USA)	(1)	New York	17	Feb

In an Olympic year, every contender arranges his season of training and racing toward that one all-important race, but in 1968 there was an added complication. The site of the Olympic Games was Mexico City, where the altitude was more than one and one-third miles above sea level.

This meant an important shortage of oxygen, and at the beginning of 1968 there was much speculation and little knowledge about its effects on distance runners. People who conducted experiments, while using real runners, arrived at erroneous conclusions because no runner would exert himself for an experiment as he would during an important race.

Thus, most people believed a 1500 meter runner would be six to ten seconds poorer, even if he became acclimatized to that altitude. And so most of the serious runners spent the year making an effort to adjust to running at a high altitude. The French established a training camp in the Pyrenees, Mexico City had many curious visitors in pre-Olympic meets and tests, the United States held its final training and trials near Lake Tahoe at an altitude equally as bad as Mexico City's, and the others did what they could. Only Keino lived normally.

Because so many important races were run at high altitudes, times were not as fast as in previous years, and most of those races were at 1500 meters. One exception to all these conditions was Tümmler, who took his place with Ryun and Keino as a super miler during 1968.

BODO TÜMMLER

As a boy of eight, Bodo walked and ran up to 25 kilometers with other "pathfinders" once a week. He favored tennis at first and never raced until he was 16. He ran 3:58.4 in 1962 at the age of 19. He prefers long runs for training.

Now 24 years old in 1968, the powerful 6'2", 159-pound West German finally began to run some fast races to go with his history of strong finishes in tactical races. His competitive record, in addition to his European Championship of 1966, included the European Cup final in 1965 and Olympic Preview victories at Mexico

City in both 1966 and 1967, but his fastest 1500 was 3:39.1.

A rumor had Tümmler out of the Olympics early in 1968 with, of all things, a heart condition, but he put an end to the speculation by running 1000 meters in 2:18.8 and 3000 in 7:59.4 in June.

Then he raced at Stockholm against De Hertoghe on July 2. After times estimated at 57 and 1:56, he passed three quarters in 2:57.2 and then pulled away with a fast last lap in 57.5. He ran 3:54.7, and De Hertoghe finished in 3:56.0.

In a great 1500 at Cologne on July 10, Tümmler ran the first lap in 56.3, took the lead at 750 meters and pushed the pace with 1:56.5 and 2:55.5 for 1200 meters. It took a last 300 in 41.0 to stay safely ahead of the little Belgian. Tümmler's 3:36.5 was only one-fifth of a second from Jazy's European record. De Hertoghe ran 3:37.1, German half-miler Walter Adams ran 3:37.5, Arnd Krüger ran 3:38.8, and Von Ruden was fifth in 3:39.4, the same fast time as Rudi Simon of Belgium.

Tümmler, who had placed third in the 1956 European Championships 800 with 1:46.3, abandoned that distance in 1968 to concentrate on the 1500. Satisfied with his condition after his 3:36.5, he went back to tactical victories until August 22 at Karlskrona. There, he followed a pace of 57 and 1:56, then ran all alone for the last lap and a half to clock 3:53.8, a time bettered only by Ryun, Keino, and Jazy.

Tümmler beat Gärderud for the third time in 1968, with a good 3:38.1 to the Swede's 3:38.7 on August 26 at Göteborg, and went to Mexico City undefeated.

RYUN IN TROUBLE

After a winter of good background running, Ryun ran 3:57.5 indoors on February 9 in New York before he had done any fast training. Then his troubles began. He injured an ankle and won a slow double in the Big 8.

He ran the same ambitious double in the NCAA, except the two-mile came first. His ankle still hurt, and now his arches were bothering him, but he outkicked Gerry Lindgren in 8:39.0 and ran a 54.7 last quarter to win the mile in an easy 4:06.8.

He was bothered by a hamstring injury but he ran 3:42.8 on April 20 and a 4:10.3 mile at Boulder, Colorado's mile-high altitude, on May 18. Then he contracted mononucleosis and was supposedly out for the "season."

He was forced to rest, but he lived in Flagstaff, Arizona, at a 6907-foot altitude and gained some acclimatization. By July 27 he was ready to test himself, and he ran an 880 in 1:47.9 at Flagstaff. There was some question as to the exact value of his time, because such an altitude aids speed as much as a full second per lap but at the same time it hinders endurance because of the oxygen shortage. But Ryun was happy with his progress.

Although not qualified for the Final Trials, Ryun had a chance to be admitted by proving his condition, and he did so at Walnut, California, on August 10. He led in 60.6, was second to Wilborn's 2:00.7, in 2:01.1, and led purposefully in 3:01.1. He finished with a lap in 54.8 for a highly acceptable time of 3:55.9.

On August 31, on the Tartan track at South Lake Tahoe, the fastest times ever recorded for short races were being made, and Ryun ran his last lap in 53.5 to finish in 3:43.0. This was 3.4 seconds faster than Tümmler's "world record" for that altitude.

The Final Trials were run on the same fast track on September 13, 14, and 15. In his heat, Ryun hustled around the last lap under 53 to finish in 3:58.3, almost even with Roscoe Divine. In the semi-final, Ryun ran 3:53.0, with a last lap in 52-flat. He called it "easy".

As in all the distance runs at the Final Trials, the final of the 1500 started cautiously. Ryun led in 67.8 and 2:13.6. Then runners rushed past him and he was last when the gun sounded. He ran wide again, as he had in losing badly in the 800-meter finals, but he was in good position on the backstretch. He burst into an eight-yard lead around the curve and won by four yards in 3:49.0 over Liquori (3:49.5) and Von Ruden (3:49.8).

His last lap was in 50.8 and his last 880 in a fastest-ever 1:50.8. The consensus of opinion was that he could win at Mexico City in any fast-finish race.

KIP KEINO (Part 4)

Afraid of reaching his peak condition too soon, Keino began slowly in 1968. He avoided indoor running and early invitations. He also had a problem of deciding which events he would run in the Olympics, for he developed into a top 10,000 meter runner.

On June 1, in the high altitude of Nyeri, he ran six miles in 28:39.0, enough to frighten any sea-level runner in the world. A week later, at Nairobi, he ran a mile in 4:01.9. He showed more aptitude at the altitude on July 6, again at Nairobi, when he won a good double—three-mile in 13:48.8 and six-mile in 28:51.8.

But when he came down to sea-level and ran in Scandinavia, he was mysteriously slower. At Oslo on July 10, he ran against Clarke in a 5000. He was running well, three laps from the end, when suddenly he felt intense pain in his stomach. He dropped back and finished third. The next day, in the 10,000, he felt the same pain and he was violently ill, but he finished in 28:51.6, far behind Clarke and Temu.

Now Keino's future was in doubt. He lost a 1500 at Stockholm to John Mason of the USA on July 17. The next day Clarke beat Keino by 30 yards in another 5000. Still, Keino refused to withdraw from his scheduled races. He was due in Russia in two days.

After a disagreeable trip to Leningrad, where their plane was fumigated while they were still in it, they were hauled away in a truck and told they could not eat because it was too late. As Keino warmed up the next day, his bag with all his gear was stolen.

Keino borrowed some uncomfortable size nine shoes and won the 5000 in the Znamenskiy Memorial in 13:36.2. The next day, the borrowed shoes caused blisters and he finished the 10,000 in agony and in second place, but his time was 28:06.4, a time bettered only by Clarke and Jürgen Haase with his winning European record time of 28:04.4. Considering the altitude to be run at Mexico City, Keino was now a favorite in the 10,000 . . . if he ran.

Two days later, in Dublin, he ran a poor 4:02.4. Four days after that, at 8000-foot altitude in Kenya, he ran 10,000 meters in a good 29:52.2. In August, he won three-mile races in the Kenyan Championships, the East African Championships, and in Zambia. His last important trial before the Olympic Games was at Kisumu on August 31 when he proved to be ready for the 1500 by running a mile in 3:55.5, last three-fourths in 2:54.3.

Keino's career had been remarkable in at least one way because of his astonishing disregard for fatigue. He ran the three-mile and six-mile on the same day, he ran Olympic heats and finals on several consecutive days, he started out at ridiculously fast paces, and he ran far faster than necessary in qualifying heats. And at Mexico City, he continued this characteristic waste of energy.

First, he started in the 10,000, which meant he would have to run six times in eight days. He was running with the leaders, ready to outkick them with his superior speed, when he again felt the mysterious pain in his stomach. He ran off the track and crumpled to the grass, doubled up with pain. But when stretch bearers approached him, he leaped to his feet like some frightened animal and almost sprinted around the track. He had been disqualified earlier, but he wasted untold energy in that wild gesture.

Runners from low countries fared badly in the 10,000, and Keino entered the 5000 as favorite, *if* his stomach did not act up again. He won his heat on October 15, two days after the 10,000, and two days later he ran in the final. He ran well, but a tactical blunder on the last lap cost him a close defeat. He lost by four feet in the mediocre time of 14:05.2 to Mohamed Gamoudi's 14:05.0.

The next day, Keino was to run in the 1500 meter heats. With hard races behind him and with his doubtful stomach condition, experts thought he could not last through the 1500. They forgot that along with his unsophisticated wasting of energy, one of his most striking characteristics was courage.

He went to a German doctor, who suspected gall bladder trouble and advised Keino to avoid running until he had been x-rayed. Keino's team managers suggested he withdraw from the 1500, but he was determined to run.

1968 OLYMPICS

Some big names were suddenly missing in 1968. Grelle retired, afraid of the altitude. Wadoux, who ran 3:37.9 on July 4, chose to run the 5000, where he placed ninth. May had defected to West Germany and was not yet eligible to represent the West Germans internationally, nor had he regained his form. Gärderud, who gained prominence in 1967, ran 3:38.7 at Göteborg on August 26, but he was eliminated in his heat here in the cruel 7,349-foot altitude.

Keino wasted more energy in his heat by running a middle 400 meters in a fantastic 56.9. He won in 3:46.9, five seconds faster than necessary.

The semi-finals on October 19 were slower than the heats. Everybody was content to let the kick finish decide it, and three "unknowns" qualified for the twelve-man final. Ben Jipcho of Kenya had run 3:59.8 behind Keino at Kisumu on August 31. Promising Henryk Szordykowski of Poland was undefeated, but his best was 3:40.3. Jacques Boxberger of France had a best of 3:40.8.

Of the others, Norpoth had run no faster than 3:40.4 this year and failed to finish in the Olympic 5000. De Hertoghe barely qualified for the final. Von Ruden did not like the thought of a moderately-fast pace at this altitude. Marty Liquori, who showed great improvement at 19, had an injured instep. And Odlozil had run no faster than 3:41.0 in eighth place on July 10 at Cologne.

On October 20, the twelve hopefuls lined up on the red Tartan track in the low, double-decked Estadio Olimpico. Ahead of them, high on the rim of the stadium, was the wondrous scoreboard. To their left, across the end of the field, was a long and narrow stairway filled with important-looking judges and timers in reddish brown coats—the finish line. Television cameras pointed at them from every angle, exposing them to millions of people all over the world.

The orange-garbed starter raised his pistol, wired to the Omega timer. At the command, in Spanish, they leaned forward tensely. At the gun, they lurched into running motion. This was no slow start, as in the semi-finals. This was a run for the medals, and they wasted no time.

Jipcho circled the track swiftly in 56 seconds, with Keino

(56.6) right behind and Ryun (58.5) near the rear of the pack. This was not an unusual pace for milers of this caliber, nor was it difficult at an altitude which aided runners by as much as a second per lap. But for sea-level runners it was frightening to consider the prospect of continuing for 2-¾ laps.

And yet Keino ran fast. He knew there was only one way to beat Ryun. He had to take every possible advantage of his body's uncommon ability to utilize oxygen, developed from a lifetime of activity at high altitude. He took the lead and came around to the white plastic starting line for the second time, in an alarming 1:55.3.

Tümmler, in great shape and very determined, was only four yards behind Keino, and he was followed by another former tactical runner, Norpoth. On Norpoth's heels was the courageous Whetton, who had run a mile in 3:58.6 this year. Behind Whetton there was an astoundingly wide ten-yard gap of the reddish track to the blue jersey of Ryun (1:58.5). Lacking confidence because of his illness and the altitude, Ryun believed 3:39 would win. "I could not have kept up with him and still have any kick left for the finish."

Then Keino actually increased his pace! To experts who believed the altitude myth, it seemed impossible, especially after his hectic days of wasted energy in the past week. But Keino ran that third lap in 58.1, racing around to the starting line in 2:53.4. This was faster than Ryun's pace in his world record race, and it was hard to believe any man could continue at this altitude.

Tümmler was now eight yards behind, still fighting mightily. Norpoth was still following Tümmler, and Ryun (2:56.0) had actually gained four yards on the third lap, but he was still a frightening 14 yards behind Keino.

At sea level, Ryun would be expected to race past Keino and leave him struggling behind, and there were many in Estadio Olimpico who still expected it. Surely Keino could not continue! Ryun moved past Norpoth on the backstretch and came alongside Tümmler. But Tümmler was running beyond all expectations, and Ryun had to run wide on the curve.

Ryun passed Tümmler on the curve and now he was twelve yards behind Keino. Now, if ever, he had to start gaining. He drove himself courageously, suffering from fatigue, but something unexpected was happening ahead of him.

Keino was forcing himself on without tying up. Keino had run 200 meters in 27.5 and he was slowing very little in the homestretch. He was showing surprised physiologists things they could never learn from their experiments. He was showing them that 1500-meter runners gained speed from the altitude, like 800 meter runners, and the fortunate altitude-trained runners lost less than they gained. He strode joyously across the finish line, the gap in his lower teeth bared in a strained smile. His courageous gamble had paid off with his first victory over Ryun—the first victory over Ryun by any miler since 1965.

Ryun saw he could never catch Keino and he eased the torture. He looked back three times in the stretch to be certain he was saving the silver medal, and he actually lost about five yards on Keino.

Whetton finished with surprising strength, closing on Norpoth at the end. Von Ruden, nearly last all the way, showed a good but useless finish at the end.

Results: Keino 3:34.9, Ryun 3:37.8, Tümmler 3:39.0, Norpoth 3:42.5, Whetton 3:43.8, Boxberger 3:46.6, Szordykowski 3:46.6, Odlozil 3:48.6, Von Ruden 3:49.2, Jipcho 3:51.2, De Hertoghe 3:53.6, Liquori 4:18.2.

Keino's Olympic record was his fastest ever, but, of course, it was his only hard 1500 at a high altitude. He certainly could have run faster without the hard runs of the previous week.

Keino also suffered his pain again, in the last half lap. Later, during a victory parade in Nairobi, he fainted, and his problem was diagnosed as a gall bladder infection.

Keino, whose last lap was in 55.9, said, "I knew Ryun had a very good kick so I prepared myself to have a big lead going into the final quarter ... I said to myself that I must run very fast all the way".

Immediately after the race, Ryun slumped on a bench, suffering more than ever before. "It hurts," he moaned.

Tümmler, the only European to win a medal in the five distance runs, could well be proud of his 3:39.0 at that altitude. In those five races, Africans won ten medals including all five of the precious gold medals. Although it is possible Keino could not have won at sea level, it required one of the greatest milers in history to run 3:34.9 anywhere. He was now second fastest 1500-meter man of all time.

1968
1,500m:

3:34.9	Kipchoge Keino (Kenya)	(1)	Mexico City	20	Oct
3:36.5	Bodo Tümmler (W. Germany)	(1)	Cologne	10	Jul
3:37.1	André De Hertoghe (Belgium)	(2)	Cologne	10	Jul
3:37.5	Walter Adams (W. Germany)	(3)	Cologne	10	Jul
3:37.8	Jim Ryun (USA)	(2)	Mexico City	20	Oct
3:37.9	Jean Wadoux (France)	(1)	Paris	4	Jul
3:38.5	Arne Kvalheim (Norway)	(1)	Oslo	28	Aug
3:38.7	Anders Gärderud (Sweden)	(2)	Göteborg	26	Aug
3:38.8	Arnd Krüger (W. Germany)	(4)	Cologne	10	Jul
3:38.9	Jürgen May (W. Germany)	(1)	Rehlingen	16	Jun
3:39.0	Francesco Arese (Italy)	(1)	Schio	13	Jul
3:39.4	Tom Von Ruden (USA)	(5)	Cologne	10	Jul
3:39.4	Rudi Simon (Belgium)	(6)	Cologne	10	Jul

Mile:

3:53.8	Bodo Tümmler (W. Germany)	(1)	Karlskrona	22	Aug
3:55.5	Kipchoge Keino (Kenya)	(1)	Kisumu	31	Aug
3:55.9	Jim Ryun (USA)	(1)	Walnut	10	Aug
3:56.0	André De Hertoghe (Belgium)	(2)	Stockholm	2	Jul
3:56.8	Dave Patrick (USA)	(1)	Philadelphia	1	Jun

1968

3:57.4	Brian Kivlan (USA)	(2)	Philadelphia	1	Jun
3:58.1	Roscoe Divine (USA)	(2)	Walnut	10	Aug
3:58.4	Dave Wilborn (USA)	(1)	Eugene, Ore.	13	Apr
3:58.5	Arne Kvalheim (Norway)	(2)	Eugene, Ore.	13	Apr
3:58.6	DeVilliers Lamprecht (S. Africa)	(1)	Stellenbosch	22	Mar
3:58.6	Jerry Richey (USA)	(3)	Philadelphia	1	Jun
3:58.6	Frank Murphy (Eire)	(4)	Philadelphia	1	Jun
3:58.6	John Boulter (Great Britain)	(1)	Motspur Park	24	Jul
3:58.6	John Whetton (Great Britain)	(1)	London	3	Aug

Noteworthy Indoor Mark:

3:57.5	Jim Ryun (USA)	(1)	New York	9	Feb

Ed Lacey

Kip Keino hits the tape in his stunning gold medal performance at Mexico City. Ryun and Tummler trail.

Jeff Johnson

Above, start of the gun lap at the 1969 NCAA mile at Knoxville. Left to right, Dickie Kleier, Chris Mason, Howell Michael, Frank Murphy, Jim Ryun, Marty Liquori. Liquori defeated Ryun, 3:57.7 to 3:59.3.

Right, Kipchoge Keino.

Don Chadez

XII

Unfinished symphony

KEINO THE CHAMPION

Keino went home to great honors. His third daughter was born on the doubly happy day he won his gold medal, and he was now a Chief Inspector. After a series of tests, he was released from the hospital with the assurance that his infection had been checked by the German doctor.

He felt wonderful, and he told his wife, "When I am away, I think of this farm and I want to give up running." He could not quit, but he did go into semi-retirement during 1969.

He ran only a few races, in Kenya. His best was 3:38.8 at Nyeri. He won the East African Championships at Kampala in 3:40.4, plus an easy 5000.

By September he wanted to take another trip, and he ran a 1500 at South Lake Tahoe, where the track had been shifted to a new site 1000 feet lower than Mexico City. Against weak opposition, he ran a typical Keino race, with a first lap in 59.6, then a killer in 56.3 to make up for his "misjudged" start. He pushed around to 1200 meters in a sensational 2:53.0, then slowed to 44.3 in the last 300 meters for a good 3:37.3.

RYUN SUCCUMBS

In his first test since the Olympics, Ryun ran 4:06.2 indoors

1969

on February 8. A series of leg injuries, each seeming to cause another, slowed him but could not stop him entirely. After dropping out of two two-mile races—a significant change in him—he ran against Liquori in the indoor NCAA.

After passing three quarters in 3:06.2, Ryun hopefully passed Liquori at the start of the last lap, but his wobbly knee did not allow him to cut in and Liquori regained the lead on the inside. Ryun challenged again in the short homestretch and gained the judge's decision in 4:02.6. He finished with a shoe full of blood from broken blisters.

Ryun apparently recovered from his injuries in time to run well—although not sensationally for him—in relay meets. At the Texas Relays he ran 880 legs of 1:46.9 and 1:47.4 in losing races. At the Kansas Relays, he ran a 4:01.2 leg on Friday, and a good 3:57.6 leg on Saturday as Kansas lowered their own "world" record. At Drake, he proved he was not himself by dropping out in the middle of a hot 880 leg, and in the four-mile relay he ran 4:11 instead of the 3:58 needed to win.

People thought he was not yet in shape, but in previous years he always ran hard if he entered a race. His injuries were not all physical. He ran only two slow miles during the dual-meet season and regretfully withdrew from the Kennedy Games at the end of May because his knee was still bothering him.

He did not have a time fast enough to qualify for the NCAA, and so he became a late entry in the Coliseum-Compton mile at Los Angeles on June 7. He loafed behind the pack through 62.3, moved to third at the half in 2:01.7, and he was still third in 3:00.4. With half a lap to go, he was still third and Liquori was a threat on his shoulder, but Ryun finished the lap in 55.5 to win.

Results: Ryun 3:55.9, Sam Bair 3:56.7, Liquori 3:57.6, Frank Murphy 3:58.1, John Lawson 3:59.3, Mason 4:00.7, Chuck LaBenz 4:02.2.

Ryun said, "Before tonight I was apprehensive about this whole season, but now I'm looking forward to all the races." His next competition was the NCAA Championships.

MARTIN LIQUORI

A sensational high school runner, Marty Liquori ran 4:17.1 in 1965 before his 16th birthday. As a junior in 1966, he lowered his time to 4:13.0. As a 17-year-old senior, he started 1967 with an unhappy bout of mononucleosis but he set a high school flat-track record of 4:16.1 on March 12, then improved to 4:13.0. At the Penn Relays, he ran a relay leg in 4:04.4.

Three months before his 18th birthday, he made his debut in major racing at the Coliseum-Compton mile on June 2. Although far behind Ryun's 3:53.2, Liquori almost took second with a strong

1969

4:01.1.

On June 10, at San Diego, he beat the ailing Dave Patrick and Tim Danielson, who had become the second high school boy to break four minutes with 3:59.4 in 1966. Liquori's time was impressive, too—4:00.1.

He ran even faster in the AAU meet at Bakersfield. While Ryun was lowering the mile record to 3:51.1, Liquori ran 3:59.8 for seventh place.

As a freshman at Villanova in 1968, Liquori's competition was somewhat limited, but he ran fast times indoors. Early marks included an 8:52.4 two-mile, a 2:10.3 1000, and a mile in 4:05.0. Outdoors, he ran a 4:02.5 relay leg with a fast last lap in 55.5.

Liquori was overshadowed at Villanova by senior Dave Patrick, who won the IC4A in 3:56.8 and was favored to make the Olympic team. Liquori ran his first major race of 1968 at the Coliseum-Compton Invitational on June 7. He ran 4:00.7 and almost caught the high respected DeHertoghe for second. He did beat Frank Murphy, an Irishman at Villanova who had run a good 3:58.6 in the IC4A.

In the AAU 1500, the pace was a lazy 3:04.3 for three-fourths mile, and then Liquori was left behind in the sprint. While John Mason was winning in 3:43.1 with a last lap in 53.5, Liquori placed a disappointing seventh in 3:44.9.

In the semi-final Olympic Trials in Los Angeles on June 30, Liquori tried other tactics. He led all the way to the homestretch, but he finished third behind NCAA champion Patrick and Bair in 3:44.2. He said, "I hadn't planned to go out in front, but the pace was so slow I had no choice. I can't finish with those fellows."

Training at the Olympic camp near South Lake Tahoe, Liquori began to adapt well to the altitude and his training progressed. In a mile race at Eugene on August 23, he ran 3:59.3, significantly close to Ryun's 3:59.0.

Then, on September 16, in the final of the 1500 in the Final Olympic Trials, Liquori reached his goal . . . a place on the Olympic team. He gained at least four yards on Ryun in an impressive homestretch drive to finish in 3:49.5 to Ryun's 3:49.0. Liquori's last 400 meters took only 51.9 seconds and his last 800 was a fast 1:51.5.

He was now an international threat, at 19. But at Mexico City he had arch trouble and finished a poor last in the final.

Liquori started his 1969 indoor season badly. At Philadelphia, on January 24, he ran against Sam Bair and Jürgen May, who was making his indoor debut in his first international meet since his dramatic escape from East Germany. May set a fast pace of 57.0 and 1:58.5, and he had a 40 yard lead with a quarter to go. Bair surprised May and won in 4:03.6, but Liquori ran only 4:10.2.

The next week, in the Wanamaker Mile, a more determined

1969

Liquori ran behind May's 57.7 and 1:58.6, then began to close the gap at three-quarters, 3:02.0 to 3:00.8, and won in 4:00.8. Then, in some good races, he won a two-mile in 8:42.2 and a 1000 in 2:08.5. He won the IC4A in 4:05.3 and gave Ryun a fright at the NCAA.

Outdoors, Liquori won the IC4A in 4:03.4 and ran his fastest ever—3:57.6—behind Ryun's 3:55.9 at the Coliseum. On June 21, at Knoxville, Tennessee, he raced Ryun again in the NCAA Championships. Marty suffered an intestinal virus six days before and he had cut his workouts by two thirds for the last two weeks because of a painfully sprained ligament at the rear of his arch.

Jim Elliott, the Villanova coach, instructed Liquori to get ahead before Ryun made his move, for it had been more than five years since anybody beat Ryun from behind.

Chuck LaBenz led around the green Tartan track in a pace which favored Ryun—60.5 and 2:02.8. Liquori stayed close and Ryun moved up from the rear, running wide on the turns. Liquori led at three quarters in 3:03.5, but Ryun threatened on his shoulder.

Down the last backstretch, Liquori was almost in a frantic sprint, and Ryun was running hard to hang on. Liquori said, "I expected him to pass me any minute. I kept waiting for him."

Ryun was on Liquori's shoulder into the homestretch, but to his dismay, Ryun could not catch up. Thirty yards from the tape, he let Liquori go. Liquori looked at the sky, shouted for joy, and waved his fists as he finished.

Results: Liquori 3:57.7, Ryun 3:59.3, Murphy 3:59.8, LaBenz 4:00.5, Howell Michael of William & Mary 4:01.4.

Ryun made no excuses, although after his heat two days before he had mentioned the humidity and his reaction to a vaccination. Coach Timmons said Ryun had the thought of coming back in the three-mile on his mind. Certainly, he was not the Ryun of 1967, who would have run the last lap at least two seconds faster. One obvious fault was his foolish insistence on running wide around the turns, which cost him ten to 15 yards and a probable victory.

Liquori said, "I just went into this race to warm up for the AAU meet. I had doubts about finishing."

They met again eight days later in the AAU final, run in the even more humid heat of Miami, Florida. Ryun had developed a pain in his hip, he was told his planned "honeymoon" trip to Europe was off unless he accepted an AAU chaperone, and he was mentally fed up with training and racing, especially compared with being a bridegroom. On the second lap, he lost his desire to fight.

When Ryun slowed surprisingly, Liquori asked him, "Is something wrong?" A few seconds later, when Liquori learned Ryun had stopped, he knew he could win. After a 3:04.8 three-quarters he went into the lead on the last backstretch and won with a last lap in a strong 54.7.

Results: Liquori 3:59.5, Mason 4:00.0, Bair 4:00.2, Day 4:00.9, LaBenz 4:01.7.

On July 19, in Los Angeles, Liquori let down in the triangular meet involving USSR and the British Commonwealth. He ran 60.2, 2:00.0, and 2:58.2 although as much as ten yards behind. His strong sprint finish won an uncomfortable homestretch battle in 3:40.1 to 3:40.4 for Mikhail Zhelobovskiy and 3:42.6 for Whetton.

Liquori ran for the Americas team against a powerful Europe team at Stuttgart on July 30. Tümmler was making a good comeback after a year off during which he had operations on both legs. He had run 3:40.7 and a 3:58.8 mile this year. Francesco Arese, a dangerous 1:47.3 800-meter man, was undefeated in his first big season at 1500 meters. He had a national record of 3:39.9, after his 3:39.0 of 1968 was rejected because it was paced.

Liquori's teammate, Mason, set the pace past 800 meters in 1:58.5. With 500 meters to go, Liquori tried to run away, but Tümmler and Arese followed. Tümmler was forced to let go on the last curve, but Arese had to be defeated in the homestretch. Liquori's 3:37.2 was second best by an American, while Arese's 3:37.6 was an Italian record. Tümmler edged Mason, 3:39.3 to 3:39.4.

Thus, Liquori ended his 1969 season as probably the third best 20-year-old in the history of mile running—behind Ryun and Elliott.

EUROPEAN CHAMPIONSHIPS

The ninth running of the European Championships, held in Athens' Karaiskakis Stadium in mid-September, disappointed with a 1500-meter race not quite up to previous standards, for several reasons.

Jürgen May was not allowed to run because he had not been a resident of West Germany long enough. Most of the unhappy West German team withdrew in protest, eliminating Tümmler and Norpoth. DeHertoghe was off form, and the heats saw the elimination of Zhelobovskiy and Jim Douglas of Great Britain, who had run 3:39.9.

And yet there were strong runners in the final, including Arese, Wadoux, Whetton, Szordykowski, and Murphy, the strong Villanova runner from Eire.

Arese, whose brilliant season included only one loss—to Liquori—became a victim of his own nerves and ran only 3:42.2 for eighth place, and Wadoux faded to sixth in 3:41.7. But four runners were good enough to leave DeHertoghe in fifth place with his 3:40.9.

One was Belgium's surprising Edgard Salvé, who had run 3:40.9 in 1968 and 3:40.1 in 1969. Salvé put up a good fight with Szordykowski, who had the fastest pre-meet races. Szordykowski broke Baran's Polish record with 3:38.2 at Warsaw on August 29.

Two days before that he ran a startling 3:36.2 on a course which turned out to be seven meters short, worth at least one second.

Pierre Viaux of France led in the final by as much as 20 yards in 56.0 and 1:56.8. At the bell, the leader in 2:44.0 was Murphy, who ran 4:01.5 for the mile after his good third place in the NCAA, then won the British AAA Championships in 3:40.9.

The fourth runner to pull away from De Hertoghe was the veteran kicker, John Whetton. A most successful indoor runner, Whetton prefers to race from behind. He says, "I am nervous before big races. I have to be alone for two hours resting. I cannot sit in the stands watching others compete before my race. When I am extra nervous I am ready for all comers."

Racing down the backstretch in fourth place, Whetton moved to second. "With 200 meters to go I managed to nip through on the inside of Arese and Szordykowski, right behind Murphy."

In a hard stretch duel, Whetton fought alongside the Irishman who had beaten him for the AAA title, 3:40.9 to 3:41.8. Whetton edged ahead, completing a victorious last lap in 55.8.

Results: Whetton 3:39.4, Murphy 3:39.5, Szordykowski 3:39.8, Salvé 3:39.9, De Hertoghe 3:40.9.

OTHER RACES

Reading, England, June 11—In a startling race, Ian McCafferty ran 3:56.8 to defeat the Stewart brothers, 20-year-old Ian (3:57.3) and Peter (3:58.7). All three great prospects were from Scotland.

Berlin, Sept. 24—Four days after the European Championships, Tümmler proved his worth by outkicking Salvé in a mile race, 3:57.0 to 3:57.4.

London, Oct. 9—Arese, who had lost a slow 1500 to Szordykowski three days after his poor race in the European Championships, won the Emsley Carr Mile in 3:57.8 by outfighting Walter Wilkinson (3:58.3) and De Hertoghe (3:58.6).

1969
1,500m:

3:37.2	Marty Liquori (USA)	(1)	Stuttgart	30	Jul
3:37.3	Kipchoge Keino (Kenya)	(1)	S. Lake Tahoe, Cal.	12	Sep
3:37.6	Francesco Arese (Italy)	(2)	Stuttgart	30	Jul
3:38.2	Henryk Szordykowski (Poland)	(1)	Warsaw	29	Aug
3:39.0	Jean Wadoux (France)	(1)	Colombes	20	Jul
3:39.1	Ian Stewart (Great Britain)	(1)	London	1	Sep
3:39.3	Bodo Tümmler (W. Germany)	(3)	Stuttgart	30	Jul
3:39.4	Jürgen May (W. Germany)	(1)	Osnabrück	21	Jun
3:39.4	John Mason (USA)	(4)	Stuttgart	30	Jul
3:39.4	John Whetton (Great Britain)	(1)	Athens	20	Sep
3:39.5	Frank Murphy (Eire)	(2)	Athens	20	Sep
3:39.7	Rudi Simon (Belgium)	(1)	Audenarde	22	Jul
3:39.8	Bernd Diessner (E. Germany)	(1)	Potsdam	10	May

1969

Noteworthy Indoor Mark:
3:41.4 Jürgen May (W. Germany) (1) Dortmund 23 Feb

Mile:
3:55.9	Jim Ryun (USA)	(1)	Los Angeles	7	Jun
3:56.7	Sam Bair (USA)	(2)	Los Angeles	7	Jun
3:56.8	Ian McCafferty (Great Britain)	(1)	Reading	11	Jun
3:57.0	Bodo Tümmler (W. Germany)	(1)	Berlin	24	Sep
3:57.3	Ian Stewart (Great Britain)	(2)	Reading	11	Jun
3:57.4	Edgard Salvé (Belgium)	(2)	Berlin	24	Sep
3:57.6	Marty Liquori (USA)	(3)	Los Angeles	7	Jun
3:57.8	Francesco Arese (Italy)	(1)	London	9	Oct
3:58.0	John Kirkbride (Great Britain)	(1)	Motspur Park	23	Jul
3:58.1	Frank Murphy (Eire)	(4)	Los Angeles	7	Jun
3:58.3	Walter Wilkinson (Great Britain)	(2)	London	9	Oct
3:58.4	Chuck LaBenz (USA)	(1)	Berkeley	31	May

KEINO THE TRAVELER

After a restful 1969 season, Keino returned to his old ways of traveling and running often. He went to the United States for two indoor races, but he was surprised by John Lawson, 4:00.6 to 4:00.7, in the Los Angeles Sunkist Invitational on January 17 after he attempted a runaway with a too-fast third quarter in 57 flat. He won the second, in Philadelphia, with 4:00.6, far ahead of undertrained Liquori's poor 4:08.9.

Keino went home and won easy 1500's in 3:42.7 and 3:42.3, then traveled to New Zealand. At Auckland, on March 18, he did not have time to recover from his trip and he faded in the last quarter. He only ran 4:02.1 to 3:57.8 for 22-year-old Dutch-born Dick Quax. Four days later, at Christchurch, Keino won a good double in 3:42.0 and 14:01.2.

Back to Africa and more victories, Keino ran one fast 1500. At Abidjan, Ivory Coast, on April 4, he ran a sparkling 3:37.5. In his third trip of the year away from Africa, he ran in the King Games on May 16 at Villanova, against a much-improved Liquori.

Keino tried to run away from Liquori with one of his special paces—59.6, 1:56.2, and 2:56.9 for three-fourths mile, but Liquori closed to about eight yards back with 2:58.1. Keino slowed badly and Liquori passed him with 50 yards to go, winning with an undistinguished 3:42.6 to Keino's 3:43.8.

Keino's important event of the year came in July when the Commonwealth Games were held in Edinburgh. He prepared with an 8:29.0 two-mile in London on July 5, then qualified, in Edinburgh's new Meadowbank Sports Center, on July 18, with a fast heat in 3:40.4.

The final was on July 22, and a determined Quax set out with a pace of 42.6 for the first 300 meters. Then Keino went into the lead and set a fantastic pace in spite of the cold wind. He passed 400 meters in 57.9, then ran one in 57.1 for 1:55.0. He ran his third 400 in 57.3 for an astonishing 1200 meter time of 2:52.3.

Amazingly, Quax stayed on Keino's heels all the way to the last curve before he had to let go. Keino's last 300 was in 44.3 while

Quax could barely run under 46.

Results: Keino 3:36.6, Quax 3:38.1, Brendan Foster of England 3:40.6, P. Stewart 3:40.6, Whetton 3:41.2, McCafferty 3:42.2.

In a great 5000, three days later, Keino ran 13:27.6, but he lost to fast finishes by Ian Stewart (13:22.8) and McCafferty.

On August 10, in Dublin, Keino edged Murphy, 3:59.2 to 3:59.3, with Liquori alarmingly far back in 4:02.1. Then Keino returned to Africa and won the East African Championships in 3:39.2 and 14:05.0.

The unquenchable Keino went back to Europe, and on September 5 he beat Peter Stewart and a good field with an 8:25.4 two-mile. Three days later, in Dublin, the traveling man won in 4:05.0. He won a 2000-meter race in 5:05.2 on September 26, fastest time of the year, as was his two-mile time. He ranked as the best miler in the world for the second time.

JEAN WADOUX

Now 28 years old, the 5'10¾", 132-pound Frenchman concentrated on the 1500 meters until 1968 when he improved to 13:29.6 for 5000 meters. A promising 1500-meter man with 3:47.0 at the age of twenty, he had never quite developed, especially in competition.

He ran a likely 3:41.7 in 1963 at the age of 21, 3:40.8 in 1964 when he was last in the Olympic 1500 final, only 3:41.8 in 1965—although he ran a 3:57.2 mile—and showed continued improvement in 1966 with 3:37.7. He ran 3:38.4 in 1967, 3:37.9 in 1968, and 3:39.0 in 1969. He chose the 5000 in the 1968 Olympics and again placed ninth. In the important European Championships, he was seventh in the 1966 1500 and sixth in 1969. His record gave no indication of the startling development of 1970.

A nervous man, he wanted to be the "escaping type of runner." His training increased from 30 to 40 kilometers a day of varied running in the Vincennes forest.

After a 7:56.4 3000 on May 17, it appeared Wadoux's future was best as a 5000 meter runner. In the meet against USA at Colombes on July 8, he missed Jazy's French record by only four tenths when he won the 5000 in 13:28.0.

But on July 18, he chose the 1500 in the French Championships and after winning in 3:38.0 he felt ready to attack Jazy's European record of 3:36.3. His attempt was made five days later, on July 23.

Like Ladoumègue and Jazy before him, it was a private test with only his hares to help him. The weather that evening was ideal, and the Colombes track was fast. The hares set the pace he wanted

and Wadoux trailed along in 56.7 and 1:55.0.
Even on the difficult third lap he had a man ahead of him running at the desired pace, and so Wadoux did not lead until he reached the bell. His time at 1200 meters was 2:52.5, and excited spectators began to hope for a world record.
Wadoux made the effort of his life over those last 300 meters. After such a pace he was still able to run 41.5 and he finished in 3:34.0, second fastest 1500 ever run and less than a second from Ryun's world record.
On August 5, in Oulu, Finland, Wadoux went after the 5000 meter record. He passed 2000 meters in 5:23, but then he developed cramps and had to drop out. Six days later at Cologne he led in 5:15 but faded to ninth in a 3000. He was still undefeated at 1500 meters, however, when he ran in the European Cup final at Stockholm on August 29 against formidable opponents—Arese, Norpoth, and Szordykowski.
Possibly because it was near the end of a hard season or because his 3:34 gave him false confidence, Wadoux allowed the pace to be set by Arese. The Italian had run a fast 3:38.7 in early June, but ten days later, in Portland, Oregon, he was beaten by LaBenz's powerful 54-second last lap, 3:59.1 to 3:59.4, although ahead of Von Ruden and Quax. Arese beat LaBenz 4:02.2 to 4:02.6 a week later at Orange, Calif. After winning in 3:39.1 on July 1 at Milan from Gianni Del Buono of Italy (3:39.3) and Liquori (3:39.9), Arese lost to Szordykowski in a fast finish, 3:43.4 to 3:43.6. He lost one more race, when he ran 3:40.7 at the Bislet Games at Oslo on August 5 behind first-raters Arne Kvalheim and Liquori.
Arese, a fast 800 man, was content to lead in 62.0 and 2:05.8. Close behind came Norpoth, who had run 3:40.0 in June during a good season in which he ran a 13:34.6 5000 and a 7:49.6 3000. Szordykowski, with a best of 3:40.4, had lost only once after his successful indoor season. In his loss, here at Stockholm on July 29, he ran 3:40.7, behind Kvalheim but ahead of 1969's best-in-the-world Liquori.
The pace in the cup final increased and Wadoux finally launched his attack at the bell. He led at 1200 meters in 3:02, with only Arese left on his heels. But Wadoux had waited too long and both Arese and Szordykowski proved too strong in the stretch.
Results: Arese 3:42.3, Szordykowski 3:42.5, Wadoux 3:42.6, Zhelobovskiy 3:42.9, Norpoth 3:43.1.

OTHER RUNNERS

CHUCK LaBENZ, who surprised by progressing to 3:58.4 in 1969, lost two early 1970 battles by inches, then ran a 54.7 last lap in the Kennedy Games at Berkeley on May 30. His unexpected

3:56.9 defeated Mason (3:58.4), John Lawson (3:59.2), and Quax (3:59.9). The next week, in the Compton Invitational, LaBenz beat top-rated Liquori with 3:59.5. Then he entered ROTC summer camp for six weeks army training, but he managed to beat Arese in 3:59.1 at Portland before he lost his conditioning. He did not run well in two later races.

MARTY LIQUORI improved rapidly after his early indoor loss to Keino. He won the Wanamaker Mile in 4:02.6, ran a fast 2:07.6 for 1000 yards, beat Szordykowski twice, including the AAU in 4:00.9 (where Liquori was almost disqualified), won the IC4A in 4:02.1, and lost the NCAA to Michael. Liquori had a sore leg and Michael built up a 15-yard lead with a 59.9 third quarter and held on to win an upset, 4:03.1 to 4:03.6.

Outdoors, Liquori won the IC4A in 3:58.5, but then his poor background—because of his arch injury—began to show. He was third at Compton. He won the NCAA in 3:59.9, but only by two-tenths of a second when a startling newcomer, David Wottle of Bowling Green, Ohio, gained five yards on him in the homestretch. In a slow-paced AAU mile, Liquori was only third, and he won only one race out of seven overseas, with a best of 3:39.9.

ANDRÉ DE HERTOGHE lost his first race of 1970, when he ran 4:02.9 for third behind Szordykowski's 4:02.3, then finished a limited season undefeated with times of 3:39.5 and 3:38.9.

JÜRGEN MAY returned to the 1500 in 1970 and lost only once—to De Hertoghe, 3:39.5 to 3:40.7. May won easily against USA in 3:40.7 and also ran 3:40.0, 3:39.9, and 3:39.2.

ARNE KVALHEIM, who ran for Oregon before returning to Norway, lost only once in 1970. He scored victories over Arese, Szordykowski, and Liquori, with a best time of 3:39.6 (He also ran 5000 meters in 13:42.4 and 3000 in 7:54.8).

1970
1,500m:

3:34.0	Jean Wadoux (France)	(1)	Colombes	23	Jul
3:36.6	Kipchoge Keino (Kenya)	(1)	Edinburgh	22	Jul
3:38.1	Dick Quax (New Zealand)	(2)	Edinburgh	22	Jul
3:38.7	Francesco Arese (Italy)	(1)	Barcelona	3	Jun
3:38.8	Henryk Szordykowski (Poland)	(1)	Warsaw	12	Sep
3:38.9	André De Hertoghe (Belgium)	(1)	Blankenberge	14	Aug
3:39.0	Peter Stewart (Great Britain)	(2)	Warsaw	12	Sep
3:39.2	Jürgen May (W. Germany)	(1)	Stuttgart	20	Aug
3:39.3	Gianni Del Buono (Italy)	(2)	Milan	1	Jul
3:39.6	Arne Kvalheim (Norway)	(1)	Oslo	26	Aug
3:39.9	Marty Liquori (USA)	(3)	Milan	1	Jul
3:40.0	Harald Norpoth (W. Germany)	(1)	Koblenz	24	Jun

Noteworthy Indoor Mark:

3:41.3	Harald Norpoth (W. Germany)	(1)	Berlin	21	Feb

Mile:

3:56.3	Roscoe Divine (USA)	(1)	Eugene, Ore.	5	Jun
3:56.9	Chuck LaBenz (USA)	(1)	Berkeley, Cal.	30	May
3:57.0	John Kirkbride (Great Britain)	(1)	London	5	Jul
3:57.4	Steve Prefontaine (USA)	(2)	Eugene, Ore.	5	Jun
3:57.4	Ian Stewart (Great Britain)	(1)	Edinburgh	13	Jun

1970

3:57.4	Peter Stewart (Great Britain)	(2)	Edinburgh	13	Jun
3:57.6	Tom Von Ruden (USA)	(1)	Toronto	25	Jul
3:57.7	John Whetton (Great Britain)	(2)	London	5	Jul
3:57.7	DeVilliers Lamprecht (S. Africa)	(1)	Stellenbosch	13	Nov
3:57.8	Dick Quax (New Zealand)	(1)	Auckland	18	Mar
3:58.1	Walter Wilkinson (Great Britain)	(3)	London	5	Jul
3:58.2	Dave Wilborn (USA)	(3)	Eugene, Ore.	5	Jun

Noteworthy Indoor Mark:
4:00.1	Tom Von Ruden (USA)	(1)	Detroit	13	Mar

RYUN'S COMEBACK

Starting his comeback in May 1970, after a year of inactivity, Ryun ran long and slow distances until his excess weight disappeared and he could increase his speed. His first competition since June of 1969 was in a San Francisco indoor meet on January 22, 1971. He ran his last quarter in 56.4 and won with a smile on his face in 4:04.4.

He moved his family to Eugene, Oregon, and began working there. His second race was on the extremely fast San Diego indoor track on February 19. LaBenz set a ridiculous pace of 54.2 for the first quarter, and Ryun was 40 yards behind. At the half, LaBenz ran 1:54.5, Mason 1:57.8, and Ryun 2:01.0. LaBenz led at three quarters in 2:57.7, now only five yards ahead of Mason. But Quax passed Ryun, who was now fourth in three minutes flat.

Ryun began his move with two laps to go and when the gun cracked for the last lap he was in the lead. He won by twelve yards.

Results: Ryun 3:56.4, Mason 3:58.0, LaBenz 3:58.1, Quax 3:58.9.

Ryun, who had hoped to break four minutes but had no thought of equaling O'Hara's world indoor record, said, "How did I do that?"

He went "Down Under" to race, but he pinched a nerve in his leg and ran only 8:41.4 for two miles in Auckland, New Zealand, far back in third place. He was forced to drop out of two races.

On April 17, before 22,000 home fans at the Kansas Relays, he had his first real outdoor test. He stayed back in seventh place for the first lap, timed in 61.2, but after 2½ laps he went to the front and pulled away with a final lap in 55.3.

Results: Ryun 3:55.8, Von Ruden 3:57.2, Mason 3:57.9.

Ryun ran 5000 meters in 13:59.4 at the Vancouver Relays on May 1.

LIQUORI PREPARES TO BE NUMBER ONE

Beginning as if he intended to take up where he left off in 1969 when he ranked first among the world's milers, Liquori ran an 8:35.8 two-mile in third place, won the Wanamaker Mile in 4:00.6, ran 2:08.8 for 1000 yards, and then had a great weekend in Houston.

Running on the fifth-of-a-mile track in the Astrodome, Liquori ran a mile heat in 4:02.6, then a relay leg in 3:57.4. The next day, February 13, he won the mile in 3:57.2 with a last quarter in 55.2.

Coach Jim Elliott had already said: "Marty is in the best shape he has ever been in at this time of the season," and now the question came up as to Liquori's chances against Ryun. Liquori said, "I'm ready for him."

He won a 1500 in 3:44.2, took the IC4A in 4:06.1, and won a double in the indoor NCAA with an 8:37.2 two-mile and 4:04.7.

Outdoors, he ran 3:59.6 on Tennessee's Tartan track, and then ran relay legs in 4:04.1, 4:07.9, and 1:48.5 at Penn. The following week at the Quantico Relays, he ran 5000 meters in 13:52.4 and then, the next day, a three-fourths mile relay leg in 3:01.2.

RYUN vs LIQUORI

For the first time since the Swedish era of the 1940's, two milers from the same country seemed to be the best in the world. On a cold (55 degrees), drizzly May 16 at the Martin Luther King Games in Pennsylvania's Franklin Field, the contest between Ryun and Liquori was ballyhooed as a super mile even though it was early in the season.

Ryun followed Liquori, but both were back in the pack, and at the quarter it was Liquori 61.1 and Ryun 61.4. At the half, Ryun and Liquori edged to the front in 2:03.3.

Liquori knew he needed a faster pace and he increased to 56.7 on the third lap with Ryun on his heels. Liquori passed three quarters in three minutes even with Ryun at 3:00.3. "I thought I was a dead duck. It was much too slow for me to win the race."

But Ryun had not yet sharpened his speed and he made no effort to pass on the backstretch. He barely hung on, much as in his NCAA loss to Liquori in 1969.

Around the last curve, Ryun moved to Liquori's shoulder, but he could not pass. He ran wide, losing a yard or two and entered the homestretch in the same position. Liquori kept watching for Ryun to appear alongside but Ryun could not make it. At the end, Liquori widened the gap to a yard and a half while running his fastest ever mile by 2.6 seconds.

Results: Liquori 3:54.6, Ryun 3:54.8, Dyce 3:59.6, McAfee 4:00.0, Colburn 4:01.1, Mosser 4:02.7.

Liquori said: "I was psyched up thinking about this race a little bit every day. If I'm not up this high I'd probably lose."

Liquori ran his final quarter in 54.6. His last 880 in 1:51.3 is evidence that he could improve even more, while Ryun's past record projected much faster times when he reached top condition.

But Ryun had a far more serious problem than lack of speed work. He had an allergy problem before, but never anything like he felt when the pollen began blowing in Eugene in early May. "I wake up during the night," he said. "I don't clog up, but I continually drain. Mostly I sound like I'm coughing all the time. I can jog, but the moment I have to begin working, to need oxygen, I'm in trouble."

He tried to run a mile in Eugene's Twilight Meet on June 6 but he ran only 4:07.6 for tenth place behind Arne Kvalheim's 3:56.4 and Steve Prefontaine's 3:57.4.

Kvalheim said: "Jim has been very bad all week. Actually since a week before Philadelphia. The morning of the King mile his eyes were almost swollen shut."

Ryun could not run in the AAU mile. He tried a few races, including two in Europe, but he failed badly (4:17.3 for tenth place at Stockholm on July 6). He moved from Eugene to Santa Barbara, California, and began preparing for the 1972 Olympics.

LIQUORI WINS

With no close competition, Liquori won the IC4A mile in 4:00.4 with his last lap in 55.2. Then he ran a 440 relay leg in 48.1. He won the NCAA in 3:57.6 with a 55.6 last lap after running 4:00.7 in a heat two days before. In the AAU, at Eugene, he ran a 54.5 final lap in a hard rain to win in 3:56.5, nine yards ahead of Jim Crawford's 3:57.7.

Three days later, Liquori began a short European tour by losing at 1000 meters in 2:18.9. Two days after that, on July 1, he ran 1500 meters against Francesco Arese.

Arese, second-ranked miler of 1970, was in great shape. Undefeated in six 1500-meter races with a fastest of 3:42.2, his best runs were at other distances. On May 1 he set an Italian 10,000 meter record of 28:27.0 and on May 20 he collected his national 5000 record with 13:40.0. On June 20 he ran 3000 meters in 7:51.2 and on June 26 he set his fourth Italian record of the season with 800 meters in 1:47.1.

It was a warm night on July 1 and 29,000 people in Milan watched half-miler Mark Winzenried set a pace of 56.8 and 1:57.6. Liquori ran 57.2 and 1:58.2 while Arese ran 57.5 and 1:58.5.

Winzenried dropped out and Jacky Boxberger led until the fast Swede, Ulf Högberg, took over at 1200 meters in 2:56.5. Liquori was on Högberg's shoulder in the same time and Arese was fourth in 2:56.8.

Down the backstretch sped Liquori, and Arese could not gain until they reached the homestretch. When Arese moved closer, Liquori increased his speed and won by two yards.

1971

Results: Liquori 3:36.0, Arese 3:36.3, Högberg 3:37.3, Brendan Foster 3:39.4, De Hertoghe 3:39.9.

Both Liquori and Arese ran last 300's in 39.5, fastest ever in such a fast race. Their personal record times were equivalent to miles in 3:54.1 and 3:54.4.

Before returning home, Liquori won a notable 2000 meters from Emiel Puttemans in a U.S. record 5:02.2 to 5:03.6. Then he won the Pan-American 1500 in Colombia in 3:42.1 and a 4:02.8 mile in Toronto on August 28.

EUROPEAN CHAMPIONSHIPS

After his battle with Liquori, Arese escaped the sweltering Italian summer in a hillside resort across the Yugoslav border and he ran only an easy 1:49.1 in the six weeks before the European Championships in Helsinki.

He had built his aerobic endurance with long, hard runs during the winter, and he had good speed, and now his 3:36.3 made him the favorite in this race.

Tümmler, Wadoux, Norpoth, and Högberg were absent from the 1500, and the heats eliminated sub-3:40 men Mikhail Zhelobovskiy and Peter Stewart, plus 1969 runner-up Frank Murphy.

The 27-year-old Arese, 6'1½" and 152-pounds, led in 57.1, then Foster took over at 800 meters in 1:57.7 and 1000 in 2:29.5. Arese returned to the lead at 1200 meters in 2:57.7.

Down the stretch to the last turn, the strongest move was by consistent Henryk Szordykowski of Poland. Szordykowski, a finalist at Mexico City, ranked No. 3 in the world in 1969, ahead of Arese. He was No. 3 again in 1970, behind Arese, and he won the 1971 indoor European Championships in 3:41.4.

He broke out of a box on the first turn of the final lap and moved to Arese's heels on the last curve even though Arese ran at a 13.3 pace down the stretch.

Into the homestretch, Szordykowski fought up to Arese's shoulder, but the Italian pulled away to a two-yard victory.

Two British comers—Brendan Foster, 3:40.6 in 1970 and a 3:58.5 mile this year, and John Kirkbride, a 3:57.0 miler in 1970—stayed ahead of Boxberger around the last curve, and Kirkbride barely held off the Olympic sixth placer at the end.

Results: Arese 3:38.4, Szordykowski 3:38.7, Foster 3:39.2, Kirkbride 3:39.5, Boxberger 3:39.6, Dufresne 3:40.7, Vasala 3:41.5.

Arese's time was a new meet record. His last 300 meters was in 40.7, his last 400 in 54.8.

Jean-Pierre Dufresne, France's 1:46.7 800 meter record holder, had beaten Wadoux 3:38.9 to 3:40.6 and Foster, 3:40.6 for both. Three weeks before the European Championships he had beaten Boxberger in the French Championships, 3:42.2 to 3:42.4.

KEINO RUNS ERRATICALLY

Still the man to beat in any 1500 or mile race, Keino continued to run more fast times than anyone else ... and to lose unexpectedly.

After two good times at Pointe-à-Pierre—3:40.6 on March 29 and a 3:58.3 mile on April 3—Keino lost badly at Tel Aviv on May 2. Obviously not himself, Keino ran only 3:45.0 behind Högberg's 3:42.0.

On June 23, at Aarhus, Keino ran 3:36.9. Later, he placed second in an 800 with a surprising time of 1:47.0. In great shape, Keino once again ran too many races. On June 30, he lost a hard 13:30.4 5000 against Wadoux and the next day, still at Helsinki's World Games, he lost to Pekka Vasala's Finnish record 3:38.6. Vasala's last lap in 55.8 defeated Keino's 3:39.2.

But the next day, at Västerås, the irrepressible Keino ran 3:38.1. Four days later, in Stockholm, Keino ran Högberg into the ground with 2:54.0 for 1200 meters, then finished the mile in 3:54.4 to Högberg's Swedish record 3:57.6.

On July 17, at Durham, North Carolina, Keino was captain of the first African team to compete against the United States. In hot weather and with Liquori absent, Keino ran at a pace of 55.3, 1:55.9, and 2:55.2 to win the 1500 easily in 3:37.5. Then, two weeks later in Nairobi, he ran only 3:46.8 to lose to Mungai's 3:44.8. He came back with his fastest race of the year—3:36.8—in the Kenyan Championships at Nairobi on August 15.

BEN JIPCHO

Best known until this year as the man who set up Keino's fast pace in the 1968 Olympics, Jipcho finally broke through as a miler.

Ben Wabura Jipcho, 28-year-old, 5'10", 155-pound Kenyan, ran miles of 3:59.8 in 1968, 4:00.4 in 1969, and 4:00.6 in 1970. He ran a steeplechase in 8:29.6 for second place in the 1970 Commonwealth Games.

On July 6, 1971, Jipcho was not considered good enough to run in the big mile race at Stockholm. He ran in a "B" 1500 and placed only third with 3:44.0. Against the USA, in North Carolina, Jipcho won the steepechase in 8:45.2, then came back the same day to run 3:43.9 for second to Keino's 3:37.5.

Next, Jipcho lost both the 1500 and 5000 to Keino in the Kenya Championships. He ran only 3:44.4 in the 1500, to Keino's 3:36.8.

In the East Africa Championships a week later, Jipcho beat

Keino 3:41.2 to 3:43.2 and also won the steeplechase. This was regarded only as another of Keino's many losses rather than a breakthrough for Jipcho.

But in early September, Jipcho suddenly became a threat for Munich, 1972. At Munich's 1971 "Pre-Olympic" meet on September 4, Jipcho fell twice in the steeplechase and yet he won in 8:29.6. The next day he won from a good 5000 meters field in 13:40.8.

In Berlin, on September 7, Jipcho faced a strong field of milers, including Keino. Arese had won a mile in Toronto in 4:00.3 in August. Norpoth ran 3:58.8 after his close third in the European 5000 but his true strength was proved by his 3:37.8 indoors in February. Jürgen May was ready for another mile effort.

The pace was slower than average, with a hare running 59.8 and 2:00.4. At 1200 meters, Keino led in 3:00.6, followed by Jipcho and Arese. Keino ran hard around to the 1500 meter mark in 3:41.8, but Jipcho moved alongside and Boxberger was on his shoulder. Arese and Norpoth came next, in 3:42.4, one tenth ahead of May.

In the sprint for home, Boxberger was slowest but he held off May. Keino ran his last 120 in 15.1 to hold off Norpoth, but Jipcho and Arese pulled away rapidly. Arese gained two yards but he could not catch the smiling Jipcho.

Results: Jipcho 3:56.4, Arese 3:56.7, Keino 3:56.9, Norpoth 3:57.2, Boxberger 3:57.6, May 3:58.0.

Arese, who had been eliminated by Jipcho from the 1968 Olympic final, attempted to beat the Kenyan on September 10 in London, but Jipcho won again, 3:57.4 to 3:58.3.

Looking ahead to the 1972 Olympics in Munich, Jipcho said, "I want to win the steeplechase gold medal. I would not mind a medal in the 1500 either."

OTHER RACES

Izmir, Turkey, Oct. 13—Mansour Guettaya of Tunisia, who had run 4:00.6 in London a month earlier while losing to Jipcho, Arese and Adrian Weatherhead, defeated Arese at 1500 meters, 3:46.5 to 3:47.6. Boxberger did not finish.

OTHER RUNNERS

TOM VON RUDEN returned to the longer distance after a season of half-miles with a fourth place 3:39.7 at Helsinki on July 1 behind Vasala, Keino, and Peter Stewart. Von Ruden won his last four races, including a 3:58.9 mile victory at Turku on July 15 over Mason (3:59.0) and New Zealand's Tony Polhill (3:59.0). On July 26 at Aarhus, Von Ruden won the 1500 in 3:38.5.

1971

1,500m:

3:36.0	Marty Liquori (USA)	(1)	Milan	1	Jul
3:36.3	Francesco Arese (Italy)	(2)	Milan	1	Jul
3:36.8	Kipchoge Keino (Kenya)	(1)	Nairobi	15	Aug
3:37.3	Ulf Högberg (Sweden)	(3)	Milan	1	Jul
3:38.5	Tom Von Ruden (USA)	(1)	Aarhus	26	Jul
3:38.6	Pekka Vasala (Finland)	(1)	Helsinki	1	Jul
3:38.7	Henryk Szordykowski (Poland)	(2)	Helsinki	15	Aug
3:38.9	Jean-Pierre Dufresne (France)	(1)	Colombes	4	Jul
3:39.1	Jürgen Haase (E. Germany)	(1)	Leipzig	26	May
3:39.1	Bram Wassenaar (Holland)	(2)	Aarhus	23	Jun
3:39.2	Brendan Foster (Great Britain)	(3)	Helsinki	15	Aug
3:39.3	Peter Stewart (Great Britain)	(3)	Helsinki	1	Jul

Noteworthy Indoor Marks:

3:37.8	Harald Norpoth (W. Germany)	(1)	Berlin	13	Feb
3:41.4	Henryk Szordykowski (Poland)	(1)	Sofia	14	Mar

Mile:

3:54.4	Kipchoge Keino (Kenya)	(1)	Stockholm	6	Jul
3:54.6	Marty Liquori (USA)	(1)	Philadelphia	16	May
3:54.8	Jim Ryun (USA)	(2)	Philadelphia	16	May
3:56.4	Arne Kvalheim (Norway)	(1)	Eugene, Ore.	6	Jun
3:56.4	Ben Jipcho (Kenya)	(1)	Berlin	7	Sep
3:56.6	Walter Wilkinson (Great Britain)	(1)	Leicester	31	May
3:56.7	Francesco Arese (Italy)	(2)	Berlin	7	Sep
3:57.2	Tom Von Ruden (USA)	(2)	Lawrence	17	Apr
3:57.2	Harald Norpoth (W. Germany)	(4)	Berlin	7	Sep
3:57.3	Dick Quax (New Zealand)	(1)	Auckland	6	Mar
3:57.4	Peter Stewart (Great Britain)	(2)	Leicester	31	May
3:57.4	Steve Prefontaine (USA)	(2)	Eugene, Ore.	6	Jun

Noteworthy Indoor Marks:

3:56.4	Jim Ryun (USA)	(1)	San Diego	19	Feb
3:58.0	John Mason (USA)	(2)	San Diego	19	Feb
3:58.1	Chuck LaBenz (USA)	(3)	San Diego	19	Feb
3:58.9	Henryk Szordykowski (Poland)	(1T)	Inglewood, Cal.	12	Feb
3:58.9	Dick Quax (New Zealand)	(4)	San Diego	19	Feb
3:59.4	Tom Von Ruden (USA)	(1)	Ft. Worth, Tex.	6	Feb

Note—On an oversized indoor track, Marty Liquori (USA) did 3:57.2, winning from Leonard Hilton (USA) 3:59.1 and Greg Carlberg (USA) 3:59.6, at Houston on 13 February.

LIQUORI DISABLED

After his excellent undefeated season in 1971, Marty Liquori was the man to beat in the Olympics, and he trained harder than ever in the fall. The long workouts improved his endurance, but he injured his left heel during a race.

All runners suffer injuries, and Liquori said, "It is one of the challenges of athletics. You have to be able to decide which injuries are serious enough for rest. In this case I made the wrong choice, and tried to run through it."

He continued to train and race. "The foot would feel better during the week, but I kept tearing it again on weekends." During the NCAA championship race he realized how severe it was, and he took a month's rest. He swam and lifted weights.

In February, he tested himself in competition. His first race was a mile at Toronto on February 4 where his 4:09.9 was edged by two Italians, Francesco Arese and 13:40.2 5000 meter man Gianni Del Buono. Eight days later, in the Houston Astrodome, Liquori ran third with a fine 8:31.6 two-mile. He seemed on his way to fast miles, but he said, "I can't remember what it's like to run without pain."

The next week, running an 880 relay leg, he reinjured his foot. He tried to rest it, still hoping to run in the Olympics, but the pain persisted. Finally, in May, he went to California for another examination. The specialist confirmed a previous diagnosis: a stretched ligament had caused a large calcium deposit. Treatment: a cast, or major surgery.

He was through for 1972. There would be no world record, no Olympic gold medal. He made the grim announcement and thought about his future. He wanted to be a broadcaster, but only if he could remain an amateur. His desire to excel still burned inside him, and he talked about competing in 1973. He said simply, "I'll be back."

FANIE VAN ZIJL

Early in 1972, Stephanus Johannes Havenga Van Zijl (called Fanie, and pronounced Fahnie Fon Sell), emerged as one of the fastest milers in the world and a definite threat to anybody. As a citizen of South Africa, however, he could not run in the Olympic Games.

Born July 7, 1948, the 5'9¾", 145-pounder began as a sprinter after an attack of polio forced him to wear leg irons and medical boots. He won his first mile race when he was 14, the fifth race he won in that meet. By 1965, when he was 17, Van Zijl was good enough to be selected for the South African team to tour Europe, but a nervous disorder ended his season. In 1967, he ran a 3:59.3 mile at the tender age of 19.

In 1968 and 1969, he raced in Europe, turning in a 3:41.1 1500 meters. Then, in March of 1970, he ran a 3:59 mile and became internationally prominent with 800 meters in 1:45.6. A hernia knocked him out of the 1971 season, but afterward he trained harder than ever and began the 1971-72 South African season in great shape.

His greatest race came on March 11, 1972, at an altitude of 4400 feet. His 3:37.9 1500 has been bettered only by Keino and Ryun at a higher altitude. Nine days later, Van Zijl ran a mile in 3:56.4.

He wanted more competition, and so he went to the United States and lived with a friend, Eastern New Mexico coach Bill Silverberg. He ran 800 meters at the Drake Relays and whipped Mark Winzenried in 1:46.4. Two weeks later, at the West Coast Relays in Fresno, the lightly built South African ran his last lap in 53.8 with beautifully swift and smooth leg action to win the 1500 in 3:39.7.

Still seeking competition, Van Zijl ran a mile at Modesto on May 27 against several four-minute milers. Again he ran away on the last lap to win handily in 3:56.0. Then he terminated his season, undefeated and unsatisfied.

His future seems more than promising. He says, "Any athlete who is more gifted than normal should set his heart on the world record. I am 23 now. At 27, I should be able to be at my peak."

KEINO TRAVELS AND EXPERIMENTS

Olympic champion Kip Keino did not know the Olympic 1500 and 5000 were to be run within 25 minutes of each other, and he talked of doubling. Then, when he was finally told the bad news, it was too late to protest the Olympic schedule.

Track and field's most enthusiastic traveler went to the United States for some indoor races, and on January 14 in College Park, Maryland, three days before his 32nd birthday, he eased past the 880 in 2:03.3, than ran impressive quarters of 58.7 and 57.4 for a 3:59.4 mile.

The next day, in Albuquerque's mile-high altitude, he won easily in 4:04.2. Six days later, in San Francisco, he ran 4:01.2 with a last lap of 63.1, content to hold off Von Ruden's late charge while he saved himself for a more important race against Jim Ryun the next night.

Keino refused to push the pace against Ryun in Los Angeles, and they passed the half in 2:10.5. Ryun's finish was superior and Keino lost, 4:07.3 to 4:06.8.

Keino returned to Kenya for three months of endurance training, then went blithely to Japan with Ben Jipcho. Still concerned about which events to run in the Olympics, Keino tested himself with a 10,000 meters in 28:48.8. On May 3, he ran a steeplechase behind Jipcho in a fast 8:30.0. Four days later, he ran 8:35.2, and in the same meet he ran 800 meters in 1:48.5 and 1500 meters in 3:45.8. Back in Kenya, at Mombasa, a hot and humid city on the coast, he ran 3:36.8. His condition was good, and he could choose from four events—either the 10,000 or steeplechase, then either the 1500 or 5000—but he wanted most to defend his 1500 championship.

RYUN UNCERTAIN

After his disastrous 1971 season, Ryun put in a fall and winter of hard endurance work in Santa Barbara. His first 1972 competition was an indoor mile against Keino in Los Angeles. Ryun won in 4:06.8 with a last quarter in 56.7. He appeared to suffer from the effort, but he said, "I felt good," and added, "I think it's a very good way to start."

1972

After running two miles in 8:47.4 for fourth place in Portland, he returned to Los Angeles on February 11 for another mile. He had a cold, but he said, "I've run with colds before. It wasn't that bad." Still, he puzzled himself and his anxious fans by running only 4:13.2 in sixth place. He said, "I was really, really tight, that's all I can say. I felt pretty good the first quarter, but then I really got tight. Afterwards I had all the effects of running a very hard race."

In desperation, he moved back to Kansas, where he could train once again under Bob Timmons. On March 4, he returned to the Los Angeles Coliseum for a mile against Von Ruden, but he was even worse. His form was bad, slow and bounding, and he was never a contender, finishing far back in 4:19.2.

People began to say he was through. One doctor said the trouble was probably a lingering effect from his 1968 mononucleosis. Others said it was all in his head. Physical examinations showed no evidence of illness, and Ryun indicated all he needed was confidence. He ran in two relays in Florida, striding through a 1:48.6 880 and three-quarters in 2:56.3. More confident, he ran the 880 in the Texas Relays and won in 1:48.1. "He looked great," said Timmons." He held his form, had good lift. There was no struggling."

Two weeks later, at the Kansas Relays, Ryun pleased his home fans by leading most of the way through a 3:03.3 pace. He outkicked Von Ruden with an excellent 53.8 last lap to win in 3:57.1.

But then he became ill and ran only 4:09.0 at Drake and 4:14.2 two weeks after that in the King Games in Philadelphia. Added to his previous failures, this convinced even more people Ryun had come to the end of his string. But in Bakersfield on May 20, he ran 5000 meters in 13:38.2 with a strong finish. He felt much encouraged.

In the Federation meet, he ran an 880 heat in 1:49.1, then withdrew from the final, again raising eyebrows. On June 9, at the Vons Classic in Los Angeles, he defeated Dave Wottle 3:57.3 to 3:58.2 with a last lap in 53.9.

He was obviously a man to contend with, and yet he no longer ran well every time out, as he had through 1967. As the Final Olympic Trials approached, he announced he would try to make the U.S. team in both the 800 and 1500. His comeback was poised precariously; it could go either way—and the Trials were to be run in Eugene, where hay fever had started his downfall in 1971.

AMERICAN OLYMPIC TRIALS

The all-important Final Trials to choose the United States Olympic team were held on July 6, 7 and 8 for 1500 meter runners. Ryun had been crushed by three runners in the stretch of the 800

1972

meter final a week earlier, casting more doubt on his ability, and Dave Wottle, the surprise winner of that race in a record-equalling 1:44.3, was now considered more than a mere threat to Ryun.

Wottle, a 6'¾", 140-pounder, came into prominence in 1970 after a mediocre record. As a high school senior in 1968, at Canton, Ohio, he ran a 1:59.4 880 and a 4:20.2 mile. As a freshman at Bowling Green in 1969, he improved to 1:54.9 and 4:06.8. He ran 3:59.0 and 1:47.8 before the 1970 NCAA mile, where he gained five yards on Liquori with an impressive stretch drive to lose, 4:00.1 to 3:59.9. A startled Liquori said, "I didn't realize he had that kind of kick."

Wottle's unhappy 1971 season included a broken left ankle and, later, a stress fracture in his right ankle. In the fall of 1971, he placed 12th in the NCAA cross country, then won the indoor NCAA 880 in 1:51.8. He edged Howell Michael in the King Games Mile, each stopping the watches in 3:58.5. Ryun trailed in 4:14.2. His charging 3:58.2 lost to Ryun's 3:57.3 in the Vons Classic, and then he won the NCAA 1500 in 3:39.7 and the AAU 800 in 1:47.3. Despite his marvelous record-tying 800 in Eugene, he still considered himself best over the mile distance.

Other promising contenders were Von Ruden, Michael, Jerome Howe, and Bob Wheeler. Von Ruden, who had run a perplexing 4:01.5 for 7th in the Vons meet, was eliminated in the 800 of the Final Trials and then lacked his kick in a 1500 semi-final and was again eliminated. Howe gave Wottle a fright in the stretch drive of the NCAA 1500, then held off Michael in the AAU 1500, 3:38.2 to 3:38.3, making them fourth and fifth best on the U.S. all-time list, ahead of Dyrol Burleson. Wheeler, a 6'1", 155-pound, 20-year-old, ran a 3:59.9 mile in 1971, then won the IC4A cross country. He twisted an ankle after that, but recovered well for a 3:59.0 relay leg in the 1972 Penn Relays. Another injury kept him out of the IC4A mile and held him to a 3:40.9 third place in the NCAA 1500. But in Eugene he said, confidently, "I wouldn't have come here if I thought I couldn't make the team."

The final was run at a lethargic pace. Ryun was sixth at 440 yards in 62.7, eighth at 880 in 2:05.7, and sixth at three-quarters in 3:04.9. Then Wottle raced for the lead, and Ryun was in an unfavorable position, outside him around the last curve, with Wheeler close behind. Ryun ran away powerfully in the homestretch to win in 3:41.5 to 3:42.3 for Wottle and 3:42.4 for Wheeler. Howe barely edged Michael in 3:43.0.

Ryun's last 440 was in 51.5, impressive after a slow start on that last lap. His last 320 yards in 36.6 was inferior to his sensational 36.4 for 300 meters in a 3:38.2 race in 1967, but his sizzling last 200 must have been close to the 24.8 he ran in that 1967 race. He crossed the line with a broad smile.

There was still some doubt about Ryun's condition for a fast-paced race, and so on the night of July 29, before 17,000 people in Toronto, he tested himself. After laps of 59 flat and 1:57.6, Ryun moved to the lead and passed three-quarters in 2:57.2. "I really didn't realize I was going that fast. But when I knew I was going to have a good time I put on the pressure."

He was a fifth of a second faster than the pace in his world record 3:51.1, and now he ran 55.6 for a time of 3:52.8, third fastest mile ever run. Grant McLaren was second in 3:59.0.

Obviously pleased, Ryun said, "I felt tired before the race, to tell the truth, but I guess I wasn't." He was ready for Munich.

THE 1972 OLYMPIC GAMES

Several good milers in addition to Liquori and Van Zijl did not run in the Olympics. Jean Wadoux, the European record holder, was injured, as was Arne Kvalheim, a 3:56.4 miler. Another 3:56.4 miler, Ben Jipcho, chose the 5000 meters, along with former 3:53.8 miler Jürgen May and 1968 Olympic fourth-placer Harald Norpoth. Britain's 3:55.3 miler, Peter Stewart, withdrew at the last moment because of a back injury.

There were even more casualties in the first round of heats on September 8, which reduced the 66 entries to 30. (Four qualified from each of seven heats, plus two more on a time basis.) Ivan Ivanov, Russia's 3:37.8 threat, was eliminated in the first heat when he could run only 3:42.3, a second and a half too slow. John Kirkbride, British 3:38.7 and 3:56.5 runner, was eliminated in the slow second heat, outkicked by six-tenths while running 3:45.3. Little André De Hertoghe of Belgium, former 3:56.0 miler, faded from third to fifth in the stretch of the third heat.

In the fourth heat, Jim Ryun was running with Kip Keino. The computer which seeded the runners had failed to recognize Ryun's 3:52.8 mile time and he went unseeded as a slow 1500-meter runner. Ryun was in excellent condition. In one practice session at Munich, he ran two 800's in 1:51 each, with only three minutes rest.

Ryun stayed near the rear in the fourth heat, clocking times of 59.8 and 2:01.8. He wanted to stay out of trouble, but with 550 meters to go, an old habit betrayed him. He became anxious too soon and began to pass on the curve. To save distance, he put out his hand and tried to go between two runners. For about 20 yards, almost to the homestretch, he ran between them. Then his foot was spiked in the air.

Ryun and Billy Fordjour of Ghana fell. Fordjour's knee struck Ryun's throat and jaw. Ryun suffered a concussion of the Adam's Apple and he was partially stunned. He fell on the curb and injured his hip, scraped his right knee, and sprained his left ankle. Fordjour fell across Ryun's legs, and the world record holder lay on his back

1972

perfectly still for several seconds as his opponents raced away from him and his Olympic chances ended.

With the field more than 100 yards ahead, Ryun wobbled to his feet and hobbled a few slow steps, holding his hip. Then, suddenly, he burst into a fast run. The stunned crowd burst into cheers, but the cheers subsided as people realized Ryun had no chance. Ryun slowed and crossed the finish line in 3:51.5. He was met by his old rival, Keino, who patted Ryun's shoulder, smiled, and tried to console him. But Ryun was inconsolable. He said, "I'm very upset." An appeal on Ryun's behalf was refused. The judges ruled it was Ryun's fault, but Ryun denied this. A second appeal was entered and Ryun prepared to run in the semi-finals the next day, in case this appeal was upheld. But no favorable decision was made. Only later did an inspection of television films indicate that Ryun appeared to be pushed from the inside into Fordjour. The fastest runner of all time was finished.

In the fifth heat, Byron Dyce of Jamaica and Cosmas Silei of Kenya could not stay close. Frank Murphy of Ireland was fourth into the stretch, but he ran the last 100 meters in only 14.7. The sixth heat was the closest: Ulf Högberg was edged out of fourth place by one-tenth, but his 3:41.5 won him the last qualifying place.

The seventh heat was the fastest for 1200 meters (3:00.1), then they slowed while they gathered for the fastest homestretch battle of the heats. Mansour Guettaya of Tunisia, a feared kicker who had run a last 800 in 1:49.5 in 1971, lost out in the speedy finish by 1.3 seconds. Tony Polhill of New Zealand moved from fifth to second with the fastest last 100 meters of the heats—12.8 seconds.

SEMI-FINALS. Three semi-final heats were run on a warm September 9, qualifying three men each with the fastest fourth placer added to make a ten-man final.

The ten runners in the first semi-final were:

MIKE BOIT, a 23-year-old, 6'1½", 150-pound Kenyan halfmiler (1:47.5 for 800 meters in 1971), moved up to 1500 meters for the Olympic year and startled everyone with 3:37.4 behind Keino's 3:36.8 on a poor track at Mombasa. Later the same day he ran 800 meters in 1:47.0.

GIANNI DEL BUONO a 29-year-old Italian, ran a 1:48.0 800 in 1968, and progressed to 3:39.3 and 4:00.3 in 1970. He ran 5000 meters in 13:40.2 in 1971.

HAILU EBBA went to the United States and added Ebba to his name when nobody would believe he had no last name. He was a 49.2 quarter-miler and 4:32 miler as an exchange student, but in 1972, his sophomore year at Oregon State, he ran 3:40.4 and 3:59.3.

CHRIS FISHER was regarded as Australia's best, off his 3:39.5 and 3:59.1 in 1971. He ran 800 meters in 1:47.0. His 1970 bests were 1:47.7 and 3:41.9.

1972

TOM B. HANSEN of Denmark, now trained by Arthur Lydiard, came into prominence on August 9 with 3:38.9 at Helsinki.

ULF HÖGBERG, 26-year-old Swede, ran 3:39.3 in 1967, his best until 1971 when he ran 3:37.3 and 3:57.6. On July 19, 1972, he ran 3:39.0.

VALDIMIR PANTYELEY, USSR, ran 3:40.5 in 1969, then only 3:40.6 in 1971. In the spring of 1972 he ran 3:39.6, barely losing to Zhelobovskiy.

THOMAS WESSINGHAGE of West Germany entered the Olympics with a best of 3:40.5 and won the first heat in 3:40.6.

DAVE WOTTLE suffered from bursitis in both knees after a hard workout in July. He lost all confidence in the 1500 and did not expect to make the Olympic 800 final, but he won the gold medal in 1:45.9 with a sensational stretch run. He seemed ready now to run well in the 1500 too.

SPILIOS ZACHAROPOULOS of Greece improved to 3:40.2 in 1972.

The pace in the first semi-final was 61.4, 2:01.9, and 3:02, with Boit leading down the last backstretch and Pantyeley staying close. Wottle strangely let runners get away from him and he was eighth coming out of the last curve. A quick move to the outside edged him into sixth place with 100 meters to go, but he was four yards behind fifth place.

Then Wottle began one of the fastest kicks ever seen in an important race. He ran the last 100 meters in 11.7, speeding past Del Buono and Fisher. But Boit and Pantyeley were far ahead and Hansen was gaining on them. Wottle dipped his head—and his white cap—at the finish line but he lost the qualifying spot by an inch or so. He had begun his formidable kick too late.

Entrants in the second semi-final were:

JACQUES BOXBERGER of France, who ran 3:39.6 and 3:57.6 in 1971, placed only second in the 1972 French Championships with 3:42.2.

KIP KEINO had proved himself to be faster than ever in a pre-Olympic tune-up by lowering his 800 meter best to 1:46.4. And his excellent condition was established by his powerful victory in the Olympic steeplechase. He ran 8:23.6 with poor hurdle form ("I am jumping like a horse."), and he looked as if he could take many seconds off the world record.

HERMAN MIGNON of Belgium showed good improvement with 3:39.6 in 1972 and a fast finish in his heat.

PEKKA PAIVARINTA of Finland looked great in his steeplechase heat, then finished eighth in the final. An 8:32.8 steeplechaser in 1971, he improved his 1500 to 3:39.3 in 1972.

TONY POLHILL of New Zealand ran 4:01.7 in 1970 and improved to 3:40.1 and 3:50.0. He won the New Zealand Championships in 3:41.7 in a hard rain. He was regarded as New Zealand's best at Munich.

SHIBROU REGASSA another Ethiopian surprise, came from nowhere to run 3:42.9 in 1972, and he won a tactical victory over Boit and Howe. A determined front runner with a pretty stride he led all the way in his heat.

HAICO SCHARN of Holland ran 3:40.8 in 1971 and in 1972 he beat Bram Wassenaar in 3:39.7.

RAY SMEDLEY of Great Britain reached international prominence in 1972 at the age of 21. After a 3:41.6, he placed second to Peter Stewart in the AAA with 3:38.5.

HENRYK SZORDYKOWSKI of Poland, ranked among the world's top six for the previous four years, but now 28, did no noteworthy racing during the spring of 1972 until a losing 3:39.5 effort.

BODO TUMMLER, West Germany's great medalist of 1968, began a comeback at 29 after two years off. Early in June, 1972, he ran 3:42.7, then he beat Pantyeley, 3:43.2 to 3:43.5, and won the West German championship in 3:41.5.

The second semi-final started with a 64.2 first lap. Then Regassa pushed the pace to 2:05.5 and 3:01.2. Keino followed Regassa, then went ahead while running his last lap in 53.5. Mignon finished well for second and Polhill outkicked Regassa for the last qualifying spot. Szordykowski lost out by seven tenths in the driving finish, but Smedley and Tümmler finished far behind.

Runners in the third semi-final were:

FRANCESCO ARESE, No. 4 in the world in 1971, ran three indoor miles in the United States early in 1972. Although he beat Liquori, Ryun, and Wottle, he lost to Mason and Dyce. He won only the slowest race—4:09.5. Suffering tendon troubles, he lost three outdoor races before Ivanov beat him soundly, 3:37.8 to 3:39.3. In early August, Arese made a strong comeback with 800 meters in 1:47.1, his fastest ever, but he did not run well afterwards.

ROD DIXON of New Zealand showed great promise with 4:00.1 early in 1971, but in February of 1972 he was not fast enough to make New Zealand's record-breaking four-mile relay team.

Still, he ran miles in 4:01.2 and 3:59.6 in January. Then he lost to Polhill, 4:02.7 to 4:01.4. In the New Zealand Championship, Dixon barely lost to Polhill, with 3:41.7 for both. Two weeks later, on March 18, Dixon won in 3:41.0, but in Oslo on August 3, he was put in the B race and lost even that one, to Paivarinta, 3:42.4 to 3:42.3. At Munich, the 6'2" 22-year-old "sprained a calf muscle" jumping over a fence during an evening workout and he thought he would be unable to run in the first heat. "I could hardly walk on it." But in his heat he came from well back to race up alongside Keino at the tape in 3:40.0, a full second under his personal record.

JEAN-PIERRE DUFRESNE of France, who ran 3:38.9 and 3:40.6 in 1971, won the 1972 French Championships from Boxberger in 3:41.4.

1972

GUNNAR EKMAN of Sweden, a 4:00.6 miler in 1971, improved to 3:57.7 in 1972.

BRENDAN FOSTER of Great Britain had a record of pushing the pace without winning. He ran 3:40.6 for third in the 1970 Commonwealth Games and placed third in the 1971 European Championships. In 1971, he ranked ninth in the world without winning. His best 1500 was 3:39.2. In 1972, he forced the pace to a 3:55.9 mile on June 10, but he lost to Peter Stewart. He was fourth in the AAA in 3:39.3.

KLAUS-PETER JUSTUS of East Germany, a 3:41.5 runner in 1970 at 19 and European junior champion, became a winner in 1972, when barely 21, with winning times of 3:39.6, 3:40.0, 3:39.0, 3:40.4, 3:41.0, and 3:39.5. His 3:41.0 at Helsinki's TOP Games beat Vasala's 3:41.7.

GERD LARSEN, Denmark's top man and a Lydiard pupil, came into prominence in 1971 with a 1:47.5 800. In 1972 he had a 3:39.4 1500, plus a victory over Foster in 3:39.9.

PEKKA VASALA a 3:41.8 runner in 1968 at 20, had improved only to 3:41.0 in 1970, but he broke through with 3:38.6 in 1971. Called "Mr. Unpredictable" in Finland, Vasala was only ninth in the 1971 European Championships. Early in 1972 he lost to Justus with 3:41.7 and ran a 3:57.2 mile behind Foster. On July 19 he followed a pace of 57.6 and 1:57.0, passing 1200 meters in 2:54.2 for a Scandinavian record 3:36.8. A week later, against Britain, he beat Foster in 3:41.2 and won the 800 in 1:46.0. After a 3:38.3, he ran a great 800 on August 20—1:44.5—but he said, "I'll stick to the 1500 for the Olympics."

PAUL-HEINZ WELLMANN of West Germany ran 3:40.8 in 1971 and had a personal record of 3:40.3 entering the Olympics. He placed second in the fifth heat in 3:41.8.

BOB WHEELER, USA, lowered his 1500 mark to 3:40.8 after the Final Trials. He qualified with 3:41.3.

In the third semi-final, Arese pushed a hard pace, 57.7, and Foster led him at 800 meters in 1:59.1. Vasala led at 1200 in 2:58.5. A fast, driving finish saw Dixon break through to the verge of greatness with a last 300 in 39.0 which edged Vasala in 3:37.9. Foster lowered his personal record to 3:38.2 for third, and Wellmann became the tenth qualifier with a good 3:38.4. Ekman and Wheeler also had personal records of 3:39.4 and 3:40.4. Arese faded to 3:41.1.

THE FINAL was run on September 10, and the day was hot, but clouds began to shield the runners before the start at 3:35 p.m. The ten finalists took their positions on a green line a meter back of the white starting line. On command, they moved quickly to the starting line and took the set position. The gun sent them running, but nobody was in a hurry.

Foster led at the end of the first lap in 1:01.39, rounded off

1972

from the electronic timing to 61.4. Keino, who was expected to set a fast pace, lagged back in eighth down the backstretch and around the curve. Then, on the homestretch, he moved quickly and led at 700 meters in 1:47.

Around the curve to the starting line, where Keino strode past majestically in 2:01.36, the bearded, black-clad figure of Dixon moved to second. Golden-haired, darker-bearded Vasala took over third place, and the tall Boit also passed Foster.

As they increased speed along the backstretch, Hansen let them go, and Mignon moved swiftly on the curve. Along the red track in the homestretch, under the tent-like roof like a giant spiderweb, Vasala ran close behind the flying Keino, and Foster ran back up to third.

Keino's tactics were obvious now as he sped past the clanging bell. He had run a lap in 55.1 and he held the pace around the curve to the starting line—1200 meters in 2:56.5. It was a powerful effort by Keino, but the slow first 600 left the others full of run. Into the last curve, Vasala followed closely and Boit moved to third ahead of Dixon, who looked surprisingly strong.

Into the homestretch, Vasala moved to Keino's shoulder, then past him by three yards while the small group of Finnish fans went mad. Dixon raced past Boit and gained on Keino. Foster barely beat Mignon, and Wellmann drove past Pantyeley.

Results: Vasala 3:36.3, Keino 3:36.8, Dixon 3:37.5, Boit 3:38.4, Foster 3:39.0, Mignon 3:39.1, Wellmann 3:40.1, Pantyeley 3:40.2, Polhill 3:41.8, Hansen 3:46.6.

Vasala's 3:36.3 was equal to sixth on the all-time list. Keino's 3:36.8 was within a fifth of a second of his non-altitude record. Dixon's 3:37.5 broke Peter Snell's New Zealand record and puts him on the threshhold of greatness. He threw his arms in the air with joy at the finish (New Zealand's lone medal winner), and on the victory stand he wept tears of happiness. Then he shook hands with Keino, his idol.

Vasala's last 400 in 53.5 was good, but his last 800, forced to 1:49.0 by Keino, has never been equalled. His last 1000 meters was about 2:19.1, second only to Ryun's world-record finish. Vasala's last 1200 meters was about 2:49.8.

Vasala, an accountant in Lohja, said, "The race went much as I expected. I remained in a good position, waiting for Keino's attack. When it came, I just glided along in his wake. I knew—on the strength of my 800 times—that I had more speed than anyone around, and so I was confident. I released my surplus energies with 150 meters to go." With the gold medal around his neck, he said he was sorry Ryun did not participate. Vasala's victory helps prove history's most obvious lesson: there will always be new champions and new record breakers... always exciting new runners and races.

1972
1,500m:
3:36.3	Pekka Vasala (Finland)	OG (1)	Munich	10	Sep
3:36.8	Kipchoge Keino (Kenya)	(1)	Mombasa	24	Jun
3:37.4	Mike Boit (Kenya)	(2)	Mombasa	24	Jun
3:37.5	Rod Dixon (New Zealand)	OG (3)	Munich	10	Sep
3:37.8	Ivan Ivanov (USSR)	(1)	Turin	2	Jun
3:37.9	Fanie Van Zijl (South Africa)	(1)	Potchefstroom	11	Mar
3:38.2	Jerome Howe (USA)	(1)	Seattle	17	Jun
3:38.2	Peter Stewart (GB)	(1)	London	15	Jul
3:38.2	Brendan Foster (GB)	OG (3)sf	Munich	9	Sep
3:38.3	Howell Michael (USA)	(2)	Seattle	17	Jun
3:38.4	Paul-Heinz Wellmann (WG)	OG (4)sf	Munich	9	Sep
3:38.5	Frank Murphy (Eire)	(1)	Athens	14	Jun
3:38.5	Ray Smedley (GB)	(2)	London	15	Jul

Mile:
3:52.8	Jim Ryun (USA)	(1)	Toronto	29	Jul
3:55.3	Peter Stewart (GB)	(1)	London	10	Jun
3:55.9	Brendan Foster (GB)	(2)	London	10	Jun
3:56.0	Fanie Van Zijl (South Africa)	(1)	Modesto	27	May
3:56.0	Jim Douglas (GB)	(3)	London	10	Jun
3:56.5	John Kirkbride (GB)	(4)	London	10	Jun
3:56.7	Steve Prefontaine (USA)	(1)	Eugene	23	Apr
3:57.0	Tony Polhill (New Zealand)	(1)	London	15	Sep
3:57.2	Pekka Vasala (Finland)	(2)	Stockholm	5	Jul
3:57.6	Len Hilton (USA)	(1)	Spring, Texas	3	Jun
3:57.7	Gunnar Ekman (Sweden)	(4)	Stockholm	5	Jul
3:57.8	Tom Von Ruden (USA)	(1)	Los Angeles	4	Mar

Noteworthy Indoor Marks:
3:57.9	Tom Von Ruden (USA)	(1)	Fort Worth	4	Feb
3:58.9	Len Hilton (USA)	(2)	Fort Worth	4	Feb
3:59.4	Kipchoge Keino (Kenya)	(1)	College Park	14	Jan
3:59.5	Bob Maplestone (GB)	(1)	San Diego	19	Feb

Mark Shearman

It's Vasala! The Finnish ace outkicks Keino to win the 1972 Olympic title.

ALL TIME WORLD LIST (As of 20 October 1972)

Here, as in the rest of the book, interpolation is made as per Portuguese Scoring Table ("Systeme rationnel pour classer les performances athletiques," by Dr. Fernando Amado). Converted marks are given in parentheses.

3:33.1	(3:51.0)	J.RYUN (USA)	(1)	Los Angeles	8	Jul	67
(3:33.2)	3:51.1	Ryun	(1)	Bakersfield	23	Jun	67
(3:33.5)	3:51.3	Ryun	(1)	Berkeley	17	Jul	66
3:34.0	(3:51.9)	J.WADOUX (France)	(1)	Colombes	23	Jul	70
(3:34.9)	3:52.8	Ryun	(1)	Toronto	29	Jul	72
3:34.9	(3:52.9)	K.KEINO (Kenya)	(1)	Mexico City	20	Oct	68
(3:35.2)	3:53.1	Keino	(1)	Kisumu	10	Sep	67
(3:35.2)	3:53.2	Ryun	(1)	Los Angeles	2	Jun	67
(3:35.4)	3:53.4	Keino	(1)	London	20	Aug	66
3:35.6	(3:53.6)	H.ELLIOTT (Australia)	(1)	Rome	6	Sep	60
(3:35.6)	3:53.6	M.JAZY (France)	(1)	Rennes	9	Jun	65
(3:35.7)	3:53.7	Ryun	(1)	Los Angeles	4	Jun	66
(3:35.8)	3:53.8	J.MAY (E Germany)	(1)	Wanganui	11	Dec	65
(3:35.8)	3:53.8	Keino	(1)	London	28	Aug	67
(3:35.8)	3:53.8	B.TÜMMLER (W.Germany)	(1)	Karlskrona	22	Aug	68
3:36.0	(3:54.1)	Elliott	(1)	Göteborg	28	Aug	58
3:36.0	(3:54.1)	M.LIQUORI (USA)	(1)	Milan	1	Jul	71
(3:36.1)	3:54.1	P. SNELL (NZ)	(1)	Auckland	17	Nov	64
(3:36.1)	3:54.1	May	(1)	Auckland	15	Dec	65
(3:36.2)	3:54.2	Keino	(1)	London	30	Aug	65
(3:36.3)	3:54.4	Snell	(1)	Wanganui	27	Jan	62
(3:36.3)	3:54.4	Keino	(2)	Auckland	15	Dec	65
3:36.3	(3:54.4)	Jazy	(1)	Sochaux	25	Jun	66
3:36.3	(3:54.4)	F.ARESE (Italy)	(2)	Milan	1	Jul	71
(3:36.3)	3:54.4	Keino	(1)	Stockholm	6	Jul	71
3:36.3	(3:54.4)	P.VASALA (Finland)	(1)	Munich	10	Sep	72
(3:36.4)	3:54.5	Elliott	(1)	Dublin	6	Aug	58
3:36.4	(3:54.5)	May	(1)	Erfurt	14	Jul	65
3:36.4	(3:54.5)	Jazy	(1)	Rennes	15	Jun	66
3:36.5	(3:54.6)	Tümmler	(1)	Cologne	10	Jul	68
(3:36.5)	3:54.6	Liquori	(1)	Philadelphia	16	May	71
(3:36.6)	3:54.7	Ryun	(1)	Lawrence	22	Apr	67
(3:36.6)	3:54.7	Tümmler	(1)	Stockholm	2	Jul	68
3:36.6	(3:54.7)	Keino	(1)	Edinburgh	22	Jul	70
(3:36.7)	3:54.8	Ryun	(2)	Philadelphia	16	May	71
(3:36.8)	3:54.9	Snell	(1)	Modesto	25	May	63
(3:36.8)	3:54.9	Keino	(2)	Wanganui	11	Dec	65
(3:36.8)	3:55.0	Snell	(1)	Compton	7	Jun	63
3:36.8	(3:55.0)	Keino	(1)	Nairobi	15	Aug	71
3:36.8	(3:55.0)	Keino	(1)	Mombasa	24	Jun	72
3:36.8	(3:55.0)	Vasala	(1)	Turku	19	Jul	72
3:36.8	(3:55.0)	Keino	(2)	Munich	10	Sep	72
3:36.9	(3:55.1)	Keino	(1)	Aarhus	23	Jun	71
(3:37.1)	3:55.2	Keino	(1)	Nyeri	24	Jun	67
(3:37.1)	3:55.3	Ryun	(1)	San Diego	27	Jun	65
(3:37.1)	3:55.3	Keino	(1)	Kingston	13	Aug	66
3:37.1	(3:55.3)	A.DE HERTOGHE (Belgium)	(2)	Cologne	10	Jul	68
(3:37.1)	3:55.3	P.STEWART (GB)	(1)	London	10	Jun	72
(3:37.2)	3:55.4	Elliott	(1)	London	3	Sep	58
(3:37.2)	3:55.4	J.GRELLE (USA) -50-	(1)	Vancouver	15	Jun	65
(3:37.2)	3:55.4	Snell	(2)	San Diego	27	Jun	65
(3:37.2)	3:55.4	Grelle	(1)	San Diego	11	Jun	66
3:37.2	(3:55.4)	Keino	(2)	Los Angeles	8	Jul	67
3:37.2	(3:55.4)	Liquori	(1)	Stuttgart	30	Jul	69
3:37.2	(3:55.4)	Keino	(1)	Munich	5	Sep	71
3:37.3	(3:55.5)	Keino	(1)	South Lake Tahoe	12	Sep	69
3:37.3	(3:55.5)	U.HÖGBERG (Sweden)	(3)	Milan	1	Jul	71
3:37.4	(3:55.5)	Elliott	(1)	Oslo	5	Sep	58
(3:37.4)	3:55.5	J.BEATTY (USA)	(2)	Compton	7	Jun	63
(3:37.4)	3:55.5	Jazy	(1)	St. Maur	2	Jun	65

(3:37.4)	3:55.5	Grelle		(3)	San Diego	27	Jun	65
(3:37.4)	3:55.5	Keino		(1)	Kisumu	31	Aug	68
3:37.4	(3:55.5)	M.BOIT (Kenya)		(2)	Mombasa	24	Jun	72
(3:37.5)	3:55.6	D.BURLESON (USA)		(3)	Compton	7	Jun	63
(3:37.5)	3:55.6	J.ODLOZIL (Czechoslovakia)		(2)	London	30	Aug	65
(3:37.5)	3:55.7	A.SIMPSON (GB)		(3)	London	30	Aug	65
3:37.5	(3:55.7)	W.ADAMS (W Germany)		(3)	Cologne	10	Jul	68
3:37.5	(3:55.7)	Keino		(1)	Abidjan	4	Apr	70
3:37.5	(3:55.7)	Keino		(1)	Durham	17	Jul	71
3:37.5	(3:55.7)	R.DIXON (NZ)		(3)	Munich	10	Sep	72
(3:37.6)	3:55.8	Ryun		(1)	Lawrence	23	Apr	66
3:37.6	(3:55.8)	Odlozil		(1)	Prague	13	Aug	66
3:37.6	(3:55.8)	Arese		(2)	Stuttgart	30	Jul	69
(3:37.6)	3:55.8	Ryun		(1)	Lawrence	17	Apr	71
3:37.7	(3:55.9)	Wadoux		(2)	Prague	13	Aug	66
(3:37.8)	3:55.9	M.LINCOLN (Australia)		(2)	Dublin	6	Aug	58
3:37.8	(3:55.9)	Jazy		(1)	Colombes	28	Jul	63
(3:37.8)	3:55.9	May		(4)	London	30	Aug	65
(3:37.8)	3:55.9	Ryun		(1)	Walnut	10	Aug	68
3:37.8	(3:55.9)	Ryun		(2)	Mexico City	20	Oct	68
(3:37.8)	3:55.9	Ryun		(1)	Los Angeles	7	Jun	69
3:37.8	(3:55.9)	I.IVANOV (USSR)		(1)	Turin	2	Jun	72
(3:37.8)	3:55.9	B.FOSTER (GB)		(2)	London	10	Jun	72
(3:37.9)	3:56.0	Beatty		(1)	Toronto	25	Jun	63
(3:37.9)	3:56.0	W.BARAN (Poland)		(1)	London	3	Aug	64
(3:37.9)	3:56.0	Grelle		(2)	Los Angeles	4	Jun	66
(3:37.9)	3:56.0	Ryun		(1)	London	12	Aug	67
(3:37.9)	3:56.0	De Hertoghe		(2)	Stockholm	2	Jul	68
(3:37.9)	3:56.0	F.VAN ZIJL (S Africa)		(1)	Modesto	27	May	72
(3:37.9)	3:56.0	J.DOUGLAS (GB)		(3)	London	10	Jun	72
(3:37.9)	3:56.1	Snell		(1)	Los Angeles	18	May	62
(3:37.9)	3:56.1	Grelle		(2)	Toronto	25	Jun	63
(3:37.9)	3:56.1	N.DUGGAN (GB)		(2)	San Diego	11	Jun	66
(3:37.9)	3:56.1	Grelle		(2)	Bakersfield	23	Jun	67
3:37.9	(3:56.1)	Wadoux		(1)	Paris	4	Jul	68
3:37.9	(3:56.1)	Van Zijl		(1)	Potshefstroom	11	Mar	72
3:37.9	(3:56.1)	Dixon		(1)sf	Munich	9	Sep	72
3:37.9	(3:56.1)	Vasala		(2)sf	Munich	9	Sep	72
3:38.0	(3:56.2)	May		(1)	Potsdam	26	Jun	66
(3:38.0)	3:56.2	D.WILBORN (USA)	-100-	(3)	Bakersfield	23	Jun	67
3:38.0	(3:56.2)	Wadoux		(1)	Colombes	18	Jul	70
(3:38.1)	3:56.3	Beatty		(1)	Helsinki	21	Aug	62
(3:38.1)	3:56.3	R.DIVINE (USA)		(1)	Eugene	5	Jun	70
3:38.1	(3:56.4)	S.JUNGWIRTH (Czech)		(1)	Stará Boleslav	12	Jul	57
(3:38.1)	3:56.4	Grelle		(4)	Compton	7	Jun	63
3:38.1	(3:56.4)	T.O'HARA (USA)		(1)	New Brunswick	28	Jun	64
3:38.1	(3:56.4)	Snell		(1)	Tokyo	21	Oct	64
(3:38.1)	3:56.4	Odlozil		(2)	Auckland	17	Nov	64
(3:38.1)	3:56.4	Snell		(1)	Los Angeles	4	Jun	65
(3:38.1)	3:56.4	Grelle		(2)	Los Angeles	4	Jun	65
(3:38.1)	3:56.4	R.DAY (USA)		(1)	Bakersfield	12	Jun	65
3:38.1	(3:56.4)	Keino		(1)	Lusaka	16	Sep	67
3:38.1	(3:56.4)	Tümmler		(1)	Göteborg	26	Aug	68
3:38.1	(3:56.4)	DICK QUAX (NZ)		(2)	Edinburgh	22	Jul	70
(3:38.1)	3:56.4	A.KVALHEIM (Norway)		(1)	Eugene	6	Jun	71
3:38.1	(3:56.4)	Keino		(1)	Västerås	2	Jul	71
(3:38.1)	3:56.4	B.JIPCHO (Kenya)		(1)	Berlin	7	Sep	71
(3:38.1)	3:56.4	Van Zijl		(1)	Stellenbosch	20	Mar	72
3:38.2	(3:56.5)	May		(1)	Oslo	12	Jul	66
3:38.2	(3:56.5)	May		(1)	Jena	24	Jul	66
3:38.2	(3:56.5)	Ryun		(1)	Düsseldorf	17	Aug	67
3:38.2	(3:56.5)	H.SZORDYKOWSKI (Pol)		(1)	Warsaw	29	Aug	60
3:38.2	(3:56.5)	J.HOWE (USA)		(1)	Seattle	17	Jun	72
3:38.2	(3:56.5)	P.Stewart		(1)	London	15	Jul	72
3:38.2	(3:56.5)	Foster		(3)sf	Munich	9	Sep	72
(3:38.3)	3:56.5	S.VALENTIN (E Germany)		(1)	Potsdam	28	May	59

(3:38.3)	3:56.5	Beatty	(1)	London	18	Aug	62
3:38.3	(3:56.5)	Jazy	(1)	St. Maur	7	Oct	62
3:38.3	(3:56.5)	Jazy	(3)	Prague	13	Aug	66
(3:38.3)	3:56.5	Liquori	(1)	Eugene	26	Jun	71
(3:38.3)	3:56.5	J.KIRKBRIDE (GB)	(4)	London	10	Jun	72
3:38.3	(3:56.5)	H.MICHAEL (USA)	(2)	Seattle	17	Jun	72
3:38.3	(3:56.5)	Vasala	(1)	Oslo	2	Aug	72
3:38.4	(3:56.6)	Jazy	(2)	Rome	6	Sep	60
3:38.4	(3:56.6)	Elliott	(1)	Göteborg	18	Sep	60
(3:38.4)	3:56.6	C.WEISIGER (USA)	(5)	Compton	7	Jun	63
(3:38.4)	3:56.6	Simpson	(1)	London	7	Jun	65
3:38.4	(3:56.6)	May	(1)	Helsinki	28	Jul	65
3:38.4	(3:56.6)	Wadoux	(1)	Sochaux	17	Jun	67
3:38.4	(3:56.6)	Arese	(1)	Helsinki	15	Aug	71
(3:38.4)	3:56.6	W.WILKINSON (GB)	(1)	Leicester	31	May	71
3:38.4	(3:56.6)	P-H.WELLMANN (W Ger)	(4)sf	Munich	9	Sep	72
3:38.4	(3:56.6)	Boit	(4)	Munich	10	Sep	72
(3:38.5)	3:56.7	Grelle	(2)	London	18	Aug	62
(3:38.5)	3:56.7	Burleson	(1)	St. Louis	22	Jun	63
(3:38.5)	3:56.7	Odlozil	(1)	London	3	Jul	65
(3:38.5)	3:56.7	S.BAIR (USA)	(2)	Los Angeles	7	Jun	69
(3:38.5)	3:56.7	Arese	(2)	Berlin	7	Sep	71
(3:38.5)	3:56.7	S.PREFONTAINE (USA)	(1)	Eugene	23	Apr	72
(3:38.5)	3:56.8	Snell -150-	(1)	Auckland	22	Feb	62
(3:38.5)	3:56.8	J.DAVIES (NZ)	(3)	Auckland	17	Nov	64
(3:38.5)	3:56.8	Ryun	(3)	Los Angeles	4	Jun	65
(3:38.5)	3:56.8	Davies	(2)	London	3	Jul	65
(3:38.5)	3:56.8	D.PATRICK (USA)	(1)	Philadelphia	1	Jun	68
3:38.5	(3:56.8)	Kvalheim	(1)	Oslo	28	Aug	68
(3:38.5)	3:56.8	I.McCAFFERTY (GB)	(1)	Reading	11	Jun	69
3:38.5	(3:56.8)	T.VON RUDEN (USA)	(1)	Aarhus	26	Jul	71
3:38.5	(3:56.8)	Keino	(1)	Nairobi	10	Oct	71
3:38.5	(3:56.8)	F.MURPHY (Eire)	(1)	Athens	14	Jun	72
3:38.5	(3:56.8)	R.SMEDLEY (GB)	(2)	London	15	Jul	72
3:38.6	(3:56.9)	D.WAERN (Sweden)	(2)	Goteborg	18	Sep	60
3:38.6	(3:56.9)	Vasala	(1)	Helsinki	1	Jul	71
3:38.7	(3:56.9)	Valentin	(1)	Potsdam	27	Aug	60
(3:38.7)	3:56.9	O'Hara	(2)	St. Louis	22	Jun	63
(3:38.7)	3:56.9	Valentin	(1)	Potsdam	26	Jun	63
3:38.7	(3:56.9)	M.BERNARD (France)	(2)	Colombes	28	Jul	63
(3:38.7)	3:56.9	Simpson	(1)	Dublin	5	Jul	65
(3:38.7)	3:56.9	Keino	(1)	Napier	4	Dec	65
(3:38.7)	3:56.9	Keino	(1)	Tokoroa	6	Dec	65
3:38.7	(3:56.9)	O.RAIKO (USSR)	(1)	London	17	Jun	66
(3:38.7)	3:56.9	Von Ruden	(4)	Bakersfield	23	Jun	67
3:38.7	(3:56.9)	A.GÄRDERUD (Sweden)	(2)	Göteborg	26	Aug	68
(3:38.7)	3:36.9	C.LaBENZ (USA)	(1)	Berkeley	30	May	70
3:38.7	(3:56.9)	Arese	(1)	Barcelona	3	Jun	70
3:38.7	(3:56.9)	Szordykowski	(2)	Helsinki	15	Aug	71
(3:38.7)	3:56.9	Keino	(3)	Berlin	7	Sep	71
3:38.7	(3:56.9)	Douglas	(1)	Athens	27	Jun	72
3:38.7	(3:56.9)	Kirkbride	(3)	London	15	Jul	72
(3:38.8)	3:57.0	Elliott	(1)	Dublin	23	Sep	60
(3:38.8)	3:57.0	Tümmler	(1)	Berlin	24	Sep	69
(3:38.8)	3:57.0	Kirkbride	(1)	London	5	Jul	70
(3:38.8)	3:57.0	TONY POLHILL (NZ)	(1)	London	15	Sep	72
3:38.8	(3:57.1)	M.HALBERG (NZ)	(2)	Oslo	5	Sep	58
3:38.8	(3:57.1)	I.RÓZSAVÖLGYI (Hun)	(1)	Budapest	30	Jul	60
3:38.8	(3:57.1)	Burleson	(2)	New Brunswick	28	Jun	64
3:38.8	(3:57.1)	Snell	(1)sf	Tokyo	19	Oct	64
(3:38.8)	3:57.1	Simpson	(2)	Kingston	13	Aug	66
3:38.8	(3:57.1)	A.KRÜGER (W.Germany)	(4)	Cologne	10	Jul	68
3:38.8	(3:57.1)	Keino	(1)	Nyeri	2	Aug	69
3:38.8	(3:57.1)	Szordykowski	(1)	Warsaw	12	Sep	70
(3:38.8)	3:57.1	Ryun	(1)	Lawrence	22	Apr	72

3:38.8	(3:57.1)	Krüger		(1)	Cologne	15	Jul	72
3:38.8	(3:57.1)	M.GUETTAYA (Tunisia)		(2)	Turku	19	Jul	72
3:38.8	(3:57.1)	J-P.DUFRESNE (France)		(1)	Warsaw	9	Aug	72
3:38.8	(3:57.1)	R.WHEELER (USA)		(1)	Aarhus	14	Sep	72
(3:38.9)	3:57.2	D.IBBOTSON (GB)		(1)	London	19	Jul	57
3:38.9	(3:57.2)	Rózsavölgyi		(1)	Budapest	22	Aug	59
3:38.9	(3:57.2)	Valentin		(1)	Varna	9	Oct	63
3:38.9	(3:57.2)	Grelle		(3)	New Brunswick	28	Jun	64
3:38.9	(3:57.2)	Baran	-200-	(2)sf	Tokyo	19	Oct	64
(3:38.9)	3:57.2	Wadoux		(2)	St.Maur	2	Jun	65
(3:38.9)	3:57.2	Divine		(5)	Bakersfield	23	Jun	67
(3:38.9)	3:57.2	Keino		(1)	Belfast	16	Aug	67
3:38.9	(3:57.2)	May*		(1)	Rehlingen	16	Jun	68
3:38.9	(3:57.2)	De Hertoghe		(1)	Blankenberge	14	Aug	70
(3:38.9)	3:57.2	Von Ruden		(2)	Lawrence	17	Apr	71
3:38.9	(3:57.2)	Dufresne		(1)	Colombes	4	Jul	71
(3:38.9)	3:57.2	H.NORPOTH (W Germany)		(4)	Berlin	7	Sep	71
(3:38.9)	3:57.2	Foster		(1)	Stockholm	5	Jul	72
(3:38.9)	3:57.2	Vasala		(2)	Stockholm	5	Jul	72
3:38.9	(3:57.2)	T.B.HANSEN (Denmark)		(1)	Helsinki	9	Aug	72
3:39.0	(3:57.3)	Jungwirth		(2)	Göteborg	28	Aug	58
(3:39.0)	3:57.3	Weisiger		(2)	Modesto	25	May	63
3:39.0	(3:57.3)	Ryun		(4)	New Brunswick	28	Jun	64
3:39.0	(3:57.3)	Grelle		(1)	Cologne	7	Jul	65
(3:39.0)	3:57.3	Burleson		(1)	Eugene	2	Jun	66
3:39.0	(3:57.3)	M.VILT (USSR)		(2)	London	17	Jun	66
(3:39.0)	3:57.3	De Hertoghe		(1)	Stockholm	4	Jul	67
3:39.0	(3:57.3)	Arese		(1)	Schio	13	Jul	68
3:39.0	(3:57.3)	Tümmler		(3)	Mexico City	20	Oct	68
(3:39.0)	3:57.3	IAN STEWART (GB)		(2)	Reading	11	Jun	69
3:39.0	(3:57.3)	Wadoux		(1)	Colombes	20	Jul	69
3:39.0	(3:57.3)	P. Stewart		(2)	Warsaw	12	Sep	70
(3:39.0)	3:57.3	Quax		(1)	Auckland	6	Mar	71
3:39.0	(3:57.3)	Högberg		(1)	Lidingö	1	Jun	71
(3:39.0)	3:57.3	Ryun		(1)	Los Angeles	9	Jun	72
3:39.0	(3:57.3)	K-P.JUSTUS (E Germany)		(1)	Potsdam	15	Jun	72
3:39.0	(3:57.3)	Högberg		(3)	Turku	19	Jul	72
3:39.0	(3:57.3)	Foster		(5)	Munich	10	Sep	72
3:39.0	(3:57.3)	H.MIGNON (Belgium)	-230-	(2)	Aarhus	14	Sep	72

*May represented West Germany in this and later years.

INDOOR MARKS:
3:37.8	(3:55.9)	H.NORPOTH (W Germany)	(1)	Berlin	13	Feb	71
(3:38.1)	3:56.4	T.O'HARA (USA)	(1)	Chicago	6	Mar	64
(3:38.1)	3:56.4	J.RYUN (USA)	(1)	San Diego	19	Feb	71
(3:38.4)	3:56.6₀	O'Hara	(1)	New York	13	Feb	64
(3:38.9)	3:57.2₀	M.LIQUORI (USA)	(1)	Houston	13	Feb	71

₀Made on oversized track.

TALLY OF MARKS AT 3:39.0/3:57.3 OR BETTER:

29 — Keino
21 — Ryun
11 — Grelle
10 — Snell
9 — May
8 — Jazy
7 — Wadoux, Elliott
6 — Tümmler, Arese, Vasala
5 — Liquori
4 — De Hertoghe, Beatty, Burleson, Odlozil, Simpson, Foster, O'Hara, Valentin
3 — P. Stewart, Högberg, Van Zijl, Szordykowski, Kirkbride, Von Ruden
2 — Boit, Dixon, Baran, Douglas, Divine, Jungwirth, Quax, Kvalheim, Weisiger, Davies, Rózsavölgyi, Krüger, Dufresne, Norpoth
1 — Adams, Lincoln, Ivanov, Duggan, Wilburn, Day, Jipcho, Howe, Michael, Wilkinson, Wellmann, Bair, Prefontaine, Patrick, McCafferty, Murphy, Smedley, Waern, Bernard, Raiko, Gärderud, LaBenz, Polhill, Halberg, Guettaya, R.Wheeler, Ibbotson, Hansen, Vilt, I.Stewart, Justus, Mignon.

INDEX

Åberg, O. (Sweden), 144, 146, 147, 149, 150, 151, 151, 152, 153, 154, 157, 158, 158, 162, 163, 164, 166, 191/192.
Adams, W. (W.Germany), 280, 285, ATL.
Agostini, M. (Trinidad), 210, 211.
Ahldén, E. (Sweden), 131, 135, 141, 143, 143.
Ahlsén, A. (Sweden), 121, 122, 126, 127, 129, 130.
Åkerberg, O. (Sweden), 129.
Albison, S. (GB), 2, 3.
Alford, J. (GB), 105, 106, 130.
Andersson, A. (Sweden), 110, 111, 114, 115, 119, 120, 121, 122, 123, 124, 126, 127, 128, 128, 129, 130, 131, 132, 133, 134, 134, 135, 136, 137, 138, 139, 140, 141, 141, 143, 144, 145, 147, 151, 164, 166, 167, 170, 170, 171, 176, 181.
Andersson, B. (Sweden), 130, 133, 134, 143.
Andersson, K. (Sweden), 126, 133.
Andersson, R. (Sweden), 147.
Anentia, A. (Kenya), 258.
Arese, F. (Italy), 278, 285, 291, 292, 292, 293, 295, 296, 296, 299, 300, 302, 303, 303, 311, 312, ATL.
Arnaud, H. (France), 19, 20, 21.
Ashby, S.T. (GB), 48.

Backhouse, G. (Australia), 105, 106.
Bacon, F. (GB), 10, 11, 11, 28.
Bailey, D. (Canada), 275, 276, 279.
Bailey, J. (Australia), 188, 189, 190, 191, 192, 193, 197, 198, 204.
Baillie, W. (NZ), 177, 234, 243.
Bair, S. (USA), 274, 279, 288, 289, 291, 293, ATL.
Baker, H. (USA), 26.
Baker, P. (GB), 19, 21, 27, 29.
Ballieux, A. (Belgium), 190.
Bannister, R. (GB), 154, 155, 156, 157, 159, 159, 161, 162, 163, 166, 167, 170, 171, 172, 173, 174, 175, 176, 177, 178, 179, 180, 181, 184, 185, 187, 190, 197, 200, 201, 202, 203, 204, 244.
Baraldi, G. (Italy), 194, 195, 209.
Baran, W. (Poland), 225, 226, 231, 232, 233, 233, 238, 238, 239, 240, 247, 248, 249, 250, 251, 252, 253, 256, 263, 270, 272, 272, 291, ATL.
Baraton, G. (France), 40, 43.
Barker, A.E. (GB), 14.
Barry, J.J. (Eire), 151.
Barthel, J. (Luxemburg), 145, 146, 149, 159, 160, 162, 163, 164, 165, 166, 170, 174, 175, 179, 181, 183, 188, 190.
Barwick, E.W. (Australia), 65.
Bauer, R. (USA), 86.
Beatty, J. (USA), 214, 221, 222, 223, 224, 225, 226, 226, 229, 230, 231, 233, 234, 235, 236, 237, 238, 239, 243, 244, 256, 262, ATL.
Beccali, L. (Italy), 50, 51, 53, 54, 58, 59, 62, 63, 64, 65, 67, 70, 71, 72, 73, 74, 77, 78, 80, 81, 82, 83, 86, 86, 87, 89, 90, 92, 93, 94, 95, 96, 96, 97, 98, 101, 105, 106, 106, 115, 194.
Bedarff, E. (Germany), 29.
Bell, S. (USA), 240.
Bell, W. (USA), 266, 276.
Bengtsson, I. (Sweden), 131, 134, 149, 150, 152.

Bennett, C. (GB), 13.
Béres, E. (Hungary), 170, 179, 188.
Bergkvist, G. (Sweden), 144, 146, 147, 148, 149, 151, 151, 152, 153.
Berisford, M. (GB), 226, 231, 233.
Bernard, M. (France), 213, 216, 217, 218, 219, 220, 221, 221, 225, 226, 232, 233, 237, 238, 247, 248, 249, 250, 251, 252, 253, 270, ATL.
Binks, J. (GB), 14, 15, 25, 25, 28, 37, 109.
Björn, E. (Sweden), 19/20.
Blagrove, M. (GB), 201, 202, 212.
Blake, A. (USA), 11.
Blotiu, C. (Rumania), 62.
Blue, T. (Australia), 216, 220, 221, 227, 228.
Böcher, H. (Germany), 39, 41, 42, 43, 46, 47, 47, 48, 49, 53.
Boit, M. (Kenya), 309, 310, 311, 313, 314, ATL.
Bolin, A. (Sweden), 24.
Bonhag, G. (USA), 15.
Bontemps, P. (France), 39.
Bonthron, B. (USA), 68, 69, 70, 70, 73, 74, 74, 75, 76, 77, 79, 80, 81, 82, 82, 83, 83, 84, 86, 87, 88, 89, 94, 96, 98, 101, 113.
Boot, P. (NZ), 105, 106.
Borel, J. (France), 12.
Borg, E., see Purje, E.
Borican, J. (USA), 107, 112, 115.
Böthling, H. (Germany), 233.
Böttcher, W. (Germany), 92, 94.
Boulter, J. (GB), 245, 286.
Bourdier, F. (France), 12.
Bowden, D. (USA), 193, 197, 198, 199, 203, 204, 214.
Bowerman, B. (USA), 214, 222, 240.
Boxberger, J. (France), 283, 285, 299, 300, 301, 302, 310, 311.
Boyd, I. (GB), 178, 180, 190, 191, 195, 196.
Boyle, M.A. (USA), 17.
Boysen, A. (Norway), 161, 162, 163, 164, 166, 171, 178, 179, 181, 186, 187.
Bradley, P. (USA), 101, 103.
Brasher, C. (GB), 167, 172, 173.
Bray, J. (USA), 13.
Bright, N. (USA), 86, 87.
Brocksmith, H. (USA), 61, 62, 64, 65, 70.
Bruni, F. (Italy), 34.
Buhl, H. (Germany), 226.
Buker, R. (USA), 36, 38, 38, 39, 39.
Bullwinkle, G. (USA), 53.
Burke, B. (USA), 34.
Burke, J.M. (USA), 22, 23.
Burleson, D. (USA), 214, 216, 219, 220, 221, 222, 223, 224, 226, 228, 230, 231, 233, 234, 235, 236, 238, 239, 240, 243, 244, 245, 246, 248, 249, 250, 251, 252, 263, 264, 265, 272, 273, 275, 307, ATL.
Burnham, D. (USA), 125, 129, 134.
Burtin, A. (France), 29.
Butterfield, G. (GB), 15, 16, 29.
Bushnell, A. (USA), 75,
Byelitskiy, I. (USSR), 238, 245.
Byelokurov, N. (USSR), 162.

Camien, J. (USA), 235, 236, 239, 240, 243, 244, 245, 251, 263, 264.
Capozzoli, C. (USA), 167.

319

Carlberg, G. (USA), 303.
Carroll, P. (Eire), 11.
Carter, E. (USA), 10.
Carter, N. (USA), 39, 46, 47, 48, 52.
Cavanaugh, T. (USA), 38.
Ceraj, Z. (Yugoslavia), 157.
Cerati, U. (Italy), 81, 82, 86.
Cerutty, P. (Australia), 172, 205, 206, 210, 216, 219, 241.
Cevona, V. (Czechoslovakia), 142, 146, 148, 149, 153, 154, 161.
Chamberlain, C. (USA), 53.
Chapman, R. (USA), 59, 61.
Chataway, C. (GB), 167, 172, 173, 176, 181, 184, 185, 187, 187, 188, 192, 200.
Chinnery, W.M. (GB), 3.
Clarke, R. (Australia), 203, 205, 206, 246, 252, 254, 254, 258, 259, 261, 268, 269, 270, 276, 281, 282.
Clarkson, R. (USA), 264.
Coan, C. (USA), 53, 65.
Coenjaerts, P. (Belgium), 50.
Colburn, K. (USA), 298.
Coleman, P. (USA), 221.
Comstock, B. (USA), 89, 90.
Conger, R. (USA), 46, 47, 48, 52, 53, 59, 72.
Conneff, T.P. (USA), 9, 10, 11, 11, 17, 25, 28, 57.
Connolly, J. (USA), 29, 34, 39.
Cornell, B. (GB), 231, 239.
Cornes, J.F. (GB), 53, 54, 56, 57, 62, 63, 64, 64, 65, 67, 78, 79, 80, 81, 82, 87, 90, 91, 92, 93, 94, 95, 96.
Courtney, T. (USA), 198.
Cox, W. (USA), 47, 48.
Craske, H.M. (GB), 80.
Crawford, J. (USA), 299.
Cregan, J. (USA), 13.
Crothers, B. (Canada), 254, 262.
Crowley, F. (USA), 53, 60, 61, 62, 63, 65, 73.
Culp, E. (USA), 116, 129,
Cummings, W.J. (GB), 4, 5, 6, 7, 8, 9, 11.
Cunliffe, E. (USA), 214, 221.
Cunningham, G. (USA), 60, 61, 62, 63, 64, 64, 65, 66, 67, 68, 70, 73, 74, 74, 75, 76, 77, 81, 82, 83, 83, 84, 86, 87, 87, 88, 89, 92, 93, 94, 95, 96, 97, 98, 100, 100, 101, 102, 103, 104, 106, 107, 108, 109, 110, 111, 111, 112, 113, 114, 114, 115, 125, 151, 168, 182, 183, 183.
Curtis, W. (USA), 29.
Curtis, W.B. (USA), 10.
Cutbill, H. (USA), 29, 34, 37.

Dahl, M. (USA), 230.
Daly, B. (USA), 88.
Danielson, T. (USA), 289.
Davies, J. (NZ), 231, 234, 238, 246, 247, 248, 249, 250, 251, 256, 260, 261, 262, 263, ATL.
Davis, C.E. (GB), 34.
Dawson, G. (USA), 66, 84, 95.
Day, B. (USA), 243, 244, 245, 246, 251, 263, 268, 273, 291, ATL.
Deckard, T. (USA), 95, 107.
De Hertoghe, A. (Belgium), 271, 278, 278, 279, 280, 283, 285, 285, 289, 291, 292, 296, 296, 300, 308, ATL.
Delaney, B. (USA), 243, 244.
Delany, R. (Eire), 190, 191, 192, 193, 195, 196, 197, 198, 200, 201, 202, 204, 207, 208, 209, 210, 212, 213, 214, 215, 220, 226, 228.
Del Buono, G. (Italy), 295, 296, 303, 309, 310.
Dellinger, B. (USA), 212, 224.
Deloge, H. (France), 13.
Depastas, E. (Greece), 193.
Devaney, M. (USA), 26.
Dianetti, J. (USA), 146.
Dickenson, E. (GB), 4.
Dickson, J.F. (Sweden), 25.
Diessner, B. (E.Germany), 292.
Divine, R. (USA), 274, 279, 281, 286, 296, ATL.
Dixon, F. (USA), 117, 130.
Dixon, R. (NZ), 311, 312, 313, 314, ATL.
Dodds, G. (USA), 116, 117, 125, 126, 129, 130, 130, 131, 134, 135, 143, 145, 146, 147, 149, 151, 183.
Dodge, R. (USA), 39.
Dohrow, G. (Germany), 161, 162, 166, 180, 181, 190, 192, 193, 197.
Dotson, B. (USA), 226, 231, 233, 238, 244.
Douglas, J. (GB), 291, 314, ATL.
Douglas, M. (USA), 34.
Druetzler, W. (USA), 158, 160, 161, 162, 163, 165, 167.
Duddle, W. (GB), 4, 11.
Dufresne, J-P. (France), 300, 303, 311, ATL.
Duggan, N. (GB), 272, ATL.
Dühne, F. (Germany), 12.
Dunn, C. (USA), 170.
Durkfeldt, Å. (Sweden), 130.
Dwyer, F. (USA), 169, 171, 175, 182, 183, 183, 188, 191, 197.
Dyce, B. (Jamaica), 298, 309, 311.

Eastman, B. (USA), 67, 75.
Easton, B. (USA), 168, 174.
Ebba, H. (Ethiopia), 309.
Eby, E. (USA), 27.
Edward VII, King of G.B., 15.
Edwards, P. (Canada), 54, 59, 62, 63, 64, 65, 87, 92, 93, 94, 96.
Efaw, F. (USA), 143.
Eischen, C. (USA), 149.
Eisenhart, L. (USA), 125.
Eklöf, N. (Sweden), 39, 43, 48.
Ekman, G. (Sweden), 311, 312, 314.
Elizabeth II, Queen of Great Britain, 234.
Elliott, H. (Australia), 204, 205, 206, 207, 208, 209, 210, 211, 212, 212, 213, 214, 215, 216, 217, 218, 219, 220, 221, 221, 222, 225, 227, 228, 229, 232, 244, 245, 250, 256, 260, 262, 267, 270, 275, 276, 278, 291, ATL.
Elliott, J. (USA), 290, 298.
Ellis, C. (GB), 39, 46, 47, 49, 50, 53, 65.
El Mabrouk, P. (France), 151, 152, 152, 153, 154, 154, 158, 159, 160, 161, 162, 163, 166.
Elmore, C. (USA), 242.
Emery, J. (GB), 101.
Ericsson, I. (Sweden), 149, 149, 153, 154, 154, 158, 162, 163, 164, 165, 166, 169, 170, 170, 174, 178, 179, 180, 181, 190, 191, 192, 193, 194, 197, 204, 204, 209, 211.
Eriksson, F. (Sweden), 43.
Eriksson, H. (Sweden), 123, 141, 142, 143,

143, 144, 146, 147, 148, 149, 149, 150, 151, 151, 153, 170.
Eyerkaufer, K. (Germany), 233.
Eyre, L. (GB), 153, 154.

Fairbairn-Crawford, I.F. (GB), 16.
Fall, E. (USA), 25, 26, 28.
Farran, G.H. (Eire), 3.
Fenske, C. (USA), 88, 89, 95, 98, 101, 103, 104, 105, 106, 106, 107, 108, 109, 110, 111, 111, 112, 113, 114, 115, 183.
Ferguson, R. (Canada), 178, 181.
Ferris, D. (USA), 124.
Fisher, C. (Australia), 309, 310.
Flack, E. (Australia), 11.
Fontecilla, E. (Chile), 195.
Fordjour, B. (Ghana), 308, 309.
Forman, K. (USA), 233, 234.
Foster, B. (GB), 294, 300, 303, 311, 312, 313, 314, ATL.
Furia, A. (Italy), 73.

Gamoudi, M. (Tunisia), 253, 282.
Garay, S. (Hungary), 142, 146, 148, 154, 159.
Gårderud, A. (Sweden), 278, 278, 279, 280, 283, 285, ATL.
Garrison, J. (USA), 255.
Gehrmann, D. (USA), 148, 149, 149, 150, 151, 152, 154, 156, 158, 167, 183.
Geis, M. (USA), 68, 70.
George, A.B. (GB), 9.
George I, King of the Hellenes, 14.
George, W.G. (GB), 4, 5, 6, 7, 8, 9, 10, 11, 22, 23, 28, 29, 43, 100.
Georgsson, L-E. (Sweden), 143.
Gerschler, W. (Germany), 160, 232.
Getz, W. (USA), 52.
Gibbs, W. (GB), 3.
Ginn, Robert (USA), 116, 128, 129.
Goix, R. (France), 82, 92, 94, 105.
Goodwin, W. (USA), 38, 39, 44.
Gordon, A. (GB), 185, 202.
Gottfridsson, S. (Sweden), 146, 154, 192.
Graham, D. (Northern Ireland), 269.
Graham, R. (GB) 86, 91, 92, 95.
Grant, A. (USA), 13, 14.
Gregson, H. (GB), 14.
Greene, N.S. (Eire), 3.
Grelle, J. (USA), 214, 214, 216, 217, 219, 220, 221, 222, 224, 226, 230, 231, 233, 234, 234, 235, 236, 238, 239, 240, 243, 244, 245, 246, 251, 254, 255, 256, 262, 262, 263, 263, 264, 265, 268, 272, 273, 274, 275, 276, 277, 278, 283, ATL.
Grodotzki, H. (Germany), 213, 221.
Groth, M. (USA), 236, 240, 241, 243, 244, 245, 251.
Guettaya, M. (Tunisia), 302, 309, ATL.
Guillemot, J. (France), 29.
Gunton, C. (GB), 3.
Gustafsson, R. (Sweden), 126, 127, 129, 130, 131, 132, 133, 134, 136, 139, 141, 142, 143, 143, 145.

Haase, J. (E.Germany), 273, 282, 303.
Hägg, G. (Sweden), 115, 117, 118, 119, 120, 121, 122, 123, 124, 125, 126, 127, 128, 128, 129, 130, 131, 132, 133, 134, 135, 136, 137, 138, 139, 140, 141, 141, 142, 143, 144, 145, 147, 150, 151, 164, 166, 167, 170, 171, 173, 174, 176, 179, 181, 187, 208, 209, 220.

Hägg, N. (Sweden), 118, 119, 123.
Hägg, S. (Sweden), 118, 123, 124.
Haglund, I. (Sweden), 126, 129.
Hahn, L. (USA), 36, 38, 39, 39, 40, 43, 44, 47, 48, 116.
Haith, D. (GB), 226.
Halberg, M. (NZ), 177, 178, 181, 188, 188, 189, 190, 193, 195, 196, 197, 207, 208, 210, 211, 212, 212, 217, 222, 223, 227, 228, 229, 235, ATL.
Hallowell, N.P. (USA), 61, 62, 63, 64, 65.
Hallows, N. (GB), 16.
Halstead, J.P. (USA), 16.
Hamarsland, A. (Norway), 178, 209, 211, 212, 214, 216, 217, 218, 219, 220.
Hamilton, B. (USA), 197.
Hampson, T. (GB), 58.
Hanavan, E.M. (USA), 17, 18.
Hansen, T.B. (Denmark), 310, 313, ATL.
Hansenne, M. (France), 50, 140, 141, 142, 143, 145, 146, 148, 149, 149, 150, 151, 152, 152, 153, 154.
Harbig, R. (Germany), 124, 160.
Hardman, W. (USA), 165.
Harmon, P.S. (USA), 29.
Harper, C. (USA), 241.
Hartikka, N. (Finland), 105, 106, 106, 110, 111, 114.
Hawtrey, H. (GB), 14, 28.
Hazen, J. (USA), 69.
Heaviside, J. (Eire), 3.
Hedlund, O. (USA), 19, 21, 29.
Heino, V. (Finland), 134.
Helgas, L. (Finland), 47.
Hellström, B. (Sweden), 120, 121, 122, 123, 128, 129.
Hellström, K. (Sweden), 15.
Henderson-Hamilton, C.C. (GB), 14, 15, 29.
Herbert, J. (USA), 103.
Herman, F. (Belgium), 154, 162, 164, 165, 166.
Herrmann, S. (Germany), 187, 188, 193, 194, 195, 197, 209, 210, 213, 213, 214, 221, 226, 226, 232, 233, 234, 238, 238, 256, 259, 262, 263, 270.
Hewson, B. (GB), 181, 184, 185, 187, 188, 191, 192, 193, 194, 195, 196, 197, 201, 203, 207, 209, 210, 211, 212, 213.
Higgins, W. (USA), 34.
Hill, A. (GB), 26, 27, 28, 28, 29, 31, 43, 85, 90, 107.
Hill, R. (USA), 53, 59.
Hill (USA), 38.
Hilton, L. (USA), 303, 314.
Hitler, Adolf, Chancellor of Germany, 93.
Höckert, G. (Finland), 119.
Hoffman, G. (Czechoslovakia), 272.
Högberg, U. (Sweden), 278, 278, 299, 300, 301, 303, 309, 310, ATL.
Holmberg, A. (Sweden), 158, 159.
Holmér, G. (Sweden), 119, 121, 155.
Holmestrand, T. (Sweden), 211.
Homer, epic poet of Greece, 1.
Horan, F. (GB), 69.
Hornbostel, C. (USA), 66, 67, 73, 83.
Horspool, T. (GB), 2.
Hoskin, G. (NZ), 161.
Howe, J. (USA), 307, 311, 314, ATL.
Hulse, B. (USA), 117, 125, 126, 129, 130, 130, 131, 134, 135, 145.
Hulthin, E. (Sweden), 34.
Hume, Bob (USA), 134.

321

Hume, Ross (USA), 134.
Huttunen, M. (Finland), 186.
Ibbotson, D. (GB), 191, 197, 200, 201, 202, 203, 204, 208, 211, 212, 213, 260, ATL.
Iglói, M. (Hungary), 92, 100, 101, 106, 178, 184, 186, 190, 213, 214, 224, 231, 243.
Iharos, S. (Hungary), 178, 179, 180, 181, 185, 186, 187, 187, 188, 189, 192, 197, 208, 213, 226.
Isberg, J. (Sweden), 129.
Isohollo, V. (Finland), 73, 119.
Ivanov, I. (USSR), 308, 311, 314, ATL.

Jackson, A.N.S. (GB), 18, 19, 20, 21, 22, 28.
Jacob, H. (Germany), 111.
Janssens, D. (Belgium), 154.
Jansson (Spångert) Å. (Sweden), 101, 110, 111, 114, 115, 120, 124, 128, 129, 130.
Järvelä, N. (Finland), 29.
Jazy, M. (France), 188, 190, 210, 213, 213, 214, 217, 218, 219, 220, 221, 225, 226, 232, 233, 233, 234, 237, 238, 245, 247, 248, 251, 252, 253, 254, 256, 259, 262, 263, 264, 270, 271, 272, 272, 278, 280, 294, ATL.
Jipcho, B. (Kenya), 283, 285, 301, 302, 303, 305, 308, ATL.
Jochman, M. (Poland), 213.
Johansson, E. (Sweden), 12.
Johnson, D. (GB), 213.
Jones, J.P. (USA), 17, 18, 19, 20, 21, 22, 23, 25, 26, 28, 28, 68.
Jones, T. (USA), 107.
Jonsson (Kälarne), H. (Sweden), 99, 100, 102, 105, 106, 106, 114, 115, 119, 120, 121, 123, 127, 128, 129, 140.
Jordan, P. (USA), 160.
Jörgensen, E. (Denmark), 142, 146, 149, 149.
Jörgensen, R. (Norway), 53, 54.
Jörgensen, T. (Denmark), 144.
Jukola, M. (Finland), 120.
Jungwirth, S. (Czechoslovakia), 158, 162, 166, 170, 178, 179, 180, 181, 186, 187, 188, 189, 190, 191, 192, 193, 194, 195, 196, 197, 199, 200, 201, 202, 204, 208, 209, 210, 211, 212, 213, 233, ATL.
Justus, K-P. (E.Germany), 312, ATL.
Juza, M. (Czechoslovakia), 253, 260.

Kaindl, L. (Germany), 111.
Kakko, J. (Finland), 180, 199.
Kälarne, H.—see Jonsson, H.
Kane, C. (USA), 128, 129.
Karlsson, B. (Sweden), 144.
Karlsson, K-E.(Sweden), 144, 146, 149, 154.
Karlsson, S. (Sweden), 158, 164, 165, 166, 169, 170, 170, 175, 179.
Karver, G. (USA), 146, 149.
Keeling, P. (GB), 245.
Keino, H.K. (Kenya), 248, 254, 257, 258, 259, 260, 261, 262, 262, 263, 264, 268, 269, 270, 271, 272, 275, 276, 277, 278, 279, 280, 281, 282, 283, 284, 285, 285, 287, 292, 293, 294, 296, 296, 301, 302, 303, 304, 305, 308, 309, 310, 311, 312, 313, 314, ATL.
Keller, J. (France), 46, 50, 51, 52.
Kent-Smith, B. (GB) 217, 221.

Kenyatta, Jomo, President of Kenya, 260.
Kerr, G. (Jamaica), 223, 234.
King, E. (Canada), 63.
Kinnunen, A. (Finland), 48.
Kiprugut, W. (Kenya), 260, 277.
Kirby, E. (USA), 34.
Kirkbride, J. (GB), 293, 296, 300, 308, 314, ATL.
Kiser, R. (USA), 48, 52, 53, 59.
Kittel, A. (Czechoslovakia), 46.
Kiviat, A. (USA), 19, 20, 21, 22, 24, 25, 25, 28, 29, 32, 36.
Kivlan, B. (USA), 286.
Kolehmainen, H. (Finland), 25, 31, 32.
Köpke, F-F. (Germany), 29.
Kovács, L. (Hungary), 209, 210, 212, 214, 218, 221.
Kraft, B. (Sweden), 52, 53,
Krause, H-H. (Germany), 46, 54.
Krüger, A. (W.Germany), 280, 285, ATL.
Kurgat, Kipkeino Arap (Kenya), 257.
Kusocinski, J. (Poland), 53, 58, 65, 82.
Kuts, V. (USSR), 184, 200, 206, 253.
Kvalheim, A. (Norway), 278, 285, 286, 295, 296, 296, 299, 303, 308, ATL.

Laaksonen (Finland), 120.
LaBenz, C. (USA), 288, 290, 291, 293, 295, 296, 297, 303, ATL.
Ladoumègue, J. (France), 44, 45, 46, 47, 47, 48, 49, 50, 51, 52, 52, 53, 54, 57, 58, 59, 62, 70, 70, 71, 72, 73, 74, 83, 96, 96, 101, 140, 294.
Lamers, R. (Germany), 161, 162, 163, 166.
Lamprecht, DeV. (South Africa), 286, 297.
Landqvist, S. (Sweden), 150, 151, 152, 152, 153, 157, 158, 158, 161, 175.
Landy, J. (Australia), 165, 166, 166, 170, 171, 172, 173, 175, 176, 177, 178, 181, 184, 186, 187, 188, 189, 191, 192, 193, 194, 195, 196, 197, 197, 198, 202, 203, 204, 206, 212.
Lang, W. (GB), 2, 3, 11.
Langenus, A. (Belgium), 179.
Langridge, J. (GB), 48.
Lanzi, M. (Italy), 105.
LaPierre, J. (USA), 168.
Larravee, L. (USA), 39.
Larsen, A. (Denmark), 53.
Larsen, G. (Denmark), 312.
Larsson, L. (Sweden), 119.
Larva (Lagerström), H. (Finland), 45, 46, 47, 47, 48, 49, 53, 54, 62, 63, 70, 70.
Lash, D. (USA), 86, 88, 92, 95, 97, 98, 100, 101, 102, 104, 107, 113, 115, 169.
Lauck, W. (USA), 73.
Law, D. (GB), 177.
Lawrenz, O. (Germany), 188.
Lawson, J. (USA), 288, 293, 206.
Lehne, H. (Norway), 101.
Lehtinen, L. (Finland), 54, 72.
Leibowitz, P. (USA), 116, 128.
Lermusiaux, A. (France), 11, 12.
Lermond, G. (USA), 53.
Lermond, L. (USA), 47, 52, 53, 56, 59, 60, 65, 70.
Leva, E. (Belgium), 192.
Lewandowski, S. (Poland), 187, 201, 202, 204, 211, 212, 213, 214, 217, 218.
Lewis, H. (USA), 73.
Liewendahl, F. (Finland), 36, 41.
Lightbody, J. (USA), 14, 15.

322

Liljekvist, H. (Sweden), 130.
Lincoln, M. (Australia), 190, 192, 193, 195, 196, 197, 201, 203, 204, 206, 207, 208, 212, 213, 215, 216, 217, 218, 222, ATL.
Lindgren, G. (USA), 242, 280.
Liquori, M. (USA), 274, 281, 283, 285, 288, 289, 290, 291, 292, 293, 293, 294, 295, 296, 296, 297, 298, 299, 300, 301, 303, 303, 307, 308, 311, ATL.
Loney, E.V. (GB), 16.
Loukola, T. (Finland), 53, 58.
Lovelock, J.E. (NZ), 54, 55, 56, 57, 58, 62, 63, 64, 64, 66, 67, 68, 69, 70, 70, 71, 72, 73, 74, 75, 78, 79, 80, 81, 82, 82, 83, 83, 84, 85, 86, 86, 87, 87, 90, 91, 92, 93, 94, 95, 95, 96, 96, 98, 99, 101, 102, 105, 113, 114, 121, 156, 163.
Lowe, D. (GB), 36, 41, 44.
Lueg, W. (Germany), 158, 159, 161, 162, 163, 164, 166, 170, 170, 171, 179, 180, 181, 187.
Lundgren, S. (Sweden), 26, 27, 29.
Lundh, U.B. (Norway), 210, 211.
Lundqvist, S. (Sweden), 147.
Lunghi, E. (Italy), 16
Luomanen, M. (Finland), 54, 63.
Lutyens, W. (GB), 10, 11.
Lydiard, A. (NZ), 189, 222, 227, 228, 229, 246, 247, 251, 310, 312.

MacDonald, B. (GB), 34, 39.
Mack, B. (USA), 149, 154.
Macmillan, D. (Australia), 158, 161, 162, 163, 164, 166, 167.
MacMitchell, L. (USA), 113, 115, 116, 125, 128, 129, 142, 143, 183.
Madeira, L. (USA), 22.
Magee, J. (USA), 99.
Mahannah, R. (USA), 104.
Mahoney, D.S. (USA), 22.
Mäki, T. (Finland), 111, 113, 124.
Malmberg, S. (Sweden), 134, 141.
Mangan, J. (USA), 61, 65, 73, 87, 88, 95.
Manning, J.L. (GB), 260.
Maplestone, R. (GB), 314.
Martin, O. (USA), 48, 52.
Martin, P. (Switzerland), 46, 53, 92.
Martin, S. (France), 43, 44, 45, 47, 48, 50, 51.
Mason, J. (USA), 282, 288, 289, 291, 292, 296, 297, 302, 303, 311.
Matilainen, M. (Finland), 87.
Matuschewski, M. (E.Germany), 278.
May, J. (E.Germany), 238, 238, 256, 260, 261, 262, 262, 263, 268, 269, 270, 271, 272, 273, 278; (W.Germany), 283, 285, 289, 290, 291, 292, 293, 296, 296, 302, 308, ATL.
McAfee, R. (USA), 298.
McCafferty, I. (GB), 292, 293, 294, ATL.
McEwen, D. (Canada), 158.
McGough, J. (GB), 15.
McInstray (GB), 2, 3.
McKniff, W. (USA), 65.
McLaren, G. (Canada), 308.
McMillen, B. (USA), 154, 158, 159, 160, 162, 163, 164, 165, 166, 183.
McWhirter, N. (GB), 173.
Meade, G.P. (USA), 15.
Meanix, W. (USA), 23.
Mehl, W. (USA), 110, 111, 113, 114, 114, 115, 116, 128, 165, 183.

Mehlhose, H. (Germany), 111.
Meiers, F. (France), 12.
Meredith, T. (USA), 18, 23, 24, 59.
Metcalf, J. (GB), 1.
Michael, H. (USA), 290, 296, 307, 314, ATL.
Mickelsson, P. (Finland), 72, 73.
Mignon, H. (Belgium), 310, 311, 313, ATL.
Mikkola, J. (Finland), 32, 33.
Milligan, V. (Northern Ireland), 178, 181.
Mills, E. (GB), 2.
Miranda, J. (Argentina), 183.
Mitchell, E. (USA), 117, 130.
Moakley, J. (USA), 17, 27.
Moens, R. (Belgium), 187, 203, 204, 204, 213, 221, 223, 225, 247.
Momotkov, Y. (USSR), 216.
Moore, A. (USA), 52.
Moore, J. (GB), 48.
Moore, P. (USA), 113, 114, 114, 127.
Moran, E. (USA), 214, 221.
Morel, R. (France), 52.
Morgan, V. (GB), 52.
Morizot, (France), 50.
Mosser, M. (USA), 298.
Mostert, J. (Belgium), 93, 96, 103, 104, 105, 106, 106, 109, 111.
Mugosa, V. (Yugoslavia), 180.
Mungai, D. (Kenya), 301.
Munski, J. (USA), 113, 114, 114, 115, 128.
Murphy, F. (Eire): 286, 288, 289, 290, 291, 292, 292, 293, 294, 300, 309, 314, ATL.
Murphy, M. (USA), 9.
Mussabini, S. (GB), 26.
Myers, L. (USA), 5, 6, 8, 9.

Nai, D. (Italy), 58.
Nankeville, B. (GB), 148, 149, 151, 153, 154, 154, 157, 158, 160, 161, 170, 170, 171.
Napoleon I, Emperor of the French, 58.
Neidnig, A. (USA), 114.
Newcomb, J. (USA), 154, 159.
Nicolas, C. (France), 253, 278.
Nielsen, G. (Denmark), 164, 166, 179, 180, 181, 181, 182, 183, 183, 187, 187, 188, 189, 191, 193, 194, 195, 196, 197.
Nilsson, L. (Sweden), 101, 115, 128.
Nordell, F. (USA), 62, 65.
Normand, R. (France), 82, 85, 86, 86.
Norpoth, H. (W.Germany), 232, 233, 233, 237, 247, 262, 268, 269, 270, 271, 272, 272, 273, 277, 283, 284, 285, 291, 295, 296, 300, 302, 303, 308, ATL.
Nurmi, P. (Finland), 29, 30, 31, 32, 33, 34, 34, 35, 36, 37, 38, 38, 39, 39, 40, 41, 42, 43, 43, 44, 45, 47, 47, 48, 50, 52, 70, 72, 88, 133, 153, 162.
Nuttall, J. (GB), 2.
Ny, E. (Sweden), 54, 63, 64, 65, 67, 81, 82, 83, 85, 86, 87, 87, 92, 93, 94, 96.

O'Connell, D. (USA), 29.
O'Connor, E. (USA), 22, 23.
Odlozil, J. (Czechoslovakia), 248, 249, 250, 251, 252, 255, 256, 260, 262, 262, 263, 265, 270, 271, 272, 283, 285, ATL.
Offenhauser, G. (USA), 52.
O'Hara, T. (USA), 234, 235, 236, 238, 239, 240, 243, 244, 245, 246, 247, 248, 251, 297, ATL.
Öhrn, B. (Sweden), 53.

Olander, G. (Sweden), 123.
Orton, G. (USA), 10, 13.
Orywal, Z. (Poland), 210, 212, 214.
Otenhajmer, A. (Yugoslavia), 154, 156, 157, 158, 159.
Overton, J. (USA), 25, 26, 29.

Päivärinta, P. (Finland), 310.
Pantyeley, V. (USSR), 310, 311, 313.
Papavassiliou, G. (Greece), 195.
Parlett, J. (GB), 157, 158.
Parnell, B. (Canada), 161.
Patrick, D. (USA), 273, 279, 285, 289, ATL.
Paull, W. (USA), 17, 18, 29.
Payne, R. (USA), 38.
Pekuri, K. (Finland), 106, 106.
Pelé, R. (France), 39, 43.
Pell, D. (GB), 109, 111.
Peltzer, O. (Germany), 32, 34, 39, 40, 41, 42, 43, 44, 45, 47, 47, 48, 49, 50, 51, 53, 63, 72.
Perry, L. (Australia), 165, 166.
Persson, R. (Sweden), 126, 131, 132, 133, 134, 136, 137, 139, 141, 141, 142, 143, 146, 147, 149, 149, 154, 157.
Peter, D. (USA), 128.
Petkiewicz, S. (Poland), 53.
Pettersson, Å. (Sweden), 136, 137.
Pettersson, O. (Sweden), 101, 122.
Peussa, A. (Finland), 36.
Pipyne, J. (USSR), 190, 204.
Pirie, G. (GB), 171, 181, 186, 189, 192, 194, 197, 200, 201, 204, 208, 215, 220, 221, 221, 225, 226.
Pohjala, T. (Finland), 54.
Polhill, T. (NZ), 302, 309, 310, 311, 313, 314, ATL.
Porter, R. (USA), 130.
Potapchenko, I. (USSR), 278.
Potter, L. (USA), 48.
Poulenard, C. (France), 45.
Poulsen, A. (Denmark), 130.
Power, D. (Australia), 221.
Powers, J. (USA), 21, 25, 29.
Prefontaine, S. (USA), 296, 299, 303, 314, ATL.
Price, D.W. (GB), 53.
Pugachovskiy, A. (USSR), 135.
Purje (Borg), E. (Finland), 34, 43, 45, 46, 47, 48, 51, 53, 54, 62, 65, 70. 72, 73, 73.
Putnam, R. (USA), 53.
Puttemans, E. (Belgium), 300.

Quax, D. (NZ), 293, 294, 295, 296, 297, 297, 303, ATL.
Quinn, T. (USA), 142, 143, 146, 149.

Rafferty, J. (USA), 135, 141.
Raiko, O. (USSR), 271, 272, 278, ATL.
Ray, J. (USA), 23, 25, 25, 26, 27, 28, 28, 29, 34, 36, 37, 38, 39, 39, 43, 44, 70.
Reese, J. (USA), 39.
Reeve, A. (GB), 78, 79, 80, 82, 83, 85, 86.
Regassa, S. (Ethiopia), 311.
Rehberg, R. (USA), 143.
Reiff, G. (Belgium), 143, 145, 146, 148, 149, 150, 151, 152, 152, 153, 154, 157, 158, 158, 160, 164, 165, 166, 168, 170, 171, 179.
Rice, G. (USA), 106, 107, 109, 113, 116, 125, 126, 133.

Richards, W. (GB), 2, 3, 11.
Richey, J. (USA), 286.
Richtzenhain, K. (Germany), 188, 189, 190, 192, 193, 195, 196, 197, 201, 209.
Riddell, T. (GB), 73, 85, 86.
Rideout, B. (USA), 103, 104, 106, 107, 108, 109, 110, 111, 111, 112, 113, 114, 114.
Rideout, W. (USA), 103, 107, 111, 114, 115.
Ringvall, T. (Sweden), 143, 146.
Ritola, V. (Finland), 35, 37, 38, 40, 41, 45, 47.
Robertson, L. (USA), 11.
Robinson, S. (USA), 46, 48.
Roelants, G. (Belgium), 259.
Romo, R. (USA), 266, 273.
Rose, R. (NZ), 39, 40, 43, 44.
Ross, B. (USA), 149.
Ross, J. (Canada), 161, 167.
Rózsavölgyi, I. (Hungary), 179, 186, 187, 187, 188, 188, 189, 190, 191, 192, 193, 194, 197, 209, 210, 211, 212, 213, 214, 214, 215, 216, 218, 219, 220, 221, 221, 224, 225, 226, 226, 232, ATL.
Rudd, B. (South Africa), 27.
Rushmer, A. (GB), 279.
Ryan, J.W. (USA), 22.
Ryun, J. (USA), 241, 242, 243, 244, 245, 246, 248, 251, 252, 254, 255, 256, 262, 263, 263, 264, 265, 266, 267, 268, 269, 272, 273, 273, 274, 275, 276, 277, 278, 279, 279, 280, 282, 284, 285, 285, 286, 287, 288, 289, 290, 291, 293, 295, 297, 298, 299, 303, 304, 305, 306, 307, 308, 309, 311, 313, 314, ATL.

Salinger, T. (Czechoslovakia), 233, 238.
Salvé, E. (Belgium), 291, 292, 293.
Salonen, O. (Finland), 193, 198, 199, 204, 213, 214, 214, 216, 224, 226, 231, 233, 247.
Salsola, O. (Finland), 190, 191, 193, 194, 197, 198, 199, 204, 210, 212.
Sandoval, R. (Chile), 193.
San Romani, A. Sr. (USA), 87, 88, 89, 92, 93, 94, 95, 95, 96, 97, 98, 99, 100, 101, 102, 103, 104, 106, 107, 108, 109, 110, 111, 111, 113, 123, 169.
San Romani, A. Jr. (USA), 240, 241, 243, 244, 245, 246, 251.
Santee, W. (USA), 167, 168, 169, 170, 170, 171, 173, 174, 175, 176, 181, 182, 183, 183, 184, 187, 188, 190.
Sarkama, T. (Finland), 105, 106, 110, 111, 114, 115.
Savinkov, V. (USSR), 223.
Schade, H. (Germany), 160.
Schärer, W. (Switzerland), 36, 38.
Scharn, H. (Holland), 311.
Schaumburg, F. (Germany), 82, 86, 86, 87, 93, 94, 99, 101.
Scholtz, C. (South Africa), 92.
Schul, B. (USA), 244, 246, 251, 254, 262.
Schwarte, A. (Germany), 218.
Scott. N. (NZ), 193, 195, 196, 197.
Seagrove, W. (GB), 38.
Seaman, B. (USA), 188, 191, 197, 203, 230, 231, 233, 235, 236, 238, 239, 243.
Sears, R. (USA), 73, 82, 86, 88.
Seidenschnur, R. (Germany), 124, 129.
Semper, H. (USA), 167.
Sheppard, M. (USA), 16, 17, 18, 19, 20, 21.

324

Shields, L. (USA), 27, 29, 34.
Shrubb, A. (GB), 14, 25, 91.
Silei, C. (Kenya), 309.
Silverberg, B. (USA), 304.
Simon, A. (Hungary), 226.
Simon, R. (Belgium), 280, 285, 292.
Simpson, A. (GB) 238, 240, 248, 249, 251, 257, 260, 262, 263, 269, 270, 271, 272, 276, 277, 279, ATL.
Sink, R. (USA), 143, 149.
Sivak, J. (USA), 48.
Sjögren, G. (Sweden), 43.
Slade, W. (GB), 3, 4, 5.
Slykhuis, W. (Holland), 143, 148, 149, 149, 150, 151, 152, 153, 154, 154, 156, 158, 159, 160, 170, 179, 181.
Smedley, R. (GB), 311, 314, ATL.
Smith, H. (USA), 174.
Smith, J. (USA), 98, 101, 106.
Snell, P. (NZ), 220, 222, 223, 226, 227, 228, 229, 230, 233, 233, 234, 235, 236, 238, 239, 243, 244, 246, 247, 248, 249, 250, 251, 253, 254, 255, 256, 261, 262, 262, 263, 264, 265, 267, 276, 278, 313, ATL.
Snook, W. (GB), 6, 11, 29.
Soalhat, M. (France), 12.
Sokolov, Y. (USSR), 192, 193, 204.
Southworth, W. (USA), 106.
Spångert, Å., see Jansson, A.
Stallard, H.B. (GB), 27, 28, 29, 31, 34, 36, 38, 47.
Stampfl, F. (GB), 172, 173, 185, 192, 194.
Staniszewski, J. (Poland), 105.
Starr, R.S. (GB), 48.
Stewart, Ian (GB), 292, 292, 293, 294, 296, ATL.
Stewart, Peter (GB), 292, 294, 296, 297, 300, 302, 303, 308, 311, 312, 314, ATL.
Strand, L. (Sweden), 132, 135, 136, 137, 139, 140, 141, 141, 142, 143, 143, 144, 145, 146, 146, 147, 148, 149, 149, 150, 151, 151, 152, 152, 153, 154, 154, 159, 170, 179, 181, 187.
Studd, I. (NZ), 269, 273.
Sukhanov, S. (USSR), 195.
Sullivan, J.E. (USA), 21.
Sullivan, J.P. (USA), 15.
Sullivan, T. (Rhodesia), 216, 220, 221, 222.
Sundin, R. (Sweden), 135, 141.
Svensson, A. (Sweden), 149.
Swan, G. (USA), 29.
Swartz, R. (USA), 53.
Szabó, M. (Hungary), 57, 67, 73, 81, 82, 87, 90, 92, 94, 96, 97, 98, 99, 100, 101, 115, 121, 129.
Szekeres, B. (Hungary), 213.
Szentgáli, L. (Hungary), 196.
Szordykowski, H. (Poland), 271, 283, 285, 291, 292, 292, 295, 296, 296, 300, 303, 311, ATL.

Taber, N.S. (USA), 18, 19, 20, 21, 22, 23, 24, 25, 25, 28, 32, 33, 43.
Tábori, L. (Hungary), 181, 184, 185, 186, 187, 187, 188, 189, 190, 191, 192, 193, 194, 196, 197, 201, 203, 207, 212, 213, 214, 220, 221, 224, 230, 231.
Taipale, I. (Finland), 152, 153, 154, 154, 157, 158, 158, 170, 176.
Tala, M. (Finland), 29, 34.
Taylor, S. (GB), 226, 231, 233.

Tegnér, T. (Sweden), 40.
Teileri, O. (Finland), 86.
Templeton, D. (USA), 113.
Temu, N. (Kenya), 269, 281.
Thomas, A. (Australia), 207, 208, 210, 211, 212, 216, 217, 220, 221, 228, 238, 247, 251.
Thomas, R. (GB), 50, 51, 53, 54, 54, 57, 62, 70, 72, 73, 90, 99.
Thomas, J. (USA), 151.
Tilbury, F. (GB), 48.
Timmons, B. (USA), 241, 242, 243, 263, 264, 273, 290, 306.
Tincler, G.B. (Eire), 11, 11.
Toft, N. (Sweden), 151, 169, 175.
Tölgyesi, V. (Hungary), 162.
Tribou, W. (USA), 129.
Trube, H.L. (USA), 15, 17.
Truex, L. (USA), 158, 171, 181.
Trutt, M. (USA), 106.
Tucker, B. (USA), 245.
Tulloh, B. (GB), 228/229, 234, 258.
Tulzer, V. (Austria), 238.
Tümmler, B. (W.Germany), 256, 262, 265, 270, 271, 272, 272, 277, 278, 279, 280, 281, 284, 285, 285, 291, 292, 292, 293, 300, 311, ATL.
Turner, S. (NZ), 228.
Twomey, J. (USA), 149, 154.

Ulzheimer, H. (Germany), 160.

Valentin, S. (Germany), 204, 213, 216, 217, 221, 225, 226, 233, 237, 238, 238, 245, 247, ATL.
Vamos, Z. (Rumania), 213, 217, 218, 219, 220, 221, 225, 226, 238.
Van Zijl, F. (South Africa), 304, 305, 308, 314, ATL.
Vasala, P. (Finland), 300, 301, 302, 303, 312, 313, 314, ATL.
Vefling, K. (Norway), 144.
Velsveebel, M. (USSR), 161.
Venzke, G. (USA), 53, 60, 61, 62, 65, 66, 70, 74, 74, 75, 76, 77, 82, 83, 84, 85, 86, 87, 88, 89, 92, 93, 94, 95, 96, 97, 98, 101, 102, 103, 106, 110, 111, 112, 114, 114, 115.
Verheuen, R. (Belgium), 209, 225, 226.
Vernier, J. (France), 146, 152, 152, 153, 154.
Vervoort, G. (France), 253, 262.
Viaux, P. (France), 292.
Vilt, M. (USSR), 271, 272, ATL.
Vohrálik, V. (Czechoslovakia), 27, 29.
Von Ruden, T. (USA), 266, 273, 274, 278, 279, 280, 281, 283, 285, 285, 295, 297, 297, 302, 303, 305, 306, 307, 314, ATL.
Von Sigel, E. (Germany), 19, 20.
Vuorisalo, O. (Finland), 176, 186, 193, 199, 203, 204, 209, 210, 212, 217, 218.

Wade, H. (GB), 11.
Wadoux, J. (France), 237, 238, 248, 250, 252, 253, 263, 270, 271, 272, 272, 278, 278, 283, 285, 291, 292, 294, 295, 296, 300, 301, 308, ATL.
Waern, D. (Sweden), 191, 192, 193, 194, 195, 197, 198, 199, 203, 204, 204, 209, 210, 211, 212, 213, 217, 218, 219, 220, 221, 221, 225, 226, 228, 244, ATL.
Walsh, E. (USA), 143.

Walters, J. (USA), 195.
Ward, P. (GB), 85.
Wartelle, A. (France), 145.
Wassenaar, B. (Holland), 303, 311.
Watson, R. (USA), 29, 34, 36, 37.
Weatherhead, A. (GB), 302.
Webster, A. (GB), 159.
Weed, L. (USA), 116, 128, 129.
Weisiger, C. (USA), 230, 231, 232, 233, 235, 236, 238, 239, 240, 241, 243, 244, 245, 247, 251, 255, 266, 268, 272, ATL.
Wellmann, P-H. (W.Germany), 312, 313, 314, ATL.
Welsh, A.R. (GB), 15.
Welsh, H. (GB), 11, 13, 28.
Wessinghage, T. (W.Germany), 310.
Westman, F. (Sweden), 119.
Wheatley, G.A. (Australia), 269.
Wheeler, Bob (USA), 307, 312, ATL.
Wheeler, K. (Australia), 269.
Wheeler, Ted (USA), 190, 191.
Whetton, J. (GB), 248, 249, 250, 251, 260, 263, 276, 284, 285, 286, 291, 292, 292, 294, 297.
White, J. (GB), 8.
Whitfield, M. (USA), 169, 174, 175, 268.
Whyte, W. (Australia), 46.
Wichmann, H. (Germany), 46, 47, 47, 48, 53, 54.
Wide, Edvin (Sweden), 29, 31, 32, 33, 33, 33, 36, 37, 39, 40, 41, 42, 43, 43, 44, 45, 46, 47, 47, 48, 72, 81.
Wide, Ernst (Sweden), 19, 20, 21, 23, 25, 28, 32.
Wiggs, M. (GB), 213, 218, 223.
Wilborn, D. (USA), 274, 276, 279, 281, 286, 297, ATL.
Wilkinson, W. (GB), 269, 292, 293, 297, 303, ATL.

Williamson, H. (USA), 82.
Wilson, D. (GB), 130, 134, 141, 142.
Wilson, H. (GB), 16, 19, 28.
Wilt, F. (USA), 116, 152, 154, 156, 158.
Windnagle, L.V. (USA), 23, 28.
Wint, A. (Jamaica), 156.
Winzenried, M. (USA), 299, 304.
Wiriath, R. (France), 34, 39, 47.
Wold, D. (USA), 143.
Wolde, M. (Ethiopia), 188, 190.
Wood, K. (GB), 181, 188, 190, 192, 193, 194, 195, 196, 201, 202, 204, 208, 226, 226.
Wooderson, A.T. (GB), 78.
Wooderson, S.C. (GB), 77, 78, 79, 80, 82, 85, 86, 86, 87, 90, 91, 92, 95, 96, 98, 99, 100, 100, 101, 105, 106, 106, 107, 108, 109, 111, 114, 122, 128, 130, 134, 138, 139, 140, 141, 142, 143, 147, 151, 155.
Wottle, D. (USA), 296, 306, 307, 310, 311.
Wyatt, F. (GB), 181.

Yancey, J. (USA), 209.
Yergovich, T. (USA), 242.
Young, G. (USA), 264.

Zacharopoulos, S. (Greece), 310.
Zamperini, L. (USA), 104, 106, 109, 110, 111, 111, 112, 113, 114, 115, 169.
Zamperini, P. (USA), 104.
Zander, J. (Sweden), 20, 21, 23, 24, 25, 27, 28, 32, 33.
Zátopek, E. (Czechoslovakia), 155, 179.
Zhelobovskiy, M. (USSR), 291, 295, 300, 310.
Zvolensky, A. (Czechoslovakia), 179.